OXFORD POLITICAL THEORY

Series Editors: Will Kymlicka, David Miller, and Alan Ryan

CRITICAL REPUBLICANISM

OXFORD POLITICAL THEORY

Oxford Political Theory presents the best new work in contemporary political theory. It is intended to be broad in scope, including original contributions to political philosophy, and also work in applied political theory. The series contains works of outstanding quality with no restriction as to approach or subject matter.

CRITICAL REPUBLICANISM

The Hijab Controversy and Political Philosophy

CÉCILE LABORDE

OXFORD

UNIVERSITY PRESS

*This book has been printed digitally and produced in a standard specification
in order to ensure its continuing availability*

OXFORD

UNIVERSITY PRESS

Great Clarendon Street, Oxford OX2 6DP

Oxford University Press is a department of the University of Oxford.
It furthers the University's objective of excellence in research, scholarship,
and education by publishing worldwide in

Oxford New York

Auckland Cape Town Dar es Salaam Hong Kong Karachi
Kuala Lumpur Madrid Melbourne Mexico City Nairobi
New Delhi Shanghai Taipei Toronto
With offices in
Argentina Austria Brazil Chile Czech Republic France Greece
Guatemala Hungary Italy Japan South Korea Poland Portugal
Singapore Switzerland Thailand Turkey Ukraine Vietnam

Oxford is a registered trade mark of Oxford University Press
in the UK and in certain other countries

Published in the United States
by Oxford University Press Inc., New York

ISBN 978-0-19-955021-0

ACKNOWLEDGEMENTS

This book is an attempt to reconcile the left-wing republican political culture I inherited from my formative years in France with the Anglo-American liberal philosophy I became acquainted with in the rigorous and inspiring atmosphere of British universities. The need for reconciliation came about as I struggled to explain—though not to justify—the bewildering recurrence of *affaires du foulard* (hijab controversies) in French political life since 1989. I came to the view that while my Anglophone interlocutors were right to think that the hijab ban (which became law in March 2004) was morally indefensible and politically dangerous, they were too quick in dismissing as illiberal the republican ideals that underpin it. Thus, I undertook to re-interpret and rescue the ideals of republican citizenship from the illiberal policy pursued by the French state. The critical republicanism I defend will probably be deemed too liberal by French republicans and too republican by Anglo-American liberals. But (for what it is worth) I am pleased to report that articulating it has helped me reduce the tension between the various prejudices that I hold.

In the process of formulating these ideas, I have incurred a number of debts. From the start, David Miller encouraged me not to worry unduly about how the work might fit in with the accepted dichotomy, in Anglophone political theory, between abstract normative philosophy and context-sensitive interpretation. He carefully read the final manuscript and offered typically searching criticism. Another series editor, Will Kymlicka, was generous in his support, and made a number of challenging comments. I also benefited from expert editorial support from Dominic Byatt, and helpful advice from an anonymous reader from Oxford University Press. No less helpful were the incisive and supportive comments I received from John Horton and Catriona McKinnon, both of whom read large sections of the draft manuscript. In addition, Catriona offered firm, friendly, and timely encouragement, which helped me through considerably.

Over the years, I have benefited from written and oral conversations with a great number of colleagues, students, and friends, and it is a pleasure to thank them here: Catherine Audard, Brian Barry, Richard Bellamy, Chris Brown, Ian Carter, Dario Castiglione, Clare Chambers, John Charvet, Jerry Cohen, Diana Coole, John Dunn, Khadijah Elshayyal,

Cécile Fabre, Éric Fassin, Matthew Festenstein, Nancy Fraser, Michael Freeden, Robert Goodin, Peter Hallward, Sudhir Hazareesingh, Axel Honneth, Itsvan Hont, Julian Jackson, Peter Jones, Stuart Jones, Paul Kelly, Chandran Kukathas, Justine Lacroix, George Letsas, Annabelle Lever, Christian List, John Maynor, Andrew Mason, Saladin Meckled-Garcia, Tariq Modood, Monica Mookherjee, Per Mouritsen, Jan-Werner Müller, Véronique Munoz-Dardé, Karma Nabulsi, Alan Patten, Emile Perreau-Saussine, Philip Pettit, Anne Phillips, Jonathan Quong, Quentin Skinner, Jean-Fabien Spitz, Marc Stears, Zofia Stemplowska, Laura Valentini, Georgios Varouxakis, Albert Weale, Stuart White, and Jo Wolff. Drafts of this project were presented to audiences at seminars in Amsterdam, Aarhus, Cambridge, Cardiff, Dublin, Exeter, Colchester, Florence, Manchester, Naples, Nottingham, Oxford, Paris, Pisa, San Francisco, Sheffield, and at various venues in London: the London School of Economics, King's College London, University College London, the Institute for the Study of Historical Research, and the Institute for the Study of Muslim Civilizations.

As a Professeur Associé at the École des Hautes Études en Sciences Sociales (EHESS) in Paris, I had the good fortune to give presentations to the seminars convened by Françoise Gaspard, Serge Paugam, and Dominique Schnapper, who generously discussed the ideas of this book. For inviting me to the École, and for still talking to me despite our many disagreements, I am grateful to Christophe Prochasson. Maud Verdier and Malika Amaouche made my stays in Paris very enjoyable, offering hospitality, friendship, endless conversations, and memorable meals. My research in Paris was funded by a Large Research Grant from the British Academy, which I was fortunate to co-hold with Jeremy Jennings, who provided continual inspiration and friendship. The final writing up was greatly assisted by an Arts and Humanities Research Council Research Leave Grant. Staff at the British Library, Fondation Nationale des Sciences Politiques, and Bibliothèque Nationale de France greatly facilitated the collection of sources necessary for this project. I also received invaluable support, and a great deal of intellectual stimulation, from my own institution, the School of Public Policy at University College London. UCL is a great place for the study of political theory, and I am proud (and pleased) to belong there.

I have other, more personal, debts. Esther Leneman and Sally Weintrobe provided vital support when it mattered. So did the continual love of my family back home: my sister Delphine and my parents, Jacques and Pierrette Laborde. My greatest debt, however, is to Mark Hewitson. Over the last 14 years, Mark has been the best reader, critic, colleague, friend, confidante, companion, father, sailor, and cook one could hope for. Our daughters, Anna and Camille, were born while the manuscript was being prepared, and made it seem far less important.

Some parts of this book have appeared elsewhere. I am grateful to the publishers for permission to reprint the following material:

'Secular Philosophy and Muslim Headscarves in Schools', *Journal of Political Philosophy*, Vol. 13, No. 3, 2005, 305–29.
'Female Autonomy, Education and the *Hijab*', *Critical Review of International Social and Political Philosophy*, Vol. 9, No. 3, September 2006, 351–77.

London
February, 2008

CONTENTS

CHAPTER 1

Political Philosophy, Social Theory, and Critical Republicanism

This book is a critical contribution to normative republican theory. It is critical in two distinct, if related, senses. First, it is critical of those interpretations of republicanism which justified the ban on the wearing of religious signs (particularly the Muslim hijab) in French schools in March 2004. Second, it is critical of a certain way of doing political theory, common to Anglo-American liberals and French republicans, which is insufficiently reflective about the relationship between normative prescriptions and social facts. My argument is primarily normative—it justifies abstract republican political ideals by reference to their moral appeal, internal coherence, and so forth—yet it is rooted in methodological engagement with the sociological, context-dependent 'pre-notions' that implicitly inform theorizing in political philosophy. Thus, my argument is critical, both methodologically (it enriches the tools of analytical, normative political philosophy with insights drawn from critical social theory) and substantively (it argues against standard interpretations of the demands of republican citizenship in existing societies).

Traditions of Republicanism

There has recently been a revival of interest in the republican tradition in Anglo-American political theory.[1] While the tradition as a whole was centrally concerned with the themes of freedom, political participation, civic virtue, and corruption, it is, perhaps retrospectively, seen as exhibiting two strands. One, magisterially brought to life by John

Pocock, endorses the Aristotelian concern for the good life and argues that human beings can only realize their nature as 'political animals' through participation in self-governing communities.[2] Alongside this neo-Athenian strand of republicanism can be discerned a neo-Roman strand whose central concern is *libertas*—the powerful ideal of freedom under the rule of law passionately defended by Roman orators such as Cicero, and carefully elucidated in the writings of Quentin Skinner.[3] The neo-Roman theory of freedom, which prima facie is more suited to the anti-perfectionist and pluralist ethos of contemporary liberalism, has been given a systematic formulation in Philip Pettit's *Republicanism. A Theory of Freedom and Government* (1997).[4] Pettit's theory of freedom as non-domination is capacious enough to encompass and link together a number of traditional republican themes: individual liberty, the rule of law, popular deliberation, civic virtue, and the common good. According to the republican view, I am free only if I am recognized by others as enjoying a status that protects me resiliently against arbitrary interference and guarantees my equal status as a citizen living in community with others. In a word, I am free as a *citizen* of a particular state, a state that promotes the common good of non-domination. Pettit's theory of non-domination thus supports Jean-Jacques Rousseau's connection between *liberté* on the one hand and *égalité* and *fraternité* on the other.[5]

In a world pulled apart by the forces of economic and technological globalization, social privatization, cultural fragmentation, and the loss of political agency, republicans eloquently speak of the perceived need to rehabilitate the political ideal of citizenship.[6] Yet, at the same time, the revived republicanism of Anglo-American political thought is ill-equipped to contribute to important contemporary political debates. Its first limitation is that, because of its focus on the ultimate value of *political* citizenship, it has had comparatively little to say about so-called multicultural[7] controversies in existing societies. Republicans assume that, in an ideal world, cultural identities, while important to people's lives, should have minimal bearing on their citizenship, because they should be transcended through political engagement in a culturally and religiously neutral public sphere, and/or subsumed by an inclusive national identity. However, republicans have not systematically engaged with the pressing question of how to deal with actual identity-related claims in the real world, where what Will Kymlicka calls the 'benign neglect' of cultural and religious conflict is not an option.[8] Kymlicka further asserts that republicans cannot maintain their commitment to unitary citizenship once they jettison the myth of the ethno-cultural neutrality of the state.[9] I shall, in response, suggest practical ways in which republicans can bridge the gap between the non-neutrality of actual states and their culture-blind normative prescriptions. The second flaw of the Anglo-American tradition of republicanism is that, in the words of its historically minded advocates, it is a 'lost' tradition which fell victim to the hegemonic rise of the natural-rights language of Lockean liberalism from the late eighteenth century onwards. As a result, republicanism's central concepts mostly survive as linguistic traces in need of 'excavation' by historians highly conscious that their patient retrieval of the connections between freedom and the law, citizenship and participation, virtue and corruption run against the liberal intuitions of their readers.[10] Yet this assumption—that republicanism is a venerable tradition but not a living model—spectacularly ignores the fact that republicanism *is* the dominant language of modern politics in France, a cultural and philosophical idiom as pervasive as that of liberalism in other countries. What is more, this is a tradition that was partially revived, and re-invented, in response to real-world cultural conflict, such as the rise of a rightist, racist party (the Front National) in the early 1980s and the first hijab controversy (*affaire du foulard*) in 1989.[11] A second ambition of this book, therefore, is to assess the contribution of contemporary French republicanism to the normative republican response to multicultural conflict.

To be sure, the relationship between the French and the Anglo-American tradition of republicanism is ambiguous. Republicanism in France may seem to have 'gone native' to the point of blurring any 'family resemblance' with other republican traditions.[12] Its emergence is bound up with the revolutionary repudiation of the lessons of history and tradition, and is better understood by reference to the particular French context of centralized and absolutist monarchy in the age of Enlightenment than by comparison with past neoclassical experiments. Thus, French republicanism displays its own singular set of commitments, focused on the centralized nation-state and its direct relationship to the individual citizen, and founded on principles of universality and equality.[13] While a hitherto dominant liberal revisionist historiography has tended to present it as the upshot of an archaic, populist, revolutionary, statist, and illiberal egalitarianism,[14] recent contributions have begun to rehabilitate its distinctive contribution to modern progressive liberal thought,[15] and seek to re-situate it within a broader European tradition of republican reflection about the social and political conditions for freedom as non-domination.[16] Where French republicanism, however, may be seen to diverge from neoclassical republicanism is in its unambiguous endorsement of central Enlightenment tenets: in contrast to neo-Athenian republicanism, it is rooted in moral universalism and political rationalism (and is comparatively less populist and participatory), and in contrast to neo-Roman republicanism, it is unashamedly perfectionist (committed as it is to a progressive, humanist, and secular conception of the person). Mapping French republicanism onto the main lines of debate between Anglo-American liberals and communitarians is a no less difficult exercise.[17] French republicanism seems to incorporate central liberal intuitions, such as commitment to the impartiality of the state, the universal and egalitarian status of citizenship, the separation between public and private spheres, preference for individual over collective rights, commitment to individual autonomy, and a civic not ethnic mode of national identity. But it also appears communitarian in its advocacy of a strong public identity transcending private preferences and identities, its emphasis on the good of popular self-government, social solidarity, and cultural assimilation, and its commitment to the unitary nation-state as the chief site of citizenship.[18] As Karl Marx so acutely saw in *The Jewish Question*, the revolutionary French state operated the simultaneous elevation of discrete individuals into a general but abstract communal existence.[19] The ideals of *liberté*, *égalité*, and *fraternité* could only be realized in a distinctive, autonomous, *political* 'community of citizens'.[20]

Prima facie, such a tradition is singularly ill-suited to look positively on contemporary demands for the recognition of cultural and religious differences in the public sphere. And yet, the question as to how the republic should deal fairly with cultural and religious demands was at the centre of the complex debates which surrounded the hijab controversy between 1989 and 2004, when arguments for and against the ban on religious signs in schools were exchanged in public debate with a mixture of passion, sincerity, and ingenuity (along with less endearing motivations such as hostility, prejudice, and bad faith). This book uses the hijab controversy as the lens through which to analyse contemporary French republicanism. In doing so, it uses both interpretive and normative methods.

Methodological Considerations

By way of methodological clarification, let me start by setting out, and then discarding, two standard ways of interpreting 'foreign'— in my case French—texts and practices. The first I call 'synthetic' (or contextualist) and the second 'analytic' (or abstracting). The first approach is a fully contextualist, synthetic approach, prevalent in much of the field of French studies, inspired by the broader Cultural Studies movement. French republican discourse is seen as embedded in a richly textured tapestry of idiosyncratic historical, political, and social practices. The problem with this contextualist approach is that, in its almost anthropological focus on the radical *strangeness* of French republican political culture, it rarely attempts to see through discursive contextualization and capture ways in which the French may address general problems common to contemporary societies. Furthermore, contextualist analysis often illicitly smuggles in normative judgements, for example, castigating the French republicans' routine rejection of such *linguistic* categories as 'liberalism', 'race', and 'ethnic minorities' as symptomatic of their *substantially* illiberal, racist, and ethnocentric biases. French discourses and practices are unconsciously measured against a particular linguistic and normative background, with little attempt made—paradoxically—to account for the actual meanings of the concepts used in French discourse and their effects on political and social practice.[21] More promising is the second, analytic or 'abstracting' approach, which uses the tools of analytical philosophy to filter out what is culturally and historically particular, and therefore irrelevant to general philosophical concerns, and to translate the rest into general categories, give it a rational grounding and a formally logical structure. The aim is to distinguish, as far as possible, culturally and linguistically mediated misunderstandings from substantive agreements and disagreements. We can extract from French debates general logical propositions whose coherence, plausibility, and desirability can then be assessed. Basically, we help the French republican thinker address a wider audience— we do with him or her what historians of philosophy do with past thinkers. The problems with such an approach are essentially those identified by contextualist critics of traditional intellectual history such as Quentin Skinner. Abstracting or analytic approaches, by leaving out untranslatable concepts, obscure references to parochial traditions and rhetorical, emotional uses of language, might thereby leave out important aspects of meaning.[22] Let me take an example. In her otherwise stimulating analyses of the French hijab controversy, Elisabetta Galeotti presents the debates over the wearing of headscarves in French schools as symptomatic of the difficulties of liberal theories of neutrality and toleration in grappling with demands for the collective recognition of minority cultures.[23] However, she makes insufficient reference to the concept of *laïcité* (secularism) which—or so I shall argue—played the central justificatory (not only explanatory) role in these debates.

Comparative political theory has to navigate between these two reductionist approaches and avoid both the Scylla of synthetic incomprehension and the Charybdis of analytic mistranslation. Because the present work has an ultimately normative purpose—it aims to defend a general theory of republican citizenship applicable beyond the French context—it adopts a primarily analytic rather than synthetic approach.[24] It does not provide a full and contextual account of where, why, and by whom certain republican ideas were articulated in France; it seeks, rather, to account for their justificatory force by interpreting and reconstructing their logic as accurately as possible. Readers might then wonder why, if the purpose of the book is primarily normative, I spend so much time reconstructing and interpreting the logic of French republican arguments, instead of moving directly to defending or criticizing them. This is because, as I suggested in my comment about Galeotti's account of the hijab controversy, normative philosophers tend implicitly to rely on an overdrawn distinction between what have been called the 'contexts of justification' and the 'contexts of discovery'. The former refer to the factors (e.g. second-order commitment to the abstract values of neutrality and toleration) that can *rationally justify* belief in a first-order principle; the latter refer to the factors (e.g. the national ideology of *laïcité* in France) that may have *actually caused* a given theorist to adopt a principle.[25] The problem is that the analytical project of bracketing off what prima facie appears as a contingent and particularist context of discovery (such as the *laïcité* tradition) underestimates the implicit, taken-for-granted historical, social, and linguistic context in which the seemingly purely rational justification of abstract ideals of neutrality and toleration itself takes place. Thus, as Skinner said of the study of past ideas, the study of foreign ideas can help us redescribe and problematize our interpretations of the world, through the understanding of the unreflected assumptions we have inherited.[26] So ideological contextualization—in comparative political theory as in intellectual history—should not be a one-way but a two-way process: it invites us to denaturalize the presuppositions of our own discourse. In providing a relatively detailed account of the context without which certain French ideas would just not make sense, I merely provide, for French republicanism, what is implicitly already present, if often invisible, in Anglo-American liberal political philosophy—a set of pervasive linguistic conventions and sociological assumptions.[27] My ultimate purpose, however, is analytic and justificatory, not anthropological and contextual: I am interested in French ideas in so far as they can help us reflect about general problems. With these brief methodological considerations in mind, let me now set out the main issues raised by the hijab controversy.

Republicanism, Laïcité, and the Hijab Controversy

The law of 15 March 2004 stipulates that 'in primary and secondary public schools, the wearing of signs or clothes through which pupils ostensibly express a religious allegiance is forbidden'. The law's targets are Muslim headscarves, though Jewish yarmulkes and large Christian crosses are also banned in state schools. The law was intended to put an end to the 15-year long *affaire du foulard* which started in the Parisian suburb of Creil in the autumn of 1989 when two pupils came to class wearing Muslim scarves.[28] The incident—quickly politicized by all sides—sparked a hotly contested national debate about religious neutrality in republican schools, the dwindling status of public education in a fragmented society, the problematic legitimacy of traditional norms of authority and social integration, the status of women in minority cultures, the protracted liquidation of the colonial legacy, the politicization of race and immigration, the seemingly difficult integration of North African immigrants, fears about a 'conflict of civilizations' pitting the West against Islamic fundamentalism, and a sense of diffuse threat to French national identity.[29] More recently, in a number of European countries, hijab-related controversies have increasingly become the catalysts for a wider questioning of the ideals of pluralism and multiculturalism.[30] Focusing (at least in the interpretive sections of this book) on the French case, and on matters of principle rather than on prudential, prejudiced, or strategic considerations, I show that the wearing of hijab to school was highly controversial because it challenged three dimensions of the republican ideal of *laïcité* (secularism) at once.[31] The origins of *laïcité* are usually traced back to the 1789 Revolution, which brutally accelerated a century-long process of autonomization of the civil government from the Catholic Church. After a century of diffuse confrontation and failed compromise between the two institutions, *laïcité* became the official doctrine of the Third Republic (1870–1940) symbolized by such landmarks as the establishment of secular state primary education in the 1880s and the disestablishment of the Catholic Church in 1905. However, it would be a mistake to reduce *laïcité* to a conception of the proper relationship between state and religion, with particular attention paid to matters of education. *Laïcité* is a broader moral and social philosophy, a complex set of ideals and commitments which constitutes the closest equivalent— or perhaps direct alternative—in France to the liberal doctrine of toleration. *Laïcité* is often translated as 'secularism', but I argue that it in fact encompasses a comprehensive theory of republican citizenship, articulated around three ideals: equality (religious neutrality of the public sphere or secularism *stricto sensu*), liberty (individual autonomy and emancipation from religious oppression), and fraternity (civic loyalty to the community of citizens).[32] Thus, the wearing of the hijab in French schools raised three distinct issues at once:

(i) Equality-as-neutrality: is the religious neutrality (or secular nature) of the public sphere the best way to show equal respect to all citizens, religious and non-religious?

(ii) Liberty-as-autonomy: should republican education aim to emancipate children from the faith and culture inculcated by their family?

(iii) Fraternity-as-community: does the public recognition of cultural and religious difference undermine civic loyalty to the community of citizens?

To these questions, 'official republicans' (as I shall call them) answer in the affirmative; this is how they justify banning religious signs (the hijab in particular) in schools. In this view, the hijab can alternatively be seen as

(i) an ostentatious religious sign, which infringes the neutrality of the public sphere, in itself a guarantee of equality between all citizens,

(ii) a symbol of sexist oppression, which denies the liberty and autonomy of the girls wearing it,

(iii) a demand of recognition of cultural difference, which undermines national identity and trans-ethnic solidarity.

In response, 'tolerant republicans' (as I shall call them) have developed a range of arguments to defend the wearing of hijab in schools. Their main argumentative strategy, however, has been to denounce the gap between abstract republican prescriptions and social realities in France. Thus, they have pointed out that, in practice, the French public sphere is not religiously neutral, the hijab is not necessarily a form of female oppression, and members of minorities are in practice excluded from participation on fair terms in mainstream French national society. Tolerant republicans, I shall argue, have been more elusive in their normative prescriptions: do such social facts (if empirically ascertainable) make the republican ideals of liberty, equality, and fraternity hopelessly utopian ideals? If it is true that French society does not live up to its republican self-image, what should be done about it in practice? What is missing in the debate is a framework for incorporating critical social theory into republican normative philosophy. This is precisely what my *critical* republicanism seeks to provide. Critical republicanism is critical in the sense that it is not an 'ideal theory' but a practical philosophy, which takes at its core concern the normative relevance of such complex sociological facts as the relationships between culture and power, modes of immigrant integration, perceptions of ethnic relations, the foundation of civic cohesion, the place of religion in contemporary societies, the transformation of Muslim identities in the West, education in a pluralist society, gender and power, and the relationship between racial, sexual, and social disadvantage. Substantively, critical republicanism strongly criticizes the hijab ban but seeks to retrieve and rehabilitate, in a progressive direction, some of the republican concerns which motivate it. It thus offers its own version of the three ideals of *laïcité*: equality as secular impartiality, liberty as non-domination, and fraternity as trans-ethnic integration. In the next section, I provide a brief sketch both of the ideals and the strategic ambitions of my normative critical republican theory.

Normative Critical Republicanism: Substantive and Strategic

My approach invites a critical turn in normative political theory. Broadly speaking, this means that, in contrast to those schools of analytical political philosophy which exclusively focus on ideal moral norms on the one hand, or institutional legal norms on the other, critical republicanism enquires into three further dimensions of 'norms' which have traditionally been at the centre of critical social theory, from Karl Marx to Pierre Bourdieu and Jürgen Habermas.[33] These concern, respectively, the relationships between ideal norms and practical norms, legal norms and social attitudes, and cultural norms and power relationships. These should, I argue, be of particular concern to thinkers of the left—thinkers, that is, who have a direct interest in progressive, egalitarian reform in the real world, and whose political theory is designed to help this purpose.[34] Let me briefly outline their significance in turn.

(i) Ideal norms and practical norms. Are ideal principles directly applicable in the real world? French official republicans think so. This is partly because they implicitly assume that French society already meets basic republican standards and is 'well ordered', in John Rawls's sense. The philosophical defence of the hijab ban is, I shall show, an example of such 'ideal-applied' theory which fails to generate fair, practical norms for the real world. Note that this critique sidesteps the current debate within Anglo-American political theory, about how 'fact-sensitive' ideal theory should be.[35] My target, rather, is the kind of theory which claims *both* to identify ideal normative principles *and* to serve as a practical guide for reform in the real world. It is the kind of theory, in a word, that consciously or unconsciously confuses ideal and practical norms.

(ii) Legal norms and social attitudes. Should practical reform exclusively seek to design the right institutions and laws, or should it also seek to alter citizens' attitudes and ethos? While many liberals are suspicious of approaches which seek to transform people's preferences and behaviour, instead of taking them as they are,[36] others, most prominently socialists and republicans, have insisted that social attitudes and citizens' ethos are as important as just institutions and laws in creating and sustaining the ideal society.[37] Jerry Cohen, for example, has argued, *contra* Rawls, that the just society is one whose citizens adhere to principles of justice in their daily life;[38] and republicans have long insisted that republics cannot survive without citizens exhibiting civic virtue.[39] This insight tallies with an important dimension of the multicultural critique of liberalism, which insists that societal norms and attitudes (such as levels of racist prejudice, inter-group civility, religious tolerance, a spirit of social equality) are as important as legal rules and institutions in shoring up the status and self-esteem of members of cultural and religious minorities.[40]

(iii) Cultural identities and power relationships. Mainstream Anglophone multiculturalist theory has taken a rather uncritical view of the claims of 'culture', seeing them as a set of interconnected values, traits, customs, and institutions inherent to particular groups and pre-existing their interaction with wider society.[41] However accurate this may be in relation to the original groups for which the theory was elaborated (Aboriginals and Québécois in Canada, notably), it is radically inadequate as a template to understand the political dimensions of immigrant multiculturalism, especially in Europe.[42] Immigrants and their children are not so much the bearers of discrete, authentic, and self-contained cultures, as they are the targets of identity assignation from the outside, finding themselves stigmatized as foreigners, Arabs, Blacks, Pakistanis, Muslims, or (generically in France) *immigrés*. The critical literature on ethnicity and the social construction of difference has shown that contemporary cultural claims are shot through with relations of power and domination and shaped by the asymmetrically distributed power of recognition.[43] What defines a minority is precisely its vulnerability to 'identity assignation' by the majority[44]—a normative power which is not incompatible with the re-appropriation of stigmatized identities by their bearers (witness the assertion of Islamic identities among second- and third-generation immigrants in Europe).[45]

One distinctive contribution of critical republicanism is to analyse the way in which different kinds of norms (practical, social, and cultural) should be incorporated into contemporary political theory. These norms are relevant on the two levels at which the theory operates: substantive and strategic, ideal and practical. Let me say a little more about these two dimensions.

Substantive Ideals

Substantively, critical republicanism links together liberty, equality, and fraternity. As we have seen, such a connection is pivotal to both the Anglo-American and the French republican traditions. To recall, on the republican view, I am free when I am recognized by others as enjoying a status that resiliently protects me against arbitrary interference and guarantees my equal status as a citizen living in community with others. Republicanism is thus essentially a theory of citizenship. Broadly speaking, critical republicanism articulates a progressive, social-democratic, and inclusive version of republicanism. In line with other theories of democratic equality,[46] its ideal is that of a society where all citizens enjoy basic but robust civic standing, in the form of political voice, basic personal autonomy, equal opportunities, material capabilities, and intersubjective mutual recognition as equal citizens. In a republic, citizens enjoy not only the objective goods that membership in a fair scheme of social cooperation brings, but they also enjoy the subjective and intersubjective goods associated with such membership. Among such goods is the feeling that they are seen by others (and that they see others) as full members of such a scheme. Such attitudes of mutual civic recognition are fostered, not through the forcible inculcation of common values, let alone through the repression of deviance and dissent, but rather through the actual sharing of genuinely *public* spaces—from political forums to mixed neighbourhoods and common secular schools—where citizens learn to live together, argue and disagree together, and continuously re-invent their imagined collective identity. Critical republicans are social egalitarians: they are concerned about the quality of the relationships that citizens enjoy with one another, and about the way in which large inequalities of condition and differences in life experiences affect the common status of citizenship.[47] They are also concerned about the way in which economic inequality and social exclusion can motivate or exacerbate the divisive politicization of ethnic and cultural differences—a connection gravely underestimated in recent multicultural writings.[48] A politically inclusive and socially egalitarian society—an ideal republican society—would (it is hoped) successfully resist the politicization of identities, whether of majorities or of minorities. My critical republicanism, therefore, neatly converges with the civic, egalitarian liberalism which claims that identity-related claims should be subjected to the test of egalitarian justice and subordinated to the ideal of inter-ethnic solidarity.[49] Its distinctively republican inspiration, however, is betrayed by the importance it places on social norms and civic attitudes on the one hand, and on a robust public sphere of interaction and participation on the other.

Strategic Principles

Where, however, critical republicanism significantly improves on existing liberal and republican theories is that it deliberately articulates strategic, practical principles as well as substantive ideals. Or, more accurately, it denies that the former can be unproblematically derived from the latter. The problem is this. Recall that I have just suggested that ideal republican polities should be 'difference-blind' and secular. Yet it is clear that actual societies fall short of such republican ideals of equality and inclusion and that, partly as a result, cultural and religious differences have become an important mode of political mobilization. In such circumstances, the 'benign neglect' of cultural and religious claims is not an appropriate response. One problem with much of republican (and liberal) normative theory is that its proposals are designed to apply to ideal well-ordered societies, but they are also offered as practical proposals designed to guide reform in the real world. Thus, typically, multicultural issues are presented as raising questions about the legitimacy of *additional entitlements* (exemptions, special rights) for members of cultural minorities, and about the extent of their required *compliance* with accepted common norms. During the hijab controversy, for example, official republicans argued, first, that a universally secular public sphere does not unfairly discriminate against Muslims and, second, that citizens of foreign origin should make an effort to integrate into the national French community. Yet, even if such ideal principles are intuitively plausible, what was too often missing from official republican reasoning was an assessment of the legitimacy and fairness of existing status quo arrangements. How secular is the French public sphere in practice? How inclusive is the national identity that minorities are supposed to endorse as 'theirs'? Official republican reasoning tends to be marred by what I shall call the problem of *status quo neutrality*. Status quo neutrality is a theoretical position which unreflectively takes some background institution or distributive pattern for granted and, as a result, fails to provide an impartial baseline from which current claims about unjust treatment, misrecognition, domination, oppression, and the like can be normatively assessed.[50] Some of the justifications for the ban on the wearing of hijab in schools are examples of unreflective 'applied-ideal' political philosophy—where abstract principles are deemed directly to generate principles of policy—at its worst. In contrast to official republicanism, critical republicanism takes seriously the gap between ideal principles and social reality, and offers a *principled strategy for reform*.

Yet, *contra* multiculturalist critics of official republicanism, I shall defend the validity of ideal republican principles such as secular impartiality, civic integration, and liberty as non-domination. From the fact that existing societies do not meet ideal standards—they are ethnocentric, biased towards majorities, ethnically and socially segregated—a number of radical critics (often influenced by the writings of Michel Foucault) conclude that such ideals are only mystifying and oppressive ideologies which perpetuate the domination of majorities over minorities.[51] Yet this is a non sequitur, and one that is particularly damaging for the emancipatory and egalitarian prospects of the left. Critics often provide accurate and relevant social diagnoses, which are a useful antidote to the naïve sociology underpinning much abstract political philosophy, but their reasoning suffers from a double normative deficit—what Thomas Spragens has called the 'fragility of its ethical base'.[52] On the one hand, their evaluation of the legitimacy of the existing state of affairs is implicitly informed by unarticulated ethical ideals which are not radically dissimilar to the liberal or republican ideals they set out to discredit; and on the other hand, their narrowly critical stance leads to practical impotence and political cynicism.[53] What the left needs is to find a way to connect facts and norms, practical reforms and substantive ideals. In this book, I explore what this might imply in the context of protracted multicultural controversies, in particular those raised during the hijab controversy.

Critical republicans, *contra* official republicans, believe that the optimal compliance of citizens with republican principles cannot legitimately be required under conditions where those principles are only imperfectly realized and upheld by state institutions. To put it in Rawlsian terms: in non-ideal conditions, where the basic structure is not fully just, citizens may have (inter alia) a duty to strive to bring about just institutions, but they are not (non-reciprocally) required to abide by ideal principles of justice.[54] To put it in perhaps more apposite republican idiom: when institutions are corrupt, citizens cannot be expected to be fully virtuous. Here is a familiar republican conundrum: while in a non-corrupt, well-ordered republic, institutions and laws are supported by appropriate civic attitudes and virtue on the part of citizens, how much virtue should citizens display when institutions fall short of republican ideals? Of course, it can be legitimately argued that citizens who most benefit from current unjust institutions have a *pro tanto* duty to seek to uphold justice.[55] By contrast, it would be counter-intuitive to suggest that this duty should disproportionately fall on those who are disadvantaged and excluded from current institutions. Yet one problem in France, as is generally true, is that the burden of maintaining standards of civic virtue, patriotic allegiance, and secular restraint has too systematically fallen on minorities. Muslims suspected of lukewarm allegiance to principles of secular restraint or gender equality, second-generation immigrants blamed for 'refusing to be French', have been asked to behave as the exemplary citizens of (an increasingly elusive and idealized) French republic. The critical republican view that I defend suggests that it is institutions, instead of citizens, that should be 'republicanized' as a matter of priority. And when demands are made on minority citizens, they should be made on a reciprocal basis, rather than in isolation from the existing structure of legal and customary rights and entitlements.

To be sure, some demands made on minorities are ipso facto illegitimate. The ban on the hijab in schools, for example, cannot be defended on any of the main grounds presented by official republicans. I shall argue, notably, that the demand of secular restraint does not apply to schoolchildren, that the forcible removal of hijab is not a defensible mode of female emancipation, and that cultural and religious assertion in the public sphere should not be equated with a refusal to integrate. So the demand that Muslim schoolgirls take off their headscarf is, in almost all contexts,[56] wrong. Yet this is not the case for a number of connected demands, which may be contextually illegitimate and unfair, yet are defensible as part of an ideal republican settlement. In such cases, reciprocity must apply. For example, it is not illegitimate to refuse to grant certain cultural and religious rights to Muslims (e.g. the right to set up faith schools out of public funds), but only if the existing system of state regulation of non-Muslim religious schools—which falls well short of secular principles—is scrutinized and reformed. It is not illegitimate to impose the universal teaching of core civic skills, such as personal autonomy, in state schools, but only if the current curriculum is made more sensitive to the different ways in which autonomy can be exercised in pluralist societies. It is not illegitimate to request members of minorities to forego special assistance in the form of ethnically based policies of affirmative action, but only if more systematic efforts are made to fight ethnic discrimination on the one hand, and economic disadvantage and social and geographical segregation on the other. I shall argue, generally, that minority demands must be evaluated and responded to against the background of the burdens and benefits entailed by existing institutions and practices. While official republicans tend to reject minority demands on the ground that they are in breach of republican principles, and multiculturalists tend to approve minority demands on the ground that republican principles act only as ideological mystifications legitimizing actual majority domination, critical republicans assess the legitimacy of minority demands in relation both to the actual distribution of burdens and benefits in society and to ideal republican arrangements.

My basic objection to official republicanism, therefore, concerns not so much its substantive ideals as its strategy for reform. Too often, official republicanism functions as an uncritical ideology which both legitimizes the status quo by idealizing it and imposes unreasonable burdens of compliance on challengers, outsiders, and minorities.[57] Seeking to provide an attractive alternative, my critical republican proposals tend to be more radical and structural than standard republican (and liberal) proposals. This is because the actual realization of the ideals of religious impartiality, cultural inclusiveness, and social integration in existing societies will require the far-reaching reform of existing arrangements. In some cases, I shall advocate multicultural-sounding measures (such as the recognition of the contribution of minorities to national history or the promotion of members of 'visible minorities' to symbolic positions), liberal-sounding measures (such as greater impartiality of the state towards religions, in the form of diminished support for traditional religions), and republican-sounding measures (such as the robust defence of common secular schools and socially mixed neighbourhoods). On one level, my strategic approach is largely consequentialist, albeit constrained by a principle of fairness. It postulates that whatever helps us approximate the realization of our normative republican standards is to be encouraged, provided the burdens of reform are shared in a fair, public, and reciprocal way.[58] Yet, in another sense, my strategic approach consistently honours and promotes a distinct ideal, both as the means and end of reform. This broad but distinctive ideal is that of non-domination.

Critical Republicanism and Non-Domination

Here, I understand non-domination in a sense more general than Pettit's well-known defence of it as a theory of *freedom,* which provides an attractive alternative to both negative and positive conceptions. Pettit claims that freedom should not be equated with non-interference (as in negative liberty) nor with self-mastery (as in positive liberty) but, rather, with the absence of mastery by others.[59] The illuminating intuition underlying Pettit's approach, for my purposes, is twofold. On the one hand, he is committed to an anti-perfectionist and pluralist view of human freedom which does not affirm a particular conception of the good life or the value of particular cultures or identities. Freedom as non-domination, we might say, is content-neutral. On the other hand, Pettit insists that interference (notably state or legal interference) is not the only constraint on such content-neutral freedom: relationships of dependency, arbitrary power, social hierarchy can, too, be freedom-limiting. Such an expansive view of the constraints on freedom points to a critical republican understanding of *citizenship as non-domination,* and gives republicans valuable resources with which to approach multicultural controversies. Thus, expanding on Pettit's dual intuition, I argue that citizens do not need to have their particular identities and cultures positively recognized and affirmed by the state; they need only not to be dominated.[60] Citizens are dominated if (inter alia) they are subjected to 'institutionalized patterns of cultural value... that prevent [them] from participating as peers in social life'[61]—they are humiliated, stigmatized, marginalized, silenced, indoctrinated, defined by others, and their capacity for what I shall call 'minimal autonomy' and democratic voice is either denied or dismissed.[62] What exactly are those institutionalized patterns of cultural value, or dominating social norms, as I shall call them? They are social norms and rules which, when pervasive, internalized and partly institutionalized, profoundly affect the free and equal status of the members of certain groups. A classic example of a dominating social norm is sexism. Imagine a liberal society where fair equality of opportunities to all is guaranteed by the state: gender equality norms apply to all spheres of law, women have equal educational rights to men, and there are provisions associated with maternity, childcare, and part-time work. Yet, traditional patriarchal and sexist norms continue to permeate society. Women are expected to shoulder the greatest share of domestic labour, there is a 'glass ceiling' which limits their career prospects in prestigious and well-remunerated professions and, in many spheres of social life, they are reduced to their bodies and appearance. In sum, despite being legally treated as citizens, they are socially dominated. In this book, I suggest that attitudes of *ethnicization*—where citizens are reduced to their presumed identity, culture, or religion, and consequently stigmatized as immigrant, Arab, or Muslim—can function in similar ways to sexism (and often operate in parallel to it, as my analysis of the double domination of Muslim women by patriarchal and neo-colonial discourse will show).

There is an important debate, within contemporary Anglo-American philosophy, about whether the liberal theory of justice—with its emphasis on just laws and institutions, rather than on the ethos and attitudes exhibited by citizens—is able to provide an account of what is wrong with dominating social norms and, if it can, whether it is equipped to combat them. Socialists claim that liberals neglect the way in which only an *ethos* of solidarity and citizenship—when non-dominating norms prevail—can make good the formally equal rights of the liberal state.[63] Some liberals dispute the charge, suggesting that a fully just 'basic structure', to use John Rawls's expression, would promote an egalitarian ethos, ensure that no one suffers from the effects of social domination, and guarantee the 'social bases of self-respect' to all.[64] Others accept the charge and defend the liberal focus on institutional design rather than social ethos. They argue that the reduction of dominating social norms would compromise the liberal commitment to pluralism, impose too burdensome duties of personal conduct on citizens, and involve the illiberal 'policing of beliefs' by the state. They also point out that the identification of dominating social norms, given their subjective and agent-relative dimension, would fall foul of the liberal commitment to the public nature and scrutiny of standards of justice.[65] How do critical republicans situate themselves in relation to this crucial debate? Like social democrats, feminists, and multiculturalist theorists of recognition, critical republicans insist that non-dominating social norms and attitudes matter as much to the status of citizenship as just laws and institutions. But they also argue that the state can combat dominating social norms without having to 'police beliefs' and without having publicly to assert and recognize the value of socially dominated identities and forms of life. There are many ways in which *institutional* change and reform, rather than the direct inculcation of norms or the punishment of non-politically correct opinions, can contribute to altering dominating social norms, in symbolic rather than coercive ways. This is particularly the case in non-ideal, existing societies where ethnocentric 'soft rules' still permeate both social life *and public institutions*.[66] Following Elisabetta Galeotti, I would argue that such soft rules are an important site of the experienced exclusion of minorities in actual societies, particularly in formerly culturally homogeneous Western European nation-states. There, minorities are *constituted* through the 'normality-defining' power of the majority: they are not so much defined by adherence to specific conceptions of the good or distinct ways of life under conditions of moral and cultural pluralism, as they are parties in a certain kind of power relationship where they are socially constructed artefacts of the beliefs and perceptions of the majority.[67] More specifically, many multiculturalist controversies, of which the French hijab case is only one example, arise out of the perceived discrepancy between the legal status of equal citizenship and the prevalence of ethnocentric social and institutional norms. Examples of such norms or 'soft rules' are the prevalence of racist and anti-Muslim prejudice in society, the objectification of 'minorities' or immigrants in public discourse (where they are its objects rather than its subjects), persistent traces of religious (Christian) establishment in social life and institutional structures, and a diffuse ethnocentrism permeating public education and historical narratives. In contrast to Brian Barry, who thinks that some degree of cultural and religious partiality is trivial provided its effects are purely symbolic and do not infringe on citizens' basic rights and opportunities,[68] I argue that symbols do matter in multicultural societies.[69] In so far as they have an impact on who is *perceived to be* a member of the community, they affect the intersubjective status of citizenship. Furthermore, many soft rules have an institutional and public component: they constitute what Nancy Fraser calls 'externally manifest and publicly verifiable impediments to people's standing'.[70] By targeting the dominating structure of institutional social arrangements, instead of diffuse discursive cultural representations, Fraser rightly seeks to avoid the illiberal consequences associated with the 'thought police' of political correctness. Yet, I also share the intuition behind Barry's polemic against theorists of multicultural recognition: in many cases, real-world multicultural conflict must be addressed, not through the granting of identity-specific group rights, but through the more consistent application of liberal, difference-blind ideals of equality and impartiality. My critical republican rejoinder merely adds that such ideals can only be realized if the impact that culturally biased soft rules and dominating social norms have on the intersubjective status of citizenship is taken seriously. And this may require more radical institutional reform than most liberals assume.

Critical republican non-domination, therefore, requires the removal of obstacles to the full participation of members of minorities as citizens. These obstacles are mostly socio-economic (in the form of substantive opportunities) and symbolic and discursive (in the form of dominating social norms and ethnocentric soft rules). Members of minorities are better served by an ideal of non-domination, which identifies the specific ways in which they are excluded from citizenship in actual societies, than by the de-contextualized application of negative principles of difference-blind equality or positive principles of identity-conferring recognition (although non-domination in practice might require both negative and positive policies). We can bring out the force of this point by drawing on Peter Jones's distinction between *unmediated merit recognition* and *mediated status recognition*, where the former refers to the direct and positive validation of particular identities and ways of life, and the latter to the more general granting of equal value to all individuals as persons or as citizens, which may also indirectly translate into respect for the identities that *they* value.[71] Jones is right to suggest that struggles for recognition should best be interpreted as demands for mediated status recognition: very often, as even proponents of the so-called politics of difference such as Iris Marion Young have recognized, 'claims for recognition usually function as part of or means to claims against discrimination, unequal opportunity, political marginalization, or unfair burdens'.[72] But what Jones underestimates is the extent of the publicly validated, institutionalized structures of merit recognition of dominant identities in existing societies. The republican ideal of universal *status* recognition, in sum, can only be achieved through the reduction of unequal *merit* recognition in existing societies. Critical republicans, therefore, advocate the scrutiny of those pervasive soft rules and customary status quo arrangements which entrench the merit recognition of majorities and thereby undermine the status recognition of minorities. Thus, in the first part of this book, I shall argue that members of religious minorities would benefit from *more* rather than *less* secularism, if this is understood as the construction of a less Christian-biased, genuinely neutral public sphere showing respect to all citizens. In the second part, I will show that members of minorities would also benefit from *more* rather than *less* autonomy-related skills, if autonomy is conceived as a culturally neutral tool with which to combat domination, whether that of the majority or of minorities (such as that embedded in patriarchal, sexist traditional arrangements). Finally, the third part will suggest that members of minorities would benefit from *more* rather than *less* national solidarity: they are not well served by ideals of 'post-national' citizenship which end up validating their status of second-class denizens excluded from the still largely ethnicized national imaginary. Critical republicanism interprets struggles for recognition as struggles for 'voice' and for participation, be it economic, social, cultural, or political.

Overall, then, critical republicanism recommends strategies of civic incorporation of minorities, mostly (though not exclusively) through the de-ethnicization of existing norms and practices. The identities of minorities may be positively validated and recognized by the state only if this is the more effective way for their members not to be dominated: stigmatized, silenced, and reduced to an ascriptive and imposed identity. Arguably, in many (though in no way all) cases of so-called multicultural controversies, members of minorities have suffered not from insufficient recognition but from an excess of recognition of the wrong kind. Too often, their presumed cultures and religions are portrayed as essentialist, anthropological, and self-contained wholes within which individuals are immersed and from which they derive their profound beliefs and motivations for action. This not only ignores the constructed, interactionist, and political dimension of most identities seeking recognition in contemporary pluralist societies, and inadequately accounts for the multifaceted, post-colonial experience of children of immigrants in Europe, but it also tends to reduce grave and complex phenomena such as the Islamist radicalization of some alienated young Muslims to a cultural 'clash of civilizations' between the abstractly defined entities of 'Islam' and 'the West'. Of course, critical republicanism makes no pretence that it can explain, let alone offer remedies to, such problems. What it more modestly seeks to show is that neither the radical multiculturalist rhetoric of the recognition of difference as an alternative to the ideal of civic inclusion nor the liberal and republican unconscious idealization of status quo arrangements in actual Western societies have helped reduce the 'citizenship deficit' of members of minorities. Both, in fact, have underestimated the appeal of the republican ideal of inclusive citizenship, when this is critically understood and applied, as I seek to do in this book, by interrogating the complex relationships between ideal and practical norms on the one hand, and the ends and means of progressive reform on the other.

To conclude this brief presentation of critical republicanism, what can be said about its contribution to contemporary normative multicultural political philosophy? It should already be clear that critical republicanism diverges, on a fundamental level, from radical, post-colonial, post-national, and post-secular forms of multiculturalism, which lack a plausible theory of common citizenship. But where exactly does my critical republican theory differ from the multiculturalism of liberal egalitarian philosophers such as Kymlicka, who advocates a range of ethno-cultural rights intended to assist the civic integration of immigrant communities in European states? Critical republicanism shares some common ground with the revised ('third-stage') multicultural theory articulated by Kymlicka.[73] First, they both focus on contextual justice and status quo reform, rather than on the abstract discussion of the legitimacy of departures from abstract neutrality, in the form of special rights or privileges for minorities. As Kymlicka points out, in the real world, minority rights can be a legitimate response to nation-building processes which unfairly advantage historical majorities. Second, both liberal multiculturalism and critical republicanism advocate fair terms of integration for immigrants. Kymlicka rightly points out that, in contrast to national minorities and indigenous groups, immigrant groups do not wish to preserve a separate, comprehensive 'societal culture' alongside mainstream society. Rather, whatever ethno-cultural rights they are granted serve to facilitate their civic integration as equal citizens.[74] Critical republicanism similarly subordinates identity recognition to the claims of the political identity of citizenship.

Where, then, does critical republicanism differ from Kymlicka's theory? Importantly, critical republicanism is not (or not primarily) a theory of culture and multiculturalism. This is because it emphatically denies that the key variable in the integration of citizens of immigrant/Muslim/post-colonial origin in Western Europe is their culture and its recognition as such. There are three dimensions to this denial. First, immigrant minority exclusion in Europe is more likely to be rooted in race and class than in culture or religion, as my analysis of the socio-economic exclusion of second- (and third-) generation immigrants in France will show. Multicultural ideology largely misdiagnoses the problem; as Kwame Anthony Appiah put it in relation to Afro-Americans in the United States: 'culture is not the problem, and it is not the solution'.[75] Second, critical republicans take seriously the specific issues raised by religion (as distinct from culture) and seek to formulate a theory of secularism sensitive to the religious non-neutrality of European states and to the need for the recognition of Islam on a par with other religions. Third and finally, critical republicans are less deferential than multiculturalists towards the claims of culture, because they harness a critical theory of the social and political construction of difference to the republican ideal of difference-blind citizenship. Thus, while Kymlicka's liberal culturalism values cultural identities as essential contexts for the exercise of individual autonomy, critical republicans worry that individual autonomy (and civic solidarity) may be threatened by the outside imposition of stigmatized identities—such as those of immigrant, Arab, or Muslim. While multiculturalists advocate the public recognition of specific groups, such as 'immigrants' (Kymlicka) or 'Muslims' (Modood), critical republicans do not single out any pre-defined and fixed group as the object of their concerns. They claim, rather, that citizens who find themselves associated with these groups have diverse citizenship entitlements which address different types of disadvantage. Thus, the book will show that *qua* members of a racialized underclass, such citizens would benefit from genuinely colour-blind socio-economic integration; *qua* Muslims, they need a revised theory of the inclusive secular state; *qua* members of post-colonial minorities, they deserve recognition of their contribution to the nation's history and culture; and *qua* 'minorities within minorities' (e.g. women), they need the robust promotion of their ability to resist multifaceted domination. Critical republicans, then, pursue no single strategy of ethno-cultural (or religious) recognition; and are more likely to advocate the de-ethnicization and disestablishment of dominant cultures and identities (when possible) as the best strategy for the civic incorporation of minorities members. Members of minorities have an overriding interest in being recognized as full citizens of the state. While this may at times require that their beliefs and practices be positively accommodated, in most cases it will demand that they are not dominated—that mainstream institutions and practices do not unduly restrict their opportunities for civic participation. In practice, some of the critical republicans' concrete proposals may converge with those of liberal multiculturalists, yet their premises, and their priorities, differ markedly from theirs.[76]

The critical republican ideal is not so much a multicultural polity where cultural diversity is valued as a public good, as a republican polity where no citizen is dominated because of their (presumed or re-appropriated) cultural identity. Critical republicanism can justify fair terms of integration to members of minorities by rectifying the dominating effect of status quo biases. Thus, while Kymlicka asks that 'common institutions provide the same degree of respect, recognition and accommodation of the identities and practices of immigrants as they traditionally have of the identities and practices of the majority group',[77] critical republicans more realistically concentrate on rectifying the most severe dominating effects of neo-colonial oppression or Christian establishment. And while Kymlicka vaguely suggests that 'robust forms of nation-building should be combined and constrained by robust forms of minority rights',[78] critical republicans advocate non-domination as the unifying ideal which informs both the ends and the means of citizenship policies. The advantage of my understanding of non-domination is that, while it captures multiculturalists' concern about the exclusionary effects of cultural symbols, discourses, and customs in existing states, it puts a premium on the identity of citizenship, thus justifying, when feasible, the disestablishment and de-politicization of cultural and religious identities, and it advocates difference-sensitive common institutions, rather than separate institutions. To the extent that Kymlicka endorses these broad ideals—to the extent, that is, that he explicitly seeks to harness minority rights to civic goals—I would argue that his revised theory is not as multicultural as he claims. Recall that Kymlicka's original multicultural defence was rooted in the thought that individual autonomy can be exercised only within distinct societal cultures, such as those exhibited by national minorities and indigenous groups.[79] Yet, as immigrants, in Kymlicka's own view, are not the bearers of such societal cultures and are expected to integrate within the dominant culture, the normative basis on which their distinct interests are accommodated at all remains unclear. Critical republicanism, as a theory of citizenship, provides such a basis, with its emphasis on the motivational foundations of civic allegiance and on the egalitarian idea of non-domination.

As a corollary of its comprehensive social approach, the contribution of critical republicanism to contemporary political theory extends beyond controversies about multiculturalism. In particular, it applies the theory of non-domination to areas hitherto ignored or neglected by Anglophone republicans such as Pettit. Let me summarize critical republican contributions in two such areas: social critique and the ideal of citizenship. First, my approach firms up the relationship between republicanism and critical theory broadly understood. On the one hand, I interpret republican reflection as rooted in non-ideal theory and political *praxis*, concerned not so much with ideal theories of justice as with the correction of actual relationships of power and domination. I expand on Pettit's insight that the ideal of non-domination helps us reflect upon the problem of the arbitrary state (*imperium*) asking how a state marked by Christian establishment and a colonial past can reduce the domination it exerts on its non-Christian, post-colonial minorities. Thus, for example, I develop a new republican theory of the secular state, as a state which does not dominate religious believers, ensures rough equality between majority and minority religions, while preserving a secular public sphere of common citizenship. On the other hand, critical republican theory builds on Pettit's insight that the most pervasive forms of domination are found in the private sphere of family, religion, and the market (*dominium*). Critical republicanism significantly improves on Pettit's theory, however, by pointing to forms of domination which, being the product of indoctrination, manipulation, and norm internalization, remain invisible to their victims. Thus, critical republicanism connects with social critics of domination, from Marxists to feminists, and brings new thoughts to the dialectic between female oppression and emancipation.

Second, critical republicanism sets out a distinctive theory of the good of citizenship. On the one hand, it strongly advocates autonomy-promoting education yet denies that the actual exercise of autonomy is an ingredient of the good life. People need not live autonomously to be good citizens, but they need to have the appropriate skills to combat servility and domination in public and private life. More generally, in religion and culture, critical republicanism favours democratic strategies of voice and dissent over liberal strategies of choice and exit. The other major critical republican contribution to citizenship is its rehabilitation of the solidaristic and egalitarian dimensions of national citizenship, both in its material (socio-economic) and imagined (intersubjective) dimensions. *Contra* post-national thinkers, I show that minority members have an important interest in belonging, and being seen to belong, to the national community, given that the latter remains an important locus of identification for the majority. To deny that they have such an interest is to validate their second-class status in existing societies—it is, for example, to validate popular perceptions that women wearing hijab are not and cannot be French. I shall argue that only a radical strategy of de-ethnicization of the republic can fairly integrate members of minorities as equal citizens

Critical republicanism, therefore, develops a radical, comprehensive, and progressive interpretation of Pettit's theory of non-domination, enriching the paradigm of neo-Roman freedom with the Rousseauian themes of citizenship, social equality, education, religion, and patriotism. As a result, critical republicanism should appeal to the Left as a political project and strategy for reform. Thus, in line with the broad social aims of feminist and anti-racist movements, it targets social and private, not only public and political, structures of domination. By politicizing some areas of interpersonal relations, critical republicanism is more open to structural social reform than political liberalism.[80] In line with social equality theorists, critical republicanism advocates not only the just distribution of goods and resources but also the expansion of basic powers, virtues, and capabilities, including those of personal autonomy, civic skills, and self-respect.[81] In line with civil society-based theories of radical democracy, critical republicanism stresses the importance of forums of contestatory democracy, both in the public and in the private sphere.[82] It also follows social democratic critiques of identity politics and of communitarian social theories in interpreting community-building and social cohesion as primarily social and political, rather than cultural and moral, processes. And, finally, it connects with a central commitment of the Left as a political movement, by presenting republican struggles as struggles to reduce the actual gap between the social fact of domination and the ideals of liberty, equality, and fraternity. These are just some of the arguments developed in this book.

By now, it should be clear that this book is not specifically about France. Or if it is, it is so in the same way that Anglo-American political philosophy implicitly speaks to the parochial public culture of the United States, Canada, and the United Kingdom. There is, admittedly, an important difference. Contemporary Anglo-American analytical liberal philosophy is an abstract, technical, and academic discipline self-consciously detached from concrete historical traditions and particular political debates. French republicanism, by contrast, is better conceived of as a 'public philosophy' or national ideology, mostly articulated and diffused by public intellectuals, politicians, and the media, and operating on lower levels of abstraction and philosophical sophistication than Anglo-American analytical liberalism.[83] Yet, French republicanism also has universalistic ambitions, and it is these that I seek to rescue and rehabilitate. But to do so, as I have suggested above, requires that proper interpretive tools be put to use. Anglo-American philosophers too quickly tend to understand the hijab controversy as being about intolerance of difference and the legitimacy of basic religious rights—important themes which, however, are only part of the story I want to tell. My normative proposals, therefore, are rooted in a critical interpretation of a rich and complex national discourse. It is also my hope that the detour *via* the French context will, in turn, bring out the sociological, context-dependent 'pre-notions' that implicitly inform abstract theorizing in Anglo-American political philosophy. Such theorizing is often based on John Rawls's method of reflective equilibrium, which seeks coherence between theoretical principles and intuitive judgements. It is the status of such intuitive judgements that a more critical, interpretive, and comparative theory unsettles. Turning finally to the last section of this introduction, I now explain how the interpretive and the normative dimensions of this book are related.

Structure of the Book

This book contains three parts, the first on *égalité* as secularist neutrality, the second on *liberté* as female autonomy, and the third on *fraternité* as national solidarity. Each part contains two interpretive chapters and one normative chapter. The interpretive chapters present an analysis of the French hijab debates, reconstructing the argument of advocates (official republicans) and critics (tolerant republicans) of the ban in turn (Chapters 2, 3, 5, 6, 8, 9).[84] In both cases, I attempt to reconstruct their strongest, most persuasive version, often filling out missing logical links and spelling out unarticulated, culturally specific assumptions. It is important to stress that those chapters do not represent my own views—they set out and reconstruct the most convincing interpretation of the views I seek to discuss. Building on the opposite sides of the argument, I then develop my own ideas in the three normative chapters (Chapters 4, 7, 10). As suggested above, my critical republicanism finds faults with the excessive 'normativism' and idealizing proclivity of official republicanism, and it also departs from the unprincipled 'sociologism' and normative deficit of their critics. Official republicans tend to be good philosophers, and tolerant republicans good social critics. Critical republicanism, in its attempt to provide a practical yet principled progressive response to multicultural conflict, seeks (optimistically) to combine good philosophy and good social theory. Quite often, this means that critical republicanism endorses the empirical findings put forward by tolerant republicans, and attempts to incorporate them into a more realistic, revised normative republican theory. At other times, critical republicanism finds that the sociological (and sometimes theological) evidence on which the respective theories rely is, at best, contestable and contested, and it articulates principles that do not presume their truth or falsity. Of course, my critical republican theory does not claim fully to address the range and complexity of the arguments exchanged by official and tolerant republicanism during the hijab controversy. But it takes a view on the most important, and the most challenging, of them, from the perspective of the (sociologically minded) political philosopher. Let me now briefly summarize the argument of each chapter in turn.

Chapter 2 presents the official republican view of secularism as a theory of neutrality and equal concern. In this view, citizens are treated fairly if they live under a religiously neutral (neither religious nor anti-religious) public sphere. Chapter 3 reconstructs the *laïcité ouverte* objection, which points out that, as the state in practice tolerates the expression of certain religions in the public sphere, all religions should benefit from an even-handed extension of recognition. In Chapter 4, I defend my own 'critical secularist' proposals, which attempt to theorize how to reduce the domination of Muslims in a non-neutral society, in a way that promotes the republican ideal of the impartial and civic public sphere. I argue that the state should, in general, not support or recognize religions unless not doing so infringes a basic religious right or gravely undermines contextual parity (the actual parity of status between majority and minority religions).

Chapter 5 introduces the official republican defence of liberty as individual rational autonomy, and the idea that the republican state must emancipate vulnerable and oppressed young girls by banning dominating, patriarchal practices in its schools. Chapter 6 presents a range of radical feminist objections, which both denounce the paternalistic imposition of a controversial conception of the good on minority members and which point out that the wearing of the hijab is not incompatible with freedom and agency. In Chapter 7, I defend my own interpretation of liberty as non-domination, which requires that citizens not be forcibly liberated from contested oppressive practices, but rather equipped with culturally neutral, autonomy-related skills, and given opportunities for effective political *voice*, so that they can resist domination, oppression, manipulation, and indoctrination in their private and social life.

Chapter 8 introduces the official republican case for requiring minorities to endorse national identity and privatize their cultural and religious differences, in the name of civic, inter-ethnic solidarity. Chapter 9 challenges the official republican account of civic solidarity, pointing out that in practice French national identity has imperialist, ethnocentric, and racist foundations. The application of a difference-blind model of integration has contributed to the ethnicization and exclusion of racially defined minorities, which should, conversely, be positively recognized. In Chapter 10, I defend a revised model of republican integration, which emphasizes the political and socio-economic prerequisites of the fair incorporation of members of minorities and, instead of the recognition of the 'Other', advocates the profound and inclusive transformation of the 'We' that underpins the imagined community of the nation.

PART 1

Égalité and Republican Neutrality

CHAPTER 2

Official Republicanism, Equality, and the Hijab

It is often remarked that the key principles of liberalism—separation between public and private spheres, religious toleration, and equality before the law—were articulated in response to the religious conflicts of post-Reformation Europe. Historically, liberalism has been committed, at least minimally, to a weak version of secularism, which requires the state to abstract from divisive religious views and to appeal to values likely to provide a common point of allegiance for all citizens, regardless of their confessional loyalties. Religion should be removed from public affairs and confined to a politically indifferent private sphere. The de-politicization and privatization of religion was not merely a pragmatic, prudential solution to the political instability brought about by the religious wars of the sixteenth and seventeenth centuries. The autonomy of the political sphere from religious institutions and beliefs became an enduring liberal ideal because it offered a powerful articulation of the Enlightenment moral vision of universal rights, freedom, and equality. By abolishing the privileges enjoyed by members of the dominant church, the state guaranteed the free exercise of religious freedoms for all in the private sphere. By establishing a non-sectarian, neutral public sphere, it ensured that all enjoyed the status of equal citizenship, as common membership in a political community transcending particular beliefs and allegiances. It can be said, therefore, that secularism as a doctrine of separation between the political and the religious spheres provided an early, paradigmatic articulation of the liberal ambition to combine the protection of individual freedoms and the diversity of conceptions of the good in society with shared norms of political membership as equal status. Central to this doctrine was the ideal of liberal equality, an ideal which also underpins most recent liberal discussions of state neutrality. Broadly speaking, a state is neutral when it refrains from appealing to controversial moral values and draws instead on principles which all citizens can endorse, thereby—on a contractualist account of political justification—treating them with equal respect.[1]

In this chapter, I argue that the French principle of *laïcité* can be seen as a version of the liberal ideal of equality as state neutrality.[2] I have sketched out this liberal ideal in its broad outlines, leaving aside the variety of its institutional embodiments (disestablishment being merely one option) as well as the complex discussions about the liberal concept of neutrality. I have merely tried to suggest that what may be called the secular core of liberalism embodies a combination of the three principles of freedom of religion, equal respect, and state neutrality. Those three principles were recently articulated as providing the central values of *laïcité* in the official report of the Stasi Commission, which was convened by President Jacques Chirac in the summer of 2003 to give advice on whether Muslim schoolgirls should be allowed to wear headscarves in state schools.[3] It is in the name of the republican principle of *laïcité* that the law of 15 March 2004 was voted, which banned 'the wearing of signs or clothes through which pupils ostensibly express a religious allegiance'. This chapter seeks to reconstruct the secular case for the ban in its most plausible form. In what follows, I spell out the implications of the French doctrine of separation of church and state, showing notably how it embodies liberal ideals of equality and neutrality.

I also suggest that *laïcité* offers a distinctively *republican* interpretation of the requirements of liberal neutrality, which notably emerged as a response to the bitter conflicts between French republican institutions and the Catholic Church. In broad terms, republican *laïcité* endorses a more expansive conception of the public sphere than political liberalism, as well as a thicker construal of the 'public selves' which make up the citizens of the republic. So, crucially, state schools are seen to be part of the public sphere and pupils, as potential citizens, are required to exercise restraint in the expression of their religious beliefs. The ban on Muslim hijab in schools, in this view, helps protect the neutral public sphere from religious interference and secure a system of equal religious rights for all. In other words, limits on the exercise of religious liberties in the public sphere are necessary conditions for the maintenance of a system of equal liberties for all. Therefore *laïcité*, like secular liberalism, attempts to weigh out the sometimes conflicting principles of freedom of religion, equality between citizens, and state neutrality. The key difference between liberal secularism and republican *laïcité* is that the latter makes greater demands on state institutions (in terms of abstention and non-discrimination) and on its citizens (in terms of restraint). *Laïcité*, like many doctrines of separation between state and religion, contains both an *institutional doctrine of separation*, which outlines what separation means for governmental institutions (Section I), and a *doctrine of conscience*, which prescribes norms of conduct both for religious organizations and for individual citizens (Section II).[4] When applied to state schools, the separation doctrine and the doctrine of conscience combine to justify the ban on Muslim headscarves (Section III). I conclude that the ban on Muslim hijab in schools furthers five central values of secular philosophy. Or so, at least, official republicans claim. The next two chapters will critically assess the cogency of the case that this chapter sets out as convincingly as possible.

I. Laïcité *as a Separation Doctrine*

On 11 December 1905, republicans in power abolished the Concordat which, since 1801, had regulated the relationships between the French state and 'recognized religions' and had, in practice, entrenched the political and social power of the dominant Catholic Church. The first two articles of the 1905 Law of Separation between Church and State read:

> Article 1. The Republic ensures freedom of conscience. It guarantees the free exercise of religions.
> Article 2. It neither recognizes nor subsidizes any religion.

The principle of separation between church and state has since been recognized as a quasi-constitutional principle, and is implicitly referred to in Article 1 of the 1946 Constitution, according to which 'France is an indivisible, *laïque*,[5] democratic and social republic'. The 1905 Law of Separation embodies a classical ideal of liberal separation between state and religion, underpinned by an individualistic and egalitarian conception of justice as best pursued through state abstention from religious affairs. As a prominent public lawyer puts it, 'In law, what is *laïcité*? It is deduced from the principle of equality: from the principle of equality follows that of the neutrality of the state and public authorities, and *laïcité* is no more than this principle applied to religious affairs.'[6] In order to clarify the sense in which the Separation Law embodies an ideal of egalitarian justice as state neutrality, I first identify four strands that make up the separation doctrine: libertarian (Section I.A), egalitarian

(Section I.B), agnostic (Section I.C), and individualistic (Section I.D).[7] When combined, they are shown to lend themselves to a conception of formal, rather than substantive, equality between religions (Section I.E). French *laïcité*, in this sense, tallies with the influential defence of liberal principles of formal equality before the law and 'the privatization of difference' recently reiterated, with characteristic vigour, by Brian Barry.[8] Where, however, *laïcité* slightly diverges from such egalitarian liberalism is in its republican emphasis on the strict preservation of the autonomy of the secular public sphere, which is regulated by an independent ethics and more expansively constructed than standard liberal understandings would allow (Sections I.F and I.G).

A. A Libertarian Principle

The state permits the practice of any religion, within limits prescribed by the requirements of public order and the protection of basic rights. It neither promotes nor combats particular religious beliefs, and refrains from interfering in the internal affairs of religious institutions. The principle of religious freedom was first (ambiguously) asserted during the 1789 Revolution: in the wording of Article 10 of the Declaration of the Rights of Man, 'no one should be persecuted [*inquiété*] for their opinions, even religious ones'. A century later, the principles both of religious freedom and of religious pluralism were entrenched by the Third Republic: the 1905 Law of Separation graphically symbolized the removal of state control of religion, and the recognition of the pluralist structure of background religious institutions in civil society.

The principle of religious freedom is 'libertarian' in the narrow sense that it chiefly requires that the state *refrain* from interfering in religious affairs. Thus, Article 1 of the 1905 law ('the republic *guarantees* the free exercise of religions') is typically understood by official republicans not to mandate positive state aid to religions: the exercise of religious freedoms should simply not be unduly constrained or burdened by the state. Religions should be allowed to flourish in the private sphere without state interference, according to the zeal and organizational capacities of their adherents and the appeal of their dogma. Only in particular cases should the state provide financial aid to support the exercise of religious freedoms. For example, the 1905 law authorized the public funding of chaplaincies in 'closed' institutions such as the army, prisons, and boarding schools, so as to guarantee rights of religious exercise to those physically unable to attend normal religious services. But this is a rare justifiable exception to the general principle of state abstention. On the whole, therefore, the combination of the provisions of Articles 1 and 2 of the 1905 Separation Law is not deemed to generate a conflict of principles similar to that between the 'non-establishment' and the 'free exercise' clause of the First Amendment of the US Constitution.[9] In American jurisprudence, the protection of the 'free exercise' clause sometimes requires relaxing the 'establishment' clause, by compelling the state to step in positively to guarantee that adequate provision is available for the exercise of (notably minority) religious rights. French official republicans generally believe that non-establishment and state abstention are in themselves sufficient guarantees of the free exercise of religious freedoms.

B. An Egalitarian Principle

Minimally understood, the egalitarian principle requires that the state does not give preference to one religion over another: the equality referred to here is equality between believers of all faiths. This goes beyond the libertarian principle, as the state can theoretically allow unlimited religious freedom and still treat some religions preferentially. Thus, French republicans typically refer to the 'weak establishment'[10] of the Anglican Church as falling short of the egalitarian principle.[11] Even though religious freedoms and religious pluralism are fully protected in the United Kingdom, establishment in itself confers material and symbolic privileges to adherents of the majority confession. In France, under the Concordat, throughout the nineteenth century, Catholicism was similarly recognized as 'the religion of the great majority of the French' (without, however, being the official religion of the state), a status which conferred benefits unavailable to the other 'recognized religions', Protestantism and Judaism. The 1905 law aimed to place all religious institutions on an equal plane.

Naturally, this entailed a *capitis diminutio* to the detriment of the Catholic Church: equality between all religions essentially meant the abolition of the privileges of the dominant church. However, strong hostility to the Separation Law by the Vatican, and reluctance by French Catholic authorities to implement it, led republicans to make a number of concessions (notably allowing free use by Catholics of state-owned churches).[12] Such historical compromises, however, are not deemed to generate obligations on the part of the state to extend such benefits to religions, such as Islam, which were not present on French soil (at least in mainland France) in 1905. They are seen as minor, historically unavoidable, infringements of the separation principle. For example, free use of state-owned religious buildings was only possible because church property belonged to the state in the first place. Today, to allow public support for the construction of Muslim mosques, for instance, would violate the spirit and the letter of the law, which postulated that, *from 1905 onwards*, all religions would be treated identically—none would be subsidized by the state. Therefore, official republicans urge the strict respect of the separation principle and reject the idea of the 'historical compensation' of Islam as incoherent and spurious.[13] In the words of the Stasi Report, 'drawing on the principle of equality, the *laïque* state grants no public privilege to any religion, and its relationship with them is characterized by legal separation.'[14]

C. An Agnostic Principle

This third principle, understood minimally without reference to its theological connotations, implies that the state should neither favour nor disfavour religion as such: it should be 'agnostic'—neutral by ignorance—vis-à-vis the respective claims of believers and non-believers. This is often contrasted with the American situation where, in spite of official non-establishment, a diffuse religious culture permeates public institutions. For French official republicans, when the state introduces religious practices and symbols into its institutions, even of a theistic nature (e.g. when it requires state officials to swear belief in God), it implicitly puts pressure on non-believers to conform, and therefore fails to treat them with equal respect. Only a fully secular public culture can adequately respect liberty of conscience, understood as permitting 'free adhesion to a religion and the refusal of any religion'.[15] The 1905 law explicitly put an end to the official recognition of the 'social utility of religion' recognized by the Concordat. Public culture did not need to rely on transcendental foundations: for the first time, the possibility of a fully secular public morality was adduced. Jules Ferry opposed religious teaching in state schools 'on principle': even though, in the 1880s, the majority of the French were believers, it was wrong to exclude non-believers from the public sphere.[16] As prominent republican Aristide Briand put it, the republican state 'is not religious, nor anti-religious: it is a-religious'.[17] Steps towards the secularization of the public sphere had already been taken in the 1880s. For example, communal cemeteries were secularized: religious signs such as crosses were removed and only discreet symbols were allowed on individual tombstones. Religious marriages are ignored by French law: only civil marriages have legal validity. Exemption from military service may be granted on non-religious conscientious grounds. The agnostic principle, in sum, requires the state not to single out religious believers for special treatment, and to ensure that the public sphere is bereft of potentially exclusionary religious references and symbols. The 'naked public square' best expresses the ideal of equality between all citizens. In the words of one commentator, 'the non-confessional nature of the state puts all citizens on a plane of rigorous moral equality vis-à-vis the state.'[18]

D. An Individualistic Principle

The individualistic principle stipulates that (i) group membership should not generate differential treatment of individuals by the state and (ii) if rights are attributed to groups, they should not override the individual rights of their members. Thus stated, of course, the principle is too general and must be refined. Principle (i) is clearly too strong: social policy, notably, is typically addressed to groups, or categories of individuals, classified in relation to their income, their occupation, and so forth; the only differences that should be ignored by the state are, to use John Rawls's phrase, 'morally arbitrary' differences. As Article 2 of the 1958 Constitution states, the republic 'ensures equality before the law of all citizens, with no distinction made on the basis of origin, race or religion'. This is the core of 'difference-blind' liberalism, which provides each individual with a uniform set of rights regardless of their culture, identity, or beliefs.[19] The French state goes as far as forbidding the collection of statistics about racial origins or religious affiliation. The use of ethnic categories (such as 'White', 'Black', or 'Arab') is banned in official discourse, and there are no reliable official statistics on the number of Catholics, Protestants, Jews, and Muslims in France. The ban on religious classification graphically symbolizes the refusal to allow 'morally irrelevant' religious affiliation either to confer a benefit or to impose a burden on individual citizens.

Principle (ii), which asserts the primacy of individual rights over group rights, should be qualified, notably in relation to religion. Religious institutions are not merely aggregates of private individuals: they are inevitably communal institutions which generate their own set of duties and obligations for their members. An overly individualist construal of religious organization (one, for example, which would require churches to be democratically organized) would clearly undermine the whole point of religious freedom, which entails respect for church autonomy. Early parliamentary drafts of the 1905 law did in fact expound such an individualistic conception, proposing that the internal structure of the Catholic Church be broken up, priests be chosen by their congregation, and dissident churches be free to establish themselves. Rightly criticized for forcing a 'Protestant' reform on the Catholic Church, those projects were shelved: the republican state recognizes the hierarchical structure of the Roman Catholic Church. Catholics, however, have complained that individualistic philosophy still permeates the state's view of the Church: the ethos and purpose of Catholic schools, for example, may be violated by the requirement that they may not select their pupils on religious grounds. Critics argue that to conflate religious discrimination with discrimination on morally arbitrary grounds betrays an unnecessarily restrictive view of collective religious rights.[20]

It is undeniable that the official republican reading of *laïcité* is strongly influenced, on different levels, by the wider individualistic philosophy of the 1789 Revolution, which strongly asserted both principle (i) and principle (ii). The 'emancipation' of Jews provided an early, paradigmatic model of the individualistic model of citizenship which was substituted for the mosaic of corporate laws inherited from medieval society. In the famous words of *député* Clermont-Tonnerre, 'Jews must be refused everything *qua* nation, and granted everything *qua* individuals.... They must no longer constitute a political body or order in the state: they acquire citizenship individually.'[21] In 1791, Jews were invited to take a civic oath and to renounce 'all privileges and exceptions formerly introduced in their favour'. They were granted full citizenship as individuals, not as members of a religious minority. In fact, the French state does not recognize the existence of 'minorities' in the nation.[22] As the Haut Conseil à l'Intégration forcefully put it in its 1991 report:

The French conception of integration should obey a logic of equality not a logic of minorities. The principles ... [of] the Revolution and the Declaration of the Rights of Man and of the Citizen permeate our philosophy, founded on the equality of individuals before the law, whatever their origin, race or religion ... to the exclusion of an institutional recognition of minorities.

Thus the French government requested a 'reservation' of Article 27 (on minority rights) of the International Covenant on Civil and Political Rights, on the grounds that 'France is a country in which there are no minorities, and where the chief principle is non-discrimination'. It also declared the 1999 European Charter of Regional or Minority Languages incompatible with the French Constitution. Hence the rejection of the legitimacy of group rights: individual rights such as religious freedom, freedom of speech, association, and so forth are sufficient to ensure that individuals are free to practise their religion and express their cultural identities in the private sphere, without express public recognition. Multiculturalism—the public recognition of collective identities and the attribution of special rights to communities—is castigated as a return to the mass of anomalies and special cases that entrenched privileges and inequalities under the *ancien régime*. The individualistic conception of *laïcité*, therefore, should be seen as an application to religious affairs of a broader model, that of the revolutionary heritage of legal uniformity,[23] combined with an Enlightenment-influenced 'liberalism of equal dignity', to use Charles Taylor's phrase.[24]

E. A Principle of Fairness

In what sense, then, does the separation doctrine articulated in the last four sections embody an ideal of fairness? The difference-blind and abstentionist neutrality of the state is fair to individuals because it treats them identically, regardless of their particular faith, identity, and affiliations. This does not mean that the separation doctrine is hostile to the expression of differences: on the contrary, a diversified, pluralist civil society can develop best under the framework of universalist common laws. It is precisely because liberal freedoms are important that the politicization of group identities should be resisted;[25] it is precisely because religious freedom is important that no religious group should be granted recognition. As legal commentator Geneviève Koubi puts it in a deliberately paradoxical phrase, 'le droit à la différence est un droit qui ne se réglemente pas' (roughly: 'the right to difference is not a legally enforceable right').[26] 'Equality between religions', she has recently added, 'can only be understood as refusal by the state to recognize any'.[27] The liberal state only establishes fair background conditions for the free development of religious and cultural identities in the private sphere. This means that liberal equality should not be taken to mean substantive equality or equality of outcome. In cultural and religious matters at least, it is best expressed through the formal equality embodied in uniform, general legislation.

So official republicans concur with Brian Barry in denying that a situation in which religious groups fare differently under a neutral state is inherently unfair. *De jure* equality need not generate *de facto* equality. It is in fact the distinctive feature of the liberal conception of justice defended by Barry and by French official republicans that it establishes fair background conditions, and lets the cards fall where they may, as it were, instead of pursuing the chimerical objective of achieving substantive equality between groups through policies of 'positive discrimination'. Such arguments were recently reiterated in response to a Muslim request that public authorities subsidize the buildings of mosques, to remedy the radically insufficient provision of adequate Muslim religious facilities. Although this is considered as a legitimate request by French authorities, which have sought to bypass the stringent ban on the public funding of religion,[28] it has been rejected by defenders of the separation doctrine on three grounds. First, as we have seen, the principle of 'historical discrimination' is seen as incoherent and spurious: that Muslims were not present on French soil in 1905 cannot justify giving them more than their fair share today. Second, to exempt Muslims from a generally applicable rule would introduce a clear inequality between them and other believers—with Islam benefiting from state funding that is denied to other religions. Third, the very idea that provision of Muslim religious facilities is 'insufficient' and 'unfair' assumes that a baseline for sufficiency and fairness can be objectively determined. However, in the absence of precise statistics about the exact number of practising Muslims in France, the actual meaning of 'substantive equality' (even as pro rata equality) remains elusive. At any rate, there might be nothing intrinsically unfair about the small number of mosques in France. As Michèle Tribalat and Jeanne-Hélène Kaltenbach pithily put it, 'the poverty of a religion may stem from the fact that its adherents are poor, too few, or ungenerous.'[29] What would be unfair is if public authorities treated Muslims differently from other religious groups—for example, if local authorities (as they too frequently do) unreasonably refuse to grant planning permission for the building of mosques to local Muslim communities, in clear breach of the principle of *laïcité*. But as long as the republic guarantees to Muslims the full and fair application of the law, republicans should not worry about how successful particular religious groups are in translating into specific outcomes the equal set of opportunities offered to them.

Thus far, I have spelt out the implications of the separation doctrine as a doctrine of formal equality. So far, we might say, so liberal. For *laïcité* closely resembles the anti-multiculturalist, egalitarian liberalism defended by Brian Barry. Interestingly, from a French perspective, Barry's doctrine, with its emphasis on equality before the law and its hostility to collective rights, would appear as more *républicain* than *libéral* (liberalism in France is often associated with minority rights, the politics of recognition and affirmative action). From an Anglo-American perspective, we could say that French republicanism is a tough-minded version of egalitarian, difference-blind liberalism. For example, the refusal to recognize the existence of minorities and to accept that religious freedom is more than a negative liberty which merely requires state abstention for its proper enjoyment would probably be seen as too uncompromising even by Barry. There are, in addition, two further features which make *laïcité* a distinctively *republican* interpretation of liberalism, influenced by Rousseauist Jacobinism and refined by the founders of the Third Republic. The reluctance to grant public recognition to differences—religious or cultural—appears all the more tough-minded in the light of both of the relative 'thickness' of the public sphere in France and the claim by the state to embody an independent secular ethics. Both combine to make the 'public' identity of citizenship an expansively constructed identity, and one that is more discrepant from the 'private' identity of citizens than political liberals, such as Rawls, would allow.

F. A Homogeneous Public Identity

Separation doctrines in general are founded on a distinction between the public and the private spheres; what characterizes *laïcité* is the relatively expansive construal of the former in relation to the latter. This should be related to the French 'state tradition'.[30] In Kenneth Dyson's words, the state in the Continental tradition appears as a

highly abstract and impersonal... political concept which identifies the nation in its corporate and collectivist capacity, as a legal institution with an inherent responsibility for regulating matters of public concern, and as a socio-cultural phenomenon which expresses a new, unique form of associative bond.[31]

Many historical factors combined in France to ensconce the view that 'the state' stands for a homogeneous, autonomous public domain: the Roman-law influenced doctrine of state sovereignty elaborated after the religious wars of the sixteenth century, the struggles of the absolutist monarchy to shake off the domination of the Vatican, the need to forge national unity out of disparate regional, corporate, and religious traditions, and the emergence of a central bureaucracy with a distinctive mission and ethos. As Alexis de Tocqueville perceptively saw, the 1789 Revolution pursued this long-standing effort of centralization, by transferring the attributes of state sovereignty from the monarchy to a homogeneous *peuple*. The Rousseau-influenced revolutionary hostility to intermediary groups and 'factions'—associated with privileges, divisiveness, and corruption—shaped a view of republican democracy as essentially unitary, and permanently fragile and under threat. The public sphere was to be protected from the interference of particular loyalties, identities, or groups, lest it allow the 'general will' to disaggregate into myriad conflicting private wills.

It is, however, the struggles of the state to establish its political hegemony against a domineering Catholic Church still wedded to the pre-revolutionary order that shaped most deeply the expansive and unitary *laïque* public sphere in the nineteenth and early twentieth centuries. There was a clear link between anticlericalism, *laïcité*, and democracy: the Church was perceived as a minority faction usurping popular sovereignty. As Buisson put it, 'a laïque state [must be] strong enough no longer to share sovereignty with the Church, and a nation strong enough to manage its own affairs.'[32] With *laïcité* and the separation of the religious and political spheres, the republican state partly took over the spiritual mission previously pursued by the Catholic Church. As republican philosopher Charles Renouvier lucidly foresaw in 1872, 'let us be aware that the separation between Church and State signifies the organization of the moral and educational state.'[33] The nineteenth-century 'conflict between the two Frances' (Catholic and republican) chiefly centred on the control of the public sphere, and notably instances of socialization such as schools, the 'laboratories of the future'.[34] Hence the central importance of education to *laïcité*. If the republic was to create 'citizens' out of 'believers', it had to engage in a strong formative project, aimed at the inculcation of the public values of democratic and egalitarian citizenship, and introduce an alternative set of civic symbols into the public sphere, so as to lead citizens to endorse a robust public identity capable of transcending more particular religious, cultural, and class loyalties.[35] The liberal egalitarian strand of *laïcité*, therefore, advocated a robust, republican implementation of the 'formative project' characteristic of the political liberalism of, for example, Stephen Macedo[36] and Eamonn Callan.[37]

G. An Independent Public Ethic

In broad terms, political liberalism seeks to identify a set of shared *political* values that all citizens can endorse whatever their particular *comprehensive* conceptions of the good. Charles Taylor has suggestively argued that such a project is at the heart of the tradition of Western democratic secularism. He identifies three 'modes of secularism'. The first, which he terms the 'common ground' approach, was based on a convergence of general but religiously derived precepts of morality shared by all Christian sects. The second, which he calls the 'independent ethic' approach, sought to abstract from religious beliefs altogether and identify general features of the human condition. Taylor then goes on to show that both approaches are unsuited to contemporary pluralist societies, the first because of its narrow Christian roots and the second because of its hidden secularist bias. Rawls's 'overlapping consensus' approach seems to him to be a truly 'free-standing' conception which can nonetheless be endorsed from a variety of—secular or religious—perspectives.[38]

It has been rightly suggested that 'French republican secularism is the clearest expression of what Taylor calls the independent ethic mode of secularism'.[39] In 1910, leading republican Ferdinand Buisson (who wrote a book significantly if ambiguously called *The Laïque Faith*) addressed the Chamber of Deputies on the subject of *morale laïque*, claiming that it proved the originality of France, the only country that had tried to found a morality outside of religion and of metaphysics.[40] The French tradition of the autonomy of the state, complemented after the Revolution by the republican ideal of a self-governing people democratically establishing the terms of its political constitution, strongly rejected the 'heteronomy' involved in subjecting political authority to religious institutions, transcendental foundations, and revealed truth.[41] More specifically, *laïcité* as an ethic independent of religion, based on reason and conscience, had roots in the Enlightenment search for a natural religion, Victor Cousin's Kantian spiritualism, and in the more radical search for '*la morale indépendante*', a morality wholly detached from religious concepts, in the works of the anarchist socialist Pierre-Joseph Proudhon, neo-Kantians Charles Renouvier and Jules Barni, positivist Émile Littré, and *solidariste* sociologists Emile Durkheim, Alfred Fouillée, and Léon Bourgeois. Protestants, Freemasons, and free thinkers were at the forefront of this attempt to establish the scientific foundations of morality.[42] Jules Ferry, the main promoter of *morale laïque* as the public philosophy of French schools, argued that such morality was 'neutral' in the sense that it was distinct from 'those high metaphysical conceptions... over which theologians and philosophers have been in discord for six thousand years'. Instead, it appealed to 'a moral truth superior to all changes of doctrine and all controversies'. This truth was compatible with—though not derived from—traditional moral views, what Ferry called 'the good old morality of our fathers'.[43] As Marcel Gauchet has suggested, the aim was to 'encompass all religions without doing violence to them, from a superior viewpoint', a project which he contrasts to American-style 'civic religion' and its 'common-ground' strategy of finding a theistic 'lowest common denominator'.[44] To put the point differently, *laïcité* was a kind of 'second-order' secularism, a set of rational, moral values upon which a variety of 'first-order' comprehensive views, including religious ones, could converge. Conservative Catholics were quick to point out the inevitably secular bias of seemingly 'second-order' rational morality (which at any rate was not morality at all, but rather 'a morality of forms in the air'). Republicans were not unduly perturbed by what they saw as an irrational and archaic rejection of a universally valid truth. And in practice, little tension was felt between the independently derived *'morale indépendente'* informed by the positivism of Littré and Quinet and the 'good old morality of our fathers' hailed by Ferry, who cleverly set aside controversial issues about the metaphysical foundations of morality to appeal to a 'practical consensus on the common content of morality'.[45] The hope was to convince Catholics that one could be a religious believer in the private sphere and a citizen in the public sphere—a project not dissimilar to the 'political liberalism' articulated by John Rawls. However, because of the particularly robust conception of civic identity endorsed by republicans, the demands of republican citizenship were fairly stringent ones, as we shall see in the next section.

II. Laïcité *as a Doctrine of Conscience*

Laïcité as a doctrine of conscience prescribes norms of conduct for religious organizations, in terms of their internal 'laïcization' (Section II.A), and for individual citizens, in terms of religious restraint in the public sphere (Section II.B).

A. The 'Laïcization' of Religions

The chief obligation that the separation doctrine imposes on religious groups is to respect the law, renounce all claims to political power, and refrain from intervening in public debate in partisan fashion.[46] Historically, *laïcité* was essentially an anticlerical doctrine in this sense. 'Clericalism, there is the enemy!' the republican leader Léon Gambetta famously exclaimed in 1877 in the Chamber of Deputies.[47] Throughout the nineteenth century, the Church had used its social power—notably its monopoly of primary education—to preach anti-republican, royalist doctrines, and fought to re-establish the *societas christiana* in place of the 'diabolical' only regime of modern democracy. It accepted republican institutions slowly and reluctantly: while Catholics had tactically 'rallied' to the Republic in 1892 (the so-called *Ralliement*), it was only in 1945 that the Assembly of Cardinals and Archbishops of France publicly accepted *laïcité*, as entailing both religious freedom and the 'sovereign autonomy of the state in temporal matters'.[48] At the 1964 Vatican II Council, the Roman Catholic Church finally renounced its ambition to bring about a confessional (Catholic) state, and fully accepted religious pluralism. Renouncing clericalism and accepting religious pluralism were not, however, the only concessions that French religions made to the *laïque* order: they also profoundly transformed their doctrine, practices, and institutions. Of course, many of these changes may not be due to *laïcité* itself but to the broader secularization of Western society; yet given the particularly strict conception of the separation of politics and religion and the robust conception of citizenship enforced by the French state, they were perhaps more profound and painful there than elsewhere.

There are three major indices of the laïcization of French religious groups. First is the privatization and individualization of religious life. This was a most difficult and protracted adjustment as far as the Catholic Church was concerned, given its claim to constitute a 'total institution' covering the whole of social, cultural, and political life. With *laïcité*, it was relegated to the status of a private institution with no legitimacy in public debate and reduced visibility in social life. *Laïcité* implicitly fostered a view of religious life as a discrete and personal activity, a view which notably looked with suspicion at forcible attempts at religious conversion. The right to engage in religious propaganda and 'proselytism' (recognized by the European Court of Justice as being entailed by religious freedom[49]) tends to be seen in France as an unacceptable breach of individual freedom and a divisive threat to public order. Incidentally, such suspicion of proselytism (which resurfaced during the hijab controversy) may be traced back to the sixteenth-century religious wars between Catholics and Protestants, with Protestants—then the only significant religious minority in France—granted an uneasy toleration (the *Edict of Nantes* of 1598), provided they kept to themselves and refrained from attempts at evangelization and propaganda.[50] The second major transformation forced onto religious believers was the revision of their dogmas, chiefly to allow the primacy of state laws over religious prescriptions. Jews, often presented by French republicans as a model of successful laïcization of religion, had in the early nineteenth century re-interpreted a number of religious obligations (e.g. family law, dietary prescriptions) to facilitate their accession to citizenship, according to the principle *Malkhuta dinah* (the country's law is the law).[51] The third transformation was thus the nationalization of religions, their recognition that believers must show full allegiance to the French state, not to foreign-based religious authorities. Gallicanism—the early monarchical effort to nationalize the French Catholic Church—was rooted in the long-standing suspicion that 'those *messieurs* [the Jesuits] are not from France, they are from Rome'. A distinctive feature of what has been called 'Franco-Judaism' stresses the convergence between the universal values of the French Revolution and those of Judaism, while toning down the national content of Jewish identity and biblical references to the 'chosen people'.[52]

Drawing on those historical examples, official republicans argue that just as traditional religions have made significant efforts to adapt to the framework of the *laïque* state, so should more recently established ones such as Islam. The suspicion is that Muslims, in contrast to Catholics, Jews, and Protestants in the past, may be unable or unwilling to reform their religion in order to ease the tension between their civic and their religious identities. Contemporary republican discussion is preoccupied with the question of the seeming incompatibility between Islam and *laïcité*.[53] The first worry is the absence of separation between spiritual and temporal spheres in Islam: in the oft-quoted words of Muslim leader Youssouf al Qaradawi, 'from the Islamic point of view, everything pertains to religion, and everything pertains to the law.'[54] As a result, Islam is seen as an all-embracing communal identity, which makes it difficult for believers to distance themselves from their religion to act as full members of democratic society. Because Islam is 'at the same time a religion and a political system', it seemingly 'contradicts the requirements of the French state'.[55] On a practical level, the lack of distinction in Islam between 'religious' activities and 'cultural' activities such as education, charity, or social work makes it difficult for Muslim organizations to avail themselves of the funding opportunities offered by French law, which authorizes public subsidy of the latter but not the former, in the name of *laïcité*.[56] The second difficulty stems from the universal scope of Islam. Membership of the *Umma* (the universal community of believers) overrides national citizenship, potentially creating a conflict of loyalties between civic and religious allegiances. Thus, doubts are cast about the sincerity of Muslim allegiance to the *laïque* state. Muslim intellectuals (such as the influential Swiss academic Tariq Ramadan) are routinely suspected of accepting *laïcité* either on partial grounds (making full use of its guarantee of religious rights without fully accepting corollary duties) or on prudential grounds (as a temporary second best to a more religiously influenced political order).[57] The Muslim attitude to the French state may therefore represent an unstable and unprincipled modus vivendi, rather than a principled endorsement of the values underpinning *laïcité.*[58] Third, republicans fear that the actively proselytizing proclivities of Islam threaten the fragile social peace historically achieved through enforced religious restraint. If France has broken with the absolutist past of 'one nation, one king, one law' and embraced religious pluralism, it is still reticent vis-à-vis the pluralism of religious militantism.

Finally, relationships between the French state and the Muslim community are made difficult by the internally divided and disorganized nature of the latter. One paradox of French *laïcité* is that, for all its commitment to the separation of church and state and its 'privatized' and 'individualized' construal of religion, it has always, of necessity, relied on state recognition of centralized religious authorities, which act as representatives of French Catholics, Jews, and Protestants and legitimate interlocutors to the government. Since the 1980s, efforts have thus been made to set up a representative Muslim Council, seen as one important step towards the creation of a truly 'French Islam' (one less dependent on foreign states). High on the agenda are schemes for the training of French-born imams and the fair distribution of the 'halal tax', both crucial in lessening the dependence of the Muslim community on foreign donors and foreign interference (notably Algeria, Morocco, and Saudi Arabia). The complex events leading to the recently created (and contested) French Council of the Muslim Cult illustrate the dilemma involved, for the French state, in avowedly respecting and even encouraging the self-organization of Muslims while discreetly seeking to entrench the authority of moderate, *laïque* leaders over the Muslim community.[59] The neutral state, therefore, is not totally indifferent to the structure of religious communities or to the content of their doctrines. In particular, it favours the laïcization of Muslim organizations along lines already followed by Catholics, Protestants, and Jews. In addition to the demands it makes of religious organizations, *laïcité* also makes specific demands on individuals, especially public agents.

B. Religious Restraint in the Public Sphere

In recent Anglo-American liberalism, debate has focused on the question of the legitimacy of religious argument in public debate. When citizens engage in public reasoning, to what extent should they bracket off their comprehensive conceptions of the good, and notably their religious beliefs? In France, while similar issues have arisen in relation to censorship, abortion, and bioethics, they have been quite marginal, given the prima facie suspicion of religious arguments in public debate.

More attention has been paid to the question of the legitimacy of the expression of religious faith by state agents. We have seen that *laïcité* postulates that only if the public sphere is kept free of all religious symbols can it treat citizens equally. This puts stringent limits on the expression of religious beliefs by public functionaries. Official republicans insist that a line be drawn between 'freedom of conscience' and the 'expression of faith in the public sphere'.[60] It is not always legitimate for citizens to 'make use of a private right in public':[61] in the public sphere, the value of religious freedom must be balanced against other values derived from the principle of *laïcité* as neutrality.[62] The first is that of equal respect of citizens as users of public services. This implies, of course, that no discrimination can be made between citizens on grounds of religion, gender, or race. But public services must also display outward signs of neutrality: they must be *seen* to be neutral.[63] Thus public agents have a *'devoir de réserve'* (obligation of restraint): they must not display any sign of religious allegiance, so as to show equal respect to all users of public services. Thus French law has been very strict about banning religious symbols in public services. On 3 May 2000 (*Marteaux* decision), the Conseil d'État reasserted that 'the principle of *laïcité* puts limits on the right [of state agents] to express their religious convictions while engaged in public functions'.[64] Recently, for example, a Muslim tax inspector was prevented from wearing a headscarf while on duty. While there have been debates in other countries about the compatibility of state uniforms with religious dress,[65] in France, the ban on the wearing of religious symbols by public agents is an uncontroversial one and applies regardless of whether state agents must wear official uniforms or not (as in the case of tax inspectors). Note too that the scope of 'public service' is expansively constructed in France as it covers, for example, postal services, public transportation systems (and of course state schools, as we shall see in the next section), and is estimated to include up to five million agents. The second *laïque* value which can override duties of faith is that of the state's interest in the application of a uniform rule to all its agents. Thus, exemptions from the normal rules of organization of public service to allow functionaries to perform duties associated with the exercise of their religious duties (daily prayers, weekly day of rest) are granted parsimoniously by administrations and courts, although the latter have been more tolerant of demands for leave for annual religious holidays. What is called in France 'the ethos of public service', in sum, imposes fairly stringent limits on the exercise of religious freedoms in the *laïque* public sphere.[66]

III. Laïque *Schools and Republican Citizenship*

It is in state schools that the doctrine of *laïcité* has found its fullest application. Given the centrality of education to the republican project, it is in that area that the obligations both of the state and of citizens (*laïcité* as separation doctrine [Section I] and *laïcité* as doctrine of conscience [Section II]) apply most strictly. Put together, they justify the ban on Muslim headscarves in schools.

A. State Obligations: Civic Schools, Neutral Schools

The Educational Laws of the 1880s are, with the Separation Law of 1905, the building blocks of the institutional architecture of *laïcité* in France. In fact, the ideals of *laïcité* were fully implemented in state schools nearly 20 years before formal separation of church and state, an indication of the utmost urgency with which republicans treated educational reform.[67] The primary objective was to take primary education out of the hands of the Catholic Church. Schools were to be *civic* institutions whose chief mission was to 'create citizens' imbued with the republican ethos; this mission could be achieved only if schools were *neutral* towards religious and other particular allegiances.

Schools, then, were central to the civic project of the Third Republic. The monopoly on primary education enjoyed by the Catholic Church meant that most children were socialized into a culture that was anathema to the liberal principles of 1789. Where religiously controlled schools had taught deference towards traditional authorities, tolerance of natural and social inequalities, and encouraged cultural and political divisiveness, republican schools would promote principles of equality, mutual respect, and national unity. The republican school, therefore, was conceived as a microcosm of republican political society: within its walls, children would learn to become citizens, a shared public identity that transcended their local, cultural, and religious affiliations. A law of 1884 established the principle of free and compulsory primary education both for boys and girls. All were to be subjected to a nation-wide uniform curriculum: in the interests of national unity, the equal right to education was construed as the right to a rigorously identical provision of educational goods to all children, with few accommodations for variations in language, culture, religion, and even (remarkably for the time) gender.[68] Throughout the country, republican schools competed with parish churches as the symbolic focal point of village life, and teachers—the *hussards noirs de la République*—were dispatched from their training colleges with a proud sense of the importance of their civilizing mission, that of making 'peasants (and Catholics) into Frenchmen'.[69] As a result, official republican educational philosophy gives little scope for parents' choice and involvement in the education of their children. The state's interest in education is constructed expansively: schools are seen as paradigmatically public spaces, not as extensions of the family or local community. In contrast to the conception prevalent in Britain, for example, where schools are broadly responsive to the needs and demands of local communities, sometimes along religious and cultural lines, in France, the 'detached school' is seen as promoting specific civic values which cut across communal divisions and even diverge from values prevalent in other spheres of social life, such as the family and the marketplace.[70] As prominent official republican intellectuals grandly put it in a 1989 Open Letter urging the Minister for Education to press for a ban on headscarves, 'in our society, the school is the only institution which is devoted to the universal'.[71] It affirms the independent ethic of *laïcité* and requires all children to be socialized into it. In 1882, Jules Ferry—the main inspirer, with Ferdinand Buisson, of the *laïque* educational laws—substituted 'moral and *civic* instruction' for traditional 'moral and *religious* instruction'. Civic education was thus a new subject in the recently designed republican textbooks: children were to be taught about basic principles of universal morality, the great principles of the 1789 Revolution, and their rights and duties as citizens of the French Republic. State schools were openly anti-monarchical and pro-republican: as Ferry put it, republicans could not, lest they give up on their civic mission altogether, promise political neutrality. The one thing they could promise, he said, was religious neutrality.

The religious neutrality of schools was achieved through the scrupulous avoidance of any reference to religion in the content of education, and the removal of any religious signs such as Christian crosses from classrooms.[72] While this was denounced as an openly anti-religious affront by many Catholics, republicans insisted that the fact that schools refrained from either endorsing or criticizing religious values meant that they could be truly inclusive and respect the diversity of private beliefs; in the words of the 1884 law, they could be open to all 'with no distinction made on the basis of opinion or religion'. In the entry on 'Neutralité' in his *Dictionnaire de pédagogie* of 1884, Buisson wrote that 'the school is neutral, in the sense that it welcomes without discrimination and on a plane of perfect equality children from all religions, and even those who do not belong to any religion'.[73] Ferry insisted that teachers be sanctioned if they disturbed the 'fragile and sacred conscience' of children or offended parental beliefs. Here are his precise instructions, as he laid them down in a famous *Letter to Teachers* in 1883:

The republic stops where conscience begins. (...) When you propose a precept or maxim, ask yourself if you know a single honest person who could be offended by what you are going to say. Ask if the father of a family...could in good faith refuse his consent to what he would hear you say. If yes, refrain from saying it; if no, speak out. (...) You are in no way the apostles of a new religion.[74]

Schools should eschew morally controversial topics and concentrate on the inculcation of so-called elementary notions based on morally neutral, scientific truths. The purpose of public education was to diffuse a corpus of objective knowledge, while neutralizing all 'partisan' or 'metaphysical' opinions. It was crucial that schools be neutral in this sense, as attendance was compulsory, intake was mixed, and young children were particularly vulnerable to external influence and indoctrination. Furthermore, because the purpose of civic education was to foster a sense of civic commonality and mutual respect between children, it was crucial that schools be insulated from the divisive sectarianism that threatened to tear apart civil society. This conception of the school as a 'sanctuary'—still widely shared by official republicans today—was further entrenched in the 1930s when, to counter the rise of fascist and communist propaganda, Education Minister Jean Zay explicitly banned all forms of 'proselytism'—both political and religious—in state schools. In the—almost Arendtian—words recently used by the Stasi Report, because children in a republic are 'expected to live together beyond their differences', schools must be 'protected from the furore of the world'.[75]

Naturally, teachers have a special duty to embody this neutrality of the state: the '*devoir de réserve*' applies to them more strictly than it does to other public agents. There is, for example, a prima facie incompatibility between the function of primary school teacher and any ecclesiastical function. While teachers cannot be discriminated against on grounds of their private religious beliefs, they should not express them in schools. Thus, a Versailles administrative court recently ruled that the wearing of a Muslim headscarf by a teacher was in breach of *laïcité*, as it would violate the freedom of conscience of the children entrusted to her care.[76] Her religious rights were therefore limited by the state's interest in the preservation of a non-sectarian, non-discriminatory public sphere.

B. *Demands on Pupils: The Ban on* Hijab

The law promulgated on 15 March 2004 stipulates that 'in primary and secondary public schools, the wearing of signs or clothes through which pupils ostensibly express a religious allegiance is forbidden'. The law's targets are Muslim headscarves, though Jewish yarmulkes and large Christian crosses are also banned in state schools. The law is intended to put an end to the 15-year-long hijab controversy which started in Creil in the autumn of 1989 when two girls came to class wearing Muslim scarves. This raised a legal challenge for *laïcité*: there are no school uniforms in French state schools, and it was unclear whether there was an explicit rule preventing pupils from wearing religious symbols. Asked by the Education Minister Lionel Jospin to provide legal advice, the Conseil d'État laid out general principles and guidelines in its 27 November 1989 *avis*.[77] It argued that headscarves were not in themselves in breach of *laïcité*: the exercise of religious freedoms by pupils could be limited only when it was an obstacle to the implementation of the statutory mission of state education. This happened when the display of religious insignia involved pressure, proselytism, propaganda, or provocation, when it disturbed the good order of the school, or posed a threat to health and safety.[78] This nuanced ruling proved difficult to implement in practice, as it left it to heads of schools to settle issues locally, on a case-by-case basis. It is this legal uncertainty that provided the most immediate incentive for the convening of the Stasi Commission and the drafting of the 2004 law. However, back in 1994, Education Minister François Bayrou had already published more specific instructions banning all 'ostentatious' signs in schools. Although this general regulation was neutralized (though not formally annulled) by the Conseil d'État, its principles were broadly those which inspired the recent law, and so it is worth quoting at length:

The school is the space which more than any other involves education and integration, where all children and all youth are to be found, learning to live together and respect one another. If, in the school, there are signs of behaviour which show that they cannot conform to the same obligations, or attend the same courses and follow the same programs, it negates this mission. All discrimination should stop at the school gates, whether it is sexual, cultural, or religious discrimination.... In schools, freedom of conscience, combined with respect of pluralism and the neutrality of public service, requires that the 'educational community' be insulated from any ideological or religious pressure.... It is not possible to accept the presence and multiplication of

ostentatious signs in school, signs whose meaning involves the separation of
certain students from the rules of the common life of the school.... Such
signs are in themselves part of proselytism.[79]

If we elucidate the meaning of this document carefully, in light of the
general principles of *laïcité* both as separation doctrine and as doctrine
of conscience, and of republican educational philosophy, we are in a
position to articulate the secular argument against the wearing of hijab in
schools. Legal commentators have observed that it is the first time that
the principle of the neutrality of public services is explicitly understood
to entail obligations for its users. The preface to the 2004 bill made this
clear: 'while pupils... are naturally free to practise their religion, they
must do so while respecting the *laïcité* of the schools of the republic. It
is precisely the neutrality of the school which guarantees the freedom of
conscience of pupils, and equal respect for all beliefs.'[80] A preliminary
point to clarify is the sense in which pupils should be in any way
subjected to a *devoir de réserve* similar to that which applies to teachers
and other public agents. Although no such stringent demand can apply
to *users* of public service who do not represent the neutrality of the
state in an official capacity, republicans argue that state school pupils
are no ordinary users of an ordinary public service. Because schools are
miniature 'communities of citizens', where pupils learn the principles
of *public* citizenship, the principles of toleration of civil society do not
apply with full force in them, and *laïcité* makes demands of religious
restraint on the part of pupils too.[81] Headscarves, as ostensible signs of
religious belief, infringe on the neutrality and civic purpose of schools
in five different but interconnected ways.

1. *Muslim headscarves introduce signs of private difference and religious divisiveness
   into the public sphere.* They constitute an 'ostensible' intrusion of religious identities into public schools, which should be protected from
   sectarian divisions. In the public space, the wearing of headscarves
   can be considered an illegitimate act of propaganda and an aggressive
   act of proselytism. The best way to deal with the destabilizing impact
   of religious differences in civil society is not to accommodate them,
   but to exclude them from the public sphere. This draws on *laïcité*
   as an 'agnostic' principle and on the 'neutral schools' arguments
   adduced in Sections I.C and III.A.
2. *Muslim headscarves symbolize the primacy of the believer over the citizen.* In
   so far as the wearing of headscarves is a religious obligation for
   Muslim girls and is 'non-detachable from the person as a believer',[82]
   it symbolizes the refusal by Muslims to separate their identity as

citizens from their private religious identity. The ban on headscarves thus signals to the Muslim community that, like other religious groups in the past, it must make greater efforts to reconcile its interpretation of its faith with the demands of *laïcité* as an ethic independent of, and superior to, particular religious prescriptions. This draws on *laïcité* as an 'individualistic' and as an 'independent' public ethic, and on the 'laïcization of religions' argument adduced in Sections I.D, I.G, and II.A.

3. *Muslim headscarves infringe on equality between pupils.* Schools are non-discriminatory and show respect to all pupils as individuals, regardless of their private affiliations and beliefs. Headscarves infringe on such difference-blind equality in two ways. First, they introduce ostensible distinctions that should be irrelevant within the school: between believers and non-believers, Muslims and non-Muslims, 'good' Muslims and 'bad' Muslims, and men and women. Second, to tolerate headscarves would be to create an unjustified exemption from a general requirement of religious restraint on the part of all believers. It is not in itself unjust that a uniform law (a ban on religious symbols) is more burdensome for some individuals than for others. This draws on the 'fairness' argument articulated in Section I.E.

4. *Muslim headscarves undermine the civic mission of schools.* The Muslim demand for girls to be allowed to wear headscarves to school is often accompanied by other requests (referred to in the Bayrou *circulaire* above) for exemptions from classes, such as physical education or biology. This raises the worrying prospect of *à la carte* schooling, whereby parents' organizations and local and religious communities seek to re-shape the universal curriculum to accommodate their particular needs.[83] This argument against parental and community involvement and *à la carte* schooling is derived from the 'civic schools' argument adduced in Section III.A.

5. *Muslim headscarves undermine the overall scheme of religious freedoms.* By wearing headscarves in the public square, Muslim pupils infringe on the liberty of conscience of others. Given compulsory attendance requirements and the mixed intake of schools, it is crucially important that children, at an age when they are particularly vulnerable, not be exposed to the ostentatious religious behaviour of others, lest their freedom of conscience be infringed.[84] Therefore, restrictions on the exercise of religious rights in the public sphere help secure a system of equal religious rights for all. In this sense, the ban on headscarves can be seen as a 'universal non-monetary tax imposed on Muslims for the maintenance of the secular state'.[85] This sums up

the principle of *laïcité*, which makes the protection of equal religious rights conditional on the maintenance of a neutral public sphere. It draws on a combination of the general separation doctrine and the 'religious restraint' argument in Sections I and II.B above.

Thus, to sum up, official republicans believe that the ban on Muslim headscarves in schools helps further five central values of the secular philosophy of *laïcité*: the preservation of a shared, non-sectarian public sphere; the distinction between the private and the public identities of individuals; equality before the law and non-discrimination; universal civic education in common schools; and the guarantee of equal religious rights for all. The ban can therefore be said to be compatible with one interpretation of the secular core of liberalism. Or so, at least, official republicans argue. The next chapter presents a range of objections to their line of argument.

CHAPTER 3

―――

Tolerant Secularism and the
Critique of Republican Neutrality

The French official republican interpretation of the secular core of liberalism, which was elucidated in the previous chapter, significantly differs from the American conception of the separation doctrine. In the constitutional tradition of the United States, freedom of conscience is seen as paramount: strong reasons are required to justify the imposition by the state of burdens on the exercise of religious rights. In France, by contrast, the protection of the secular public sphere is paramount, because of the greater historical threat posed by the Catholic Church to liberal democracy. Today, however, critics of official *laïcité* question whether traditional French secularism provides adequate protection for religious freedom, in a new context where religious groups can act as pillars of, rather than threats to, the democratic settlement. It is their argument—the *laïcité ouverte* or tolerant secularism argument—that I present and reconstruct in this chapter. Two versions of the critique of the secular argument for the ban on hijab in schools can be identified. The first challenges the official republican interpretation of *laïcité* as a *doctrine of conscience:* it endorses the broad aims of *laïcité* but argues that they are compatible with the wearing of religious signs by pupils (I). The second is sceptical of *laïcité* as a *separation doctrine*. It notes that in practice the French public sphere falls short of the secular ideal of separation (II) and from this fact of non-neutrality of the public sphere it deduces a norm of even-handed recognition of all religious groups—including Muslims—by the state (III). Once the ideal of strict separation between religion and politics is abandoned, the rationale for the ban on religious signs in schools collapses. As one commentator concisely put it, 'The ban on headscarves makes no sense at a time when religion massively returns to the public sphere, as a moral reference, as a locus of consultation or decision for the great issues that divide society.'[1]

The Compatibility of Headscarves with Laïcité

According to the first line of argument, advocates of the ban on Muslim headscarves in schools endorse too stringent an interpretation of *laïcité* as a doctrine of conscience. They interpret the neutrality of the public sphere to require such an expansive construal of the public identity of citizenship that they jeopardize the very values that *laïcité* is intended to protect, namely, religious liberty, civic inclusion, and fair treatment. This section argues that allowing Muslim pupils to wear headscarves to schools is compatible with the constitutional principle of *laïcité*, suitably interpreted.

Religious Liberty

Official republicans present *laïcité* more as a limit to, than as a guarantee of, religious freedom. Yet this is to misunderstand the original point and subsequent interpretations of the separation doctrine. The institutional separation of state and church aimed not only to secure the autonomy of the public sphere from religious interference, but also to ensure the freedom of religions from state control. While it is true that in the early years of the establishment of the republican order, the anti-clerical republican state struggled to impose a secular, autonomous political order on a reluctant church, by 1945 the 'conflict between the two Frances' was appeased and the republican order secured. By then, it was clear to most that *laïcité* primarily meant 'respect [by the republic] of all faiths', as solemnly proclaimed in Article 1 of the 1958 Constitution. Most legal theorists, following the interpretation proposed by constitutional lawyer Jean Rivero in a seminal article written in 1949, insist that religious freedom is the fundamental value protected by *laïcité*, and separation between church and state is merely the institutional mechanism designed to secure it.[2] Not only is religious liberty in general granted prominent constitutional value, but it is also firmly protected through an array of judicial decisions against discrimination on religious grounds. In sum, the protection of religious liberty in French law is fully guaranteed by the constitutional value of *laïcité*, with no need for supplementary principles (such as that of toleration, for example).[3]

Laïcité thus understood has found additional support in international law, which—to the dismay of official republicans—gives prominent place to religious freedom and ignores that of *laïcité* as such.[4] France's Conseil d'État, declaring in 1989 that Muslim headscarves were not in themselves incompatible with *laïcité,* made copious reference to international law, notably the European Convention for the Protection of Human Rights and Fundamental Freedoms (Article 9 in particular), the International Convenant on Civil and Political Rights (Article 18 in particular), and the Convention against Discrimination in Education.[5] The right to express one's religious convictions, including in the public sphere, is increasingly construed as a basic human right which all states must respect. When Dalil Boubakeur, the *recteur* of the Paris Mosque, declares that 'If a girl asks to have her hair covered, I believe it is her most basic right', he is framing a religious practice in terms of a basic individual right, thus appealing both to the 'libertarian' and 'individualistic' principle of *laïcité* derived from the 1789 Declaration of the Rights of Man, and to the universal rights regime which should override more particularistic, local traditions such as that of the neutrality of state schools in France.[6] The strict distinction established by official republicans between the private sphere of religious expression and the public sphere of religious restraint is also challenged by the recognition, in international and domestic law, of the social, collective, and therefore unavoidably public dimension of the exercise of religious freedoms.[7]

Given the special constitutional protection afforded to religious freedom, any infringement of the right of individuals to manifest their religious beliefs publicly would require a strong justification. Religious freedoms, classically, can be limited only if their exercise infringes the rights and liberties of others or pose a threat to public order.[8] Two points can be made here. First, it is implausible to assert that the wearing of hijab in schools is in itself an act of proselytism and propaganda likely to infringe on the religious freedom of other children or threaten the school's order. The Conseil d'État, repudiating the official republican position outlined in Chapter 2, was clear on this point. In law, religious signs should not be presumed to have any intrinsic meaning above and beyond that of symbolizing the faith of their bearer, unless—and this was an important qualification—they are accompanied by actions which perturb the normal functioning of the school.[9] Thus, of the 49 cases of school regulations banning headscarves brought to the attention of the Conseil d'État between 1992 and 1999, the great majority (41) were annulled on the grounds that they established too absolute a prohibition.[10] The Conseil pointed out that the headmasters had too readily endorsed the official republican position that any external manifestation of religious belief was in itself likely to perturb schoolchildren. Yet, in a democratic society, it is important 'not to sacrifice the freedom of those who believe to the fear of offending those who do not believe', to borrow the expression of Rivero in his 1949 comment on moves to ban Christian crosses in schools.[11] The Conseil d'État agreed to the ban on headscarves only in the rare cases when veiled Muslim girls had actively engaged in proselytizing or otherwise disruptive behaviour, or had refused to comply with compulsory attendance requirements.

The law of 15 March 2004 regrettably overrides this well-established and consistent—if difficult-to-apply—case law. It dispenses with the distinction between the mere display of religious symbols and disruptive behaviour threatening the good order of the school, and substitutes 'a principle of prohibition' for a 'principle of regulated freedom'.[12] The law forbids 'the wearing of signs or dress through which pupils ostensibly manifest allegiance to a religion', singling out Muslim headscarves, Jewish yarmulkes and large Christian crosses, in the name of the religious neutrality of state schools. There is (at the time of writing) a question mark over the compatibility of such a ban with the European Convention on Human Rights. Official republicans point to a number of decisions by the European Court of Human Rights which have recognized that states such as Turkey, which is the only other *laïque* state in Europe, may have a legitimate interest in preserving a secular public sphere and prohibiting religious (Muslim) dress in public institutions. French official republicans hope that European judges will similarly be persuaded that the paramount value of the religious neutrality of French schools can justifiably limit pupils' religious rights.[13]

The second question to consider, therefore, is whether the neutrality of state schools *itself* requires that pupils exercise restraint in the expression of their religious beliefs. Here again, the Conseil d'État explicitly criticized the official republican position, arguing in its 1989 *avis* that schoolchildren have 'the freedom to express and manifest their religious beliefs within educational institutions'.[14] It drew not only on the Convention against Discrimination in Education and other relevant international covenants but also on recent domestic legislation, such as the Jospin educational law of 10 July 1989, which notably gave pupils new rights of information, expression, and rights of association within schools. To some extent (as we shall see below), this was a new departure in official educational philosophy, but it also provided an interpretation of *laïcité* fully consistent with the intentions of the republican founders such as Jules Ferry. For neutrality in schools, from the start, was meant to apply to teachers, the content of teaching, and school buildings, not to pupils themselves. As the Haut Conseil à l'Intégration put it in its 2001 report on 'Islam in the Republic', teachers and pupils are in a 'radically different position' vis-à-vis *laïcité* in schools: the former have a *duty* to guarantee the neutrality of the public service they provide, so that the latter can *benefit* from such guarantee, as it is there precisely to protect their own freedom of conscience.[15] Official republicans, therefore, are mistaken to extend the '*devoir de réserve*' from teachers to pupils: while it is true that pupils must refrain from acting in such a way that the expression of their beliefs has divisive, obtrusive, or proselytizing effects on the school community, they should not be prevented from displaying mere signs of religious allegiance. Ferry himself had insisted that schools must be *laïque* precisely so as not to 'disturb the fragile and sacred conscience of children'[16] (he had, for example, insisted that all schools be allowed a weekly day off for parents to provide religious instruction to their children).

Critics conclude that it is wrong, therefore, to assimilate schools to fully public spaces in which individuals should act primarily from their shared identity as citizens, on the basis of public, secular reasons: children are not (yet) citizens, and nor are they agents of the state. Schools provide a neutral, non-discriminatory public space which is inclusive of all children regardless of their particular allegiances, and they should scrupulously avoid discriminating against pupils on religious grounds. This, after all, is the civic mission of schools.

Civic Inclusion

For Muslim pupils, the penalty for refusing to remove the hijab is nothing less than exclusion from the school. Advocates of the ban conveniently overlook the fact that it has the effect of denying children the very education that the republic placed at the heart of its civic mission.[17] When (primary) education was made free and compulsory in the 1880s, it was intended to be inclusive of all children, 'with no distinction made on the basis of religion or opinion'. As Education Minister Lionel Jospin reminded critics in 1989, 'schools are there to welcome, not to exclude, children'.[18] It is indeed no small paradox, given the centrality of the right to education and the strongly universalist ethos of common schooling shared by official republicans, that they should hardly pause to consider the damaging consequences of a ban on headscarves. If the point of compulsory common schooling is to inculcate all children with the public norms of citizenship, it is difficult to see how expelling some children from state schools will in any way further the goal of civic inclusion. Nor is this all. The consequences of the ban for Muslim pupils—critics point out—are all the more profound because there are only a handful of Muslim private schools in France.[19] So, contrary to Catholic or Jewish families who can opt for forms of private schooling that better accommodate their religious commitments, Muslims have (as yet) little alternative to state schooling. Many official republicans feel uncomfortable with the very existence of private religious schools in the first place. Yet the fear that the ban on headscarves might precipitate the emergence of separate Muslim schools displaying only tenuous allegiance to the principles of *laïcité* has not proved disturbing enough to unsettle them. The Stasi Report bizarrely notes, with relief, that the law will not necessarily make matters worse as some Muslim families already send their children to Catholic schools,[20] which are known to be more tolerant of the expression of religious beliefs (and because of their 'special character', are exempted from the 2004 law). The majority of expelled Muslim girls, however, have tended to resort to distance-learning schemes validated by the Ministry for National Education. Official republicans have failed to explain how either alternative (private schooling or distance learning) is ultimately preferable to keeping veiled Muslim girls in state schools, where they can be integrated within the 'community of citizens'.[21] The implicit assumption, of course, is that most pupils will accept removing their headscarves, and endorse the identity of undifferentiated citizen in the public sphere.

But here, too, official republicans end up advocating a self-defeating strategy, one that undermines rather than promotes the civic mission they attribute to state schools. If schools are to be genuine microcosms of republican society, they must foster the virtues of toleration and mutual respect that citizens are expected to demonstrate in their interaction with one another. And they can only do this if children are truly exposed to a diversity of lifestyles and beliefs, instead of having their private identities subsumed under a homogenous public identity. The problem is that the official republican conception of civic education takes too easy a route towards civic inclusion. As Meira Levinson has felicitously put it, 'the French model shifts the brunt of liberal education from teaching toleration of *private others* to inculcating mutual respect for *public similars.*'[22] In a useful (if necessarily schematic) comparison, she notes that, in contrast to the English divided, 'privatized' model of public schooling which primarily responds to parental and communal preferences, and in contrast to the American unstable reconciliation of identity politics and common public schooling through the equal accommodation of differences within a pluralist national sphere, the

French republican conception seeks to achieve neutrality through the equal exclusion of differences. This, she rightly notes, frees up the public space of the school, and the public identity of the individual, to be shaped in the service of citizenship more fully than either the American or the English model allow, while preserving in liberal fashion the integrity of private identities.[23] Yet French republicanism makes the achievement of these two objectives of political liberalism conditional on the complete public invisibility of private differences. This is a high price to pay for children forced to leave behind their religious beliefs when they cross the gates of the schools: the demands of citizenship seem unreasonably stringent. In addition, and more to the point here, it is unclear how the public virtue of restraint and avoidance will translate into a private virtue of toleration and mutual respect. In schools, children are implicitly asked to treat Muslim girls with equal respect *despite their being Muslim*, as it were; whether they will be capable, upon leaving the school, to show respect to Muslim girls *as Muslims* is open to question. Banning difference in the public sphere might make respect for difference in the private sphere more hazardous: it is undeniable that the highly publicized hijab controversies have reinforced suspicion—and sometimes stigmatization—of Muslim women wearing the scarf outside the public sphere. The ban on the expression of religious identities in schools, therefore, might unwittingly foster discriminatory attitudes towards them outside schools. Despite official republican claims to the contrary, fostering a strong public identity is an unreliable shortcut to the goal of fostering mutual respect between citizens: a more tortuous, but ultimately more reliable, route would involve teaching toleration through actual confrontation with private differences.

Fairness

Finally, the official republican account can be challenged on the ground that the ban on headscarves in schools is not fair to Muslims, and falls short of the *laïque* aim to treat all citizens with equal respect. Two claims can be made. First, the prohibition on religious signs in schools is not a generally applicable rule mandated by the legal regime of *laïcité* but an ad hoc discriminatory measure against Muslim symbols; second, even when the ban takes the form of a general law universally applicable to all signs (as the 2004 March law does), it is still unfair as it constitutes a form of indirect discrimination against Muslims.

Let me start with the first point. When the first headscarf affair erupted in 1989, there was no legal rule against the wearing *by pupils* of religious signs in schools. At least since 1945, no significant legal case had been brought to the attention of the courts, and necklaces with Christian crosses were (one can presume) widely tolerated in state schools. In 1989, it became clear that the 'problem' with Muslim headscarves was not merely that they were a religious symbol, but that they were a particularly *visible* one. The Conseil d'État, which in its carefully crafted *avis* drew a distinction between the permissible display of religious belief and disruptive actions or attitudes, ambiguously interpreted the *ostentatious* wearing of headscarves as a possible instance of the latter (making references to a 1937 *circulaire* prohibiting proselytism and propaganda in schools). This opened the way to the rather less subtle distinction established by Education Minister François Bayrou in a 1994 *circulaire,* which banned ostentatious religious signs in schools, making it clear that Muslim headscarves but not Jewish yarmulkes nor Christian crosses fell into that category. This measure was nullified by the Conseil d'État on the grounds that it established too absolute a prohibition. Yet until 2004 it was left to headmasters to apply the Conseil d'État regulations by deciding whether particular instances of headscarves-wearing were 'ostentatious' or not. Leaving aside the often intractable difficulties involved in this potentially highly arbitrary decision, it is obvious that the criterion of 'ostentation' was designed specifically to target Muslim signs, and that it relied on a highly contestable notion of unacceptable visibility in the public sphere. Few official republicans paused to consider whether it is legitimate for a neutral, *laïque* state to discriminate between discrete and ostentatious social practices, given that such judgements are inevitably made against the backdrop of specific, non-neutral, cultural contexts. A Muslim hijab is 'ostentatious' in Paris in a way in which it is not in Casablanca where, by contrast, smaller Christian crosses are likely to stand out. The suspicion of 'ostentation', 'proselytism', or 'propaganda' often relied on no more than an impression of visual aggression by the outward expression of an unfamiliar and foreign religion. Yet as J. S. Mill eloquently put it, in a liberal society, the law should never act upon mere social dislike or disgust vis-à-vis a minority practice.[24] It is no small irony, of course, that a religious sign—the headscarf—that is intended to symbolize the modesty and discretion of Muslim women should be considered in France as sign of public assertion and aggressiveness. All in all, those rules unfairly single out the practices of some minorities, and by defining the signs that minorities are allowed to wear in public, indulge in precisely the kind of 'politics of identity' that *laïcité* claims to eschew.[25] A public sphere which in effect prescribes norms of social invisibility to members of religious minorities is not neutral. The 1990s rulings against headscarves, therefore, openly infringe the egalitarian norm of *laïcité*.

The law voted in March 2004 prima facie rectifies this blatant inequality of treatment between Muslims and members of other religious groups, in so far as it prohibits the wearing of 'ostensibly religious' signs, of which Muslim headscarves are just an instance, in the name of the neutrality of the public sphere.[26] So we have a general, universal rule, which applies equally to all, and which is justified by appeal to a legitimate common interest in the maintenance of a secular public space. However, while it is true that the law does not directly discriminate against Muslims, it might constitute a case of indirect discrimination. According to the conception of equality spelt out by the European Court of Justice, discrimination can occur either directly, when similar situations are (wrongly) treated differently, *or* indirectly, when different situations are (wrongly) treated identically.[27] More specifically, indirect discrimination on ethnic or religious grounds occurs when a uniform rule imposes a disproportionate burden on some individuals by unfairly preventing them from complying with obligations that arise from their ethnic or religious membership. Thus, for example, in English law, a claim of indirect discrimination on ethnic grounds is required to show that the proportion of members of a given group who can comply with the regulation is 'considerably smaller' than the proportion of other individuals not of that group who can comply with it.[28] The concept of equality endorsed by French law is incapable of dealing with such indirect discrimination. This is because it postulates that no unfair discrimination can (*ex hypothesi*) occur when individuals (even when situated differently) are treated identically.[29] Thus, a legal decision of 1996 confirmed that a municipal regulation specifying that 'no particular food or diet will be served' in schools was not in breach of republican equality, and did not indirectly discriminate against those religious believers with specific dietary requirements, such as Muslims or Jews.[30] Furthermore, in France, while religious freedom and religious non-discrimination are constitutionally guaranteed, their exercise is subject to *lesser* protection in the public sphere: *laïcité* postulates that religious expression in the public sphere be subjected to prima facie disapprobation. Interestingly, this means that if headscarves are presented not as a sign of religious piety but as traditional, ethnic dress, or as a fashion item, they do not infringe on the *laïcité* of the public sphere and, given the lack of school uniform requirements in French schools (in contrast to England), they cannot be prohibited. Some Muslim groups have thus sought to 're-brand' headscarves as fashion items, and some pupils have come to school wearing what is called a *bandana*, a strip of scarf across the head that leaves hair visible and a popular adolescent fashion accessory. In response, the governmental *circulaire* of 18 May 2004, which specifies the conditions of application of the March law, allows headmasters to prohibit the wearing of 'signs [that are] ostensible in intent' (*par destination*). This power granted to headmasters subjectively to assess the individual motives of headscarves-wearers, regardless of their expressed intentions or their actual behaviour, opens the door to arbitrary and potentially discriminatory decisions. As one legal commentator recently put it, 'between a blond-haired pupil wearing a *bandana* on her head and a Maghrebi [*beur*] pupil wearing the same bandana, it is easy, too easy, to see which of the two will catch the attention of the [school] administration'.[31] This provision therefore opens the way to forms of ethnic or racial discrimination.

Nor is the apparently more general, neutral prohibition on 'objectively' (*par nature*) religious signs immune from discriminatory effects, albeit of a more indirect kind. If, as some Muslims claim, the hijab is a religious obligation, and not merely a symbolic and perfunctory sign of allegiance to a religion, then the cost of obeying the law for pious pupils might be deemed unreasonably high, and an infringement on their religious liberty. No such dilemma, it can be argued, arises for Christians asked to remove 'crosses of manifestly excessive size', as the displaying of the latter is no religious obligation (nor is it a Christian tradition to exhibit 'large' crosses, which reinforces the impression of absurdly ad hoc legislation). Jewish yarmulkes are arguably in a similar position to headscarves but, again, the existence of private Jewish schools makes it easier for Jews to lessen the costs of exclusion from state schools. A charge of indirect discrimination,[32] therefore, could be levelled against the law, on the grounds that Muslim schoolgirls are unfairly deprived both of their right to education[33] and of their right of religious exercise.[34] The European Court of Human Rights might consider that, even if the aim pursued through the prohibition of religious signs—the maintenance of a secular public sphere—is a legitimate one, it cannot pursued in a discriminatory way.[35]

Critics, therefore, challenge the official republican account of the *laïque* doctrine of conscience, and argue that given *laïcité*'s fundamental commitment to religious freedom, civic inclusion and fairness, it should accommodate the wearing of religious signs in state schools. Some critics, however, have gone further, and have also challenged the validity of the ideal of *laïcité* as a separation doctrine. We saw in Chapter 2 that official republicans justify the ban on headscarves in schools through appeal to principles of state neutrality and separation between state and religion. Yet if, as critics argue, the latter are only partially applied in France, and are in any case normatively flawed, then the request that Muslims abide by them becomes difficult to justify. The 'universal non-monetary tax for the maintenance of a secular state' that the ban is supposed to represent is no more than an ad hoc, arbitrary measure which, to use the language of game theory, requires Muslims to cooperate when in practice others defect. Or, to put it differently, it is unfair to ask Muslims to contribute to the maintenance of an ideal secular state if the latter is no more than a myth.

Laïcité *in Practice: The Myth of Separation*

There are two chief problems with the official republican account of the separation doctrine. The first is that it is a normativist account, in the sense that it pays little attention to its actualization in concrete institutions and practices.[36] Official French republicans implicitly assume that the ideals of *laïcité* are already embodied in institutions and practices, and thus make little room for the critical confrontation of the chasm between the strict ideal of separation and the messy reality of actual state–church relationships in France. The ideology of *laïcité*-as-separation functions simultaneously as a descriptive and as a normative category; as descriptive category, it is flawed because it only selects from reality those aspects which fit its normative tenets; as normative category, it is impotent because it cannot act as a criticism of actual practices. Second, the official republican account is anachronistic. Its habitual, almost incantatory, references to a heroic, rather idealized, picture of the achievements of the *laïque* founders of the Third Republic tends to obscure both the reality of the past (that the separation between church and state was far less complete, and far more pragmatic, than official historiography assumes) and the reality of the present (that relationships between state and religions have substantially altered over the last century). In all these different ways, the separation doctrine has become an official republican myth. Thus, critics point out that a fully secular public sphere was never historically achieved in France (1) and that recent developments have further facilitated a *rapprochement* between public and private spheres, and between state and religion, notably in schools (2). Instead of strict separation, what has been emerging in France is 'tolerant' separation, or 'open secularism' (*laïcité ouverte*).[37]

A Historically Incomplete Separation

One chief inspirer of *laïcité ouverte* has been Jean Baubérot, the holder of the Chair in the Sociology of Religions at the Paris École Pratique des Hautes Études. Much of his historical work has sought to debunk the official republican historiography of *laïcité*. In his account, France underwent a gradual process of secularization, of which the 1905 law was only one contingent 'threshold' and not, as official republicans portray it, the *nec plus ultra* of enlightened secular rationality. The first 'threshold', that of the 1801 Concordat, had already achieved significant recognition of religious pluralism and of the autonomy of the state from religious interference. Further, Bauberot thinks it is inaccurate to present *laïcité* as the forcible imposition of a secular order by republicans onto a recalcitrant church. Instead, he writes of a series of '*laïque* pacts', in which pragmatic compromises were reached between republican rulers and religious institutions. Lastly, he insists that the Separation Law embodied a 'tolerant separation', that promoted by socialist leaders Jean Jaurès and Aristide Briand (who were keen to appease religious conflict, which they saw as a distraction from social problems), instead of the more militant anticlerical proposals of Émile Combes and Ferdinand Buisson.[38] The upshot of this revised account is that the French pattern of secularization is not as unique as official republicans claim; the separation between church and state was a contingent and not a necessary outcome; and it took more moderate forms than is often claimed. Thus, the exceptionality of the French experience is relativized: French-style institutional separation is not a pure form of secularism of which other countries only offer pale imitations. Instead, it is more useful to identify a general pattern of Western secularism (the non-confessional nature of the state, recognition of religious freedom, and so forth) and to see French *laïcité* as one parochial version of it. Specific national experiences—the impact of the radical Enlightenment, strong Catholic hostility towards the principles of the 1789 Revolution, the strength of the state tradition, and the pronounced distrust towards the public role of intermediary groups—account for the historical association of French secularism with the strict exclusion of religions from the public sphere.[39] Now that these conflictual ideological legacies have lost their raison d'être, it is time for official republicans to take a more objective, less-biased look at the actual legal and administrative powers historically granted to religions by the French, instead of focusing on the formal structure of church–state relationships and the separation doctrine.[40]

The first thing they should take note of is that the French state has not refrained from subsidizing religions, directly or indirectly.[41] It is in this area that the gap between 'legal *laïcité*' and 'imagined *laïcité*'[42] is most pronounced. Some exceptions to the neutrality-as-abstention principle have already been referred to: they concern state provision of chaplaincies in closed institutions (to guarantee the actual exercise of religious rights to prisoners, soldiers, etc.) and the public maintenance of—some—religious buildings (which may be justified through a concern for the preservation of the national heritage). In addition, religious associations, when they are recognized as promoting a 'public interest', benefit from a generous system of tax breaks on donations (laws of 1959 and 1987) which closely aligns them with the status of charities in other countries. Religious associations can also obtain public support for their charitable, educational, social—though not their religious—activities. Some legal commentators go as far as comparing the French situation to that of Britain and the Netherlands, where public support for religion is mostly indirect,[43] or even to an 'implicit system of recognised cults'[44] closer to the German system. It has even been suggested that, regardless of the formal differences between systems of church–state separation, concordatarian arrangements, and national churches, a fairly distinctive and homogeneous 'Western European model of church and state relations' could be discerned, whereby basic religious freedoms are available to all, but state support is greater for those religious groups that share the principles and values upheld by the majority.[45]

It would seem that formally secular and separationist France bears this out. Most strikingly, for example, the French Republic subsidizes private (mostly Catholic) schools (up to 10 per cent of their budget). While historically the *laïque* Left had rallied to the slogan 'state funds for state schools, private funds for private schools', Catholics retorted that respect for freedom of religion and for freedom of teaching (*liberté d'enseignement*) required that the state step in to ensure that such freedoms were effectively realized. The Debré Law of 1959 made public funding conditional on private schools entering into a 'contract of association' with the state, which compelled them, inter alia, to follow the national curriculum and welcome all children regardless of their religious background. While, as a result, little remains of the 'special character' of private schools, which about 17 per cent of French schoolchildren attend, this uneasy compromise sheds doubts over the republican claim that only common schooling in state-run, fully secular schools can adequately fulfil the civic purposes of education. The anomalous situation of state-funded private schools in *laïque* France remains bizarrely under-theorized in official republican writings. Even more damaging to the official republican case, given its commitment to legal uniformity, is the exceptional status of religious groups in

Alsace-Moselle. Those regions became French again in 1918 but were not subjected to the legal regime of *laïcité*: as a result, ministers are paid by the state, religious teaching (Catholic, Protestant, and Jewish) is offered in schools, and Catholic bishops are appointed by the President of the Republic (the only head of state in the world to do so).[46] The Stasi Report—the most recent, comprehensive statement of the official republican view of *laïcité*—saw no need to introduce any but cosmetic alterations to this historical anomaly.[47]

Yet the entanglement of the French public sphere with religions is not merely an exotic phenomenon relegated to the outer fringes of the national territory. French public life is still permeated, in more or less direct ways, by Catholic culture, as testified by national holidays which include such specifically Catholic dates as All Saints' or Assumption Day. The diffuse hegemony of Catholic culture—an estimated 65 per cent of the French population still refer to themselves as culturally Catholic—means that few eyebrows were raised when the official burial ceremony for Socialist President François Mitterrand took place at the Notre Dame Cathedral in Paris, or when the republic celebrated in great pomp the anniversary of the baptism of the first medieval Christian King, Clovis. Nor is this all. It is often noted that republican *laïcité* modelled itself on the organizational and ideological structures of the Catholic Church. As if through mimetic assertion, republicans set up an alternative comprehensive system of values and institutions, which shared the centralization, hierarchy, and dogmatism of their Catholic adversary. No wonder republicans often unconsciously use religious language to refer to the 'sacred' mission of state schools, 'sanctuaries' where children become enlightened through the selfless devotion of teachers, the 'priests' of the *laïque* 'faith'. As Baubérot states in a trenchant criticism of the official republicans' dogmatic view of schools: 'as the unique and obligatory path towards the universal, the school becomes the mediating institution which dispenses knowledge-as-salvation and, alone, fights off the hellish demons present everywhere in society. Their school is a counter-church. But it is a church that is typically Catholic (word which precisely signifies "universal").'[48] The rhetoric of the school as a 'sanctuary'—a sacred space that can be entered only with awe and restraint, and often bareheaded—also echoes religious imagery. It is as though, historically, the material and symbolic power of the Catholic Church was such that republicans had to establish a counter-society able to replicate the level of affective mobilization previously achieved by the Catholic *Zeitgeist*.[49] Commentators have astutely referred to 'Catho-*laïcité*', or to 'Catholicism without Christianity' as the official doctrine of the French Republic.[50] The legal order of *laïcité* was chiefly elaborated in relation to the Catholic Church.[51] Hence, for example, its bias towards tightly structured, centralized religious groups, and its inability coherently to deal with the claims of new religious movements. Danièle Hervieu-Léger has convincingly demonstrated that the French antipathy towards new religious movements and cults (*sectes*) partly derives from this narrow conception of religious pluralism, whose recognition stops at the borders of traditional religions, and notably those which, like Catholicism, exhibits a clear hierarchical structure and clergy.[52] The religious representatives of the traditional 'recognized cults' have, even after 1905, remained the 'privileged interlocutors of public authorities'.[53]

As we shall see, the de facto non-neutrality of the French public sphere considerably weakens the official republican claim that the regime of *laïcité* treats Muslims fairly. Meanwhile, it is worth pointing out that, historically, Islam, as the dominant religion in colonial territories such as Algeria (which was officially a French *département*), was always granted special—discriminatory—treatment.[54] The 1905 Separation Law was not applied in Algeria. Colonial authorities sought to exercise tight control over Islam, and despite repeated requests, refused Algerian Muslims the benefits of the Separation Law. Note too that one condition of access to French citizenship for Algerians was that they give up their 'personal status' (under which they were subject to Islamic family law)—a unfortunate signal that allegiance to Islam and French citizenship were incompatible.[55] The official republican assumption of the 'citizenship deficit' of Muslims seems, therefore, to have long-standing, if unconscious, colonial roots.[56] Nor did the republic, for all its commitment to *laïcité*, wholeheartedly foster the '*laïcization*' and 'nationalization' of the mainland Muslim community. The tortuous history of the Great Mosque of Paris (funded by the state through an exceptional 1920 law suspending the provisions of the 1905 law, and later controlled by the Moroccan and then the Algerian governments) is ample testimony of the competition between the French and foreign states for the control of the Muslims of France. This made difficult the emergence of an independently organized 'French Islam', subject to the same legal regime as other religious groups. In sum, there was, from the start, a 'Muslim exception to *laïcité*',[57] which did not, contrary to official republican claims, exclusively stem from Muslims' presumed inability to adapt to the secular order.

Careful examination of the historical regime of *laïcité* therefore, reveals a mass of anomalies, exceptions, and compromises which sit awkwardly with the descriptive-cum-normative separation doctrine expounded by official republicans.

The Transformations of the Public Sphere

Since 1945, the ideological foundations of *laïcité* have been further undermined by a multifaceted movement of profound redefinition of the relationship between public and private spheres. As Rivero pointed out, *laïcité* was elaborated in a society characterized by the coexistence of and separation between a centralized but hardly interventionist state and a fairly autonomous civil society.[58] By the mid-twentieth century, increased public regulation of social and economic life, coupled with greater involvement of social groups in the design and implementation of public policy, blurred well-established boundaries between public and private spheres. By the 1980s, it became clear to many that the state could no longer claim to be the *instituteur* of social life; it had become a more modest *régulateur*.[59] The official ideology of *laïcité*, which was originally conceived as an 'anti-theology' asserting the autonomy of the political state against the social power of Catholicism, lost much of its raison d'être and motivational appeal as its traditional adversary, the Catholic Church, crumbled.[60] Church authorities publicly accepted *laïcité* and the republican order, and had to contend with accelerating secularization and the 'de-regulation' of religious life, as evidenced by the proliferation of new religious movements. The internal transformation of religions and the pluralization and fragmentation of the religious landscape were accompanied by new claims for the public recognition of religions as valid forms of both of personal identity and social bond. The 'conflict between the two Frances' was over, it was held, and *laïcité* had entered into a new phase, where religions were no longer excluded from the public sphere but, rather, recognized as legitimate partners in collective discussion and decision-making.[61] Religions have been increasingly recognized as having a 'social' and 'cultural' role, and have to that effect been supported by state institutions, in breach of the strict separation doctrine.[62]

Not surprisingly, education has not been immune from the broad shift in the boundaries between public and private sphere. When official republicans defend the ban on hijab as a way to preserve the integrity of the 'detached school', they conjure up an unrealistic and anachronistic picture of the school as an egalitarian 'counter-society', a kind of sanctuary wholly insulated from civil society. Yet, even during the heyday of the Third Republic, *laïque* schools were less meritocratic and egalitarian, and more tolerant of family cultural and religious identities, than republican mythology implies.[63] More significantly, since the generalization of mass education in the 1960s, the whole republican model of education has been shaken to its core.

Critical sociologists pointed out that seemingly democratic schooling reinforced rather than undermined existing social hierarchies.[64] Post-1968 libertarians stressed that its centralized, uniform, and disciplinary organization was oppressive both of the personality of children and of their cultural identities. Individuals have rightly become suspicious of the arrogant, rationalist, and scientist domination exercised by official republican educational experts.[65] More recently, the rise of 'educational consumerism' on the part of (middle-class) parents has accentuated the chasm between the official doctrine of common schooling and widespread practices of strategic uses of increasingly diversified resources in an educational 'black market'.[66] Schools are being urged to open up to the values of the family and the marketplace and, inevitably, to be more tolerant of the expression of religious identities. They no longer transform society, but are transformed by it.[67] In this changed context, with the secular character of schools no longer seen as a bulwark against the forces of illiberal conservatism, the *laïque* fear of the 'intrusion of religions' into schools seems wholly misplaced. In an increasingly secularized society, the differences between a (formally) religious education in a private school and a secular education in a state school have become immaterial: in practice, both public and private schools compete to meet parental demands of educational performance and responsiveness. Among those demands is that for greater tolerance of children's cultural and religious identities: far from a reassertion of clerical control over the nation's youth, such demands must be related to the extension of a number of citizenship rights (information, rights of association, and expression) to schoolchildren and to the growing de-institutionalization and individualization of religious claims and practices. Education specialists have even worried about the profound ignorance on the part of French children of the religious dimension of their society's historical heritage and, significantly, recent proposals have been made to introduce basic exposure to the main world religions into the national curriculum.[68] Thus, it is time (for critics of official *laïcité*) to substitute a '*laïcité* of intelligence' for the traditional '*laïcité* of indifference', in Régis Debray's felicitous words. As *laïcité ouverte* advocate and legal adviser to the government, Kessler states, 'schools are *laïque*, not because they forbid the expression of different faiths but because they tolerate all of them.'[69] Official republicans, then, cling to an ideal that has lost all credibility in contemporary society. By interpreting the wearing of Muslim headscarves through the lenses of late nineteenth-century anticlerical struggles, they are oblivious to the profound changes that religion, the public sphere, and schools have undergone over the last decades. Those changes invite a re-conceptualization of the relationship between state and religion.

From Fact to Norm: 'Tolerant Secularism'

Advocates of *laïcité ouverte* or 'tolerant secularism' argue that the profound historical changes briefly charted in the previous paragraph mean that the separation ideal defended by official republicans has lost its normative appeal. The time has come for the French to develop a 'new paradigm'[70] which takes seriously the ethical pluralism of contemporary society, recognizes the contribution that religions can make to public debate, and ensures fair treatment to minority religions such as Islam. *Laïcité* should not be about the strict separation between the state and religion, but about the even-handed tolerance and recognition of religious groups by the state.

Recognizing the Public Role of Religions

The transformations of the public sphere and of religion charted above have momentous consequences for the normative critique of *laïcité*. As we shall see in Chapter 6, the publicization of religious faith as a valid expression of authentic personal identity raises deep questions about the *laïque* commitment to individual emancipation from traditional allegiances; and, as we shall see in Chapter 9, the emergence of religiously based identities as alternative forms of communal membership deeply challenges the *laïque* conception of national identity. This section concentrates on the particular challenge such transformations pose to *laïcité* as a *shared secular ethic*. Advocates of *laïcité ouverte* (tolerant secularism), or 'deliberative *laïcité*'—grouped notably around the Ligue de l'Enseignement[71] and the liberal Catholic journal *Esprit*—have since the mid-1980s sought to rethink the ethical foundations of *laïcité*. In this, they were encouraged by the broad renewal of interest in moral and political philosophy in academic circles.[72] They make two related claims. First, traditional *laïcité* is ill-equipped to confront the deepest ethical issues of the time. In its attempt to found a wholly secular morality, either it merely replicated the Christian-influenced 'good old morality of our fathers'—a set of vague precepts of civil behaviour—or it became entangled with purely instrumentalist uses of the grand nineteenth-century ideals of reason, science, and progress. Today, in a world scientifically disenchanted and characterized by a deep pluralism of conflicting worldviews, the *laïque* morality of the founders of the Third Republic appears to be, at best, ineffective and, at worst, bankrupt.[73] It is, notably, unable to inform public debate about such divisive and uncharted areas as bio-ethics. So contemporary moral philosophers rightly begin their enquiries from the 'fact of pluralism'—or, in Weberian terms, the 'war of the gods'[74]—and from the refusal to assert the superiority of any conception of the good life. If common values are to be found in contemporary societies, they can only be ascertained through the procedural, dialogical means of the exercise of public reason.[75] In this conception of 'deliberative *laïcité*',[76] moral values should not be deduced monologically from a starting point located in human reason, as in the 'independent ethic' logic charted in Chapter 2, they should be elaborated dialogically through the confrontation of conflicting but overlapping ethical perspectives.

The second claim made by advocates of *laïcité ouverte* is that religious groups can make valuable contributions to public debate and public policy.[77] Their commitment to a comprehensive view of the good life is a useful antidote to the secularist bias towards instrumental rationality and the damaging separation of social life into private and public spheres. Furthermore, religious leaders are increasingly willing and able to address both believers and non-believers on key issues of social life in non-confessional fashion. They therefore can act as the moral consciences of the nation and as 'civic voices' in an ongoing public deliberation about the content and implications of the new *laïque* ethos. Some, like Jean Baubérot, have identified the latter as the 'ecumenical religion of human rights'—a 'religion' that even the Catholic Church now professes to embrace, thus allowing the 'non-clerical involvement of Catholicism in the public sphere'.[78] The 'new *laïque* pact' called for by Jean Baubérot and Jean-Paul Willaime breaks with *laïcité* as a 'counter-system' opposed to religions to define it as 'the regulating framework of the pluralism of worldviews'.[79] 'Reasonable comprehensive doctrines', including religious ones, should be 'recognized' as legitimate participants in 'public reason'.[80] Tellingly, the National Consultative Committee on Ethics presented its own work as such an exercise in Rawls-inspired public reason.[81] The composition of this Committee—four out of its 41 members come from prominent 'spiritual families'—is one striking instance of the growing (and unprecedented) legitimacy of religious representatives in official republican institutions, and of the state's recognition of 'the social utility of religions in moral reflection'.[82] Sociologist of religion Hervieu-Léger has advocated the creation of a 'High Council of *Laïcité*' made up notably of religious representatives and responsible for adjudicating 'struggles over values' arising from the multifaceted claims made in the name of religion in the public sphere—and she predictably cited, as one of those 'struggles', the conflict over the permissibility of hijab in schools.[83] Religious groups, in sum, have a growing role to play in the democratic redefinition of the norms of *laïcité*.

In what sense, then, is *laïcité ouverte* still a regime of *laïcité*? For its advocates, it preserves the central insights of republican *laïcité*, in its commitment to respect for religious pluralism and religious freedoms, to a shared (if overlapping) public ethic, and to the confessional neutrality of the state. Yet such neutrality—which, it must be recalled, embodies an ideal of equality—is achieved, not through strict separation between state and religions but, rather, through inclusive and even-handed treatment of all religions. As Charles Taylor puts it, 'the goal is a state which is even-handed between religious communities, equidistant from them, as it were, rather than one where religious reasons play no overt role.'[84] Given the unavoidably prominent influence of Christian traditions in France, including in the public sphere, only a conception of neutrality as even-handedness can guarantee fair treatment for Muslims.

Fair Treatment for Muslims

The historical non-neutrality of the French public sphere and the de facto recognition of religious organizations by the Republic raise serious doubts about the coherence of the official republican rejection of a number of Muslim demands. In 1994, the Muslim Representative Council (CORIF) adopted a 'Charter of the Muslim Cult in France' whose Article 31 dealt with 'equality between religions'. It notably requested state measures towards the building of mosques, the appointment of Muslim 'chaplains' [*aumôniers*] in schools, the army, hospitals and prisons, 'Muslim areas' in cemeteries, and private schools under contract of association with the state. Official republicans, in their eagerness to discount many Muslim requests as moves towards the unacceptable publicization of religion, and as involving breaches of republican equality, fail to see that most religious demands are not compensatory or exemption-based, but simply require the application of the current regime of *laïcité* to Islam. Thus, Muslim demands such as public help towards the building of mosques and recognition of (some) Muslim holidays are not demands for unacceptable 'visibility in the public square', 'positive discrimination', or 'special treatment',[85] but are merely requests of *comparable visibility* and equal rights between majority and minority religions. The Stasi Report, for its part—perhaps to compensate for its tough stance on headscarves—accepted that legitimate demands (such as the provision of pork-free meals in schools, prisons, and the army, or the creation of 'Muslim areas' in communal cemeteries) should be acceded to, even if they implied special provisions and exemptions from the common law.[86] Genuine respect of freedom of religion by the *laïque* state requires that Muslim-sensitive 'reasonable accommodations' be made.[87] Yet the report failed to frame such demands within a coherent account of equality between religions. For example, it grudgingly conceded that 'no legal disposition prevents the creation of Muslim [private] schools'[88]—an embarrassedly negative formulation which signalled a less than ringing endorsement of the mere extension of rights already enjoyed by Christians and Jews. Even more troubling is the report's confused justification of some glaring breaches of the secular neutrality of the state. One example is its unexpected defence of the existing exceptional regime of Alsace-Moselle. Given the report's insistence on the need to reaffirm the 'founding' principles of the 'separation between state and religion', which ultimately justify the proposed ban on headscarves in schools, it could be expected that it would at least have questioned the justifiability of this regional exception. Not so. While it recommended that the teaching of Islam be introduced in Alsatian schools, along with that of other religions, it defended the 'special status' of Alsace-Moselle, on the grounds that those regions were 'not present on French soil in 1905' and that 'local populations are attached to it'.[89] Such arguments—the 'historical argument' and the 'communal consent' argument—sit awkwardly with the neutrality-oriented philosophical foundations of the separation doctrine. They also unwittingly provide argumentative ammunition for other groups—such as Muslims—who were 'not present in 1905' either, and who might be similarly 'attached' to the application of non-*laïque* provisions to them. As Baubérot has wrily commented, 'it is difficult to justify conceding everything to Alsatians and nothing to Muslims.'[90]

Such inconsistencies reveal that official republicans find it difficult to conceptualize what equality between religions requires in a society that does not live up to the ideal theory of separation. When confronted with demands of equal recognition by minority faiths (notably Islam), they resort to an implicit default position which we might characterize as a 'regime of toleration', not a regime of equality. A regime of toleration (in the strict sense) operates against the background of a public culture permeated by majority (mainly Catholic) traditions, from which decisions about how to respond to minority demands are made. Toleration then refers to grudging acceptance (or forbearance) of unfamiliar or strange behaviour or attitudes of minority groups by majority groups. We have seen that normative *laïcité*, by contrast, is based on an assumption of absolute neutrality between majority and minority religions (in fact, it need not even acknowledge the existence of majorities and minorities). In many cases (as in the ban on headscarves), official republicans appeal to normative *laïcité* to repudiate Muslim demands, but when faced with the messy reality of the actual *laïcité* regime in France, they resort to a confused, almost embarrassed appeal to pragmatic compromises and the unavoidable permeation of the French public sphere by century-long Christian traditions.

Advocates of *laïcité ouverte,* for their part, are more candid about the need positively to recognize and value such traditions (it is no coincidence that many of them have a Christian background), but they are also more worried about how minority religions fare under such a regime of toleration. They would probably endorse a version of what Joseph Carens and Veit Bader have called 'equality as even-handedness'—where equality stands for rough, prorated, equivalent support for all religious groups and is partly measured through assessment of substantive outcomes (e.g. actual provision of religious facilities).[91] Evidently, substantive equality between religions does not mean that all religious groups should have the same number of religious facilities or benefit from identical amounts of state support, but it means that they should enjoy official recognition in rough proportion to their social 'representativeness' (as measured, for example, by the number of their members).[92] While *laïcité ouverte* advocates freely concede that this should mean a greater willingness on the part of the state to give support to the dominant religion, Catholicism,[93] they also plausibly suggest that Islam would also fare better (in absolute terms) under their system than under the current system. In this way, 'the most debatable feature of the European model of church and state relations—its inborn degree of unequal treatment—can be kept under control and the balance between basic freedom for all and selective cooperation can assure a reasonable integration between old and new Europeans.'[94] For example, Muslims could be compensated for the fact that, in contrast to Catholics, they did not benefit from extensive state support *prior to* the Separation Law of 1905, and therefore found it difficult subsequently to gather enough funds to build mosques. There is a case, therefore, for 'historical compensation' for Muslims, which would take the form either of a relaxing of the distinction between 'cult-related' and 'cultural' activities (thus allowing state support to Islamic centres containing a prayer room or even a fully fledged mosque) or, alternatively, of an exceptional suspension of the 1905 law to authorize publicly funded mosques.[95] Because formal equality and state abstention often perpetuate historically entrenched inequalities, measures of 'compensatory inequalities' can be justified, thus bridging the gap between the 'normative *laïcité*' praised by official republicans and the reality of structurally unfair treatment of recently established religions. Demands for the public recognition of religion and equality as even-handedness have culminated in the Archbishop of Strasbourg's proposal that the regime of Alsace-Moselle be extended to the whole of France—offering to all religions, including Islam, the benefits of public funding and religious teaching in schools.[96]

Advocates of *laïcité ouverte* further argue that official republicans fail to treat Muslims fairly when they impose stringent demands of laïcization on them. The charge is twofold. First, if it is true that the French separation regime is in practice a form of 'Catho-*laïcité*', then the presumed incompatibility between *laïcité* and Islam may have as much to do with the historical particularism of the French system as with the presumed allergy of Muslims to liberal universalist norms. As Dalil Boubakeur, the *recteur* of the Paris Mosque, and Soheib Bencheik, the moderate Marseilles *mufti*, have insisted, Muslims can smoothly integrate into confessionally neutral Western states respectful of religious freedoms.[97] Suggestions that Muslims are congenitally unable to separate the public and private dimensions of their lives smack of orientalist clichés about the essentially pre-modern nature of Islam. In practice, the integration of Muslims into Western society requires pragmatic adjustments on both sides and, as Carens and Williams have noted, 'for the most part, a commitment to equality would seem more strongly to support a modification of Western attitudes towards Muslim immigrants than a demand that Muslims modify their practices.'[98] Second, even if it were true that Islam is an all-embracing worldview intrinsically hostile to secularism, this is hardly a Muslim peculiarity. All monotheistic religions have endorsed secularist norms slowly, painfully, and reluctantly, as the protracted conflicts between the Catholic Church and the French state amply testify. Nor have they—or indeed can they—endorse the substantive norms of secularism: many religious believers opine that God's law is superior to man-made law, that true morality can only be religiously derived, that abortion is morally wrong, and so forth. Yet as long as they do not seek to use the state to act upon those views or impose them upon others, and they accept to distinguish, for purposes of peaceful social cooperation, their 'political' identity as citizens from their 'comprehensive' values (to borrow Rawlsian terms used to make this point by *laïcité ouverte* advocate Françoise Lorcerie[99]), they conform to the civic norms of *laïcité*. To require more of Muslims (to ask them to become substantively secular) is in effect to apply a double standard to them. By analogy, *laïcité* never forbade the Bishop of Paris from declaring in his Sunday sermons that abortion was wrong: what it forbade him from doing was to support attacks against abortion clinics.[100] Religious believers are not required to 'love' republican laws but merely to 'respect' them.[101] While some commentators explicitly endorse what Rawls would call a modus vivendi view of *laïcité*,[102] others hope to preserve *laïcité* as a sincerely shared public ethic, but one whose content becomes the product of democratic deliberations in which Muslim organizations should be actively engaged. Thus, Hervieu-Léger has suggested that Islam be 'included among the "great spiritual families" which do not merely accept the republican legal order, but which contribute to providing its moral and symbolic foundations'.[103] More than a century after the 1905 law was passed, many in France agree with her that the separation doctrine should be given up and that traditional *laïcité* should give way to a more tolerant secularism. This tolerant secularism, to sum up the findings of this section in Hervieu-Léger's words, should strive to 'combine the public recognition of the "great spiritual families" with respect for equality between all religious groups'.[104]

CHAPTER 4

Critical Republicanism, Secularism, and Impartiality

Let me summarize my arguments so far. Chapter 2 set out the official republican case for the ban on religious signs (particularly, Muslim headscarves) in schools. Muslims are required to respect the secular (non-religious) neutrality of schools, which are seen to be part of the public sphere. According to the official republican ideal of *laïcité*, republican equality is best promoted through maintenance of the secular nature of the public sphere and non-interference by the state in religious matters. The separationist and abstentionist dimensions of *laïque* neutrality are held to protect the values of equal citizenship, religious freedom, and universalist inclusion. Chapter 3 rebutted this official republican argument and examined two versions of the tolerant republican case for allowing religious signs in schools. According to the first version, secular *laïcité* might be an appealing ideal, but on no plausible interpretation does it mandate that schoolchildren's rights to wear religious clothing be restricted. The ideals affirmed by *laïcité* (religious freedom, inclusion, and equal respect) are violated rather than promoted by the ban on headscarves. The second version of the tolerant republican challenge goes further, and cast doubts on the *laïque* ideal itself. As separation is no more than a historical myth, and the French public sphere is far from neutral in the *laïque* sense, contextual fairness demands that the privileges historically granted to Catholics be extended to minority religions such as Islam. Tolerant republicanism, therefore, substitutes pragmatic even-handedness between religious groups for abstentionist neutrality, and allows for the recognition of collective religious identities in the public sphere.

In this chapter, I attempt to adjudicate between these two contrasting approaches by defending a critical republican theory of secularism.

Briefly put, I shall argue that opposition to the ban on religious signs does not imply opposition to secularism per se. Thus, critical republicanism finds no fault with the first version of the tolerant republican argument as it applies to the ban on hijab. If secularism is properly understood, as the idea that public institutions must be religiously neutral in order not to dominate citizens of all faiths, it cannot justify a ban on schoolchildren wearing religious signs. Critical republicanism, by contrast, is more sceptical of the second version of the tolerant republican challenge, which rejects secular separationism on the grounds that, as existing arrangements fall short of the ideal of *laïcité*, it would be unfair to require Muslims to abide by them. Critical republicanism interrogates the relationship between facts and norms, with a view to articulate what treating Muslims fairly means under a non-neutral regime. In a first section, I argue that both official and tolerant republicanism suffer from a form of 'status quo neutrality' (to use Cass Sunstein's expression[1]) which fails to assess the legitimacy of existing church–state arrangements. In a second section, I set out critical republican principles of secular impartiality, which identify a baseline from which practical claims of fairness between religions can be evaluated. In a third section, I show how these principles help us respond to a range of Muslim demands for public recognition, in France and elsewhere. What matters to critical republicans is that Muslims, like all citizens, enjoy a status of non-domination in the secular state.

Before proceeding, let me note that although my critical republican principles have primarily been elaborated in the context of French *laïcité* (as the structure of this book makes clear), they are designed to be general enough to be relevant to a range of controversies about the place of religion in contemporary politics. Of course, the political theory of multiculturalism and secularism needs to attend to the context of its elaboration and application, if only to avoid implicitly generalizing the North American experience.[2] To that extent, it is important to keep in mind that the politics of religious accommodation are (and should be) deeply influenced by the historical structure of church–state relations in individual countries. Thus Muslim politics in France, England, and Germany have been profoundly influenced by, respectively, the traditions of separationist *laïcité*, Anglican establishment *cum* tolerance, and multiple public incorporation.[3] They therefore uneasily lend themselves to the application of abstract normative guidelines. Yet attending to context does not mean giving up on the ambition to articulate general principles valid across different contexts. Thus, my critical republicanism is able to shed light on national controversies such as the UK debate about faith schools, the German debate about Muslim incorporation, and the US debate about the legitimacy of religious arguments in politics.[4] One ambition of critical secularism is precisely to keep a delicate balance between contextual relevance and normative generalization.

Religious Neutrality and the Status Quo

In Chapters 2 and 3, we saw that official and tolerant republicans propound almost opposite interpretations of the proper relationship between state and religion. Here, I want to argue that, despite their profound differences, they share one central flaw: they both endorse a version of 'status quo neutrality'.[5] Status quo neutrality refers to a theoretical position which takes the existing distribution of burdens and benefits in society for granted or, more precisely, which fails to provide an impartial baseline from which current claims about inequalities or unjust treatment can be normatively assessed. Neither official nor tolerant republicans are sufficiently critical of existing church–state arrangements, and their potentially dominating effect. Their respective attitude towards the status quo is problematic, although for opposite reasons—or so I shall argue in this section. The next sections will explicate more fully the demands of critical republican secularism as impartiality and non-domination.

Official republicans conduct their defence of *laïcité* through *abstraction from* the status quo. Focusing exclusively on explicating how things should be, they pay no attention to justifying or criticizing how things are. Thus, they respond to Muslim demands for recognition with a principled and abstract defence of the separation between state and religion, wilfully ignoring the fact that the French state is neither indifferent towards religious groups nor neutral between them. Thus, they expose themselves to two connected charges of inconsistency. The first is that of double standards: the state should not make demands on Muslims that it does not make on other religious believers. The second is a version of the *tu quoque* ('you too') objection: the state should not impose on Muslims the application of principles (of *laïcization*) that it itself does not fully honour. Now, in logic seminars and in law courts, *ad hominem* arguments of this kind tend to be dismissed as argumentative fallacies, because they undermine the authority of the speaker rather than address the substance of her argument. When it comes to assessing the fairness of political decisions, however, consistency over time and even-handed treatment of different groups are far from irrelevant considerations. So even if, for example, it is thought that no public money should (ideally) be used to build religious facilities, it might be difficult, in practice, to justify denying Muslims any kind of financial support, given the fact that Catholic churches are, by historical agreement, subsidized by the state. At the very least, official republicans would have to admit that the current regime of state–church relations in France exhibits anomalies which are troubling from the perspective of the French state's proclaimed commitment to neutralist separation. Failing that, the demand that Muslims abide by principles of *laïcité* as neutrality when, under status quo arrangements, *laïcité* is only imperfectly realized, cannot plausibly be construed as a fair demand. Note that my critique of neutrality here differs from standard perfectionist, communitarian, multiculturalist, and feminist critiques. I am not claiming that the ideal of neutrality itself should be abandoned because states in the real world are, necessarily and pervasively, non-neutral. Nor am I proposing that we substitute consequentialist neutrality (whereby actual end-state results are taken into account as a measure of fairness) for justificatory neutrality (whereby the fairness of the rule is justified independently of its practical impact on different individuals and groups). It is my belief that justificatory neutrality captures an important value of fairness, one which focuses on providing people equal opportunity sets for the pursuit of their various ideals, instead of ensuring that people are equally successful in their pursuits.[6] The chief problem with justificatory neutrality, and the separationist conception of *laïcité* that it inspires, is that it is wrongly expected by official republican to generate directly applicable principles of treatment of minorities. Yet, as Marxists and critical theorists have long pointed out, directly and uncritically applying rules of neutrality under non-neutral institutional conditions only perpetuates the status quo and legitimizes existing inequalities between dominant and minority groups. In the words of Dutch sociologist Jan Rath, 'the shift to state neutrality [is] like drawing up the bridge in front of the newcomers'.[7] To put the point differently. The problem with official republican neutrality is *not* that it is an impractical 'ideal theory', to use John Rawls's term. It is, rather, that while (in contrast to Rawlsian ideal theory) it claims to be a set of directly applicable, or at least action-guiding, principles, it nonetheless (by contrast to Rawlsian non-ideal theory) completely abstracts from the concrete conditions to which they are supposed to apply. It is the combination of high-minded abstraction, action-guiding ambition, and fact-insensitivity that makes official republicanism vulnerable to the charge of status quo neutrality.

Tolerant republicans, for their part, suffer from an opposite problem. They justify their critique of neutralist *laïcité* through *idealization of* (not abstraction from) the status quo. Their claim, at its simplest, is that the existing rights and privileges enjoyed by the historically dominant church should be extended, in the name of fairness, to more recently established minority religions such as Islam. In the words of Tariq Modood in the context of English debates about whether the established status of the Anglican Church can benefit religious minorities, we should aim to 'equalize upwards' (i.e. multi-faith recognition) rather than 'equaliz[ing] downwards' (i.e. disestablishment).[8] French tolerant republicans, likewise, argue that Islam will benefit from an extension and generalization of the implicit 'system of recognized cults' prevalent in France. They take an openly practical approach to the even-handed treatment of minorities under non-neutral conditions, and are much more aware than official republicans of the complexity of demands for contextual fairness. Yet, I would suggest, they tend to idealize the status quo and to make virtue out of necessity. In their eagerness to ensure some kind of equity between majority and minority religions, they gloss over the need for the proper justification of the existing entitlements and privileges of the historically dominant church. Thus, they argue that the right to set up their own schools cannot consistently be denied to Muslims, given that it has been granted to Christians and Jews. Yet, they have not established whether faith schools are legitimate in the first place (I briefly discuss this below, as well as in other parts of the book). Thus, they are vulnerable to the charge of status quo neutrality: they, no more than official republicans, make a systematic effort to justify or criticize existing state–religion relationships. While official republicans' theory of separation is too abstract and too disconnected from reality to provide fair and practical guidelines for reform, tolerant republicans' theory of even-handed fairness is too ad hoc, and lacks principled criteria with which to distinguish between legitimate and illegitimate forms of political recognition of religion. Furthermore, their theory of equality as even-handedness between groups runs into familiar problems attendant to consequentialist neutrality and the conception of outcome equality it generates (problems of measurement, problematic concept of 'representativeness', fairness for non-religious citizens, notably).

This is not to deny that these are complex issues. Treating different religious groups fairly in existing societies, where historical contingencies, rather than principles of justice, have left their mark on state–church relationships, is far from straightforward. But I have suggested that the terms of the current debate between secularists and their critics are themselves fraught. Both sides, for different reasons, fail to identify and defend a benchmark of religious equality against which the status quo can be criticized and reforms justified. In what follows, I sketch a revised theory of republican secularism which is both *critical* and *normative*, thus avoiding the defaults of status quo neutrality.

In Defence of (Critical) Secularism as Impartiality

Most liberals take it for granted that liberal democracies have a secular core. Even multiculturalist critics such as Will Kymlicka argue that while politics and culture cannot, and should not, be kept apart, a separation should be maintained between the state and religion.[9] Yet this intuitive liberal separationism is in need of proper justification and defence—a need made more acute by the recent, multifaceted assault on secular ideals and practices.[10] In what follows, I attempt to identify and defend the kernel of truth contained in the ideology of *laïcité* set out in Chapter 2. At the simplest level, a democratic state is secular in the sense that it does not affirm any religious creed, and does not seek to confer special benefits or burdens to citizens affirming any religious creed (or none). In this way, it is fair to all: it shows equal respect to adherents to the majority religion, minority religions, and adherents to no religion at all. For critics of secularism, the claim that secularism treats religious believers fairly is based on a rhetorical sleight of hand.[11] The secular state is supposed to provide neutral common ground, yet it is also the favoured substantive position of those who do not embrace any religion. As a result—the argument continues—the secular state cannot avoid being biased towards non-religious people, and the ideal of secularism violates the liberal injunction that the state should not favour any conception of the good in particular.[12] I think that there is something to the charge, but the case is overstated. A secular public order cannot claim to be equally suited to religious and non-religious peoples, but it is nonetheless the closest we can get to being an order that most, if not all, citizens can endorse. Secularism seeks common ground; *ex hypothesi*, this cannot lie in controversial conceptions of the good. Among such conceptions are the belief that God exists and the belief that God does not exist. A secular state, by eschewing all references to God, avoids taking sides between these two conceptions. Unquestionably, making no reference to God is more problematic for those who believe in God's existence than it is for those who do not. But this is an unavoidable—if regrettable—asymmetry, not a hypocritical sleight of hand on the part of secularists intent on foisting their substantive (agnostic or atheistic) way of life on others. Historically, secularism did not succeed primarily because it suited atheists. Rather it suited believers, because it allowed the state to be neutral towards the merits of competing religious views. So the onus of proof, in my view, lies with critics of secularism: they must show that there is an alternative, non-secular, basis on which the common ground of citizenship can be based.[13] To put the question thus is to imply that, in pluralist societies, genuinely common ground cannot have a religious basis, for such basis would fail to be publicly intelligible, and therefore would fail to offer adequate justifying reasons for the exercise of state power.[14] That the content and form of common ground principles must be secular does not mean, however, that they cannot be endorsed from the perspective of religious conceptions of the good, as in Rawls's overlapping consensus. Republicanism, no more than political liberalism, need endorse a comprehensive 'independent ethic' conception of secularism.[15]

More complicated is the question of the appropriate reach of what I have called 'common ground' secular principles. Challenges to secularism raise anew the question of where to draw the line between the public sphere, where secular principles of exclusion of religion apply, and the private sphere, where they do not.[16] While critics of secularism implicitly accept that constitutional essentials and state policy must be secular, and that citizenship rights must be independent of religious membership, they have questioned the *laïque* implication that religious belief can have no place in political argument and civic life more broadly. *Laïcité*, in their view, is too demanding if it requires the complete privatization of belief. Thus an important debate within recent (notably American) liberal theory has centred on secularism as a *doctrine of conscience* prescribing norms of conduct both for religious organizations and for individual citizens. In particular, liberal neutralists such as John Rawls and Robert Audi have been challenged by critics such as Kent Greenawalt and Paul Weithman for seeking to exclude religious convictions from public reason.[17] Critical republicans occupy an intermediary position in this debate. They suggest that while it is natural and acceptable for citizens to enter politics out of religious conviction, and to introduce religious arguments in broad public debate, it is not acceptable for the constitution to be theologically inspired, or for public officials to justify public decisions by reference to religious views; in both cases, 'common grounds' principles should be appealed to.[18] Generally, critical republicans tend to be fairly tolerant of the religious expression of ordinary citizens, but they adopt a less tolerant stance towards display of religious allegiance or support by state institutions.

A more difficult issue, from a critical republican perspective, is that of the religious freedom of individual state officials (as distinct from the religious neutrality of institutions or policies).[19] Does the institutional doctrine of separation prevent civil servants from exercising their basic rights of religious practice when on duty? We saw, for example, that the principle of the religious neutrality of the state prevented French and German schoolteachers (along with other public officials) from displaying signs of religious allegiance. In a critical republican view, such prohibitions can never be general in form, and should be a function of the importance of the public function and of the vulnerability of the users of the service. Thus, government ministers but not tax inspectors, primary school teachers but not university lecturers, may be subjected to an obligation of religious restraint while on duty. But leaving this important complication aside, the basic insight of critical republicanism is clear enough: secularism is primarily an *institutional* doctrine of separation, prescribing the extent to which state institutions, and the public sphere more generally, must remain secular *so that* citizens can freely follow their conscience. A tough institutional doctrine is therefore the condition for a tolerant doctrine of conscience. Recall that republican secularism aims to show equal respect to all religious and non-religious citizens by guarding against majoritarian infringements on freedom of conscience (of adherents to minority religions and non-adherents). It is primarily concerned about the potentially conformist, divisive, or discriminatory effects of the material and symbolic recognition of religion in the public sphere. Thus, it constructs the public sphere fairly expansively, as a space where citizens can meet as citizens. A non-sectarian, non-confessional public space best embodies the ideal of democratic impartiality by showing respect to, and thus motivating the allegiance of, all citizens regardless of their particular beliefs. One central space where civic and secular principles take most of their force is school. Schools, in the republican view, are central *loci* of civic socialization and transmission of knowledge. Their function, in particular, is to promote tolerance and respect for difference, which are conditions for the respect of religious freedoms. Classrooms, therefore, must be (as far as possible) diverse and inclusive, and must be free of religious orthodoxy or divisive sectarianianism. That public schools must (preferably) be secular, therefore, follows from the republican ideal of citizenship.

This, I think, is the kernel of truth contained in the separationist ideal of *laïcité*. In many areas of common life, the best way to institutionalize the ideal of republican equality is to erect a 'wall of separation' between public institutions and religion. However—and here is a crucial qualification—in some cases, official republican separationism is *not* the best way to institutionalize equal respect. As we saw in our analysis of the hijab controversy, official *laïcité* fails to treat religious believers fairly when it imposes unreasonable burdens on the exercise of basic religious rights, and it fails to treat minority believers fairly when it endorses a form of status quo neutrality which in practice advantages majority religions. Thus, critical republicanism, in an effort to provide a benchmark of religious equality against which religious claims can be assessed, adds two crucial provisos to the *laïque* defence of separationism. It posits that *the state should not support religion, unless such abstention (i) unreasonably burdens the exercise of basic religious freedoms or (ii) legitimizes status quo entitlements which unduly disadvantage minority religious groups.* Only then will the secular state be a non-dominating state. Let me briefly spell out the two provisos. The first—let us call it the 'basic free exercise' proviso—is rooted in the thought that a secular state is fair to, and inclusive of, all citizens in so far as it does not unreasonably burden or advantage them in virtue of their religious or non-religious beliefs. Religious citizens can be considered to be unreasonably burdened if existing arrangements make it impossible or very difficult for them to practise the basic tenets of their religion (provided these do not impose unreasonable burdens on the rest of society).[20] Thus, *contra* the strictly 'libertarian' interpretation of the demands of free religious exercise, religious exercise may need to be assisted by the state: for example, the state has a duty to provide religious chaplaincy services in enclosed public institutions such as prisons, boarding schools, hospitals, and the armed forces. Thus, the institutional doctrine of separation does not automatically mandate a stringent interpretation of separation as a doctrine of conscience. Secular institutions must be inclusive and should not dominate religious citizens: they should not unreasonably deprive them of basic rights of free exercise.

The second proviso—let us call it the 'contextual parity' proviso—addresses the fairness of secularist demands on minorities. Official *laïcité*, in so far as it urges religious minorities to respect the principle of separation, imposes unfair burdens on them, in cases when historically established religious groups have benefited from favourable treatment by the state. The problem, here, is how to achieve equality between religions under status quo, non-ideal conditions. The basic critical republican intuition is that status quo entitlements which do not meet the demands of justificatory neutrality and significantly burden minority religious groups must be corrected or compensated for. Only then can we guarantee the (roughly) equal opportunity to practise Islam under institutional conditions which, while requesting that minorities abide by the 'hard rules' of secular restraint, entrench customary 'soft rules' which in practice favour historically established religions. Critical republicans—in contrast to both official and tolerant republicans—explicitly confront this complex question, and believe that answering it would go a long way towards addressing the legitimate grievances of Muslims in relation to the existing practices of European states. The shift from abstentionist neutrality to non-dominating impartiality requires a broader justification of existing benefits and burdens than either official or tolerant republicans are able to provide. Critical republican impartiality does not require endorsement of a substantive, consequentialist conception of religious equality, but it imposes a fairly stringent test on what counts as fair background for the exercise of religious liberties. In this way, secular impartiality can be said to apply to religious affairs the 'wide' conception of equality of opportunity that has become current in the egalitarian literature on social justice.[21] To borrow Peter Jones's useful distinction, (justificatory) neutralists are right to say that people should bear the internal *burdens* attached to the pursuit of their conceptions of the good and beliefs, but this does not mean that they should bear all the *consequences* that follow from the intersection between internal burdens and the effect of non-neutral historical institutions.[22]

Critical Secularism in Practice: Addressing Muslim Demands

Critical secularism, then, upholds the secular character of the public sphere unless doing so infringes a basic religious free-exercise right (on a weakly consequentialist view) or entrenches exorbitant majoritarian historical privileges (on a wide justificatory view). The 'basic free exercise' and 'contextual parity' provisos are deliberately qualified: the free-exercise right must be 'basic',[23] the privileges have to be 'exorbitant'. In other words, there is a prima facie assumption that public institutions must promote secular policies, unless such policies have a demonstrably dominating effect on religious believers. My claim is that critical secular principles offer broad but clear guidelines about how to weigh conflicting values and adjudicate the complex claims brought in the name of religion in contemporary societies.[24] They do so without either abstracting from or idealizing status quo arrangements, and to that extent considerably improve on both official and tolerant republicanism. In this section, I seek to make good this claim by focusing on four particular Muslim demands: multi-faith establishment, religious schools, public funding for mosques, and the wearing of religious dress (an example of religious exemption from general rules). I shall argue that while critical republicans accept the legitimacy of the latter two demands (under certain conditions), they are more sceptical about the former two. They object to extending a number of existing privileges to Muslims not because Muslims are not deserving of them, but because the privileges are not legitimate in the first place. Muslim demands, then, should not be acceded to or rejected *simpliciter*, as under a conception of status quo neutrality. They pose deep questions of systemic impartiality and prompt the re-evaluation and reform of existing regimes of religious recognition.

Multi-faith establishment refers to the demand that the organic links between the state and historically dominant churches be extended to Islam (and other minority religious groups). By organic links, I refer to persisting traces of the historical establishment of religion within the state, dating back to the times when the state, in accordance with the principle of *cujus regio, ejus religio* (whose realm, their religion), upheld the public function, moral truth, and social value of Christianity. Thus, for example, the Church of England is still formally linked to the British Crown, and Anglican bishops sit in the House of Lords; the Catholic, Protestant, and Jewish public corporations in Germany are entitled to federally collected church taxes; in the French region of Alsace-Moselle (where the 1905 law does not apply) churches receive public funding, and priests, rabbis and pastors are paid by the state. In many European countries, religious (mostly Christian) education is compulsory in state schools; and religious beliefs enjoy special respect and protection from the law (in the form of blasphemy laws or special conscientious objection rights).[25] Advocates of multi-faith establishment argue for the extension of these privileges to Muslims.[26] Thus, in England, proposals have been made for the appointment of Muslim representatives to the House of Lords and for the extension of blasphemy laws to Islam;[27] in Germany, there have been attempts to recognize Islam as a public corporation entitled to church tax; and in France, some have argued for the extension of the Alsatian regime to the rest of the country. Such proposals, in my view, fail to meet both the main clause and the free-exercise proviso of the critical republican standard of impartiality. Establishment regimes infringe the religious neutrality of the public sphere in ways that dominate non-religious citizens. While it is true that establishment is mostly symbolic and cannot be said to put anyone at a serious disadvantage,[28] symbols do matter when the basic identification of citizens with their institutions is concerned. Just as Muslims are likely to be alienated by the distinctively Christian religiosity permeating public institutions, so non-religious citizens are likely to be alienated by any official display of religiosity by institutions. Now, citizens' interest in maintaining the secular character of the public sphere could be overridden, according to my first proviso, if a basic free-exercise interest was at stake. No such interest, I submit, is protected by religious establishment. In a republic, religious citizens should be given ample opportunities to practise and express their faith, including in public, but they do not require privileged—material or symbolic—access to state institutions in order to do so. In these particular cases, then, critical republicanism would favour disestablishment ('equalizing downwards') rather than multi-faith establishment ('equalizing upwards').

It is important to note that none of this is meant to imply that the secular state should offer no recognition to religious groups. It should, but exclusively for the purpose of protecting citizens' right to free exercise, not in order to entrench the public function of religion in its institutions. Let me illustrate this important distinction, which is often overlooked, with two examples. Public institutions such as hospitals and prisons should be secular in character, so as to respect the freedom of conscience of their (religious and non-religious) users, but they must offer facilities for religious worship for the patients and inmates who require them. Similarly, the state should not entrench the social, institutional, or political role of religious groups by formally integrating them into its institutions. However, it should grant recognition and status to representatives of religious groups, so that religious needs whose fulfilment requires state authorization, organization, and funding (such as the provision of adequate religious facilities in enclosed institutions, to use the previous example) can be identified and responded to. Thus, it is perfectly legitimate for state officials to consult and negotiate with Christian, Muslim, Jewish, and other religious authorities about how best to organize worship. There is, therefore, a fundamental distinction to be made between establishment and the institutional guarantee of free exercise rights—a distinction overlooked both by *laïcité* advocates and their critics.

The right to set up *Muslim schools* is the second demand I examine. Undeniably, it would be unfair to refuse to extend to Muslims rights already granted to other religions. But are such rights legitimate in the first place? Can status quo arrangements be justified? Critical republicans are deeply sceptical about the permissibility, or at least the value, of separate religious education. It is one area, they believe, where the secularist case should be made most forcefully. French republicans, like American political liberals, are right to see educational policy as a privileged way of 'creating citizens',[29] of inculcating those civic virtues of toleration, mutual respect, and civility which guarantee the survival and stability of democratic arrangements. In this view, schools are not purely extensions of the family home (as they would be on a libertarian or communitarian account), they are appropriately public spaces which should be importantly 'detached'[30] from parental and local control in virtue of their special role in 'cultivating common democratic values among all children, regardless of their academic ability, class, race, religion or sex'.[31] Republicans and political liberals make the plausible assumption that these values can be cultivated only through sustained exposure to, and engagement with, ethical and social diversity. As a result, they tend, rightly, to be partial towards common, comprehensive, secular schools. The extent to which particular religious schools are willing and able to pursue appropriate civic educational goals greatly varies in practice, and it would be rash to generalize. Yet if, by religious school, we mean a school whose interactions with those outside the community of faith remain limited, and whose pedagogy, rules, structures of authority, and large parts of the curriculum are designed to encourage children's belief in a particular religion, it is undeniable that such a school ipso facto denies children exposure to ethical diversity and sufficient training in secular reasoning, and thus provides preparation to citizenship inferior to that of a common secular school.[32]

What should follow from this, in terms of public policy, is more contested. School reform in the real world is a particularly fraught endeavour. Parents may opt for religious schools partly because existing secular state schools fall well short of the ideals of secular inclusiveness, academic excellence, and ethical purpose. For example, state schools may, by design or by default, foster crassly materialistic, consumerist, and substantively secularist world views. Thus, in itself, the abolition or regulation of religious (private or state-funded) schools might do nothing to improve the quality of state schools or their appeal to religious parents. On consequentialist grounds, therefore, many republicans and liberals have legitimately been cautious in their criticism of religious schools. Debate has, instead, centred on the question of school regulation.[33] A critical republican approach to those debates would stress three main points. First, as Harry Brighouse has recently argued, religious schools should be incorporated into state systems so that they can be made to adhere to democratic standards (including a ban on selection) and pursue civic goals.[34] The philosophical and principled case has recently been made by Ian MacMullen, who argues that while there is no justification for a blanket prohibition on religious schools, there are grounds for suspicion of arrangements that tend to reproduce the home environment of the child in the school, shielding students from ethical, cultural, and social diversity. 'Moderate religious schools', whose curriculum, pedagogy, and admission policies foster respect of diversity and the cultivation of autonomy (about which more will be said in Chapter 7) may be allowed, provided they are tightly regulated. Second, and again following MacMullen, critical republicans will probably have to concede that the very grounds that make a religious school acceptable on civic grounds also make it qualify for public funding. While the French practice of public funding of private schools and the British granting of charity status to independent schools may appear gravely to undermine secular ideals, in fact, it would be arbitrary and indefensible for religious schools to be available only and always to those who can afford private education. Thus, MacMullen's conclusion seems to me incontrovertible: 'on pain of inconsistency and unfairness, governments cannot justify the general policy of permitting the operation of a wide range of private religious schools while refusing to fund a similar education in the faith for those who cannot afford it'.[35] In sum, the civic ideals of republicanism demand that, if religious schools are to be tolerated, they be tightly controlled and funded by the state. In later chapters (7 and 10), I shall explore whether the other ideals underpinning critical republicanism—autonomy and solidarity—warrant the prima facie toleration of even moderate religious schools.

Third, and as importantly in the critical republican view, state schools must be reformed. Secular education should not be too burdensome for religious children. Secular education involves, not the inculcation of a substantive humanist doctrine but, rather, reasoned agnosticism and exposure to the value of different worldviews, religious and non-religious. Secular schools need not aim to eliminate or even to discourage religious belief: they are called secular because of the absence of a religious purpose, not because of any opposition to religion. Drawing on the distinction drawn earlier between secularism as an institutional doctrine and secularism as a doctrine of conscience, we can say, in line with the former, that state schools should neither impose school prayers nor dispense religious education, but that they should, in line with the latter, accept the wearing of religious signs by pupils, accommodate their religious needs as far as possible (dietary requirements, religious holidays) and include knowledge about religions, including minority religions, in the curriculum.[36] Within state schools, Muslim pupils must be respected not *despite* their being Muslim (as official *laïcité* suggest), but *as* Muslims. Such reforms would go a long way towards accommodating Muslim unease about state education. This would certainly be the case in France, where there is little demand for separate Muslim schools. Even in Britain, surveys have shown that while a majority of Muslims support Muslim schools, only a minority would actually want to send their children to them.[37] This suggests that separate schooling is not as important to Muslims as, on the one hand, symbolic parity with other religions and, on the other, good (state) schools. This is in line with critical republican proposals, which suggest that in some cases symbolic parity can be best achieved by reducing existing privileges and providing good quality 'common ground' provision.

In my third example—the demand for *public subsidy for the building of mosques*—parity would, by contrast, be best achieved by 'equalizing upward'. From a French *laïque* perspective, this is an unexpected and almost unorthodox proposal. Article 2 of the 1905 Separation Law is often interpreted as strictly prohibiting the use of public funds for the building or maintenance of places of worship. Yet, as far as Muslim places of worship in France are concerned, a convincing case for allowing an exception to this general principle can be made. Recall that critical secularism advocates policies of separation between state and religion unless they infringe a basic religious free-exercise right or entrench exorbitant majoritarian historical privileges. I shall argue that the demand that the state help Muslims build mosques meet both provisos—the 'basic free exercise' and the 'contextual parity' provisos. Arguably, the availability of suitable places of worship is central to the actual exercise of religious rights. Scholars agree that the establishment and maintenance of a place of worship is part of the fundamental rights of religious freedom enjoyed by everyone living in Europe.[38] While the first generation of Muslim migrants practised their religion within the confines of family homes or communal prayer rooms, the permanent settlement of Muslims on European soil has rendered the need for adequate, public religious facilities particularly acute.[39] Note that the qualification 'adequate' points to a sufficientarian, rather than strictly egalitarian, criterion of fairness (there is no point building a large mosque everywhere there is a cathedral) thus avoiding complicated issues of what substantive equality requires, and focusing on guaranteeing minimum standards of non-domination. In the case of financially poor yet demographically significant religious groups such as Muslims in France, the legitimate interest they have in getting access to minimal religious facilities overrides the 'libertarian' principle of state abstention, and justifies that the state step in to guarantee actual conditions for free exercise. This is all the more legitimate, I would argue, because Catholics still benefit from pre-1905 advantages: as we noted in Chapter 3, houses of worship built before 1905 continue to be state property and are maintained by local municipalities. Thus, it is incorrect to speak of compensating Muslims for the fact that they did not benefit from state help *before* 1905: strictly speaking, Muslims should be compensated for *present* disadvantage, as public money is being channelled towards the maintenance of (mostly Catholic) churches. Helping Muslims build mosques, then, would rectify this exorbitant historical privilege while facilitating their exercise of religious rights. These are two necessary, and in this case sufficient, conditions for allowing an exception to the separationist clause of critical republicanism. They are sufficient because they are not overridden by a compelling state interest in keeping the public sphere free of religion: while hospitals and schools can be said to be relevantly public (in the sense that they concern the fair distribution of primary goods in non-voluntary associations), town streets (where mosques are built) are not.

A similar balance of considerations (public interest, importance of the particular religious freedom, contextual fairness) should be applied to most Muslim demands for *religiously based exemptions from general rules*— my fourth example. The issue has received extensive coverage in the so-called multiculturalist literature in Anglophone political theory. One position can be identified with Brian Barry (and, as we saw, French official republicans). It posits that individuals are treated fairly when they are subjected to the same (legitimate) rules: liberals should not pre-occupy themselves with uneven burdens or unequal outcomes. At the other end of the spectrum stand multiculturalist advocates of pragmatic even-handedness and substantive equality, as epitomized by Bhikhu Parekh (and French tolerant republicans).[40] They argue that a prima facie neutral rule can be indirectly discriminatory if it is unreasonably burdensome for members of some group. Critical republicans, for their part, occupy an intermediate position between those two theories, one which critically interrogates the nature of the general rules to which exemptions are sought.

On the one hand, the problem with Barry's approach is that it does not pay adequate attention to what counts as a legitimate rule. Barry discusses the legitimacy of general health-and-safety regulations, to show that if the law is legitimate and furthers an important public interest, no religious exemption should be granted; and if exemptions are legitimate, this shows that the general law had no rationale in the first place. But he barely discusses the impact of what may be called customary 'soft' rules: rules which have not been democratically discussed nor subjected to stringent public interest tests. For example, he argues that most customary 'local norms' (e.g. norms of 'public order' and 'decency') do not raise any issue of (liberal, universal) justice.[41] Thus, it is not illegitimate for majoritarian conventions to be enforced, according to the adage 'this is the way we do things here'. What Barry underestimates is how customary rules have implications for fairness when they unreasonably favour the preferences and values of the historical majority *and* infringe the basic religious rights of minorities.[42] Thus, it may be difficult to practise Islam in a public space created and occupied by non-Muslim citizens. Consider cemeteries, which are perceived to be secular (in so far as Christian crosses, for example, are removed from common areas) and hence public and inclusive. Yet many cemeteries are run following customary, unreflected pre-Christian or Christian norms: for example, burial plots traditionally face East. The problem is that this relatively trivial customary rule makes European cemeteries unsuited for Muslim burials, where the dead must imperatively be lying on their side and have their face turned towards Mecca (south-east). In such cases, it is not illegitimate that public funding be set aside to set up Muslim cemeteries, or at least burial spaces within existing cemeteries, allowing for the correct alignment of graves.[43] Critical republicanism, therefore, is open to the questioning of customary rules when they have dominating effects, when, for example, they entrench the unreflected cultural norms of the majority while infringing the basic religious rights of minorities.

On the other hand, multiculturalists such as Parekh tend to construe the concept of indirect discrimination far too broadly. A democratic law which serves a legitimate public purpose should not routinely be discarded as an arbitrary customary rule, and exemptions to it should not be allowed, even if it generates disproportionate burdens on members of minorities. I see no rationale, for example, for granting religious groups exemptions from the civil law of marriage and filiations, in so far as these typically enforce a restrictive interpretation of women's rights.[44] (Of course, people may feel symbolic allegiance to religious or customary law, but this should complement and never override their civil rights.) The application of gender equality provisions may be burdensome for a number of religiously minded people, but it would be absurd to argue that this ipso facto amounts to illegitimate indirect discrimination against them. In addition, some multiculturalists fail to recognize that the cultural permeation of the public sphere is only a problem if it has worrisome dominating effects—for example, if it unreasonably burdens the exercise of basic religious rights. Much will revolve, of course, around how to identify which basic religious requirements give rise to rights claims, who is entitled to make this judgement, and how to assess what an unreasonable burden is. On one interpretation, members of religious minorities should be allowed (or enabled) to do what members of the majority can already do unaided (e.g. thanks to a Christian-influenced calendar, celebrate major annual holidays, and attend religious services once a week).[45] One problem with this is that it artificially homogenizes the demands of religious ritual and overlooks the fact that some religions, such as Islam and Orthodox Judaism, are more ritual-based than Christianity, and their adherents would see the performance of visible and regular rituals as basic to the practice of their faith. Fortunately, the great majority of Muslims do not intend to impose an unreasonable (maximalist or integralist) conception of the demands of their religion. Rather, as I have suggested above, they legitimately seek to remove the most blatant inequalities in basic opportunities for the practice of Islam in Western countries. They should thus welcome a critical republican approach to secularism, for three reasons. *First*, critical republicans endorse secularism as the best guarantee of equal citizenship. Many Muslim demands are demands of access to the equal status of citizenship: they are not demands for exorbitant, special rights. Yet, *second*, critical republican equality is not the formal equality of official republicans or of liberal egalitarians like Barry; nor does it necessarily mandate state abstention from intervention in religious affairs. Critical republicans recognize that a secular state respects equal citizenship only if it does not dominate its religious citizens. Thus, a critical republican state would ensure that Muslims (like other believers) are able to follow the basic tenets of their religion: it is committed to what I called basic free exercise. *Third*, and in contrast to both official and tolerant republicanism, critical republicanism rejects status quo neutrality and normatively scrutinizes existing church–state arrangements. Its commitment to what I called contextual parity follows from the thought that the status quo can dominate members of minority religions, and it prescribes how to treat religious minorities fairly in formally secular, but historically Christian-dominated, societies.

Interestingly, a version of critical republicanism appears to be endorsed by a substantial number (about a quarter) of the European Muslims interviewed by Jytte Klausen. She describes their position, which she calls 'secular integrationism', in the following way: 'the sentiment is that what applies to other faiths should also apply to Islam. Many secularists prefer the strict separation of church and state and, if this was already the established rule, their first preference is that the state provides no assistance to religion. But given that state neutrality is generally not an option, the secularists want equity.'[46] Where my critical republicanism differs from this 'secular integrationism' is in its belief that neutrality at times can and should be an option. In some cases, what Modood sceptically calls 'equalizing downward' is the right course of action, even if historically dominant religions lose out in the process. In fact, if republicans were actively to militate—as I have argued they should—against status quo arrangement regarding faith schools or Christian establishment, they would undermine the suspicion, held by members of minority religions, that Western secularism is no more than an ideology entrenching majority domination. The critical republican approach can rescue secularism from the charge of status quo neutrality.

PART 2

Liberté and Republican Autonomy

CHAPTER 5

———

Official Republicanism, Liberty, and the Hijab

> The degree of equality in education that we can reasonably hope to attain, but that should be adequate, is that which excludes all dependence, either forced or voluntary (Condorcet).[1]

For the state, through its educational system, to seek to 'exclude all dependence, either forced or voluntary' is not an aim that many contemporary Anglo-American liberal philosophers would want to make their own. The Enlightenment utopia that individuals should be freed from their dependence on alienating and oppressive systems of thought, through the liberating power of rational education, is one which has been seemingly discredited by the collapse of authoritarian socialism in the twentieth century. Liberals, following John Rawls's retreat to a modestly 'political' liberalism in 1993, have become wary of the risks of state oppression involved in the imposition of a conception of the good life as self-determination or autonomy. If the state appeals to the truth of, say, Concorcet's secular and individualistic rationalism, it fails to show respect to those citizens holding values (perhaps deeply held religious or communal values) which may well be false, and oppressive, but which are still reasonable for purposes of liberal justification. Liberals should take ethical pluralism seriously, lest their liberalism ends up justifying state oppression in the name of a sectarian conception of the good.

Two important premises of this argument are rarely commented upon. The first is that anti-perfectionist liberals like Rawls implicitly assume that, *ceteris paribus*, state oppression is a worse evil than other forms of social oppression, on the important grounds that the coercive use of state power deserves special justification. Second, they assume that individual autonomy or rational self-determination are sectarian moral values whose promotion is inevitably oppressive. Neither premise would be unconditionally accepted by the French *laïciste* thinkers whose argument I reconstruct in this chapter. Instead, they tend to assume that the democratic state is potentially a benevolent, emancipatory force, and that some of the major sources of oppression are rooted in private institutions such as the family and religious institutions. They further take it for granted that the liberation of individuals from such oppression, mainly through autonomy-promoting state education, is a precious achievement of liberal modernity. By *laïcisme*, therefore, I refer to a modernist, emancipatory, and perfectionist strand of *laïcité* that has remained relatively immune from the profound reconsideration of the metaphysical and epistemological tenets of Enlightenment philosophy which, in the context of post-totalitarian, post-colonial, pluralist societies, has taken most of Western thought away from 'grand narratives', 'foundationalist', or 'comprehensive' ideologies.[2] The *laïciste* argument remains rooted in the progressive, modernist philosophy of history endorsed by the humanist secular Left of the nineteenth and early twentieth centuries, with its conception of progress as liberation from traditionalist, obscurantist systems of beliefs. While the dominant view of *laïcité* is captured by the liberal ideal of neutrality discussed in Chapter 2, a more militantly *laïciste*, perfectionist interpretation of *laïcité* has recently come to the fore, in relation to the wearing of hijab in schools. Thus, Marc Sadoun has noticed a tendency, on the part of official republicans, 'to shift from mere separation [of religion and politics] to the expulsion of beliefs from the sphere of the mind'[3]— which is what *laïcisme* refers to. More specifically, *laïcistes* have deployed rationalist, emancipatory, and autonomy-based arguments against the wearing of hijab by young women.[4]

We can say that *laïcistes* are liberal perfectionists, to use a term familiar to Anglo-American philosophy. They believe that the state should promote worthwhile forms of life, and that worthwhile lives are those that exhibit a high degree of individual autonomy.[5] They also point out that Muslim headscarves are symbols of female and religious oppression, which gravely infringe on their wearer's autonomy. I shall show, however, that *laïcistes* are only hesitantly paternalist: faithful to liberal intuitions about the dangers of state oppression and the paradox involved in 'forcing people to be free', they are reluctant directly to prohibit oppressive practices and rely, instead, on the emancipatory power of education. Within state schools, Muslim girls should be provided with a comprehensive education in rational autonomy, so that they are in a position to emancipate themselves from the restrictive gender roles inculcated by their family, community, and religious leaders. Yet, because of the special status of schools as freedom-promoting institutions, they should also provide Muslim girls with an opportunity to experiment with forms of substantive autonomy—hence the ban on hijab within schools themselves.

In this chapter, I use 'liberty' and 'autonomy' interchangeably, because the conception of liberty which is implicit in most *laïciste* writings is one that identifies liberty with rational self-determination. One is not free when one mindlessly follows the opinions, ideals, goals, and values of others: one's life must be lived 'from the inside'[6] and is, further, not compatible with voluntary servitude. Thus *laïcistes*, in contrast to contemporary anti-perfectionist liberals, express concern about the content of the social norms in which individuals—notably children—have been socialized into.[7] They believe that acceptance of authoritarian religion, communal tradition, or oppressive gender roles is incompatible with being autonomous, and they go on to lay stress on the need for rationality to direct the autonomous person's behaviour. As philosopher of education Harry Brighouse has averred, 'broadly speaking, the capacities involved in critical reflection help us to live autonomously', either by rationally reflecting on, revising, and repudiating the values we have been socialized into, or at the very least by being able to identify with them 'from the inside'—in a way that reflects our capacity for agency and autonomy.[8] The *laïciste* conception of freedom as autonomy is, as a result, deeply rationalist, intellectualist, and often anti-religious.

This chapter is structured as follows. In the first section, I provide an account of the modernist vision of the 'emancipatory state', linking together the *laïcistes'* suspicion of religion, commitment to anti-traditionalist modernization, rejection of the ethical relativism of contemporary multiculturalism, and defence of education as providing the means to self-emancipation. In the second section, I explain the sense in which Muslim headscarves can be considered symbols of female subservience, drawing on the republican imaginary about citizenship, gender and religion, and on the analysis of the contemporary Muslim revival as a traditionalist, patriarchal backlash. The third section brings those findings together and tries to reconstruct a coherent case for banning headscarves within schools.

The Emancipatory State

This section elucidates the philosophical premises of the *laïciste* (anti-religious, anti-traditionalist, perfectionist) strand of *laïcité*. It surveys in turn its commitment to freedom of thought (1), state-led social modernization (2), defence of the individual against oppressive groups (3), and belief in education as self-emancipation (4).

Freedom of Thought versus Religious Belief

According to Jean Baubérot, the hijab controversy has revived the tension, inherent to the concept of *laïcité*, between respect for 'freedom of conscience' and promotion of 'freedom of thought'.[9] The former (*la liberté de conscience*) refers to the constitutionally guaranteed protection of religious freedom. As we saw in Chapter 2, in this view, a secular state is a neutral state, which respects and guarantees equal religious rights to all its citizens. The latter ideal (*la liberté de penser*) refers to 'the right to independently re-examine beliefs received from family, social groups, and society as a whole'; it implies rational self-determination, and points out the emancipation of the human mind from religious beliefs and prejudices. Such emancipation requires a secular state which is not a neutral state but which, instead, openly promotes a conception of the good life as the life lived according to substantively secular, rationalist standards.

While this substantively anti-religious, secularist strand of *laïcité* has not been the object of a comprehensive philosophical statement, its historical roots are not difficult to trace. For most of the eighteenth and nineteenth centuries, the powerful alliance between the Catholic Church and counter-Enlightenment, illiberal forces was such that religion itself was inevitably looked on with suspicion by progressive thinkers bent on advancing the cause of reason, progress, and individual liberty. The French Catholic Church had successfully resisted the liberalizing forces of the Reformation, and pitted the claims of faith and tradition against those of reason and critical enquiry: consequently, the French Enlightenment was markedly more anti-religious than its German, Scottish, or English counterparts.[10] The perception that 'reason' and 'faith' stood in unavoidable tension was reinforced by the anti-religious attacks of 1789 revolutionaries, and by the Church's rearguard attempt, throughout the nineteenth century, to retain its grip on the nation's minds.[11] Chapter 2 argued that this 'conflict between the two France' wedded all republicans to anticlericalism (criticism of the Church's political and social influence) and to universal civic education (inculcation of the basic political values of the republic into the citizenry). But a minority of more advanced republicans, influenced by a radicalized Kantian ethics or by secular positivism, went further, and concluded that religious belief per se was incompatible with republican citizenship.

What, then, was wrong with religious belief? At bottom, it was deemed to conflict with the republican commitment to individual autonomy. Catholics, in particular, were taught uncritically to accept the dictates of God, the pope, and priests, and to live by rules that they could neither comprehend nor scrutinize. Religious belief, then, represented an abdication of the human capacity for rational, autonomous self-determination. As Protestant free thinker Ferdinand Buisson put it, 'anyone who accepts a credo... renounces his freedom of thought and becomes a believer. This is a man who warns us that at some point he will stop using his reason to rely on an already-there (*toute faite*) truth that he is not allowed to control.'[12] Free thinkers like Buisson were not necessarily atheists, but they insisted that religious belief should be left to individual reason and conscience, and not be moulded by externally imposed dogma.[13] Socialist Jean Jaurès, in a famous speech to the Chamber of Deputies in 1895, startled his audience when he proclaimed that 'all truth that does not stem from us is a lie... No dogma should limit the perpetual effort and perpetual search of human reason.'[14] Further still, the content of religious dogmas itself encouraged subservience and dependency, as evidenced in the Catholic Church's teaching on the inherently sinful and corrupted nature of human beings, its scriptures against the arrogance of human reason, and its theological justifications for the inequalities of *ancien régime* society. The Church maintained the populace in a state of ignorance and servitude and, as both Condorcet and Rousseau had pointed out, only self-determining, autonomous citizens could form and sustain a republic. Because the republic's legitimacy was rooted in public opinion, it must 'establish the moral conditions which guarantee the rightness and the independence of this opinion, notably in relation to prejudices and dogmas that claim to direct it'.[15] Thus, the republic could not be neutral vis-à-vis the doctrines that enslaved the people; as neo-Kantian philosopher Charles Renouvier put it, *laïque* morality should 'aim to take minds away from superstitious beliefs, and above all from doctrines which contradict [the ideal of] justice'.[16] To those *laïciste* republicans, *laïcité* implied emancipation of the human mind from *obscurantisme*.

This secularist, militantly anti-religious interpretation of *laïcité* was much in evidence in the repression of religious congregations (such as Jesuit teaching orders) in the early twentieth century, and has recently resurfaced in the debate about the risks of 'mental manipulation' involved in membership of 'harmful cults' (*sectes nocives*) such as the Church of Scientology. In both cases, republicans pointed to the dangers of the 'exploitation of dependency' and 'alienation of moral autonomy', and to the need to protect vulnerable individuals from the 'so-called right to alienate their liberty'.[17] In both cases, the French republic's high-handed treatment of religious groups in the name of the protection of individual freedom was internationally castigated as intolerant and illiberal 'thought police'. In truth, in the absence of unambiguous instances of reprehensible acts by sectarian groups, the charge of 'mental manipulation' is notoriously difficult to prove and, at any rate, the legal regime of *laïcité*, given its fundamental commitment to freedom of conscience, prevents the courts from repressing 'manipulative' cults on paternalistic grounds.[18] Despite high-profile prosecutions of such groups as the Church of Scientology, the 'anti-cult' law voted in 2002, therefore, turns out to have mainly a symbolic, educative, and preventive, rather than repressive, function. Even sympathizers of the emancipatory ambitions of *laïcisme* concede that the state can do no more than equip citizens with the knowledge and skills they need to resist the most pernicious forms of religious indoctrination. As foremost *laïciste* apologist Henri Pena-Ruiz states, 'the eradication of the dangers of irrationalism would be salutary, but it can only happen through education and public information, to the exclusion of all measures which restrict freedom of conscience.'[19] We can say, therefore, that the *laïciste* state is a *perfectionist* state—it does not refrain from passing moral judgements about the content of individual conceptions of the good— but it is wary of *paternalistic* coercion—which would conflict with both freedom of conscience and freedom of thought. In the spirit of John Stuart Mill's perfectionist liberalism, French *laïcistes* castigate religious doctrines that infringe on human dignity and autonomy,[20] recommend that individuals who endorse them be 'guided, reasoned with, educated', rather than forcibly coerced into behaving autonomously, and only allow state paternalist intervention in the case of children, who must be protected against premature indoctrination by their parents or community. Where French *laïcistes* diverge from Mill, however, is in their belief that the state, unlike any other social institution, is an inherently benevolent, progressive, and modernizing institution, that traditional identities pose a threat to autonomy, and that state-controlled education holds the key to rational self-emancipation.[21] These points are elucidated in the next three sections.

The State, Modernity, and Tradition

Laïcisme is one manifestation of a wider modernist philosophy of the state, which sees it as the chief agent of the historical emergence of individualist, liberal society. French revolutionaries, in contrast to their English and American predecessors, were convinced that liberal society did not emerge naturally out of the unfettered development of commercial society and parliamentary democracy: theirs was a rationalist and voluntaristic project, which aimed at wrenching individuals free from the corrupt state of servility they had found themselves under in the *ancien régime*.[22] The liberal autonomous individual was not a natural or historical given: it was to be brought into existence by the rational, civilizing influence of the modernist state.[23] As sociologist Émile Durkheim reflected a century later, in the French tradition, 'the stronger the state, the more respected the individual'.[24] Jean-Fabien Spitz has recently drawn attention to the 'classical *topos* of French republican thought, which asserts that social inequalities and the possibility of private oppression stand in inverse proportion to the power of the state'.[25] Republicans were not unaware of the dangers of state oppression, but deemed it generally more benign than forms of social oppression perpetuated in the name of tradition or religion—not an unreasonable assumption in a pre-liberal, deeply conservative society where only the alliance between a modernizing bourgeoisie and a strong state was able to break the hold of feudal, aristocratic interests.[26] In the republicans' historical imaginary, therefore, the state had 'unashamedly' imposed its 'social authority' in the interests of 'promoting the autonomy of persons':[27] it had, notably, liberated individuals from the grip of traditional loyalties and identities. The state, therefore, was the chief agent in the transition from *Gemeinshaft* to *Gessellschaft*, from status to contract, from a communitarian order to an individualistic one.[28] According to the influential sociological paradigm of social integration first adduced by Durkheim, citizens were to be—literally—'acculturated to modernity'[29] by the state: it was a functional requirement of modern industrial society that they leave behind their particular bonds and primary allegiances (to local cultures, family traditions, and religion) to avail themselves of opportunities for social and geographical mobility. The modernist story of 'integration' was one of autonomization, individualization, and unavoidable cultural disenchantment.[30] Nation-building involved uprooting individuals from 'archaic' regional cultures,[31] a 'civilizing mission' which, notwithstanding the salience of ethnocentric, racist assumptions about the intrinsic 'difference' and backwardness of non-European peoples, was also tentatively pursued in French colonies such as Algeria and Senegal.[32] Republicans were confident in the universality in the values of progress, individualism, and autonomy, and in their corrosive effects on archaic, illiberal traditions. Republican philosopher Alain Finkielkraut thus reformulated this classic Enlightenment-influenced account of modernity thus: 'it is *at the expense of his culture* that the European individual has conquered, one by one, all his liberties, it is also, and more generally, the critique of tradition which constitutes the spiritual foundation of Europe.'[33] This valuable Enlightenment modernist heritage, he believes, is threatened by contemporary multiculturalism.

Multiculturalism, Relativism, and Oppression

One central strand of criticism of contemporary multicultural philosophy, in the writings of French official republicans, is that, in its rehabilitation of the legitimacy of 'cultures', 'traditions', and 'collective identities', it turns its back on the modernist, progressive project of individual emancipation. Philosophers such as Finkielkraut, Régis Debray,[34] Pierre-André Taguieff,[35] and Catherine Kintzler[36] have interpreted the contemporary revival of cultural identities, and claims for the recognition of difference, as a regression to an anti-liberal, counter-Enlightenment, communitarian social philosophy which postulates that individuals are primarily defined through their group membership. The Left, in its generous impulse to make amends for the complicity of Western universalism with cultural imperialism, colonial atrocities, and the heavy-handed repression of sub-national identities by the state, ended up endorsing the age-old anti-universalist, anti-individualistic prejudices of conservatives and reactionaries. The latter—from Joseph de Maistre to Maurice Barrès—had argued that the abstract individual hailed by revolutionary republicans was a fiction, that liberal education tragically 'uprooted' children from their cultural milieu, and that moral values were not universal but community-relative. It is this relativistic, anti-individualistic philosophy that the post-colonial, multicultural Left has—albeit unwittingly—inherited. In its commitment to show respect to traditional cultures, notably those of immigrants from former colonies, it ends up reducing the latter to a fixed, essentialized 'identity', denying their basic individual dignity, and legitimizing the collective oppression of vulnerable individuals in the name of tradition, culture or religion. Throughout the 1990s, official reports of the Haut Conseil à l'Intégration repeatedly pointed to the dangers of *communautarisme* (which, in French, stands for the tendency of cultural groups to control and restrict the lives of their members by isolating them from wider society) and recommended that opportunities be provided to individuals to stand back from, or exit, from their communities.[37]

In a commentary on recent Anglophone liberal writings about cultural and moral pluralism, Yves-Charles Zarka takes both John Rawls and

Will Kymlicka to task for playing down (in different ways) the centrality of individual autonomy to liberalism. Rawls fails to recognize that making 'reasonableness' a condition of liberal justification necessarily excludes those groups which unreasonably reject core liberal values such as respect for individual autonomy.[38] Kymlicka, for his part, is more committed to autonomy but does not convincingly show that granting cultural rights to groups will not ipso facto introduce restrictions of their members' rights and liberties.[39] Both, Zarka suggests, should be more candid about asserting substantive liberal values, and unambiguously state that toleration should not be extended to those groups which do not respect individual autonomy. If there is a 'right to difference', it cannot encompass a right to endorse 'obscurantist forms of conscience, mores and life'.[40] 'The state, he concludes, must guarantee and protect individual liberties against the possible oppression of religious orthodoxies or community constraints.'[41] Customary practices such as female genital mutilation, polygamous or forced marriages, and—as we shall see below—the wearing of hijab are routinely offered as instances of such oppression. One salient feature of the French, by contrast to Anglophone, debates about multiculturalism and feminism,[42] however, is that they have revolved less around the legitimacy of the legal accommodation of cultural practices than about the purpose and content of state education and the 'public philosophy' of the republican state exhibited therein. It is on the educational battlefield that the French 'cultural wars'—the conflict between universalism and relativism, between individualism and *communautarisme*, between 'reason' and 'identity'—have mostly been played out.

Education, Reason, and Self-Emancipation

Throughout the 1980s and 1990s, a highly polarized, acrimonious, and often intellectually confused debate about which education best promoted the republican ideals of freedom and equality pitted 'pedagogues' against 'republicans'.[43] The former, critical of the elitism and social exclusivity of abstract, one-size-fits-all schooling, advocated child-centred pedagogy, sensitive to the particular social and cultural background of children. The latter, by contrast, insisted that all children, regardless of their family and social circumstances, be equipped with classical humanist instruction, centred on the mastery of universal skills and knowledge contents (*les savoirs*), which in themselves were liberating and egalitarian. For 'republicans', child-centered, culturalist pedagogy only legitimized a 'dumbed down' education for disadvantaged children, which were patronizingly reduced to their 'culture' and thus denied the benefits of genuine, humanist, universal, intellectual 'culture'. In *The Undoing of Thought* (1987), Finkielkraut launched a powerful attack on the culturalist philosophy underpinning the *réforme pédagogique*, elucidating in the process the foundational principles of the emancipatory state conjured up by *laïcistes*. In his view, *la culture*, that is, high or classical culture, founded on individual critical reappropriation of the humanist canon, should be defended against *le culturel*, a more anthropological, relativist, and anti-intellectual notion. Multiculturalists had perversely praised 'culture' *qua* origin or particular collective identity (the German *Kultur*) instead of 'culture' *qua* individual cultivation of the mind and transcendence, through rational reflection, of common sense and social and cultural determinism (the German *Bildung*).[44] Yet only the latter—enlightened rational education—holds the key to individual emancipation.

Many republicans thus endorse an almost Platonist, humanist doctrine of knowledge as freedom. Knowledge-acquisition—the process of learning itself—fosters an ability to abstract from the bonds of social habit, unreflected prejudices, and oppressive ideologies.[45] Thus, the philosophy dissertation—a compulsory subject in the final year of French secondary school—is the *nec plus ultra* of republican education: there, students are taught to seek to transcend 'common sense' (*le sens commun*) to reach 'common reason' (*la raison commune*). (Not surprisingly perhaps, many republican educationalists are themselves philosophers or philosophy teachers, in contrast to their *pédagogue* adversaries who are more likely to have been trained in the social sciences, notably sociology.) Thus, philosophers write about the emancipatory power of enlightened knowledge, and of learning as the conquest of true autonomy and the breaking away from servitude and dependency.[46] They typically hold fast to a positivist distinction between 'knowledge' and 'belief'—the former essentially freedom-enhancing, and the latter oppressive.[47] How, then, is this knowledge to be acquired? How are the forces of 'nature' and 'society' to be tamed by the force of 'knowledge' and 'reason'? Republicans, influenced by the modernist and rationalist paradigms outlined above, have no qualms in firmly asserting that only the state can deliver such emancipatory knowledge. Nowhere does the ideology of political rationalism manifest itself more starkly than in the conception of the state as an *instituteur* (the telling French word for teacher). The modern state is perceived as the holder of science, of reason, the 'principal agent of the institution of truth'[48] in society. Neo-Kantian philosopher Catherine Kintzler argues that 'in a society characterized by ubiquitous relationships of domination—cultural, religious and economic—state schools are a privileged locus for the inculcation of the habit of independence through the exercise of critical judgment'.[49] Republican education, she claims, should ideally be 'anti-social': it should substitute for non-voluntary forms of social membership a rational capacity for individual self-determination.[50] Historian Yves Deloye notably has demonstrated that the educational philosophy of the Third Republic was consciously designed to substitute rational persuasion for the moral indoctrination long dispensed by the church.[51] The pivotal difference between republican and Catholic education was that while the former involved submission to the authority of a 'master' (the teacher), it was one whose role it was to teach children to 'live without a master'. As an official report of the General Inspectorate grandly noted, education should teach children to 'find in themselves the resources to break free from subjection'.[52] By contrast, 'social authorities' such as families, churches, cultural communities, and the media merely perpetuate the domination of heteronomous systems of thought. Within schools, pupils 'learn not to have to endure spiritual subjections, and lucidly to reflect on their ideological and religious conditioning'.[53] Writing in the midst of the 1994 headscarves affair, Kintzler argued that to educate children is to encourage them to distance themselves from their family or community beliefs and to reflect critically on them. 'Children', she wrote, 'should forget their community and think of something other than that which they are in order to think by themselves.'[54] This is what republican historian Claude Nicolet calls '*inner laïcité*'—the capability for self-emancipation fostered by (state) education to rational autonomy.[55] This capability, *laïcistes* argue, is denied and negated by the wearing of such symbols of subservience as the Muslim hijab.

Muslim Headscarves as Symbols of Female Religious Subservience

This section elucidates the feminist critique of hijab, first by retrieving a deeply rooted republican imagery about the links between citizenship, gender, and religion, then by interpreting the recrudescence of the wearing of headscarves as a practice central to today's traditionalist, patriarchal backlash within Muslim communities worldwide.

The Republic, Gender, and Religion

The veiled Muslim woman has revived a potent imaginary about republicanism, gender, and religion. In the early twentieth century, at the height of the republic's struggle against religious congregations, the veiled Catholic nun was perceived as the antithesis of the republic. She was the 'anti-Marianne',[56] whose irrational religiosity and forced confinement ostensibly symbolized rejection of the republican ideal of secular progress, female autonomy, and rationality. As women in general were deemed highly vulnerable to the influence of the Catholic Church, their liberation from the grip of religion was a pivotal republican mission. As Jules Ferry unambiguously claimed, 'women must belong to Science, or else they will belong to the Church.'[57] In truth, French republicans' optimism about the possibility of female enlightenment, notably through state education, did not extend as far as granting them political rights: while male universal suffrage was secured in 1848, women were allowed to vote only in 1945. Conflicting accounts of this troubling anomaly—which goes to the heart of the connection between citizenship and republican conceptions of individual autonomy—have been offered. While radical feminist historians have argued that the representation of women as irrational and non-autonomous was instrumental to the republican construction of the public sphere as a gendered, 'fraternal' community of (male) citizens,[58] republican historiography has pointed out that it is, paradoxically, because republicans embraced a universalist, progressive notion of gender equality—as equal capacity for reason and autonomy—that they were reluctant to open up partial 'spaces of citizenship' for women in patronizing deference to their traditional functions—as wives and mothers, for example—and instead kept alive the promise of their full recognition as autonomous citizens, once they had acquired the necessary independence, through education and participation in the labour force.[59] Be that as it may, the burgeoning feminist movement did not hesitate to rally round the anticlerical republican camp.[60] For all the latter's ambivalence about the 'gender of citizenship', its explicitly universalist, emancipatory discourse opened up the promise of women's liberation from traditional, particularly religious, forms of social domination.

The natural affinity between the French feminist movement and *laïcité* was further premised on the denunciation of the historical manipulation of religion by patriarchal power. All monotheistic religions historically contributed to entrench the domination of women. Crucially, male domination was often played out on women's bodies, and particularly on the legitimate modes of physical appearance that faithful women should display as symbols of their loyalty to God (and to their husbands). In this context, veiling must be seen as an 'antique alienation', in the words of Kacimi, expressing '3,000 years of hatred of women', notably in semitic cultures.[61] Did not St Paul himself argue that women must wear on their heads the symbol of their subservience: 'man must not cover his head because he is the glory of God; as for woman, she is the glory of man'?[62] The control of women's bodies was tightly linked to the control of their sexuality, seen as a potential threat to the order of socially regulated procreation and family transmission. To those feminists who in the 1970s had fought for women's rights over their own bodies, the hijab raises the spectre of regression towards age-old constraining impositions on women, reminiscent of the nineteenth-century Victorian corset or of the twentieth-century ban on women wearing 'masculine' trousers.[63] While some argue that Islam is not inherently more sexist than Christianity or Judaism,[64] others point to its specific 'theological complex' inclined to repress feminine sexuality as such,[65] and its historical association with deeply patriarchal societies, notably Middle Eastern and Mediterranean.[66] More to the point, however, the contemporary reassertion of patriarchal norms within Muslim communities worldwide is symptomatic of the way in which women and their status become primary targets of the traditionalist, religious backlash experienced in societies confronted with rapid social change and the widespread social destabilization it brings in its wake. This neo-traditionalist backlash provides the context against which the wearing of hijab has been interpreted in contemporary France, and it has bought new life into the *laïciste*, anti-traditionalist, anti-religious, and feminist strand of French republicanism.

A Neo-Traditionalist, Patriarchal Backlash

As early as 1936, British feminist Ruth Frances Woodsmall observed that 'veiling is a barometer of social change in the Muslim world'.[67] Throughout the nineteenth and twentieth centuries, the issue of women's dress became a pivotal site of struggle between modernizers and traditionalists. While modernizers (such as Mustapha Kemal in Turkey or the Shah in Iran) castigated the backward and oppressive practice of veiling as a potent symbol of archaic myriad restrictions on women's freedom, notably their confinement outside the public sphere of education and work, traditionalists (such as Egypt's Muslim Brothers or Ayatollah Khomeiny in Iran) fought a rearguard battle to fend off the forces of modernization and preserve (or reinvent) an idealized Muslim community.[68] As feminists have long argued, while collective identities are typically androcentric, the burden of maintaining their continuity and integrity through time is chiefly placed on women. 'Fallen women'—those women who are tempted and corrupted into 'modern', foreign, ways of life—are blamed for failing to preserve the group's (men's) honour. In times of rapid change, defensive male-dominated communities feel a need to control women in their midst, usually through appeal to a rigidly sexist interpretation of a sacred religious text. Thus, religious fundamentalism often takes the form of a 'patriarchal protest movement'.[69] Its neo-traditionalist rejection of secular modernity is principally expressed through control of women's bodies and movement (through scriptures against sexuality, contraception, or abortion, or against the breakdown of families caused by female work)[70] and, in the case of Islam, through control of women's dress.[71] The hijab is deliberately used as a powerful marker of vital separations: between the sacred and the profane, intimacy and visibility, men and women, husbands and other men, and faithful and 'fallen' women.[72] Arguably, claims that veiling is central to Islamic faith are complete perversions of Islam, based either on a misunderstanding of the historical context of the Qur'an or, more cynically, on a deliberate distortion of the sacred text by patriarchal power.[73] Above all, they express a wish to stem the destabilizing impact of women's entry into traditionally male public spaces, such as universities and paid work. As Morrocan feminist Fatima Mernissi states, the headscarf is 'a symbol revealing a collective fantasy of the Muslim community: to make women disappear, to eliminate them from communal life, to relegate them to an easily controllable terrain, the home, to prevent them from moving about, and to highlight their illegal position on male territory by means of a mask'.[74] The enhanced visibility of hijab in Muslim countries since the 1970s can be interpreted as a patriarchal backlash against the (failed) modernization of Middle Eastern and North African societies by secular nationalist movements, a backlash which seeks to re-establish a traditionalist social order centred, above all else, on the reaffirmation of traditional gender roles and on women as chief guardians of cultural, family, and religious values.

It is this feminist interpretation of fundamentalism as a patriarchal religious movement that is (implicitly) endorsed by French *laïcistes*. While concerns about female subordination were raised mezza voce during the first two 'headscarves affairs' of 1989 and 1994, they have come to the fore in recent years, in official circles, against the background of the growing audience found by fundamentalist Muslim movements in French-deprived neighbourhoods. Many socialists, notably, recently supported the ban on the grounds that they had been naïve about the worsening of women's status in deprived neighbourhoods—a cause taken up by such organizations as the Ligue des Droits de la Femme and the Grand Orient de France. Meanwhile, an alliance had been formed between the 'grassroots feminism' of young second-generation immigrants from the *quartiers* (deprived immigrant neighbourhoods) and the 'middle class feminism' of republican *laïciste* intellectuals,[75] which created an 'extraordinary pro-feminist consensus'.[76] Women and their bodies were perceived as the chief site of preservation of an idealized 'Muslim identity', and headscarves were held to symbolize the inferiorization of women. Fundamentalists, exploiting Muslims' feelings of humiliation, in a tense international context, have actively sought the 're-Islamization' of immigrant-dominated areas, precipitating a dramatic 'regression' of the status of young women.[77] Republican hopes for the emancipation of *beurettes* (young women of Maghrebi origin), through educational and work opportunities, were dashed when it appeared that an increasing number of them were being forced by their families or spiritual leaders to wear Muslim headscarves and conform to traditional gender roles. As Rachel Bloul has noted, the honour of women is 'not just an armature of stable systems of cultural reproduction', but also acts as a 'surrogate for the identity of embattled communities of males': men shore up their humiliated sense of identity (and virility) through control of 'how their women look'.[78] Women's appearance is a powerful signifier of specifically female virtues such as modesty, chastity, and obedience. Thus, headscarves should not be seen in isolation but connected to such deplorable trends as the recrudescence among Muslim groups of oppressive practices like polygamy, repudiation, and forced marriages,[79] as well as a recent spate of sexual violence and harassment against women. In the spring of 2003, young women from the *quartiers* organized a country-wide march to denounce the humiliating blackmail to which they were routinely subjected by their male peers: 'dress decently and wear a scarf or else you are fair game for sexual harassment'—thus conjuring up two age-old figures of female alienation, the 'saint' and the 'whore'. Against those men— fathers, brothers, and imams—who claimed to define the legitimate parameters of 'Muslim womanhood', they defiantly proclaimed that they intended to be 'neither prostitutes nor slaves' (Ni Putes Ni Soumises is the name of their association).[80] Hanifa Cherifi, the mediator appointed by the government to solve headscarves dispute in schools, summed up the critics' view when she asserted, during parliamentary auditions, that the headscarf was 'more than a piece of clothing' and referred to a 'restriction of mixity, of individual liberty, and of gender equality'.[81]

If this is the case, republicans should heed the warnings of feminists living in Muslim countries who urge the French not to see the hijab as a mere manifestation of cultural particularism or private religious piety, and to show solidarity to women who have opposed veiling, from the Syrian and Iraqi women who publicly took off their veil in the 1920s, to Algerian and Iranian women today who resist fundamentalist oppression.[82] Algerian feminist Wassyla Tamsali has urged her French counterparts not to use double standards in criticizing the subordination of women in culturally different contexts. Feminists should denounce 'everything that reduces women to their reproductive sexuality and to their exclusive dependency on the community that decides their fate', and should not be intimidated by the religious claims made on behalf of hijab: after all, the feminist struggle for abortion in the 1970s attacked a dogma that was more fundamental to the Catholic Church than veiling has ever been to Islam.[83] Misguided post-colonialist scruples should not stand in the way of the universalist promotion of female emancipation against the regressive force of religious, counter-Enlightenment forces.[84] For in addition to the imposition of a patriarchal interpretation of the Qur'an, the wearing of headscarves symbolizes a broader religious, obscurantist protest against Western modernity, not least the rationalist and emancipatory ambitions of state education.[85] Not only have attempts been made to deny schoolgirls the benefits of 'mixed' school activities such as physical education, but the hijab has also been associated to rejection by Muslim students (or their families) of such subjects as biology, history, and some philosophy classes, on the grounds that they contradicted the teachings of Islam. The headscarf symbolizes, at best, a profoundly ambivalent attitude towards the benefits of secular free enquiry and, at worst, an obscurantist and oppressive assertion of the primacy of communal tradition or divinely ordained command over individual reason.[86] It denies young girls the very benefits that republican education had promised them, namely, the possibility of emancipation from their condition through the critical re-examination of beliefs inculcated by their families or communities.

Education and Autonomy: The Liberty-Based Case against Hijab *in Schools*

The previous two sections have elucidated two central premises of the *laïciste* case. The first is that the emancipatory ambitions of the republican state are best pursued through education to autonomy, which fosters in children a capacity to distance themselves from the traditional, often oppressive values transmitted by their family and community of origin. The second is that Muslim headscarves in themselves are symbols both of female and of religious oppression, and infringe on the republican conception of liberty as rational self-determination. It is not immediately obvious, however, that the combination of these two premises is sufficient to justify banning headscarves in schools. There are, in particular, two missing links in the argument. First, why should pupils be required to take off their headscarves *prior to* their being educated in autonomy? Second, if the wearing of hijab is incompatible with a life of autonomy, why ban headscarves *only* in schools? Coherent answers to these—admittedly central—questions are, unfortunately, not readily available in the French literature. In this section, I attempt to reconstruct a coherent and plausible *laïciste* case, putting special emphasis on its distinctive republican conception of education. Prima facie, the *laïciste* case is compatible with liberal educational paternalism: it states that the state has a special duty to inculcate in children the skills associated with the exercise of autonomy. While this explains the *laïcistes*' exclusive focus on *children*'s education in autonomy (and their repudiation of state paternalism for adult headscarves-wearers), it does not account for the ban on headscarves in schools. This is because, on a standard liberal account, what should suffice for paternalistic purposes is that veiled schoolgirls, like all children, benefit from a comprehensive autonomy-promoting education. To understand why they need, in addition, to take off their headscarves while receiving such education, we need a more robust republican conception of education. This suggests that state schools are not only spaces in which children acquire a *capacity* for autonomy, they are—unique—spaces in which children can *exercise* (some form of) (relevant) autonomy.

Paternalism, Socialization, and Children

If we assume, on the one hand, that the wearing of headscarves infringes individual autonomy and, on the other, that the emancipatory state has a duty to promote individuals' interest in their own autonomy, why not ban hijab in society altogether?[87] Why be concerned merely with children, and with school regulations? Admittedly, as Mill argued, the legitimacy of state paternalistic intervention (i.e. infringement of someone's liberty in order to promote their interest in liberty) cannot be posed in the same terms regarding adults and children. Adults should generally be considered the best judges of their own interests, and should be left free to make mistakes, pursue valueless forms of life, or follow a life of blind devotion to others or to God (but not, Mill noted, permanently to enslave themselves). The state may encourage, in a number of non-coercive ways, the pursuit of autonomy by its citizens, but what it cannot do is to *coerce* adult citizens into behaving autonomously. As we saw during our brief discussion of the French state's attitude towards cults (*sectes*), the state can alert citizens to the dangers of sectarian membership, but it cannot ban cults altogether. By the same token, arguably, the state can legitimately criticize the oppressive patriarchal order which requires women to cover their heads, but it cannot forcibly prevent Muslim women from wearing headscarves. To use *laïc* vocabulary, the state may promote freedom of thought but cannot enforce its exercise, because of its prior commitment to respect for freedom of conscience. By contrast, and crucially, a perfectionist commitment to the value of individual autonomy can legitimize paternalistic action in the case of children. This is because children have not yet formed their conception of the good and moral character, and must be protected from premature indoctrination by their parents or community. Through education, they should be given the rational skills required critically to assess the values they have been brought up with, so they are in a position to choose for themselves which to endorse, revise, or repudiate. Families cannot be trusted to provide autonomy-promoting education to their children; the state, with its public commitment to autonomy and citizenship, is a more reliable paternalist agent, at least as far as children's interest in their own autonomy is concerned.[88]

If this is the case, why should the state not forbid all under-age *children* from wearing religious headscarves (leaving it up to them, when they become adults and have acquired the tool of autonomy, to make an informed, independent decision about the demands of their religion)? The basic answer is that this would fall outside the bounds of justifiable paternalistic intervention. To see why this is so, let us compare Muslim headscarves with another customary practice of female oppression, female genital mutilation. For our purposes here, two differences between the two practices stand out.[89] First, while genital mutilation causes direct and measurable harm to young girls— gravely infringing on their physical integrity and health and damaging their sexual capabilities—headscarves do not so much *cause* particular harms as act as a *symbolic marker* of female inferiority and subservience.[90] Thus, paternalistic intervention is more difficult to justify in the latter than in the former case. Second, and crucially here, while girls are subjected to genital mutilation at a young age, Muslim headscarves are typically worn by girls after they have reached puberty, when they can be presumed to have willingly consented to wearing them. Of course, all prohibitions to which under-age children, but not adults, are subjected to on paternalistic grounds (such as prohibitions on the sale of alcohol) rely on inevitably arbitrary decisions about what constitutes the 'age of reason' in particular cases. Yet in so far as informed consent is what underpins the pre-emption against paternalistic intervention against adults, the fact that mature adolescents are capable of it clearly provides grounds for caution regarding the legitimacy of a blanket ban on headscarves. That the hijab may be consented to, then, provides a prima facie argument against 'direct' paternalism.

However, I now want to suggest that this fact also provides a strong argument for 'indirect' paternalism—whereby all children are provided with a comprehensive autonomy-promoting education. This can be seen by probing further the connection between autonomy and socialization in the writings of the *laïcistes*. A preliminary observation is that some would concede that the wearing of headscarves can at times be a clear instance of coercion of hapless young children or adolescents by their parents or community leaders. Indeed, there is abundant evidence of Muslim girls as young as 12 or 13 being forcibly coerced into covering their heads. However, *laïcistes* insist that even in the more common cases when older adolescents *voluntarily* decide to wear headscarves on religious grounds and are not subjected to obvious coercion or threats by either their parents or religious leaders, doubts must be cast about the authenticity and validity of their choice. Two arguments have been offered. First, even if adolescents autonomously decide to affirm their religious or cultural identity by wearing a Muslim headscarf, they are deceiving themselves about the implications of their choice. Too frequently, women are instrumentalized by Islamist groups operating in the *quartiers*, and the 'chosen scarf' swiftly becomes a 'forced scarf', as young veiled women are then required to live up to standards of 'Muslim womanhood' defined by patriarchal norms.[91] So even if their initial decision to wear the headscarf is autonomous, it impairs their future capacity for autonomy. Second, and more importantly, the decision to wear a headscarf may itself be a rationalization of the limited range of options opened to Muslim girls: it may be, to use the term favoured by (some) Anglo-American liberals, an 'adaptive preference'.[92] Adaptive preferences are preferences that have—consciously or otherwise—been altered to fit unjust background conditions, so that their holder can conceal the injustice of her situation from herself. If the actual choice opened to young Muslim women in certain *quartiers* is either to wear a headscarf and be shown respect by their male peers, or opt for 'Western' clothing and be subjected to abuse and harassment, they may seek to maintain their dignity and self-esteem by convincing themselves that their choice to veil is a free one. Yet as Finkielkraut puts it, 'those who do it to protect themselves from misogyny and sexism cannot be said to be free.'[93] For, in the words of another commentator, such insidious, 'internalized pressure' is an 'expression of consent only by proxy' and expresses 'the silent alienation of a human being whom it is difficult to see as autonomous'.[94] This is because, while their freedom of action may not be externally limited, their desires and preferences have been internally shaped and constrained in unjust ways. As sociologist Pierre Bourdieu pointed out (albeit in a different context), in line with well-established feminist literature, 'male domination', like all forms of 'symbolic domination', works essentially by being 'invisible' and 'gentle' to its victims, who 'internalize' its categories through a form of 'enchanted subjection' that primarily inscribes itself through 'things and bodies'.[95] The choice to veil, on the *laïciste* view, may be interpreted as an instance of *dominated choice*, whereby choosers are subjected neither to interference with their actions nor to direct coercive threats, but where (i) the options open to them are equally unattractive and (ii) their option set has been framed by an unjust, patriarchal normative order. Thus, in the words of feminist Zelenski, 'the fact that girls claim the headscarf does not make any difference [to the reality of their domination]'.[96]

One difference the girls' prima facie consent does make, however, is that a blanket ban on headscarves would be unduly coercive and would not address the root cause of female oppression—the internalization by women of pervasive norms of patriarchal socialization. What is required, instead, is an alternative socialization, and this is precisely what state education is designed to provide. A number of *laïcistes* and feminists appeal to Article 5 of the UN Convention on the Elimination of all Forms of Discrimination against Women, which focuses, not only on legal reform and prohibitions but also on the 'modification of social and cultural patterns of conduct of men and women' with a view to 'eliminate prejudices of female inferiority'.[97] In *laïque* schools, young Muslim girls benefit from a thoroughly non-sexist education, which exposes them to the variety of gender roles that can be freely taken up in French society, and they are taught autonomy-related skills, which empower them to reflect on, and question, the broader cultural and religious norms they have been brought up with. They are, for example, taught methods for evaluating the truth and falsehood, or relative probability, of various claims about the world; they are taught how to resist manipulation and made to understand that adaptive preferences can be avoided by 'stepping back' from their commitments and reflecting on how they were formed; they are taught that good lives are lives lived autonomously.[98] As Condorcet put it (in the phrase cited in the epigraph to this chapter), one chief purpose of education is to 'exclude all dependence, either forced or voluntary'. Education, in other words, allows the only emancipation that is worth the name (because it is not brought about through coercive paternalism): self-emancipation.

So the education favoured by *laïcistes* is what John Rawls would call a 'comprehensive' liberal education, in contrast to his favoured 'political' liberal education. In broad terms, a political liberal education fosters the political virtues of citizenship: the ability to see one's conception of the good as only one among a range of reasonable views, the ability to distinguish, for purposes of political deliberation, one's comprehensive doctrine from the public requirements of mutual respect, reciprocity and so forth. In French *laïque* terms (as set out in Chapter 2), secular civic education fosters in children a capacity to separate their public from their private selves, and to endorse a '*laïcized*' interpretation of their religious commitments. By contrast, a comprehensive liberal education, in Rawlsian terms, explicitly cultivates substantively liberal virtues such as autonomy and individuality; it shapes the whole of the self, not merely the self in its 'political', civic capacity, and thoroughly alters the relationship of the self to its ends and values. In *laïque* terms, such an education provides children with the skills required for 'self-emancipation' from oppressive value systems inculcated in the private sphere of family and community life. Now, as a number of liberal theorists of education have argued, and Rawls himself has conceded, a political education is in practice hardly distinguishable from a comprehensive education in autonomy.[99] This is because, as Amy Gutmann has neatly put it, 'the skills of political reflection cannot be neatly differentiated from the skills of evaluating one's one way of life.'[100] Nor should liberals 'regret'—as Rawls does[101]—the wide-ranging impact that a liberal education will have on how individuals relate to the sometimes illiberal, traditional, religious comprehensive doctrines they have been brought up to believe. While liberals are committed to respect for the pluralism of ethical doctrines in society, they should only respect those that are 'reasonable' and, arguably, doctrines that advocate the oppression of certain members of society are not doctrines that liberals should seek to accommodate.[102]

All French *laïque* thinkers would, I suspect, be in broad agreement with Eamonn Callan, Amy Gutmann, and Meira Levinson's suggestion that all liberal education is inevitably autonomy-promoting. As we have seen, even the neutralist strand of *laïcité* elucidated in Chapter 2 comprises a robust conception of the 'detached school' as promoting values discrepant from those of the family and society at large, and fostering, for the purposes of citizenship, a capacity to adopt reflective distance vis-à-vis one's upbringing. That all *laïque* defenders are committed to education as promoting at least a weak version of autonomy is not surprising, given their foundational commitment to disentangle citizenship from the grip of Catholicism. So even advocates of a strictly 'neutral' education, such as Jules Ferry, acknowledged (and sometimes privately welcomed) the fact that the inculcation, through state education, of an a-religious public morality and of a capacity for rational critical thinking would unavoidably encourage children to step back from unthinking religious commitments. If there is a difference between the neutralists and *laïcistes*, therefore, it is *not* that the latter but not the former are committed to autonomy-promoting education. The difference is more subtle. While a neutralist state fosters the capacity for formal autonomy without specifying how autonomy should be used to the good ('a republican can think what he likes, provided he thinks by himself', in Nicolet's words[103]), a *laïciste* state is a more openly perfectionist one: it does not refrain from identifying and promoting substantive forms of the good, autonomous life, and is more suspicious of the compatibility of religious beliefs with full autonomy. Thus, it may inform citizens about the risks of 'mental manipulation' involved in membership of particular religious groups, and may publicly denounce Muslim headscarves as 'symbols of female oppression'. Furthermore, *laïcistes* present schools as special institutions where the good life of autonomy must be experimented with, and hence argue that religious headscarves have no place in them. While, as we saw, neutralists appealed to the secular doctrine of separation between public and private spheres to justify the ban on hijab in schools, *laïcistes*, more bluntly and more controversially, appeal to the intrinsic value of the non-religious life. The ban on hijab in schools, then, graphically symbolizes the normative, autonomy-driven order of state schooling.

Schooling as an Experiment in Autonomy: The Case for Banning Hijab *in Schools*

Assuming, as we have thus far, that headscarves are symbols of female oppression, and that Muslim girls should be provided with a comprehensive education in autonomy, why should they be required to take off the hijab upon entering the school? Republican philosopher Charles-Yves Zarka puts it thus: 'nothing prevents a woman from wearing the headscarf when and where she wishes. This is not what is at stake. What is at stake is the wearing of the headscarf by adolescents within state schools, that is, within institutions where they have to be taught the principles of liberty and autonomy.'[104] It is, therefore, because of the particular nature of schools as institutions shaped by the norms of autonomous reasoning that headscarves should not be tolerated in their midst. Schools are not only spaces in which children acquire a *capacity* for autonomy, they are—unique—spaces in which children can *exercise* and *experiment with* autonomous thinking and behaviour. Note that, within schools, children are routinely subjected to paternalistic authority, often of a coercive kind, not merely on educational grounds (as with standards of discipline, for instance) but also on more general perfectionist grounds. For example, while the state does not ban the sale of unhealthy, processed foods to children in shops and supermarkets, it may legitimately, on public health grounds, teach children about the benefits of healthy eating *and* forbid the sale of 'junk' food within its schools. By the same token (the *laïciste* argument would continue), the state does not ban the wearing of headscarves in civil society, but it may legitimately forbid it within schools. The first argument put forward by *laïcistes* to this effect is that it is incoherent for state schools to promote values such as gender equality and autonomous critical enquiry while tolerating in their midst symbols that ostensibly contradict those values. In so far as Muslim headscarves symbolize both the assertion of the claims of faith against those of reason and learning, and those of patriarchal subjection over those of women's self-determination, they should not be tolerated within schools, as they deny schoolgirls the basic independence, agency, and autonomy that it is the schools' mission to promote.

Second, *laïcistes* argue that schools must provide a place where young Muslim girls can experiment with alternative constructions of female, Muslim, and personal identity. Within schools, they come to realize that they do not need to cover their head in order to be respected by others, they learn to think for themselves without having to second-guess what their spiritual leader or father would expect them to think, and they learn to interact freely with members of both sexes. Schools, therefore, provide a safe, domination-free environment where young women can try out and experience the various goods that the exercise of personal autonomy brings. If the hijab was tolerated in schools, the fear is that veiled Muslim schoolgirls would only partially benefit from education in autonomy. The wearing of headscarves, associated as it is with attitudes of subservience, humility, and reserve, in itself hinders the development of the virtues associated with autonomy, namely, self-belief, assertiveness, and a critical mind. Third, schools as 'spaces of liberty' must act as a counterweight to family and community pressure. They should be seen as allies by those Muslim girls who seek to escape from the restricted choices offered by their family or community. The ban gives them arguments to refuse to wear headscarves altogether, and therefore contributes to undermine the powerful grip of neo-traditionalist, patriarchal groups in the *quartiers*.[105] Prominent feminist Elizabeth Badinter thus made the case for this paternalistic duty of state schools: 'Putting a veil on the head is an act of submission. It burdens women's whole life. Their fathers or their brothers choose their husbands, they are closed up in their own homes and confined to domestic tasks, etc. . . . Without this public rule [the ban in schools], [the girl] finds herself alone again, and she loses.'[106] *Laïcistes* frequently insist that, were schools to tolerate headscarves, they would fail in their duty to protect vulnerable girls in their (often subdued and silent) struggle to assert their independence against community and religious dictates. Schools have a special duty to help the emancipation of *beurettes*.

It is time to conclude this chapter. *Laïcistes* are unrepentant perfectionists (they believe that the state should promote substantive values such as individual autonomy, understood principally as rational self-determination from religious dogmas and traditional identities) and they further believe that the hijab gravely infringes on the autonomy of young Muslim girls. *Laïcistes*, however, are more hesitant paternalists, aware as they are that individuals cannot be *coerced* into behaving autonomously, all the more so given the pervasiveness of their socialization into family, religious, and community norms. At best, individuals can be *educated* in autonomy—hence the pivotal role of education as a precondition of self-emancipation. Within the unique institutions of state schools, children not only acquire the tool of autonomy but can also experiment with some forms of substantive autonomy. Schools provide a space structured by norms different from those of family and religion, and it is in children's interest to be thoroughly *socialized into* (not simply exposed to) forms of autonomous behaviour and thought appropriate to modern individualistic societies. Such alternative socialization into autonomy, which justifies the ban on headscarves in schools, promotes children's interest in autonomy without being unduly coercive (given the inevitably coercive nature of most school rules and regulations). Such, then, is the (reconstructed) liberty-based case against headscarves in schools. It has been subjected to powerful criticisms, which I consider in the next chapter.

CHAPTER 6

─────

Female Agency and the Critique
of Republican Paternalism

The *laïciste*, autonomy-based argument for the ban on hijab in schools has been subjected to a range of criticisms by advocates of the toleration of headscarves. This chapter reconstructs the most persuasive version of them, critically addressing the sociological, conceptual, and normative foundations of the *laïciste* case, and providing a comprehensive alternative account. The first section interprets the paternalistic ban on hijab as a form of state oppression, which claims to coerce individuals into being free, in the name of a highly contestable conception of individual autonomy as secular liberation from religion. The second section sets out an alternative sociology of contemporary religion to the modernist paradigm implicitly endorsed by *laïcistes*, showing that the contemporary religious revival is not necessarily a traditionalist and anti-individualistic backlash but is, rather, compatible with postmodern agential individualism. Bringing these conceptual and sociological arguments to bear on the moral and normative case, the third section shows that toleration of the hijab in schools expresses respect for Muslim female agency.

Republican Paternalism and State Oppression

Although they have fallen short of advocating a full ban on Muslim headscarves, *laïcistes* are committed to the view that the state, through its educational system, can and should emancipate Muslim girls from patriarchal, religious oppression. Critics retort that, while the provision of an autonomy-promoting education to all children may be justifiable on liberal (Millian) paternalistic grounds, the forcible prohibition of the wearing of symbols of heteronomy in schools falls outside the scope of permissible paternalist intervention. *Laïcistes* cannot at the same time argue that the only valuable emancipation is self-emancipation *and* justify coercing young girls into behaving autonomously. As Hector Yankelevich puts it, 'if it is true that all servitude is voluntary, the only way for girls and women to stop wearing the veil is ... to take it off themselves.... Any "liberation" from above will be rejected for what it is: colonialist and coercive.'[1] *Laïcistes* have not faced up to the liberal paternalist paradox so eloquently formulated by J. S. Mill: the state gravely infringes on individual liberty if it prohibits certain individual actions merely on the grounds that they jeopardize the autonomy of those who engage in them.[2] At most, the state may educate *children* so as to enhance their capacity for autonomy and self-emancipation, and it may also prohibit practices that cause obvious and durable harm to them, in a way that compromises their future capacity for autonomy. The ban on headscarves in schools in practice contradicts the first objective, and it does not fall under the scope of the second, as I shall show in the following two sections. The third section radicalizes the critique and suggests that the ban itself reproduces forms of colonialist oppression.

Exclusion, Emancipation, and the Purposes of Education

Critics point out that *laïcistes* are caught in an unrecognized contradiction. By defending the ban on headscarves in schools as facilitating the emancipation of young Muslim girls, *laïcistes* conveniently forget that banning headscarves in many cases means excluding Muslim girls from schools. Although the 2004 law provided for extensive 'consultations' between school authorities and young Muslim girls and their parents, it remains the case that the ultimate sanction for refusing to comply with the ban is exclusion.[3] There are two obvious problems with this. First, it is an unfair, disproportionate, and discriminatory sanction: it affects pupils who are widely recognized to be serious, studious, and trouble-free,[4] it punishes those very girls who are the victims of the sexism of their male peers, and therefore perpetuates the very gender inequality it claims to combat,[5] and it condemns Muslim girls to an almost certain 'educational death' (*mort scolaire*).[6] As Jean-Fabien Spitz has asked, 'what bizarre conception of punishment must one endorse to say that those who are subjected to it in no way deserve it?'[7] Because *laïcistes* hardly pause to consider that the ban affects persons and not only religious symbols—that it involves a very real sanction, exclusion from school—they do not reflect on the oddity of punishing those they consider to be victims. Second, and importantly, exclusion from school is no ordinary punishment. It is a self-defeating form of punishment which openly contradicts its declared aim, namely, the emancipation of Muslim girls. As leftwing intellectuals claimed in a manifesto published in *Libération*, 'it is by welcoming [the girl] within schools that we can help to emancipate her, by giving her the tools of autonomy, and it is by excluding her that we condemn her to [oppression].'[8] The ban, in other words, is counterproductive. It is marred by a 'blatant contradiction': 'it burdens girls, their life, their future, their flesh, with the punishment of the injustice of which they are victims, by sending them back to a community-dominated [*communautaire*] space permeated by the religious sexism' that it was precisely meant to combat.[9] Note that this consequentialist argument prima facie accepts two central premises of the *laïciste* case: that veiled girls are subjected to oppression, and that schools are emancipatory spaces. It argues that there is no contradiction involved in being 'against headscarves *and therefore* against exclusion', as 'the construction of autonomy is only possible through the institution of the school'.[10]

Others, however, challenge the *laïcistes*' irenic and utopian conception of schools and education. The latter's elevated, Platonic belief in the liberating power of knowledge is belied by the more prosaic lessons drawn from the history and sociology of education in France. Even during the heyday of the idealized Third Republic, when schooling offered some promise of emancipation for disadvantaged social groups, it fell short of the comprehensive and universal education in autonomy conjured up by *laïcistes*. Not only were the values of obedience and conformity given primacy over those of free critical enquiry, but schools also contributed to entrench existing class and gender inequalities. The apparent democratization of the educational system in the twentieth century was denounced by critical sociologists such as Pierre Bourdieu as a sham.[11] The seemingly neutral and universal autonomy-related skills (paradigmatically inculcated through the philosophy dissertation) turned out to form part of the culturally acquired *habitus* of the educated bourgeoisie. Schools, in a word, contributed to the reproduction of social domination more than to emancipation from structures of domination. The cultural codes implicitly transmitted through education closely matched those acquired at home by children of French-born, urban, educated middle-class families, while other children were forcibly uprooted from their background and taught abstract, formalist skills and knowledge that hardly connected to their life experiences. As critics of *laïcisme* put it in an Open Letter of 1989, 'one cannot demand that children and adolescents abruptly break with their families, with their origins. One would not transplant a tree by cutting its roots.'[12] Critical reflections about the relationship between individual autonomy and cultural identity shaped the *pédagogique* movement of the 1970s. Wrongly derided by *laïcistes* as a 'dumbed down' and patronizing education, *pédagogisme* laid stress on the need to respect children's cultural coherence, and on the cultural preconditions of the exercise of individual autonomy. In its emphasis on children's authentic self-expression and intercultural dialogue, and in its view of schools as 'laboratories of civility'[13] and not only as providers of abstract knowledge, this educational philosophy was influenced by wider philosophical reconsiderations of postmodern identity and individualism (as we shall see below). The ideal of the school as a privileged space where children can experience autonomy and detach themselves from archaic, pre-modern social structures and beliefs is seen to have lost all credibility in an increasingly globalized cultural world where children are subjected to a plurality of social influences, from youth culture to reconstructed family traditions.[14] Hence, critics also challenge the *laïcistes'* simplistic account of harm, autonomy, and socialization.

Harm, Autonomy, and Socialization

The *laïciste*, liberty-based argument against headscarves relies, at bottom, on a version of at least one of the following claims: headscarves-wearing is intrinsically a harmful practice; all religious belief is suspect on the grounds of autonomy; and individuals can be oppressed by social norms. These three claims are both elusive and contentious.

First, *laïcistes* explicitly justify the ban on the wearing on headscarves on the grounds that the practice infringes individual autonomy. It is a harmful practice, even when consented to, as it implies subjection to oppressive religious and patriarchal norms. Yet in so far as headscarves are only religious symbols, and not objectively and directly harmful practices, they are 'interpreted as an infringement on female dignity only on the basis of a reconstruction of what is known, or is thought to be known, about Islamic religion and civilisation'. In themselves, though, headscarves 'express nothing',[15] and it is wholly illegitimate for state authorities to indulge in subjective interpretations of the meaning of particular religious and cultural practices, especially in cases where the harm they supposedly cause is exclusively of a psychological and symbolic kind. While *laïcistes* suggest that the hijab signals the likelihood of more tangible harms being done to the girls (forced marriages, for instance), the link between them is at best tenuous and contingent. At any rate, as liberal philosophers Monique Canto-Sperber and Paul Ricoeur, as well as radical feminist Christine Delphy have insisted, it is not permissible to restrict one liberty (the liberty to wear headscarves) in order to protect possible future liberties which are not directly infringed by the banned practice.[16] The Conseil d'État has always insisted that it was not within its remit to interpret the meaning of religious signs. Neither the Stasi nor the Debré commission have taken heed of those precautionary warnings, and they have not hesitated to rally round one-sided and controversial interpretations of the hijab as the oppressive symbol of traditionalist patriarchy. Yet (as we shall see in the last section), the wearing of headscarves is a complex (post)modern practice, with a variety of meanings, and it is not incompatible with forms of female agency.

Second, *laïcistes* occasionally convey the impression that adhesion to a religion, and obedience to religious prescriptions, in itself indicates a posture of heteronomy and servitude. Spitz has noted the absurd 'enormity' of the claim that 'full adherence to a religion is incompatible with the status of citizen and the autonomy this implies'.[17] In truth, the *laïciste* discussion of the implications of respect for freedom of conscience has been somewhat loose and unfocused. Yves Charles Zarka, for example, in his recent treatise on toleration, approvingly discusses classical arguments for toleration derived from Locke and Bayle (to the effect that there is no rational metric of the good life, or that conscience cannot be forced, for example) and then, when discussing the case of the *hijab,* conflates it with obviously non-voluntary practices such as 'forced marriages' as well as with 'inequality of rights', and goes on to posit with no justification that 'voluntary servitude' cannot be tolerated.[18] Throughout, he avoids the difficult question of whether freedom of conscience does not precisely entail freedom voluntarily to enslave oneself. The concept of 'mental manipulation' or 'psychological subjection', which is used by *laïcistes* to castigate the wearing of hijab as well as membership of dangerous cults, is thus highly problematic. Religious belief by definition entails the partial renunciation of autonomous reasoning, as well as forms of psychological dependency.[19] As Hervieu-Léger has critically commented, the *laïciste* invocation of autonomy-driven freedom of thought is in fact too often used as a selective filter separating good from bad religiosity, with bad religiosity referring to new or unfamiliar religions, which are more easily suspected of mental manipulation than traditionally established religions such as Catholicism. Yet, she argues, the right to religious radicalism must be defended as firmly as the right to change or repudiate religion. Individuals must be able freely to choose to be poor, chaste and obedient, to defer to a spiritual master or to take the veil [*se cloîtrer*] for the glory of God without being subjected to paternalist tutelage for mental weakness or social inadequacy.[20]

A life of heteronomy, then, might be a good, fulfilling life, provided it is 'lived from the inside', that is, appropriated by individuals as being authentically 'their' lives. *Laïcistes* have been worryingly elusive on the crucial question of whether one can autonomously decide to lead a heteronomous life. This is because their chief focus has been on children, who *ex hypothesi* are not deemed capable of full autonomy, subjected as they are to a host of formative and coercive influences, some of which justify paternalistic concern.

Yet this raises the question, third, as to whether it makes sense exclusively to single out the wearing of hijab as a form of false consciousness or adaptive preference to an oppressive normative order. *Laïcistes* tend to deploy a thoroughly de-contextualized concept of autonomy as the capacity to distance oneself from social norms and live by one's own rules. From this perspective, the veiled Muslim girl is castigated as a social conformist, who mindlessly follows the precepts of her religion or the demands of her community. As republican feminist Elizabeth Badinter has stated, 'wearing torn jeans or pink hair is an act of autonomy. Putting a veil on one's head is an act of subservience.' Leaving aside the highly contestable notion that following the latest youth fashion is a sign of anti-conformism, 'it is remarkable how this sort of construction treats all the pressures within French society *not* to wear the hijab (...) as background conditions of free choice and only pressures from parents or others to wear the hijab as coercive'.[21] From this perspective, wearing the hijab and displaying a high level of personal piety may appear as 'a rather comfortingly moral and autonomous choice, perhaps even a mark of bold individualism'.[22] While it may signal conformist subservience in a society comprehensively structured around strict traditional or religious norms, in a society such as France, where there is a plurality of conflicting normative orders, a more complex account of autonomy and agency is required. Nor should the assumption that the norms structuring dominant French society (autonomy, individual equality, and so on) are intrinsically liberating, go unchallenged. Thus, critics have also compared the forced 'unveiling' of Muslim girls in the name of Western feminist understandings of emancipation to practices of colonialist domination.

A Selective and Colonialist Feminism

The *laïcistes'* republican feminism is paradoxical in two ways: it is highly selective, focusing exclusively on the marginal issue of the hijab as the chief symbol of female oppression in French society, and it unconsciously replicates the forced unveiling of Arab women which was the hallmark of the so-called civilizing mission in North African colonies. I develop these two criticisms in turn.

While it is true that French feminists historically rallied round republicans in the latter's struggle against clericalists and conservatives, it would be a great exaggeration to claim that republicans have been champions of women's rights. The strong republican distinction between the public sphere of reason and autonomy and the private sphere of dependency and domesticity neatly mapped onto gender lines, confining women to natural or social inferiority. The perfectionist commitment to autonomy as the hallmark of citizenship, then, often justified the exclusion from citizenship of those deemed to lack autonomy. Women obtained the right to vote only in 1945, and it is only in the 1960s that the patriarchal conception of the family was challenged in law (notably allowing wives to manage the family budget or work outside the home without asking for their husbands' permission).[23] While gender equality as non-discrimination is now secured in French law, the persistence of profoundly sexist norms throughout society is amply testified by the dramatic underrepresentation of women in political office, and the persisting lack of questioning of the traditional division of labour within the family. This state of affairs has been perniciously legitimized by the resurgence of a quasi-official 'feminine neo-feminism' which, in opposition to the radical 'second-wave feminism' of the 1970s, emphasizes the complementarity rather than the equality between the sexes and naturalizes sexist constructions of gender norms.[24] In this context, the Stasi Commission report's proud statement that 'French society does not accept breaches in gender equality'[25] is historically selective, confuses high-minded principles and practices and, most ironically, takes Muslims to task for not undertaking what the French Republic itself had spectacularly failed to do, beyond the limited confines of its schools: challenging deeply ingrained norms of gender socialization.[26]

One concern that *laïcistes* paradoxically share with their presumed adversaries (patriarchal male Muslims) is concern about how women appear in public. *Laïciste* feminists tend to focus on visible symbols of oppression, such as headscarves. More harmful and widespread, but far less visible, practices of gender oppression such as domestic violence, wage inequality, the work/family balance, genital mutilation, or polygyny, have not provoked as much public outcry as Muslim headscarves. Headscarves are notably perceived as a denial of women's freedom to control their own sexuality. Yet female sexuality and bodily appearance in France is powerfully framed by pervasive norms of beauty, fashion, dress, figure, makeup, and so on, as diffused through the hegemonic 'feminine neo-feminism' of women's magazines and the media. The hijab controversy must be placed within a context of heightened sexualization of women's (mainly adolescent) bodies in French society, and it intriguingly coincided (in 2003) with public concern about female fashion clothing as a graphic symbol of their sexual availability. The *laïciste* injunction on Muslim girls to 'uncover' and reveal their bodies, in this view, is less about the promotion of female autonomy and sexual liberation as it is about the assertion of dominant norms of femininity. Thus, radical feminists have not been slow in interpreting the headscarves controversy as a male contest over women's bodies, and to argue that the 'right to one's own body' should be defended, not only against minority practices such as veiling but also against the sexist norms of female appearance in mainstream French society.[27]

Not only do *laïcistes* exclusively focus on the practices of minority groups, to the detriment of critical scrutiny of the sexist practices of their own society,[28] but they also unconsciously reproduce the sexual politics of the colonial civilizing mission.[29] For the ban on headscarves is eerily reminiscent of colonial measures against veiling in Arab societies. Between the sixteenth and nineteenth centuries, the hijab had emerged as a symbol of status among the Muslim ruling classes. To Western colonialists, the hijab came to symbolize the oppression of women and the backwardness of Eastern societies. Nineteenth-century orientalist writers constructed an image of the Arab as an uncivilized male whose masculinity relied on the mistreatment of women. Thus, the colonizers imposed unveiling and female education in one 'civilizing' package—a strategic mistake which had the unintended effect of promoting the hijab as a powerful symbol of patriotic and anti-colonial struggle and resistance.[30] A late episode of the recurrent colonial politics of veiling and unveiling took place during what the *New York Times* in 1958 called the 'battle of the veil' in Algiers, when French soldiers forcibly and publicly took off women's veils, a violent act which was experienced by Algerians as literal and figurative rape.[31] Arguably, the (partly repressed) memory of this painful episode casts a long shadow on the headscarves controversy in post-colonial France. Just as during the Algerian war, women's bodies were perceived as territories to conquer, to liberate, and to occupy, in France today, the bodies of Muslim women similarly symbolize those 'lost territories of the republic' which the latter must reclaim from the grip of Arab males demonized as uncivilized and aggressive chauvinists.[32] The female body has again become a metaphor for (post)-colonial occupation, and *laïciste* feminism can be seen as an instance of what post-colonial critic Gayatri Chakravorty Spivak has called 'white men saving brown women from brown men'.[33] In line with Michel Foucault's analyses of the body as the main site of power contests, it has been argued that unveiling, far from liberating women by revealing the 'naturalness' of the unveiled body, is merely yet another oppressive practice of corporal inscription.[34] The attempt to liberate women by removing the veil simply re-inscribes women's bodies as symbols of culture rather than as individual agents.[35] Women, as contests for male power, are caught between alternative contradictory injunctions and silenced.

A remarkable but barely noticed feature of the extensive consultations undertaken by the Stasi Commission in the autumn of 2003 is that hardly any veiled woman was heard, on the grounds that the commission, assuming they were manipulated and alienated, would 'not be sensitive to their arguments'.[36] Only Saïda Kada, a Lyons-area activist and co-author of a thoughtful book about French Muslim women,[37] was invited on the last day, almost as an afterthought; the questions put to her tended to be accusatory and suspicious rather than informational, in tone and content.[38] Female Muslims, like all 'subaltern women', are thus written, represented, argued about, and even legislated for (in the French case), but they are allowed no discursive position from which to speak.[39] The commission had no qualms silencing veiled women because it assumed they had no authentic voice of their own, being the hapless victims of a Muslim patriarchal order. Similarly, as Shahnaz Khan has noted, Muslim feminist voices were not solicited during the Canadian veil controversy, which 'reinforced the binaries of us and them, oppressed and free, thereby strengthening the distance between the orientalist view of the veil as oppressive and the Islamist view of it as liberating'.[40] The Stasi Commission often displayed an astonishing ignorance of contemporary French Islam, relying instead on journalistic constructions of Islam influenced by post-9/11 'clash of civilizations' theses, which themselves mirrored colonialist assumptions about the backwardness of Muslim societies, or at best naïve misunderstanding. (When, for example, the Commission looked for a 'discrete' Muslim sign which could be tolerated in schools, on a par with small Christian crosses and stars of David, it came up with 'Fatima's hands'.[41] The choice could not have been more inept. Fatima's hands are not religious signs but a kind of talisman traditionally called *khomsa* and worn by older Maghrebi women. The *khomsa* was renamed 'Fatima's hand' by the French colonists, presumably because 'Fatima' was the homogenizing, depersonalizing, and racist name given indiscriminately to Algerian women. No doubt few young French Muslims rejoiced at being officially allowed to wear what at best was a meaningless and non-Islamic sign, and at worst reminded them of colonial paternalism.)[42] The commission barely took notice of the best sociological works on contemporary French Islam, and gave disproportionate attention to second-rate works castigating Iranian or Algerian Islamism and replicating the *laïciste* enchanted story of Western modernity fighting off the obscurantist forces of essentialized 'Muslim societies'. Thus, the Commission was not well equipped to understand the profound changes that affected religion and identity in post-colonial, postmodern conditions. These changes have put into question the *laïciste* modernist advocacy of individual emancipation from obscurantist traditionalism, as the next section will show.

Postmodernity, Authenticity, and Religion

Republican *laïcistes*, by harking back to an ideal of individual autonomy drawn from the Enlightenment humanism of Condorcet and Kant, seem strangely unperturbed by the profound philosophical, anthropological, and sociological reconsiderations of the nature of individualism and modernity in Western twentieth-century thought.[43] Their commitment to individual autonomy understood as emancipation, through rational reflection, from the shackles of religious beliefs and traditional identities, sounds an almost naïve, ironic tone in an age thoroughly disenchanted with the 'grand narratives'[44] of progress, rationality, and emancipation. Any accurate assessment of the prospects for individual freedom in contemporary societies must take account of the profound critique of the foundationalist illusions of Enlightenment philosophy. Reflecting on the insidious complicity of modern humanist thought with the twentieth-century horrors of fascism, Stalinism, and colonialism, post-war thinkers (from Louis Althusser to Michel Foucault) drew on the critical philosophies of Marx, Nietzsche, Heidegger, and Freud to cast doubts on the Enlightenment emancipatory project and the rationalist individualism that underpinned it. They deconstructed every residue of the subject understood as being capable of self-reflection and autonomous thought and action. The 1968 protesters energetically proclaimed that the republican ideal of rational citizenship had only fostered individual submission to the dehumanizing logic of bureaucratic rationalization, and repressed the plurality of cultural, gender, and sexual identities in the name of a one-sided account of modern individualism. Republican confidence in the emancipatory powers of the state was further dented as increased social complexity, the decline of the privileged *loci* of citizenship—schools, parliament, political parties, and unions—and the multifaceted crisis of political representation signalled a profound 'crisis of the institutions which used to guarantee the correspondence between national norms and individual motivations'.[45] Collective ideologies of emancipation (or salvation), such as communism, Catholicism, and *laïcisme*, lost their grip on an increasingly privatized and depoliticized citizenry. The bold progressive ambitions of *laïcisme* were tainted by their association with the discredited Enlightenment grand narratives of science, reason, and progress. In a thoroughly 'disenchanted world',[46] permeated by profound ethical pluralism,[47] *laïcisme* appeared as a controversial and repressive 'secular religion',[48] committed to a metaphysical conception of reason. *Laïcisme* implicitly mirrored the Catholic paradigm of revelation and conversion, whereby individuals had to transcend their empirical and material contingencies to gain access to a deeper form of transcendental knowledge; as in Catholicism, freedom of conscience was subordinated to the claims of metaphysical truth.[49] The time had now come, as Jean-Paul Willaime has put it, to 'laïcise *laïcité*',[50] to rid it of its rationalist, scientist, and metaphysical undertones; in Edgar Morin's words, it should be harnessed to a more modest and self-reflexive form of reason, one which, 'while demystifying myths, does not make a myth of demystification'.[51]

While, in the 1970s and 1980s, there was a marked revival of interest in liberal notions of individual freedom and human rights,[52] few thinkers (apart from *laïciste* official republicans) reverted to the rationalist, metaphysical, almost Promethean picture of individual autonomy evinced by the Enlightenment. In a move not wholly dissimilar to the 'anti-foundationalist and anti-metaphysical rupture in Anglo-American political philosophy, many French thinkers stressed the need to take seriously the deep pluralism of contemporary societies and to repudiate controversial Enlightenment assumptions about progress as rational emancipation. As the republican conception of the autonomous citizen was anachronistic, biased, and potentially oppressive, an alternative account of prospects for individual freedom in postmodern societies was required. A number of observers, reflecting on the collapse of traditional modes of social integration and the post-1968 multifaceted liberalization of society, mused about the emergence of a hedonistic, consumerist, narcissistic, politically apathetic postmodern individual, free of collective constraints, deep attachments, and ideological loyalties.[53] In such circumstances, the republican call for individual emancipation from sources of oppression was singularly misplaced. In lieu of the rational, autonomous, positive individualism hailed by republicans, what was emerging was an 'individualism veering towards *anomie*'.[54] 'In a disenchanted democracy and a society of individuals, the main challenge is no longer the conquest of the autonomy of the subject through emancipation from constraining and alienating collective frameworks; it is that of the construction of the subject in a situation of political and religious *anomie* where the individual finds itself in search of connections and meaning.'[55]

Resisting the cultural pessimism often associated with denunciations of the *anomie* and moral vacuity of postmodern society, liberal political philosophers Luc Ferry, Sylvie Mesure, and Alain Renaut have sought to salvage the moral content of the new individualistic society. Against the 1960s prophets of radical and agonistic subjectivity, they sought to articulate a non-metaphysical, Enlightenment-influenced moral individualism, influenced by Kant and Rousseau, and rooted in an appreciation of the intersubjective, dialogical nature of contemporary identity.[56] The 'new individualism' of the 1980s liberal revival[57] was distinctively less Promethean, less rationalist, more rooted, more pluralist than the individualism of *laïcistes*, and notably made room for the cultivation of cultural, religious identities. Interestingly, many French thinkers found faults with both sides of the Anglo-American 'liberal-communitarian' debate, at least in the schematized form in which it was received in France.[58] While Rawls's *Theory of Justice* was criticized for its use of a seemingly a-historical and self-interest-based rationalism in the construction of principles of justice, communitarians were blamed for their anachronistic and potentially reactionary idealization of traditional communities and stable, immutable personal identities. Some found in the work of Canadian philosopher Charles Taylor a more congenial articulation of their own historical reflections on the transformations of individual identity in modern times.[59] In *Sources of the Self*, Taylor had described a profound shift from the politics of dignity and autonomy (as emancipation from ascribed identities) to those of honour and authenticity (as the recognition of the singular integrity of the self as creator of its own cultural and ethical experiences).[60] As Marcel Gauchet has (less approvingly) glossed, the modern ideal of freedom as 'transcendence of particularity' has given way to an ideal of 'the authentic self' which emerges from the subjective appropriation of objective identities.[61]

This picture of postmodern subjective identification offers a distinct alternative to three other models of the self: the communitarian picture of selves encumbered with thickly constituted, bounded, and unchosen allegiances, the anomic and agonistic self of '1968 philosophers' and the institutionally produced autonomous citizen conjured up by official republicans. It found support in the works of the sociologists associated with Alain Touraine at the CADIS of the École des Hautes Études en Sciences Sociales. This generation of sociologists had broken with classical paradigms of social integration, whether Durkheimian, functionalist or Marxist, and sought to account for the disintegration of the systemic coherence of modern societies. As Max Weber and the Frankfurt School had correctly anticipated, the enlightened political rationalism appealed to by official republicans has degenerated into a purely instrumental rationality (of which the globalized economy is the latest incarnation) which has been unable to shape, or contain, the defensive emergence or reassertion of local, national, cultural, and religious identities. What Touraine calls 'demodernization' refers to the growing split between the rational, instrumental demands of the market and bureaucratic society and the satisfaction of affective, expressive, and cultural needs.[62] In the light of the growing disjunction between the 'life world' and the 'system' (to use Jürgen Habermas's terms), 'the problem of socialisation is no longer that of conformism versus autonomy, it becomes that of reflexivity, of justification, of distance between roles and individual motivations.'[63] Where classical sociologies (such as Durkheim's) postulated a 'fit' between the institutional structures of modernity (and notably state institutions) and individual motivations, through a dialectical process of socialization and autonomization, those theorists argue that contemporary subjectivity emerges from the reflective reappropriation of the tension between institutionally defined social roles and self-generated, authentic cultural, and personal identities. In Touraine's formulation, 'to the utopian image of the rational, ideal society, is substituted the pragmatic image of the individual ... striving to construct and defend its individuation against, on the one hand, the impersonal logic of the market and, on the other, the personalized power of the community.'[64]

Thus, while official republicans tend to portray the contemporary assertion of particularist identities (Arab, immigrant, Muslim) as residues of, or regressions to, pre-modern, anti-individualist communitarian forms of social life, multiculturalist sociologists such as Touraine, Michel Wieviorka, Françoise Gaspard, Farhad Khosrokhavar, and Nacira Guénif-Souleimas lay stress on the active agency of the (post)modern subject.[65] The postmodern 'actor' constructs, from the plurality of incommensurable, fragmented, and disconnected cultural, economic, and social orders in which she is immersed, her own way of being in the world. In contrast to the rather static references to individuals' 'conceptions of the good' favoured by Anglo-American philosophers, this sociological approach also draws attention to the way in which contemporary identities are shaped through processes of intersubjective recognition and misrecognition. The growing literature on ethnicity, for example, shows that contemporary ethnic claims are shot through with relations of power and domination and are framed through confrontation between dominant norms and 'minorized' and dominated forms of life.[66] Such an approach also contradicts the republican modernist account of the integration of immigrants as a linear and progressive process of individual acculturation to modernity. Post-colonial accounts of ethnicity point out that immigrants, *despite* being perfectly integrated into the rational system of modernity, still find themselves subjectively 'colonized' and 'racialized' by the host society.[67] The more they are 'acculturated', 'autonomized', and integrated into modern economic and social structures, the more, it seems, they find themselves externally defined and ethnicized by the gaze of others. They become 'strangers to themselves': while the typical socio-psychological affliction of modernity was disenchantment and nevrosis (caused by the institutionalized repression of archaic, irrational impulses), the affliction of postmodernity is more likely to be alienation and schizophrenia (caused by the tensions between objective role-allocation and subjective and intersubjective perception).[68] Under such circumstances, the cultivation (or reinvention) of ethnic identities allows immigrants to initiate a process of 'reversal of stigma'[69] and restore their wounded self-esteem. On this view, ethnicity does not denote pre-modern backwardness but is, rather, constitutive of postmodern identity, an uncertain *bricolage* of individually reappropriated references and narratives. It is the product of the search, by the fragmented subject or actor, of a pragmatic reconciliation between the two spheres of existence (rational instrumentality and affective identity) which have been torn apart by the twin processes of de-institutionalization and de-socialization.[70]

Those processes have similarly affected religious life. Sociologists of religion have rejected simplistic interpretations of the contemporary religious revival as an assertion of anti-modern, collectivist, tightly structured faith communities. Instead, widespread individualization and de-socialization have eroded individuals' allegiance to traditional religious institutions while, at the same time, feeding their existential need to make sense of their lives. Individuals no longer inherit religious affiliations; they choose whether, when, and how to consume the diverse religious goods on offer in an increasingly deregulated 'religious market', characterized by the proliferation of 'new religious movements'.[71] These movements—evangelical Protestant, charismatic Catholic, *sufi* Islam, spiritualist Hindu, and so forth—lay stress, not so much on the content of metaphysical beliefs, obedience to strict God-given laws or compliance with traditional rituals, as on the authenticity of the individual's religious experience. Religions have become vehicles for self-fulfilment and self-realization, and have answered profound yearnings, in a rapidly changing, technologically advanced society, for the re-establishment of affective bonds and collectively shared meaning. Thus, the two figures of the postmodern believer, as Danièle Hervieu-Léger has shown, are the 'converted' and the 'pilgrim'.[72] While expressing deep ambivalence vis-à-vis the anonymous, rationalizing, and globalizing tendencies of modern life, the contemporary religious revival is a by-product of them, even, as many observers have noted, in its radical fundamentalist incarnations.[73]

Islam has been far from immune from these broad trends. Students of Western Islam, repudiating orientalist readings of Islam as stuck in a pre-modern, communitarian past, have noted that the relation of young Muslims to their parents' religion is as individualistic, as eclectic and as selective as that of Christians and Jews. Contemporary Western Islam is, in a sense, a 'new religious movement', distinct from the customary, traditional Islam still practised by older generation of immigrants, and it broadly replicates the individualistic, subjectivist tendencies of other religious movements.[74] This means that Muslim identity is as much a chosen as an inherited identity, one which lays stress on a privatized, emotional, cultural, and ethical relationship to faith and ritual, selectively and critically appropriated by young Muslims, including by those who opt for an integralist and fundamentalist interpretation of the demands of religion.[75] Young European Muslims, therefore, are more 'born again Muslims' than traditional 'ethnic Muslims'. Furthermore, contemporary Islam is a global identity, one which breaks with its ethnic and traditional incarnations in the Maghreb or Middle East, for example, and projects itself onto an imagined voluntary global community of the true believers. Contemporary Islam is de-ethnicized, globalized, and deeply implicated with the contradictory forces of modernity and Westernization, as Olivier Roy has shown.[76] Radical Islamism, while often cast as 'traditionalist' or 'anti-modern' is in fact an 'alternative modernity: like third-world nationalism before it, it is often shaped by the very discourses of modernity and Westernization it seeks to counter'.[77] As Roy has noted, Western Islam demands '*hallal* fast food, not camel's milk couscous'.[78] It favours modest clothing, but has developed styles of dress that are essentially quite new, combining Arabic, Turkish, or East Asian features on the one hand and Western features on the other.

Can we go further and, in line with the postmodern approaches charted in this section, interpret the resurgence of hijab among young European Muslims as a sign of 'growing individualization and the desire of all to be recognized for what they wish to be'?[79] Is it possible that, pace *laïcistes*, the headscarf represents not a traditionalist backlash, but a complex postmodern identity claim; not communal oppression, but individual authenticity; not patriarchal power, but female agency? The problem, of course, is that the hijab has historically been so tightly associated with patriarchal power that we need to understand why Muslim women would deliberately *choose* to wear it. To do this, we need to move away from *laïciste* understandings of female *autonomy* and develop an alternative account of female *agency*.[80]

Muslim Headscarves and Female Agency

Feminist notions of agency are informed by a criticism of the traditional liberal (and *laïciste*) understanding of autonomy as denoting individuals' ability to question and repudiate the cultural contexts and norms they have been socialized into. We saw in Chapter 5 that *laïcistes* took seriously the way in which social norms shaped individual preferences and desires, but insisted that, notably through autonomy-promoting republican education, individuals (e.g. Muslim women) should learn to reject constraining and unjust norms (e.g. the Islamist patriarchal order) and thereby become free, self-directing agents. Radical feminists, drawing notably on the analyses of Michel Foucault, are sceptical about this possibility. They suggest that social norms shape individuals' preferences through and through, that there is no detached, free-floating subject outside the discourses that produce and constitute it, and that the liberal discourse of autonomous subjectivity is itself a discourse of power. Feminists have, however, repudiated Foucault's early determinist approaches (as in *Discipline and Punish*, where he seemed to negate human freedom altogether in his account of docile bodies entirely disciplined by the operations of ubiquitous power[81]) and have drawn on his later attempt to offer a more sophisticated account of the interaction between power, resistance, and agency.[82] The intuition here is that power is not only oppressive but also creative: every relation of subordination and domination also creates a capacity for action and resistance, whereby dominated individuals assert their selfhood through the adaptation to, manipulation or subversion of the normative order they are subjected to. Thus, radical feminists endorse a notion of individual agency as the ability to reflect on existing (heteronomously acquired) attachments and values. What, then, are the differences between radical feminist agency and republican feminist autonomy (as defined in the previous chapter)? Female agency, in the radical feminist view, is relational, content-neutral, and interstitial. It is relational not only in the weak sense that its exercise implies pre-existing relations and attachments but also in that it is not the solliptical exercise of *rational* examination of, and demarcation from, such attachments called for by *laïcistes*. Instead, individuals show agency in the way in which they reflect on and reappropriate their deepest existing commitments, including those connoting emotional connectedness, such as loyalty, commitment, piety, devotion, benevolence, and so forth. They do not overcome the effects of socialization to function as autonomous persons; instead, they make choices within the relational contexts in which they find themselves, choices which reflect their sense of self. Second, agency is content-neutral in that it need not accord with a substantive notion of the self-directed, autonomous life. Thus, free agents may choose a heteronomous life, so long as they do so with minimum procedural competency and this life represents what they affirm as deeply important to them upon reflective consideration.[83] Thus, for a woman to choose a life of religious devotion or domestic servility might reflect appropriate levels of agency if it is a real choice that is congruent with her deepest values and perspectives, even as it falls short of the more demanding ideal of *laïciste* autonomy. Third, agency is interstitial in that, by contrast to the *laïcistes'* almost Promethean view of emancipation, it operates in the interstices of power: hence the Foucaldian references to 'resistance', 'bargaining', 'manipulation', or 'subversion' by individuals of existing power relationships which cannot be entirely escaped from.

Adopting an agency-based view of liberty, rather than an autonomy-based one, allows us to see that Muslim women are not the passive victims of their religion and culture: they are also—in ways that *laïciste* accounts of autonomy fail to capture—agents of their own lives.[84] They make choices about their religious practice, their professional activity, their family, and so forth, and they do so within the particular contexts which make choices meaningful to them and to the community (or communities) to which they belong. Thus, women typically 'bargain with patriarchy' (in the specific form patriarchy takes in different cultural settings): the voluntary wearing of hijab may signify the 'recuperation and affirmation' of a 'heretofore marginalized identity'.[85] In a reflection on female agency in relation to Muslim practices of veiling, Nancy Hirschmann notes that 'rather than having power over the terms of customs like veiling that set the parameters of individual choice, women instead manoeuvre within male-defined terms to negotiate their preferences, make their choices, or assert their identity'.[86] Thus, women may not have 'taken part in constructing the *framework within which* decisions about dress take place', but within that framework, they make space to 'establish identity and agency, and resist patriarchy'.[87]

Therefore the decision to wear the hijab may not represent, as *laïcistes* believe, the 'silent alienation' of a dominated, humiliated woman but,[88] rather, be the sign of a more or less 'accommodating protest'[89] towards the status of subservience and humility that the veil symbolizes. This point can be illustrated through the identification of three degrees of female agency as expressed in the choice to veil, from the most accommodating to the most subversive. First, covering one's head can have a protective and dignity-enhancing function: in keeping with the original spirit of the wearing of hijab by the Prophet's wives, it is a sign of social status and respectability. For many Muslim women, the veil signifies, not a position of humiliating submission, but one of safety, status, and respectability. It shields women from the lustful gaze of men and affords them a valuable space of dignity and respectability. Wearing the hijab allows girls to gain the respect of their family and peers and shore up their self-esteem, as it is a visible symbol of admired virtues such as piety, chastity, and modesty. It also liberates them from the per-ceived dictates of Western fashion and from the pervasive sexualization of women's bodies, especially at a time—during and after puberty—when adolescents often experience feelings of discomfort and shame towards their bodies. The hijab offers a practical coping strategy in the face of the stresses of public appearance.[90] By wearing a headscarf, Muslim girls assert their determination to be perceived, not as sexualized bodies, but as human beings deserving of respect. Arguably, in this case, women's agency is rather limited, as the decision to veil is merely the outcome of the uncritical internalization of constraining sexist norms and of a conscious rationalization of, and adaptation to, a narrow set of available options. Yet to argue, as *laïcistes* do, that it is therefore an illegitimate 'adaptive' preference to conditions of oppression is to fail to respect the integrity of women's own choices and perspectives. Muslim women may genuinely value the privacy, respectability, and self-esteem that they derive from being veiled. The choice to veil expresses agency if it accords with their reaffirmation of deeper wants and commitments.

Second, wearing the hijab can permit and facilitate women's free circulation into public space and their unhindered pursuit of a range of autonomously chosen activities. Observers have noted that, even in societies formally ruled by *sharia* law, such as Iran, the effect of compulsory veiling for women has been more mixed than is often recognized. It has notably rendered socially acceptable women's access to universities, the job market, and public office: paradoxically, veiling has enhanced the public presence of women who would otherwise be confined to private domesticity.[91] In this view, veiling can be likened to an (expensive) entrance ticket to an otherwise inaccessible public sphere. *Ceteris paribus*, such compromises between public and private existence are also negotiated by Muslim adolescents in the very different context of French society. There, they are often confronted by a pernicious 'double bind' or 'contradictory injunction'[92] stemming from their dual membership: French society urges them to emancipate themselves from oppressive communal traditions, while their families and community enjoin them to be faithful and loyal to them. The wearing of headscarves is one symbolic way to meet both demands and thereby ease the strains of multiple allegiances. It is often strategically used by adolescents to reassure their families about their loyalty to tradition and community as they simultaneously enjoy the benefits of free movement outside the home. Wearing the hijab allows them freely to study, work, socialize, and even strike up friendships with men without the fear that their reputation will be damaged. In this view, headscarves provide families with a symbolic and emotional guarantee of communal allegiance, while simultaneously authorizing and legitimizing girls' autonomous behaviour.[93] Paradoxically, then, the adoption of the hijab may not declare women's place to be in the home but, on the contrary, legitimize their presence outside it.[94] As sociologists Françoise Gaspard and Farhad Khosrokhavar have shown, young *beurettes* opt to wear the hijab to facilitate their transition from the world of 'identity and tradition' to that of 'alterity and modernity': it allows them to cultivate 'the illusion of continuity' when it is in fact 'a factor of discontinuity'.[95] Muslim adolescents are therefore able to manipulate the cultural meanings of traditional symbols such as headscarves to their advantage, while minimizing the emotional and social costs involved in renouncing either personal independence or communal attachment. Yet this agential strategy comes at a cost, especially when it takes the form of a schizophrenic commitment to, and perilous reconciliation between, two seemingly separate and discrete worlds, one perceived to embody modernity, emancipation, and independence (mainstream

French society) and the other perceived to embody individual allegiance and submission to communal rules (the Muslim community).[96]

The wearing of hijab can, however—third—also be symptomatic of individual reappropriation of the precepts of Islam by women themselves, and symbolize female empowerment. In this case, women gain personal dignity and independence *through* their embrace of Islam and in doing so, they reform Islam from within. They implicitly or explicitly contest both the distortion of the egalitarian message of Islam by patriarchal traditions, and dominant Western notions of female emancipation as a necessarily secular process. This connects with the movement of 'Islamic feminism', which emerged in Iran in the 1990s and has since been used to refer to the broader redefinition of gender relations taking place within the Islamic diaspora, especially in Western Europe and North America.[97] The pivotal assumption of Islamic feminists is that patriarchal domination, far from being a Qur'anic injunction, must be related to pre-Islamic customs and to the subsequent monopolization of the elaboration of the *fiqh* (Islamic jurisprudence) by men. Muslim feminists have pointed out that the Prophet Muhammad had sought to emancipate women, and had surrounded himself with independent, intelligent, and resourceful women. Even as Islam instituted a hierarchical structure as the basis of relations between men and women, it also preached, in its ethical voice, the moral and spiritual equality of all human beings.[98] The sacred text of the Qur'an contains a powerfully egalitarian message, notably stressing that both men and women should, through personal effort of education and reflection, cultivate their understanding of the demands and rewards of the pious life. Adhesion to Islam signifies voluntary submission to God's will, not blind allegiance to the legalistic precepts of traditionalist *ulema*. Women may thus engage in feminist *ijtehad* (independent reasoning, religious interpretation) and deconstruct *sharia*-related rules in a women-friendly egalitarian fashion (e.g. in terms of birth control, personal status law, and family code). Women who decide to wear the hijab do so freely, out of personal engagement with religious texts, and thereby assert their direct relationship with God. They take their cue from the writings of Muslim intellectuals such as Tariq Ramadan, who argues both that veiling is an obligation for the believers *and* that it can only be the outcome of a personal choice and self-development.[99] Adoption of Islamic dress in this case denotes not affiliation with conservative ethical and social habits of male domination and female subservience but, rather, commitment to advance women's opportunities in education, employment, professional achievement, and equal political rights, while asserting specifically female virtues in the private sphere of personal relationships and family. As Nadine Weibel has written of these often well-educated, young women, 'puritan and rebel at the same time, they undoubtedly innovate when they claim to liberate themselves from the authority of men to submit, instead, to that of Allah'.[100] Women thus use practices, such as veiling, which have historically underpinned patriarchal oppression to subvert patriarchy, and assert themselves as autonomous believers.[101]

Nor is this all. Young Muslim women further carve out a space of agency by repudiating their schizophrenic dual location within the two normative parameters of Muslim traditionalism and Western feminist modernity. To put it bluntly, they proclaim that their parents' Islam is not the true Islam, and that Western feminism is not true feminism. They criticize the oppression of generations of Muslim women with the same virulence as they denounce the sexual exploitation of Western women.[102] The reformist Islam they endorse is as critical of the archaism of the 'ethnic' Islam practised by their parents' generation[103] and preached by ignorant, traditional *ulema*, as it is of Western modernity. Veiled women implicitly denounce the simplistic and reified normative alternative that dominant discourse presents them with—an injunction to choose between 'tradition' and 'modernity', between 'religion' and 'female emancipation'—and they creatively shape the contours of a new Muslim feminist identity.[104] Little wonder therefore that they have been (somewhat provocatively) enlisted by some radical feminists to the 'queer' cause.[105] The queer movement seeks to destabilize fixed gender and sexual identities and to assert the radical indeterminacy and contingency of postmodern selves. Hijab-wearing in this view can be an expression of queer agency, the provocative manipulation and subversion of the twin discourses of Western feminism and traditional Islam. It opens up what Homi Bhabha calls a 'third space', a space where the individual's negotiation of contradictory demands and polarities effectively creates a hybridized subjectivity. Muslim women cannot escape the structural bind within which the construct 'Muslim women' places them, but they can manipulate the diverging yet overlapping significations it has acquired in Muslim and Western imaginaries.[106]

Thus, women who decide to wear the hijab do so for a variety of reasons, which reflect varying degrees of female agency, conceived as reflective reappropriation (and sometimes subversion) of the dominant meanings of the Muslim headscarf. The *laïcistes'* attempt to reduce this complex social phenomenon to a simple, unambiguous instance of internalized male domination simply is not tenable.[107] The veiled woman for *laïcistes* conjures up an image of an individual wholly subservient to an oppressive, communitarian patriarchal order—the paradigmatic example of such oppression being policies of forced veiling in Iran, Saudi Arabia, or Taliban Afghanistan. Yet in a Western pluralist society such as France, the wearing of hijab can hardly signal conformist subservience to a comprehensively structured normative order: it is often the outcome of a voluntary decision taken by young Muslim women, to help them reconcile conflicting demands emanating from the various sub-worlds in which they navigate, as well as progressively defining the contours of a new, modern European Muslim identity. *Laïcistes* are profoundly insensitive to the diversity of ways of being Muslim in the contemporary world. They might be right to point out that the wearing of headscarves has deep patriarchal foundations, but they should pay more attention to the ways in which such foundations are internally challenged by Muslims themselves, and in particular by hijab-wearing young women. Furthermore, while *laïcistes* exclusively concentrate on one general feature of the hijab—its historical association with patriarchy—they tend to misinterpret another crucial historical feature of the hijab—its association with anti-Western protest. They see it as further proof of the anti-modern, backward, and immobile tendencies of Islam. What this disregards is the responsibility of the West in promoting the veil—which it castigated as a symbol of Muslim otherness and backwardness—as a modern flag of resistance to colonial rule, forced Westernization and cultural and social marginalization. A number of traditional signs, customs and traditions were politicized through encounters with the West, and then used as symbolic weapons and markers of cultural pride for Muslims. Contemporary post-colonial France is no different. There too, the hijab has been a powerful symbol of the re-islamization of Arab (and Berber) youth over the last two decades or so, often in protest against the broken promises of the French model of integration. As we shall see in Part III of this book, the headscarves affair raises difficult issues relating to the cultural and socio-economic integration of Muslim minorities in France, and the hijab has become a symbol of resistance to forced assimilation into French culture, just as, elsewhere in the world, it has come to symbolize anti-Western protest.

What are the implications of all this for Muslim female agency? This chapter has chiefly concentrated on women's struggles to assert themselves in relation to alternative gender models, that of traditional Islam on the one hand and Western models of female sexual emancipation on the other. The problem is, given the growing polarization between the discourses of 'Western modernity' and 'Islam', and the defensive reassertion of Muslim identity in the face of Western hostility, women's attempt to assert a hybridized female subjectivity in the 'third space' (to use Homi Bhabha's words again) might be doomed. Guénif-Souleimas and Macé's playfully 'queer' interpretation of the deconstruction of gender roles by Muslim women underestimates the force of the injunction to belong, and to be seen to belong, in a context of perceived clash of civilizations. In fact, the more Islam is portrayed by the Western media as a backward, oppressive, and uncivilized religion, the more Muslims will feel victimized and stigmatized, and the more Muslim women will feel the need to close ranks and defensively assert their cultural pride as Muslims, if necessary by toning down their feminist demands. Hence the ultimately self-defeating effect of *laïciste* paternalism: it might well reinforce the very patriarchal tendencies that it denounces, as women prioritize the struggle against perceived Western imperialism and islamophobia over that against Muslim patriarchy. Muslim women, therefore, can express agency in complex different ways, although their assertion is much more fragile and uncertain than queer radical feminists suggest. For it looks as if Muslim women ultimately have to choose between asserting their identity as women (against sexism and patriarchy) *or* as Muslims (against Western stereotypes and islamophobia), and this choice may often be experienced as a choice 'between betrayal and betrayal'.

The normative upshot of all this—to round up the argument of this chapter—is that republican paternalism, as embodied in the ban on headscarves in schools, is both wrong in principle and counterproductive. It is wrong in that it fails to respect the agency of those women it claims to emancipate in the name of an elitist, decontextualized and imperialist conception of individual autonomy. It is counterproductive in that, *even if* the struggle against patriarchy is a legitimate one for Muslim women, it is not helped by measures of stigmatization and coercion, and might even exacerbate the defensive assertion of patriarchal norms by Muslims.[108] Thus, critics of *laïcisme* tend to concur with philosopher Étienne Balibar's overall assessment of the case for the ban. Balibar points out that in a globalized, transnational society characterized by the erosion of the power of the patriarchal family and the existence of a plurality of models of female agency, individuality, and autonomy are no longer defined in opposition to rigid, uniform, imposed social roles. Muslim women should thus not be forcibly 'liberated' but 'left free' to wear headscarves in schools: as they are caught in the 'crossfire of two dominations', sexist and imperialist, any attempt to undermine the former might be experienced as an instance of the latter.[109] Contemporary postmodern, post-colonial societies are too complex to exhibit the simple patterns of social domination that might, in the past, have justified paternalistic intervention in the interests of individual autonomy and emancipation. In Nacira Guénif-Souleimas's words, young female Muslims should be left to experiment with the fragile 'tempered liberties' they derive from their contradictory entanglement in 'multiple dominations'.[110]

In the next chapter, I examine whether such a laissez-faire approach is the most appropriate way to tackle potential domination in civil society and attempt to defend, instead, a version of republican autonomy and non-domination which empowers vulnerable members of society without, however, endorsing the perfectionist paternalism of the *laïciste* ban on hijab.

CHAPTER 7

Critical Republicanism,
Non-Domination, and Voice

In the previous two chapters, I reconstructed the strongest version of the opposite sides of the feminist debate about the wearing of hijab in the French context, spelling out its (seldom explicit) sociological and historical assumptions, and filling out its (often missing) logical links. In this chapter, I provide my own normative assessment of the terms of this debate. I argue that while the radical feminists discussed in Chapter 6 are right to denounce the ban on hijab, the *laïciste* feminists discussed in Chapter 5 are right to worry about oppression and domination in civil society, and I elaborate a concept of republican non-domination which formalizes and extends these conclusions beyond the case study of the French hijab controversy.

Autonomy and Non-Domination

It is difficult to deny that banning the hijab from schools on paternalistic, autonomy-related grounds is wrong, self-defeating, and misguided. It is wrong because it fails to respect the agency of those women it claims to emancipate in the name of a contested conception of secular autonomy and a misguided, neo-orientalist interpretation of Islam. The fact that wearing the hijab is not in itself a harmful practice should have been sufficient to ward *laïcistes* off any paternalistic measure. Even if we construe the hijab as a harmful, *because* autonomy-impairing, practice, the republican commitment to self-emancipation militates against a coercive ban, even (indeed, especially) in autonomy-promoting spaces like schools. The ban is also self-defeating because, even if the struggle against patriarchy is a legitimate one for Muslim women, it is not assisted by measures of stigmatization and coercion, and might even exacerbate the defensive assertion of patriarchal norms and practices within sections of the community, in a process of what Ayelet Shachar has called 'reactive culturalism'.[1] And as the hijab is in practice being transformed from a symbol of female submissiveness into one of assertive contestation both of the cultural domination of the French state and of patriarchal power, it should be clear that the state is misguided when it forcibly seeks to liberate French adolescents wearing a Muslim headscarf to school. Thus, even if it may be conceded that the 2004 law 'worked' in practice, in the sense that more schoolgirls took off their headscarves than left schools, and some of them were undeniably encouraged by the ban to resist peer pressure to wear headscarves outside schools, it is still questionable whether a blanket ban on hijab is, in general, a defensible mode of female emancipation. So even if we concede that the ban is not entirely self-defeating (in the sense that it may have fulfilled its declared objectives), it is still wrong and misguided.[2]

Yet I shall argue that it does not follow from this that we should repudiate the republican *laïciste* project *in toto*. While critics are right to argue against the ban on the *hijab,* the philosophical and sociological resources they mobilize in support of their conclusions have unwelcome implications for those on the Left still committed to the progressive project of emancipation (albeit in a form compatible with recognition of the pluralism and complexity of contemporary society). At bottom, the critics' case relies on a combination of a modestly political liberalism averse to using the state to promote the value of autonomy with a postmodern sociology of subjectivity which reduces agency to the individual negotiation and manipulation of a plurality of normative social orders. Such a combination potentially legitimizes the perpetuation of domination and oppression in civil society. It makes individual agency compatible with very constrictive life situations, of the kind that *laïciste* feminists are right to worry about: situations of seeming consent to relationships of subservience and servility. What radical feminists and multiculturalists lack, therefore, is a positive theory of domination, and an account of when and how it is legitimate for the state to further non-domination. In this respect, *laïciste* feminists offer valuable resources, although they have mobilized them towards the wrong cause: the hijab ban. First, *laïcistes* rightly worry about the abuses of private power, in institutions such as the family or religious groups; second, they point out that such power can take the form of socialization, indoctrination, and manipulation, rather than overt interference or coercion; and third, they champion state education as providing an alternative socialization (to autonomy). In what follows, I develop these crucial *laïciste* insights by integrating them into a critical republican theory of non-domination.

The first insight has been formalized by Philip Pettit as the distinction between two classical modes of domination, drawn from Roman law: *imperium*, the arbitrary power exercised by the state and its agents, and *dominium*, the arbitrary power exercised by private and collective persons in civil society.[3] By suggesting that republicans should worry about relations of domination in individuals' public and private lives, in formal and informal settings, Pettit joins in with socialists, feminists, and radical democrats in expanding the scope of the political to spheres long considered to be immune from public scrutiny, notably the family, the workplace, and religious groups. Yet he does so without idealizing the existing state, concerned as he is with the dangers of arbitrary power that public authorities in practice yield over individuals and social groups. In its attempt simultaneously to curb *imperium*- and *dominium*-related forms of arbitrary power in existing society, Pettit's framework can be used to illuminate two key problems, which have thus far been regrettably peripheral to Anglophone multiculturalist political theory. One is the *arbitrary state* problem, which asks under which conditions states, which have a history of colonialism, oppression, and imperialism, can legitimately force liberal reform on those very groups (First Nations or post-colonial minorities) which perceive themselves to be the victims of the state's illiberal and ethnocentric past.[4] The second problem is the *internal minority* problem, which concerns the negative impact that multicultural accommodation or toleration can have on the most vulnerable members of the groups that benefit from it, in particular women.[5] It is the combination of these two problems that makes the feminist controversy about the hijab so intractable. While *laïcistes* focus on the internal minority problem and seek to emancipate Muslim women from intra-group patriarchy, radical feminists are acutely aware of inter-group domination and the arbitrary state problem, particularly in post-colonial settings. Yet what the alternative masks is the complex ways in which gender and racial oppression operate and interrelate, both within and between majority and minority groups.[6] Building on Pettit's framework, I shall explore ways to take seriously Muslim women's 'double domination' (inter- and intra-group, ethnocentric, and patriarchal).

The second and third *laïciste* insights concern norms of socialization and the importance of education in equipping individuals with tools with which to resist domination. This, I will suggest, is insufficiently captured by Pettit's account, which concerns itself too narrowly with domination as a *subjectively experienced* harm, thus neglecting phenomena of restrictive socialization and the development of adaptive preferences under oppressive conditions, whereby individuals prima facie consent to living under relations of domination. Thus, Pettit's republican theory is no better equipped than standard liberal accounts to tackle the hard cases of multicultural domination, which involve customary practices and norms that are neither legally sanctioned nor coercively imposed, but are based on informal arrangements within seemingly consensual relationships. Examples of such practices and norms are pressure to wear restrictive clothing, arranged marriages, socialization into gendered roles, and sex-segregated religious education. The critical republicanism I advocate, by contrast, shares the feminist concern for the dominating impact of sexist norms, and as a result endorses the *laïciste* advocacy of robust forms of autonomy-promoting education. I shall argue, however, that the good life is not one of full autonomy and self-determination, but rather one in which autonomy-related skills can (but do not have to) be used by individuals to combat the most pernicious forms of domination. What matters is that individuals have minimum discursive control or 'voice'—that they can contest the power that is exercised over them. My defence of autonomy-promoting education, then, complements Pettit's emphasis on contestability and voice as guarantees of the non-arbitrariness of power. While French *laïcistes* tend to rely on an educational, rationalist, almost intellectualist solution to the problem of domination, Anglophone republicans and deliberative democrats have rightly put their faith in the empowerment that comes with democratic engagement in both formal politics and informal social spheres. Thus I shall show that the 'double domination' problem can be best addressed through the identification of the proper conditions for adequate *voice* in both public and private settings.

Let me start, then, with a clarification of my understanding of domination. On a broad level, and following Iris Marion Young, domination refers to 'institutional conditions which inhibit or prevent people from participating in decisions and processes that determine their actions and the conditions of their actions. Persons live within structures of domination if other persons or groups can determine without reciprocation the conditions of their actions'.[7] Domination is a useful concept for feminists because it suggests that the mere condition of being vulnerable to others' actions, decisions, and opinions, without necessarily being coerced or otherwise interfered with by them, may be freedom-limiting, and that such condition has importantly structural and institutional features. There are, however, different ways in which people can be 'inhibited' or 'prevented'—to use Young's expressions—from participation in the determination of the conditions of their actions. One aspect of domination that I shall bring to light in this section combines elements from the classical sociological definition of Max Weber and the normative definition of Philip Pettit. On the Weberian account, domination (by contrast to other forms of power) works at least partly through consent; it is based on 'a minimum of voluntary compliance, that is, an *interest* (based on ulterior motives or genuine acceptance) in obedience'.[8] Weber's is a descriptive account which captures the power at work in relationships as diverse as the parent–child, teacher–pupil, employer–employee relationships. More normative definitions of domination include a value-based component which accounts for the badness or wrongness of domination: thus Pettit specifies that domination refers to a capacity for *arbitrary* interference. An interference is arbitrary, according to Pettit, if it does not track the 'relevant... interests and ideas of the person suffering the interference'.[9] Can people, then, consent to domination? For Pettit, an arbitrary power is not necessarily a power that has not been consented to (it is, rather, a power that is exercised without possibility of recourse or contestation). Pettit rightly insists that 'consent to a form of interference is not sufficient as a guard against arbitrariness' and points to the example of workers forced to 'consent' to iniquitous working conditions.[10] But note that in this case, even though workers *consent* to iniquitous contracts, they are *aware* that the contracts are iniquitous. Pettit has less to say about situations where domination is consented to in the stronger sense of the term: in the sense, that is, that it is not perceived for what it is by its victims. Cases of 'backroom manipulation', where domination is 'not a matter of common knowledge', are described as 'one exception' to his otherwise explicitly subjectivist account of domination.[11] Domination, for Pettit, is a 'grievance', a 'complaint',[12] a 'feeling' of vulnerability and powerlessness: dominated people 'bristle under the yoke' of domination. Thus, Pettit does not give sufficient thought to the possibility that domination may affect a person's interests even though she might be unaware of it, as in the well-known examples of the submissive housewife or the contented slave.[13]

I submit that one basic interest which domination violates is our interest in minimal autonomy. Thus, the republican ideal of non-domination is connected with our status as free and autonomous,[14] although it does not entail full-blown autonomy. The thought is that domination involves a (systematic and intentional) denial of a person's capacity for minimal autonomy. When we are dominated, we are either deprived of the ability to form our own perspective (we are indoctrinated, manipulated, socialized into submissive roles) or, if we possess the capacity, we are prevented from using it (we are silenced, humiliated, threatened). Emphasizing the way in which a capacity can be *denied* and not only *dismissed* through domination allows us to take into account phenomena of unjust (in Pettit's phrase, arbitrary) preference formation or 'backroom manipulation'. Thus, we can understand how domination can be partly consented to, by being invisible to its victims. John Stuart Mill brilliantly captured the workings of the subjection of women:

> the masters of women wanted more than simple obedience, and they turned the whole force of education to effect their purpose. All women are brought up from the very earliest years in the belief that their ideal of character is the very opposite to that of men; not self-will, and government by self-control, but submission, and yielding to the control of others.[15]

Thus, women can be dominated both by being denied the opportunity to develop their own perspective (autonomy-denial) *and* by being led to adopt attitudes of subservience, self-denial, and servility, which make them vulnerable to further domination (autonomy-dismissal). Unsurprisingly, the republican concept of domination appealed to feminist writers such as Mary Wollstonecraft and Mill, as it neatly encapsulates the complex and insidious ways in which the subjection of women was psychologically experienced (as damaged self-respect) and socially maintained (as an ideology or internalized social norm). Because domination works partly through the successful internalization of norms, the extent to which dominated individuals are able to articulate a specific grievance varies; all the same, they suffer a specific wrong, that of being deprived of their own voice.

That social beliefs or ideologies play a central role in sustaining relationships of domination has long been obvious to sociologists, whether Marxist, Weberian, or Foucauldian. It should be a thought also congenial to normative republicans, for three important reasons. The first is that republicans have historically been suspicious of utilitarian accounts of the prima facie value of existing preferences, beliefs, and norms.[16] Given that the latter are formed under the structural constraints of existing, non-ideal conditions, some of them are likely to be partly expressive of relationships of domination. The second reason why republicans have an interest in the content of existing beliefs and norms is that they are granted as important a role as good laws in sustaining the republican polity. Norms that foster the domination of some citizens over others are unlikely to be supportive of the egalitarian, cooperative ethos essential to the republic: they undermine civic virtue. Third, they also negate citizens' independence, a foremost republican virtue. Citizens who are unduly dependent on the wills and opinions of others are unlikely to display the critical faculties, sense of impartiality, and self-esteem (a stable sense of one's own separate identity and a confidence that one is worthy enough to participate in political life) required by citizenship.[17] Citizens' independence, importantly, is not merely an objective and subjective state but relies on intersubjective patterns of social recognition: it connotes the 'ability to look at each other in the eye', confident of one's social status as a 'person in [one's] own legal and social right'.[18] To be non-dominated is to be recognized as having a voice of one's own. To use a recent formulation of Pettit's, domination infringes on our freedom understood as 'discursive control': 'to enjoy discursive control is to be proof against being silenced, or ignored, or refused a hearing, or denied the final say in one's own responses. It is, on the contrary, to be given recognition as a discursive subject with a voice and an ear of one's own'.[19] More precisely, republican citizens have discursive control when they are entitled and capable of contesting (or at least asking for a justification of) the power that is exercised over them. We can say that someone is a 'discursive subject' when he or she is considered worthy of being given justifying reasons for others' actions or injunctions towards them.[20]

Non-domination as discursive control is a more attractive ideal than either the rationalist conception of autonomy of *laïciste* feminists or the Foucauldian conception of agency developed by radical feminists. Nothing about non-domination requires that individuals break free from their religious or communal attachments; nor does the ideal imply that the good life is a life of autonomy. The autonomy critical republicans value is more akin to a basic capability: a skill which, up to a threshold (minimum discursive control), is essential to the good life, but which, above the threshold, individuals do not have to develop further, let alone to exercise fully. Conceived as a *minimum capability*, autonomy is best understood not as an intrinsic but as an instrumental, yet primary, good. It is an essential ingredient to living a successful life—a life that is good for oneself—but it is not necessarily a part of that success. The capacity for ongoing rational reflection about one's beliefs and values is an effective way of detecting false or inadequately supported beliefs and identify the presence of inconsistent values, as well as being an important safeguard against exploitation and manipulation by others.[21] Note that autonomy thus conceived is compatible with what I called (in Chapter 6) the 'relational' and 'content-neutral' features of the concept of agency favoured by radical feminists and multiculturalists. Where non-domination theorists differ from the latter is in their willingness to scrutinize the workings of 'interstitial' agency— agency which expresses itself as resistance to power—in order to assess whether it is sufficient to protect our interest in minimum discursive control. In other words, they worry that certain forms of power can suppress basic human interests, even when they are seemingly accepted, negotiated, or subverted by those who live under them. Non-domination, therefore, offers a normative yardstick of evaluation, thus avoiding the moral indeterminacy of the Foucauldian understanding of power and resistance. To illustrate: a concept of non-domination allows us to say that, while the meaning of headscarves in contemporary France is contested, subverted, and reappropriated in ways that undermine univocal patriarchal domination, it is not clear that veiling practices in countries such as Saudi Arabia or Iran can be so easily defended as *adequate* expressions of female agency, *even though* they are endorsed, resisted, or manipulated by Muslim women. Arguably, women in such countries do not have enough 'discursive power' to be able effectively and publicly to contest the dress codes they are supposed to follow. Thus, non-domination theorists respect the deep attachments valued by individuals, whether religious, traditional, or communal; what they fear is their potentially disempowering, oppressive, and dominating features. These can be ascertained, not through abstract discussions of the meaning of cultural practices or the content of conceptions of the good, but through careful contextual analysis of actual power relationships. The guiding philosophical principle is clear enough, though: we do not have an (basic and universal) interest in pursuing a life of autonomous assertion, but we do have a (basic and universal) interest in combating ethical servility.

How, then, do we test for absence of ethical servility? Marilyn Friedman, who coined the concept of content-neutral or procedural autonomy, herself recognizes that such autonomy is not necessarily an expression of genuine, non-dominated consent. She highlights three tests for the validity of expressed consent. Women, she says, must be 'able to choose among a significant and morally acceptable array of alternatives', they must be 'able to make choices relatively free of coercion, manipulation and deception', and they must 'have been able to develop, earlier in life, the capacities needed to reflect on their situations and make decisions about them'.[22] I would argue that the first two conditions are too strong, and are in fact incompatible with respect for the myriad non-autonomous lives that Friedman's theory of content-neutral, procedural autonomy is designed to accommodate.[23] The first condition underwrites the traditional liberal emphasis on individual choice and the availability of attractive options. Liberal theorists of multiculturalism have tended to focus on the right to exit as the guarantee of consent to seemingly oppressive and restrictive practices.[24]

Yet the alternative of 'staying or leaving' misconstrues, or at least radically simplifies, what is at stake for women in their (often grudging) endorsement of traditional cultural practices such as arranged marriages or the wearing of hijab. Arguably, Muslim women, for example, have no interest in leaving their community or stopping being Muslim, although (I shall suggest) they may have an interest in being able to contest interpretations of it which deny them discursive voice. Friedman's second condition is also too demanding: we just cannot free ourselves from all kinds of manipulative interference, ranging from parental pressure, religious education, or capitalist advertising. Overall, by arguing, in effect, that people must be fully autonomous before they make their life choices (which may themselves not involve the exercise of substantive autonomy), Friedman's liberal approach sets too high standards for the respect of non-autonomous lives. An alternative and preferable approach is *not* to conceive of autonomy as a pre-condition for respect of choices, but as a capability that all must be equipped with, at least minimally, so that they can best exercise their judgement when faced with particularly pernicious forms of domination. This capability approach, in effect, is what Friedman's third condition, on education, alludes to. But the first two conditions, by making autonomy a condition for being heard and respected as a moral agent capable of genuine consent, get the relations between voice and autonomy wrong. Women must not prove they are autonomous to be heard: being heard is part of what it means to be (minimally) autonomous, that is, non-dominated. A republican and democratic, rather than liberal, approach sees the promotion of autonomy as an a priori tool of empowerment and democratic engagement, rather than as an *ex post* test of the validity of individuals' choices and perspectives.

Critical Republicanism and Education

Given the centrality of socialization, consensual norms and adaptive preferences to my account of domination, the emphasis I put on education as a privileged means to combat—or at least pre-empt—domination should not be surprising. For consider the ways in which coercive law can be ill-suited to combat the evils of servility and domination. If it focuses on punishing acts of arbitrary interference by those in positions of power (for example, coerced marriages), it misses the ways in which individuals can be dominated without being interfered with (witness the more subtle coercion involved in some 'arranged' marriages). If it focuses on prohibiting harmful practices performed because of the internalization by consenting adults of norms of domination (for example, female genital mutilation), it is on the fairly demanding condition that the harm they cause to their practitioners considerably outweighs the autonomy-infringing effects of paternalistic intervention.[25] At any rate, coercive legislation can be counterproductive and does not address the root causes of domination. It could be argued at this point that addressing the 'root causes' of domination would require a radical programme of social and economic reform, which would effectively rebalance power between dominant and dominated groups. French republicans have (rightly in my view) been castigated for glossing over the need for such structural reform. By contrast, because they take seriously the ideological and cultural underpinnings of domination, they have been unrepentant in their advocacy of robust autonomy-promoting education.

Educational paternalism avoids many pitfalls of legal paternalism. It seeks indirectly to influence, rather than directly to coerce; and it is primarily aimed at children, to whom the classic anti-paternalist injunction (that people's autonomy must be respected) does not fully apply, as children's autonomy must be promoted before it can be respected. There are two kinds of reasons—negative and positive— why republicans should champion autonomy-promoting education. A negative argument points to the fact that autonomy-denying education can be a form of domination, if it makes children dependent upon, and subservient to, their educators; if it shapes what Eamonn Callan has called 'ethically servile' children.[26] A more positive defence points out that education should actively promote autonomy-related skills because they are essential to ward off potential domination in future life. By autonomy-related skills, I mean an extensive set of skills encompassing practical reason, moral courage, critical skills, awareness of the 'burdens of reason', exposure to a diversity of ways of life, understanding of the full range of one's rights, and so forth.

Note that there is an asymmetry between the fairly comprehensive nature of the autonomy-related skills taught in schools and the minimalist nature of our basic interest in minimal autonomy or non-domination. This asymmetry, far from being worrisome, is pivotal to the critical republican strategy. We saw earlier that republicans do not attribute special value to autonomous choice as such: citizens can follow traditions, practise their faith, devote their lives to others, or take their cue from parents and priests. But citizens should not have to endure relationships of domination—relationships of subordination, indoctrination, manipulation, humiliating dependency, and the like. The line between legitimate interdependence and harmful dependency is notoriously difficult to draw, especially as it is, at least partly, dependent on the distribution of a rather intangible form of power: discursive power. For these very reasons, the best hope we have of combating domination is by equipping individuals with extensive discursive power: individuals need to have a fairly secure sense of self, of their own status, and need to be taught how to '[resist] impulses or social pressures that might subvert wise self-direction'.[27] My claim, then, is that even a minimalist understanding of autonomy as non-subordination to the will and opinions of others requires, to acquire its fair value, that individuals be comprehensively equipped with autonomy-related skills. The asymmetry between means and ends is a deliberate one. Education in autonomy, we may say, provides extensive immunization against the risk of domination. But the question immediately arises: is it *too* extensive? Might it not kill off not only the virus of domination but also the benign interdependencies which make our lives valuable? To some extent, this echoes a familiar worry about all forms of liberal education— the worry that, *nolens volens*, they are biased towards individualistic ways of life. John Rawls, as we have seen, had to concede 'with regret' that his favoured political liberal education would affect the way in which individuals related to their personal ends and commitments.[28] Critical republicans are more unrepentant, but also more sanguine, about this possibility. They are more unrepentant about a degree of unavoidable 'overspill': the minimum independence which republican citizens must exhibit has both political *and* personal dimensions, which cannot therefore be neatly separated.[29] But republicans are also more sanguine about the possibility that the inculcation of autonomy-related skills above and beyond this minimum threshold does not amount to an injunction to place autonomy at the centre of one's life. If, as the old republican adage has it, the price of liberty is eternal vigilance, then autonomy-related skills are what keep us alert and vigilant. Being vigilant, however, should not prevent us from enjoying the good inherent in living a non-dominated life—in particular, the good inherent in our pursuit of a diversity of goals and commitments, including non-autonomous ones.

Autonomy-facilitating education furthers the critical republican ideal of non-domination in a number of ways: it brings children to the minimum level of independence essential to republican citizenship; it further inculcates in them broad autonomy-related skills, leaving them free to shape the course of their own lives if they wish; it does not claim to eradicate all domination from social life, but empowers individuals to resist its most pernicious forms. It is compatible with the wearing of hijab by young schoolgirls in schools. This is because it seeks to equip students with generic, content-neutral skills rather than with substantive beliefs about the good life, yet provides them with tools with which to resist the dominating imposition of a conception of the good life on them. A more difficult question is whether autonomy-facilitating education is necessarily a secular education, or whether it can be provided within religious schools.[30] Clearly, in so far as autonomy requires some critical distance from inherited beliefs and dispositions, schools must 'foster an atmosphere of reflection detached from the constitutive commitments of the other arenas of the child's life'.[31] Religious schools are prima facie unlikely candidates for this task, as they do not expose children to, or encourage, open-minded, rational engagement with ethical diversity.[32] Yet this does not necessarily mandate a blanket prohibition of all types of religious schools, which are infinitely diverse. But what it suggests is that the schools that are permitted should be tightly regulated and forced to balance religious instruction with non-religious and other-religious perspectives.[33] Thus, it is clear that the combined force of civic (Chapter 4) and autonomy-based (Chapter 7) reasons is sufficient to justify more stringent regulation of religious secondary schools than we see today. Note, too, that the critical republican state's endorsement of autonomy does not undermine its opposition to paternalism of adults: autonomy can and should be publicly encouraged in children through schools, but adults must not be discriminated against if they choose not to exercise autonomy in their own lives.[34]

To sum up the findings of this section: educational paternalism avoids the paternalist pitfalls of *laïcisme* without resigning itself to leaving individuals unaided in the face of domination. In contrast to much recent multiculturalist discussion, critical republicanism does not attempt to adjudicate the respective claims of abstractly conceived 'autonomy', on the one hand, and 'culture' or 'religion', on the other, but draws attention to the exercise of illegitimate social *power* in general, and not only within cultural and religious minorities. Further, autonomy-facilitating education is not primarily about securing a right for individuals to exercise autonomy by leaving their communities (the 'right to exit' defended by liberals).[35] It is, rather, a way to help individuals resist domination *within* the cultural and normative frameworks they recognize as their own. Instead of the right to 'exit', therefore, critical republicans emphasize the right to 'voice'. Arguably, most Muslim women do not want to leave their religion; but they have an interest in being able to challenge those interpretations of it which deny them discursive power. Autonomy-facilitating education is a necessary (though, evidently, not a sufficient) condition for this to take place. What are also required are effective channels for voice and contestation, so that both inter-group and intra-group domination can be challenged and combated.

Critical Republicanism and Voice

Thus far, I have implicitly concurred with republican *laïcistes* in assuming that non-domination is best pursued through state-controlled education. It is now time to introduce an important caveat to this general republican presumption in favour of the state. It is this: the state can promote non-domination only if it is not itself an arbitrary state, a dominating power. What does it mean for the state to dominate cultural and religious minorities, such as Muslims? Recall the grievances expressed by Muslims about the way in which public deliberations leading to the scarf ban were conducted in the winter of 2003–4: no hijab-wearing Muslim woman was interviewed, on the grounds that the Nationality Commission would 'not be sensitive to their arguments'; and the official report in favour of the ban unashamedly peddled orientalist clichés about veiling and the backwardness and misogyny of Islam.[36] The state engages in cultural domination when it marks some groups out by stereotypes and, at the same time, silences them and renders them invisible. Such domination deprives Muslims of minimum discursive control: they are not allowed to speak for themselves, they are subjected to demeaned images of their identity, they are made to feel vulnerable to the decisions and opinions of others. In other words, they are spoken about but not spoken to; they are not considered worthy of being given reasons. So even in the absence of interference, discrimination, or otherwise unjust treatment, they are not secure in their status as citizens: the price of liberty, for them, is eternal discretion.[37] Institutional silencing (the state pays no regard to the views of group members about the meaning of one of their practices, the *hijab)* and institutional misrecognition (the state officially validates stereotypical, essentialist, and demeaning prejudices about Islam) are cases of unacceptable institutional domination, because they undermine the very conditions for the minimum public standing of Muslims. The normative upshot of this is that citizens should not have an identity imposed upon them by the state, and they are entitled to contribute to, or at least to contest, the public decisions that concern them directly. In educational terms, the 'non-imposition' requirement means that state schools should teach autonomy without stigmatizing certain children as being potentially oppressed or dominated by their religion or culture; they must teach gender equality without castigating the intrinsic misogyny of any particular group; and they must expose children to the plurality of ways of life compatible with the exercise of discursive autonomy, including religions. They must avoid making autonomy (and any other value they impart) the hallmark and characteristic feature of any particular conception of the good or cultural heritage. Only then will the (true) claim that all children, regardless of the culture of their parents, have a basic interest in acquiring discursive autonomy be likely to be accepted as reasonable by members of culturally dominated groups.

In political terms, how can cultural domination be curbed? I shall argue that Anglophone republicans are right to favour a democratic, rather than a legalist and a priori solution to problems of cultural conflict. Generally, republicans are committed to the view that, for the state not to dominate them, the people must in some way be involved in its government. There are, however, different versions of this claim. Advocates of contestatory democracy, of which Pettit is the most prominent, endorse a fairly minimalist version of popular involvement, seeing majority tyranny and 'populism' as one of the chief forms of domination. In the old republican adage, the people want not to be a master, but to have no master. Thus, power should be dispersed, not concentrated at any point, and there should be constitutional constraints on its exercise.[38] Pettit's republic is designed to ensure that the government can reliably track the common interests of its citizens, who can then contest and review decisions through judicial, tribunal, ombudsman-like, multicameral, and local institutions. The people should be able to act as 'editors' of policy in addition to the more traditional authorial role they play through their elected representatives.[39] Pettit specifically makes space for the input of minorities: by contrast to Rousseauian republicanism where the people should only be considered 'collectively', Pettit argues that the government should not ignore the people considered 'severally or distributively': not only the majority but also 'relevant minorities' should be heard through impartial procedures.[40] Advocates of participatory democracy, for their part, doubt that contestatory democracy is sufficient to guarantee the non-dominated status of all citizens, and have argued for more robust forms of self-government. Diversified avenues for the political involvement of citizens—proposals include referendums, Internet democracy, workplace democracy, town meetings, citizens' juries, compulsory voting—are necessary for the voice of disadvantaged groups to be heard.[41] Advocates of deliberative democracy share Pettit's concerns about the dangers of untamed majoritarianism, but believe that democracy, conceived as rational deliberation about ends and values or 'public autonomy'[42] has internal self-correcting tendencies. In a democracy organized deliberatively, all have a fair chance to speak, decisions are publicly made on the basis of the best argument presented, and citizens' initial preferences and values are transformed in the process of interacting with others, generating virtuous circles of trust and participation.[43] Deliberative democracy has recently come to the fore as one of the most promising way to address protracted cultural conflict, by bringing minority citizens into inclusive forums of public deliberation where their claims can be heard and democratically scrutinized.[44]

The republican ideal of public, deliberative process of decision-making and/or contestation of state policy clearly has a number of attractive features relevant to the hijab—and similar—debates. In particular, it helps address what I earlier called the *arbitrary state* problem, in two crucial ways. First, in the real world, any intervention by the state in the practices of a particular cultural or religious group, even if justified by standards of human rights or gender equality, is likely to be perceived as an instance of neo-colonial imposition, if it is undertaken by a state with a colonial past over members of a minority who still perceive themselves (and are perceived) as erstwhile colonial subjects. In such cases, top-down decision-making is neither fair nor prudent, and democratic consultation is a better way to shore up the legitimacy of reforms. Some political theorists have even suggested that, while the state may legitimately impose liberal reform on non-oppressed groups, it should tread more carefully, and proceed more democratically, in the case of groups which can legitimately claim to have been oppressed by it in the past.[45] Second, and more importantly, deliberative interaction is essential to bring out the way in which the well-rehearsed antinomies between 'autonomy' and 'tradition', or between 'gender' and 'culture', serves to gloss over the culturally biased and imperfectly realized nature of the valued ideals of Western societies. Deliberative engagement helps reduce the spontaneously ethnocentric double standard which judges majority cultures according to their ideals, and minority cultures according to their practices. Third, the case for a democratic, instead of liberal or a priori approach, is even clearer in the case of practices which are mostly symbolic, such as dress and the wearing of distinctive signs of religious allegiance. While *laïcistes* are right to suggest that, in blatant cases of slavery and oppression, the state need not consult with the slaves and the oppressed in order to emancipate them, they are wrong to take the wearing of hijab as such an unambiguous instance of harm and oppression, conceived independently of the meanings given to it by those who wear it. Non-democratic, *ex cathedra* judgements made by the state or its representatives risk hiding from view and often aggravating phenomena of reactive culturalism, whereby members of dominated groups close ranks around the denigrated practice, precipitating a defensive retreat into conservative cultural forms and identities. In such cases, there is no short cut to the inclusion of minorities in deliberative forums. The claim is not the epistemological one that the 'authentic' meaning of practices can be ascertained only through the hermeneutic uncovering of the self-understanding of its practitioners. It is, rather, the political one that the actual meanings of particular practices is not a variable independent of existing inter-group dynamics: the illiberality of a group's norms and practices is often a strategic response to the political, legal, and cultural environment in which it finds itself.[46] In so far as such environment contributes to the silencing of group members' voice, only democratic deliberation will bring the complex meanings of the contested practices to the open. Thus, the inclusion of minority members in deliberative forums can help lessen both the arbitrary state and the reactive culturalism problem.

Does this mean, however, that minorities' cultures and religions must be positively recognized and validated, given formal and permanent representation in the organs of the state, and granted a right of veto over decisions that affect them? Critical republicans are sceptical about the compatibility of such strong politics of recognition with republican ideals. Three main points can be made. First, as many deliberative democrats and republicans have pointed out, the entrenchment of fixed group identities may not facilitate the reflexive transformation of citizens' identities and preferences through deliberative engagement, and may also hamper multiple identifications by citizens. Second, mainstream theories of recognition and deliberative democracy have wrongly tended to present cultural conflict as essentially marked by deep pluralism and profound moral disagreement. This has shifted attention away from the political and interest-led nature of cultural conflict. The zero-sum game language of cultural and religious authenticity often distracts from the more pragmatic politics of strategic positioning within both inter-group and intra-group dynamics, whose outcome is more liable to bargaining and compromises than to the moral consensus sought for by some deliberative democrats.[47] Granting minorities a right of veto would prevent the search for mutually acceptable solutions and undermine the sense of common citizenship essential to republican community. A republican state is fair in so far as it gives adequate, impartial consideration of all views in open forums.[48] Third, and connectedly, the entrenchment of group identities risks shoring up the authority of traditional, unrepresentative leaders demanding deference to claims phrased in the vocabulary of identity recognition. To the extent that the politics of recognition would insulate groups from deliberative scrutiny, it is at odds with republican deliberative democracy.[49]

This leads to what is, for my purposes here, the most important objection to the strong politics of recognition: that, in lessening the *arbitrary state* problem, it risks aggravating the *internal minority* problem. Shachar has thus highlighted the problem of 'multicultural vulnerability': 'multiculturalism presents a problem when state accommodation policies intended to mitigate the power differentials between groups end up reinforcing hierarchies within them... and may leave members of minority groups vulnerable to severe injustices within the group'.[50] In the case of the French hijab controversy, insufficient consultation with Muslims about the meaning of hijab was compounded by the near-total absence of input from women wearing the hijab. In dominant public discourse, girls of Muslim origin were perceived either as oppressed and silent victims of religious and patriarchal oppression in need of emancipation by the state, or as autonomous, non-religious *beurettes* fully assimilated to the individualistic, secular, and egalitarian norms of French society. Such paralysing alternatives, by ignoring the complexity of female Muslim identities, did little to lessen the conservative backlash which saw many women naturally close ranks with their communities, in defiant rejection of the perceived paternalism of the French state.[51] Lack of internal democracy, therefore, contributes to reactive culturalism. Another scenario, that of 'empowering at-risk group members',[52] does, here again, commend itself as the only fair and legitimate way to curb the dual domination experienced by Muslim women. An excellent illustration of the need for two-level democratic engagement, both with the group as a whole, and with internal minorities within it, is provided by Monique Deveaux's analysis of the arranged marriage debate in Britain.[53] She shows how a liberal, choice-based interpretation of arranged marriages risks missing out much of the meaning of the practice. The 2000 report of the governmental task force, entitled 'A Choice by Right', singled out individual choice as the chief distinguishing feature between (legitimate) arranged marriages and (reprehensible) forced marriages. On the one hand, democratic input from representatives of Asian communities was essential in 'de-ethnicizing' the practices, making it less exotic by drawing fruitful analogies with accepted Western practices, such as dating introduction agencies. Yet, on the other hand, the recasting and normalization of arranged marriages as fully consensual marriages diverted attention away from the more complex relationships which underpinned them. In particular, what dropped out of sight were the hidden forms of community pressure and manipulation which made 'exit' or resistance unattractive options, especially as arranged marriages further valued goods such as parental love and support, group loyalty, and social status. In such circumstances, more spaces, formal and informal, should be created for the expression, by women in particular, of their grudging acceptance of practices such as arranged marriages. In particular, Deveaux suggests that we should see what social changes and support might make it possible for girls who may not want an arranged marriage to express this desire without incurring the serious psychological costs of exit. The strategy, then, is one of encouraging voice over choice, dissent over exit—a typical critical republican strategy.

A legitimate worry, at this stage, might be that this democratic and republican approach is no more sensitive than the liberal approach to the need to respect the internal authority structures of voluntary groups, particularly those, such as religious groups, which by their very nature eschew electoral representation and democratic debate as legitimate modes of organization. Would a critical republican approach, for example, force the internal democratization of the Catholic Church, so that internal minorities such as women and homosexuals are adequately represented in its authority structures? Such an approach would be deeply unattractive, as it would undermine the legitimate diversity of associational goods in civil society. However, this should not lead us to the conclusion that there is no alternative to the standard corporatist arrangements whereby state authorities consult only with the self-appointed, traditional representatives of cultural and religious groups. A distinction should be drawn between internal structure and external representation. In matters that relate to the citizenship status of members of minorities, there is no reason why the state, in its attempt to find legitimate and fair solutions to particular conflicts, should not seek out the views and perspectives of group members who are not traditionally or formally represented in the group's hierarchical structure. In matters of non-discrimination in employment and access to public goods and services, or in matters of reform of personal and family law, the state should encourage the external representation of a range of affected parties, including internal minorities. This, Deveaux's case studies of gendered cultural conflict suggest, is precisely what was at stake in the democratic reform of customary law in Canada and South Africa. In the former case, the Natives Women's Associations of Canada (NWAC) struggled—unsuccessfully—to be involved in deliberations over the

Charlottetown Accord concerning the application of the Charter of Rights and Freedoms to First Nations peoples; and in the latter case, the ANC's Women's League and the Federation of African Women sought to advance their own understanding of the seemingly intractable conflict between African customary law and constitutional sex equality provisions. In both cases, a delicate balance had to be struck between respect for the cultural autonomy of the group and gender justice—a balance, Deveaux suggests, which could only be achieved through the actual confrontation, within democratic forums, between affected participants' views and interests. It was crucially important to give external voice to women's groups in public forums, even as respect for group autonomy was held to imply respect for its internal (traditional and non-democratic) structure. Furthermore, Deveaux suggests additional ways of empowering and giving voice to vulnerable minority members: the amplification of existing sites of internal, grass-roots democratic contestation, the provision of substantive resources—educational, organizational, and material—and use of the law.[54] The issue arises, of course, as to how best to identify and represent vulnerable members: in the absence of internal democratic procedures, women's groups are a priori no more legitimate than traditional male elites. While the issue is ultimately intractable, democratic and republican theorists tend to put their faith in the bottom-up emergence and validation of contestatory practices and groups, however informal, within traditional communities. They note, too, that the provision of external democratic forums and internal empowerment schemes will have a knock-on effect on the internal structure of the group, thus triggering or furthering self-validating processes of internal democratization. This is in line with the critical republican approach, which does not advocate paternalistic top-down reform, but rather grass-roots democratic empowerment; and which does not encourage the far-reaching implementation of participatory democracy, but rather the stimulation of vibrant practices of democratic contestation. Thus, within cultural and religious groups in civil society, Pettit's weak principle of the possibility of contestation is more promising than the stronger principle of participatory democracy advocated by other republicans. This means that Native, Muslim or Catholic women's groups can be empowered and given political voice without fully undermining the integrity of religious and traditional organization. Delicate balances must be struck, but Pettit's general principle is right: 'what is required for non-arbitrariness in the exercise of a certain power is . . . the permanent possibility of effectively contesting it'.[55]

Conclusion

It is time to sum up my rejoinder to the feminist controversy about the ban on headscarves in schools. Substantively, my conclusion has been that Muslim schoolgirls should be allowed to wear the hijab to school but have a basic interest in autonomy-promoting education and in the democratic contestation of ethnocentric and patriarchal domination. This conclusion is supported by a critical republican understanding of non-domination as 'discursive control'. Like *laïciste* feminists, critical republicans argue—*contra* political liberals—that we should worry about the invisible and seemingly consensual nature of certain forms of social and personal domination and—*contra* Foucauldians—that we should seek a normative yardstick with which to distinguish between pernicious and benign domination. But, like critics of the hijab ban, they are concerned that forcibly to liberate individuals from consensual forms of domination might be unacceptably ethnocentric and paternalistic, especially if coercive intervention is justified by appeal to a thickly constituted, controversial value such as personal autonomy. The republican ideal of non-domination as discursive control does justice to both intuitions and offers an alternative to both *laïciste* and radical feminism. It asserts that, while individuals do not have a basic interest in autonomous assertion, they have a basic interest in avoiding situations of servility, subservience, and domination—situations, that is, where they are unable (barred from or incapable) to contest, or at least to be given justifying reasons for, the power that is exercised over them. Because individuals who thus lack discursive power have often been socialized into thinking that discursive power is not something that they should have, their emancipation will be more effectively assisted by an alternative socialization and education than by paternalistic coercion. Critical republicans then claim that autonomy-promoting education is one privileged way (non-coercively) to empower children to resist present and future domination. The inculcation of autonomy-related skills does not amount to the imposition of a comprehensive vision of the good life as a life of autonomy. Rather, it provides individuals with skills with which to detect, and contest, the ways in which their legitimate ties and commitments can be distorted by illegitimate and oppressive uses of power over them. Thus, autonomy-promoting education avoids the paternalist and perfectionist pitfalls of *laïcisme* without resigning itself to leaving individuals unaided in the face of domination.

Yet education is not sufficient, and dominated individuals must also be provided with effective political voice. This is not to say that republican theorists should therefore espouse the 'politics of recognition', if we mean by this that for people to be secure in the enjoyment of a non-dominated status, their particular identities must be given special protection and public recognition. Republican non-domination is a less demanding ideal: it does not aim to guarantee that all are equally esteemed and honoured, but only to secure the self-respect that comes with minimum discursive control. These proposals avoid the pitfalls of the arsenal of special protections and group representation defended by advocates of the politics of recognition, while addressing the most basic way in which members of cultural and religious minorities are deprived of voice in contemporary Western societies. Furthermore, they are sensitive to the double domination to which intra-group minorities are subjected, and are careful not to solve the 'arbitrary state' problem through aggravating the 'internal minority' problem. Vulnerable individuals—in particular female members of minority groups—must be equipped to resist the multiple forms of domination they are potentially subjected to: public and private, secular and religious, ethnocentric and patriarchal.

PART 3

Fraternité and Republican Solidarity

CHAPTER 8

Official Republicanism, Solidarity, and the Hijab

The first two sections of this book explored two distinct interpretations of *laïcité*. The first was associated with a neutral state respectful of religious difference in the name of equality, and the second with a more perfectionist state committed to the promotion of individual autonomy in the name of liberty. The third and last section explores the third dimension of *laïcité*, which calls for a communitarian state fostering a civic sense of loyalty to a particular historical community. Thus, as one commentator observes, 'one cannot be *laïque* in France unless one accepts an important part of our national-republican heritage.'[1] Historically, this understanding of *laïcité* underlaid the republican ambition to substitute for traditional Catholic-inspired sociability a new civic bond, which would unite citizens in common love of the secular republic. In this view, a society whose only public commitments are to neutrality, individuality, or autonomy would be inherently fragile and incapable of sustaining a sense of mutual concern and solidarity between its citizens. In other words, the new *laïque* civic bond should not be solely based on *liberté* and *égalité*: it would also have to inspire feelings of *fraternité*. As Régis Debray has eloquently written: 'every man, every woman has a right to belong to a community. Republicans more than others, because they have a duty to *create* one (...). They must subordinate the natural community, that of blood (*la lignée*), to a cultural community (...). *Laïcité must be a culture, or it will not be.*'[2] Abstract citizenship must be complemented with allegiance to a republican public culture, a strong sense of national identity which has recently become associated with suspicion towards the divisive politics of cultural and religious (primarily Islamic) difference. Thus, a communitarian, culturalist interpretation of the demands of *laïcité* has been increasingly mobilized by official republicans to contest the wearing of Muslim headscarves to school.[3] The hijab is seen as symptomatic of a broader demand of recognition of cultural and religious difference in the public sphere which, official republicans fear, risk undermining national unity and patriotic fraternity (or solidarity, to use a less archaic and gendered expression).

In this chapter, I reconstruct the official republican case to this effect, and in this way set the scene for my own critical engagement (in Chapter 10) with the fraternity-based argument for the hijab ban. The chapter contains three sections. The first argues that, historically, republican solidarity had non-ethnic foundations but relied on fairly high levels of cultural convergence, as shared nationality was expected to function as a civic and democratic bond. The second section shows how the historical model of national assimilation served as a template for the integration of immigrants and their children in the 1980s. The third section suggests that the public wearing of hijab has been perceived by official republicans as a symptom of a crisis of the national model of integration, one that sets divisive identity politics against the republican politics of inclusive solidarity.

The Foundations of Republican Solidarity

The Rejection of Ethnicity

It is a long-standing theme of nineteenth-century republican historiography that French identity was never rooted in racial or ethnic homogeneity. A large, heterogeneous country originally made up of a variety of 'Celtic, Iberic, Germanic'[4] components, France—it was argued—lacked 'a community of origins, customs, languages and laws'.[5] Whatever 'national' unity was achieved through the efforts of successive rulers from the Middle Ages onwards, it was forcibly created out of an unusual degree of social and cultural diversity: France, republican historian Michelet applauded, had always been a fusion of races.[6] Under the influence of the moral universalism of the Enlightenment, 1789 revolutionaries believed in the irrelevance of citizens' cultural inheritance in creating an inclusive modern political nation. Frenchness, as the *député* Lamourette strikingly put it in the early years of the revolution, required no bond more concrete than 'philosophical consanguinity'.[7] It was, however, in the late nineteenth century, amidst the rise of biological and racial theories of identity, that republicans fully elaborated their 'anti-ethnic' theory of the nation. In a famous speech of 1882 entitled 'What is a Nation?', historian Ernest Renan—himself no progressive republican, but nonetheless a significant influence on republican understandings of the nation—empathically denied that the French nation had a concrete, objective foundation such as shared racial or ethnic descent.[8] No doubt his alternative vision of the nation as a 'daily plebiscite' was a polemical construct chiefly intended to legitimize French claims on the linguistically and culturally 'German' province of Alsace-Lorraine. No less polemical, but more heartfelt and possibly more enduring, was the principled rejection of ethnic nationalism by turn-of-the-century republicans in the aftermath of the Dreyfus affair. Republicans sought to falsify and discredit the deterministic, organicist, and inegalitarian theories of racial identity propounded by rightist ideologues stirring up xenophobic, racist, and anti-Semitic sentiments across France.

Foremost among those republicans, sociologist Émile Durkheim showed that in complex modern societies characterized by the growing division of labour and the development of abstract forms of 'organic' solidarity, primordial ethnic attachments became less salient and were progressively supplanted by superior, more rational forms of solidarity, of which the highest was attachment to the democratic nation.[9] Little wonder, as Dominique Schnapper has suggested, that it is patriotic, assimilated Jews such as Émile Durkheim and Marcel Mauss who laid the theoretical foundations of the French sociological model of 'national integration', which they saw as the most effective bulwark against the pernicious denial of the 'Frenchness' of Jews by the racialist Right.[10] Schnapper goes on to suggest that there lies the root of the long-standing suspicion of French sociologists (and, we may add, political theorists) towards the use of the concepts of 'race' and 'ethnicity' in academic and political discourse. As abstract sociological concepts partly create the reality they purport to describe, talk of race and ethnicity might in practice reinforce anthropologically elusive and morally irrelevant divisions within society. Undoubtedly, the nation is no less anthropologically elusive, as it too is a non-objective, 'imagined community',[11] but at least it should be morally salient, as it is 'imagined' as a universal, inclusive grouping predicated on the 'transcendence of ethnic particularism'.[12] Thus, the French reluctance to refer to 'race relations' or 'ethnic minorities' should not be too quickly dismissed as naïve or wrong-headed: it is rooted in what Schnapper approvingly calls the 'anti-racist project of national sociology'.[13] The upshot, it has been (perhaps wishfully) noted, is that 'France is one of the countries where racial prejudice has been the least strong',[14] as the definition of national identity always contained a weak, almost inexistent, ethnic component.[15] Citizenship, French republicans have consistently argued, should be based on universal attachment to the non-ethnic nation. Now, if national identity does not draw on ethnic bonds or shared descent, what is it based upon? Our next step is to clarify the French conception of citizenship as nationality.

National Culture as Civic Bond

Nationality laws are often presented as crude but fairly reliable indicators of national conceptions of citizenships, as they specify who the state considers in law to be citizens.[16] For national republicans, France stands out—at least in the standard comparison with the archetypical 'ethnic' German nation—both for its wide and almost automatic application of *jus soli* (award of citizenship on the basis of residence not descent) to children of immigrants, and for the relative ease of naturalization upon request by resident foreigners.[17] This may suggest that the chief conditions for becoming a French national are to live in France (residence) and to desire to be French (consent).[18] This, however, is a misguided, if common, interpretation of the spirit of French nationality laws, for two main reasons. First, mere residence in the country has rarely been deemed a sufficient condition for acquiring French citizenship. The generous cosmopolitanism of the early years of the 1789 Revolution was quickly overshadowed by a growing divide between 'national' and 'foreigner', and concomitant overlap between 'national' and 'citizen'.[19] By the Third Republic, French nationality had come to acquire a substantive content, in terms of socialization into a common national culture. Prolonged (five-year) residence in the country—to which was added a minimum level of linguistic proficiency—sufficed only in so far as it was an *indicator* of such socialization and enduring attachment to the country;[20] it established a 'presumption of integration'.[21] The insistence that citizenship is based on socialization into national culture explains the recent republican rejection of 'post-national' proposals for the separation of nationality and citizenship.[22] Schnapper, for example, has argued against the attribution of political rights of citizenship to (non-EU) non-nationals on the grounds that temporary residence and mere participation in economic and social life are no substitute for the political and cultural affinity required by the status of full citizenship.[23] The 1988 report of the Commission de la Nationalité (Nationality Commission) similarly insisted that the French conception was not one of 'integral *jus soli*', but rather one that set pre-requisites of education and socialization to the acquisition of nationality.[24]

Second—*pace* common interpretations—consent and will have historically played a marginal and contested role in the attribution of French citizenship. Significantly, controversy surrounded a 1993 reform of nationality laws which, for the first time, required second-generation immigrants to make a formal request for French nationality upon reaching 18.[25] While advocates of the bill appealed to the revolutionary tradition of the patriotic civic oath and to Renan's voluntaristic ideal of nationality as a 'daily plebiscite', with its emphasis on will and consent rather than culture and origin,[26] critics argued that the reform was in breach of the republican tradition: it unfairly singled out, *because of their ethnic or national origin*, children who, like their French-born peers, had been thoroughly socialized in French schools and wider society. Whatever their ethnic origin, those children had become culturally French, and to require them to *request* French nationality was an unnecessary, burdensome, and discriminatory demand.[27]

Thus, official republicans may disagree over the relative weight of passive socialization and expressed desire as conditions for the naturalization of foreigners. Yet, they all agree that French nationhood, while excluding objective blood ties or common descent, involves a mixture of 'cultural belonging and political will'.[28] Renan himself, in his 1882 speech, combined references to the nation as a voluntary contract (a 'daily plebiscite') and as a 'spiritual principle' which connected past and present generations through shared historical memories (and amnesias). Later republicans confidently argued that this 'spiritual principle' could be endorsed by all prospective citizens, based as it was on subjective appropriation of the founding myths of an inclusive political community.[29] As nationhood was thus a matter of collective invention and social *becoming* and rather than intrinsic and primordial *being*, it was conceived both as an inclusivist and an assimilationist ideal. As Schnapper recently put it, 'the nation is open to all those who, whatever their race, their religion or their presumed "cultural difference", have the ability and the will to acquire the means to participate in its economic activity and to share its political ideals': it is 'neither blood, nor residence' as such which determine Frenchness, but 'socialization' into national culture.[30]

So much, then, for the French conception of nationhood, as partly expressed through the laws governing the acquisition of nationality. Why, then, did French republicans, distancing themselves from the universalist and contractual conception of the nation inherited from the Enlightenment and the 1789 Revolution, insist on shared socialization into national culture? Why should the cultural bond of nationality, instead of purely political citizenship, be promoted in this way? The answer, I argue, is that national culture was intended to function as a *civic and democratic* bond, the foundation for the affective solidarity binding together the 'community of citizens'. The relationship between cultural affinity and political membership, in other words, was an instrumental one: the ideal was political citizenship, and the means to achieve this ideal was shared cultural membership.[31] The aim of state-promoted cultural assimilation, in republicans' eyes, was not to express and enhance French cultural identity *via* state action but, rather, to harness cultural identity to the political purpose of constituting a democratic self-governing community. While the French tradition of state-centred assimilation is a complex and long-standing one,[32] there is a distinctively republican interpretation of it, which is rooted in a long-standing tradition of reflection about the social and cultural preconditions of democratic self-government: the tradition of republican patriotism. As, in a republic, political sovereignty lay exclusively with the people, high and sustained levels of trust, solidarity, and civility are required to motivate citizens to engage in democratic self-government. In order to be able to determine their collective fate, citizens must feel they belong together: they must develop what Jürgen Habermas has called a 'we-perspective of active self-determination'.[33] Polities where individuals are strangers to one another and are bound to their state only through vertical bonds of legal subjection (as in the monarchies and empires vilified by classical republicans) lack—or rather do not need—such an affective bond between their members. Such polities are intrinsically corrupted, dedicated as they are to the pursuit of the honour and self-seeking interest of the ambitious and the powerful, to the detriment of the disenfranchised and alienated masses. Republics, by contrast, are dedicated to the pursuit of the common good, which is ascertained through the full and undistorted expression of the collective will of the people, which Rousseau called the 'general will'. Because republics are rooted in popular participation—or deliberation—they need popular civic virtue for their stability and legitimacy. Thus, republics cannot afford to be indifferent to the mores and dispositions of their members, and they should foster not the minimal virtues of civility and toleration, but the more demanding virtues of mutual empathy and even altruistic devotion to the community of citizens. To keep the threat of corruption (the erosion of the common good) at bay, citizens need to be willing to put common interests over and above the pursuit of their individual or factional interests.[34]

During the French Revolution, this republican fear of the corrupting effect of 'factions' was exacerbated by the perceived association between corporatist and regionalist movements and counter-revolutionary forces.

The will of the people could only fully and freely express itself, Jacobins believed, if the political powers of the 'nations within the nation'—be they regional, occupational, religious, or linguistic—were drastically reduced.[35] The French republic was to be 'one and indivisible', or it would fall prey to factionalism and corruption, as well as inequality. For republicans made a strong connection between unity and equality, and between pluralism and inequality. The diversity of orders and statuses under the *ancien régime* had meant, not only that individuals were deprived of equal rights but also that the wide disparity of their social conditions made it impossible for them to feel part of the same nation. The 'nation', for revolutionaries, was primarily a call for social unity and the abolition of socially divisive differences. Thus, equality was associated not only with equality before the law and the separation between public and private spheres (as seen in Chapter 2) but also with broad convergence in citizens' dispositions and mores, as well as in their opportunities and life-prospects. From Machiavelli to Rousseau, republicans had insisted that citizens must be in a position of relative economic and social equality vis-à-vis one another, so that no poor man could be bought and corrupted by a rich man, and the rich and the poor knew that their fates were bound together. Republican equality, therefore, has an importantly economic and social, not only political and legal, dimension: the reduction of inequalities and the expression of social solidarity are essential to guarantee the equal status of citizenship. In the early twentieth century, a group of French republicans, the Solidaristes (Léon Bourgeois, Émile Fouillée) grounded progressive schemes of social welfare and insurance on ideas of social interdependence and solidarity, as a republican alternative both to liberal individualistic laissez-faire and socialist class-based politics.[36]

What, then, were the sociological and affective foundations of republican solidarity? In a society where traditional intermediary groups—in particular the once hegemonic Catholic Church—had lost much of their influence, what could provide an effective substitute to the social glue long provided by the traditional Christian social ethos? Citizens' rational endorsement of the values of the revolution (democracy, human rights, etc.) was, it was feared, too 'thin' to replicate the level of affective mobilization previously achieved by the hegemonic Catholic *Zeitgeist*. Instead, republicans turned to shared nationality as the social bond suitable to a modern democratic society. Just as classical republicans had believed that patriotism was the 'fountain' of all virtues, modern French republicans insisted that shared nationality underpinned republican solidarity, civic virtue (*le civisme*), and mutual identification. As Maurizio Viroli has shown, patriotism had long been a central republican virtue, and encompassed commitment to the democratic ideals of the republic as well as attachment to the history, memories, traditions, customs, culture, and language of a particular place: attachment, not to this or that republic *qua* republic, but to one's own republic in its concrete manifestations.[37] In contrast to the 'philosophical consanguinity' conjured up by early revolutionaries (of which a recent reformulation is Habermas's cerebral 'constitutional patriotism'[38]), republican patriotism—as evinced, notably, in Jean-Jacques Rousseau's writings about Geneva and Poland—was rooted in a sense of mutual identification towards a concrete *peuple* constituted as a *sui generis* and self-determining entity. While in the classical, medieval, and Renaissance republics, such as Sparta, Athens, Venice, Florence, and Geneva, this sense of identification was achieved through geographical proximity and social homogeneity, in modern large-scale societies, national identity came to provide a functional equivalent to them in the nineteenth century. There is, therefore, some continuity between the old city-state patriotism and the modern civic nationalism articulated by nineteenth-century republicans. This means, of course, that not every 'culture' will be effective as the foundation of democratic solidarity: only beliefs, memories and traditions which express—or at least are compatible with—the universalist and democratic values of the republic can legitimately be promoted by the state. Thus, republicans had few qualms about promoting an idealized and heroic view of national history, one which was destined to make citizens proud of the achievements of the *Grande Nation*, while encouraging selective amnesias about the more sombre and conflictual episodes of France's past (Renan in his 1882 address had deliberately praised 'amnesias' and 'forgetting' as essential to national solidarity). The French republican state thus cultivated a strong sense of national solidarity among its citizens, chiefly by implementing active policies of cultural assimilation from above, thus shaping a pervasive and relatively stable 'national habitus', to use Norbert Elias's terms.[39] Nor was this cultural nationalism deemed incompatible with the universalist ethos of the revolution. French culture harboured credible aspirations to universality, chiefly because, in the spirit of the Enlightenment, it was self-consciously expressed as a product of the human mind *qua* human, not *qua* French, and because it was promoted by a highly centralized, rational state able to foster the type of social bond required by modern society (as suggested by Durkheim).

To sum up, France can be described as the typical Western European nation-state, with high levels of congruence between nation, state, and culture.[40] Such congruence has been given a republican (Jacobin) justification through reflection on the sociological and affective conditions of republican democracy. French republicans believed that the bond of shared nationality—socialization into national culture—would provide the motivational anchorage for the voluntary discharge of the duties of citizenship. The affective bond of nationality underpins 'adhesion to a political project, loyalty towards a civilization which is a common good, and the intense feeling of sharing in each other's fate [*faire partie de la même aventure*]'.[41] Thus, in their view, the link between democracy and nationality is—*contra* Habermas—more than a historically contingent link. Unless high levels of mutual identification and feelings of solidarity are maintained among citizens, no polity can remain truly democratic.[42] Because homogenous national culture was thus intended to function as a *civic* bond (in an oft-repeated phrase, 'in France, the national bond is the social bond'[43]), it was fostered and promoted by French state institutions to an unprecedented degree.

The Institutions of National Solidarity

It is chiefly during the Third Republic that the 'nationalization' of French society took place on a significant scale. The regime engaged in an ambitious programme of nation-building which was designed (in Eugen Weber's famous phrase) to transform 'peasants into Frenchmen',[44] and more generally to 'nationalize identity':[45] the nation was to become a central cognitive and ethical category for the citizens of the republic. Participation in the newly republicanized and nationalized institutions of, notably, school and army was encouraged. Schools, in particular, were pivotal to the republican project of nation-building (which partly explains why they still are the neuralgic point of the hijab controversy). The national strand of republicanism examined in this chapter promoted a distinctive understanding of the aims of republican education. We saw in Chapter 2 that neutralist republicans saw the civic purpose of schools as the inculcation of basic principles of *political* citizenship, in themselves neutral towards children's cultural (and religious) attachments. We saw in Chapter 5 that *laïciste* republicans, for their part, tended to endorse a more *comprehensive* conception of liberal education, one that openly fostered the exercise of rational autonomy and encouraged individual emancipation from the constraints of social and religious life. What, then, distinguishes 'national' republicans, whose argument the present chapter reconstructs? *Contra* neutralists, they insist that democratic principles and values must be rooted in a particular culture to have the required motivational force. Thus, civic education must be patriotic in a 'thicker' cultural sense than neutralists believe.

Contra laïcistes, national republicans argue that education should promote, not so much the dubious virtues of a-social individuality and
unfettered choice, as the more properly civic-minded virtues of self-
restraint, responsibility, solidarity, and the ability to abide by common
rules. Thus, civic education must, of necessity, find the right balance
between individuality and sociability, criticism and compliance, self-
assertion and self-restraint.[46]

   In previous chapters, we saw that the educational project of the
Third Republic fulfilled central neutralist and *laïciste* purposes. Yet
standard historical accounts—such as Weber's seminal *Peasants into
Frenchmen*—have rightly portrayed it primarily as a nationalist, or *nation-
building* project. Republican schoolteachers (aptly named *instituteurs,* as
they were expected to 'institute' the nation) taught children about the
genius of the *Grande Nation,* whose great achievement was to have
discovered and spread the universal values of the Enlightenment. Thus,
'the republican school was patriotic and universalist at the same time,
universalism being channelled though a particular language and culture,
that of... Parisian civil servants'.[47] Children from *patois*-speaking rural
families across the French provinces were to be thoroughly socialized
into a national culture which was as foreign to them as it may
have been to foreign immigrants.[48] Attachment to the nation was not
merely fostered through civic education classes: subjects such as history,
geography, and literature were taught so as to enhance children's sense
of identification with, and pride in, the *grandeur* and special destiny of
France. Thus, *laïcité* in the eyes of 'national' republicans took the form
of a kind of Rousseauian 'civic religion',[49] complete with founding
myths,[50] revolutionary rituals and patriotic celebrations,[51] and promoting an ethically charged feeling of national belonging and a consensualist
conception of democracy. Patriotic education had an unashamedly
moral and civic purpose, that of 'moralizing... citizens, motivating them
to respect the laws..., encouraging certain forms of sociability, in a
word, educating... mores for political ends'.[52] This religion of the *patrie*
was not only diffused through schools: the conscript army—the other
republican institution par excellence—was also a pivotal site of patriotic
citizenship. During military service, youngsters from different social and
regional backgrounds were socialized into the same national language
and culture, taught about the greatness of French democracy, taught
the virtues of solidarity and devotion to their co-citizens, and ultimately
called upon to defend their *patrie.*

   Less dramatically and more routinely, the bonds of cultural fraternity provided the foundations for the expression of socio-economic
solidarity between citizens. It is sometimes assumed that republicans'

eulogy of civic community was a conservative, anti-socialist alternative to radical policies of socio-economic distribution.[53] While there is some truth in this, the reality is more complex. As we have seen, historically, republican polities aspired to be socially egalitarian as well as culturally homogeneous, at least to a point, as republicans worried about the corrosive impact of social and economic inequalities on citizenship. In France, early twentieth-century Durkheimian Solidaristes and republican socialists such as Jean Jaurès repudiated Marxist class politics but argued that the ties of social interdependence, most fully developed within national society, gave rise to bonds of mutual obligations between citizens. The nation was to be the natural site of social justice and economic redistribution. As Étienne Balibar has shown, the new sphere of 'the social' was constructed according to national criteria,[54] and large sections of the republican Left came to see the post-1945 welfare state as a constitutive element of French national identity.[55] It embodied the 'national republican' intuition that membership in the national community guaranteed access to the egalitarian status of citizenship. This status included universal economic and social benefits and services which, combined with relatively high levels of taxation of the middle and upper classes, ensured that the life-experiences of the rich and the poor were not so radically discrepant as to undermine their sense of 'being in the same boat'. The realization of equal opportunities and social mobility was also facilitated by universalized access to a nation-wide public culture and language: for national republicans, an accessible, democratic culture was a public good which furthered egalitarian ends.

In recent years, two features of the post-1945 welfare state have been hailed as central to the much-invoked republican social model—a favoured alternative to the neo-liberal 'Anglo-Saxon' model.[56] The first is the pivotal role of the state in guaranteeing social cohesion through provision of a full range of nationalized public services, both traditional social services and public infrastructural services.[57] The second is the universality and uniformity of state provisions: the right to social welfare is attached to the quality of citizen (or even resident),[58] not to membership of a particular group. Thus, many benefits are available on an unconditional, universal basis, instead of being means-tested. Most significantly, when resources *are* targeted towards the worst-off, the latter are identified exclusively in economic and social terms, thus excluding any policy of 'positive discrimination' in favour of racially or culturally defined groups. For example, the *Zones d'Education Prioritaire (ZEPs)*, which allow schools located in impoverished areas to benefit from extra educational resources and support, are only 'coincidentally' located in immigrant areas: people of (say) North African origin benefit from special provision only by virtue of being economically disadvantaged, not by virtue of being North African.[59] For national republicans, the rationale for excluding 'ethnic targeting' is to generate solidarity between the different ethnic and cultural components of the French state. Particularist policies (especially those which combine the rectification of social inequalities with the recognition of cultural difference) might exacerbate morally arbitrary differences, lock the worst-off in a vicious circle of discrimination and disadvantage, set groups against one another in endless competition for 'ethnic advantage', and undermine the ideal and institutions of republican solidarity.[60] Positive discrimination policies, then, threaten the ideal of fraternity on national republican grounds (we saw in previous chapters than they were seen to undermine the ideal of equality on neutralist, difference-blind grounds; and the ideal of liberty on individualistic, anti-collective rights grounds). The imperatives of national solidarity exclude any recognition of ethnic or cultural particularity—and therefore any recognition of the distinct culture of immigrant communities.

National Integration: Making Immigrants into Citizens[61]

Reviving a French Tradition

The theory of republican solidarity sketched out above provides the relevant context against which to understand the French model of the integration of immigrants. The basic principle is simple. There is no specificity of immigrant integration: immigrants are expected to assimilate into the French nation exactly in the same way as nineteenth-century *patois*-speaking peasants. As Brubacker put it, 'if school and army could turn "peasants into Frenchmen", they could turn native-born foreigners into Frenchmen in the same way.'[62] Thus, immigrants *qua* immigrants are not seen (at least retrospectively) as posing any particular problem to the French assimilationist model. This is because, as we have seen, ethnic origins were historically deemed irrelevant to the acquisition of French nationality, and so everyone could potentially become French; education into French culture involved unavoidable uprooting and 'acculturation' for all children; French culture was seen as prestigious and attractive enough to be willingly endorsed by foreigners; and, finally, the prosperous post-war 'social state' ensured that most could benefit from the tangible, material goods promised by the status of national citizenship. Immigrants, it was believed, spontaneously and willingly became French, at least from the second generation, when they become socially and economically integrated.[63] The acquisition of nationality—not purely in a legal but in a substantive sense, referring to the acquisition of a 'national habitus' made up of specific social roles, moral outlook, and cultural dispositions—took place through a combination of forcible socialization and benign assent (albeit mixed with feelings of self-hatred and guilt).[64] Thus, not surprisingly, the massive, successive waves of immigration into the country did not occupy a central role in French collective memory: they were not seen as altering the profound structures of French culture and society, but merely as yet another dissolvable ingredient into the capacious 'melting pot' that France had been for centuries.[65] As Donald Horowitz puts it, 'immigrants could come to a France already established, but they could neither make nor remake it.'[66] Once they were Frenchified, immigrants' ethnic origin became irrelevant. Of course, Polish or Portuguese immigrants had often partially recreated community-based networks of solidarity in France, to preserve 'fragments' of their culture, smooth their integration into French society, and protect themselves from xenophobia, but such 'communities' dissolved after the second generation and—crucially—were never granted public recognition.[67] The French state never recognized ethnic or cultural communities in its midst.

Such assimilationist model, it must be stressed, is not historically unique to France, although it was pursued there with more vigour, consistency, and purpose than elsewhere. Where France departed from other countries, such the United Kingdom, was in the *revival* that the assimilationist model enjoyed in the 1980s and 1990s, when it was theorized as the centrepiece of a celebrated 'French model of national integration'. For a while, in the 1970s and early 1980s, it looked as though a more pluralist understanding of national identity might be gaining ground. The anti-colonial and regionalist movements had profoundly discredited the uniformizing, ethnocentric, and oppressive tendencies of the Jacobin state. Members of oppressed minorities— regional, ethnic, immigrant, sexual—were claiming 'cultural rights' and the newly elected Socialist government, supported by the youth orga- nization SOS Racisme, officially proclaimed (in the words of President François Mitterrand) the 'right to be different, the right to an identity sustained by the promotion of [immigrants'] homeland languages and cultures'.[68] The multiculturalist experiment was however limited in theory and practice and, above all, it was short-lived. As the economic and social crisis deepened, the rightist National Front exploited popular discontent to stir up racist feelings of resentment against immigrants, and cynically appropriated the rhetoric of cultural and ethnic difference to assert the right of the French to protect their identity against the 'invasion' of foreign peoples. This, for all intents and purposes, killed off the burgeoning multiculturalist movement in France. The rhetoric of ethnic and cultural differentialism, historian of racism Pierre-André Taguieff warned, was dangerously prone to being manipulated to the service of inegalitarian and divisive ideologies, and thus should be banned from republican discourse.[69]

It is in this context that the 'French model of integration' was articulated in the mid-1980s, as an alternative to the exclusive discourse of the Far Right and the multiculturalist praise of the 'right to be different'.[70] Both, it was argued, indulged in divisive *communautarisme*, emphasized differences instead of resemblances between citizens, illegitimately politicized ethnic identities, and misleadingly perpetuated the myth of the impossible assimilation of foreign populations. The multiculturalist eulogy of difference had had disastrous effects in other Western countries, notably in the United States where, it was believed, the unchecked development of identity politics had contributed to relegate disadvantaged minorities to social 'ghettos' and set ethnic groups against one another in an accelerating spiral of mutual mistrust, thus undermining the foundations of nation-wide solidarity, notably social and economic.[71] France, by contrast, should build on its tradition of full integration of all into a common culture, economy, and society. This was strongly asserted by Prime Minister Michel Rocard during the first hijab controversy in 1989. France, he said, should avoid becoming 'a juxtaposition of communities'; it must be founded on 'common values' and must not follow the 'Anglo-Saxon model which allows ethnic groups to barricade themselves inside geographical and cultural ghettos' leading to 'soft forms of apartheid'. Republicans' response to the National Front was thus two-pronged. On the one hand, they passionately reaffirmed the age-old 'taboo of origins' which—as we have seen—had been the hallmark of the Durkheimian and Dreyfusard critique of the anti-Semitic Right.[72] Thus, the French should revive their tradition of republican integration and national citizenship, instead of uncritically endorsing the ideologically suspect (in a French context) discourse of multiculturalism and inter-ethnic relations.[73] On the other hand, republicans insisted that 'the nation should not be left to the National Front', and stressed the need to assert a 'strong, ... but non-ethnic ... French identity'[74] capable of providing a focus of affective solidarity in a context of fears of social breakdown and national decline. The nation, it was held, was the only progressive—because democratic—bulwark against the divisive and regressive forces of globalization and multiculturalism. A central French republican tenet—echoing the concerns of American 'strong democrats' such as Benjamin Barber—was that the neo-liberal politics of economic and social deregulation on a global scale and the neo-communitarian politics of identity on a local (or transnational) scale were intimately connected, and only within the nation could the democratic impetus be found to stem such divisive and inegalitarian forces. A democratic and inclusive theory of the nation was thus proffered as a response to the exclusive discourse of the Far Right, a response that endorsed the latter's concern for the crisis of national identity and seeming 'de-sacralization' of French citizenship.

It is in this context that the idealized historiography of the French 'melting pot' and republican solidarity—of which I provided a theoretical account in the first section of this chapter—was produced, as an explicit political intervention by republican intellectuals concerned about the growing influence of the Far Right.[75] Over just a few years, there emerged an unprecedented consensus over what Miriam Feldblum has rightly called the 'nationalist politics of citizenship'.[76] This consensus took institutional shape in the composition and findings of the Commission de la Nationalité (Nationality Commission), which (as we saw) was convened in 1986 to reform nationality laws.[77] Against the National Front's claim that French nationality should not be 'given away' to immigrants on pains of creating millions of disloyal *Français de papier* ('fake French'), the commission's report explicitly asserted that French nationality should be open to all residents whatever their origin, provided they were willing fully to 'integrate' into the French nation.[78] On this, the Left (e.g. Alain Touraine, New Left sociologist of multiculturalism) and the Right (e.g. Pierre Chaunu, conservative Gaullist) could agree. As commission member Schnapper reminisced, 'the Right admitted the massive fact of the definite presence of Maghrebis, the acculturation of the generation educated in France, and the necessity to do all to integrate them. The Left... renounced the mirages of multiculturalism.'[79] The consensual celebration of what was perceived as a transhistorical French 'model of integration' only excluded the National Front and a section of the post-national and multicultural Left committed to integral *jus soli* and cultural pluralism. This consensus I have called in this chapter 'national republican'.[80] It was articulated in such aptly titled works as Dominique Schnapper's *The France of Integration* and *Community of Citizens*, Jacqueline Costa-Lascoux's *Immigrants into Citizens*, Emmanuel Todd's *The Fate of Immigrants. Assimilation and Segregation in Western Democracies*, Pierre-André Taguieff's *The Strength of Prejudice*, Gérard Noiriel's *The French Melting Pot* and Michèle Tribalat's *Making France* and *From*

Immigration to Assimilation.[81] These works—along with the official reports of the Nationality Commission and the Haut Conseil à l'Intégration (High Council for Integration)—set out what came to be called the 'French model of integration'.

Integrating Immigrants

'In France, the Report of the Nationality Commission noted approvingly, national unity rests on cultural unity.'[82] France was held together by a much-invoked—if rarely spelt out—*culture commune* which immigrants were expected to acquire. What, then, was this common culture, and what precisely were immigrants (and their children) expected to endorse? Throughout the 1980s, much semantic confusion surrounded terms such as 'integration' and 'assimilation', as ways of describing processes of immigrant adaptation to the host society. While usage varied, assimilation commonly referred to the 'loss of [immigrants'] original features' (in the words of the Nationality Commission[83]) and integration signalled full 'participation to society' compatible with 'preservation of cultural, social and moral specificities' (in the words of the High Council for Integration).[84] Both reports opted for 'integration' over what they saw as the repressive and colonial overtones of 'assimilation'. Integration was, supposedly, less coercive and less pervasive than assimilation; it was, as a result, more respectful of immigrants' cultures. Yet, I shall argue, closer analysis of official writings on immigrant integration betrays a slightly different, if more diffuse, expectation than that of integration thus defined. Of course, while all agree that any voluntarist policy towards immigrants should emphasize 'resemblances and convergences', not differences,[85] not all republicans shared an identical understanding of legitimate demands put on immigrants: hard-liners advocated cultural assimilation as full and comprehensive 'Frenchification',[86] while 'tolerant republicans' such as Schnapper defended the 'right to cultivate particularities in personal as well as social life', alongside endorsement of French public identity.[87]

Yet all republicans importantly embraced two tenets of the 'French integration model'. The first was that, in practice, and over (at most) a few generations, most immigrants became assimilated into French culture. A team of demographers led by Michèle Tribalat made the point forcefully in a ground-breaking study published in 1995. This showed that immigrants of Maghrebi origin—those whose successful integration into French society raised most doubts—were well-advanced on the path to full cultural assimilation. Tribalat's methodology was to measure the extent to which the social practices of people of non-French origin differed from a synthetic set of median variables interpreted as 'averagely French'. She then noted that the gap between ethnic immigrants and *'français de souche'* (indigenous French)[88] was steadily reducing on all variables: marital status, intensity of religious practice, length of children's schooling, occupational specialization, affective link to another country, and so forth.[89] The Nationality Commission report thus approvingly observed the 'erosion of the traditional [Maghrebi] family structures'.[90] Contrary to the claims of the Far Right, then, neither ethnic origin nor presumed 'cultural distance' were insuperable obstacles to assimilation into French culture.[91] In Tribalat's study, as in other sociological studies of the same type,[92] three features were typically highlighted as emblematic of the efficacy of the French 'melting pot': adoption of French as the immigrants' main language, endorsement of a privatized (*laïque*) interpretation of their religion, and willingness to enter into 'mixed' (i.e. inter-ethnic) marriages. While rejecting the claim that individuals' origin was an insuperable obstacle to assimilation, national republicans still speculated that the particular difficulties encountered by the latest wave of immigrants into France—coming from North Africa in particular—stem from the greater 'cultural distance' between French culture and—notably—Islamic traditions.[93]

The second tenet embraced by most—if not all—national republicans was that integration had been a success because immigrants had genuinely wanted to participate in French society and become French. Thus, as Pierre-André Taguieff and Patrick Weil noted, 'for integration to succeed,...it must be willed [by immigrants].'[94] Historically, to become French was a process of 'moral ennobling'[95] for the impoverished and uneducated immigrant who cherished the opportunities for economic participation, social mobility, and cultural enrichment promised by access to French culture. Today, the success of the French model still depends on the strength and prestige of French nationality, and on the availability of the goods, material and symbolic, associated with it. The more the French are confident about, and proud of, their collective identity—the argument goes—the more immigrants will want to assimilate into French society. It is a truism of national republican discourse that the construction and transmission of a strong sense of national identity and the spread of common cultural forms can only help immigrant integration. In the telling words of Alain Touraine (who tends to be associated with the 'multicultural' strand of republicanism), 'the integration of immigrants must be constantly associated with the affirmation of the French identity'.[96] Thus, contrary to claims of the Far

Right, immigration is compatible with a vibrant and confident sense of national identity[97]—an interpretation enthusiastically embraced by anti-racist immigrant associations such as SOS Racism and France-Plus.

Thus, the understanding of integration defended by national republicans relies on a sociological and psychological theory of the development of patriotic loyalty and 'affection' (the socio-psychological explanation of 'the will to be French') and of cultural resemblance (the social process of 'assimilation' studied by sociologists). Immigrants over time come to 'adopt behaviours and attitudes explicitly or implicitly requested by the host society',[98] and the difference between assimilation and integration is, *in fine*, largely immaterial.[99] In other words, immigrants are not forcibly coerced into giving up their culture; yet the disintegration of immigrant cultures takes place anyway, and at a fast pace, merely through daily exposure to, and participation in, French society.[100] So it is illusory to seek to maintain a hard-and-fast distinction between a shared 'public' culture and a multiplicity of thick and comprehensive 'private' cultures'—as some republicans of a more 'neutralist' and 'liberal' dispositions seek to do.[101] As Noiriel asks rhetorically, 'does the nation ... stop at the doors of the family, of the group, of the individual ... or does it permeate them through and through, and transform them entirely?'[102] Assimilation into French society, then, happens in a way that is non-coercive but pervasive. This, I believe, is what gives its distinctiveness and coherence to the much-praised (but thinly defined) 'French model of integration'.

What happens, then, to immigrant cultures? The 1995 Report of the High Council for Integration addressed the issue of 'cultural links and integration' and, in an innovative move, recognized that the cultivation by immigrants of their cultures and traditions could be 'a factor of integration'.[103] Yet this concession to a pluralist understanding of immigrant integration was followed by a number of provisos and nuances which, put together, eloquently testify to the force of the national republican model of integration. Thus, the council noted that the cultivation of foreign cultures should be only a transitory measure, which should not consolidate immigrant communities into segregated 'ghettos' only likely to exacerbate the 'marginalization' and 'stigmatization' of already disadvantaged individuals.[104] When immigrant communities were, like the Chinese community, spatially concentrated and tightly knit, they should remain 'discrete' and refrain from all claims to the public recognition of their cultural specificity.[105] Overall, the council noted approvingly, most immigrants did not wish to maintain their original culture in other than a 'fragmentary' and symbolic way: the 'dominant culture' for them too was that of the French 'school, television, and *cité* [neighbourhood, town]'.[106] Thus, the council drew on the main conclusions reached by national republican sociologists: that, at most, citizens of foreign origin in France kept alive a 'residual', 'symbolic', and often 'imaginary' sense of belonging to their home (or parents') culture, which for the most part did not underpin dual allegiance or genuine conflict of loyalty, as the 'national reference' remained paramount.[107] Through routine exposure to the national institutions of education, the army, the universal welfare state, national parties, trade unions and media, and neighbourhood associations, second-generation immigrants were automatically socialized into mainstream French culture.

Whatever social disparities remained between them and 'indigenous French' should be attributed to the predominantly lower-class origins of migrants, not to (illusory and receding) cultural difference nor to (almost negligible) racial prejudice. This, national republicans implicitly assert, is the real 'French exception' which makes multiculturalism and identity politics distinctly unsuited to national conditions. Economic and social disadvantage still disproportionately affects immigrants and their children, but it is best addressed through universal, difference-blind, egalitarian policies. Immigrants must be granted genuine equality of opportunity, and this requires that they be educated in common schools, taught in French, and so forth. Thus, the 1970s multiculturalist policy of inviting foreign teachers to teach second-generation children with their 'languages and cultures of origin' within French schools is widely condemned for having hampered rather than facilitated integration.[108] On the whole, then, it can be concluded that the official theory of republican integration requires immigrants, for all intents and purposes, to become culturally French, save for the cultivation of 'fragments' of their original culture in a private or familial setting. So the distinction here is not—as in 'neutralist' republicanism—between a neutral public sphere and a pluralist private (in fact social) sphere; it is, rather, between a culturally homogenous public and social sphere and a reduced private (in fact familial) sphere. The Nationality Commission recognized it was moved by an 'instinct to transform... foreigners into French citizens, speaking *the same language*, sharing the *same* culture and patriotic *values*, participating in the national life like the others, *even if they retain in the private order their religious and cultural loyalties*'.[109] Yet such private attachments and loyalties should in no way be recognized publicly through the attribution of 'collective rights', as this would further slow down the natural process of assimilation, encouraging community closure, and constituting 'a serious risk of segregation'.[110]

The distinctiveness of the French national republican approach can be discerned through comparison with the 'liberal nationalist' positions of Will Kymlicka.[111] Although their mode of argument is more sociological and historical than ethical and normative, French national republicans would concur with Kymlicka in asserting that immigrants have no collective right of cultural self-preservation, on the grounds that their culture of reference—what Kymlicka calls their (self-contained, comprehensive) 'societal culture'—is not their home culture but the culture they have acquired—or will acquire—upon migrating. Thus—crucially—immigrants (or foreigners, or ethnic minorities) should have no right of special political representation. French republicans would, by contrast, be more ambivalent than Kymlicka vis-à-vis respect for what he calls 'poly-ethnic rights'—rights attached to the preservation of key cultural and religious practices on grounds of equality between majority and minority groups.[112] And of course, given their commitment to national unity, they would deny that non-immigrant, regional communities within France (Basque or Corsican, for example) have rights of national self-determination. On a national republican account, to sum up, France is not made up of immigrant (and regional) minorities coexisting alongside a culturally dominant majority. It is made up of *Français* all sharing in the same culture, a status which *étrangers* and *immigrés* are invited to acquire and expected to aspire to.

Muslim Headscarves, Identity Politics, and the Crisis of Integration

In 1997, the High Council for Integration published a report with a title which, in its inimitable French socio-political jargon, perfectly captured the national republicans' response to the headscarves crisis. The report was entitled 'Weakening of the social bond, entanglement within particularisms, and integration in the *cité*'.[113] It thus set out a diagnosis of the problem—the affective bond between citizens had been loosened—identified its causes—individuals had taken refuge in their particular identities—and hinted at a solution—the national and local *polis* must restore its capacities of integration of disaffected citizens. Thus, the French model of integration was rehabilitated and praised precisely at the moment when it seemingly had lost much of its force and efficacy. Not only did state institutions find it increasingly difficult to socialize citizens into a common culture (Section 'The Crisis of Integration'), foreigners themselves no longer aspired to be French and, instead, defiantly asserted their separate identity (Section 'The Hijab Ban as Rejection of Identity Politics'). Thus, national republicans tended to see the headscarves affair as a regrettable symptom of the erosion of the dual model of integration, based both on institutional socialization and on individual consent. In this view, the ban on hijab signifies a reassertion of the continued validity of the republican model of integration.

The Crisis of Integration

As Didier Lapeyronnie has shown, 'national society', with its highly integrated economic, social, cultural, and political systems, has given way to a fragmented society in which a prosperous and mobile middle class, integrated into the world economy, coexists—but hardly interacts—with a marginalized and ghettoized population, which the French call the 'excluded' (in English, the underclass), cut off from any hope of social mobility and cultural integration into the society of the 'included'. In an increasingly globalized world, social-economic modernization and national assimilation have come apart, in what sociologists have called the 'end of national society'.[114] As the prospects for social mobility and the sense of a solidarity provided by a shared culture wane, excluded groups develop their own references and identities, often in defiant response to the unfulfilled promise of their social promotion and emancipation. While this is of course a general trend, it has taken a particular force in France, where the efficacy of national integration was long seen to depend on a strong conception of republican citizenship backed up by a centralized state—the chief promoter of the 'national society'. The erosion of the French model of integration has taken three main forms: the decline of national patriotism and civic virtue, the thinning out of the socio-economic content of republican citizenship, and the discredit of universalist state institutions.[115]

Let me start with the first point. Citizenship has, over the last few decades, been concomitantly de-nationalized and de-sacralized. The nation-state has lost the ethical and cognitive centrality which late nineteenth-century republicans had ennobled it with, as it has come under the twin pressures of transnational globalization and supra-national (notably European) integration. Nationality—and the range of statuses and roles it implied—has been displaced as individuals' chief point of reference, as it competes with a whole set of sub-national and post-national, cultural, religious, occupational, and sexual attachments. The naïve and unreflected patriotism of the Third Republic has given way to a reconsideration of the darkest episodes of French history, notably those which—like the revolutionary Terror, Vichy years, and colonial atrocities—shake to its core the heroic and elegiac '*roman national*', to use Paul Yonnet's phrase. This more critical approach to national identity, combined with the rise of the hedonistic and right-based individualism in the aftermath of May 1968, makes it increasingly difficult to mobilize individuals' sense of civic virtue, as loyalty to the French 'community of citizens'. Thus, republican writings in the 1980s and 1990s abounded on the very Durkheimian themes of the 'crisis of the social bond' and the development of social anomie and *incivilités* (anti-social behaviour). Second, national republicans were well aware that this decline of citizenship was not unconnected to the deepening socio-economic crisis, and rising levels of unemployment, inequalities and social exclusion from the late 1970s onwards. The crisis had two main effects: it thinned out the material content of citizenship, considerably reducing its attractiveness as a status promising access to equal opportunities, material well-being and intergenerational social mobility, and it eroded the 'social consensus' around (relative) redistribution of wealth and social welfare guaranteed by republican *solidariste* institutions. Immigrants found themselves both victims of, and scapegoats for, the rarefaction of the economic and social goods of citizenship, as the Far Right cynically exploited feelings of social relegation and resentment of the white working class. To those 25 per cent of youngsters of immigrant origin unable to find a job, the promise of republican integration seemed understandably hollow.

Nor, third, were traditional institutions of national integration able to withstand the wider disintegration of the republican settlement, and proved less and less able to 'integrate' individuals. Military service (abolished in its traditional form in 1995) proved to be an anachronistic, authoritarian, and inefficient institution. Leftwing parties and trade unions, which had played a unique role in fostering solidarity between French-born and immigrants workers by promoting inter-ethnic values of proletarian internationalism and republican patriotism, saw their membership collapse as France entered into a profound and multifaceted 'crisis of representation'. The Catholic Church—that centralized and authoritarian institution reviled by *laïciste* republicans, as we saw in Chapter 5—was (retrospectively) hailed by national republicans as having successfully mobilized and integrated generations of Poles, Italians, Spaniards, and Portuguese; yet it had seen its integrative powers significantly reduced. Above all, the national institution of integration most dramatically weakened in France was the state school. The intensity of successive 'headscarves affairs' in France cannot be understood unless it is related to a long-standing and deep-seated *malaise des enseignants* (teachers' malaise). Teachers have had to deal with more homogeneous publics, reduced resources, and new socio-cultural claims, and their authority as *instituteurs de la nation* has been shaken to its core. As a result, as the Nationality Commission report put it, the state educational system is 'less authoritarian, less demanding, less sure of its values and of its mission',[116] notably that of socializing all children into a common culture. In fact, schools find themselves on the front line of all the social problems that have derailed the French 'model of integration': discredit of traditional authorities, patriotism and civic virtue, social breakdown and violence, ethnic segregation, inequalities, and social exclusion.

One aggravating factor, in national republicans' eyes, is the tendency, on the part of local and national authorities, to give ground to the centrifugal forces of social disintegration, by encouraging the segmentation and ethnicization of public policy. Human rights, anti-racist associations and their supporters on the Left, are blamed for their postcolonial, guilt-ridden idealization and 'victimization' of Arab-Muslim youth.[117] Thus schools have become too accommodating of the 'right to difference' and too tolerant of substandard education for the most disadvantaged, thus failing in their mission of providing all children with access to the same cultural 'baggage'.[118] The welfare state, too, is less and less universal and unconditional, and in its attempt to address specific situations of disadvantage and exclusion, has segmented the citizenry into diverse, dependent and often ethnically defined 'clients'.[119] As local authorities have recruited Maghrebi social workers to act as intermediaries to the disaffected youth in the *banlieues*, and used implicitly ethnic quotas to manage housing or educational problems, local politics have been worryingly sensitive to 'ethnic' logics. Worst of all, a number of French institutions—the police, places of higher education—have practised forms of covert 'positive discrimination', attributing benefits, places and posts to citizens of foreign origin, not on grounds of need or merit but in the name of the promotion of 'diversity' and the 'dignity of immigrant cultures'. National institutions of integration have, thus, been permeated by a pernicious differentialist ideology,[120] which undermined their—already weakened—powers of republican integration and accentuated, rather than narrowed, the 'social fracture' between the included and the excluded. The right to difference could only lead to the perverse ethnicization of social problems and to accelerated social disintegration.

Thus, the solution to the multifaceted 'crisis of integration' diagnosed by national republicans is a simple one. It implies the revalorization of republican citizenship and the reassertion of the validity and authority of the republican order. In an emblematic manifesto of 1998, eight prominent intellectuals (all broadly from the Left, but of different persuasions) articulated the central concerns of the national republican politics of citizenship: a defence of the French model of integration against both asocial individualism and ethnic particularism, a repudiation of 'foreign' models and influences (notably the 'Anglo-Saxon' ethnic model), an appeal to the restoration of the 'republican order' through the enforcement of basic norms of civility and cooperative behaviour and the coercive apparatus of law, and the invocation of the socializing role of traditional institutions such as schools, complemented by the restoration of basic networks of sociability in civil society. 'We must', they wrote in nostalgic vein, 'restore the long chain of citizenship whose links were, in the old days, the father, the teacher, the mayor, the lieutenant, the factory mate, the [local Communist Party] cell or trade union secretary.'[121] Institutional forms must be found which can insert individuals into a coherent and *solidaire* society animated by an 'ambitious collective project',[122] restored basic law and order, civility and law-abidingness, and successfully transmitted a common culture. A central belief of national republicans is that social breakdown, crime and insecurity, and doubts about national identity adversely affects the worst-off disproportionately, and therefore truly egalitarian and progressive politics should not leave those traditionally 'rightwing' themes to the dangerously exclusive and reactionary nationalism of the Far Right.[123] At the same time, while only strong institutions could successfully integrate individuals, particularly those of foreign origin, their very strength and success relied on the willingness of individuals to abide by their demands. This two-pronged strategy of reassertion of the republican order was concisely summed up in the Nationality Commission Report: while institutions must develop 'new capacities of organization and integration', individuals, for their part, must show 'clear adhesion to the essential common values of French society'.[124] Nowhere was this more necessary than within schools: as they are the traditional 'locus of construction of the social bond', it is in their midst that the 'communitarian drift' (*dérive communautaire*), symbolized by the emergence of separatist Islamic identities, must be resisted. In this view, demands for the right to wear Muslim headscarves in schools 'reveal the difficulties of the school's integrative mission': they are both a consequence of, and a contributing factor to, the crisis of integration. Therefore, it is not only institutions that are failing to integrate individuals: individuals are also unreasonably refusing to 'integrate themselves' (*s'intégrer*).[125]

The Hijab Ban as Rejection of Identity Politics

As we have seen in previous chapters, the wearing of the hijab is seen by neutralist republicans as an ostentatious religious sign and by *laïciste* republicans as a symbol of sexist oppression. National republicans, for their part, see it as a claim for the recognition of ethno-cultural particularity. The public and provocative endorsement of an Islamic identity by young Maghrebi is perceived as a profound challenge to the French model of integration. The wearing of headscarves has become the most visible symbol of the (re-)islamization of youth of North African origin.[126] More specifically, the turn to 'identity politics' of second-generation immigrants has been seen, against the background of the reassertion of the national model of integration, as symbolizing *unreasonable free-riding, divisive cultural affirmation, hostile provocation*, and *illusory refuge*. I analyse these arguments in turn.

Unreasonable free-riding

The argument here is that immigrants default on the 'duty of integration' which befalls them by virtue of their having settled into a country with a strong republican commitment to high levels of cultural solidarity. There are two versions of the argument. According to the first, it is not unreasonable for a host society to expect its 'guests' (migrants) to conform to some extent to local ways and customs ('behaviours and attitudes explicitly or implicitly requested by the host society'),[127] especially as the fact that they voluntarily migrated created legitimate expectations about their willingness to acculturate. Thus, a parallel is drawn between immigrant integration and hospitality rules; as Julia Kristeva puts it, 'respect for immigrants should not erase the gratitude due to welcoming hosts'.[128] In this view, immigrants' willingness to publicize their Muslim identity through, for example, ostentatious veiling is seen as 'contrary to assimilation', for assimilation implies 'openness to the host society as manifested in private or public sociability, respect for [local] mores and customs, loyalty towards France'.[129] Non-European immigrants may practise their culture and religion, but must do so quietly and discreetly—not only out of respect for the *laïque* separation between public and private spheres (as neutralist republicans argue) but on the more 'communitarian' grounds of respect for the host culture, including its European (some even say Judeo-Christian) heritage.[130] A second, less openly communitarian argument, suggests not so much that immigrants who assert their particular identity abuse the laws of hospitality, but that they, more specifically, free ride on the benefits of living in a republican state. The 'republican pact' (*pacte républicain*) implies a reciprocal relationship between state and citizens: the state provides all, including immigrants, with the full rights of citizenship, in return for citizens' endorsement of the shared identity which underpins republican solidarity. Note that this goes beyond the 'laws of hospitality'-interpretation of the requirement of assimilation, as it applies to all citizens, not only immigrants. One oft-repeated tenet of national republicanism is that integration—the acquisition of 'standard' French cultural norms—required a considerable effort on the part of *patois*-speaking peasants from remote areas in the nineteenth century, just as it can today prove a painful acculturation for socially disadvantaged and excluded groups. Thus, citizenship implies not only the enjoyment of rights (notably the positive social and educational rights offered by the republic) but also the performance of duties and 'effort' on the part of those who aspire to it. National republicans often present the wearing of hijab and identity politics as symptomatic of the advent of a 'right-based' and 'me-first' society, and of the erosion of the virtuous politics of republican self-government, and blame advocates of 'the right to be different' for it.[131]

Divisive cultural affirmation

Claims for the 'right to be different' also contribute to the corruption of the republican ideal of the common good: contemporary ethnic politics are assimilated by national republicans to the destructive advancement of sectional interests by self-interested 'factions'. Thus, the 1994 Bayrou *circulaire*, which provided advice about religious signs to schools, firmly asserted:

The French idea of the nation and of the Republic . . . refuses to countenance any splintering of the nation into separate communities indifferent towards each other, concerned only with their own rules and laws, in a mere state of coexistence. The nation is not simply a collection of citizens holding individual rights. It is also a community with a shared destiny.

National republicans note that headscarves are one of the most visible symbols of the presumed cultural 'separateness' of Franco-Maghrebi communities. In a typical construction of 'identity politics', Islamic references are used as identity markers, community mobilizers, and legitimizing discourses for group leaders, and provide the foundations for claims for public recognition and collective rights.[132] Not surprisingly, the Muslim hijab has become the most effective and provocative emblem of this new 'communitarian politics'.[133] It is a *'voile identitaire'*, one that symbolizes the exclusive primacy of a separate Arab-Muslim identity over French identity. It also symbolizes the willingness of the Franco-Muslim community to be 'recognized as such, as a political community, on the model of American ethnic groups', in a way that would 'challenge the confusion between nationality and citizenship which is at the foundation of political legitimacy'.[134] Thus, many national republicans assert that the wearing of hijab is a political statement more than an authentic cultural and religious practice that should be respected as such: in contrast both to the 'modernizing' argument used by *laïciste* republicans, and the laws-of-hospitality argument referred to above, they do not believe that migrants—or their children—are the authentic bearers of a 'culture of origin'. By contrast to *laïcistes*, national republicans fear, not so much the archaic, authoritarian and misogynist tendencies of traditional Islam as the disruptive effects of the provocative 're-islamization' (in fact first-time Islamization) of alienated French youth. Taking their cue, notably, from Tribalat's work on the success of sociological assimilation into France, they assume that second-generation migrants are thoroughly 'Frenchified', that their knowledge of Islam is fragmentary and partial, and that their new Islamic identity is, as a result, a purely instrumental and artificial one, one self-consciously adopted as an ethnically divisive claim for recognition of difference as such. By proclaiming themselves 'Muslims', or 'Arabs', and by referring to indigenous French as 'white', '*Gaulois*', or '*Séfrans*',[135] they introduce categories of ethnic politics into the republican polity. National republicans fear a *repli communautaire*, whereby communities assert their distinctiveness and separateness, refuse to live by common rules and endorse common values, and attempt to use their 'artificial identity' to 'appropriate public spaces', in the revealing words of the High Council of Integration.[136] The assertion of the right of difference in schools is thus a symptom of the worrying 'Balkanization' of society. Demands to wear headscarves in schools, along with other *commmunautaire* requests for the recognition of Arab-Muslim difference, reveal 'strategies hostile to integration'[137] and should be resisted in the name of the republican model of integration.

Hostile provocation

The wearing of headscarves is also taken by many national republicans as a 'symbol of Islamic expansionism' and anti-Western fundamentalism.[138] While in 1989 and 1994, the headscarves affair could plausibly have been interpreted chiefly in terms of the balancing of freedom of conscience and the demands of secularism, in the aftermath of the World Trade Centre terrorist outrage and the rise of anti-Western feelings around the world, this very French (or Franco-Algerian) affair should be situated within the broader context of the rise of international Islamism.[139] The Stasi Report was clear on this point: 'the question is no longer freedom of conscience but public order', as Islamism is 'not only a religion but a global and comprehensive political project' which opposes 'France and its values'.[140] Significantly, politicians with notable multicultural sympathies, such as socialist Jack Lang, rallied round the ban in 2004, having (in their words) taken the measure of the dangers of 'Islamist penetration and propaganda'.[141] Thus, the rhetoric of 'republican defence'—the defence of the republic against its enemies successfully employed against the fascist Right in the past—was mobilized through a French version of the 'conflict of civilizations'. The worrying rise of violence, anti-social behaviour, and anti-Semitic provocations in deprived *banlieues* was associated with the hold that Arab-Muslim culture has over increasing numbers of French children, who turn to Islamic sources for their authoritative knowledge.[142] These radicalized youth show basic hatred for republican values, refuse to be French, see themselves as implicated into a global conflict pitting Israel and the West against Muslims worldwide, and are sometimes prone to use violence to pursue their destructive ends. It is those fanatical 'brothers' who are often at the forefront of local 'headscarves affairs', putting pressure on local authorities as a way of infiltrating and destabilizing the republican state.

Illusory refuge

National republicans do not deny that the turn towards Islamic ethnic politics is partly a response to the disappointment felt by many immigrants over the unmet promises of their social and economic integration within French society. As Taguieff has noted, the deeply rooted social crisis of the 1970s contributed both to the 'Lepenization'[143] of the white working class and the 'Islamization' of second-generation Arab immigrants.[144] Republicans do not deny that in a context of widespread 'discrimination and loss of sense of belonging to the republic' among immigrant youth, Islam can be seen as a 'refuge'.[145] The appeal to ethnicity and the demand for recognition of one's culture and identity may be interpreted as an assertion of basic dignity and 'compensation for social exclusion'.[146] Yet, national republicans further argue, the cultural response to the social crisis is a profoundly misguided one. First, it is counter-productive: it aggravates exclusion by locking immigrants into a cycle of social and economic disadvantage. Thus, the Stasi Report likened the wearing of hijab by young Muslim girls to a form of 'self-exclusion', which in effect made a number of jobs and positions inaccessible to them.[147] Second, the cultural response to the social crisis is illegitimate: social exclusion cannot be an 'excuse' for the most divisive and provocative behaviour of defiant young Muslims. As the Stasi Report put it, 'social oppression is no excuse for anti-social behaviour'. Social problems must be given social solutions, and the principles of national cultural solidarity reaffirmed. Integration may prove a difficult task in practice, but it is still an ideal worth striving for. 'The baseness of practices', the Stasi Report proclaimed, 'does not invalidate the greatness of principles.' Thus, the ban on headscarves in schools is a powerful symbol of the reassertion of the 'republican order' and the continued validity of the ideal model of integration, even—or we might say particularly—in a time of crisis.

Such, then, is the fully reconstructed argument for the hijab ban on the grounds of national republican solidarity. It is a highly contested line of argument, as the next chapter will demonstrate.

CHAPTER 9

Social Exclusion and the Critique
of Republican Nationalism

La République est une menteuse (the Republic is a liar)[1]
Our fraternity is real and their citizenship is fake.[2]

National republicans are right to interpret the public endorsement of an Islamic identity by young French Maghrebi as a profound challenge to the republican model of integration. What they fail to see is that this is an understandable response to the failure of this model. Defiant Islamization is a form of ethnic and social protest which denounces the 'lies' of the republic, in particular its broken promises of integration of all its members regardless of ethnic origin. Instead of the oppressive and ethnocentric politics of national integration, a more identity-sensitive and discrimination-centred approach to ethnic relations should be adopted. Or so, at least, is the line of reasoning of critics of national republicans, which I fully reconstruct in this chapter. The first section suggests that the demands of cultural integration are too burdensome on immigrants who already suffer from socio-economic exclusion. The second section mounts a more radical ideological critique and denounces the invisible yet ubiquitous ethnicization of social relations that is both tolerated and generated by the apparently 'ethnic-blind' discourse of integration. The third section shows that the assertion of Muslim identities in the public sphere can be symptomatic, either of defiant disaffiliation from the republic (the 'Islam of the excluded') or of a claim of integration without cultural assimilation (the 'Islam of the included'). The appropriate response in both cases is not the reassertion of an archaic and ethnocentric model of national integration but, rather, the implementation of tougher anti-discrimination policies and the positive recognition of ethno-cultural differences in the public sphere.

A Critique of Cultural Assimilation and National Integration

To urge immigrants to integrate into French common culture is problematic on two grounds. First, it gravely underestimates the moral costs of cultural assimilation, especially when the content of the presumed common culture is ambiguous and unspecified—as the first section will show. Second, it wrongly assumes that immigrants' obligations are unconditional: that their duty to integrate into French society is unrelated to how successfully they have been integrated and accepted by wider society—as the second section will argue.

Uncommon Culture, Assimilation, and Xenophobia

In a critique of the multiculturalist proposals of Will Kymlicka and Charles Taylor, Dominique Schnapper notes that 'the state is never really neutral. The common culture must impose itself upon particular cultures, but is this not the price to pay for all citizens fully to participate in national society?'[3] Yet to speak, as national republicans routinely do, of a 'common culture' is to beg many questions. What is this common culture, how common is it, and how is it acquired? The first problem is that of the content of the cultural norms and practices that immigrants are expected to endorse; and the second is that of the moral justification of immigrant acculturation. I address these two issues in turn.

Recall that the republican argument for a common culture—that it facilitates democratic communication and fosters the appropriate virtues among citizens—sees cultural affinity as an instrumental not an intrinsic good. As it is a means (to democratic communication and mutual commitment) instead of an end in itself (as more conservative versions of nationalism would have it), it only needs to be 'thick' enough to fulfil that end. As Schnapper cautiously puts it, democratic communication merely requires 'a common language, a certain culture, some common values'.[4] Yet these cautionary words are also vague words, and are symptomatic of the reluctance of national republicans to provide a clear normative account of the kind and level of cultural affinity required for political solidarity. Schnapper is in fact one of the few republicans to show awareness of the problem. Most writers tend to take sociological accounts of the historical efficiency of cultural assimilation as proof of its moral legitimacy, thus confusing descriptive and normative argument. In part, of course, this is because they inherited a wider belief in the intrinsic superiority of French 'high' culture, in the universalistic ambitions of the *Grande Nation*, and in the merits of cultural centralization—all beliefs central to French political culture, but not easily reconcilable with the republican instrumental argument for cultural solidarity. Yet if the point of cultivating a common culture is to reinforce solidaristic feelings between all citizens, it is crucial that the overarching national culture be sufficiently accessible and inclusive. The problem, critics point out, is that the much-invoked French common culture turns out to be worryingly uncommon, in two senses: it is elitist, not popular, and it is controversial, not consensual. First, then, the common culture praised by republicans is often blamed for its elitist, Parisian, and intellectual bias.[5] The ideal-type of the well-integrated immigrant is the highly educated, softly spoken, Parisian-accented member of the middle class, a pure and proud product of republican meritocracy—but a hard act to follow for disadvantaged children of working-class North African families. Such a highbrow conception of citizenship has the perverse effect of humiliating those deemed incapable of meeting its standards, and of hiding from view the real causes of the exclusion of the underclass.[6]

Second, the common culture implies cultivation of a 'shared historical memory', in Schnapper's terms.[7] The problem, of course, is that a national history that deliberately silences the viewpoints and experiences of minorities—regional, sexual, colonial[8]—and occludes the contribution of immigrants to national identity is unlikely to be easily shared, and therefore is an unsuitable candidate for an inclusive focus of patriotic allegiance. In fact, national republicanism fosters an uncritical patriotism which deliberately encourages selective amnesias about the sombre and conflict-ridden episodes of France's past.[9] The bloody and imperialist episodes of colonial repression, for example, were long erased from national memory, making it difficult for Maghrebi immigrants and their children to associate with the official view of France. Worse still, as the national (and colonial) myth is that the *grandeur* of France lay in it 'anthropophagic'[10] ability to assimilate foreigners, it is difficult for immigrants not to perceive the contemporary injunction to integrate as a repatriation of the colonial project into mainland France, as if what could not be achieved in French Algeria should be achieved with Algerians in France. The unreflected-upon colonial undertones of French national identity undoubtedly alienate migrants from former colonies. National republicans argue that a strong and confident national identity facilitates immigrant integration by providing a common focus of loyalty and pride, but they have not given sufficient thought to the *content* and *type* of national identity that would be adequate to the task. This uncertainty as to the actual contours of so-called common culture generates confusing and unspecified expectations as to which French norms immigrants are specifically required to endorse, especially at a time when the national community itself is becoming more and more heterogeneous and pluralist. Can one, for example, be a devout Muslim and a good French citizen?[11]

The second issue raised by the demand of integration is that of the moral acceptability of the acculturation of immigrants. By positing that there is no specificity of immigrant integration, in the sense that all citizens of France must in one way or another integrate into society— that is, acquire the national *habitus,* the social norms, that will allow them to be functioning citizens—republicans gravely underestimate the difficulty involved in *changing* cultures.[12] Acculturation is a fraught and difficult process: as Charles Taylor has insisted, the loss of one's cultural identity, whether it occurs through repression, forced invisibility, or as a side-effect of integration into another culture, can be a deep moral wound.[13] Thus, the acculturation of immigrants and their children raises ethical difficulties of a different order to those of the socialization of children born in France of French parents. Such difficulties are even more salient when they are accompanied by an implicit stigmatization of immigrant cultures. Because high moral stakes are associated with integration into the national culture, other cultures are comparatively devalued and despised: they are merely what immigrants must shed to be 'promoted' or 'elevated'[14] to Frenchness, to be 'as French as us as possible'.[15] The common culture becomes the culture of reference against which all are forced to define themselves. This assumption of cultural superiority is aggravated by some national republicans' tendency to conflate the universal values of freedom, reason, and equality with every particularity of French ways and customs, in an unthinking display of naïve ethnocentrism, and concomitantly to reduce foreign cultures to barbaric and illiberal practices.[16] Islam in particular tends to be portrayed as an alien civilization. Thus, the ideology of cultural assimilation implicitly or explicitly promotes a caricatured view of immigrants' culture, encourages xenophobia and public disapproval of foreign cultural practices *qua* foreign, and thus fails to show respect to their bearers. It falls short of the ideals and purposes of republican citizenship: as Patrick Simon has pointed out, citizenships has come to refer to 'the adoption of norms, values and practices which have everything to do with culture and very little with political citizenship'.[17]

To sum up, the national republican model of integration, for all its generous and inclusive rhetoric, can be shown in practice to rely on a highly contestable construal of French common culture, which turns out to be uncomfortably close to the unreflected-upon beliefs and prejudices of the historic majority. If immigrants are to be patriotic towards a national community that they genuinely feel is 'theirs'—as the theory of republican patriotism enjoins—such beliefs and prejudices cannot be the foundation of nation-wide solidarity.

Integration, Compliance, and Reciprocity

As we saw in Chapter 8, national republicans argue that today's immigrants should conform to the national model of integration because of its proven historical effectiveness and because it guarantees access to tangible opportunities and benefits. Yet, on both those grounds, the fairness of the injunction to integrate into French society can be called into question.

First, it can be argued that the historical model of integration that immigrants are expected to comply with is a highly inaccurate reconstruction, and to this extent cannot generate obligations of compliance. Thus, critics of the national republican interpretation of the French melting pot have pointed out that, historically, the integration of immigrants into French society was not so much a politico-cultural as a socio-economic process. National republicans have tended to exaggerate the role played by state-run national institutions such as schools and the military in the integration of immigrants. Immigrants participated in French society mainly through intermediary groups such as neighbourhood and community associations, religious groups, left-wing parties, and trade unions. Marxist historians and others have stressed that 'integration was conflict-ridden and inegalitarian and mainly achieved through the workplace'.[18] Immigrants were actively involved in the two chief mass organizations of twentieth-century French society—the Communist Party and the Catholic Church—two organizations which articulated internationalist and militant doctrines often deliberately at odds with the consensual national ideology of the official republic. Nor was French society free from discrimination on ethnic or racial grounds. Again, national republicans have tended to take republican rhetoric at face value and idealized the ethnicity-blind conception of national identity. Every wave of immigration—Polish, Italian, Portuguese—was historically met by xenophobic protest and racial violence,[19] and post-1945 immigration officials did not hesitate to resort to 'ethnic quotas' of immigrants to minimize racial tensions, in contravention of the official discourse about the irrelevance of cultural or racial origins. Overall, immigrant integration has been a slow, painful, and conflict-ridden process, whose success can only be assessed retrospectively.[20] Thus, today's immigrants are urged to comply with a retrospectively reconstructed, highly idealized model which bears only a tenuous relation with historical reality. If previous immigrants did not integrate into French society through unconditional allegiance to politico-cultural state institutions, why should today's immigrants?

The extent of immigrants' obligations can be brought into shaper focus, second, by looking at the balance sheet of integration today. Even assuming that the model of integration is a broadly accurate characterization of past trends (even, that is, if successful immigrant integration was the outcome of deliberate state policies), is it still valid today? National republicans, as we have seen, do accept that there is a profound crisis of integration in France. They recognize, first, that national institutions of integration such as schools are no longer able to 'forge the social bond' (to use an oft-quoted French expression) in a context of pluralization, de-nationalization, and globalization and, second, that the tangible benefits associated with national citizenship have thinned out considerably, especially for second-generation North African immigrants whose prospects of educational achievement, economic integration, and social mobility have been *reduced* over the last 20 years or so. For *banlieue* youth, the agents of socialization are more likely to be social workers, policemen, and local housing officials than the sainted universalist national institutions, a situation brought to the attention of the French public through a wave of suburban protest in the 1990s, and more recently in November 2005.[21] So economic, social, and political institutions are not as successful as they were in the past in integrating immigrants. Yet, if this is the case, is it fair to place the chief burden of integration on the shoulders of immigrants? Is it fair to ask immigrants to 'integrate themselves' (*s'intégrer*) if the state and wider society have failed to provide them with the means of integration? As Philippe Genestier states, 'identification with the symbols of national unity and compliance with [the host society's] lifestyles and behaviour can only be demanded if it is reciprocated with the protection of the law,... active participation in the political system and attendance to basic demands for equality and social mobility.'[22]

The question of whether socio-economic disadvantage and political exclusion provides, if not a justification, at least a mitigating circumstance for immigrant disaffection vis-à-vis the republic is at the heart of the disagreement between national republicans and their critics. National republicans imply that the current injustices suffered by immigrants and their children do not affect the validity of the principles of national integration. The Stasi Report, for example, accepted that the headscarves crisis was a symptom of the social and economic disaffection of second-generation immigrants, who suffered from chronic lack of opportunities and widespread ethnic discrimination. But, as we have seen, it also suggested that social injustice should not be a 'pretext' for refusing integration: 'the greatness of principles, it proclaimed somewhat grandly, is not invalidated by the baseness of practices'.[23] Yet this is precisely what critics challenge.[24] At least the Stasi Report could have insisted more strongly on the rectification of the 'baseness of practices':[25] it could have urged the state to take concrete measures to reduce the multiple forms of disadvantage suffered by immigrants, so as to restore a balance of rights and duties between them and the state. Instead, the bulk of the report lamented the 'communitarian drift' and 'refusal of integration' of immigrants, thus blaming the latter for the sorry state of integration in France. One way to phrase the critics' complaint is to draw a contrast between ideal and non-ideal theory. In an ideal world, where the institutions of republican integration function well and treat individuals justly, it may be fair to require immigrants to comply with the demands of cultural assimilation in return for the benefits of social inclusion: the model of integration is directly applicable on a reciprocal basis. By contrast, in non-ideal conditions, where state institutions fail to deliver on the promises of integration, it is unclear whether the disadvantaged have a duty of full compliance with the ideal model of integration.

To put it in perhaps more apposite republican language. If the republic is corrupt—if it fails to promote the common good in an inclusive and egalitarian way—how much virtuous conformity can it legitimately demand of its citizens? This demand, to be seen as fair, must be underpinned by reciprocity of entitlements and duties, lest it appears as an unconditional injunction, backed by the threat of repression. Critics have thus deplored the repressive turn of national republicanism, which 'demands conformity' while 'denying integration'.[26] It is true that national republicans have adopted an increasingly moralistic approach to the perceived failure of integration, attributing diverse phenomena characteristic of deprived *banlieues*—anti-social behaviour, urban violence, anti-Semitic attacks, disciplinary problems in schools, revival of Islamic practice, demands for respect of the 'right to difference'—to a 'corrupt' disposition on the part of ungrateful immigrants increasingly defaulting on their duties of civility and compliance. North African youth are routinely blamed for 'not being integrated'—a doubly ambiguous statement which on the one hand conflates *socio-economic* and *cultural* integration, and on the other confuses French society's *institutional* responsibility to integrate immigrants with immigrants' *personal* failure to integrate into society.[27] As a result, despite gesturing at necessary social and economic solutions to the crisis of integration, republicans' responses have chiefly been moralistic, culturalist, and repressive. They have focused on the symbolic re-sacralization of citizenship (revival of civic education, more restrictive nationality laws), the appeal to a stronger sense of French national identity, and the restoration of the 'republican order' (school discipline, tougher security laws, repressive control of the *banlieues*).[28] Against a backdrop of high levels of unemployment, ethnic discrimination, and social exclusion, the national republican suspicion of immigrant disloyalty and the injunction to virtuous citizenship and respect of *laïcité* are both unfair and ineffective: they add insult to injury. As Joël Roman has put it, 'the invention of a republican model [is] primarily intended to oppose the demands for recognition and justice of categories of population which are routinely suspected of lacking loyalty towards national institutions and values'.[29] In this context, the ban on Muslim headscarves can only be seen as a 'brutal and discriminatory measure which magnifies the injustices already suffered . . . by youth from disadvantaged backgrounds, notably those originating from post-colonial immigration'.[30]

A Critique of Republican Implicit Ethno-Nationalism

The previous section has taken the moral purpose of the doctrine of national integration seriously. It has taken at face value national republicans' hope that immigrants could be fully integrated into French society, but has shown that the means employed towards that end were unsuitable or illegitimate. Thus, for example, national republicans have not sufficiently specified the exact content of the common culture that immigrants are expected to endorse, and nor have they elucidated the broader economic and social conditions under which immigrants could legitimately be expected to comply with their demands. This section moves to a more radical form of critique, which reveals the implicit assumptions, unconscious motives, and unforeseen consequences of the discourse of integration. Unlike the more analytical and rational form of political *philosophy* deployed so far (a critique of national republicanism on its own terms), this section offers a more comprehensive critique of the *ideology* or *discourse* of integration (a critique of national republican-ism's own terms). This section brings out the ways in which the national republican discourse of integration, for all its militantly *ethnicity-blind* credentials, is in fact compatible with, and at times reliant on, an ethnic conception of the nation and growing ethnicization of social relations.

Thus, national republican discourse unwittingly dissimulates and hides from view the processes of ethnicization at work in French society Section 'The Invisibilization of Ethnicization' and—more seriously yet—generates or at least contributes to those very processes Section 'The Ubiquity of Ethnicization'. Ethnicization in national republican discourse is, paradoxically, both invisible and ubiquitous. This is a radical challenge to the theory of national integration because it shows national integration to be literally *impossible* for immigrants of non-French ethnic origin. In such circumstances, only a break with integration policy and move towards discrimination-centred policies can address the problems of immigrants Section 'From Integration to Discrimination-Centred Policies'.

The Invisibilization of Ethnicization

The first charge against the 'ethnicity-blind' doctrine of national integration is that it may be an attractive ideal but offers no guidelines about how to deal with the reality of the pervasive ethnicization of social relations in France. By banning all references to *race* in public discourse, official doctrine has been incapable of tackling *racism* in French society; by banning all references to ethnic *difference*, it has been blind to ethnic *discrimination*. Not only does the abolition of talk of race not mean the abolition of racism, but it also makes it much more difficult to confront. National republicans tend to put their faith into the inherently positive virtue of the iteration of abstract norms (such as the moral irrelevance of racial origins)[31] without realizing that in conditions where such norms are systematically violated (where discrimination on racial grounds is rife) such iteration is more likely to function as 'performative denial'—a wishful conflation of the claim that 'France should not be racist' with the claim that 'France is not racist'. While race would be a morally irrelevant category in a justly organized, ideal society, it has been made politically relevant by racists in the non-ideal society in which we live: to deny this is in effect to deprive oneself of the means effectively to combat racism and ethnic discrimination. National republicanism, then, is a philosophy without *praxis*, an ideal theory with little purchase in the non-ideal world in which we live. Worse still, 'the invisibilization [*occultation*] of ethnic and racist discriminations ends up *de facto* legitimizing them'.[32]

The invisibilization of ethnic discrimination is a perverse side-effect of the republican 'taboo of origins'. First, by reducing racism to an ideology rooted in scientifically inaccurate and morally unacceptable beliefs about biological (or cultural) difference and hierarchy, which must be combated philosophically,[33] national republicans underestimate the practical effects of racial stereotypes in society. These are much more diffuse and pernicious than the openly racist practices advocated by the Far Right, and include widespread practices of ethnic discrimination, whether direct or indirect, intentional or institutional. Thus, the abstract condemnation of racism does little to address the myriad ways in which racial prejudice underpins pernicious and diffuse practices of unfavourable treatment and is thus intimately connected to social inequality.[34] It does nothing, for example, to address the systematic—if hidden—discrimination suffered by Black or North African youth in the labour market, where employers too often justify their hiring (and firing) practices by referring to the tastes and preferences of their customers. Similarly, it does little to combat the pernicious 'institutional racism' of public administrations, such as the police, marred not necessarily by the racism of individual actors, but rather by a systematic and systemic discriminatory bias. In short, it misses the ways in which racism is not only a political ideology which loudly proclaims theses of racial inequality but also a discrete, pervasive social practice of discriminatory treatment of individuals implicitly perceived as different and inferior. This practice cannot be apprehended, let alone combated, within the naively colour-blind categories of national republican discourse, which focuses on combating openly racist speech rather than routine discriminatory practices, and rejects any form of ethnic statistical monitoring.

As a result, national republicans occlude the way in which the failings of integration may be caused by ethnic discrimination against immigrants. In the theory of national integration, inequalities between 'French' and 'immigrants' are either reduced to initial socio-economic disparities, or are blamed on immigrants' culture and attitudes, or else are explained by the inability of French institutions to inculcate a common culture. As we saw, some critics have pointed out, in response, that the common culture cherished by national republicans contains unreasonably elitist and residually ethnocentric components, which make it an unlikely focus for immigrants' loyalty. Yet the majority of critics focus, not on the official, high-brow culture dispensed by state institutions and intellectuals, but rather on the 'lived' culture and social experience of integration into French society. Integration, in other words, has a sociological as well as a cognitive dimension. Sociological studies have shown that the social practices of people of non-French origin largely converged towards a set of median variables interpreted as 'averagely French', ranging from language, marital status, intensity of religious practice, length of children's schooling, occupational specialization, affective link to another country, exposure to mainstream media, and willingness to enter into 'mixed' (i.e. inter-ethnic marriages).[35] Thus, second-generation immigrants do not suffer from a significant cultural handicap (most of them have been socialized in French schools and feel French); and their initial socio-economic handicap is not sufficient to account for the extent of their social exclusion. For example, the unemployment rate of youth of African or Maghrebi origin born in France is three times as high as those of European origin in the same generation, same neighbourhood, and with the same qualifications.[36] This, at the very least, should make for a prima facie presumption of unjust discrimination.[37] National republican ideology, because it repudiates all references to the social relevance of ethnicity, is conceptually incapable of accounting for the structural connection between economic disadvantage and ethnic discrimination. The successful integration of immigrants is closely dependent on overall prosperity and opportunities; in times of economic and social crisis, immigrants (and their children) are the first victims of, and the scapegoats for, large-scale unemployment, exclusion, and segregation.[38] The complex causes for the formation of this racial underclass are ignored by national republicans.[39]

Second, and paradoxically, the official 'taboo of origins' has a particu-larly perverse effect, that of giving free play to the unofficial and uncon-trolled use of ethnic categories by public agents and social actors.[40] Officially and publicly, the latter refer to universalist and colour-blind criteria of social analysis, either social (poverty, unemployment) or territorial (Zones of Priority Education, 'deprived *banlieue*', etc.). But privately and implicitly, such categories are increasingly decoded in ethnic terms by local officials, social workers, and teachers, who are faced with the (literally) 'unspeakable truth' that visible minorities tend to be disproportionately represented among socially and territorially disadvantaged groups. Thus, public officials covertly engage in the local management of ethnic diversity.[41] Housing authorities, for example, in their attempt to increase what is euphemistically called 'social mixity' in disadvantaged areas, routinely make use of unofficial quotas of immigrants in the granting of new homes.[42] School officials, likewise, attempt to control the (perceived) deleterious effects of the concen-tration of children of foreign origin in particular schools or classes, so as to prevent 'white flight'. Regardless of whether the rationale of such policies can be justified, it is clear that the lack of transparency and hypocritical '*double jeu*' in their implementation undermines their legitimacy. Worse still, the illicit and uncontrolled dissemination of ethnic categories reinforces the impression that 'Arabs' or 'Africans' are the causes of social problems and—further still—that this is somehow attributable to their 'culture'.

Unfortunately, the national republican discourse of integration does little to prevent or alter such popular misperceptions. Michèle Tribalat's ground-breaking study, which repudiated the traditional dichotomy between 'national' and 'foreigner' to take account of the effects of ethnic origins on immigrant integration, only considered how the latter may hamper individuals' capacity to adapt to French culture, and did not seriously contemplate the possibility that the failure of integration could be attributed to racism or discrimination on the part of the host society.[43] In the national republican paradigm, in sum, the only 'culture' that poses a problem of integration is that of minorities, never that of the majority. As French culture is presumed to be anti-racist, inclusive and universalist, the reality of anti-minority discrimination on ethnic grounds is hidden from view, and the popular perception that minorities are responsible for their failure to integrate is implicitly validated. One difference between national-republican and popular perceptions is that the former would emphasize the malleability of cultures (and therefore the possibility that all immigrants, whatever their origin, can eventually become French) while the latter would perceive differences between 'French' and 'immigrants' as essential, primordial, in a word, 'ethnic' (in the sense used by republicans). Yet, in the next section, I will suggest that national republican discourse itself is not as impermeable to logics of ethnicization as it claims to be. Critics have argued that the theory of national integration relies on the very assumptions it seeks to eschew (an ethnic conception of the nation and of immigrants) and as a result produces precisely what it claims to combat (exclusive and defensive *communautarismes*).

The Ubiquity of Ethnicization

I have already suggested that the French common culture invoked by national republicans is uncomfortably close to the historic majority's culture, and to that extent had an unavoidably particularist content.[44] Radical critics go further, and argue that any appeal to a shared identity such as nationality is per se exclusive: identity defines itself through what it defines itself against. The thought is not merely that theories of the nation are by definition theories of bounded communities, which of necessity specify criteria of membership and exclusion; it is, rather, that nations are communities that are essentially constructed in opposition to an imagined 'Other'. In the case of France, the figure of the North African Muslim has come to represent the Other of the republican citizen. North African immigrants are thus implicitly ethnicized—reduced to essential and unchangeable traits—while the content of Frenchness is similarly essentialized.

The exclusivist tendencies of the French republican theory of the nation have complex historical roots, which can only be alluded to here. The 1789 Revolution simultaneously invented the 'citizen' and the 'foreigner', and in the ensuing struggle to preserve the sovereignty and unity of the newly emancipated nation at war with the rest of Europe, the distinction took on an increasingly moralized dimension. Members of the nobility, suspected of contacts with European aristocracies, were seen as the 'foreigners within'; republican virtues were nationalized (one was expected to be a *'bon français'* before being an *'honnête homme'*), and *fraternité* between citizens was, at the height of the Terror, seen to depend on the exclusion and repression of foreigners, traitors, and aristocrats (terms routinely used as synonyms).[45] Thus, foreigners were not only outside the geographical and legal boundaries of the state, but they were also strangers within. The nationalization of political ethics, and the suspicion of foreigners that it implied, took place at an accelerated pace in the late nineteenth century, which witnessed what Gérard Noiriel has called 'the tyranny of the national' (with 'identity cards', for example, acting as markers of difference).[46] While republicans openly rejected biological theories of the French 'race', they endorsed an implicitly genealogical and substantialist understanding of national identity. By the end of the nineteenth century, national solidarity was promoted as a vehicle of social cohesion and a foil to domestic class conflict,[47] and was imbued with strongly organic and naturalistic dimensions. This was already apparent in Renan's celebrated definition of the nation. For all his efforts at demarcating the French 'daily plebiscite' from the German emphasis on racial or ethnic descent, his references to the nation as a 'spiritual principle' and transhistorical bond between generations traced the contours of a seemingly natural community of citizens.[48] Thus even republicans drew on the mystical and intangible dimensions of 'eternal Frenchness'. The recent Stasi Report did not refrain from appealing to the *'laïque instinct'* of the French people.[49] Such naturalistic language dissolves the distinction, cherished by republicans, between 'culture' and 'race', if the latter is seen, not as a set of objective (e.g. phenotypical) features pertaining to individuals, but as a series of subjective, inherited, or transmitted dispositions which make particular individuals believe that they naturally belong together. Thus, republican nation-building must be seen (in Étienne Balibar's terms) as a process of 'fictive ethnicization'.[50] The ethnicization of the nation—appeal to a seemingly eternal, unchanging and natural community—reinforces the solidarity between the 'established/insiders' by maintaining a clear boundary between them and the 'foreigners/outsiders'.

Thus, foreigners may acquire French nationality, but can they ever (to use the telling legal expression) be 'naturalized'? National republican discourse is permeated by this foundational ambiguity. Witness the ambiguous way in which those who are requested to integrate into the French nation are designated: the *immigrés*. The advantage of the term is to avoid both an ethnic designation ('Arab', 'African', etc.) and a narrowly legalistic one ('foreigner'). It is intended as a purely sociological and historical term, and stresses that immigration is the main source of the ethno-cultural diversity of French society. The problem is that the term has no fixed meaning, and ends up reproducing the implicitly ethnic categories of common sense.[51] It tends to be reserved for individuals of African or North African (instead of, say, European) origin. Yet most of those designated as *immigrés* have not (by contrast with their parents or even grandparents) migrated from anywhere; they are French nationals and have lived all their lives in France. Thus, the label of *immigré* 'marks one out definitely with the seal of exteriority according to a criterion which is more likely to be that of skin colour, facial features, or social conditions, than that of one's real origin'.[52] It is 'a category of social judgement... associated with practical and symbolic relationships of domination... or, more precisely, a category of ethnic judgement... which refers to a status of exclusion [*non-appartenance*] from the national community'.[53] Thus, naturalization—the acquisition of French nationality—does not make one less of an *immigré*, a 'foreigner within', one who is physically here but belongs elsewhere.[54] While the term *immigré* is avoided in the most careful academic writings, it appears in a number of official publications, and is often counterposed to that of *français*.[55] This is clearly a senseless categorization, which arbitrarily identifies an 'object group of integration' among the general population—the 'youth of immigrant origin' or 'young immigrants'—and stigmatizes them for their refusal or inability to 'become French'. Yet as Gérard Noiriel has put it, '"youth of immigrant origin" do not exist' (as a culturally distinct group).[56] If they have one shared attribute, it is social disadvantage and discrimination on ethnic grounds. The discourse of integration, by using an 'insidiously binary framework'[57] setting *francais* against *immigré*, ends up—not unlike the 'race relations' discourse it criticizes—objectifying ethnic categories, without however laying bare the social mechanisms of the production of ethnicity, notably discrimination by the host society. Instead, it designates *immigrés* through an essentialized view of their 'culture of origin'—a euphemism for ethnic essence. Intriguingly, it is precisely at the time when the so-called *immigrés* are becoming fully assimilated into French culture that irrational fears about their 'assimilability' are voiced.[58] A paradox often noted by theorists of identity and ethnicity is that perception of ethnic difference becomes most salient when the outsider group objectively appears more similar to insiders. Much anti-Semitism, for example, has been motivated by the fact that Jews were fully acculturated and therefore dangerously invisible. It is the Other *in our midst* that triggers fears about our own identity: the young, assimilated yet religious Muslim claiming equal access to French society, rather than the discrete, Mandarin-speaking Chinese shopkeepers whose lives are entirely structured around their community of origin. Thus, the discourse of integration is marred by a fundamental *aporia*: it highlights the very differences it claims to want to reduce and it 'blames individuals for the very exteriority to which it relegates them'.[59] The demand to integrate is an inherently 'paradoxical injunction': however integrated the *immigré*, by definition he can never be 'naturalized' and always remains perceived as the inassimilable Other.[60]

In contemporary France, the Algerian Muslim is the 'absolute foreigner', 'the most *immigré* of *immigrés*', to use Adbelmalek Sayad's phrase.[61] To understand the 'North African problem' of French society, of which the virulence of the hijab controversy is but one symptom, it is important to recall the forgotten memories of colonialism in general, and the French-Algerian connection in particular.[62] Recent historiography has begun to re-evaluate the centrality of the colonial project to French republican ideology and practice, and suggested that the deeply inegalitarian colonial system was not an anomaly, but rather, a laboratory for republican experiments. The doctrine of assimilation was a 'profoundly republican and profoundly colonial ideology',[63] which paradoxically institutionalized the ethnic distinction between 'citizen' and 'subject' (*indigène*). In the colonies, nationality and citizenship were kept distinct: the 'natives' were French nationals but were denied citizenship rights, and were subjected to a derogatory legal regime, the infamous Code de l'Indigénat.[64] The population of Algeria (which was officially a French *département*) was divided between 'Europeans' and 'Muslims', with the former enjoying all the rights of citizenship and the latter promised an elusive 'assimilation' if they proved sufficiently deserving. In practice, French citizenship was more accessible to a Pole moving to France than to a Muslim resident of French Algeria. The native Arab and Berber population—tellingly referred to by its religion—was thus irremediably ethnicized. Muslims were internal

Others whose assimilation into France was endlessly promised and infinitely delayed.[65] This 'lie', in the eyes of radical critics, is inherent to republican citizenship. Because the republic is imagined as a civilizing mission, a 'work in progress', it needs an uncivilized Other as continued proof of its validity. 'The republic has always needed its colonies, its slums and its *banlieues* as sites of exotic and radical otherness, in order to continue to believe in its universal mission.'[66] Thus, assimilation is paradoxically both an aspirational promise and a practical impossibility, at least on a large scale.[67]

The traumatic events of the Algerian war—including the brutal repression of the independentist movement by French authorities— meant that French colonial policy was not critically re-examined in the aftermath of decolonization. As a result, the relationship between France and its former colonial subjects (notably Algerian) replicated many of the ambiguities of the colonial setting.[68] In the 1960s, *immigrés* were chiefly treated as cheap and transient labour and not considered part of the nation. In the 1970s and 1980s, their permanent settlement in France coincided with a deep economic and social crisis which went to the heart of national identity and solidarity. In response to the National Front's claim that mass immigration undermined French identity, republicans reasserted the continued validity of the French *mission civilisatrice*: the promise of immigrants' full cultural assimilation was to be held up as proof of the continued *grandeur* of France. Yet the republican reaction had more in common with that of the racist party than met the eye: an a priori assumption that France suffered from a 'crisis of national identity' which immigrant-directed policies could remedy, a profound suspicion of cultural difference, and a tendency to separate out and essentialize both the national community ('*les français*') and the *immigrés*.[69] Furthermore, in the absence of official reconsideration of the legacy of colonialism in France, republican imaginary re-imported into the post-colonial world the mental structures of the colonial order. Thus, the *immigrés*, like their ancestors, the *français musulmans* of Algeria, are urged to assimilate and become invisible, with their non-compliance attributed to their suspect culture of origin and repressed as deviant and dangerous. Colonial imaginary permeates republican discourse: the re-establishment of the republican order in the *banlieues* is likened to a territorial conquest, riots, and violence are associated with 'ethnic conflict', delinquent youth of immigrant origin are referred to as *sauvageons* (uncivilized natives), and so forth. As in the colonies, therefore, the demand of assimilation is intimately connected both to the threat of repression and to the ethnicization of social problems.[70]

While national republican discourse eschews openly ethnic language, it has found a substitute in the form of Islam. As François Burgat has put it, 'from a French perspective, Islam is first and foremost the identity marker of the "Other's " culture and thus simply of the Other'.[71] The designate of Muslim has, over recent years, supplanted that of *immigré*, and been used indiscriminately to refer collectively to people of North African origin. In the post–Cold War (and post-9/11) world, as in the colonial era, Islam is implicitly imagined as the frontier of French citizenship.[72] Recall that the native Algerian population was referred to as *musulman*, that Islamic personal status was seen as the greatest obstacle to assimilation, and that there always was a Muslim exception to *laïcité*. Little wonder therefore that culturalist and orientalist theses about a 'clash of civilizations' (promoted in the United States by neo-conservatives such as Bernard Lewis and Samuel Huntington) pitting 'Western values' against an essentialized view of 'Muslim culture' have found favour in France (although the so-called clash is interpreted as a domestic rather than an international conflict).[73] Thus, even such an official report as the Stasi Report echoed widely exaggerated fears about the creeping Islamization of France, and did not refrain from carelessly associating Islam *in toto* with anti-Semitism, terrorism, crime, sexism, and sexual violence.[74] The hijab controversy therefore, gave a respectable gloss (the defence of *laïcité*, women's rights, and citizenship) to rather crude forms of Islamophobia.[75] This refers not to critique of Islam *qua* religious belief, but to hostility towards Muslims *qua* racialized group. In Europe generally, the headscarf also seems to have become the primary visual identifier as a target for hatred, with Muslim women being routinely abused and attacked.[76] The rise of Islamophobia is one symptom of the growing ethnicization of social relations in France. Critics have blamed the national republican discourse of integration— with its binary oppositions between *français* et *immigré*, *laïcité* and Islam, the civilized and the barbarians—for fostering what some have called 'republican racism'[77] or 'ethnonationalism'.[78]

No wonder therefore that the target group of republican ethno-nationalism—youth of North African origin—have over recent years increasingly turned away from the mirages of integration and defiantly reappropriated the ethnic categories to which they had been relegated. In a well-known process of 'reversal of stigma',[79] they increasingly refer to themselves as 'Arabs' or 'Muslims', by opposition to the 'Séfrans'[80] or 'Gaulois', and indulge in provocative identity statements, which testify to the rise of a defensive *communautarisme* on both sides. A recent manifesto highlighted the plight of the 'natives [*indigènes*] of the republic'—those young French nationals whose families migrated from former colonies and who find themselves (like their grandparents) openly discriminated against and implicitly relegated to second-class citizenship. In a country where race and colonialism have long been taboo, and where post-colonial critique remains marginal, the suggestion that France's integration policies amount to 'internal colonialism' predictably provoked an outcry.[81] It is time, however, that French republicans draw lessons from the increased polarization of the integration debate around the repressed categories of race and ethnicity. For it is obvious that if there is a specificity of the integration of citizens of North African origin, it is not that their culture is too distant from French culture, or their religion incompatible with the republic. It is, rather, that they still suffer from the painful heritage of colonial racism and discrimination. It is also obvious that national republican discourse has perversely contributed to the ethnicization of social relations that it vigorously denounces. It pits ethnicized *immigrés* against a no less ethnicized construal of Frenchness, making its proclaimed aim—integration—an endlessly receding prospect. Thus it would be wise, as Michel Wieviorka has urged, to 'give up on the notion of integration'[82] and address the real causes of immigrants' problems: widespread discrimination on ethnic grounds. The salience of ethnicity in French society must be taken seriously, not hypocritically denied.

From Integration to Discrimination-Centred Policies

According to their critics, national republicans have thus far misunderstood the nature of ethnicity in contemporary societies. They implicitly endorse an essentialist or 'primordialist' view of identity, according to which *immigrés* (notably) exhibit cultural dispositions acquired chiefly through in-group socialization.[83] Those dispositions pre-exist, and shape, their interaction with wider society, and may hinder their integration into French culture. Most contemporary accounts of ethnicity, however, have moved away from such primordialist assumptions and instead developed interactionist or constructivist approaches. In this view, ethnic identity does not pre-exist but is shaped by social interaction between groups, notably between majority and minorities.[84] Thus, it makes sense for critics to talk (as we did in the previous section) of dynamic processes of *ethnicization*, whereby social relations are interpreted as relations between groups socially defined by their real or presumed origin, and where such origin is a determining factor of action and interaction, marked by simultaneous alterization and hierarchization. The content and thickness of ethnicity is also shaped by the asymmetrically distributed power of recognition: what defines a minority is precisely its vulnerability to 'identity assignation' by the majority. Ethnicity has no objective 'hard core' but is fluid and contingent, as it is based on intersubjective identification—what we feel we are is partly defined by the gaze of others. Witness how the same ethnic groups are the object of different stereotypes in different Western societies. Bengladeshi, Maghrebi, or West Indian identities are experienced very differently in France and in Britain—to say nothing of how they are actually 'lived' in the countries where they originated. The historical relationship between home and host country, the complex and peculiar patterns of immigration, settlement, position in the labour market, and so forth, shapes the way in which immigrant communities are subjectively positioned. National republicans' unease about concepts of race and ethnicity has blinded them to the analysis of the real effects which follow from social belief in their existence.

Sociologists and anthropologists have identified different contexts for the emergence of ethnicity. First, ethnic minorities can come to existence through being discriminated against—'treated differentially'—because of the skin colour, general appearance, name—or any other 'illegitimate criterion'—of the individuals who are seen to compose it. Given the strong tradition of national integration in France, it has been noted that collective identities there have primarily emerged, not through prior awareness of ethnic distinctiveness, but through the experience of racism and exclusion.[85] Second, minorities are not merely passively acted upon, but actively seek to shape their sense of collective identity and self-esteem within those constraints. Their lack of recognition by the majority provokes feelings of hurt pride, defiant hostility, radical demarcation from the despised identities or, instead, demand for positive recognition of them. Thus, ethnicized individuals often reappropriate the negative identities they have been attributed with and turn them into positive ones—witness the Black power movement in 1960s America or today's reassertion of 'Muslim pride' by Asians and North Africans in Europe. Nor, third, is the contemporary ethnic revival exclusively or necessarily a response to stigmatization and misrecognition. Culturalist and less power-centered approaches have pointed out that cultural and ethnic identities are important resources of affective mobilization in an increasingly fragmented and globalized world. Ethnic consciousness is not incompatible with objective cultural integration into wider society: as a number of American sociologists have shown, second- and third-generation immigrants often (re)discover their ethnic roots, and seek to assert more complex hyphenated identities than would have been available to their parents, who struggled to assimilate into the host society.[86] Institutionalist approaches for their part point to the ways in which the political use of ethnic categories can be a strategic resource both for groups and for public officials.[87]

From the 1990s, the hitherto taboo themes of ethnicity and ethnic discrimination have been increasingly used in French debate, not only by critical sociologists[88] but also by prominent sociologists of the republic,[89] official bodies[90] as well as successive governments.[91] As a result, 'the question of the abandonment of the republican model of official blindness towards "origin" and "race" is now posed.'[92] A discrimination-focused approach breaks with the national republican theory of integration in a number of crucial ways. It substitutes a sociological analysis of actual practices in the real world for an abstract normativist model only suited to already just institutions.[93] It makes connections between racism and inequality which national republican discourse is conceptually unable to apprehend.[94] It shifts the blame for the difficulties of integration away from *immigrés* and towards the host society. It renames *immigrés* 'minorities', thereby acknowledging their status, not as indefinite outsiders or guests, but as bona fide citizens suffering from a particular kind of disadvantage. Finally, it recognizes that taking ethnic origin into account is the only way to tackle ethnic discrimination. As the 1998 Belorgey Report put it, 'one can only tackle what one names'.[95] In the late 1990s, French authorities for the first time recognized the extent of racial and ethnic discrimination in the country—a discursive break whose real effects should not be underestimated. Under the impetus of European legislation, France has set up an array of legal and administrative anti-discriminatory instruments, notably an expert board, telephone hotline, and local commissions to hear and advise plaintiffs.[96] Legislation and case law reversed the burden of proof (from employee to employer) in discrimination cases, and sought to track forms of indirect (non-intentional) discrimination.[97]

Such legislation was overdue: the normativist, abstract bias of French national republicanism, combined with its eschewal of any form of ethnic monitoring, meant that actual practices of discrimination on ethnic grounds long tended to be underestimated and left unchecked. However, in so far as anti-discrimination policies address situations where, in breach of the law, individuals are wrongly treated differentially, they nicely complement the republican emphasis on 'colour-blind' equality before the law.[98] In recent years, however, an even more serious challenge to the republican paradigm has emerged. This is the idea that individuals' ethnic origin may justify that they be treated differentially in law. For example, minority racial groups in the United States benefit from policies of affirmation action intended to rectify the past and present injustices they have suffered. In France, such policies have long been dismissed as misguided 'positive discrimination' and deemed—as we saw in Chapter 8—inegalitarian, anti-meritocratic, divisive, and above all morally dubious, as they give official recognition to the illegitimate attributes of race and ethnic identity. Recently, however, voices have been heard in France to defend *la discrimination positive*.[99] This evolution was facilitated by a prior broad reconsideration of the nature of republican equality. As welfare policies began to shift, against a background of declining resources, from universal, uniform state provision towards targeted support for disadvantaged groups, it became clear that equal (i.e. uniform) treatment might not necessarily imply treating individual as equals (i.e. fairly). In some cases, differential rights are the only way to equalize opportunities between differentially situated individuals.[100] While leftwing republicans feared—not unreasonably—that the substitution of *équité* (fairness) for traditional republican *égalité* might be used to undermine the *solidariste* ethos of the welfare state,[101] it soon appeared that 'justified discriminations' on ground of *équité* were sometimes the only way to correct the deeply inegalitarian effects of market competition, and as such fitted neatly with the interventionist tradition of the republican state.[102] Thus, a number of groups benefited from 'positive discrimination' policies: the disabled in the labour market, women in politics (the *parité* constitutional reform of 1996), civil service candidates in overseas French territories, disadvantaged children living in *Zones d'Education Prioritaire* (ZEP), and so forth.

The next step for advocates of ethnic positive discrimination was to suggest that such rectificatory policies inadequately addressed one central and specific source of disadvantage, discrimination on ethnic grounds.[103] The most developed forms of positive discrimination in France have a *territorial* basis: they provide special help to neighbourhoods which suffer from multiple socio-economic disadvantages.[104] Yet as ethnic minorities tend to be socially disadvantaged and spatially segregated, they are the *de facto* recipients of such policies. To target some policies specifically at ethnically defined minorities would put an end to official hypocrisy and introduce more transparency into public policy, while directly addressing a particularly serious and pervasive form of disadvantage.[105] Thus, a recent report advocated targeted measures to help members of 'visible minorities' (Maghrebi and Blacks) to get employment and training.[106] Already, government policies have offered local jobs to 'youth of immigrant origin', major companies and elite universities have announced their determination to 'diversify their recruitment' on ethnic grounds,[107] and recently a 'Muslim *préfet*'[108] was appointed by the Minister of the Interior.[109] Such (tentative and contested) acclimatization of affirmation action policies to the French context does not only aim at reversing the effects of discrimination on equality grounds but is also intended to reduce racism and ethno-centrism and to promote cultural and ethnic diversity at all levels of French society.[110] As minorized groups have reclaimed features of their despised identities (Arabic, Berber, Muslim, African, Caribbean), they want to be recognized for what they (feel they) are, not only judged on their ability to live up to a thickly defined ideal of cultural Frenchness. Thus, positive discrimination policies are also intended as a challenge to French ethno-nationalism, and as instruments of positive recognition of the value of minority cultures and celebration of cultural diversity itself. Multiculturalist thinkers argue that the monocultural republican model should give way to what Alain Touraine has called 'cultural democracy'.[111]

Muslim Headscarves, Social Protest, and the Redefinition of National Identity

National republicans are right to see the public endorsement of an Islamic identity by young French Maghrebi as a profound challenge to the republican model of integration. What they fail to see—critics point out—is that it is a response to the failure of this model. Defiant Islamization is a form of ethnic and social protest which denounces the 'lies' of the republic, or at least its broken promises of *solidarité* towards all its members regardless of ethnic origin. Muslim youth reject the republican injunction of cultural assimilation as unfair, and denounce the implicit ethno-nationalism of the republic as exclusive. They seek to transform their 'unchosen and imposed ethnicity' (*ethnicité subie*)—as the Arab, immigrant or Muslim Other of the French citizen—into a positive assertion of proud identity. Yet it would be a mistake to see the Muslim revival among the youth, of which the hijab is the most visible symbol, as necessarily expressing a strategy hostile to integration. We hinted above at the complex meanings of contemporary ethnicity, and it has been rightly noted that 'the ambivalence of identity claims is nowhere better illustrated than by in the practice of headscarves-wearing'.[112] Taking the risk of over-simplification, this section suggests that endorsement of a public Muslim identity can take two broad forms. To borrow Farhad Khosrokhavar's terms, the 'Islam of the excluded' expresses a defiant ethno-religious disaffiliation from the republic; whereas the 'Islam of the included' seeks to redefine the terms of immigrant integration into the republic. I analyse these two in turn.

Ethno-Religious Protest and Disaffiliation from the Republic

The Islamization of immigrant youth came out of the failure of the *Beur*[113] movement of the 1980s. The *Marche des Beurs* of 1983 mobilized *banlieue* youth around slogans of equal opportunities, anti-racism, human rights, an open conception of national identity and campaign for the exercise of political rights. It pointed to a pluralist, grass-roots, participatory, and egalitarian inflexion of the theory and practice of republican integration. The movement however soon fell victim to its own divisions, manipulation by political parties, disconnection between the *Beur* elite, and an increasingly disaffected grass-roots, the rise of the Far Right and defensive national republican reaction on the part of the political class.[114] The next generation of *banlieue* leaders—that of the *petits frères* (little brothers)—had lost faith in the possibility of integration through traditional republican channels (education, political rights, social mobility) as they found themselves socially and territorially relegated to increasingly stigmatized and ethnicized *banlieues*.[115] Feeling 'excluded from the universal' [of citizenship], they began to 'reclaim the particularism to which they were relegated'.[116] In the void left by absence of political leadership and erosion of local public services, Muslim associations moved in. They offered welfare, educational, and other social services to the local population and channelled the feelings of frustration and resentment of disaffected youth. Embrace of the Muslim faith gave young people the strength to bear their sense of despair and stay away from drugs, crime, and violence. It gave life to the ideals of solidarity and *fraternité* which the republic had inculcated but not practised,[117] endowed with spiritual meaning the ordinary acts of their life, and restored their sense of dignity and self-esteem: 'at the mosque, at least, I am someone'.[118] The life of those *'néo-communautaire'* young Muslims (to use Nancy Venel's expression[119]) revolves almost exclusively around religion: their comprehensively Islamic existence acts as a defiant testimony to their status of non-integration into mainstream French society.[120]

Yet the 'Islam of the excluded' does not amount only to an apolitical retreat into spiritual, personal, and local spheres of existence (the local mosque, the *quartier* Muslim association) but is also associated with demands for the recognition by French authorities of the collective, distinct needs of the Muslim community. *Néo-communautaire* Muslims are keen to emphasize their radical difference from the rest of society, and seek to carve out a distinct 'sacred place' for their 'community' within the secular public square.[121] Their participation in French political life does not extend beyond using political rights to ensure that the Muslim voice is heard, and lobbying for the granting of special community rights.[122] Such instrumental and community-centred approach to citizenship, which substitutes identity politics for the republican search for the common good, may coexist with deliberatively provocative statements of indifference or hostility towards national citizenship and the republic. As one of those young Muslims neatly put it, 'I am a practising Muslim and a non-practising French.'[123] *Néo-communautaire* Muslims do not identify with the national community, which they typically refer to as an external 'they' ('the French'), and nor do they associate with consensual patriotic events (such as the multi-ethnic national football team's victory in the World Cup of 1998). Feeling radically excluded from the society in which they live, they have invented for themselves a de-territorialized identity.[124] As we saw in Chapter 6, the new Islam is a globalized and de-ethnicized Islam, which can motivate radical disaffiliation from national citizenship in the name of allegiance to the *Umma* (global community of believers). The mental world of the *néo-communautaires*, influenced by such spontaneously global ideologies as Salafism,[125] has a dual—local and global—anchorage, completely bypassing the national reference so central to French republicanism. As French Muslims are urged to 'take sides' during every international crisis[126] and routinely made to feel they do not fully belong to the nation, it is small wonder that a growing number of them have come to interpret the world through the lenses of a worldwide 'clash of civilizations', a war between 'the West' and 'Islam', which they see as raging in countries such as Israel and Iraq. Occasionally, such feelings are successfully exploited by radical *jihadist* movements seeking to harness to their murderous and nihilist political agendas the 'negative religiosity'[127] of disaffiliated youth.[128] Yet such violent radicalization remains a minority phenomenon.[129] The 'Islam of the excluded' mainly expresses defiant disaffiliation from the republic, rather than violent hostility towards it.[130] It is, as Olivier Roy has suggested, more akin to youth rebellion and social protest than to the assault of an organized, anti-Western 'enemy within'.[131] It is, moreover, not the dominant form of Islamization of second-generation youth in France. In particular, it is rarely the Islam that hijab-wearing adolescents stand for. Paradoxically, while Muslim schoolgirls and students tend to be well integrated within French society, they are somehow blamed for the integration problems of their brothers. Their distinct challenge to the national republican ideology of integration comes from a stance not of radical exclusion but of a 'conflicts between [visions of] integration'.[132]

Integration without Assimilation

Thus, the second form of Islamization concerns well-integrated youth who, in defiance of the national republican injunction of cultural assimilation, claim the right to be French *and* Muslim in the French public sphere.[133] This is a phenomenon characteristic of second-generation immigrants. In contrast to their parents who were not fully integrated into French society *and* practised the Muslim religion as discreetly as they could, the young's visible and vocal Islam is—however paradoxical this may sound to national republicans—a sign of their *de facto* integration within French society.[134] It may in fact be as a symbol of integration that the hijab is frowned upon by sections of French society: 'one of the many meanings of the headscarf, and not the least of them, is undoubtedly: "we are here, we are from here, whether you like it or not".'[135] French-born Muslims do not see themselves as guests who should abide by the laws and mores of the country out of respect for hospitality rules: they are *bona fide* full members of a society that they want to make their own. As one interviewee explained, in a comment about public appearance that could also apply to the hijab:

> my father, he did not dare wear his *djellabah* when he went out because he did not want to shock the neighbours. He behaved like a guest. But me, when I want to wear my *djellabah* to go to the market, I don't think twice. Yet the neighbours, what do they think? That my father was integrated, and that I refuse to integrate! It's the opposite that's true. What do you want me to integrate into? It's my country, France![136]

Those young Muslims seek to escape the paralysing alternative, fostered by national republican discourse, between assimilation and multicultural separatism, and the accompanying suspicion of their inability to comply with its terms. Instead of the ethnicized terms of *immigré* or *Beur*, which suggest an uneasy, deficient, or transitional membership in French society, they proudly claim a coherent, albeit hyphenated, identity as 'Franco-Muslim'.[137] They define themselves as fully French and endorse the rights and duties of citizenship, notably political and social participation. They seek a voice in public debate, one which would empower them to speak as subjects, rather than being spoken of as a 'problem group'—as the Stasi Commission proceedings, for example, tended to do. Those *accommodateurs*, as Nancy Venel has called them (in contrast to the *néo-communautaires* described in the previous section) want to participate in French society.[138] Yet they want to do so, not as undifferentiated citizens, but as Muslims. They recognize the separation between the temporal and the spiritual spheres, do not seek to create a Muslim political party or change the laws of the state in an Islamic direction, but they want their faith openly to inform their social commitments. Thus, Dounia Bouzar is correct to liken them to those Christian Democrat reformists of the early twentieth century, who broke with the anti-modern, anti-republican strands of Roman Catholicism to engage in social and associational activism as *citoyens chrétiens*.[139] Many educated young French Muslims are influenced by the writings and speeches of reformist Muslim intellectuals such as Tariq Ramadan. The latter seeks to redefine the terms of citizenship for Muslims in Europe, encouraging them to become active citizens in their societies, take full advantage of the opportunities offered by liberal freedoms to religious minorities, and 'bear testimony' to their faith by being model but critical citizens, fighting for the improvement of social conditions for all. The *accommodateurs'* conception of citizenship has thus been said to be more 'civil' than 'civic', more centred on civil society than on the state and official institutions.[140] Over recent years, thousands of religiously inspired social associations have mushroomed in French *banlieues*, which provide a range of services to the local population—from education to sporting activities through to legal services—or militate in favour of human rights, charity, anti-racism, fair trade, environmental issues, all in the name of the 'social message' of Islam, but not necessarily through direct reference to the practice or teaching of religion itself.[141]

While young Muslims thus redefine the terms of their participation into French society, they also interrogate the content of French national identity, and can into question the thickly cultural content of the normative Frenchness appealed to by national republican intellectuals. Their protest thus illustrates the decomposition of the nation-state model of integration, which postulated a systemic fit between social, economic, and cultural spheres within bounded national communities. The injunction on immigrants to integrate culturally is all the more paradoxical because French society—like many national societies—is widely seen to be disintegrating under the pressures of globalization and cultural pluralism: it is as though immigrants (and their children) were asked to bear the burden of keeping alive an ideal of Frenchness on behalf of an insecure French society fearful of losing its national identity. Repudiating this 'hysterical'[142] demand, young Muslims increasingly seek to distinguish their claim to French citizenship from their embrace of the majority's way of life. Thus, what national republicans take to be a crisis in the integration of immigrants reveals itself to be a crisis of French ethno-nationalism.[143] The in-depth interviews with veiled Muslim students undertaken by French sociologists over the last few years[144] have all confirmed that contemporary Muslim identity in France has shaped itself principally in response to the crisis (and radicalization) of the traditional model of republican integration. They have all revealed, further, how the themes of social protest, reversal of stigma, citizenship as grass-roots involvement in local associations, demand for collective recognition, and a pluralistic national identity are at the heart of the new 'Muslim identity politics' of which the hijab has become the most visible emblem in France. Whether such new developments justify a shift towards the politics of identity and recognition will be considered in the next chapter, where I critically assess the claims both of national republicans and of their critics, with a view to articulate and defend an attractive critical republican alternative.

CHAPTER 10

Critical Republicanism, Civic Patriotism, and Social Integration

In Chapter 9, the official republican theory and practice of immigrant integration was found problematic on two grounds. On the one hand, it confuses the denial of the moral relevance of ethnicity with the denial of its social existence, and as a result inadvertently deprives itself of the means to tackle discriminatory practices. The application of difference-blind policies in conditions of widespread racial discrimination only contributes to the legitimization of ethnicized social relationships. On the other hand, official republicans' conception of nationality as shared common culture is inherently exclusive: it downplays the ethnic-like, particularist components of French culture and underestimates the moral costs of acculturation and assimilation for immigrants and their children. For critics, therefore, the politics of republican solidarity are oppressive of difference: they bring some citizens together only at the cost of excluding others. Now, this is the recognizable starting point of multiculturalist Anglo-American political philosophy, if by multiculturalism we mean the positive advocacy of policies of public recognition of group difference. Interestingly, however, few French commentators are self-declared normative multiculturalists, for two main reasons. The first is professional: most of the critics cited in Chapter 9 are sociologists or historians, not philosophers, and they are generally adverse to what they see as abstract and moralistic simplifications by political philosophers, or as unscientific and partisan interventions in political debate on the part of public intellectuals. The second reason is ideological: even critics of the French official republican model of integration implicitly share its fundamental principles, such as the refusal to see national society as composed of self-contained groups, suspicion vis-à-vis the political use of racial and ethnic statistics, emphasis on the nation as the relevant unit of citizenship, and the primacy of social and political over cultural and racial issues. Yet critics have so far failed to combine their philosophical intuitions with their sociological observations: if it is true that the ethnicization of social relations has gravely undermined the prospects of republican integration, what should be done about it? Is ethnically based positive discrimination an acceptably 'republican' response? And should the national model of integration be replaced with a post-national citizenship more open to cultural difference? Even the most astute critics have been frustratingly evasive in their constructive answers to such fundamental questions.[1]

It is such questions that I aim to address in this chapter. The critical republicanism I advocate endorses most of the critical sociological findings presented in Chapter 9, and it also seeks to contribute positive prescriptions towards the reform of the national republican model of integration. Its main targets are multiculturalist responses to the failure of this model, as expounded, notably, by Anglo-American commentators on France.[2] Multiculturalists can be said to advocate a two-pronged response: positive discrimination on racial grounds (as a way to rectify the socio-economic exclusion of children of immigrants) and the substitution of ethnic and religious identity politics for national integration (as a way to lessen their cultural oppression). In this chapter, I defend a critical republicanism which upholds the republican ideal of trans-ethnic solidarity and national integration, while addressing the legitimate concerns of multiculturalists. In particular, I argue that both official republicans and multiculturalists, in different ways, tolerate or aggravate the damaging ethnicization of social relations in France, and that only a radical strategy of *de-ethnicization* of the republic can fairly integrate members of minorities as equal citizens. De-ethnicization does not mean turning a blind eye on the pervasiveness of ethnicized norms and practices in contemporary society, or blaming minorities for unreasonably stressing their ethno-cultural particularism at the expense of national citizenship. Rather, de-ethnicization refers to the elimination of institutional, cultural, and social obstacles to the fair incorporation of minorities: the onus is on mainstream institutions radically to reform themselves in ways that promote the political and social participation of all. In this chapter, I illustrate this critical republican strategy of de-ethnicization in relation to two highly contested areas of controversy, in France and elsewhere: affirmative action policies in higher education, and the compatibility between national and Muslim identities. In both cases, I distinguish between the politics of recognition, which involves the positive validation of ethno-cultural difference, and the politics of non-domination, which involves the removal of cultural and socio-economic obstacles to minority incorporation. And, in both cases, I argue that the politics of non-domination, rather than those of recognition, help promote the republican ideals of solidarity and inclusion. Before I illustrate what the politics of non-domination as de-ethnicization would mean in practice, let me sketch out, in a first section, the broader theoretical perspective—both *critical* and *republican*—which underpins it.

Critical Republicanism: Strategies of De-Ethnicization

Republicans of all persuasions harbour legitimate doubts towards radical (or separationist) multiculturalism. In Iris Marion Young's terms, such multiculturalism demands 'institutions that promote reproduction of and respect for group difference',[3] and it advocates policies such as the attribution of rights of self-government to cultural and religious minorities, the setting up of separate educational systems, group representation with a right of veto on issues of concern to the group, transnational minority politics, and wide exemption rights from general laws on religious and ethnic grounds. The main problem with these policies is that, in many cases, it is not clear whether they are defended as ideals of coexistence between different groups, or as ideals of equal citizenship for all individuals. Republicanism, for its part, is primarily a theory of citizenship which asserts, first, that individuals have a fundamental interest in living in a polity which treats them as equal citizens, regardless of their particular loyalties, identities, and beliefs (the legal dimension of citizenship) and, second, that individuals also have a fundamental interest in being seen as equal citizens by others (the motivational dimension of citizenship). The politics of identity recognition advocated by radical multiculturalists bear a problematic relationship to the ideal of citizenship, on two grounds. First, the politics of recognition can be at best ineffective, and at worst counter-productive, as a policy of citizenship. This is the case when policy and discourse concentrate on the promotion of cultural difference at the expense of the reduction of socio-economic inequalities, and thus aggravates the real and felt separation between self-contained and exclusive cultural groups.[4] Thus, multicultural politics in Britain and the Netherlands have recently been blamed for fostering a permissive environment for the rise of extremist separatist religious movements among disaffected Muslim youth.[5] Geographic segregation, limited educational and work opportunities, and community isolation are mutually reinforcing, and compounded by a multiculturalist discourse which tends to essentialize differences, notably those between the 'Muslim community' and 'us' ('the West'). Official republicans too easily ignore the fact that Muslims may suffer from injustices of recognition as well as distribution (to use Nancy Fraser's useful distinction[6]), but they are right to point out that recognition of their Muslim identity, in and by itself, does nothing to improve their socio-economic opportunities.

Second, the politics of recognition are self-defeating at best, and unattractive at worst, as an ideal of republican citizenship. The very idea of the 'public recognition' of an identity is incoherent in the absence of a recognition-granting 'public'. Even such a radical advocate of the politics of identity as Young conceded that 'a heterogeneous public, however, is a public, where participants discuss together the issues before them and come to a decision according to principles of justice'.[7] Thus, the politics of recognition rely on the presence of a civil sphere where citizens recognize one another as worthy of equal respect and display attitudes of mutual trust and good will towards one another. Radical advocates of 'difference' implicitly take for granted what they explicitly want to deny, namely, that the recognition of cultural and ethnic difference presupposes the existence of feelings of trans-ethnic and trans-cultural solidarity.[8] Such republican feelings are in fact essential to the stability and health of the republic. For republican citizenship is (reasonably) demanding: it requires that people willingly share in practices of social cooperation (such as wealth distribution), be able to make compromises for the sake of the common good, and be ready to defend the institutions of their common liberty. For people to discharge their duties as citizens, they must feel that their fates are, at least partially, bound together. In this respect, patriotism (of the right sort) can, on the republican account, have an instrumental value, in so far as it underpins practices of solidarity (or fraternity, to use old republican language). The politics of recognition, when they unduly stress group difference, and see the wider civic polity merely as a framework for peaceful coexistence, undermine republican patriotism. This is not to say that republican patriotism cannot accommodate extensive cultural and ethnic diversity. Solidarity should have a primarily political, social, and economic foundation: it motivates participation in a community of equal citizens. This means, in particular, that republican solidarity should not have a narrowly 'ethnic' basis—if by 'ethnic' we mean here a set of traits and features that are inherited and cannot be transmitted and acquired. The point and purpose of republican patriotism is to frame a 'civil sphere',[9] an inclusive and impartial sphere within which all resident individuals, regardless of their particular origins and identities, can be included as equal citizens.

In sum, the substantive ideals pursued by official republicans are persuasive and attractive. However, the strategic principles they defend are problematic. To put it simply, they fail to recognize that existing public spheres do not live up to this attractive ideal of the civil sphere. They assume that existing bonds of solidarity can be extended to historically excluded groups without having to question the particular ways through which the civil sphere took shape. Yet, as the most acute observers put it, all 'civic' nations are rooted in a particular 'ethnic' experience. As a result, civic competences and virtues have historically been associated with the traits of dominant groups (white, male, middle class, Christian, Parisian, and so forth) and, as we saw in Chapter 3, secularism in France took the unmistakable form of 'Catho-*laïcité*'. This is what leads radical multiculturalists to contend that the politics of republican solidarity are inherently exclusive. There are, however, two ways to interpret the multiculturalist contention. In a strong interpretation, republican ideals of impartiality, inclusiveness, and solidarity are ideological myths dissimulating and legitimizing the domination of majority groups. In a weak interpretation, the fact that republican ideals have been imperfectly realized does not mean that they are incoherent or illusionary, and that they cannot be used by minorities to challenge the status quo. The difficulty is that the historical ethnicization of the public sphere, as we might call it, still weighs heavily on the present, and creates often intangible obstacles to the fair incorporation of minorities. This, it seems to me, is the most powerful insight offered by multiculturalists, and the most powerful challenge to difference-blind republican politics. The incorporation of stigmatized ethnic groups into the civil sphere can only take place through the de-ethnicization of the actually existing civil sphere and the de-stigmatization of the traits associated with minority groups. Thus, *pace* official republicans, closing the gap between the ideal civil sphere and the pervasive ethnicization both of majority and minority identities will involve taking issues of cultural and ethnic identity seriously—and critically. In the real world in which we live, 'benign neglect' of ethnicity is just not a (fair) option.[10]

Thus, official republicans and multiculturalists suffer from symmetrical failings. Both of them, paradoxically, can be shown to aggravate the divisive ethnicization of social relations, either by denying or by reifying them. Official republicans identify an attractive ideal, that of inclusive trans-ethnic solidarity. Yet by assuming that this ideal is already embodied in existing institutions, they end up tolerating, and sometimes aggravating, the implicit ethno-nationalism which in practice permeates them, and the ethnicization of minority groups which accompanies it. In this respect, it is fair to say, as multiculturalists do, that the French public philosophy of 'indifference to differences' has in practice contributed to the conflict-ridden ethnicization of social relations. Unfortunately, the politics of recognition that radical multiculturalists advocate would merely exacerbate this problem. The politics of recognition risk merely setting groups against groups, unless they are motivated by a wider sense of trans-group solidarity, one that can only be underpinned by the ideals of the civil sphere. I want to go further, and suggest that only a *critical republicanism* can successfully reconcile the claims of solidarity and inclusion in the real world. The real world I have in mind is contemporary French society but my prescriptions in this chapter, like those of Chapters 4 and 7, are general enough to apply to other relevantly similar societies, notably Western European nation-states in relation to their treatment of immigrant groups. The critical republican theory of solidarity draws on, and combines, two chief sources of inspiration: the post-Marxist tradition of critical theory, and the republican tradition of the primacy of politics.

From the post-Marxist tradition of critical theory, I draw the insight that political philosophy, if it is going to make a practical difference, should concern itself with the effective critique of existing structures of domination and social norms, not only with the design of ideal institutions and laws; and yet it should not (as postmodernists do) give up on the ideal of domination-free communication and solidarity.[11] It should seek to combine 'a theory of injustice with a theory of justice'.[12] From the republican tradition of citizenship, I draw the insight that it is through actual participation in common life that citizens experience and give substance to republican citizenship and solidarity: participation (political, social, and economic) is the best way to secure the shared republican good of non-domination.[13] Selectively interpreted and combined, these two traditions suggest a progressive way out of the impasses of multicultural theory and practice, by pointing to a fair, practicable, yet far-reaching strategy of de-ethnicization of politics, which is central to my critical republicanism. Let me say a little more about this critical republican strategy.

First, it is a strategy, in the sense that it aims to offer an integrated approach to the ends and means of social reform. Thus, critical theorists charge normative theorists, such as Anglo-American liberal philosophers and French official republicans, for reasoning as if just institutions were already in place, and for not placing the question of social change and transformation at the heart of their theory.[14] The problem is not—as conservative communitarians and radical postmodernists have it—that abstract normative reasoning per se is illegitimate: it is a useful and indispensable way to articulate and justify our deep moral convictions. But, critical theorists suggest, normative philosophers too often fail to interrogate the relationship between ideal principles and the facts they are expected to guide. We saw in Chapter 9, for example, that French official republicans confuse colour-blindness as a means and as an end of policy. While colour-blindness might be the ideal morality for an ideal society, it is not necessarily the appropriate response to racial discrimination in existing colour-coded societies. Thus, colour-conscious policies might well be the best way to de-racialize society in the long term.[15] Such judgements are consequentialist in nature and depend on assessment of relevant social facts, which are likely to differ from society to society. The preferential treatment of racially defined individuals might be the only way to reverse situations of long-standing structural, institutionalized discrimination (such as that affecting Afro-Americans in the United States). On the other hand, it might have perverse side effects in other contexts, such as Europe, where it might neither improve the socio-economic position of minority members nor—importantly for our purposes here—alter the social norms (prejudices, stigmatization) that underpinned and maintained their exclusion in the first place.

Second, and connectedly, critical republicans take as their starting point existing forms of social interdependence, and the norms and beliefs which sustain them. Not all of the latter will be conducive to relationships of solidarity and justice between citizens; some will positively undermine them. This is overlooked by many liberal theorists of justice who tend to take people's existing identities or conceptions of the good as constitutive of the normal pluralism of social life: in the words of Brian Barry, the liberal state should be 'an instrument for satisfying the wants that men happen to have rather than a means of making good men'.[16] Critical theorists, by contrast, are concerned about the unfair genesis of, and the unjust consequences that may follow from, some of the social norms and wants that 'men happen to have'. For example, our discussion of sexist socialization in Chapter 7 alluded to the presence of illegitimate 'adaptive preferences' (preferences adaptive to restrictive or oppressive social relationships) on the part of members of dominated groups. Our discussion of religious domination in Chapter 4 revealed how seemingly secular institutions embodied conventional and invisible Christian norms, with adverse effects on the fair treatment of members of minority religions. And Chapter 9 suggested that the contemporary ethnicization of Muslim identity may be, at least in part, a defiant response to the exclusivist ethnicization of norms of Frenchness (and, more broadly, of Western culture). Such experiences of restrictive socialization, domination, stigmatization, mutual mistrust, reversal of stigma, misrecognition, indirect discrimination, and the like concern the beliefs that people hold, and the power relationships within which they are inscribed, as much as the laws and institutions that govern their interactions. When such beliefs and attitudes are prevalent, they are corrosive of the civic bond: a society in which citizens harbour feelings of intense mistrust towards others cannot be a republic. Recall that citizenship, on the republican account, refers to both a legal status and a psychological, intersubjective disposition: citizens feel themselves to be equal, to be sharing in the same fate, they do not think that other citizens are radical 'Others', people with ways of life, cultures, that they want nothing to do with. A republic cannot tolerate (or let develop) the perception of a 'conflict of civilizations' or a 'war between cultures' in its midst; if it does, it has become corrupt. So the ethnicization of group difference is symptomatic of a breakdown of republican social equality. Social equality obtains when disparities in life experiences are not so large that citizens do not see one another as equals.[17] The thought is that in a society where social equality obtains, perceptions of cultural and ethnic difference do not become damagingly salient. In a critical republican view, one privileged way to foster social equality is through the creation of incentives to participation in social and public life, notably in socially and racially mixed neighbourhoods. Critical republicanism is a 'territorial republicanism', which relies on urban de-segregation for the promotion of social mixity and equal opportunity.[18]

Third, and connectedly, critical republicanism does not insulate the cultural politics of recognition and identity from issues of social injustice. Current debates about multiculturalism tend to underestimate the fact that the politicization of cultural, ethnic, and religious difference becomes particularly salient when, as is often the case, difference is bound up and overlaps with socio-economic inequalities and injustices. Note that this is different from saying (with traditional Marxists) that identity-related conflict is merely expressive of underlying socio-economic trends, nor is it (with liberal social democrats such as Barry) to blame New Left identity politics for having functioned as an ideological distraction from the Old Left's traditional concern for social justice. The claim is, rather, that in many contemporary cases of cultural conflict, misrecognition (a consequence of the ethnic partiality of the actual civil sphere) tends to become politicized when it is experienced as an 'insult added to injury': when, that is, it compounds and exacerbates existing socio-economic exclusion and relegation. Defiant Muslim politics in France must be explained as a response to a multifaceted experience of 'social contempt'[19] felt by Muslims, not exclusively or necessarily *qua* religious believers, but *qua* presumed members of a marginalized working class and racial (post-colonial) underclass. The excessive culturalization of politics and ethnicization of social conflict has tended to obscure this essential fact. This does not mean to say that the specific harm caused by misrecognition should not be addressed, but it means that purely symbolic recognition would fail to reveal the structural causes of domination and inequality. These are rooted in institutions and processes which, while openly universalist and meritocratic, in practice exhibit intangible obstacles to the fair integration of members of disadvantaged minorities. Thus, critical republicanism concurs with the powerful thought underlying the republican vision of the founders of the Third Republic: that it is not so much lack of virtue but, rather, lack of justice which leads to the corruption of the republic and attendant problems of factionalism and egoism. The provision of fair system of equal opportunities, Durkheim and other insisted, promotes feelings of solidarity between citizens by protecting the most vulnerable from the domination of the powerful and fostering mutual trust in the justice of basic institutions.[20]

In addition to the promotion of 'really equal' opportunities,[21] one central way in which republics pursue solidarity is through political inclusion and 'voice' strategies—already discussed in Chapter 7. As many French critical theorists have pointed out, struggles for recognition in contemporary society are best interpreted as struggles for voice. Those whose particular experience and identity are despised and stigmatized are typically those who are, in philosopher Jacques Rancière's terms, *sans-voix* (voiceless): they are those who are spoken about and spoken for, but who cannot speak for themselves.[22] A strategy of political inclusion of 'voiceless' individuals and groups furthers central republican ideals. First, it lessens their sense of misrecognition without necessarily validating and reinforcing their 'authentic' group identity. In a republican view, participation has a transformative effect, whereby citizens' interests and perspectives are altered and enlarged through their confrontation with others'. Second, it reduces the perceived ethnic partiality of the public sphere, by pluralizing the range of possible identities that can be publicly endorsed by citizens as citizens. Thus, through participation, minority citizens resist domination by others: they resist being reduced to an essentialized identity on the one hand, and being subjected to an ethnicized conception of civic identity on the other. Critical republicanism shares with theories of recognition an emphasis on the intersubjectively and agonistically constructed nature of identity, but sees politics as a way of resisting, rather than recognizing, particularist identification.[23] Non-domination, instead of recognition, is the objective of republican participation.

Thus, critical republicanism reconstructs struggles for recognition as struggles against domination and for fair incorporation into the republic. A legitimate Muslim demand, for example, is to be integrated into French society on fair terms, and to have Muslim identity accepted as one of the normal ways of being French. Leaving aside the accommodation of specifically *religious* needs mandated by the principle of secular impartiality (discussed in Chapter 4), this mostly requires the de-ethnicization and 'mainstreaming' of Muslim identity. Muslims should not be seen as the 'Others' that 'we' have to integrate, as a special and different group bearer of an alien civilization—an alterization encouraged, in different ways, by both multiculturalists and official republicans. In fact, sociological studies in France show that Muslims, and citizens of immigrant origin generally, are '*des Français comme les autres*' (to borrow the title of a recent study), and there is growing evidence that Muslims are progressively integrating into European societies.[24] The (undeniable) radicalization of a minority of young alienated Muslims can only be worsened by playing into the Islamist rhetoric of a 'clash of civilizations', which over-emphasizes the role of beliefs and religion as major causal factors of international and domestic conflict.[25] Yet, if there is a specificity of Muslim integration, it is twofold. First, Muslims still disproportionately suffer from socio-economic disadvantage, a reflection of the fact that most came from working class immigrant backgrounds, have been relegated to poor urban neighbourhoods and have suffered from racial discrimination in the labour market. However, there is little evidence that *religious* discrimination is the chief cause of Muslims' social exclusion. On this ground alone, it is absurd to contemplate schemes of positive discrimination for Muslims (as anticipated in the appointment by the then Minister of the Interior Sarkozy of a 'Muslim prefect' in 2004):[26] such schemes would not address the real cause of Muslims' problems, while contributing to their collective ethnicization. In the next section of this chapter, I analyse the forms of affirmative action that a critical republican theory of social integration would support.

The second specificity of Muslim integration in Europe is that they live in societies where existing institutions and norms, while seemingly neutral, have historically been framed by non-Muslims, in ways that still affect their incorporation on fair terms. In Chapter 4, I showed how Western secularism was in practice biased towards Christian religions, and I suggested practical ways to 'neutralize' the public sphere so as to promote its impartiality. In the last section of this chapter, I turn to the more cultural (as opposed to religious) dimensions of the public sphere, where the secular solution of separation or 'neutralization' is not an available option. I look at how processes of publicization of Muslim identity (such as the wearing of the hijab in state schools) contribute to the pluralization of French national identity, and to the mainstreaming of Muslim identity. Thus, both in the socio-economic and the cultural spheres, critical republican strategies of incorporation of Muslim citizens are strategies of de-ethnicization of existing institutions and norms. Instead of asking that Muslims or people of immigrant origin make greater efforts to integrate (as official republicans do), or that their special identity be collectively recognized and positively validated (as multiculturalists do), critical republicans ask that existing institutions remove obstacles to their participation as equal citizens. It is only through actual participation (in schools, in universities, in neighbourhoods, in politics, in the labour market, in the media) that Muslims and other members of disadvantaged minorities can resist domination—in this case their pernicious ethnicization and alterization by others.

Republican Affirmative Action and Social Integration

We saw in Chapters 8 and 9 that official republicans and multiculturalists disagree about the legitimacy of affirmative action on ethnic grounds. While official republicans argue that only socio-economic disadvantage can be a justifiable ground for exemptions from the principle of equality before the law, multiculturalists advocate preferential treatment for members of racially or religiously defined groups. The affirmative action debate is highly relevant to critical republicanism, for two reasons. First, it is centrally concerned with increasing the participation of ethnic minority members in mainstream society, and to this extent furthers republican ideals of egalitarian social integration. Second, it directly engages with the *strategic* question of how to integrate the ends and means of social policy; in this particular case, how best to pursue colour-blind ideals of equality and solidarity in 'non-ideal', colour-conscious societies. In this section, I defend the basic official republican proposition that focuses on socio-economic disadvantage, rather than ethnic origin, is an effective way to promote both equality of opportunity and social equality. Yet I also argue that official republicans underestimate the extent to which existing institutions exhibit structural obstacles to the fair incorporation of disadvantaged groups. The removal of these obstacles will (directly and indirectly) facilitate the integration of ethnic minority members into French society, without requiring that they be preferentially promoted.

To illustrate what a critical republican strategy would mean in practice, and as a fitting counterpoint to the implicit background to affirmative action debates in Anglo-American political philosophy (the US educational system), I discuss the best-known example of affirmative action in higher education in France, the '*ZEP* conventions' at the Paris Institut d'Études Politiques (also known as Sciences Po).[27] For generations, Sciences Po has trained young people to fill the upper echelons of France's civil service, business world, and political establishment. Like other publicly financed yet largely autonomous *grandes écoles* (elite schools), Sciences Po has prided itself on its selective yet meritocratic recruitment procedure, based on a gruelling *concours* (universal competitive entrance exams). In practice, however, Sciences Po's student body has displayed a striking (and increasing) social homogeneity, with more than 80 per cent coming from the upper and upper middle classes, most of them from white, urban, professional backgrounds. The *grandes écoles* taken together have become more socially elitist over time (the proportion of students from working-class backgrounds fell from 29 per cent in the 1950s to 9 per cent in 1995),[28] a shocking indictment of republican meritocracy and social mobility. Thus, in 2001, Sciences Po, in an attempt to shake off its socially exclusive image, created a special admission track for the students of seven secondary schools located in economically disadvantaged areas (*ZEPs*). These students are exempted from the *concours*, preselected by their schools on the basis of two written papers, and then undergo a 45-minute oral exam by a Sciences Po jury. The experiment was considered a success, both in terms of recruitment and results. Over half of *ZEP* students came from working-class backgrounds and nearly all of them came from immigrant backgrounds. Their academic performance once at Sciences Po was comparable to that of their peers, and their success proved inspirational for similarly situated students. The *ZEP* conventions have since been extended to a number of other *ZEP* schools and *grandes écoles*.

Practical success did not prevent political controversy, however. Was Sciences Po-style affirmative action compatible with republican principles? The onus was on its defenders to show that the programme is essentially different from US-style positive discrimination, which in France is widely believed to be based on explicit quotas for racial minorities. In my view, the Sciences Po programme has a number of attractive features. In line with the republican tradition of the *boursier* ('scholarship boy'), it attempts to diversify and democratize recruitment without breaching meritocratic principles. It builds on well-established republican policies of urban development which tackle the territorial concentration of disadvantage, thus promoting both social mixity and mobility. And as ethnic origin per se plays no part in the identification of its beneficiaries, the programme avoids the perverse stigmatization effects associated with positive discrimination on morally arbitrary grounds such as racial origin. If (as it does) it disproportionally benefits children of immigrant families, it does so coincidentally, as a result of the fact that ethnic minorities disproportionally suffer from socio-economic disadvantage. To this extent, the programme works as a republican 'functional equivalent' to colour-conscious positive discrimination policies: it promotes members of ethnic minorities but only as a side-effect of colour-blind social policies.[29] It is also better suited to the French situation where studies show that while ethnic discrimination is endemic in the labour market, schools and public services have been relatively open to ethnic minorities.[30] There would therefore appear to be little justification for introducing reverse discrimination on racial grounds in higher education.

Yet while the Sciences Po programme is far preferable to colour-conscious positive discrimination, it remains, from a critical republican perspective, deeply ambiguous and radically deficient. It is deeply ambiguous because, in so far as it alludes to the ethnic (or religious) origin of its beneficiaries, it does so in connection with the equivocal notion of 'cultural diversity', not with that of equality and anti-discrimination. Thus, the programme itself is titled '*L'excellence dans la diversité*'; it applauds the recruitment of candidates with 'different forms of cultures and conceptions of the world'; and it points out that the selection process to Sciences Po has never been uniform, with exemptions from the *concours* already granted to foreign students.[31] These unfortunate analogies implicitly validate common perceptions to the effect that *ZEP* students (like foreign students) are less able to succeed through the normal selection procedures because of their 'culture'.[32] Thus, they are ethnicized in the worst possible way: not as members of potentially disadvantaged and discriminated against groups, but as bearers of purported cultural difference (which can be turned into an asset for diversity-conscious businesses and elite schools). From a critical republican perspective, the Sciences Po rhetoric of 'diversity' combines the worst of official republicanism and multiculturalism: it perpetuates the former's denial of the link between social disadvantage and ethnic discrimination, while gesturing at the latter's equivocal notion of the recognition of cultural difference. Little wonder that the programme has reinforced precisely what it purported to avoid: the implicit alterization of *ZEP* students as 'visible minorities'.

Thus, the Sciences Po programme is radically deficient: it falls short of a thorough democratization and de-ethnicization of the selection process in elite schools. The provision of a separate admission track for disadvantaged students only perpetuates perceptions of their difference from other students and validates the legitimacy of the normal admission procedure. What is missing is a critical examination of the fairness of existing procedures, and notably of the social and cultural bias inherent in the *concours*.[33] For in addition to traditional school subjects such as history, applicants are tested on their 'general knowledge' (*culture générale*) and their mastery of foreign languages, two skills which cannot be fully acquired in schools, and which reward what Pierre Bourdieu called the 'cultural capital' of the upper and upper middle classes.[34] The *concours* indirectly discriminates against applicants from working-class and immigrant background, regardless of their previous educational achievements. And as studies have shown that ethnic origin is not an independent predictor of educational achievement in French schools (pupils of immigrant origin do not do less well than French-born pupils *from a similar class background*),[35] the rectification of the class bias inherent in the admission procedure, of the *grandes écoles* should suffice to de-ethnicize it too. There is no need to break with the meritocratic, colour-blind republican ideal of equal opportunity and to promote an ideologically suspect 'diversity' in the *grandes écoles*.

However, it can be doubted whether reforming the *concours* would be sufficient to open up the *grandes écoles*. The problem is that well-off students from the most reputed urban secondary schools are inculcated with the confidence and ability to sit for an otherwise daunting two-day-long written and oral examination. In this respect, one virtue of the *ZEP* conventions is to 'reach out' to socially and ethnically segregated secondary schools where students' expectations and ambition are not necessarily commensurate with their potential and results. Yet, clearly, the conventions programme does nothing to challenge or undermine the deeply entrenched system of school segregation; on the contrary, it institutionalizes it through its two-tiered selection procedure. Thus, in a proposal inspired by similar experiments in Texas, California, and Florida, Patrick Weil has recently suggested that places in the *grandes écoles* be instead reserved for the top 5 per cent of secondary school graduates across the whole country.[36] This radically innovative proposal perfectly illustrates critical republican strategy, in a number of respects. First, it addresses problems of systemic and structural injustice, not contenting itself with cosmetic reform designed to inject a small dose of 'diversity' into socially exclusive institutions. Second, it is based on a context-specific diagnosis of the deep causes of the under-representation of ethnic minorities: in the case of French higher education (but not, as we shall see, in the labour market), the problem is social elitism rather than ethnic discrimination as such. Third, it avoids a mismatch between the means and the ends of reform, not taking the risk of aggravating the ethnicization of social perceptions through hazardous policies of promoting 'diversity'. Fourth, it honours the principle of colour-blind equality of opportunity central to republican public philosophy, taking seriously the real effect that public norms have on social perceptions and behaviour. Fifth, it has profound transformative effects, as it aims to 'break processes of urban segregation through which well-off families congregate in reputed secondary schools':[37] it provides incentives for them to leave the 'chic ghettos' and move to poorer areas, where their children might stand a better chance of obtaining a place at a *grande école*.

Weil's proposal thus goes beyond the democratization of elite schools and points towards more radical social transformation, one which would deliberately break up social and racial ghettos. From a critical republican perspective, the growing social, cultural, and ethnic segregation of French (and Western) society, often driven by white middle class parents' schooling strategies, should be combated as a matter of priority. Studies have shown that the broad social environment in which children are brought up significantly affects their future life chances: the mere fact of living in a socially disadvantaged neighbourhood diminishes the worth of available educational opportunities.[38] Thus, ghettoization adversely affects republican hopes of social mobility through meritocracy. Furthermore, racial prejudice tends to be the lowest in racially mixed neighbourhoods, at least those where ethnic origin is not a predictor of socio-economic status. Thus, territorial segregation adversely affects republican hopes of trans-ethnic solidarity and social equality.[39] Official republicans are right to promote social integration through urban policies of territorial integration, instead of ethnic policies of positive discrimination. Yet their policies of preferential help for disadvantaged neighbourhoods (of which *ZEP* are the best known) aim to 'improve territories, not move people',[40] whereas critical republican strategies should be geared towards generating structural incentives both to social mobility and social mixity. Weil's '5 per cent proposal' is just one example of such strategy.

In sum, critical republicans support radical forms of socio-economic affirmative action which aim to reverse structural processes of accumulation of advantage and disadvantage, notably through territorial de-segregation and the de-ethnicization of urban spaces. Phenomena of urban segregation and ghettoization are the most worrisome obstacles to republican social integration, and they are symptomatic, not of the 'communitarian drift' (*repli communautaire*) of identity-conscious Muslims, as official republicans tend to assume but, rather, they are the upshot of cumulative and explosive processes of social relegation and 'white flight'. As France's November 2005 riots spectacularly revealed, the *banlieues* suffer more from socio-economic relegation than from ethnic, cultural, or religious misrecognition.[41] Does this mean, however, that critical republicans find no use at all for ethnic categories as legitimate categories of public policy? Far from it. Official republicans have gravely underestimated the connections between social disadvantage and ethnic discrimination, and have wrongly assumed that colour-blind social integration can dispense with vigorous anti-discrimination polices. Yet, as we saw in Chapter 9, ethnic discrimination in the private sector of employment and housing is the chief cause of the specific disadvantage suffered by well-qualified graduates of immigrant origin. By castigating any form of 'ethnic monitoring' as illegitimate, official republicans deprive themselves of effective tools for punishing dis-criminatory practices, tools which need not increase the social salience of ethnic categories. Anonymous curriculum vitae and generalized 'testing' practices, for example, can prevent the most blatant forms of ethnic discrimination; while positive actions such as 'outreach' can improve the position of ethnic minorities, without challenging republi-can colour-blind meritocracy. Affirmative action, in a word, need not imply counter-discrimination on morally arbitrary, and socially divisive, grounds.[42]

Critical Patriotism and Civic Integration

In this section, I explore the cultural, or rather *identificatory*, dimension of immigrant integration. I argue that we should take seriously the way in which discourses of national identity affect the prospects of civic integration of immigrants (and racialized minorities in general). Instead of giving up on national integration, as advocated by post-national and multiculturalist thinkers, critical republicans advocate a deliberative transformation of existing constructions of collective identity. To clarify the issues at stake, let me first identify the central problem, and examine and reject one possible response to it.

The problem is this. As the argument of Chapter 9 amply showed, the republican discourse of national integration, while officially inclusive, in practice relies on highly moralized and ethnicized constructions of the national community, which paradoxically confirm the position of the foreigner, Muslim, or *immigré* as perpetual outsiders. Thus, it is by singling out the veiled Muslim girl as 'refusing to be French' that ethnonational constructions of Frenchness are affirmed and entrenched. Appeals to shared identity are used to distinguish 'them' from 'us': hence the centrality of the 'Muslim problem' to the current perceived crisis of French (and Western) national identity. The official discourse of national integration ethnicizes its target categories, as *immigrés* or *Arabo-Musulmans* whose culture of origin or religion is stigmatized as a potential obstacle to integration. Ironically, as many observers have noted, the target categories of contemporary integration (second- or even third-generation 'immigrants') are highly integrated culturally, if not economically.[43] As Joël Roman has noted, 'never have "immigrants" been so well-integrated: francophone, accustomed to France for generations, and profoundly Francophile.'[44] Born and brought up in France, they are still stigmatized as permanent *immigrés*, ethnicized outsiders: their full civic status is denied. Paradoxically, revival of interest in Islam among the younger generations signals their willingness to make France their home: while a minority of Muslims—the *néo-communautaires* referred to in the previous chapter—defiantly wish to separate themselves from mainstream society, most Muslims are *accommodateurs* who seek to reconcile their Muslim beliefs with their 'Frenchness'. Unfortunately, doubts about their Frenchness are insistently voiced: an ethno-nationalist construal of the nation has erected Islam as its internal boundary, and the hijab controversy is symptomatic of the difficulties felt by many in France in accepting that Muslims can be French.

Now, how should we respond to this real-world problem, which we could call the 'ethno-nationalist exclusion' problem? The dominant response, at least among liberal political theorists, has been relatively straightforward. They argue that the ethno-nationalist exclusion problem shows only that liberal politics should, as far as possible, steer away from appeals to culture and identity, and that citizenship should be understood primarily as a legal, socio-economic, and political status. Some have gone further, and advocated the dissociation of citizenship rights from national membership. For advocates of post-national citizenship, citizens' entitlements should be grounded in the universal status of personhood and detached from their historical connection with national membership.[45] In parallel, the plurality of citizens' authentic cultural, religious, local identities and attachments should be promoted and recognized. In a globalized world where national identity is experienced as an increasingly irrelevant, artificial and exclusive bond, post-national 'universal' citizenship and multicultural 'partial' citizenship are seen to complement each other. In the seminal picture of the New Europe drawn by Yasemin Soysal, for example, Berlin's Turkish migrants symbolize the new post-national citizens: 'sharing a social space with foreigners from other countries and with German citizens..., they...invoke, negotiate, and map collective identities as immigrant, Turk, Muslim, foreigner and European.'[46] From this post-national perspective, the republican discourse of national integration appears as an archaic, regressive, and repressive ideal.

Soysal's is undoubtedly an attractive vision, but how adequate is it as a response to what I have called the 'ethno-nationalist exclusion' problem? I think it is radically inadequate, because it does not take it seriously as a real problem. By adopting a position of benign neglect towards existing constructions of national identities, it fails to take seriously the way in which they negatively affect the status of immigrants and minorities. What Soysal underestimates is that immigrants may have a legitimate interest in being members of the imaginary construction of the nation. Among the identities that she sees Turkish Berliners as displaying, she mentions 'immigrant, Turk, Muslim, foreigner and European' but, revealingly, not 'German'. Yet, as she herself recognizes, the movement of universalization of rights has not displaced the nation-state as the primary site of allocation of benefits and protection of rights.[47] If this is true, then all beneficiaries have a prima facie interest in being citizens of the state they live in, so that they can shape public debate about how rights are interpreted and implemented. And as existing discourses of citizenship are (*pace* post-national theorists) still primarily discourses of *national* citizenship, citizens of foreign origin also have an interest in being seen to belong to the national community. To deny that they have such an interest is to validate their second-class status in existing societies. It is, for example, to validate perceptions that Turkish guest-workers, regardless of their legal status, are not and cannot be German; or that women wearing hijab are not and cannot be French.

Recall that in a republican view, citizenship has crucial intersubjective and motivational underpinnings: citizenship is not simply a legal status but also a matter of mutual recognition. For citizens to adopt what Jürgen Habermas calls the 'we-perspective of active self-determination',[48] they must feel that they belong together, that they are engaged in a cooperative enterprise, and that they identify with (some of) their shared institutions and practices.[49] Historically, feelings of 'love of country' or patriotism have been instrumental to the promotion of such feelings of republican solidarity. From this republican perspective, the ethno-nationalist exclusion problem is particularly worrisome, for two reasons. First, ethno-nationalist exclusion undermines the very purpose of republican patriotism, which is to underpin inclusive practices of solidarity within shared institutions. As Michael Walzer and David Miller have insisted, a republic cannot tolerate the presence of denizens in its midst, and on this ground should extend citizenship to all its (long-term) residents.[50] Second, on an intersubjective understanding of citizenship, one may enjoy the formal rights of citizenship and yet, by virtue of one's perceived or assigned cultural or religious identity, be arbitrarily excluded from the imaginary construction of the *patrie*. Thus, in a republican view, people's civic standing can be affected by discursive constructions of collective identity. They can be denied citizenship by being denied symbolic membership in the nation. *Contra* multiculturalists, this happens not so much through misrecognition of their 'authentic' identity as through the arbitrary imposition of an externally defined identity, that of Muslim or *immigré*, over which they have little control. Thus, the ethno-nationalist exclusion problem is also a problem of domination *lato sensu*. Muslims and immigrants, while not necessarily arbitrarily interfered with or denied basic rights, are reduced to an assigned, fixed identity; their presumed culture is reified as a comprehensive explanatory framework for all their ideas and actions; and their willingness and ability to integrate into society is a priori suspect.[51] Such domination deprives them of minimum 'discursive control': they are spoken about but not spoken to, they are subjected to demeaned images of their identity, and their full status of co-citizen is denied. Arguably, what Muslims in today's Europe suffer most from is not lack of recognition, but rather an excess of the wrong kind of recognition.

What, then, is the appropriate strategy to respond to the ethno-nationalist exclusion problem? In a critical republican view, Muslims have a legitimate interest in being accepted as full members in the imagined national community of Frenchness. So, instead of denying the importance of 'we-ness' to citizenship, and instead of resigning ourselves to the exclusivist effects of existing appeals to collective identities, we should work to expand our sense of 'we'. The critical (or civic) patriotism I advocate thus resembles Habermas's advocacy of a 'constitutional patriotism' as the motivational basis of republican democracy in pluralist societies. Habermas's intentions must be carefully interpreted, however. He is usually seen as proposing a fully post-national separation of national identity from shared commitment to universal principles, thus allowing the extension of patriotic solidarity to people of diverse cultural origins.[52] Yet closer analysis of the foundations of his 'constitutional patriotism' reveals that it is based on the interpretation of 'a particular national history and tradition'.[53] Thus, national legacies are not irrelevant to the legitimate modes of present patriotic identification. Confronting his rightwing opponents in the seminal *Historiskerstreit* (Historians' debate), Habermas in fact argued that a German liberal democratic national identity could only be elaborated through critical confrontation with the nation's past (in particular the Holocaust). The constitutional patriotism he called for implied not the denial of the particular historical legacy that the German Republic inherited but, rather, the adoption of a 'scrutinizing attitude towards one's own identity-forming tradition'.[54] Extending the point, Habermas should have made it clearer that his constitutional patriotism could not be a self-standing abstract identity a priori detached from existing national heritages. He should have insisted (in line with his deliberative ethics) that constitutional patriotism could only emerge as a *process,* through collective confrontation with repugnant legacies, and through the deliberative transformation of existing perceptions of 'we-ness'. The civic patriotism I advocate, by contrast, directly starts from existing legacies—such as the French ethno-nationalist construction of the nation—and seeks to 'de-ethnicize' their content, instead of substituting an abstract post-national loyalty for them.[55]

Civic patriots argue that existing modes of national identification should be critically scrutinized and de-ethnicized. In parallel, immigrant and Muslim identities should be 'mainstreamed', as it were, that is, presented and perceived as normal (if plural) ways of being French. 'Mainstreaming' is about removing symbolic obstacles to equal citizenship; it does not so much involve the positive validation of Muslim identities as it requires the transformation of dominant perceptions of shared identity. In this sense, it appeals more to a negative ideal of non-domination than to a positive ideal of recognition. The multicultural politics of recognition have tended to rigidify and essentialize 'cultures' and 'identities', and paradoxically denied individuals minimum discursive control, which involves (some) ability to define the terms of one's public appearance. As we have seen, the promotion of cultural diversity has too often gone hand in hand with the ethnicization of difference.

My republican defence of the politics of non-domination over those of recognition shares the concerns of egalitarian critical theorists such as Nancy Fraser and Anthony Laden. Laden's 'deliberative liberalism' emphasizes the way in which social norms shape individual and collective identifications, and more specifically the way in which 'identity imposition' renders impossible the formation of reciprocal relationships of citizenship, even in the absence of barriers to legal inclusion.[56] Similarly, at the heart of Fraser's theory is the (republican-sounding) ideal of parity of participation. Parity of participation, she argues, is impeded, inter alia, by the institutionalization of dominating patterns of cultural value. While, *pace* advocates of the politics of recognition such as Axel Honneth and Charles Taylor, no one has a right to be equally esteemed and honoured, Fraser claims that everyone has a right not to face disproportionate, institutionalized obstacles in the quest for social esteem. Non-recognition is not about the depreciation of a group's identity; rather, it refers to a form of social subordination whereby certain individuals are prevented from participating as peers in social life, in virtue of institutionalized cultural and social representations which constitute them as undeserving of respect or esteem.[57] Which people need what kind of recognition in which context depends on the nature of the obstacles they face with regard to participatory parity: the positive affirmation of misrecognized identities is only one option, others being the universalization of existing entitlements or the transformation of dominant self-understandings through the destabilization of existing status differentiations. The objective is parity of participation, and the favoured strategy is the removal of institutional obstacles to it.[58]

What would civic patriotism and participatory parity imply in the context of Muslim and immigrant integration into the symbolic community of the nation? Let me draw on four main suggestions, to conclude. First, the current terms of the discourse of national integration must be jettisoned. The injunction on *immigrés* to become *français* is a perversely paradoxical request, as both terms are implicitly ethnicized. Such language is incompatible with participatory parity: it permanently casts suspicion on the bona fide claim to membership of *immigrés*. The British language of 'race relations' and 'ethno-cultural diversity' is more satisfactory, in so far as it implicitly shifts the burden on the society's main institutions to rectify the exclusivist effects of racialized social relations. Yet in unreflectively endorsing the language of 'race' and 'cultures', it also ends up reifying collective identities and depriving individuals of minimum discursive control. Clearly, the 'naming' of the targets of social integration is a fraught exercise, but one whose importance it would be difficult to underestimate. The way social integration is talked about has a direct effect on how much it is perceived to be a reality. Critical republicans are particularly sensitive to the 'politics of naming', both because of the traditional republican intersubjective conception of citizenship and because of a critical theory-influenced concern for the real social effect of norms and beliefs. Note, however, that this concern does not necessarily mandate the politically correct 'policing of language' advocated by some multiculturalists. As Fraser has insisted, it is institutionalized, state-enforced, 'externally manifest and publicly verifiable impediments to people's standing' that should be of concern. Avishai Margalit concurs: 'a decent society has no obligation to present anyone in the positive light, even vulnerable groups and individuals...A society is decent only if its hegemonic culture does not contain humiliating collective representations that are actively and systematically used by the society's institutions.'[59] Thus, for example, critical republicans are sceptical of speech restrictions designed to protect vulnerable religious minorities from offence, humiliation, and disrespect. Freedom of speech implies that citizens are entitled to mock, offend, or criticize other citizens' religious beliefs, but it does not entitle state institutions to use prejudiced and controversial views of a religion as a basis for policy—as was the case during the French hijab controversy.[60] In civil society, critical republicans advocate not less but more speech: instead of being protected from majority views, minorities should be empowered to resist and combat them.

Second, and connectedly, the participation of minority members at all levels of society must be encouraged. While, as we saw in the previous section, access to higher education and the labour market must be facilitated through aggressive policies of non-discrimination and affirmative action on social (not ethnic) grounds, more proactive policies of symbolic representation of racial and religious pluralism can be implemented in areas such as the media. Here the approach should be overtly consequentialist: individuals who inhibit stigmatized features (skin colour, religious symbols) should be promoted to positions of public visibility. The point of representation is not positively to assert their difference but, on the contrary, to de-stigmatize their public mode of appearance. They should not be seen as spokespeople of religious or ethnic communities, but as representatives of ordinary citizens in their diversity. The point is not to hear the 'Muslim voice'; it is to give Muslims minimum discursive power so that they can (individually and collectively) find their voice(s) in public. Muslim citizens have a 'right to indifference'—to use the well-known slogan of the anti-racist organization SOS Racisme—but they can, paradoxically, only achieve it through positive policies of visibility. Participation, as republicans say, is the best way to resist domination by others.

Third, and in line with critical patriotism, the narratives of the nation must be told in a way which does not alienate or exclude minorities. Undoubtedly, national identity has an irreducibly 'ethnic' core and, to that extent, its 'de-ethnicization' should be imagined less as a fixed endpoint than as a process. Recall that in a critical republican view, the ethno-nationalist exclusion problem can only be taken seriously if one adopts a 'scrutinizing attitude towards one's own identity-forming tradition'.[61] Instead of denying the relevance of national identity, critical republicans seek to expand the modes of national identification. They do so by fostering the progressive transformation of existing constructions of 'we-ness'. Thus, the mainstreaming of Muslim identity in the French public sphere will detach dominant constructions of Frenchness from association with particular cultural traditions, be they secular lifestyles, particular culinary habits, or clothing styles. To be French, in the end, should become a primarily political identity, making reference, for example, to the (yet imperfectly realized and continuously contested) ideals of the 1789 Revolution. Thus abstract, 'constitutional' patriotism emerges *ex post*, instead of being asserted a priori. This is not to say that the French should idealize French history and reduce it to a few glorious episodes such as the revolution. As we have seen, critical republicans take responsibility for 'their' past. Now, undoubtedly, there is a tension between taking responsibility for one's collective past, on the one hand, and fostering a sense of 'we-ness' that newcomers can feel at home with, on the other. For example, if atonement for the Holocaust is central to contemporary German national identity, it is unclear how it can be made relevant to new citizens of Turkish origin. But in other cases, the two processes go hand in hand. For example, if the French were able to tell themselves a more honest and more complete story of their colonial past, and reincorporate immigrant memories into their collective memory, they could elaborate a common (if plural) story out of a divisive history. A number of recent French works have thus reflected on dialogical and deliberative conceptions of national identity, contrasted to the official, patriotic, and 'memorial'-style national history.[62]

Fourth and lastly, it should be clear by now that the acceptance of Muslim hijab in state schools promotes critical republican ideals in a number of ways. It shuns premature and prejudiced judgements about the cultural and religious practices of minority members, and to that extent avoids their ethnicization and domination. It removes institutional obstacles (in this case a misguided interpretation of educational *laïcité* as requiring the religious restraint of pupils) to participatory parity. And it normalizes the presence of Muslims in public places, thereby contributing to the de-ethnicization of perceptions of both French and Muslim identities. Young Muslims, provocatively breaking with the integration model which tolerated cultural differences only as long they remained in the private and traditional realms of family life, demonstrate that one can be French and pray five times a day, not enjoy wine and ham and wear Islamic clothing to school, university, and the office.[63] They demonstrate, in other words, that a sense of national belonging and solidarity in contemporary societies need not rely on thick cultural similarities but must take seriously the pluralism of the ways of life and commitments of their members. Many of those young *accommodateurs*, while refusing the terms of the official injunction to assimilation, endorse the broad republican theme of national identification and solidarity: they seek to reclaim their own Frenchness. They do not see themselves as post-national denizens, de-territorialized 'global Muslims' with only a tenuous attachment to their country of residence; on the contrary, they want to feel fully integrated as French nationals. Yet their public Islamic assertion disrupts the homogeneous and ethnocentric conception of national identity implicitly championed by national republican discourse. In particular, it points towards a reintegration of Islamic and North African history into a persistently amnesiac French national memory.[64] Public recognition of a Muslim component to French identity—both past and present, in its conflict-ridden as well as its consensual dimensions—would allow Muslim symbols to appear, not as the defiant rejection of republican fraternity, but as pointing towards the deliberative elaboration of a more inclusive conception of national identity, one which does not rely on the essentialization and domination of minorities.

Yet, while acceptance of the hijab in schools promotes the negative politics of non-domination, it should not be seen as opening the way to the more positive and difference-sensitive politics of recognition of Muslim identity. Undoubtedly, it is not always easy to draw hard-and-fast lines between the politics of non-domination and the politics of recognition. As we saw, a de-ethnicized national history needs positively to incorporate the memories of immigrant, Muslim and colonial peoples; and the normalization and mainstreaming of Franco-Muslim identity may require the forcible promotion of ('visible') Muslims in culturally sensitive areas such as the media. In both these cases, some positive recognition appears to be a prerequisite for non-domination and civic integration. Yet critical republicans advocate recognition of identity only in cases when non-recognition accentuates the social salience of identity-based differences: the long-term objective of policies of recognition is always de-ethnicization, the destabilization of the 'assigned identities' through which citizens are denied membership in the community of citizens. In most cases, I have argued, civic inclusion merely requires the negative removal of obstacles to participation, and need not encompass the positive recognition of separate cultural and religious identities.

Thus, while critical republicans welcome the *hijab*, and other signs of minority identification in state schools, they are strongly sceptical of the need for, and value of, separate education for Muslims (and Christians and Jews). In earlier chapters, I argued that commitment to secular (neither religious nor anti-religious) egalitarianism and civic virtues (Chapter 4) and to individual autonomy and non-domination (Chapter 7) already inclined critical republicans towards such scepticism, and motivated their defence of a tight regulation by the state of religious schools, along lines recently suggested by Ian MacMullen.[65] However, the strongest arguments against so-called faith schools— even the 'moderate religious schools' defended by MacMullen—are not based on the ideals of *égalité* nor *liberté,* but rather on *fraternité.* While the first two ideals could arguably be accommodated through state regulation of religious schools, the latter ideal—I would argue— can only be promoted through actual social mixing, within common state schools, between children of different social, cultural, and religious origin. Whether far-reaching reform of the admission policies of religious schools will be sufficient for this purpose is a moot point. But what is clear is that the republican virtues cannot simply be acquired cognitively, through curriculum changes. They must be—as Aristotle knew—learned through practice; in this case, the practice of engaging with concrete social diversity. 'Imaginary interlocutors', as Eamonn Callan felicitously put it, 'are a pallid substitute for the real thing.'[66] It is difficult for students to learn to be tolerant and respectful of other people, traditions, and ways of life unless they are actually exposed to them: only common schools concretely embody reciprocity in their daily institutional life.[67] In a republic, children are brought up together, in mixed and diverse schools and neighbourhoods where concrete bonds of inter-ethnic and inter-religious solidarity can be forged. Central to the republican ideal is that of social, cultural, and religious mixity: as I argued in Chapter 4, keeping veiled Muslim girls in schools is the best way to foster mutual tolerance and respect between Muslims and non-Muslims. Thus, critical republicans reassert the traditional republican ideals of social and civic integration, while insisting that such ideals can only be realized in truly public spheres where members of minorities are not ethnicized, segregated, and dominated but, on the contrary, made to feel that they, too, belong to the community of citizens.

Conclusion

In this book, I have defended a critical republican theory of citizenship. Its central concerns and concepts have emerged out of sustained engagement with the specific debates surrounding the hijab controversy. This means that, in contrast to standard Anglo-American interpretations of French debates, I have sought to take seriously the historical and ideological background against which the ideals of *laïcité* were articulated and debated. Further, I have shown that such detailed interpretive work is essential for the formulation of a sociologically sound normative political philosophy. My critical republicanism, then, reconstructs, criticizes and improves on the official republican philosophy which purported to justify the 2004 ban on hijab and, more broadly, points to a progressive solution to multicultural controversies in Western societies. In this conclusion, I briefly summarize its main findings.

Critical republicanism endorses the distinctive republican ideals of secularism, non-domination, and civic solidarity, yet suggests that, suitably interpreted, they do *not* justify the ban on hijab in schools. Secularism, properly understood, does not require pupils to remove signs of religious allegiance; female emancipation is not assisted by the prohibition of religious symbols; and civic solidarity depends not on cultural conformism but on social equality and the politics of participatory inclusion. Yet republican ideas, while mobilized for the wrong cause in the hijab case, are undeniably appealing and—I have further suggested—should be attractive to members of cultural and religious minorities. Republicanism is at bottom an ideal of progressive, egalitarian, and social-democratic citizenship, which points to a society where all citizens enjoy basic but robust civic standing, in the form of political voice, minimum personal autonomy, material capabilities, equal opportunities, and intersubjective mutual recognition as equals. The quality of the intersubjective relationships that citizens enjoy is adversely affected both by large inequalities of condition and life experiences and by social perceptions of incommensurable and divisive religious and cultural difference. A politically inclusive and socially egalitarian society should be able successfully to resist the divisive politicization of identities, whether of majorities or of minorities. Citizens of different cultural, social, and religious allegiance should be allowed and encouraged to 'dwell together' in genuinely public spaces—from political forums to mixed neighbourhoods and common secular schools—learn to argue and disagree together, and continuously reinvent their imagined (fictitious yet potent) sense of collective identity.

It is difficult to deny that in its official French formulation, as invoked during the *hijab* controversy, the republican ideal has proved to have exclusionary effects on minorities such as Muslims and youth of immigrant origin. Yet, I have argued, this is not because (as some multiculturalists would claim) republican citizenship is an intrinsically exclusionary ideal. It is rather because, in public discourse, the ideal of republicanism has functioned as a social ideology that purports to describe, and thereby legitimizes, existing arrangements in actual society. Thus, official republicans implicitly assume that French society already meets republican standards, and then urge members of minorities to comply with them. In common with many early Anglo-American liberal multicultural theories, French official republicans have been primarily concerned about the legitimacy of additional entitlements (exemptions, special rights) for members of cultural minorities, and about the extent of their required compliance with accepted common norms. In doing so, they have tended to assume that existing laws and norms already conform to republican ideals; they have not sufficiently reflected on the fairness of the balance of existing burdens and benefits. Critical republicanism seeks to rectify this status quo bias and asks difficult, strategic questions about how best to achieve republican ideals in actual societies. The republicanism that I defend is influenced by critical theory, broadly understood, on two levels: in its interest in social critique and practical reform on the one hand and in its focus on social norms and ethos, ideologies, and social attitudes on the other. Thus there is a natural—if hitherto largely unnoticed—connection between critical theory and the republican tradition. Republicans have, too, been interested in citizens' virtues and dispositions as much as in laws and institutions; and they have centrally been concerned with the practical, strategic question of how to create and maintain the fragile political edifice of the republic. Critical republicanism, then, departs from the dominantly idealistic and legalistic tendencies of mainstream political philosophy. It is by interrogating the complex relationships between ideal and practical norms, and between the ends and means of reform, that it seeks to rehabilitate the inclusive ideal of citizenship.

While critical republicanism endorses the broad ideals of difference-blind, egalitarian citizenship, it suggests that they do not necessarily generate direct duties of restraint and compliance on the part of minorities. Instead, existing institutions and norms should be, as a matter of priority, made more difference-blind and thoroughly 'republicanized': they need to be more secular, more respectful of citizens' autonomy, and more proactive in pursuing policies of egalitarian integration and social cohesion. Thus, in Part I of this book, I argued that members of religious minorities would benefit from *more* rather than *less* secularism, if this is understood as the construction of a less Christian-biased, genuinely neutral public sphere showing respect to all citizens. Contemporary Muslim demands raise questions about the systemic impartiality of the current republican settlement, and should not be assessed independently of historical practices of religious recognition. Even in self-professed secular states such as France, the rectification of the institutional and symbolic bias in favour of historically dominant religions would go a long way towards lessening Muslim unease about the 'really existing' republic. In Part 2, I argued that members of minorities would benefit from *more* rather than *fewer* autonomy-promoting policies and practices, if autonomy is conceived as a culturally neutral tool with which to combat domination, whether that of the majority or of the minorities (such as that embedded in patriarchal, sexist traditional arrangements). I showed how critical republicanism pointed to a non-paternalistic solution to the problem of the 'double domination' suffered by Muslim women, which involves the promotion of discursive control or voice, through both state education and democratic empowerment. In Part 3, I suggested that members of minorities would benefit from *more* rather than *less* national solidarity, if this is understood as requiring the de-ethnicization of constructions of collective identity and the removal of structural—socio-economic and cultural—obstacles to the fair incorporation and participation of all.

Throughout, I showed that neither multicultural recognition nor the liberal abstraction from difference are suitable as *general* approaches to the resolution of real-world religious and cultural controversies. Instead, I defended republican strategies of non-domination. These are sensitive to the constructed, intersubjective nature of collective identities, to the complex and diffuse forms of power in contemporary societies, and to the dialectic between the means and the ends of reform. The practical ideal of non-domination typically requires negative, structural policies of removal of socio-economic and cultural obstacles to minority incorporation; yet at times it may demand the positive, symbolic recognition of minority identities, when this assists their members in achieving participatory parity with other citizens. In all cases, I have argued, civic participation in the public sphere is the best way to combat social, cultural, and political domination. The republican tradition, in sum, contains powerful resources with which fairly to address the claims of religious and cultural minorities. These can only be exploited, however, if republicans are prepared to enrich their political philosophy with a social theory that critically interrogates the republican credentials of existing institutions and norms. The problem with French society (and, I would argue, many similarly situated societies) is not that it is *too* republican to accommodate cultural and religious minorities. It is, rather, that it is not republican enough. As the Marquis de Sade provocatively urged his compatriots as early as 1795, '*Français, encore un effort si vous voulez être républicains.*'

NOTES

Notes to Chapter 1

1. Recent surveys include Cécile Laborde and John Maynor (eds), *Republicanism and Political Theory*. Oxford: Blackwell, 2007; Jeremy Jennings and Iseult Honohan (eds), *Republicanism in Theory and Practice*. London: Routledge, 2005; Richard Dagger, 'Communitarianism and Republicanism', in Gerald Gaus and Chandran Kukathas (eds), *Handbook of Political Theory*, London: Sage, 2004, pp. 167–79; Iseult Honohan, *Civic Republicanism*. London: Routledge, 2002; Knud Haakonssen, 'Republicanism', in Philip Pettit and Robert Goodin (eds), *Handbook of Contemporary Political Philosophy*. Oxford: Blackwell, 1993, 568–74.
2. John Greville Agard Pocock, *The Machiavellian Moment. Florentine Political Thought and the Atlantic Republican Tradition*. Princeton, NJ: Princeton University Press, 1975.
3. Quentin Skinner, 'Machiavelli's *Discorsi* and the Pre-humanist Origins of Republican Ideas', in Gisela Bock, Quentin Skinner, and Maurizio Viroli (eds), *Machiavelli and Republicanism*. Cambridge: Cambridge University Press, 1990; Quentin Skinner *Liberty before Liberalism*. Cambridge: Cambridge University Press, 1997; Quentin Skinner, *Visions of Politics*. Vol. 2: *Renaissance Virtues*. Cambridge: Cambridge University Press, 2002.
4. Philip Pettit, *Republicanism: A Theory of Freedom and Government*. Oxford: Oxford University Press, 1997.
5. Jean-Fabien Spitz, *La Liberté Politique*. Paris: Presses Universitaires de France, 1995; Pettit, *Republicanism*, ch. 4.
6. Benjamin Barber, *Strong Democracy. Participatory Politics for a New Age*. Berkeley, CA: University of California Press, 1984; Quentin Skinner, 'The Paradoxes of Political Liberty', in Sterling M. McMurrin (ed.), *The Tanner Lectures on Human. Value*, Vol. 7, Salt Lake City, UT: University of Utah Press, 1986, pp. 227–50; Quentin Skinner, 'On Justice, the Common Good and the Priority of Liberty', in Chantal Mouffe (ed.), *Dimensions of Radical Democracy*. London: Verso Press, 1992, pp. 211–24; Adrian Oldfield, *Citizenship and Community: Civic Republicanism and the Modern World*. London: Routledge, 1990; Richard Dagger, *Civic Virtues: Rights, Citizenship and Republican Liberalism*. Oxford: Oxford University Press, 1997; Maurizio Viroli, *Republicanism*. New York: Hill and Wang, 2001; Michael Sandel, *Democracy's Discontent: America in Search of a Public Philosophy*. Cambridge, MA: Harvard University Press, 1996; Richard Bellamy, *Liberalism and Pluralism: Towards a Politics of Compromise*. London: Routledge, 1999; Philip Pettit, 'Republican Political Theory', in Andrew Vincent (ed.), *Political Theory: Tradition, Diversity and Ideology*. Cambridge: Cambridge University Press, 1997, pp. 112–32; Philip

Pettit, 'Republican Freedom and Contestatory Democratization', in Ian Shapiro and Casiano Hacker-Cordon (eds), *Democracy's Value*. Cambridge: Cambridge University Press, 1999, pp. 63–90; John Maynor, *Republicanism in the Modern World*. Cambridge: Polity, 2003; Luc Ferry and Alain Renaut, *From the Rights of Man to the Republican Idea*. Chicago: Chicago University Press, 1992.

7. I shall later make it clear why I think that the term 'multicultural' should be treated with caution. However, following common usage, and for the sake of simplicity, I will from now on dispense with the sceptical commas.

8. Will Kymlicka, *Multicultural Citizenship. A Liberal Theory of Minority Rights*. Oxford: Oxford University Press, 1995, p. 108. But see David Miller *On Nationality*. Oxford: Oxford University Press, 1995; David Miller, *Citizenship and National Identity*. Cambridge: Polity Press, 2000; Jürgen Habermas, 'Citizenship and National Identity: Some Reflections on the Future of Europe', *Praxis International*, Vol. 12, No. 1, 1992, pp. 171–206; Jürgen Habermas, *The Inclusion of the Other: Studies in Political Theory*. Cambridge: Polity Press, 1999.

9. Will Kymlicka, *Politics in the Vernacular. Nationalism, Multiculturalism, and Citizenship*. Oxford: Oxford University Press, 2001, p. 43.

10. Skinner, *Liberty before Liberalism*; Quentin Skinner, 'The Idea of Negative Liberty: Machiavellian and Modern Perspectives', in his *Vision of Politics*, Vol. 2, *Renaissance Virtues*. Cambridge: Cambridge University Press, 2002; Ronald J. Terchek, *Republican Paradoxes and Liberal Anxieties: Retrieving Neglected Fragments of Political Theory*. Lanham, MD: Rowman and Littlefield, 1996; Duncan Ivison, *The Self at Liberty: Political Argument and the Arts of Government*. Ithaca, NY: Cornell University Press, 1997; Oldfield, *Citizenship and Community*.

11. Dominique Schnapper, *La Communauté des Citoyens*. Paris: Gallimard, 1994 [English translation: *Community of Citizens. On the Modern Idea of Nationality*. Piscataway, NJ: Transaction, 1998]; Alain Finkielkraut, *La défaite de la pensée*. Paris: Gallimard, 1987 [English translation: *The Undoing of Thought*, London: Claridge Press, 1988]; Régis Debray, *Que vive la République*, Paris: Odile Jacob, 1989; Pierre-André Taguieff, *La Force du préjugé: Essai sur le racisme et ses doubles*. Paris: La Découverte, 1987; Catherine Kintzler, *La république en questions*. Paris: Minerve, 1996; Blandine Kriegel, *Philosophie de la Republique*. Paris: Plon, 1996; Michel Wieviorka (ed.), *Une société fragmentée? Le multiculturalisme en débat*. Paris: La Découverte, 1996; Françoise Gaspard and Farhad Khoroskhavar, *Le Foulard et la République*. Paris: La Découverte, 1995. For a critical overview of the relationship between republicanism and the left, see Denis Sieffert, *Comment peut-on être (vraiment) républicain?* Paris: La Découverte, 2006.

12. On the notion of family resemblance, see Ludwig Wittgenstein, *Philosophical Investigations*. Oxford: Blackwell, 2001, para. 67. For important attempts to situate French revolutionary republicanism within the broader European republican tradition, see Johnson K. Wright, *A Classical Republican in the*

XVIIIth Century: The Political Thought of Mably, Stanford, CA: Stanford University Press, 1997; Dale Van Kley (ed.), *The French Idea of Freedom. The Old Regime and the Declaration of Rights of 1798.* Stanford, CA: Stanford University Press, 1994; Keith M. Baker, *Inventing the French Revolution.* Cambridge: Cambridge University Press, 1990.

13. On the French republican tradition, see, notably, Sudhir Hazareesingh, *Political Traditions in Modern France.* Oxford: Oxford University Press, 1994, pp. 65–97; Keith M. Baker (ed.), *The French Revolution and the Creation of Modern Political Culture.* Oxford: Pergamon Press, 1987; Mark Hulliung, *Citizens and Citoyens: Republicans and Liberals in America and France.* Cambridge, MA: Harvard University Press, 2002; Jason Neidleman, J., *The General Will is Citizenship. Inquiries into French Political Thought.* Oxford: Rowman & Littlefield, 2001; Claude Nicolet, *L'idée républicaine en France (1789–1924). Essai d'histoire critique.* Paris: Gallimard, 1982; Claude Nicolet, *Histoire, Nation, République.* Paris: Odile Jacob, 2000; François Furet and Mona Ozouf, *Le siècle de l'avènement républicain.* Paris: Gallimard, 1993; Pierre Rosanvallon, *Le Peuple introuvable: Histoire de la représentation démocratique en France.* Paris: Folio, 1998; *La Démocratie inachevée. Histoire de la souveraineté du peuple en France.* Paris: Gallimard, 2000; *Le Sacre du citoyen. Histoire du suffrage universel en France.* Paris: Folio, 2001.

14. See, notably, the seminal works of François Furet on the centrality of revolutionary thought to French republican political culture: *Penser la Révolution française* (with Denis Richet). Paris: Fayard, 1978; *La gauche et la Révolution au 19ème siècle. Edgar Quinet et la question du jacobinisme.* Paris: Hachette, 1986; (ed., with Mona Ozouf.) *Le siècle de l'avènement républicain.* Paris: Gallimard, 1993. See also Lucien Jaume, *L'individu effacé, ou le paradoxe du libéralisme français.* Paris: Fayard, 1997; Marcel Gauchet, *La révolution des droits de l'homme.* Paris: Gallimard, 1989.

15. See, notably, Sudhir Hazareesingh, *From Subject to Citizen: The Second Empire and the Emergence of Modern French Democracy.* Princeton, NJ: Princeton University Press, 1988; Sudhir Hazareesingh, *Intellectual Founders of the Republic. Five Studies in Nineteenth-Century French Political Thought.* Oxford: Oxford University Press, 2001.

16. Spitz, *La Liberté politique;* Jean-Fabien Spitz, *Le Moment Républicain en France.* Paris: Gallimard, 2005. For a rare, excellent short survey which integrates Francophone and Anglophone republican theories, see Serge Audier, *Les théories de la république.* Paris: La Découverte, 2004.

17. For attempts to locate French republicanism in relation to communitarian philosophy, Rawlsian political liberalism and Anglophone republicanism, see the works of Alain Renaut, notably: (with Sylvie Mesure) *Alter Ego. Les paradoxes de l'identité démocratique.* Paris: Aubier, 1999; 'Les discussions républicaines du républicanisme moderne', in Alain Renaut (ed.), *Histoire de la philosophie politique,* Vol. 4. Paris: Calmann-Lévy, 1999, pp. 317–59; *Qu'est ce qu'une politique juste? Essai sur la question du meilleur régime.* Paris: Grasset, 2004; *Qu'est ce qu'un peuple libre? Libéralisme ou républicanisme.* Paris: Grasset, 2005.

18. See Cécile Laborde, 'Republican Citizenship and the Crisis of Integration in France', in Richard Bellamy, Dario Castiglione, and Emilio Santoro (eds), *Lineages of Citizenship*. Basingstoke: Palgrave, 2004, pp. 116–23; Jeremy Jennings, 'L'Egalité', 'La Liberté', 'L'Universalisme', in Vincent Duclert and Christophe Prochasson (eds), *Dictionnaire Critique de la République*. Paris: Flammarion, 2002, pp. 169–76, 216–23, 275–82; Cécile Laborde, 'La citoyenneté', in *ibid.*, pp. 116–23.

19. Karl Marx, 'The Jewish Question', in David McLellan, *Karl Marx: Selected Writings*. Oxford: Oxford University Press, 1977, pp. 51–7. On this theme, see also J. C. Isaac, 'Republicanism vs. Liberalism? A Reconsideration', *History of Political Thought*, Vol. 9, No. 2, Summer 1988, pp. 349–77.

20. I borrow the term from Dominique Schnapper, *La Communauté des Citoyens*.

21. See, for example, Max Silverman, *Deconstructing the Nation. Immigration, Racism and Citizenship in Modern France*. London and New York: Routledge, 1992; Alec G. Hargreaves, *Immigration, 'Race' and Ethnicity in Contemporary France*. London: Routledge, 1995.

22. Quentin Skinner, 'Meaning and Understanding in the History of Ideas', *History and Theory*, Vol. 8, 1969, pp. 3–53.

23. Elisabetta Galeotti, 'Citizenship and Equality. The Place for Toleration', *Political Theory*, Vol. 21, No. 4, 1993, pp. 585–605; Elisabetta Galeotti, *Toleration as Recognition*. Cambridge: Cambridge University Press, 2002, ch. 4.

24. Further, its explanatory ambitions are limited: in particular, it does not attempt to give a full account of the *causes* of the hijab controversy. Thus, it does not rely on the idealist claim that the law of Mar. 2004 can be explained by the influence of the French republican tradition. Clearly, international and domestic factors, not all mediated (or ideologically justified) by appeal to high-minded moral principles, played a crucial role. For more comprehensive critical analyses, see, notably, Françoise Lorcerie (ed.), *La politisation du voile en France, en Europe et dans le monde arabe*. Paris: Harmattan, 2005; John R. Bowen, *Why the French don't like Headscarves. Islam, the State and Public Space*. Princeton NJ: Princeton University Press, 2007.

25. On the distinction, and its relevance to political philosophy, see Hans Reichenbach, *Experience and Prediction*. Chicago: University of Chicago Press, 1961, pp. 6–7, Alan Nelson, 'Explanation and Justification in Political Philosophy', *Ethics*, Vol. 97, No. 1, Oct. 1986, pp. 154–76.

26. Quentin Skinner, 'The Idea of Negative Liberty: Machiavellian and Modern Perspectives', in his *Visions of Politics*, Vol. II, *Renaissance Virtues*. Cambridge: Cambridge University Press, 186–212, at pp. 190–5; Quentin Skinner, *Liberty before Liberalism*, pp. 109–20.

27. One excellent example of contextual yet analytical political theory is Adrian Favell, *Philosophies of Integration. Immigration and the Idea of Citizenship in France and Britain*. Basingtoke: Macmillan, 1998. For a methodological statement, see Adrian Favell and Tariq Modood, 'Multiculturalism and Normative Political Theory' in Alan Finlayson (ed.), *Contemporary Political Thought: a Reader and Guide*. Edinburgh: Edinburgh University Press, 2003,

pp. 484–513. See also Joseph H. Carens, *Culture, Citizenship and Community. A Contextual Exploration of Justice as Even-Handedness.* Oxford: Oxford University Press, 2000, and Bikhu Parekh, *Rethinking Multiculturalism.* Basingstoke: Macmillan, 2000.

28. Throughout the book, I use the terms 'Muslim headscarf' and 'hijab' interchangeably, and I also occasionally refer to the practice of 'veiling', by which I simply mean the wearing of a scarf covering the hair and neck. This is done for ease of presentation, and is not intended to deny the variety and contestability of the cultural and religious meanings associated with the terms 'hijab' and 'veiling'. For more details, see Fadwa El Guindi, *Veil. Privacy, Modesty and Resistance.* Oxford: Berg, 1999; Christian Jambert and Abdelwahab Meddeb, 'Voile et dévoilement', *Esprit*, Vol. 305, June 2004, pp. 131–47; Fawzia Zouari, *Le voile islamique*; Dounia Bouzar, Saida Kada, *L'une voilée, l'autre pas. Le témoignage de deux musulmanes françaises.* Paris: Albin Michel, 2003; Gaspard, Khoroskhavar, *Le Foulard et la république.* I do not take side in the theological dispute as to whether Islam mandates the hijab at all, or merely prohibits immodesty. There are two passages in the Qur'an that deal with the correctness of women's clothing: 'Prophet, tell your wives, your daughters, and women believers to make their outer garments hang low over them [*adna al-jilbab* has also been translated as 'wrap around them'] so as to be recognized and not insulted.' (33:59). 'And tell believing women that they should lower their gaze, guard their private parts and not flaunt their charms beyond what [ordinarily] shows.' (24:31). A core aspect of freedom of religion is that religious groups have the right to interpret their own religious texts and then follow the derived meaning. Courts generally consider it undesirable to enter into a debate as to whether a particular practice is central to a religion; problems arise, however, when there is an internal dispute as to the centrality of the practice, as is the case with hijab. Fortunately, my own arguments against the ban on hijab avoid taking a stance on this controversial theological issue. They are valid, that is, whether or not the hijab is a compulsory requirement or not. Note, too, that I do not refer to the *jilbab*, a headscarf and gown that leave only the face and hands exposed, nor to the *niqab* which also covers the face, nor to the *burka* which additionally covers the eyes, as these are not commonly worn by Muslims in France. In the UK, the full covering of the face by Muslim women (*niqab*) has recently been criticized as an obstacle to face-to-face communication, interpersonal identification, and smooth community relations. These are fairly distinct issues from those examined in this book, related as they are to the legitimacy of social and cultural conventions (such as the benefits of facial exposure); they do not directly touch upon my central themes of secularism, non-domination, and civic solidarity (although, arguably, the argument that people are more trusting of one another if they can see one another's face could be brought under this heading). Other disputes in the UK and elsewhere have centered on the acceptability of Muslim dress as an alternative to standard (school, state, or corporate) uniform requirements. This relates to the broader

question of the legitimacy of religious exemptions from general rules, which I discuss at various places in the book, notably in Chapter 4. The French hijab controversy is distinctive and challenging because there is no uniform policy in French state schools.

29. Good extended discussions or surveys include Bowen, *Why the French don't like Headscarves*; Dominic McGoldrick, *Human Rights and Religion: the Islamic Headscarf Debate in Europe*. Oxford and Portland: Hart, 2006, pp. 34–106; Lorcerie, *La politisation du voile*; Jean-Michel Helvig (ed.), *La laïcité dévoilée. Quinze années de débat en quarante Rebonds*. Paris: Libération and Éditions de l'Aube, 2004.

30. Tariq Modood, Anna Triandafyllidou, and Ricard Zapata-Barrero, *Multiculturalism, Muslims and Citizenship. A European Approach*. London: Routledge, 2006; McGoldrick, *Human Rights and Religion: The Islamic Headscarf in Europe*.

31. On the ideals of *laïcité*, see Marcel Gauchet, *La religion dans la démocratie. Parcours de la laïcité*. Paris: Gallimard, 1998; Henri Pena-Ruiz, *Dieu et Marianne. Philosophie de la laïcité*. Paris: Presses Universitaires de France, 1999; Emile Poulat, *Liberté-Laïcité? La guerre des deux France et le principe de modernité*. Paris, Cerf/Cujas, 1987; Jean Baubérot, *Histoire de la laïcité en France*. Paris: Presses Universitaires de France, 2000; Jean Baudouin and Philippe Portier (eds), *La laïcité, valeur d'aujourd'hui? Contestations et renégotiations du modèle français*. Rennes: Presses Universitaires de Rennes, 2001.

32. On the internal coherence of *laïcité*, see Cécile Laborde, 'On Republican Toleration', *Constellations. An International Journal of Critical and Democratic Theory*, Vol. 9, July 2002, pp. 167–83. That the wearing of hijab in school raised three distinct sets of issues has also been perceived by John Bowen, who notes that official republicans hoped that a law stating publicly that the hijab 'had no place in the "Republican sanctuary"', as President Chirac referred to the public school, might just reset the republic on the right path towards '*integrating immigrants, privatizing religion, and giving women equal public and social rights*'. (italics added). Bowen, *Why the French don't like Headscarves,* 157.

33. See, in particular, Karl Marx, 'The Jewish Question'; Karl Marx (with Friedrich Engels), *The German Ideology*. Amherst, NY: Prometheus Books, 1998; Pierre Bourdieu and Jean-Claude Passeron, *Reproduction in Education, Society and Culture*. London: Sage, 1990; Pierre Bourdieu, *La domination masculine*. Paris: Seuil, 1998; Jürgen Habermas, *The Theory of Communicative Action*. Boston: Beacon Press, 1987; Jürgen Habermas, *Between Facts and Norms*. Boston: MIT Press, 1996.

34. The need to complement the abstract ideals of republicanism with a critical social theory, and notably a sociology of domination, is also emphasized in Vincent Bourdeau and Roberto Merril (eds), *La république et ses démons. Essais de républicanisme appliqué*. Paris: Éditions Eres, 2007.

35. Gerald Allan Cohen, 'Facts and Principles', *Philosophy and Public Affairs*, Vol. 31, No. 3, 2003, pp. 211–45; Andrew Mason, 'Just Constraints', *British Journal of Political Science*, Vol. 34, 2004, pp. 251–68; David Miller, *Principles of Social Justice*. Cambridge, MA: Harvard University Press, 2001; Colin

Farrelly, 'Justice in Ideal Theory: A Refutation', *Political Studies*, Vol. 55, No. 4, Dec. 2007, pp. 844–64; Andrea Sangiovanni, 'Justice and the Priority of Politics to Morality', *Journal of Political Philosophy*, forthcoming, 2008.

36. See, for example, Brian Barry, who suggests that the liberal state should be 'an instrument for satisfying the wants that men happen to have rather than a means of making good men'. *Political Argument*. London: Routledge, 1965, p. 66.

37. Cass R. Sunstein, 'Preferences and Politics', in his *Free Markets and Social Justice*. Oxford University Press, 1997, pp. 13–31; Joshua Cohen, 'Taking People as They Are?', in *Philosophy and Public Affairs*, Vol. 30, No. 4, Fall 2001, pp. 363–86; Jonathan Wolff, 'Fairness, Respect, and the Egalitarian Ethos', *Philosophy and Public Affairs*, Vol. 27, No. 2, Spring 1998, pp. 97–122.

38. Gerald Allan Cohen, 'Incentives, Inequality, and Community', in Grethe Peterson (ed.), *The Tanner Lectures on Human Values*, Vol. 13. Salt Lake City, UT: University of Utah Press, 1992; 'Where the Action Is: On the Site of Distributive Justice', *Philosophy and Public Affairs*, Vol. 26, No. 1, 1997, pp. 3–30; *If You're An Egalitarian, How Come You're So Rich?* Cambridge, MA: Harvard University Press, 2000.

39. For a recent re-statement, see Richard Dagger, *Civic Virtues*.

40. Jonathan Seglow, 'Theorizing Recognition', in Bruce Haddock and Peter Stuch (eds), *Multiculturalism, Identity and Rights*. London: Routledge, pp. 78–93; Nancy Fraser, 'Social Justice in the Age of Identity Politics: Redistribution, Recognition and Participation', in N. Fraser and A. Honneth *Redistribution or Recognition? A Political-Philosophical Exchange*. London: Verso, 2003, pp. 7–109.

41. For broad critiques of the use of culture in political theory, see Seyla Benhabib, *The Claims of Culture: Equality and Diversity in the Global Era*. Princeton NJ: Princeton University Press, 2002; David Scott, 'Culture in Political Theory', *Political Theory*, Vol. 31, No. 1, Feb. 2003, pp. 92–115 and, more recently, Anne Phillips, *Multiculturalism without Culture*. Princeton, NJ: Princeton University Press, 2007. Phillips's analyses converge with some of mine; unfortunately, I read her book too late fully to incorporate and discuss her critique of standard accounts of culture and identity.

42. Favell and Modood, 'Multiculturalism and Normative Political Theory'.

43. Phillipe Poutignant and Jocelyne Streiff-Fenant, *Théories de l'ethnicité*. Paris: Presses Universitaires de France, 1995.

44. For a rare attempt to bring this insight to bear on normative multicultural philosophy, see Galeotti, *Toleration as Recognition*; and for a broader analysis of the strategic and political uses of culture in so-called multicultural conflict, see Monique Deveaux, *Gender and Justice in Multicultural Liberal States*. Oxford: Oxford University Press, 2006.

45. For the claim that political multiculturalism is not incompatible with an anti-essentialist view of culture and identity, see Tariq Modood, 'Anti-Essentialism, Multiculturalism and the "Recognition" of Religious Groups', *Journal of Political Philosophy*, Vol. 6, No. 4, 1998, pp. 378–99.

46. Elizabeth Anderson, 'What is the Point of Equality?', *Ethics*, Vol. 109, 1999, pp. 287–337.

47. On social equality, see David Miller, 'Complex Equality', in David Miller and Michael Walzer (eds), *Pluralism, Justice and Equality*. Oxford, Oxford University Press, 1995, pp. 197–225; David Miller, *Principles of Social Justice*, pp. 15–6, 240–41.

48. For a critical analysis of the (slightly different) claim that multicultural policies negatively impact on social solidarity, see Keith Banting and Will Kymlicka (eds), *Recognition and Redistribution in Contemporary Democracies*. Oxford: Oxford University Press, 2006.

49. For different versions of this claim, see Brian Barry, *Culture and Equality*, Cambridge: Polity, 2001; Amy Gutmann, *Identity in Democracy*. Princeton, NJ: Princeton University Press, 2003.

50. My account of status quo neutrality is indebted to Cass R. Sunstein. *The Partial Constitution*. Cambridge, MA: Harvard University Press, 1993, *passim*.

51. See, for example, William Connolly, *Identity/Difference: Democratic Negotiations of Political Paradox*. Ithaca: Cornell University Press, 1991; Iris Marion Young, *Justice and the Politics of Difference*. Princeton, NJ: Princeton University Press, 1990.

52. Thomas A. Spragens, *Civic Liberalism. Reflections on our Democratic Ideals*. Lanham, MD: Rowman and Littlefield, 1999, p. 100.

53. For an insightful critique of Michel Foucaut's theory of power on both these counts, see Nancy Fraser, 'Foucault on Modern Power: Empirical Insights and Normative Confusions', *Praxis International*, Vol. 1, No. 3, 1981, pp. 272–87.

54. John Rawls, *A Theory of Justice*. Cambridge, MA: Harvard University Press, 1971 (1973 ed.), p. 334.

55. Colin Farrelly, 'Dualism, Incentives and the Demands of Rawlsian Justice', *Canadian Journal of Political Science*, Vol. 38, No. 3, Sept. 2005, pp. 675–95. For a more general, sophisticated discussion of the demands of compliance and reciprocity in non-ideal theory, see Liam B. Murphy, *Moral Demands in Nonideal Theory*. Oxford: Oxford University Press, 2000.

56. More problematic is the case of countries such as Turkey, where the wearing of hijab has been widely interpreted as the powerful and visible symbol of an Islamist onslaught on the secular republic. The ban on hijab in universities was consequently found permissible by the European Court of Human Rights, in the name of respect for Turkey's national secularist tradition. In the *Leyla Sahin v Turkey* case, the European Court of Human Rights held with the University of Istanbul which had refused admission to a student wearing an 'Islamic-style headscarf'. See McGoldrick, 'Comparative State Practice: Turkey', in his *Human Rights and Religion: the Islamic Headscarf Debate in Europe*, pp. 132–72.

57. On idealization, see Onora O'Neill, *Towards Justice and Virtue: A Constructive Account of Practical Reasoning*. Cambridge: Cambridge University Press, 1996, p. 41.

58. For an exploration of some problems related to the pursuit of justice in the non-ideal world, see George Sher, *Approximate Justice. Studies in Non-Ideal Theory*. Lanham: Rowman & Littlefield, 1997.

59. Philip Pettit, 'Negative Liberty, Liberal and Republican', *European Journal of Philosophy*, Vol. 1, No. 1, 1993, pp. 15–38; Philip Pettit, 'Freedom as Antipower', *Ethics*, Vol. 106, No. 3, 1996, pp. 576–604; Pettit, *Republicanism*.

60. Thus, the republican strategy of non-domination shares similarities with 'negative' approaches to politics, which prioritize the reduction of evils such as cruelty and humiliation over the achievement of a fully just society. See Judith Skhlar, 'The Liberalism of Fear', in Nancy Rosemblum (ed.), *Liberalism and the Moral Life*. Cambridge, MA, Harvard University Press, 1989; Avishai Margalit, *The Decent Society*. Cambridge, MA: Harvard University Press, 1996; Jacob T. Levy, *The Multiculturalism of Fear*. Oxford: Oxford University Press, 2000.

61. Nancy Fraser, 'Social Justice in the Age of Identity Politics', p. 29.

62. On the broadening of the concept of domination in recent political philosophy, see Melissa S. Williams and Stephen Macedo (eds), *Political Exclusion and Domination. Nomos*, Vol. 46. New York: New York University Press, 2005.

63. For recent and influential formulations, see Cohen, 'Incentives, Inequality, and Community', 'Where the Action Is', *If You're An Egalitarian...*

64. Cohen, 'Taking People as They Are?'

65. Andrew Williams, 'Incentives, Inequality and Publicity', *Philosophy and Public Affairs*, Vol. 27, No. 3, Summer 1998, pp. 225–47; David Estlund, 'Liberalism, Equality and Fraternity in Cohen's Critique of Rawls', *Journal of Political Philosophy*, Vol. 6, 1998, pp. 99–112.

66. Michael Billig, *Banal Nationalism*. London: Sage, 1997; Veit Bader, 'The Cultural Conditions of Transnational Citizenship. On the Interpenetration of Political and Ethnic Cultures', *Political Theory*, Vol. 25, No. 6, 1997, pp. 771–813.

67. Elisabetta Galeotti, *Toleration as Recognition*. Cambridge: Cambridge University Press, 2002, *passim*. For an illuminating discussion, which explicitly connects Galeotti's theory of liberal recognition to the debate about the role of dominating social norms in liberal thought, see Sune Lægaard, 'Galeotti on Recognition as Inclusion', *Critical Review of International Social and Political Philosophy*, Vol. 2, No. 3, September 2008.

68. Brian Barry, *Justice as impartiality*. Clarendon Press Oxford, 1995, 165n.

69. Levy, *The Multiculturalism of Fear*, Chapter 8: 'Ethnic Symbolism and Official Apologies', pp. 222–48.

70. Clearly, this only partially applies to the prevalence of anti-racist and anti-Muslim prejudice in society. Yet it must be immediately noted that many liberal states criminalize certain types of offensive or humiliating speech, in particular racial or religious 'hate speech'. See Bhikhu Parekh, 'Hate Speech', *Public Policy Research*, Vol. 12, No. 4, Dec. 2005–Feb. 2006, pp. 213–23.

71. Peter Jones, 'Equality, Recognition and Difference', *Critical Review of International Social and Political Philosophy*, Vol. 9, No. 1, Mar. 2006, pp. 23–46.
72. Jones, 'Equality, Recognition and Difference', p. 42, citing Young, *Justice and the Politics of Difference*. Princeton, NJ: Princeton University Press, 1990, p. 104.
73. See, notably, Will Kymlicka, 'The New Debate Over Minority Rights' in his *Politics in the Vernacular*, pp. 17–38.
74. Will Kymlicka, *Multicultural Citizenship. A Liberal Theory of Minority Rights*. Oxford: Oxford University Press, 1995, *passim*.
75. Anthony Appiah, 'Multicultural Misunderstanding', *New York Review of Books*, Vol. 44, No. 15, 9 Oct. 1997: 30–6, p. 36, quoted in Barry, *Culture and Equality*, p. 306.
76. For a list of Kymlicka's proposals for 'immigrant multiculturalism', see his 'Immigrant Multiculturalism', in *Politics in the Vernacular*, 152–76, at p. 163.
77. Kymlicka, *Politics in the Vernacular*, p. 30.
78. *Ibid.*, p. 3.
79. Kymlicka, *Multicultural Citizenship*, pp. 82–4.
80. Pettit, *Republicanism*, 138–40; Maynor, *Republicanism in the Modern World*, pp. 110–14; Alice Le Goff, 'Néo-républicanisme et féminisme: La question de la parité', in Merril Bourdeau, *La république et ses démons*, pp. 65–84; Phillips, A. (2000). 'Feminism and Republicanism: Is this a Plausible Alliance?', *Journal of Political Philosophy*, Vol. 8, No. 2, pp. 279–93.
81. Anderson, 'What is the Point of Equality?'; John Maynor, 'Without Regret: the Comprehensive Nature of Non-Domination', *Politics*, Vol. 22, 2002, pp. 51–8 and ch. 4 of his *Republicanism in the Modern World*.
82. For a suggestive parallel between Pettit's theory of contestatory democracy and Jacques Rancière's theory of radical democracy, see Vincent Bourdeau, 'Un républicanisme du gaz et de l'eau courante', in Bowdenn and Merril, *La république et ses démons*, 13–41, at pp. 39–41. On the history of contestatory democracy in France, see Pierre Rosanvallon, *Le modèle politique français. La société civile contre le jacobinisme de 1789 à nos jours*. Paris: Seuil, 2004; *La contre-démocratie, la politique à l'age de la défiance*. Paris: Seuil, 2006.
83. For a discussion of the distinction between philosophy and ideology, and a powerful defence of the contribution of ideologies to political theory in general, see Michael Freeden, *Ideologies and Political Theory. A Conceptual Approach*. Oxford: Clarendon Press, 1996, especially at pp. 27–33.
84. It is important to stress that neither official republicans nor tolerant republicans necessarily refer to clearly identifiable groups of people, but rather to specific lines of arguments brought forward either for or against the ban on hijab.

Notes to Chapter 2

1. For a synthetic account of the 'liberalism of reasoned respect' in relation to religion, see Paul J. Weithman (ed.), *Religion and Contemporary Liberalism*.

Notre Dame, IN: University of Notre Dame Press, 1997, pp. 1–37; on the link between political liberalism and post-Reformation religious conflicts, see John Rawls, *Political Liberalism*. New York: Columbia University Press, 1993, pp. xiv–vi; on liberal principles of equality as requiring the 'privatization' of differences and uniform rights see Brian Barry, *Culture and Equality*. Cambridge: Polity, 2001, pp. 24–5; and for an articulation of the 'separation doctrine' as being underpinned by libertarian, egalitarian, and neutralist ideals, see Robert Audi, 'The Separation of Church and State and the Obligations of Citizenship', *Philosophy and Public Affairs*, Vol. 18, No. 3, Summer 1989, pp. 259–96.

2. For good analyses of how the liberal ideal of neutrality informs various institutional regimes of church–state relations, see Stephen V. Monsma and J. Christopher Soper, *The Challenge of Pluralism. Church and State in Five Democracies*. Lanham, MD: Rowman and Littlefield, 1997; John T. S. Madeley, 'European Liberal Democracy and the Principle of State Religious Neutrality' *West European Politics*, 2003, Vol. 26, No. 1, pp. 1–22.

3. Named after its president, the *médiateur de la république* (ombudsman) Bernard Stasi, the Commission was made up of 20 experts (mostly academics and lawyers) and interviewed, between Sept. and Dec. 2003, a number of political, religious, educational, and associational representatives. For the full report, see Bernard Stasi, *Laïcité et République. Rapport de la commission de réflexion sur l'application du principe de laïcité dans la République remis au Président de la République le 11 décembre 2003* Paris: La Documentation Française, 2004, thereafter 'Stasi Report'. Available at <http://www.iesr.ephe. sorbonne.fr/docannexe/file/3112/rapport_laicite.Stasi.pdf> (last accessed 27 July 2007). For a good analysis, see Alessandro Ferrari, 'Laïcité et voile islamique en France au début du nouveau millénaire', *Migrations Société*, Vol. 16, No. 96, Nov.–Dec. 2004, pp. 63–129.

4. Here I follow Audi, 'The Separation of Church and State'.

5. *Laïque* is the adjectival form of *laïcité*.

6. Michel Bouleau, 'La démission du Conseil d'État dans l' *affaire du foulard*', in Charles Zarka (ed.), *L'Islam en France*. Special issue of *Cités*, Mar. 2004, pp. 277–85, at p. 278.

7. The first three are adapted from Robert Audi, 'The Separation of Church and State…'. What Audi refers to as a 'neutralist' strand, however, I prefer to call an 'agnostic' one, to avoid confusion with the more general theory of state neutrality represented by *laïcité*.

8. Barry, *Culture and Equality*.

9. For stimulating reflections about this conflict, see 'Developments in the Law: Religion and the State', *Harvard Law Review*, Vol. 100, 1987, pp. 1606–781.

10. The expression is Veit Bader's, 'Religious Diversity and Democratic Institutional Pluralism', *Political Theory*, Vol. 31, No. 2, Apr. 2003, pp. 265–94, at p. 269.

11. Jacques Zylberberg, 'Laïcité, connais pas: Allemagne, Canada, États-Unis, Royaume-Uni', *Pouvoirs*, Vol. 75, 1995, pp. 37–52, at pp. 42–3; Jacqueline Costa-Lascoux, *Les trois âges de la laïcité. Débat avec Joseph Sitruk, Grand Rabbin de France*. Paris: Hachette, 1996, pp. 8, 96–100.

12. For details, see Alain Boyer, *Le droit des religions en France*. Paris: Presses Universitaire de France, 1993, pp. 125–40.

13. Henri Pena-Ruiz, Deliberative Democracy, the Discursive Dilemma, and Republican Theory', in James Fishkin, and Peter Laslett (eds.), *Philosophy, Politics and Society*, Vol. 7, New York: Cambridge University Press, 2003. 159–63; Jeanne-Hélène Kaltenbach, Michèle Tribalat, *La République et l'Islam. Entre crainte et aveuglement*. Paris: Gallimard, 2002, p. 118.

14. Stasi Report, p. 13.

15. Henri Pena-Ruiz, *Dieu et Marianne. Philosophie de la laïcité*. Paris: Presses Universitaires de France, 1999, p. 138.

16. Pierre Hayat, *La passion laïque de Ferdinand Buisson*. Paris: Kimé, 1999, p. 43.

17. Cited in Soheib Bencheikh, *Marianne et le Prophète. L'Islam dans la France laïque*. Paris: Livre de Poche, 2003, p. 52.

18. L. De Naurois, cited in Stéphane Pierré-Caps, 'Les "nouveaux cultes" et le droit public', *Revue de Droit Public*, Vol. 4, 1990, pp. 1073–119, at p. 1076. For a general defence of 'laïcité as equality', see Henri Pena-Ruiz, *La laïcité pour l'égalité*. Paris: Mille et Une Nuits, 2001.

19. For a recent statement, see Barry, *Culture and Equality*.

20. Jean-Michel Lemoyne de Forges, 'Laïcité et liberté religieuse en France' in Joël-Benoît d'Onorio, *La liberté religieuse dans le monde. Analyse doctrinale et politique*. Paris: Editions Universitaires, 1991, pp. 149–70, at pp. 153, 164–5.

21. Cited in Danièle Lochak, 'Les minorités et le droit public français: du refus des différences à la gestion des différences', in Alain Ferret and Gérard Soulier (eds), *Les minorités et leurs droits depuis 1789*. Paris: Harmattan, 1989, pp. 111–84, at pp. 111–12.

22. See Lochak, 'Les minorités et le droit public'.

23. Norbert Rouland, 'La tradition juridique française et la diversité culturelle', *Droit et Société*, Vol. 27, 1994, pp. 381–419.

24. Charles Taylor, 'Multiculturalism and the "Politics of Recognition"', in Amy Gutmann (ed.), *Multiculturalism and the Politics of Recognition*. Princeton, NJ: Princeton University Press, 1994, pp. 25–36. Taylor famously contrasts the Enlightenment-influenced 'liberalism of equal dignity' with the Romantic-influenced 'liberalism of authenticity' revived by contemporary multiculturalists.

25. Barry, *Culture and Equality*, p. 25.

26. Geneviève Koubi, 'Le droit à la différence, un droit à l'indifférence?', *Revue de la Recherche Juridique. Droit Prospectif*, Vol. 2, No. 53, 1993, pp. 451–63, at p. 462.

27. Geneviève Koubi, 'Le juge administratif et la liberté de religion', *Revue francaise de droit administratif*, Nov.–Dec. 2003, pp. 1055–61, at p. 1061.

28. See the recommendations of the Haut Conseil à l'Intégration, *L'Islam dans la République. Rapport au Premier Ministre.* Paris: Documentation Française, 2001, p. 50, *passim.*

29. Tribalat Kaltenbach, *La République et l'Islam,* p. 140.

30. Kenneth H. F. Dyson, *The State Tradition in Western Europe: A Study of An Idea and Institution.* Oxford, 1980; Pierre Rosanvallon, *L'État en France. De 1798 à nos jours.* Paris: Seuil, 1990 and for a comparative analysis of French and British concepts of the state, Cécile Laborde, 'The Concept of the State in British and French Political Thought', *Political Studies,* Vol. 48, 2000, pp. 540–57.

31. Dyson, *The State Tradition,* p. 43.

32. Pierre Hayat, *La Passion laïque de Ferdinand Buisson.* Paris: Éditions Kimé, 1999, pp. 31–2.

33. Marcel Gauchet, *La religion dans la démocratie. Parcours de la laïcité.* Paris: Gallimard, 1998, p. 47.

34. To borrow Gauchet's felicitous expression, *La religion dans la démocratie,* p. 52.

35. Mona Ozouf, *L'école de la France: Essais sur la Révolution, l'utopie et l'enseignement.* Paris: Gallimard, 1984; Yves Deloye, *Ecole et citoyenneté. L'individualisme républicain de Jules Ferry à Vichy.* Paris: Presses de la Fondation Nationales des Sciences Politiques, 1994.

36. Stephen Macedo, *Diversity and Distrust. Civic Education in a Multicultural Democracy.* Cambridge, MA: Harvard University Press, 2000.

37. Eamonn Callan, *Creating Citizens. Political Education and Liberal Democracy.* Oxford: Oxford University Press, 1997.

38. Charles Taylor, 'Modes of Secularism', in Rajeev Bhargava (ed.), *Secularism and its Critics.* Delhi: Oxford University Press, 1998, pp. 31–53.

39. Bhargava, *Secularism and its Critics,* 'Introduction', p. 17.

40. Cited in Phyllis Stock-Morton, *Moral Education for a Secular Society. The Development of* Morale Laïque *in Nineteenth Century France.* New York: State University of New York Press, 1988. p. 174.

41. See the stimulating analyses of Gauchet, *Religion dans la démocratie,* pp. 31–60.

42. Stock-Morton, *Moral Education*; Jacqueline Lalouette, *La République anticléricale. XIX-XXème siècles.* Paris: Seuil, 2002, pp. 142–60, 227–61. For anthologies of laïcité, see Guy Gauthier and Claude Nicolet (eds), *La laïcité en mémoire.* Paris: Edilic, 1987, and on republican philosophy generally, see Claude Nicolet, *L'idée républicaine en France (1789–1924). Essai d'histoire critique.* Paris: Gallimard, 1982.

43. Cited in Stock-Morton, *Moral Education,* p. 99.

44. Gauchet, *Religion dans la démocratie,* p. 51.

45. Thibaud Collin, 'Quel enseignement moral dans une societe laïque?', *Liberté Politique,* Vol. 24, Winter, 2003–4, pp. 71–85, at p. 78.

46. For a discussion on this point, see Audi, 'The Separation of Church and State', Paul J. Weithman, 'The Separation of Church and State: Some

Questions for Professor Audi', *Philosophy and Public Affairs*, Vol. 20, No. 1, Winter 1991, pp. 52–65, and Robert Audi, 'Religious Commitment and Secular Reason: A Reply to Professor Weithman', *Philosophy and Public Affairs*, Vol. 20, No. 1, Winter 1991, pp. 66–76.

47. On the anticlericalism of the Third Republic, see Lalouette, La *République anti-cléricale.*

48. Boyer, *Le droit des religions*, p. 65.

49. For details, see Véronique Fabre-Alibert, 'La loi française du 15 mars 2004 encadrant, en application du principe de *laïcité* le port de signes ou de tenues manifestant une appartenance religieuse dans les écoles, collèges et lycées publics: vers un pacte social laïque?', *Revue Trimestrielle des Droits de l'Homme*, Vol. 59, July 2004, pp. 575–609, at pp. 603–4.

50. The Édict was 'revoked' in 1685, putting an end to this early experience in toleration.

51. Martine Cohen, 'L'intégration de l'Islam et des musulmans en France: modèles du passé et pratiques actuelles', in Jean Baudouin and Philippe Portier (eds), *La laïcité, valeur d'aujourd'hui? Contestations et renégotiations du modèle français*. Rennes: Presses Universitaires de Rennes, 2001, pp. 315–30, at pp. 316–18; Boyer, *Le droit des religions*, p. 18.

52. Cohen, 'L'intégration de l'Islam'. On the commitment to republicanism and *laïcité* of the Jewish political elite during the Third Republic, see Pierre Birnbaum, *Les fous de la République. Histoire politique des Juifs d'Etat de Gambetta à Vichy*. Paris: Fayard, 1992, and for a nuanced account of the historical 'assimilation' of Jews in France, see Esther Benbassa, *Histoire des Juifs de France*. Paris: Seuil, 1997.

53. This preoccupation is not of course specifically French. For an analysis of the problems posed by Muslim demands to British 'secular multiculturalists', see, for example, Tariq Modood, 'La place des musulmans dans le multiculturalisme laïc en Grande-Bretagne', *Social Compass*, Vol. 47, 2000, pp. 1, 41–55.

54. Cited in Michel Renard, 'Lois de l'islam, lois de la République: l'impossible conciliation', in Zarka, *L'Islam en France.* pp. 387–95, at p. 390.

55. Dominique Schnapper, *La France de l'intégration. Sociologie de la nation en 1990*. Paris: Gallimard, 1990, p. 143.

56. For a legal analysis of the associational laws of 1901 and 1905, see Boyer, pp. 87–105.

57. See, for example, Caroline Fourest, *Frère Tariq: Discours, stratégie et méthode de Tariq Ramadan*. Paris: Grasset, 2004. Ramadan's views are made explicit in Tariq Ramadan *Les Musulmans dans la laïcité*, Lyon: Éd. Tawhid, 2004.

58. Rawls, *Political Liberalism*, pp. 148, 303.

59. See the articles by Hervé Terrel, Franck Frégosi, Nacira Guénif-Souilamas and Danièle Hervieu-Léger in Zarka, *L'Islam en France*, and for a good analysis, Jonathan Laurence and Justin Veisse, *Integrating Islam. Political and Religious Challenges in Contemporary France*. Washington, DC: Brookings Institution Press, 2006.

60. Pierre Mazet, 'La construction contemporaine de la laïcité par le juge et la doctrine', in Baudouin and Portier, *La laïcité, valeur d'aujourd'hui*, pp. 263–83, p. 270.
61. Gauchet, *La religion dans la Democratie*, p. 84.
62. Gilles Pellissier, *Le principe d'égalité en droit public*. Paris: Librairie Générale de Droit et de Jurisprudence, 1996, p. 54.
63. Laurent Wauquiez-Motte, 'Laïcité et neutralité de l'État', *Les Cahiers de la Fonction Publique*, Apr. 2004, pp. 7–9, at p. 8; Ludivine Delsenne, 'De la difficile adaptation du principe républicain de laïcité à l'évolution socio-culturelle française', *Revue du Droit Public*, Vol. 2, 2005, pp. 427–62, at pp. 442–4.
64. Cited in Stasi Report, p. 22.
65. See, for example, the debate about the wearing of Sikh turbans by the Royal Canadian Mounted Police.
66. For a detailed exposition of recent case law about the conciliation between public service and freedom of conscience, see Jean Barthélémy, 'La liberté de religion et le service public', *Revue française de droit administratif*, Nov.–Dec. 2003, pp. 1066–73.
67. For a presentation of those early laïque laws, see Dominique Gros, 'La séparation de l'Église et de l'École (1878–1886). Principes juridiques fondateurs de la laïcité scolaire' in Jean Baudouin and Philippe Portier (eds), *La laïcité, valeur d'aujourd'hui? Contestations et renégotiations du modèle français*. Rennes: Presses Universitaires de Rennes, 2001, pp. 51–63.
68. For subsequent case law, see Olivier Dord, 'Laïcité à l'école: l'obscure clarté de la circulaire "Fillon" du 18 mai 2004', *Actualité Juridique du Droit Administratif*, 26 July 2004, 1523–29.
69. Weber Eugen, *Peasants into Frenchmen*. Stanford, CA: Stanford University Press, 1976. For wonderful testimonies of teachers' experiences, see Jacques and Mona Ozouf, *La République des Instituteurs*. Paris: Gallimard, 1992.
70. For an instructive comparison along those lines see Meira Levinson, 'Liberalism versus Democracy? Schooling Private Citizens in the Public Square', *British Journal of Political Science*, Vol. 27, 1997, pp. 333–60, and on 'detached schools', see her *The Demands of Liberal Education*. Oxford: Oxford University Press, 1999, pp. 65–82.
71. Elizabeth Badinter, Régis Debray, Alain Finkielkraut, Elisabeth de Fontenay and Catherine Kintzler, 'Profs, ne capitulons pas', *Nouvel Obser-vateur*, 27 Oct. 1989.
72. For a legal analysis of neutrality in schools, see Agnès Thiriot, 'Le principe de neutralité et l'enseignement', *Savoir-Education–Formation*, Vol. 3, 1993, pp. 403–23.
73. Hayat, *Passion laïque*, p. 94.
74. Jules Ferry, 'Lettre aux instituteurs' (27 Nov. 1883), reprinted in *Pouvoirs*, Vol. 75, 1995, pp. 109–16, at 111 and *passim*.
75. Stasi Report, p. 56.

76. Delafaye, *Laïcité de combat*, p. 80.

77. See Conseil d'État, Section de l'intérieur, 27 novembre 1989, n°346893, Avis, 'Port du foulard islamique', at <http://www.rajf.org/article.php3?id_article=1065> (last accessed 17 July 2007).

78. See Jean-Claude William, 'Le Conseil d'État et la laïcité. Propos sur l'avis du 27 novembre 1989', *Revue Française de Science Politique*, Vol. 41, No. 1, Feb. 1991, pp. 28–57 and, for an analysis in English, see Sebastian Poulter, 'Muslim Headscarves in School: Contrasting Legal Approaches in England and France', *Oxford Journal of Legal Studies*, Vol. 17, No. 1, 1997, pp. 43–71. Likewise, in *Dahlab v Switzerland*, the European Court of Human Rights considered the issue of a schoolteacher in a Swiss primary school who was prohibited from wearing an Islamic scarf when teaching. It found no violation. It stressed, inter alia, the impact that the 'powerful external symbol' conveyed by a 'representative of the state' wearing a hijab could have. It also questioned whether it might have some kind of proselytizing effect. See Dominic McGoldrick, *Human Rights and Religion: the Islamic Headscarf Debate in Europe*. Oxford and Portland: Hart, 2006, pp. 121–31.

79. Circulaire Bayrou, reprinted in William, 'Le Conseil d'État et la laïcité', pp. 51–7.

80. Laurent Wauquiez-Motte, 'Laïcité et neutralité de l'État', *Les Cahiers de la Fonction Publique*, Apr. 2004, pp. 7–9, at p. 9.

81. For forceful arguments to this effect, see Catherine Kintzler, 'Aux fondements de la laïcité scolaire. Essai de décomposition raisonnée du concept de laïcité', *Les Temps Modernes*, Vol. 527, 1990, pp. 82–90, and Pena-Ruiz, *Dieu et Marianne*, p. 285.

82. Alain-Gérard Slama, 'La peur du conflit engendre la violence', in Zarka, *L'Islam en France*. pp. 151–57, at p. 157.

83. There is no possibility to opt out of subjects on religious grounds, and no systematic exemption from classes on a weekday can be granted. See Delafaye Francois, *Laïcité de combat. Laïcité de droit*. Paris, Hachette 1997, p. 110. However, following late nineteenth-century republicans who had not wished the demands of *laïque* education unduly to burden religious practice (notably by allowing a weekly day off for religious instruction, and funding chaplaincies to provide religious instruction in boarding schools), efforts have been made to accommodate minority religions, notably through allowing exceptional absences for religious festivals and the provision of alternatives to pork in school canteen's menus. Cf. Dord, '*Laïcité* à l'école, p. 1528, Yves Madiot, 'Le juge et la *laïcite*', *Pouvoirs*, Vol. 75, 1995, pp. 73–84.

84. On the importance of this consideration for the Stasi Commission, see Patrick Weil, 'Lever le voile', *Esprit*, Vol. 311, Jan. 2005, pp. 45–53.

85. Catriona McKinnon, 'Democracy, Equality and Toleration', *Journal of Ethics*, Vol. 11, No. 2, June 2007, pp. 125–46.

Notes to Chapter 3

1. Danielle Sallenave, cited in Fawzia Zouari, *Ce voile qui déchire la France*. Paris: Ramsay, 2004, p. 139.
2. Jean Rivero, 'La notion juridique de laïcité', *Chronique du Recueil Dalloz*, Vol. 31, 1949, pp. 137–40; Emile Poulat, *Notre laïcité publique. La France est une République laïque*. Paris: Berg International, 2003.
3. Geneviève Koubi, 'La laïcité dans le texte de la Constitution', *Revue de Droit Public*, Sept–Oct 1997, pp. 1301–22, at p. 1320. See also her 'Des propositions de loi relatives à la laïcité dans les établissements publics scolaires', *Revue de la Recherche Juridique. Droit Prospectif*, Vol. 73, 1998, pp. 577–85.
4. Yves Madiot, 'Le juge et la *laïcité*', *Pouvoirs*, Vol. 75, 1995, pp. 73–84.
5. See Conseil d'État, Section de l'intérieur, 27 novembre 1989, n°346893, Avis, 'Port du foulard islamique', at <http://www.rajf.org/article.php3?id_article=1065> (last accessed 17 July 2007).
6. Yasemin Nuhoglu Soysal, 'Changing Parameters of Citizenship and Claims-Making: Organized Islam in European Public Spheres', *Theory and Society*, Vol. 26, No. 4, Aug 1997, pp. 509–27. The Boubakeur quote is at p. 516.
7. Article 9 of the European Convention on Human Rights, for example, guarantees the 'freedom, either individually or in community with others, and in public or in private, to manifest one's religion or belief'. For a good survey, see Carolyn Evans, *Freedom of religion under the European Convention on Human Rights*. Oxford: Oxford University Press, 2001.
8. According to Article 9, second paragraph, freedom of religion can only be restricted if (a) its manifestations are 'prohibited by the law', (b) restrictions are seen as 'necessary in a democratic society', or (c) necessary to protect 'public safety, order, health or morals, or the fundamental rights and freedoms of others'.
9. Conseil d'État, Avis 'Port du foulard islamique', <http://www.rajf.org/article.php3?id_article=1065> (last accessed 17 July 2007). For an analysis of the Council's 'reasonableness', see Alessandro Ferrari, 'Laïcité et voile islamique en France au début du nouveau millénaire', *Migrations Société*, Vol. 16, No. 96, Nov.–Dec. 2004, pp. 63–129, at pp. 84–96.
10. Haut Conseil à l'Intégration, *L'Islam dans la République. Rapport au Premier Ministre*. Paris: La Documentation Française, 2001, p. 66.
11. Rivero, 'La notion juridique de laïcité', p. 138.
12. Véronique Fabre-Alibert, 'La loi française du 15 mars 2004 encadrant, en application du principe de laïcité, le port de signes ou de tenues manifestant une appartenance religieuse dans les écoles, collèges et lycées publics: vers un pacte social laïque?', *Revue Trimestrielle des Droits de l'Homme*, Vol. 59, July 2004, pp. 575–609, at pp. 578–9. For a discussion of the compatibility of *laïcité* with European and international law, see Dominic McGoldrick, *Human Rights and Religion: the Islamic Headscarf Debate in Europe*. Oxford and Portland: Hart, 2006; Michel De Salvia, 'La laïcité française et les

principes du droit européen', in *Tranversalités*, Vol. 93, Jan.–Mar. 2005, pp. 1–16; J. -F. Flauss, 'La laïcité et la Convention Européenne des Droits de l'Homme', *Revue du Droit Public*, Vol. 2, 2004, pp. 317–29; Alain Garay, 'La laïcité, principe érigé en valeur de la Convention européenne des droits de l'homme', *Recueil Dalloz*, Vol. 2, 2006, 103–10.

13. Bernard Stasi, *Laïcité et République. Rapport de la commission de réflexion sur l'application du principe de laïcité dans la République remis au Président de la République le 11 décembre 2003* Paris: La Documentation Française, 2004, thereafter 'Stasi Report'. Available at <http://www.iesr.ephe.sorbonne. fr/docannexe/file/3112/rapport_laicite.Stasi.pdf> (last accessed 27 July 2007), p. 59. In the *Leyla Sahin v Turkey* case, the European Court of Human Rights held with the University of Istanbul which had refused admission to a student wearing an 'Islamic-style headscarf'. See McGoldrick, 'Comparative State Practice: Turkey', in his *Human Rights and Religion: the Islamic Headscarf Debate in Europe*, pp. 132–72; Aernout Nieuwenhuis, 'European Court of Human Rights: State and Religion, Schools and Scarves. An Analysis of the Margin of Appreciation as Used in the Case of Leyla Sahin v. Turkey, Decision of 29 June 2004, Application Number 44774/98, *European Constitutional Law Review*, Vol. 1, 2005, pp. 495–510.

14. Conseil d'État, Avis 'Port du foulard islamique', at <http://www.rajf.org/article.php3?id_article=1065> (last accessed 17 July 2007).

15. Haut Conseil à l'Intégration, *Pour un modèle français d'intégration*. Paris: Documentation Française, 1991, p. 77. For a similar position, see Guy Bedouelle, Jean-Paul Costa, *Les laïcités à la française*. Paris: Presses Universitaires de France, 1998, p. 106.

16. Jules Ferry, 'Lettre aux instituteurs' (27 Nov. 1883), reprinted in *Pouvoirs*, Vol. 75, 1995, pp. 109–16, at 111 and *passim*.

17. According to a June 2004 report by the General Inspector and Heasdcarf mediator Hanifa Chérifi, there were 639 attempts to wear religious signs in contravention of the 2004 law, down 50% on previous year. 626 were Islamic headscarves, 11 turbans, 2 large crosses. 550 incidents were reportedly resolved through 'dialogue', 96 pupils left public schools for private schools, distance learning courses or to enrol in another country. 47 were excluded: 44 for wearing a hijab and 3 for wearing a turban. McGoldrick, *Human Rights and Religion*, p. 100; John R. Bowen, *Why the French Don't Like Headscarves. Islam, the State and Public Space*. Princeton, NJ: Princeton University Press, 2007, pp. 150–1.

18. Cited in Danièle Hervieu-Léger, *Le pélerin et le converti*. Paris: Flammarion, 1999, p. 232.

19. The only state-maintained (*sous contrat*) Muslim school is in the Indian Ocean island of La Réunion. In mainland France, there are two independent (*hors contrat*) schools, in Lille and Aubervilliers. Zouari, *Ce voile qui déchire la France*, p. 223.

20. Stasi Report, p. 59.
21. For a criticism of the Stasi Report along these lines, see Emmanuel Terray, 'L'hystérie politique', in Charlotte Nordmann (ed.), *Le foulard islamique en questions*. Paris: Editions Amsterdam, 2004, pp. 103–17, at pp. 114, 116.
22. Meira Levinson, *The Demands of Liberal Education*. Oxford: Oxford University Press, 1999, p. 125.
23. Levinson, *Demands of Liberal Education*, p. 124.
24. John Stuart Mill, *On Liberty*. Cambridge: Cambridge Universtiy Press, 1989 (1859), ch. 4.
25. Patrick Simon, 'L'encombrante visibilité', in Jean-Michel Helvig (ed.), *La laïcité dévoilée. Quinze années de débat en quarante Rebonds*. Paris: Libération and Editions de l'Aube, 2004, 91–5; Nordmann, *Le foulard islamique en questions*, p. 11.
26. Note, however, that the law still maintains a distinction between prohibited 'ostensible' and permissible 'discrete' signs. For a criticism of the term 'ostensible' used in the law, see Fabre-Alibert, 'La loi française du 15 mars 2004', p. 591.
27. Gouvernement de la République Italienne v. Commission, 17 July 1963, cited in Elsa Forey, 'L'égalité des cultes: un principe en évolution?', in Claude Courvoisier and Patrick Charlot (eds), *Actualité politique et juridique de l'égalité*. Dijon: Editions Universitaires de Dijon, 2003, pp. 41–65, p. 61.
28. Sebastian Poulter, 'Muslim Headscarves in School: Contrasting Legal Approaches in England and France', *Oxford Journal of Legal Studies*, Vol. 17, No. 1, 1997, pp. 43–71. Note that until recently there was no concept of discrimination on *religious* grounds in English law, which made it difficult for Muslims to raise indirect discrimination cases, unless, like the Sikhs and Jews, they could demonstrate that they were discriminated against on ethnic grounds. See Tariq Modood, *Multiculturalism, Muslims and the British State*. London: British Association for the Study of Religion, 2003, pp. 2, 7.
29. However, the law of 16 Nov. 2001, on discrimination in the labour market, introduced the notion of indirect discrimination for the first time in French law, although it remains ill-defined and difficult to apply. For a survey, see Sophie Latraverse, 'Le Droit français en matière de discrimination', at <http://iom.fi/files/legal_training/french/french_anti-discrimination_handbook_chap4.pdf> (last accessed 31 July 2007).
30. Forey, 'L'égalité des cultes', p. 61.
31. Olivier Dord, 'Laïcité à l'école: l'obscure clarté de la circulaire "Fillon" du 18 mai 2004', *Actualité Juridique du Droit Administratif*, 26 Juillet 2004, pp. 1523–29, at p. 1525. For a different account of the significance of the distinction between 'objective' and 'subjective' religious signs, see Ferrari, 'Laïcité et voile islamique en France', pp. 121–9. For doubts over the wisdom of legislating on such matters, see Florence Bussy, 'Le débat sur la laïcité et la loi', *Recueil Dalloz*, Vol. 37, 2004, pp. 2666–74.

32. Under the terms of Article 14 of the European Convention of Human Rights.

33. Protected by Article 2 of the Additional Protocol of the European Convention on Human Rights.

34. Protected by Article 9.

35. Fabre-Alibert, 'La loi française du 15 mars 2004', p. 605. A similar conclusion was already reached in Haut Conseil à l'Intégration, *L'Islam dans la République. Rapport au Premier Ministre.* Paris: Documentation Française, 2001, pp. 11, 97.

36. As sociologist François Dubet mischievously puts it, 'in France, debates about *laïcité* quickly take a religious form: they more readily engage with principles than with practices'. Francois Dubet, 'La laïcité dans les mutations de l'école', in Michel Wieviorka (ed.), *Une société fragmentée? Le multiculturalisme en débat.* Paris: La Découverte, 1996, pp. 85–112, at p. 85.

37. For a critical approach to the terms of this debate, see Etienne Balibar, 'Faut-il qu'une laïcité soit ouverte ou fermée?', *Mots*, Vol. 27, June 1991, pp. 73–9.

38. Jean Baubérot, *Vers un nouveau pacte laïque?* Paris: Seuil, 1990; *La morale laïque contre l'ordre moral.* Paris: Seuil, 1997; *Laïcité 1905–2005, entre passion et raison.* Paris: Seuil, 2004; *Histoire de la laïcité en France.* Paris: Presses Universitaires de France, 4e édition, 2007.

39. Jean-Paul Willaime, *Europe et religions. Les enjeux du XXème siècle.* Paris: Fayard, 2004, p. 46.

40. Katherine Pratt Ewing, 'Legislating Religious Freedom: Muslim Challenges to the Relationship between "Church" and "State" in Germany and France', *Daedalus*, Vol. 129, No. 4, Fall 2000, pp. 31–54, at p. 34.

41. Émile Poulat, *Notre laïcité publique. 'La France est une République laïque'.* Paris: Berg, 2003, chs. 3 and 4.

42. Francis Messner, 'Laïcité imaginée et laïcité juridique', *Le Débat*, Vol. 77, 1993, pp. 88–94. See also Jean-Michel Lemoyne de Forges, 'Laïcité et liberté religieuse en France', in Joël-Benoît d'Onorio (ed.), *La liberté religieuse dans le monde. Analyse doctrinale et politique.* Paris: Éditions Universitaires, 1991, pp. 149–70, the legal analyses of Jacques Robert, 'La notion juridique de laïcité et sa valeur constitutionnelle', in Hubert Bost (ed.), *Genèses et enjeux de la laïcité. Christianismes et laïcité.* Paris: Labor et Fides, 1990, pp. 89–100; Roland Drago, 'Laïcité, neutralité, liberté?', *Archives de Philosophie du Droit*, Vol. 38, 1993, pp. 221–30.

43. Messner, 'Laïcité imaginée et laïcité juridique', p. 94.

44. Jean Paul Willaime, 'Églises, *laïcité* et integration européenne' in Alain Dierkens (ed.), *Pluralismes religieux et laïcité dans l'Union européenne.* Bruxelles: Éd. de l'Université de Bruxelles, 1994, pp. 153–65.

45. Silvio Ferrari, 'Islam and the Western European Model of Church and State Relations', in Wasif Shadid and Sjoerd van Koningsveld (eds), *Religious Freedoms and the Neutrality of the State: the Position of Islam in the European Union.* Leuven: Peeters, 2002, pp. 6–19; Silvio Ferrari, 'The Secularity of the

State and the Shaping of Muslim Representative Organizations in Western Europe', in Jocelyne Cesari and Seán McLoughlin (eds), *European Muslims and the Secular State*. Aldershot: Algate, 2005, pp. 11–23.

46. For details, see Jacques Miet, 'Le droit local des cultes en Alsace-Moselle', *Les Cahiers de la Fonction Publique*, Apr. 2004, pp. 14–16.

47. Stasi Report, p. 51.

48. Baubérot, *Vers un nouveau pacte laïque?*, p. 188.

49. On *laïcité* as a civil religion, see Jean-Louis Willaime, 'La religion civile à la française et ses métamorphoses', *Social Compass*, Vol. 40, No. 4, 1993, pp. 571–80; Joël Roman, 'La laïcité comme religion civile', *Esprit*, Vol. 175, 1991, pp. 108–15; Jean Baubérot, 'La religion civile, impensé de la laïcité française', in his *Laïcité 1905–2005, entre passion et raison*. Paris: Seuil, 2004, ch. 10, pp. 163–86.

50. The first expression is by Edgar Morin, 'Le trou noir de la laïcité', *Le Débat*, Jan.–Fev. 1990, No. 58, pp. 38–41, at p. 38; Jean-Louis Willaime, 'La religion civile à la française et ses métamorphoses', p. 576; and the second by British sociologist David Martin, cited in Danièle Hervieu-Léger, *La religion en miettes ou la question des sectes*. Paris: Calmann-Lévy, 2001, p. 29. Cf. also Jean Carbonnier, 'La culture française: une culture 'catholique' laïcisée?', *Parole et Société*, Vol. 34, 1993, pp. 173–87.

51. Roland Drago, 'Laïcité, neutralité, liberté?', *Archives de Philosophie du Droit*, Vol. 38, 1993, pp. 221–30, at p. 222.

52. Hervieu-Léger, *La religion en miettes*, p. 25, *passim*. We will see in Chapter 5 that this antipathy should be also be related to a particular understanding of the vulnerability of freedom of conscience to exploitation through 'mental manipulation'.

53. P.-H. Prélot, cited in Ludivine Delsenne, 'De la difficile adaptation du principe républicain de laïcité à l'évolution socio-culturelle française', *Revue du Droit Public*, Vol. 2, 2005, pp. 427–62, at p. 450.

54. Soheib Bencheikh, *Marianne et le Prophète. L'Islam dans la France laïque*. Paris: Livre de Poche, 2003, pp. 108–18.

55. Patrick Weil, *Qu'est ce qu'un Français? Histoire de la nationalité française depuis la Révolution*. Paris: Grasset, 2002, pp. 225–44.

56. Vincent Geisser, *La nouvelle islamophobie*. Paris: La Découverte, 2003, p. 87.

57. Frank Frégosi, 'L'Islam d'Europe', *Esprit*, Vol. 1, Jan. 1998, pp. 109–35, at p. 110.

58. Rivero, 'La notion juridique de laïcité'.

59. For the implications of these changes for *laïcité*, see Jean Baudouin and Philippe Portier (eds.), *La laïcité, valeur d'aujourd'hui? Contestations et renégotiations du modèle franais*. Rennes: Presses Universitaires de Rennes, 2001, pp. 22–34.

60. Marcel Gauchet, *La religion dans la démocratie. Parcours de la laïcité*. Paris: Gallimard, 1998, p. 113.

61. See Jacqueline Costa-Lascoux, *Les trois ages de la laïcité. Débat avec Joseph Sitruk, Grand Rabbin de France*. Paris: Hachette, 1996.

62. Elsa Forey, 'Du "cultuel" au "culturel": vers une remise en cause du principe de séparation de 1905?', in Baudouin and Portier, *La laïcité, valeur d'aujourd'hui?*, pp. 285–96.

63. Dominique Julia, 'La République, l'Eglise et l'immigration. La laïcité dans l'histoire', *Le Débat*, Vol. 58, Jan.–Feb. 1990, pp. 33–7.

64. Pierre Bourdieu and Jean-Claude Passeron, *Reproduction in Education, Society and Culture*. London: Sage, 1990.

65. Sophie Audidière, 'L'école républicaine à l'épreuve d'une révision républicaine', in Vincent Bourdeau and Roberto Merril (eds), *La république et ses démons. Essais de républicanisme appliqué*. Paris: Éditions Eres, 2007, pp. 85–107.

66. François Dubet, 'La laïcité dans les mutations de l'école', in Michel Wieviorka (ed.), *Une société fragmentée? Le multiculturalisme en débat*. Paris: La Découverte, 1996, pp. 85–112; Martine Barthélémy, 'La logique d'ouverture de l'école publique: une fragilisation de la laïcité française', in Baudouin and Portier, *La laïcité, valeur d'aujourd'hui?* pp. 297–314.

67. Mona Ozouf, *L'école de la France*. Paris: Gallimard, 1984; Edwy Plenel, *La République Inachevée. L'État et l'école en France*. Paris: Stock, 1997.

68. Régis Debray, *L'enseignement du fait religieux dans l'école laïque*. Paris: Odile Jacob, 2002.

69. David Kessler, 'Neutralité de l'enseignement public et liberté d'opinion des élèves (à propos du port des signes distinctifs d'appartenance religieuse dans les établissements scolaires'. Conclusions du Conseil d'État, 2 novembre 1992', *Revue Française de Droit Administratif*, Vol. 9, No. 1, Jan.–Feb. 1993, pp. 112–18, at p. 114.

70. Françoise Lorcerie, 'Laïcité 1996. La République à l'école de l'immigration?', *Revue Française de Pédagogie*, Vol. 117, Oct.–Nov.–Dec., 1996, p. 72.

71. Once the advocate of a militant *laïcité*, the Ligue, under the leadership of Michel Morineau, drew the consequences of the erosion of the left-wing project of the abolition of private schools in 1984 and engaged in consultation with Catholics, Protestants, Muslims, and Freemasons over the redefinition of a more tolerant *laïcité*. See Jean Boussinesq, 'Une nouvelle laïcité?', *Projet*, Vol. 225, Printemps 1991, pp. 7–15 and Yves Palau, 'La Ligue de l'enseignement depuis les années 1980: nouvelle réflexion sur la laïcité et position dans l'espace politique', in Baudouin and Portier, *La laïcité, valeur d'aujourd'hui?* pp. 205–19.

72. See, for example, Monique Canto-Sperber (ed.), *Dictionnaire d'éthique et de philosophie morale*. Paris: Presses Universitaires de France, 1996; Alain Renaut and Sylvie Mesure, *La guerre des dieux. Essai sur la querelle des valeurs dans la philosophie contemporaine*, Paris: Grasset, 1996; Paul Ricoeur, *Soi-même comme un autre*, Paris: Seuil, 1990.

73. Paul Valadier, *Inévitable morale*. Paris: Esprit, Seuil, 1990, pp. 210–13.

74. Mesure and Renaut, *La guerre des dieux*.

75. Thibaud Collin, 'Quel enseignement moral dans une société laïque?', *Liberté Politique*, Vol. 24, Winter, 2003–4, pp. 71–85, at p. 80; Arnauld Leclerc, 'La contribution de la théorie procédurale de John Rawls à la redéfinition de la laïcité', in Baudouin and Portier, *La laïcité, valeur d'aujourd'hui?*, pp. 229–46; Jean-Marc Ferry, *Philosophie de la communication*. Paris: Cerf, 1994. Vol. 2: *Justice politique et démocratie procédurale*; Pierre Hayat, *La laïcité et les pouvoirs. Pour une critique de la raison laïque*. Paris: Kimé, 1998, Chap. 4; Alain Touraine, *Pourrons-nous vivre ensemble? Egaux et différents*. Paris: Fayard, 1997.

76. Valadier, *Inévitable morale*, p. 213.

77. See, notably, Jean-Paul Willaime, 'Le religieux dans l'espace public', *Projet*, Vol. 225, 1991, pp. 71–9.

78. Bauberot, *Vers un nouveau pacte laïque?*, p. 205.

79. Willaime, *Europe et religions*, p. 329.

80. Arnauld Leclerc, 'La contribution de la théorie procédurale de John Rawls à la redéfinition de la laïcité', in Baudouin and Portier, *La laïcité, valeur d'aujourd'hui?* pp. 229–46, at p. 238.

81. Jean-Pierre Changeux, Comité Consultatif National d'Ethique, *Une même éthique pour tous?* Paris: Odile Jacob, 1997, pp. 10, 20.

82. Jean Baubérot, 'Le débat sur la *laïcité*', *Regards sur l'Actualité*, Mar.–Apr. 1995, pp. 51–62, at p. 57. Other moves towards *laïcité ouverte* have included: consultation of religious groups about the reform of nationality laws; the public stance taken by religious authorities against racism and the National Front in 1985; public ackowledgement of the contribution of religious groups to social work and charity in disadvantaged neighbour-hoods, and the unprecedented 'Mission of Reconciliation', made up of prominent members of a number of 'spiritual families', which was sent on a official peace mission to the Pacific island of Nouvelle Calédonie in 1988.

83. Hervieu-Léger, *Religion en miettes*, pp. 263–4, conclusion. See, more gener-ally, Anne-Sophie Lamine, *La cohabitation des dieux. Pluralité religieuse et laïcité*. Paris: Presses Universitaires de France, 2004.

84. Charles Taylor, 'Modes of Secularism', in Rajeev Bhargava (ed.), *Secularism and its Critics*. Delhi: Oxford University Press, 1998, pp. 31–53, at p. 35. Cf also Brian Barry, 'it is compatible with neutrality that religions should be publicly recognized: the only constraint is, again, that they should be treated equally' Barry, *Culture and Equality*. Cambridge: Polity, 2001, p. 29.

85. Charles Zarka (ed.), *L'Islam en France*. Hors série de revue *Cités*, Mar. 2004, p. 160.

86. Stasi Report, pp. 64–5.

87. *Ibid.*, p. 64.

88. *Ibid.*, p. 28.

89. *Ibid.*, p. 51.

90. Jean Baubérot, 'Laïcité, le grand écart', *Le Monde*, 4 Jan. 2004. A rarely commented upon fact is that of the 170 schoolgirls who refused to take

off their scarf in Sept. 2004, a majority were in Alsace. Cf *Libération*, 'Au premier jour de classe, la plupart des filles voilées ont accepté de se plier à la nouvelle loi sur le port des signes religieux', 3 Sept. 2004.

91. Joseph Carens, *Culture, Citizenship and Community: A Contextual Exploration of Justice as Evenhandedness.* Oxford: Oxford University Press, 2000. Carens thus describes the ideal: 'not neutrality in the form of equal indifference but evenhandedness in the form of comparable support' (p. 13). See also Veit Bader, 'Religious Pluralism: Secularism or Priority for Democracy?' *Political Theory*, Vol. 27, No. 5, Oct. 1999, pp. 597–633; Veit Bader, 'Religious Diversity and Democratic Institutional Pluralism', *Political Theory*, Vol. 31, No. 2, Apr. 2003, pp. 265–94.

92. On 'représentativité' as a criterion for religious equality, see Forey, 'L'égalité des cultes', 43–6.

93. Jean-Paul Willaime, 'Le religieux dans l'espace public', *Projet*, Vol. 225, 1991, pp. 71–9.

94. Silvio Ferrari, 'Islam and the Western European Model', p. 12.

95. See, for example, Brigitte Basdevant-Gaudemet, 'The Legal Status of Islam in France', in Silvio Ferrari and Anthony Bradney (eds), *Islam and European Legal Systems.* Aldershot: Ashgate, 2000, pp. 97–124. For a critical survey of these proposals, see Forey, 'L'égalité des cultes', pp. 53–8. Proposals towards the public funding of mosques have recently been made in the official report of Jean-Pierre Machelon, *Les relations des cultes avec les pouvoirs publics.* Paris: La Documentation Française, 2006, 19–36.

96. Advocates of tolerant secularism have found a (perhaps unexpected) ally in Nicolas Sarkozy's *La République, les religions, l'espérance.* Paris: Cerf, 2004, who argues—albeit from a more Bonapartist and Gallican than liberal perspective—for the recognition of the social role of religion, the public funding of major religions, even-handed treatment for minority religions, public support towards the organization of religious groups, state contributions towards the building of mosques, and the 'Frenchification' of Islam.

97. Dalil Boubakeur, 'L'État et les cultes: le cas de l'Islam', *Administration*, Vol. 161, Oct.–Dec. 1993, pp. 133–45; Bencheikh, *Marianne et le Prophète*, p. 44. See more generally, Tariq Ramadan, *Les Musulmans dans la laïcité*, Lyon: Ed. Tawhid, 2004; Abdou Filali-Ansary, 'Islam, laïcité, démocratie', *Pouvoirs*, Vol. 104, 2003, pp. 5–19; Abderrahim Lamchichi, 'Les musulmans de France à l'épreuve de la laïcité', *Cahiers de l'Orient*, Vol. 71, 2003, pp. 35–53; F. Fouad Zakariya, *Laïcité ou islamisme: les Arabes à l'heure du choix.* Paris: La Découverte, 1990.

98. Joseph Carens and Melissa Williams, 'Muslim Minorities in Liberal Democracies: The Politics of Misrecognition', in Rajeev Bhargava (ed.), *Secularism and its Critics.* Delhi: Oxford University Press, 1998, pp. 137–73, at p. 162. For a European perspective on the changes required to integrate Islam into traditional systems of church–state relations, see Shadid and van Koningsveld, *Religious Freedoms and the Neutrality of the State.*

99. Françoise Lorcerie (ed.), *L'école et le défi ethnique. Education et intégration.* Paris: Institut de la Recherche Pédagogique/ESF, 2003, p. 137.

100. Olivier Roy, 'Fondamentalisme et *laïcité* en miroir', in Zarka, *Islam en France*, pp. 143–50.

101. Catherine Kintzler, *La République en questions*, Éditions Minerve, 1996, pp. 112–13.

102. Cf. Olivier Roy, 'laïcité is not about common values but about acceptance of the rules of the game.... Politics has nothing to do with sincerity... [Muslims] do not have to say that the hijab is not a religious obligation, but they must obey the law... They should not give up their values but they must submit to the law.' Roy, *La laïcité face à l'Islam*. Paris: Stock, 2005, pp. 160–5, *passim*. For a presentation of the debate between 'pluralist' (modus-vivendi), 'monist' (*laïque*-style independent ethic) and 'overlapping consensus' (associated with Tariq Ramadan) views of Islam's integration into the republic, and an alternative interpretation of Roy's own views, see John R. Bowen, 'Two Approaches to Rights and Religion in Contemporary France', in Richard Ashby Wilson and Jon P. Mitchell (eds), *Human Rights in Global Perspective. Anthropological Studies of Rights, Claims and Entitlements*. London: Routledge, 2003, pp. 33–53. For a good general philosophical discussion, see Andrew F. March, 'Liberal Citizenship and the Search for an Overlapping Consensus: the Case of Muslim Minorities', *Philosophy and Public Affairs*, Vol. 34, No. 4, 2006, pp. 373–421.

103. Hervieu-Léger, *La religion en miettes*, p. 193.

104. *Ibid.*, p. 191.

Notes to Chapter 4

1. Cass R. Sunstein. *The Partial Constitution*. Cambridge, MA: Harvard University Press, 1993, *passim*.

2. Adrian Favell and Tariq Modood, 'Multiculturalism and Normative Political Theory' in Alan Finlayson (ed.), *Contemporary Political Thought: A Reader and Guide*. Edinburgh: Edinburgh University Press, 2003, pp. 484–513.

3. On these traditions, see Joel S. Fetzer and Christopher Soper, *Muslims and the State in Britain, France and Germany*. Cambridge: Cambridge University Press; 2005; Riva Kastoryano, *La France, l'Allemagne et leurs immigrés. Négocier l'identité*. Paris: Armand Colin, 1996; Riva Kastoryano, 'Religion and Incorporation: Islam in France and Germany', *International Migrations Review*, Vol. 38, No. 3, Fall 2004, pp. 1234–55 and, generally, Rex Ahdar and Ian Leigh, *Religious Freedom in the Liberal State*. Oxford: Oxford University Press, 2005, pp. 67–97. For the view that such national divergences are subsumed under what is, in practice, a fairly homogeneous European model, see Silvio Ferrari, 'Islam and the Western European Model of Church and State Relations', in Wasif Shadid and Sjoerd van Koningsveld (eds), *Religious Freedoms and the Neutrality of the State: the Position of Islam in the European Union*. Leuven: Peeters, 2002, pp. 6–19.

4. For an attempt at a context-sensitive normative theory of religious accommodation, see Veit Bader, 'Religious Diversity and Democratic Institutional Pluralism', *Political Theory*, Vol. 31, No. 2, Apr. 2003, pp. 265–94.

5. Sunstein. *The Partial Constitution*.

6. I will suggest below, however, that justificatory neutrality cannot be made to justify unreasonable burdens on the exercise of basic religious rights, and that in such cases we should adopt a weakly consequentialist conception of neutrality.

7. Cited in Jytte Klausen, *The Islamic Challenge. Politics and Religion in Western Europe*. Oxford: Oxford University Press, 2005, p. 146.

8. Tariq Modood, *Multiculturalism, Muslims and the British State*. London: British Association for the Study of Religion, 2003, p. 164.

9. Will Kymlicka, *Multicultural Citizenship. A Liberal Theory of Minority Rights*. Oxford: Oxford University Press, 1995, pp. 3, 111.

10. See, for philosophical defences of secularism, Robert Audi, 'The Separation of Church and State and the Obligations of Citizenship', *Philosophy and Public Affairs*, Vol. 18, No. 3, Summer 1989, pp. 259–96; Charles Taylor, 'Modes of Secularism', in Rajeev Bhargava (ed.), *Secularism and its Critics*. Delhi: Oxford University Press, 1998, pp. 31–53.

11. (Critically) Anne Phillips, 'In Defense of Secularism', in Tariq Modood (ed.), *Church, State and Religious Minorities*. London: Policy Studies Institute, 1997, pp. 23–8, at. p. 27.

12. See, for example, Michael McConnell, 'Believers as Equal Citizens', in Nancy L. Rosemblum (ed.), *Obligations of Citizenship and Demands of Faith. Religious Accommodation in Pluralist Democracies*. Princeton, NJ: Princeton University Press, 2000, pp. 90–110 and Graham Walker, 'Illusory Pluralism, Inexorable Establishment', in *ibid.*, pp. 111–26.

13. Michael McConnell suggests that instead of a 'secular' state, we should aim for a 'pluralist' state which 'makes everyone at home': 'to the Protestant it is a Protestant country, to the Catholic a Catholic country, to the Jew a Jewish country'. However, he recognizes that pluralism 'dilutes the concept of "citizen"', making it difficult to identify what being an "American" is all about'. See his 'Believers as Equal Citizens', at pp. 103, 105.

14. Robert Audi, *Religious Commitment and Secular Reason*. Cambridge: Cambridge University Press, 2000.

15. On the 'independent ethic' view of secularism, see Chapter 1.

16. Tariq Modood, *Multicultural Politics. Racism, Ethnicity and Muslims in Britain*. Edinburgh: Edinburgh University Press, 2005, Chapter 7.

17. John Rawls, 'The Idea of Public Reason Re-Visited', *The University of Chicago Law Review*, Vol. 64, pp. 765–807; Kent Greenawalt, *Religious Convictions and Political Choice*. Oxford: Oxford University Press, 1988; Audi, *Religious Commitment and Secular Reason*. Paul J. Weithman, *Religion and the Obligations of Citizenship*. Cambridge, Cambridge University Press, 2002.

18. For a similar position, see Jürgen Habermas, 'Religion in the Public Sphere', *European Journal of Philosophy*, Vol. 14, No. 1, 2006, pp. 1–25.

19. Thanks to Saladin Meckled-Garcia for pressing me on this point.
20. For a fuller discussion, which however does not in my view sufficiently spell out this reasonableness requirement, see Jonathan Quong, 'Cultural Exemptions, Expensive Tastes and Equal Opportunities', *Journal of Applied Philosophy*, Vol. 23, No. 1, 2006, pp. 53–71, at 60–62.
21. For a survey, see Anne Phillips, '"Really" Equal: Opportunities and Autonomy', *Journal of Political Philosophy*, Vol. 14, No. 1, 2006, pp. 18–32.
22. Peter Jones, 'Bearing the Consequences of Belief', *Journal of Political Philosophy*, Vol. 2, No. 1, 194, 24–43.
23. By basic free exercise rights, I mean rights which guarantee freedom of religious belief, worship (minimally, a right of peaceable religious assembly as well as prayer) and freedom to engage in the rites and rituals of one's religion, provided these practices do not violate certain basic moral rights and their respect only impose reasonable burdens on other members of society. This is compatible with a mainstream understanding of what the practice of Islam in Europe requires. See Klausen, *The Islamic Challenge*; Tariq Ramadan, *Western Muslims and the Future of Islam*. Oxford: Oxford University Press, 2003. However, it is not compatible with 'integralist' conceptions of the demands of religion. On integralism, see Nancy Rosenblum, 'Introduction. Pluralism, Integralism, and Political Theories of Religious Accommodation', in Rosemblum, *Obligations of Citizenship and Demands of Faith*. pp. 3–31.
24. Current discussions of state–church relations underestimate the different levels on which state and religious groups intersect and, as a result, drastically simplify the complexity and heterogeneity of the issues involved. We can identify at least five different issues raised by the state–religion nexus.

    i. Free exercise. Does the exercise of religious freedoms require state abstention or state intervention? Can religious believers be exempted from general laws on conscientious grounds? Should religious beliefs enjoy special protection in law?

    ii. Equal protection. Are religious believers disproportionately burdened or assisted by existing laws? Do status quo arrangements discriminate (directly or indirectly) against minority religions?

    iii. Self-government. How far should respect for the autonomy of religious groups extend? Should religious groups be allowed to apply religious law in civil matters (family law, for example)? Should they be exempted from anti-discrimination legislation (on gender and sexuality grounds, for example)? Are they entitled to dispense compulsory education to children?

    iv. Public role. Should religious groups formally contribute to public debate and decision? Should their social role (charity, education, etc.) be supported out of public funds?

    v. Formal representation at state level. Should the main religious groups enjoy formal 'establishment' in the institutions of the state? Should consultative bodies be set up to advise the government on religious affairs?

Should such bodies also claim to represent the more broadly cultural and political needs of religiously defined minority groups (e.g. Muslims)?

In what follows, I address some, but by no means all, of these issues from a critical republican perspective.

25. For details on various forms of European establishment of religion, see Klausen, *The Islamic Challenge*, pp. 42–48.

26. See Tariq Modood, 'Establishment, Multiculturalism and British Citizenship', *The Political Quarterly*, Vol. 65, No. 1, 1994, pp. 53–73; Tariq Modood, (ed.), *Church, State and Religious Minorities*; Bhikhu Parekh, *Rethinking Multiculturalism. Cultural Diversity and Political Theory*. Basingstoke: Macmillan, 2000, pp. 258–60.

27. The issue was partly settled by the Racial and Religious Hatred Act 2006, which extends legislation on 'dangerous speech' and does not entrench any form of multi-faith establishment. I shall have more to say on hate speech restrictions in Chapter 10.

28. Cf Brian Barry: 'Strict adherence to justice as impartiality would, no doubt, be incompatible with the existence of an established church at all. But departures from it are venial so long as nobody is put at a significant disadvantage, either by having barriers put in the way of worshipping according to the tenets of his faith or by having his rights and opportunities in other matters (politics, education, occupation, for example) materially limited on the basis of his religious beliefs'. Barry, *Justice as Impartiality*. Oxford: Clarendon Press, 1995, 165n. For a discussion of the compatibility of establishment with religious freedom, see Rex Ahdar and Ian Leigh, *Religious Freedom in the Liberal State*. Oxford: Oxford University Press, 2005, pp. 127–54.

29. Eamonn Callan, *Creating Citizens. Political Education and Liberal Democracy*. Oxford: Oxford University Press, 1997. See also Stephen Macedo, *Diversity and distrust. Civic Education in a Multicultural Democracy*. Cambridge, MA: Harvard University Press, 2000.

30. Meira Levinson, *The Demands of Liberal Education*. Oxford: Oxford University Press, 1999, p. 144.

31. Amy Gutmann, *Democratic Education*. Princeton: Princeton University Press, 1987, p. 116.

32. See Ian MacMullen, *Faith in Schools? Autonomy, Citizenship, and Religious Education in the Liberal State*. Princeton, NJ: Princeton University Press, 2007. I have used MacMullen's proposed definition of a religious school (p. 31). Religious schools are also looked on sceptically by American liberal political theorists Gutmann, Callan and Levinson. For a (rare) argument made in the British context, see Humanist Philosophers' Group, *Religious Schools: the Case Against*. London: British Humanist Association, 2001.

33. For a comparative perspective on the diversity of national experiences, see Patrick J. Wolf and Stephen Macedo (eds), *Educating Citizens. International Perspectives on Civic Values and School Choice*. Washington, DC: Brookings Institution Press, 2004.

34. Harry Brighouse, 'Faith-Based Schools in the United Kingdom: An Unenthusiastic Defence of a Slightly Reformed Status Quo', in Roy Gardner, Jo Cairns, and Denis Lawton (eds), *Faith Schools. Consensus or Conflict?* London: Routledge, 2005, pp. 83–9.

35. MacMullen, *Faith in Schools?* p. 5. For the full argument, see pp. 50–4.

36. See, in France, the recommendations of Régis Debray, *L'enseignement du fait religieux dans l'école laïque,* Paris: Odile Jacob, 2002 and, in the UK, the Government's Swann report, officially called 'Education for All', of 1985.

37. Modood, *Multicultural Politics*, pp. 160–1.

38. Ferrari, 'Islam and the Western European Model of Church and State Relations', p. 13.

39. For a suvey, see Xavier Ternisien, *La France des mosquées.* Paris: Albin Michel, 2002.

40. Parekh, *Rethinking Multiculturalism.*

41. Brian Barry, *Culture and Equality*. Cambridge: Polity, 2001, p. 288.

42. For parallel criticisms of Barry's position, see John Horton, 'Liberalism and Multiculturalism. Once More Unto the Beach', in Bruce Haddock and Peter Stuch (eds), *Multiculturalism, Identity and Rights*. London: Routledge, 2003, pp. 25–41; Quong, 'Cultural Exemptions, Expensive Tastes and Equal Opportunities'.

43. On Muslim burials, see Yassine Chaïb, 'Le rite funéraire de l'intégration', in Yves-Charles Zarka (ed.), *L'Islam en France. Hors série de la revue Cités*, Paris: Presses Universitaires de France, Mar 2004; John R. Bowen, *Why the French Don't Like Headscarves. Islam, the State and Public Space.* Princeton, NJ: Princeton University Press, 2007, pp. 43–8; Ternisien, *La France des mosquées*, pp. 116–25. As Ternisien notes, the lack of suitable burial places means that 90% of bodies of Muslims are sent back to their 'country of origin'—where many of them never actually lived (p. 117). A recent official report suggested ways to reconcile the religious neutrality of cemeteries with Muslim burial rites: see Jean-Pierre Machelon, *Les relations des cultes avec les pouvoirs publics.* Paris: La Documentation Française, 2006, pp. 59–66.

44. Klausen, *The Islamic Challenge*, 195; Ayelet Shachar, 'On Citizenship and Multicultural Vulnerability', *Political Theory*, Vol. 28, No. 1, Feb. 2000, pp. 64–78.

45. For an equal-opportunity-based defence of religious exemptions, see Jonathan Quong, 'Cultural Exemptions, Expensive Tastes and Equal Opportunities'.

46. Klausen, *The Islamic Challenge*, p. 89.

Notes to Chapter 5

1. Condorcet, *Esquisse d'un tableau historique des progrès de l'esprit humain.* Paris: Flammarion, 1988, p. 274.

2. For a survey of these trends, somewhat paradoxically entitled the 'return of grand theory', see Quentin Skinner (ed.), *Return of Grand Theory in the Social Sciences.* Cambridge: Cambridge University Press, 1990.

3. Marc Sadoun, 'La démocratie française au risque du monde', in Marc Sadoun, (ed.), *La démocratie en France*. 2 vols, Paris: Gallimard, 2000, Vol. 1, pp. 27–137, at p. 118.

4. Thus, I use the term in a more descriptive and less pejorative way than it is sometimes used in France, usually by critics, to designate a dogmatic and narrow-minded defender of *laïcité*. It is worth noting that feminist authors Anne Zelensky and Anne Vigerie have positively embraced a similar term in an influential anti-hijab article. See Anne Zelensky and Anne Vigerie, 'Laïcardes, puisque féministes', *Le Monde*, 30 mai 2003, reprinted in *Pro-Choix*, Vol. 25, Summer 2003, pp. 11–13.

5. For an excellent survey of the debates between neutralists and perfectionists in Anglo-American liberalism, see Steven Wall and George Klosko, *Perfectionism and Neutrality. Essays in Liberal Theory*. Lanham, MD: Rowman and Littlefield, 2003.

6. The expression is Will Kymlicka's, *Multicultural Citizenship*. Oxford: Oxford University Press, 1995, pp. 80–4.

7. On autonomy and socialization generally, see Robert Young, 'Autonomy and Socialization', *Mind*, Vol. 92, No. 365, 1983, pp. 120–3.

8. Harry Brighouse, 'Civic Education and Liberal Legitimacy', *Ethics*, Vol. 108, No. 4, July 1998, pp. 719–45, at p. 728.

9. Jean Baubérot, 'La laïcité comme pacte laïque', in Jean Baudouin and Philippe Portier (eds.), *La laïcité, valeur d'aujourd'hui? Contestations et renégotiations du modèle français*. Rennes: Presses Universitaires de Rennes, 2001, pp. 39–50 at pp. 47–9; *La morale laïque contre l'ordre moral*. Paris, Seuil, 1997, pp. 305–14.

10. For a classic study, see Peter Gay, *The Enlightenment: An Interpretation*. London: Weidenfeld and Nicolson, Vol. 2, pp. 1967–70.

11. See, for example, Sadoun, *La Démocratic en France*. pp. 99–120.

12. Cited by Antoine Prost, 'La République et l'école', *Projet*, Vol. 213, 1988, pp. 85–95, p. 86.

13. Pierre Hayat, *La passion laïque de Ferdinand Buisson*. Paris: Kimé, 1999, p. 86.

14. Cited in Yves Lequin, *Histoire de la laïcité*. Besancon: CRDP de Franche-Comté, 1994, p. 9.

15. Yves Déloye, 'L'instruction', in Vincent Duclert and Christophe Prochasson (eds), *Dictionnaire Critique de la République*. Paris: Flammarion, 2002, pp. 183–8, at p. 185.

16. Cited in Marcel Gauchet, *La religion dans la démocratie. Parcours de la laïcité*. Paris: Gallimard, 1998, p. 49. On Renouvier's neo-criticism, see Marie-Claude Blais, *Au principe de la République. Le cas Renouvier*. Paris: Bibliothèque des Idées, Paris: Gallimard, 2001.

17. On 'sectes' see Alain Vivien, *Les Sectes en France. Expression de la liberté morale ou facteurs de manipulation? Rapport au Premier Ministre*. Paris: Documentation Française, 1983; Danièle Hervieu-Léger, *La religion en miettes ou la question des sectes*. Paris: Calmann-Lévy, 2001, 15, 18, 26, *passim*; Patrice Rolland, 'Le phénoméne sectaire au regard de la laïcite française', in Baudouin

and Portier, *La laïcité, valeur d'aujourd'hui?* pp. 331–44. For a comparative European perspective see Francis Messner, 'La législation cultuelle des pays de l'Union européenne face aux groupes sectaires', in Françoise Champion et Martine Cohen (eds), *Sectes et démocratie*. Paris, Seuil, 1999, pp. 331–58. On the ban on congregations, see François Delafaye, *Laïcité de combat. Laïcité de droit*. Paris: Hachette, 1997, pp. 37–8, and statements by Ferdinand Buisson, cited in Danièle Hervieu-Léger, *Le pélerin et le converti*. Paris: Flammarion, 1999, p. 219 and in Jacqueline Lalouette, *La République anti-cléricale. XIXème-XXe siècles*. Paris: Seuil, 2002, p. 62.

18. See Rolland, 'Le phénoméne sectaire au regard de la laïcite française'.

19. Henri Pena-Ruiz, *Dieu et Marianne. Philosophie de la laïcité*. Paris: Presses Universitaires de France, 1999, p. 267.

20. Mill excoriates Calvinism as an 'insidious... theory of life' that creates a 'pinched and hidebound type of human character' and adds that 'many persons, no doubt, sincerely think that human beings thus cramped and dwarfed, are as their Maker designed them to be'. John Stuart Mill, *On Liberty*. Cambridge: Cambridge University Press, 1989, (1859), p. 62.

21. According to Mill, 'A general State education is a mere contrivance for moulding people to be exactly like one another... it establishes a despotism over the mind'. *On Liberty*, p. 106.

22. Hannah Arendt, *On Revolution*. London: Faber, 1963; Patrice Higonnet, *Sister Republics. The Origins of French and American Republicanism*. Cambridge MA: Harvard University Press, 1988; Marcel Gauchet, *La Révolution des Droits de l'Homme*. Paris: Gallimard, 1989.

23. Claude Nicolet, *L'idée républicaine en France (1789–1924). Essai d'histoire critique*. Paris: Gallimard, 1982, 2nd edn, 1994, p. 483; Pierre Rosanvallon, *L'État en France. De 1798 à nos jours*. Paris: Seuil, 1990, pp. 93–135.

24. Émile Durkheim, *Professional Ethics and Civil Morals*. Transl. C. Brookfield, preface B. S Turner. London: Routledge, 1957, pp. 57, 72, *passim*. On the republican *topos* that modern individualism is inextricably bound up with the emergence of the modern state, see Jean-Fabien Spitz, *Le Moment Républicain en France*. Paris: Gallimard, 2005, *passim*. On the connection between citizenship and individualism, see Jean Leca, 'Individualisme et citoyenneté', in Pierre Birnbaum and Jean Leca (eds), *Sur l'individualisme*. Paris: Presses de la Fondation Nationale des Sciences Politiques, 1986, 2nd edn 1991, pp. 185–98.

25. Spitz, *Le Moment Républicain en France*, p. 393.

26. Although there is historiographical support for this view, I am less interested here in the accuracy of this account than in the historical self-understanding of French republicans.

27. Gauchet, *La religion dans la démocratie*, ch. 2, *passim*.

28. Alain Touraine, *Critique de la modernité*. Paris: Fayard, 1992.

29. Dominique Schnapper, *La France de l'intégration. Sociologie de la nation en 1990*. Paris: Gallimard, 1991, p. 171.

30. Didier Lapeyronnie, 'Les deux figures de l'immigré', in Michel Wieviorka (ed.), *Une société fragmentée. Le multiculturalisme en débat*. Paris: La Découverte, 1996, pp. 251–65.

31. Eugen Weber, *Peasants into Frenchmen*. Stanford, CA: Stanford University Press, 1976.

32. Alice L. Conklin, *A Mission to Civilize. The Republican Idea of Empire in France and West Africa, 1895–1930*. Stanford: Stanford University Press, 1997.

33. Alain Finkielkraut, *La défaite de la pensée*. Paris, Gallimard, 1987, pp. 143–4. Italics in the original.

34. Régis Debray, 'Etes-vous démocrate ou républicain?', *Nouvel Observateur*, Vol. 30 Nov.–6 Dec. 1989, 115–21; Régis Debray, *Vive la République*. Paris: Odile Jacob, 1989.

35. Pierre-André Taguieff, *La République menacée*. Paris: Textuels, 1996.

36. Catherine Kintzler, *La république en questions*. Paris: Minerve, 1996.

37. Haut Conseil à l'Intégration, *Pour un modèle français d'intégration*. Paris: Documentation Française, 1991; Haut Conseil à l'Intégration, *Liens culturels et intégration*. Paris, Documentation Française, 1995; Haut Conseil à l'Intégration, *Affaiblissement du lien social, enfermement dans les particularismes et intégration dans la cité*. Paris: La Documentation Française, 1997.

38. Yves-Charles Zarka, and Cynthia Fleury, *Difficile Tolérance*. Paris: Presses Universitaires de France, 2004, pp. 83, 85–9.

39. *Ibid.*, pp. 138–44.

40. *Ibid.*, p. 154.

41. *Ibid.*, p. 75.

42. See, notably, Susan Moller Okin, with respondents. *Is Multiculturalism Bad for Women?* Princeton, NJ: Princeton University Press, 1999. Monique Deveaux, *Gender and Justice in Multicultural Liberal States*. Oxford: Oxford University Press, 2007.

43. Jean-Claude Milner, *De l'école*. Paris: Seuil, 1984; Marie-Claude Blais, *Pour une philosophie politique de l'éducation*. Bayard 200; J. Manuel de Queiroz, 'Pédagogie et pédagogues contre le savoir', in Agnès Van Zanten (ed.), *L'école. L'état des savoirs*. Paris: La Découverte, 2000, pp. 374–80.

44. Finkielkraut, *Défaite de la pensée*, 113, *passim*. Along the same lines, see Henri Pena-Ruiz, *La laïcité. Textes choisis et présentés*. Paris: Flammarion, 2003, pp. 229–31, and for a critical analysis, Eric Fassin, 'Two Cultures? French Intellectuals and the Politics of Culture in the 1980s', *French Politics and Society*, Vol. 14, No. 2, Spring 1996.

45. For an analysis, see Denis Meuret, 'Intérêt, justice, laïcité', *Le Télémaque*, Vol. 14, 1998, pp. 67–77, at p. 68.

46. Generally, see Catherine Kintzler, 'Aux fondements de la laïcité scolaire. Essai de décomposition raisonnée du concept de laïcité', *Les Temps Modernes*. No. 527, June 1990, pp. 82–90; Pena-Ruiz, *Dieu et Marianne*; Henri Pena-Ruiz, *Qu'est ce que la laïcité?* Paris: Gallimard, 2003; Patrick Canivez,

Eduquer le citoyen? Paris: Hatier, 1995; Marcel Voisin, *Vivre la laïcité. Essai de méthodologie de la philosophie et de la morale laïque.* Bruxelles: Éditions de l'Université de Bruxelles, 1981; Thibaud Collin, 'Quel enseignement moral dans une société laïque?', *Liberté Politique*, Vol. 24, Winter, 2003–4, pp. 71–85, at pp. 76–7.

47. See, for example, Pena-Ruiz, *Dieu et Marianne.* p. 213.
48. Etienne Balibar, 'Dissonances dans la laïcité', *Mouvements*, Vol. 33–4, May–June–July–Aug. 2004, pp. 148–61, at p. 154.
49. Kintzler, *La République en questions*, 29–33. 78–81, 85; 'Aux fondements de la laïcité scolaire', 88–90, *passim*.
50. *Ibid.*, 18, 88, 109; 'Aux fondements', 89. See also Régis Debray, 'La laïcité: une exception française', in Hubert Bost (ed.), *Genèses et enjeux de la laïcité. Christiannismes et laïcité.* Paris: Labor et Fides, 1990, 199–208; Jacques Muglioni, 'Philosophie, école, même combat?', in Charles Coutel (ed.), *La République et l'école. Une anthologie.* Paris: Presses Pocket, 1991, pp. 74–80; Jean-Louis Poirier, 'Troisième République', in *ibid*, pp. 65–71; Prost, 'La République et l'école'.
51. Yves Deloye, *Ecole et citoyenneté. L'individualisme républicain de Jules Ferry à Vichy.* Paris: Presses de la Fondation Nationales des Sciences Politiques, 1994.
52. Cited in Françoise Lorcerie, 'L'école pourrait être un laboratoire de civilité', *Hommes et Migrations*, Vols. 1129–30, Feb.–Mar. 1990, pp. 41–6, at p. 45.
53. Pena-Ruiz, *Dieu et Marianne.* p. 288.
54. Catherine Kintzler, *La république en questions.* Paris: Minerve, 1996, pp. 78–81, 85; 'Aux fondements de la laïcité scolaire', pp. 88–90, *passim.* See also Elizabeth Badinter, Régis Debray, Alain Finkielkraut, Elisabeth de Fontenay, and Catherine Kintzler, 'Profs, ne capitulons pas', *Nouvel Observateur*, 2–8 Nov. 1989, reprinted in Kitnzler, *La République en Questions*, pp. 78–81; Martine Barthélémy, 'La logique d'ouverture de l'école publique: une fragilisation de la laïcité française', in Baudouin and Portier, *La laïcité, valeur d'aujourd'hui?* pp. 297–314, p. 298.
55. Claude Nicolet, *L'idée républicaine en France (1789–1924). Essai d'histoire critique.* Paris: Gallimard, 1982, p. 49.
56. Florence Rochefort, 'Foulard, genre et laïcité en France', *Vingtième Siècle, Revue d'Histoire*, Vol. 75, July–Sept. 2002, pp. 145–56, at p. 148. See also Caroline Ford, *Divided Houses. Religion and Gender in Modern France.* Ithaca, NY: Cornell University Press, 2005.
57. Cited in François Caron, *La France des patriotes, de 1851 à 1918.* Paris: Fayard, 1985, p. 196.
58. See, notably, Joan W. Scott, *La citoyenne paradoxale. Les féministes et les droits de l'homme.* Paris: Albin Michel, 1998. American edition: *Only Paradoxes to Offer.* Cambridge, MA: Harvard University Press, 1996.
59. Pierre Rosanvallon, *Le Sacre du citoyen. Histoire du suffrage universel en France.* Paris: Gallimard, 1992, pp. 130–45, 393–412.

60. Paul, Smith, *Feminism and the Third Republic.* Oxford: Oxford University Press, 1996; Claire Goldberg Moses, *French Feminism in the Nineteenth Century.* New York: State University of New York Press, 1984.

61. Mohamed Kacimi, 'Voile, une antique aliénation', in Jean-Michel Helvig (ed.), *La laïcité dévoilée. Quinze années de débat en quarante Rebonds.* Paris: Libération and Éditions de l'Aube, 2004, pp. 79–84, at p. 66.

62. Leïla Babès, *Le voile démystifié.* Paris: Bayard, 2004, p. 28.

63. Gisèle Halimi, 'Laïcité: une loi pour la cohésion', 23 Oct. 2003, at <www.Sisyphe.org/article.php3?id_article=730.> (last accessed 20 July 2007); Fawzia Zouari, *Le voile islamique.* Paris: Favre, 2002, p. 44.

64. Farida Shaheed, cited in Nancy J. Hirschmann, 'Western Feminism, Eastern Veiling, and the Question of Free Agency', *Constellations,* Vol. 5, No. 3, 1998, pp. 345–68, at p. 364; Kacimi, 'Voile, une antique aliénation'.

65. Fethi Benslama, *La psychanalyse à l'épreuve de l'islam.* Paris: Aubier-Montaigne, 2002. For an alternative view, which connects patriarchy to socio-political, rather than to psychologico-theological, factors, see Fatima Mernissi, *The Veil and The Male Elite. A Feminist Interpretation of Women's Rights in Islam.* Oxford: Blackwell, 1991 and *Beyond the Veil. Male-Female Dynamics in a Modern Muslim Society.* Bloomington: Indiana University Press, Revised edition, Apr. 1987.

66. Leïla Ahmed, *Women and Gender in Islam. Historical Roots of a Modern Debate.* New Haven and London: Yale University Press, 1992.

67. Cited by Meyda Yeğenoğlu, 'Sartorial Fabric-ations: Enlightenment and Western Feminism', in Laura E. Donaldson and Kwok Pui-lan (eds), *Postcolonialism, Feminism and Religious Discourse.* London and New York: Routledge, 2002, pp. 82–99, at p. 83.

68. Yvonne Yazbeck Haddad and John L. Esposito, *Islam, Gender and Social Change.* New York & Oxford: Oxford University Press, 1998; Valentine M. Moghadam, *Modernizing Women. Gender and Social Change in the Middle East.* London and Boulder, CO: Lynne Rienner, 2003.

69. Jane H. Bayes and Nayereh Tohidi, *Globalization, Gender and Religion. The Politics of Women's Rights in Catholic and Muslim Contexts.* Basingstoke: Palgrave, 2001, p. 18. For feminist critiques of religious fundamentalism in Britain, see Gita Sahgal and Nira Yuval-Davis (eds), *Refusing Holy Orders. Women and fundamentalism in Britain.* Paris: Virago, 1992.

70. Bayes and Tohidi, *Globalization, Gender and Religion,* p. 2.

71. Hala Shukrallah, 'The Impact of the Islamic Movement in Egypt', in Darlene M. Juschka (ed.), *Feminism in the Study of Religion. A Reader.* London: Continuum, 2001, pp. 190–2.

72. Nadine B. Weibel, *Par-dela le voile. Femmes d'Islam d'Europe.* Paris: Editions Complexe, 2000, pp. 57, 77–9.

73. Babès, *Le voile démystifié,* Mernissi, *The Veil and the Male Elite; Beyond the Veil.*

74. Cited in Hirschmann, 'Western Feminism, Eastern Veiling, and the Question of Free Agency', p. 351.

75. As revealed in the Open Letter to President Chirac published by the women magazine *Elle* on 8 Dec. 2003. See <http://www.ac-versailles.fr/PEDAGOGI/ses/themes/laicite/elle_petition.html> (last accessed 11 Dec. 2005).

76. Nacira Guénif-Souilamas and Eric Macé, *Les féministes et le garçon arabe*. Paris: Éditions de l'Aube, 2004, pp. 8–10.

77. Mimouna Hadjam, 'L'islamisme contre les femmes, partout dans le monde'. *Respublica, Journal de la Gauche républicaine*, Septembre 2004, last accessed on 10 July 2007 at <http://www.manifeste.org/article.php3?id_article=87>.

78. Rachel Bloul, 'Engendering Muslim Identities: Deterritorialization and the Ethnicization Process in France', in Barbara Daly Metcalf, *Making Muslim Space in North America and Europe*. Berkeley, CA: University of California Press, 1996, pp. 234–50.

79. Pena-Ruiz, *Qu'est ce que la laïcité?*, p. 108.

80. Fadela Amera, *Ni putes, ni soumises*. Paris: La Découverte, 2003.

81. Audition of Hanifa Cherifi, transcribed in Jean-Louis Debré, *La laïcité à l'école: un principe républican à réaffirmer. Rapport fait au nom de la mission d'information sur la question du port des signes religieux à l'école*. Paris: Assemblée Nationale, 2003, pp. 23–42.

82. The book that most influenced public debate about headscarves was by Iranian feminist Chahdortt Djavann, *Bas les voiles*. Paris: Gallimard, 2003. For a short history of veiling and unveiling, see Homa Hoodfar, 'The Veil in their Minds and on our Heads: Veiling Practices and Muslim Women', in Elizabeth A. Castelli (ed.), *Woman, Gender, Religion: A Reader*. Basingstoke: Palgrave, 2001, pp. 420–40, p. 428.

83. Wassyla Tamsali, 'Féministes, je vous écris d'Alger. Le port du voile n'est pas une affaire de culture', *Libération*, 14 Jan. 2004.

84. Zelensky and Vigeries, 'Laïcardes, puisque féministes'.

85. See, generally, Elisabeth Altschull, *Le voile contre l'école*. Paris: Seuil, 1995.

86. Alain Finkielkraut, 'Le foulard et l'espace sacré de l'école', *L'Arche*, Vol. 544–5, 2003, at <http://lmsi.net/spip.php?article192> (last accessed 27 July 2007), Pena-Ruiz, *Qu'est ce que la laïcité?*, *passim*; Altschull, *Le voile contre l'école*.

87. Zelensky and Vigerie, 'Laïcardes, puisque féministes', are among the rare authors who have defended this radical measure.

88. For an argument to this effect, see Amy Gutmann, 'Children, Education and Autonomy: A Liberal Argument', *Philosophy and Public Affairs*, Vol. 9, No. 4, Summer 1980, pp. 338–58.

89. On female autonomy and genital mutilation, see Clare Chambers, 'Are Breast Implants Better than Female Genital Mutilation? Autonomy, Gender Equality, and Nussbaum's Political Liberalism', *Critical Review of International Social and Political Philosophy*, Vol. 7, No. 3, Autumn 2004, pp. 1–33.

90. Hirschmann, 'Western Feminism, Eastern Veiling, and the Question of Free Agency', p. 353.

91. Hadjam, 'L'islamisme contre les femmes; Babès, *Le voile démystifié*, p. 114.

92. Jon Elster, *Sour Grapes. Studies in the Subversion of Rationality*. Cambridge: Cambridge University Press, 1983; Martha Nussbaum, 'Adaptive Preferences and Women's Options', *Economics and Philosophy*, Vol. 17, 2001, pp. 67–88.

93. Finkielkraut, 'Le foulard et l'espace sacré de l'école'.

94. Pena-Ruiz, *Dieu et Marianne*. p. 296.

95. Pierre Bourdieu, *La domination masculine*. Paris: Seuil, 1998, pp. 55, 63, 94.

96. Zelensky and Vigerie, 'Laïcardes, puisque féministes'.

97. Halimi, 'Laïcité: une loi pour la cohésion'; Henri Pena-Ruiz, *Qu'est ce que la laïcité?* Paris: Gallimard, 2003, 110. See also Sebastian Poulter, 'Muslim Headscarves in School: Contrasting Legal Approaches in England and France', *Oxford Journal of Legal Studies*, Vol. 17, No. 1, 1997, pp. 71–2.

98. Brighouse, 'Civic Education and Liberal Legitimacy', p. 728.

99. Amy Gutmann, 'Civic Education and Social Diversity', *Ethics*, Vol. 105/3, Apr. 1995, pp. 557–79; Meira Levinson, *The Demands of Liberal Education*. Oxford: Oxford University Press, 1999, ch. 1, Sec. 1.2; Eamonn Callan, *Creating Citizens. Political Education and Liberal Democracy*. Oxford: Oxford University Press, 1997, ch. 2; John Rawls, *Political Liberalism*, 199–200. For a defence of 'political' yet broadly conceived liberal education, see Stephen Macedo, *Diversity and Distrust. Civic Education in a Multicultural Democracy*. Cambridge, MA: Harvard University Press, 2000, p. 239 and *passim*.

100. Gutmann, 'Civic Education and Social Diversity', p. 578.

101. 'The unavoidable consequences of reasonable requirements for children's education may have to be accepted, often with regret'. Rawls, *Political Liberalism*, 200.

102. As Callan puts it, 'if the reason for taking the challenge of pluralism seriously is our interest in avoiding oppression, as it certainly is in Rawls's case, then our accommodation must be morally discriminating'. Callan, *Creating Citizens*, 21.

103. Nicolet, *L'Idée républicaine en France*, p. 503. Cf also Catherine Kintzler, 'Aux fondements de la laïcité scolaire. Essai de décomposition raisonnée du concept de laïcité', *Les Temps Modernes*, Vol. 527, 1990, pp. 82–90, at 88.

104. Zarka, *Difficile Tolerance*, p. 226.

105. Caroline Fourest and Fimetta Venner, 'Les enjeux cachés du voile à l'école', *Pro-Choix*, Vol. 25, Summer 2003, pp. 19–31, at p. 27.

106. Cited in Norma Claire Moruzzi, 'A Problem with Headscarves: Contemporary Complexities of Political and Social Identity', *Political Theory*, Vol. 22, No. 4, 1994, pp. 653–72, at p. 662.

Notes to Chapter 6

1. Hector Yankelevich, 'Trois fillettes voilées peuvent-elles émouvoir Marianne?', in Jean-Michel Helvig (ed.), *La laïcité dévoilée. Quinze années de débat en quarante Rebonds*. Paris: Libération and Éditions de l'Aube, 2004, pp. 103–7, at p. 107.

2. Irène Jami, Anne-Sophie Perriaux, Yves Sintomer, and Gilbert Wasserman, 'Ne pas émanciper les filles de force', in Helvig, *La laïcité dévoilée*, pp. 59–62, at p. 59.

3. In Dec. 2004, out of 640 'problematic cases', 595 were considered 'resolved' by the Minister of Education (presumably, this means that pupils were convinced to take off their scarves). 30 pupils were excluded for refusing to comply. Among those who left school (willingly or not) about 40 opted for state-validated distance learning courses, others chose private schooling. The situation of yet another 40 was still being discussed within school disciplinary committees. See <http://www.politis.fr/article1180.html> (last accessed 20 July 2007).

4. Pierre Tevanian, 'De la *laïcité* égalitaire à la *laïcité* sécuritaire', *Les mots sont importants*, 15 May 2004 (accessed at <http://www.lmsi.net>); Pierre Tevanian, *Le racisme républicain. Réflexions sur le modèle français de discrimination*. Paris: L'Esprit Frappeur, 2002.

5. Haut Conseil à l'Intégration. *L'Islam dans la République. Rapport au 1er ministre*. Paris: Documentation Française, 2001, p. 11.

6. Femmes Publiques, 'Etre féministe, ce n'est pas exclure !', at <http://lmsi.net/article.php3?id_article=181> (last accessed 20 July 2007).

7. Jean-Fabien Spitz, 'Voile au lycée: non à l'intolérance!', *Le Monde*, 17 Oct. 2003.

8. Collectif 'Oui a la laïcite, non aux lois d'exception!', <http://lmsi.net/article.php3?id_article=162> p. 15. This was notably signed by Etienne Balibar, Daniel Borrillo, Saïd Bouamama, Jocelyne Césari, Françoise Gaspard, Éric Fassin, Gérard Noiriel, Jacques Rancière, Alain Touraine, Pierre Tévanian.

9. Etienne Balibar, 'Dissonances dans la laïcité', *Mouvements*, No. 33/34, May–June–July–Aug. 2004, pp. 148–61, at p. 150.

10. Bernard Defrance, 'Contre le voile *et donc* contre l'exclusion de l'école des jeunes filles qui le portent' <http://www.bernard-defrance.net/bin/imprim.php?from=textesperso&where=156&PHPSESSID=896ffc5882745d667b5738e4ed087973> (last accessed 27 July 2007).

11. Pierre Bourdieu and Jean-Claude Passeron, *Reproduction in Education, Society and Culture*. London: Sage, 1990.

12. Brunerie-Kauffmann, Joelle, Harlem, Désir, René, Dumont, Gilles, Perrault, Alain, Touraine, 'Pour une laïcité ouverte', *Politis*, Vols. 9–15 Nov. 1989.

13. Françoise Lorcerie, 'L'école pourrait être un laboratoire de civilité', *Hommes et Migrations*, Vols. 1129–30, Feb.–Mar. 1990, pp. 41–6.

14. François Dubet, 'La laïcité dans les mutations de l'école', in M. Wieviorka (ed.), *Une société fragmentée? Le multiculturalisme en débat*. Paris: La Découverte, 1996, pp. 85–112, p. 100.

15. Denis Kessler, 'Laïcité: du combat au droit', *Le Débat*, Vol. 77, 1993, pp. 95–101, p. 99.

16. Christine Delphy, 'La suppression d'une liberté contre la défense d'une *autre* liberté?', *Revue Politique Virtuelle*, Jan.–Feb. 2004, at <http://www. alencontre.org/France/france16.html> (last accessed 20 July 2007), Monique Canto-Sperber, Paul Ricoeur, 'Des philosophes contre une loi', *Le Monde*, 10 Dec. 2003.

17. Spitz, 'Voile au lycée: non à l'intolérance'.

18. Yves-Charles Zarka and Cynthia Fleury, *Difficile Tolérance*. Paris: Presses Universitaires de France, 2004, p. 105.

19. For critiques of the anti-cult law along these lines, see Raphaël Verrier, 'Loi anti-secte. Le remède empoisonné d'un mal imaginaire', Site *Les mots sont Importants*, at <http://lmsi.net/spip.php?article58> (last accessed 20 July 2007) and Elsa Forey, 'L'égalité des cultes: un principe en évolution?', in Claude Courvoisier and Patrick Charlot (eds), *Actualité politique et juridique de l'égalité*. Dijon: Éditions Universitaires de Dijon, 2003, pp. 41–65, at pp. 46–51.

20. Danièle Hervieu-Léger, *La religion en miettes ou la question des sectes*. Paris: Calmann-Lévy, 2001, p. 185.

21. Joseph H. Carens and Melissa S. Williams, 'Muslim Minorities in Liberal Democracies: the Politics of Misrecognition', in Rajeev Bhargava (ed.), *Secularism and its Critics*. Delhi: Oxford University Press, 1998, pp. 137–76, at p. 161.

22. Adrian Favell, *Philosophies of Integration. Immigration and the Idea of Citizenship in France and Britain*. Basingtoke: Macmillan, 1998, p. 178.

23. François Dubet and Danilo Martucelli, *Dans quelle société vivons-nous?* Paris: Seuil, 1998, p. 204.

24. Guénif-Souilamas Nacira and Eric Macé, *Les féministes et le garçon arabe*. Paris: Editions de l'Aube, 2004, pp. 33–41; John R. Bowen, *Why the French Don't Like Headscarves. Islam, the State and Public Space*. Princeton, NJ: Princeton University Press, 2007, pp. 219–22.

25. Stasi Report, p. 54.

26. For a criticism of the French state's official 'gender equality ideology', see Christine Delphy, 'Égalité, équivalence et équité: la position de l'État français au regard du droit international', *Nouvelles Questions Feministes*, Vol. 16, No. 1, Feb. 1995, pp. 5–58.

27. Christine Delphy, 'Le foulard islamique: une affaire française', *Hommes et Libertés*, Vol. 125, Jan.–Feb.–Mar. 2004, pp. 40–1; Etienne Balibar, 'Dissonances dans la laïcité', *Mouvements*, No. 33/34, May–June–July–Aug. 2004, pp. 148–61; Alain Badiou, 'Derrière la loi foulardière, la peur', *Le Monde*, 21 Feb. 2004; Florence Rochefort, 'Foulard, genre et laïcité

en France', *Vingtième Siècle. Revue d'Histoire*, Vol. 75, July–Sept. 2002, pp. 145–56.

28. Homa Hoodfar, 'The Veil in their Minds and on our Heads: Veiling Practices and Muslim Women', in Elizabeth A. Castelli (ed.), *Woman, Gender, Religion: A Reader*. Basingstoke: Palgrave, 2001, pp. 420–40, at p. 441 goes further: 'mostly man-made images of the oriental Muslim women are used to tame women's demands to equality in the Western world by subtly reminding them how much better off they are than their Muslim counterparts'.

29. Rachel Bloul, 'Engendering Muslim Identities: Deterritorialization and the Ethnicization Process in France', in Barbara Daly Metcalf, *Making Muslim Space in North America and Europe*. (Berkeley, CA: University of California Press, 1996), pp. 234–50, at p. 238. On the racist overtones of republican anti-sexism, see Chouki El Hamel, 'Muslim Diaspora in Western Europe: The Islamic Headscarf (Hijab), the Media and Muslims' Integration in France', *Citizenship Studies*, Vol. 6, No. 3, 2002, pp. 293–308.

30. Leïla Ahmed, *Women and Gender in Islam. Historical Roots of a Modern Debate*. New Haven and London: Yale University Press, 1992, ch. 8, 'The Discourse of the Veil', pp. 144–68; Hoodfar, 'The Veil in their Minds and on our Heads'; Meyda Yeğenoğlu, 'Sartorial Fabric-ations: Enlightenment and Western Feminism', in Laura E., Donaldson and Kwok Pui-lan (eds), *Postcolonialism, Feminism and Religious Discourse*. London and New York: Routledge, 2002, pp. 82–99.

31. Todd Shepard, 'La "bataille du voile" pendant la guerre d'Algérie', in Charlotte Nordmann (ed.), *Le foulard islamique en questions*. Paris: Éditions Amsterdam, 2004; Frantz Fanon, *A Dying Colonialism*. New York: Grove Press, Inc, 1965, pp. 35–67, Fadwa El Guindi, *Veil. Modesty, Privacy and Resistance*. Oxford: Berg, 1999, pp. 169–73; Zouari, *Le voile islamique*, pp. 118–19.

32. Macé Guénif-Souilamas, *Les féministes et le garçon arabe*. Paris: Éditions de l'Aube, 2004.

33. Gayatri Chakravorty Spivak 'Can the Subaltern Speak?', in Cary Nelson and Lawrence Grossberg (eds), *Marxism and the Interpretation of Culture*. Champaign, IL: University of Illinois, 1988.

34. Yeğenoğlu, 'Sartorial Fabric-ations: Enlightenment and Western Feminism'.

35. Nancy J. Hirschmann, 'Western Feminism, Eastern Veiling, and the Question of Free Agency', *Constellations*, Vol. 5, No. 3, 1998, pp. 345–68.

36. In the words of Bernard Stasi, cited in Christine Delphy, 'La suppression d'une liberté comme la défense d'une *autre* liberté?'.

37. Dounia Bouzar and Saïda Kada, *L'une voilée, l'autre pas. Le témoignage de deux musulmanes françaises*. Paris: Albin Michel 2003.

38. John R. Bowen, *Why the French don't Like Headscarves. Islam, the State and Public Space*. Princeton, NJ: Princeton University Press, 2007, pp. 114, 118.

39. Kwok Pui-Lan 'Unbinding our Feet: Saving Brown Women and Feminist Religious Discourse', in Pui-lan Donaldson, *Postcolonialism, Feminism and Religious Discourse.* pp. 62–81, at p. 67.
40. Shahnaz Khan, 'Muslim Women: Negotiations in the Third Space', in Therese Saliba, Carolyn Allen, and Judith A. Howard (eds), *Gender, Politics and Islam.* Chicago: University of Chicago Press, 2002, pp. 305–36, at p. 314.
41. Stasi Report, p. 68.
42. Sophie Bessis, 'Pauvre main de Fatma!', *Le Monde*, 15 Mar. 2004.
43. For an anthology and a survey, see Joël Roman, *Chronique des idées contemporaines.* Rosny: Bréal, 2000.
44. Jean-François Lyotard, *La Condition post-moderne.* Paris: Éditions de Minuit, 1979.
45. Didier Lapeyronnie, *L'individu et les minorités. La France et la Grande-Bretagne face à leurs immigrés.* Paris: Presses Universitaires de France, 1993, p. 51. On the crisis of representation generally, see Pierre Rosanvallon, *Le people introuvable. Histoire de la représentation démocratique en France.* Paris: Gallimard, 1998, pp. 322–34.
46. Marcel Gauchet, *Le désenchantement du monde. Une Histoire Politique de la Religion.* Paris: Gallimard 1985.
47. Sylvie Mesure and Alain Renaut, *La guerre des dieux. Essai sur la querelle des valeurs.* Paris: Grasset 1996.
48. Jocelyne Césari and Jean Baubérot, 'Laïcité, communautarisme et foulard: vrais et faux débat', *Libération*, 4 Sept. 2003.
49. François Roussel, 'Le sens du commun: dissonances des voix laïques', *Rue Descartes*, Vol. 42, 2003, pp. 64–83, at pp. 74–5.
50. Jean-Paul Willaime, *Europe et religions. Les enjeux du XXème siècle.* Paris: Fayard, 2004, p. 206.
51. Cited in Willaime, *Europe et religions.* p. 207.
52. Mark Lilla, 'The Legitimacy of the Liberal Age', in Mark Lilla (ed.), *New French Thought: Political Philosophy.* Princeton, NJ: Princeton University Press, 1994, pp. 3–34.
53. Gilles Lipovestsky, *L'ère du vide. Essai sur l'individualisme contemporain.* Paris: Gallimard, 1983; Alain Ehrenberg, *L'Individu Incertain.* Paris: Calmann-Lévy, 1995; Cornelius Castoriadis, *La Montée de l'insignifiance. Les carrefours du labyrinthe IX.* Paris: Seuil, 1996; Marcel Gauchet, 'Essai de psychologie contemporaine, Vol. I. Le nouvel age de la personnalité', in *La démocratie contre elle-même.* Paris: Gallimard, 2002, pp. 229–62.
54. Haut Conseil à l'Intégration, *Affaiblissement du lien social, enfermement dans les particularismes et intégration dans la cité.* Paris: La Documentation Française, 1997, p. 15.
55. Willaime, *Europe et religions*, pp. 268–9.
56. Luc Ferry and Alain Renaut, *La Pensée 68. Essai sur l'anti-humanisme contemporain.* Paris: Gallimard, 1985; Luc Ferry and Alain Renaut, *68-86. Itinéraires de l'individu.* Paris: Gallimard, 1987; Alain Renaut, *L'ère de l'individu.*

Paris: Gallimard, 1989; Sylvie Mesure and Alain Renaut, *Alter Ego. Les paradoxes de l'identité démocratique*. Paris: Flammarion, 1999. For an analysis of the 'new humanism' see John Scott and Robert Zaretsky, 'Rousseau and the Revival of Humanism in Contemporary French Political Thought', *History of Political Thought*, Vol. 24, No. 4, Winter 2003.

57. Cf. Joël Roman, *La démocratie des individus*. Paris: Calmann-Lévy, 1998.

58. See Catherine Audard, 'Rawls in France' in Cécile Laborde (ed.), 'Rawls in Europe', *European Journal of Political Theory*, 2002, Vol. 1, No. 2, pp. 215–27.

59. For a survey, see André Berten and Hervé Pourtois (eds), *Libéraux et communautariens*. Paris: Presses Universitaires de France, 1997.

60. Charles Taylor, *Sources of the Self. The Making of Modern Identity*. Cambridge: Cambridge University Press, 1989.

61. Marcel Gauchet, *La religion dans la démocratie. Parcours de la laïcité*. Paris: Gallimard, 1998, pp. 90–1.

62. Alain Touraine, *Pourrons-nous vivre ensemble? Egaux et différents*. Paris: Fayard, 1997, Chapter 1.

63. Martucelli Dubet, *Dans quelle société vivons-nous?* Paris: Seuil, 1998, p. 48. See also François Dubet, *Sociologie de l'expérience*. Paris: Seuil, 1994. For an influential analysis of the spheres of social 'justification', see Luc Boltanski and Laurent Thévenot, *De la justification. Les économies de la grandeur*. Paris: Gallimard, 1991.

64. Alain Touraine, 'Faux et vrais problèmes', in Wievorka, *Une Société Fragmentée*, pp. 291–319, at p. 303.

65. See, for example, Alain Touraine, *Le retour de l'acteur*. Paris: Fayard, 1984; Wieviorka, *Une Société Fragmentée*; Michel Wieviorka and Jocelyne Ohana (eds), *La différence culturelle. Une reformulation des débats*. Paris: Balland; Nacira Guénif Souilamas, *Des beurettes*. Paris: Grasset et Fasquelle, 2000. See also Ahmed Boubeker, *Les mondes de l'ethnicité. La communauté d'expérience des héritiers de l'immigration maghrébine*. Paris: Balland, 2003.

66. P. Poutignant, J. Streiff-Fenant, *Théories de l'ethnicité*. Paris: Presses Universitaires de France, 1995.

67. Didier Lapeyronnie, 'Les deux figures de l'immigré', in Wieviorka, *Une Société Fragmentée*, pp. 251–66, at pp. 260–5. See also Françoise Gaspard and Farhad Khoroskhavar, *Le Foulard et la République*. Paris: La Découverte, 1995; Farhad Khosrokhavar, *L'islam des jeunes*. Paris: Flammarion, 1997; Guénif Souilamas, *Des Beurettes*; Michel Wieviorka, *Racisme et Modernité*. Paris: La Découverte, 1993, Didier Lapeyronnie, *L'individu et les minorités. La France et la Grande-Bretagne face à leurs immigrés*. Paris: Presses Universitaires de France, 1993; Dominique Schnapper, *La relation à l'autre. Au cœur de la pensée sociologique*. Gallimard Paris, 1998; P. Poutignant and J. Streiff-Fenant, *Théories de l'ethnicité*; Jim Cohen, 'Intégration: théories, politiques et logiques d'Etat' in Philippe Dewitte (ed.), *Immigration et Intégration. L'état des savoirs*. Paris: La Découverte, 1999, pp. 32–55.

68. Martucelli Dubet, *Dans quelle société vivons-nous?*, 49.
69. On stigma, see Erving Goffman, *Stigmate*. Paris: Éd. de Minuit, 1975.
70. Touraine, *Pourrons-nous vivre ensemble?*, chs. 1 and 2.
71. Admittedly, such religious transformations are less noticeable in countries, such as the USA, which are characterized by traditions of religious pluralism and Protestant individualism, than they are in France, characterized by the long-standing hegemony of the Catholic Church.
72. Danièle Hervieu-Léger, *Le pèlerin et le converti*. Paris: Flammarion, 1999. See also, on the broader transformation of religious identities, Hervieu-Léger, *La religion en miettes*.
73. Gilles Kepel, *La Revanche de Dieu*. Paris: Seuil, 1991.
74. Leïla Babès, *L'islam positif. La religion des jeunes musulmans en France*. Paris: Editions de l'Atelier, 1997. See also Olivier Roy, *L'Islam mondialisé*. Paris: Seuil, 2004 (1st edn 2002), Chapter 3; Khoroskhavar, *Islam des jeunes*, pp. 30–1, 57–9; Jocelyne Césari, *Musulmans et républicains: les jeunes, l'Islam et la France*. Paris: Complexe, 1998; Césari, 'Muslim Minorities in Europe: the Silent Revolution', in John L. Esposito and François Burgat (eds), *Modernizing Islam. Religion in the Public Sphere*. London: Hurst & Co, 2003, pp. 251–70; Nancy Venel, *Musulmans et citoyens*. Paris: Presses Universitaires de France, 2004.
75. Danièle Hervieu-Léger, 'Le miroir de l'Islam en France', *Vingtième siècle. Revue d'histoire*, Vol. 66, Apr.–June 2000, pp. 79–89, at p. 85.
76. Roy, *L'Islam mondialisé*; *La laïcité face à l'Islam*. Paris: Stock, 2005.
77. Lila Abu-Lughod, cited in Therese Saliba, 'Introduction' to Saliba, Allen, Howard, *Gender, Politics and Islam*, pp. 1–14, at p. 5.
78. Olivier Roy, 'L'islam est le miroir où la société française se regarde aujourd'hui', *Libération*, 6 Nov. 2004.
79. Ahmed Boubeker, 'Sous le voile, la mascarade de l'identité', in Helvig, *La laïcité dévoilée*, pp. 168–71, at p. 169.
80. For this shift, I partly draw on Monique Deveaux, *Gender and Justice in Multicultural Liberal States*. Oxford: Oxford University Press, 2006, p. 177.
81. Michel Foucault, *Discipline and Punish. The Birth of the Prison*. New York: Vintage Books, 1979.
82. See especially Michael Foucault, 'Afterward: The Subject and Power', in Hubert Dreyfus and Paul Rabinow (eds), *Michel Foucault: Beyond Structuralism and Hermeneutics*. Chicago: University of Chicago Press, 2nd edn, 1983.
83. I borrow the notion of 'content neutral' agency from Marylin Friedman, who distinguishes between content neutral and substantive autonomy on similar grounds. See her *Autonomy, Gender and Politics*. Oxford: Oxford University Press, 2003, pp. 19–25. For a stimulating reflection on harmful norms and the distinction between 'first-order' and 'second order' autonomy, see Clare Chambers, 'Are Breast Implants Better than Female

Genital Mutilation? Autonomy, Gender Equality, and Nussbaum's Political Liberalism', *Critical Review of International Social and Political Philosophy*, Vol. 7, No. 3, Autumn 2004, pp. 1–33.

84. For studies of Muslim female agency, see Saliba, Allen, Howard, *Gender, Politics and Islam*.

85. Anouar Majid, cited in Friedman, Autonomy, *Gender and Politics*, p. 187.

86. Hirschmann, 'Western Feminism, Eastern Veiling, and the Question of Free Agency', p. 358.

87. *Ibid.*, pp. 351, 355. Emphasis in the original.

88. Henri Pena-Ruiz, *Dieu et Marianne. Philosophie de la laïcité*. Paris: Presses Universitaires de France, 1999, p. 296.

89. Arlene MacLeod, cited in Hirschmann, 'Western Feminism, Eastern Veiling, and the Question of Free Agency', p. 357.

90. Horia Kebabza, 'Au croisement de la "race" et du "genre": les "jeunes de quartiers"', *Migrations Société*, Vol. 17, No. 99–100, May–Aug. 2005, pp. 77–89, p. 87.

91. Hoodfar, 'The Veil in their Minds and on our Heads', p. 10. Hoodfar argues that prior to the 1979 Revolution, the Shah's ban on veiling in public in effect restricted the movements of many veiled women. The suggestion that women's rights were enhanced by the 1979 Revolution is a deeply controversial one, but Hoodfar's general point, as I understand it, is that it is not so much the wearing of hijab in itself that is coercive and agency-limiting, but rather its manipulation by patriarchal power through state injunction (whether to veil or to unveil).

92. Guénif-Souilamas, *Des beurettes*, p. 25 and *passim*; Guenif-Souilamas, 'La fin de l'intégration, la preuve par les femmes', *Mouvements*, Vols. 29–30, May–Aug. 2005, pp. 150–7.

93. Nancy Venel, *Musulmanes françaises. Des pratiquantes voilées à l'université*. Paris: Harmattan, 1999, pp. 77–99; *Musulmans et Citoyens*, pp. 87–92, 188–9, 229–33; Etre Jocelyne Cesari, *Musulman en France aujourd'hui*. Paris: Hachette, 1997, pp. 157–62.

94. Ahmed, *Women and Gender in Islam*, p. 224.

95. Gaspard and Khosrokhavar, *Le Foulard et la republique*. p. 44. As Leila Ahmed has also remarked, 'far from indicating that the wearers remain fixed in the world of tradition and the past,... Islamic dress is the uniform of arrival, signalling entrance into, and determination to move forward in, modernity'. Ahmed, *Women and Gender in Islam*. p. 225.

96. Khoroskhavar, *Islam des jeunes*. pp. 118–31.

97. See notably Valentine Moghadam, 'Islamic Feminism and its Discontents: Toward a Resolution of the Debate', in Saliba, Allen, Howard, *Gender, Politics and Islam*, 15–51; Tariq Ramadan, *Les Musulmans dans la laïcite. Responsabilités et droits des musulmans dans les sociétés occidentales*. Lyon: Tawid, 1994, pp. 238–43.

98. Ahmed, *Women and Gender in Islam*, p. 238.

99. Tariq Ramadan, *Les Musulmans dans la laïcité*, p. 121. See also Simona Tersigni, 'La pratique du hijab en France. Prescription, transmission horizontale et dissidence', in Françoise Lorcerie (ed.), *La politisation du voile en France, en Europe et dans le monde arabe*. Paris: Harmattan 2005, pp. 37–52.

100. Nadine B. Weibel, *Par-dela le voile. Femmes d'Islam d'Europe*. Paris: Editions Complexe, 2000, p. 210. See also Khoroskhavar, *Islam des jeunes*, pp. 137–42; Kada Bouzar, *L'une voilée, l'autre pas*, 199, *passim*.

101. Hoodfar, 'The Veil in their Minds and on our Heads', p. 421.

102. Weibel, *Par-dela le voile*, p. 67.

103. Dounia Bouzar, '*"Monsieur Islam" n'existe pas. Pour une déislamisation des débats'*. Paris: Hachette, 2004, pp. 56–64.

104. On the role of charismatic religious leaders such as Tariq Ramadan in this process, see Dounia Bouzar, *L'Islam des banlieues, les prédicateurs musulmans, nouveaux travailleurs sociaux*. Paris: Syros-La Découverte, 2001; Tersigni, 'Prescription, transmission horizontale et dissidence'.

105. Guénif-Souilamas and Macé, *Les féministes et le garçon arabe*, p. 21, pp. 51–5.

106. For an application of Bhabha's notion of 'third space' to the understanding of female Muslims living in Canada, see Khan, 'Muslim Women: Negotiations in the Third Space'.

107. On the complex meanings of headscarves, see Fawzia Zouari, *Le voile islamique*; Kada Bouzar, *L'une voilée, l'autre pas*; El Guindi, *Veil. Privacy, Modesty and Resistance*, Gaspard, Khoroskhavar, *Le Foulard et la république*, Sonia Dayan-Herzbrun, 'The Issue of the Islamic Headscarf', in Jane Freedman and Carrie Tarr (eds), *Women, Immigration and Identities in France*. Oxford: Berg, 2000, pp. 69–82.

108. Farhad Khosrokhavar, 'L'universel abstrait, le politique et la construction de l'islamisme comme forme d'altérité', in Wieviorka, *Une Société Fragmentée*, pp. 113–51, at p. 142. Leila Ahmed has similarly noted that 'Western Criticism of Veiling runs the Danger of Undermining Islamic Women's Attempt to Affect their Own Culture'. Ahmed, *Women and Gender in Islam*, p. 162.

109. Balibar, 'Dissonances dans la laïcité', pp. 156–7. For a dense and subtle sociological exploration of the 'multiple dominations' suffered by *beurettes* en France, see Guénif-Souleimas, *Des beurettes*. See also Kebabza, 'Au croisement de la "race" et du "genre"', El Hamel, 'Muslim Diaspora in Western Europe'.

110. Guénif-Souleimas, *Des beurettes*, 345, *passim*.

Notes to Chapter 7

1. Ayelet Shachar, 'On Citizenship and Multicultural Vulnerability', *Political Theory*, Vol. 28, No. 1, Feb. 2000, pp. 64–78, p. 73.

2. Thanks to David Miller for pressing me on this point.

3. Philip Pettit, *Republicanism: A Theory of Freedom and Government*. Oxford: Oxford University Press, 1997, ch. 5.

4. On this, see Jeff Spinner-Halev, 'Feminism, Multiculturalism, Oppression and the State', *Ethics*, Vol. 112, Oct. 2001, pp. 84–113.
5. Avigail Eisenberg and Jeff Spinner-Halev (eds), *Minorities within Minorities*. Cambridge: Cambridge University Press, 2005.
6. Christine Delphy, 'Antisexisme ou antiracisme? Un faux dilemme', in Nacira Guénif-Souilamas (ed.), *La république mise à nu par son immigration*. Paris: La Fabrique Édition, 2006, pp. 81–108; Éric Fassin, 'Questions sexuelles, questions raciales. Parallèles, tensions et articulations', in Didier Fassin and Eric Fassin (eds), *De la question sociale à la question raciale. Représenter la société française*. Paris: La Découverte, 2006, pp. 230–48.
7. Young, *Justice and the Politics of Difference*. Princeton, NJ: Princeton University Press, 1990, p. 37.
8. Max Weber, *Economy and Society: An Outline of Interpretive Sociology*, New York: Bedminster Press, 1968, p. 212.
9. Pettit, *Republicanism*, p. 55. On this, see Marylin Friedman, 'Pettit's Civic Republicanism and Male Domination', in Cécile Laborde and John Maynor (eds), *Republicanism and Political Theory*. Oxford: Blackwell, 2007, pp. 246–68.
10. Pettit, *Republicanism*, p. 62.
11. *Ibid.*, p. 60. The dialectic between constraint and consent is often seen to be at the heart of the classic concept of domination. See, for example, Danilo Martucelli, 'Retour sur la domination', *Recherches Sociologiques* 2003/2, pp. 3–11. See also his *Dominations Ordinaires. Explorations de la condition moderne*. Paris: Balland, 2001.
12. Philip Pettit, 'The Domination Complaint', in Melissa S. Williams and Stephen Macedo (eds), *Political Exclusion and Domination. Nomos*, Vol. 46. New York: New York University Press, 2005, pp. 87–117.
13. Thomas E. Hill, *Autonomy and Self-Respect*. Cambridge: Cambridge University Press, 1991, pp. 4–18; Catriona McKinnon, *Liberalism and the Defence of Political Constructivism*. New York: Palgrave, 2002, Section 3.3.
14. Richard Dagger, 'Domination and the Republican Challenge to Liberalism', in John Christman and Joel Anderson (eds), *Autonomy and the Challenges to Liberalism*. Cambridge: Cambridge University Press, 2005, pp. 177–203.
15. John Stuart Mill, *The Subjection of Women*. London: Dent/Everyman, 1985, pp. 15–16.
16. Cass Sunstein, 'Beyond the Republican Revival', *Yale Law Journal*, Vol. 97, 1988, pp. 1623–31; 'Preferences and Politics', *Free Markets and Social Justice*. Oxford: Oxford University Press, 1997, pp. 13–31.
17. Susan James, 'The Good-Enough Citizen: Female Citizenship and Independence', in Gisela Bock and Susan James (eds), *Beyond Equality and Difference. Citizenship, Feminist Politics and Female Subjectivity*. London: Routledge, 1992, pp. 48–65.
18. Pettit, *Republicanism*, p. 71.
19. Philip Pettit, *A Theory of Freedom: From the Psychology to the Politics of Agency*. Cambridge: Polity Press, 2001, p. 140.
20. McKinnon, *Liberalism and the Defence of Political Constructivism*, 3.3.

21. For a forceful argument defending autonomy as an instrumental primary good, see Ian MacMullen, *Faith in Schools? Autonomy, Citizenship, and Religious Education in the Liberal State*. Princeton, NJ: Princeton University Press, 2007, pp. 88–112.

22. Marilyn Friedman, *Autonomy, Gender, Politics*. Oxford: Oxford University Press, 2003, p. 188.

23. For similar critiques, see Monique Deveaux, *Gender and Justice in Multicultural Liberal States*. Oxford: Oxford University Press, 2006, pp. 174–8; Susan Moller Okin, 'Multiculturalism and Feminism: No Simple Question, No Simple Answers', in Spinner-Halev Eisenberg, *Minorities within Minorities*, pp. 67–89, at pp. 75–9.

24. For defences of the 'plain exit right' see Chandran Kukathas, 'Are There Any Cultural Rights?', *Political Theory*, Vol. 20, No. 1, 1992, pp. 105–39; Chandran Kukathas, 'Cultural Toleration', in Will Kymlicka and Ian Shapiro (eds), *Ethnicity and Group Right*s. *Nomos*, Vol. 39. New York: New York University Press, 1997, pp. 69–104. For the claim that formal exit rights are insufficient and that vulnerable individuals need more substantive *capacities* to exit, see Susan Okin, '"Mistress of their Own Destiny". Group Rights, Gender and Realistic Rights of Exit', *Ethics*, Vol. 112, No. 2, 2002, pp. 205–30; Brian Barry, *Culture and Equality*. Cambridge: Polity, 2001, pp. 148–51, pp. 239–45; Shachar, 'On Citizenship and Multicultural Vulnerability'; Spinner-Halev, 'Feminism, Multiculturalism, Oppression and the State'.

25. Clare Chambers, 'Are Breast Implants Better than Female Genital Mutilation? Autonomy, Gender Equality and Nussbaum's Political Liberalism', *Critical Review of International Social and Political Philosophy*, Vol. 7, No. 3, Autumn 2004, pp. 1–33.

26. Eamonn Callan, *Creating Citizens. Political Education and Liberal Democracy*. Oxford: Oxford University Press, 1997, pp. 152–7.

27. *Ibid.*, p. 152.

28. John Rawls, *Political Liberalism*. New York: Columbia University Press, p. 200.

29. John Maynor, 'Without Regret: the Comprehensive Nature of Non-Domination', in his *Republicanism in the Modern World*. Cambridge: Polity, 2003, pp. 90–116; Richard Dagger, *Civic Virtue. Rights, Citizenship and Republican Liberalism*. Oxford: Oxford University Press, 1997, pp. 181–92.

30. To recall: by religious school, we mean a school whose interactions with those outside the community of faith remain limited, and whose pedagogy, rules, structures of authority, and large parts of the curriculum are designed to encourage children's belief in a particular religion. By secular education, we mean an education that lacks a specific religious purpose but is not opposed to religion, and aims to expose students to a diversity of ethical beliefs.

31. Meira Levinson, *The Demands of Liberal Education*. Oxford: Oxford University Press, 1999, p. 61.

32. MacMullen, *Faith in Schools?* pp. 162–9.

33. MacMullen advocates the following autonomy-promoting measures within religious schools: 'commitment to secular reason-giving inside and outside the classroom, balance religious instruction with critical perspectives on the faith, insulate significant parts of the academic curriculum from the religious ethos of the school, teach about other ethical doctrines in a way that makes children aware of viable alternatives to their family's faith, and demonstrate a sincere willingness to open the school to teachers and students outside the community of faith'. Despite these far-reaching changes, he argues, schools can still retain their religious character, and do not need to be radically 'detached' from family and community: they may be allowed to 'reserve a majority of places to students and teachers who belong to the community of faith, emphasize religious justifications for school rules and structures so long as they are accompanied by secular reasons... and run mandatory classes of instruction in a particular religious doctrine, so long as these classes include some secular, critical perspectives by way of balance'. MacMullen, *Faith in Schools?*, p. 175. Such regulations, however, would only apply to secondary schools and not to primary schools, which should be allowed to shape children's ethical framework more comprehensively, as a way to structure their personality and build the foundations for future exercises of autonomy.

34. *Ibid.*, pp. 134, 161.

35. See note 22 above.

36. Louisa Larabi Hendaz, *Le Voile humilié ou les auditions manquées de la Commission Stasi*. Paris: Éditions Marjane, 2004.

37. I borrow the phrase from Pettit, who also uses it in relation to the precarious status of immigrant communities. Pettit, *A Theory of Freedom*, 137. On the connection between domination and invisibility, see Danielle Allen, 'Invisible Citizens: Political Exclusion and Domination in Arendt and Ellison', in Melissa S. Williams and Stephen Macedo (eds), *Political Exclusion and Domination. Nomos*, Vol. 46. New York: New York University Press, 2005, pp. 29–76.

38. Pettit, *Republicanism*, p. 181.

39. Pettit, *A Theory of Freedom*, pp. 162–3. See also Philip Pettit, 'Democracy, Electoral and Contestatory', *Nomos*, Vol. 42, New York: New York University Press, 2000, pp. 105–44; Phillip Pettit, 'Deliberative Democracy, the Discursive Dilemma, and Republican Theory', in James Fishkin and Peter Laslett (eds), *Philosophy, Politics and Society*, Vol. 7, New York, Cambridge University Press, 2003, pp. 138–62.

40. Philip Pettit, 'Republican Freedom and Contestatory Democratization', in Ian Shapiro and Casiano Hacker-Cordon (eds), *Democracy's Value*. Cambridge: Cambridge University Press, 1999, pp. 163–90, at p. 178.

41. Nicholas Southwood, 'Beyond Pettit's Neo-Roman Republicanism: The Deliberative Republic', *Critical Review of International Social and Political Philosophy*, Vol. 5, No. 1, 2002, pp. 16–42; John Drysek, *Deliberative Democracy and Beyond. Liberals, Critics, Contestations*. Oxford: Oxford University Press,

2000; Benjamin Barber, *Strong Democracy. Participatory Politics for a New Age*. Berkeley, CA: University of California Press, 1984.

42. Henry S. Richardson, *Democratic Autonomy: Public Reasoning about the Ends of Policy*. Oxford: Oxford University Press, 2002.

43. Sunstein, 'Beyond the Republican Revival'; Joshua Cohen, 'Deliberation and Democratic Legitimacy', in A. Hamlin and P. Pettit (eds), *The Good Polity*. Oxford: Oxford University Press, 1989, pp. 17–34; Jurgen Habermas, 'Three Normative Models of Democracy', *Constellations*, Vol. 1, No. 1, 1994, pp. 1–10; Jürgen Habermas, *Between Facts and Norms: Contributions to a Discourse Theory of Law and Democracy*. Cambridge: Polity Press, 1996; David Miller, 'Citizenship and Pluralism', *Political Studies*, Vol. 43, 1995, pp. 432–50.

44. David Miller, *Citizenship and National Identity*. Cambridge: Polity Press, 2000, ch. 3, ch. 9; Richard Bellamy, *Liberalism and Pluralism: Towards a Politics of Compromise*. London: Routledge, 1999; Seyla Benhabib (ed.), *Democracy and Difference. Contesting the Boundaries of the Political*. Princeton, NJ: Princeton University Press, 1996; Seyla Benhabib, *The Claims of Culture: Equality and Diversity in the Global Era*. Princeton, NJ: Princeton University Press, 2002; James Bohman, 'Public Reason and Cultural Pluralism', *Political Theory*, Vol. 23, No. 2, 1995, pp. 253–79; Drysek, *Deliberative Democracy and Beyond*; Melissa Williams, *Voice, Trust and Memory. Marginalized Groups and the Failings of Liberal Representation*. Princeton, NJ: Princeton University Press, 1998; Anthony Simon Laden, *Reasonably Radical: Deliberative Liberalism and the Politics of Identity*. Ithaca, NJ: Cornell University Press, 2001; James Tully, *Strange Multiplicity: Constitutionalism in an Age of Diversity*. Cambridge: Cambridge University Press, 1995.

45. Spinner-Halev, 'Feminism, Multiculturalism, Oppression and the State'; Gurpreet Mahajan, 'Can Intra-Group Equality Co-Exist with Cultural Diversity? Re-examining Multicultural Frameworks of Accommodation', in Spinner-Halev Eisenberg (ed.), *Minorities within Minorities*, pp. 90–112; Okin, 'Multiculturalism and Feminism', in *ibid*. There might be, therefore, a principled reason for the much derided leftwing 'post-colonial guilt', which is often criticized for the 'double standards' it applies to the treatment of religious groups such as Christians and Muslims.

46. Daniel Weinstock, 'Beyond Exit Rights: Reframing the Debate', in Spinner-Halev Eisenberg, *Minorities within Minorities*. pp. 227–47; Shachar, 'Citizenship and Multicultural Vulnerability', pp. 37–8.

47. Deveaux, *Gender and Justice in Multicultural Liberal States*.

48. David Miller, 'Is Deliberative Democracy Unfair to Disadvantaged Minorities?', in David Miller (ed.), *Citizenship and National Identity*. Cambridge: Polity Press, 2000; Pettit, 'Republican Freedom and Contestatory Democratization'; Bellamy, *Liberalism and Pluralism*; Richard Bellamy, *Political Constitutionalism*. Cambridge: Cambridge University Press, 2007.

49. Cillian McBride, 'Deliberative Democracy and the Politics of Recognition', *Political Studies*, 2005, pp. 497–515.

50. Shachar 'Citizenship and Multicultural Vulnerability', p. 65.
51. Nacira Guénif-Souilamas, *Des beurettes*. Paris: Grasset & Fasquelle, 2000.
52. Shachar, 'Citizenship and Multicultural Vulnerability', p. 80.
53. Deveaux, *Gender and Justice in Multicultural Liberal States*. pp. 163–85.
54. *Ibid.*, pp. 109, 227, *passim*.
55. Pettit, *Republicanism*, p. 63.

Notes to Chapter 8

1. Jean-Pierre Sylvestre, 'Les fondements de la conception laïque du lien social', *Raison Présente*, Vol. 122, 1997, pp. 79–96, at p. 91.
2. Régis Debray, *Ce que le voile nous voile. La République et le sacré*. Paris: Folio/Gallimard, 2004, pp. 37–43, italics added.
3. For a good analysis of the 'culturalisation' of *laïcité*, see Joël Roman, 'Pourquoi la laïcité?', in Nacira Guénif-Souilamas (ed.), *La république mise à nu par son immigration*. Paris: La Fabrique Édition, 2006, pp. 62–80, at pp. 62–3.
4. In Ernest Renan's phrase, cited in Gérard Noiriel, *Le creuset français. Histoire de l'immigration, XIX-XXème siècles*. Paris: Seuil, 1988, p. 27.
5. In Charles Seignobos's phrase, cited in Dominique Schnapper, *La France de l'Intégration. Sociologie de la nation en 1990*. Paris: Gallimard, 1990, p. 78.
6. Cited in Rogers Brubaker, *Citizenship and Nationhood in France and Germany*. Cambridge, MA: Harvard University Press, 1992, p. 101. See also Noiriel, *Le Creuset Français*, 102, ch. 2. For an argument to the effect that this 'fusional' conception of the nation assumes rather than negates the pre-existence of separate 'races', see Jean-Loup Amselle, *Vers un multiculturalisme français. L'empire de la coutume*. Paris: Aubier, 1996.
7. Cited in Pierre Rosanvallon, *Le Sacre du Citoyen. Histoire du suffrage universel en France*. Paris: Gallimard, 1994, p. 74.
8. Ernest Renan, 'Qu'est ce qu'une nation?' (extracts in English), in John Hutchinson and Anthony Smith (eds), *Nationalism*. Oxford: Oxford University Press, 1994, pp. 17–18.
9. Dominique Schnapper, *La Relation à l'Autre, Au cœur de la pensée sociologique*. Paris: Gallimard, 1998, pp. 102–8, pp. 396–400; Jim Cohen, 'Intégration: théories, politiques et logiques d'État', in Philippe Dewitte (ed.), *Immigration et intégration. L'état des savoirs*. Paris: La Découverte, 1999, pp. 32–55, at p. 37.
10. Dominique Schnapper, *La Relation à l'Autre*, p. 402. See also Noiriel, *Le Creuset francais*, p. 32.
11. Benedict Anderson, *Imagined Communities. Reflections on the Origins and Spread of Nationalism*. London: Verso, 1991.
12. Dominique Schnapper, *La Communauté des citoyens. Sur l'idée moderne de nation*. Paris: Gallimard, 1994.
13. Schnapper, *Relation à l'autre* 102, ch. 11. For a historical survey of French research on 'inter-ethnic relations', see Véronique De Rudder, 'Jalons pour

une histoire socio-politique sur les relations interethniques en France', in Ida Simon-Barouch and Véronique de Rudder (eds), *Migrations Internationales et Relations Interethniques*. Paris: Harmattan 1997, pp. 73–96.

14. Noiriel *Le Creuset français* p. 337. See also, for a eulogy of 'colour-blind' France; Emmanuel Todd, *Le destin des immigrés. Assimilation et ségrégation dans les démocraties occidentales*. Paris: Seuil, 1994, ch. 12.

15. This is the main theme of Brubaker's classic comparison, *Citizenship and Nationhood in France and Germany*.

16. Brubaker, *Citizenship and Nationhood in France and Germany*, p. 3, *passim;* Schnapper, *La France de l'Intégration*, p. 151. This was also the starting point of the work of the Nationality Commission, convened in 1986 to reform nationality laws. See the 'Long report': Commission de la Nationalité, *Etre Français aujourd'hui et demain. Rapport présenté par Marceau Long au Premier Ministre*, 2 Vols. Paris: Union Générale d'Éditions, 1988, Vol. 2, p. 82, thereafter 'Long report'. For a contrary view, see Patrick Weil, who argues that 'nationality laws do not reflect a particular conception of the nation'. Patrick Weil, *Qu'est ce qu'un Français? Histoire de la nationalité française depuis la Révolution*. Paris: Grasset, 2002, pp. 13, 197.

17. Brubaker, *Citizenship and Nationhood in France and Germany*, pp. 77–84. Other good surveys of French nationality laws include Weil, *Qu'est ce qu'un Français?*; Smaïn Laacher (ed.), *Questions de Nationalité. Histoire et enjeux d'un code*. Paris: Harmattan 1987.

18. Note, however, that the most common means of acquisition of French citizenship is through *jus sanguinis*—the automatic acquisition of the nationality of one's parents.

19. Only residents of colonies could be French nationals without being full citizens.

20. Schnapper, *France de l'Intégration*, p. 56.

21. Long report, Vol. 2, p. 92.

22. Dominique Schnapper, 'Citoyenneté européenne et démocratie providentielle', in Patrick Savidan (ed.), *La République ou l'Europe?* Paris: Livre de Poche, 2004, pp. 337–60. See also Weil and Taguieff, 'Immigration, fait national et citoyenneté'. For defences of the 'new citizenship' and 'post-national citizenship' see Saïd Bouamama, Albano Cordeiro, and Michel Roux, *La citoyenneté dans tous ses états. De l'immigration à la nouvelle citoyenneté*. Paris: L'Harmattan, 1992; Saïd Bouamama, *Vers une nouvelle citoyenneté. Crise de la pensée laïque*. Lille: La boîte de Pandore, 1991; Catherine Wihtol de Wenden (ed.), *La citoyenneté et les changements de structures sociales et nationales de la population française*. Paris: Edilig/Fondation Diderot, 1988. For a discussion of the impact of those ideas on European citizenship, see Justine Lacroix, *L'Europe en procès. Quel patriotisme au-delà des nationalismes?* Paris: Éditions du Cerf, 2004.

23. Dominique Schnapper, 'Citoyenneté européenne et démocratie providentielle', in Patrick Savidan (ed.), *La République ou l'Europe?* Paris: Livre de Poche, 2004, pp. 337–60. See also Pierre-André Taguieff, Patrick Weil,

'Immigration, fait national et citoyenneté', *Esprit*, May 1990, pp. 245–81. For an analysis of the debate over immigrants' voting rights, see Jane Freedman, *Immigration and Insecurity in France.* Aldershot: Ashgate, 2004, pp. 90–4.

24. Long report, Vol. 2, p. 93 (Long ii, 93).

25. This law was only partially overturned by the Socialist administration in 1997. Nationality is now *automatically* granted at 18 to children born in France of foreign parents, but it can be *requested* by them when they reach 16.

26. Alain Finkielkraut, *La défaite de la pensée.* Paris: Gallimard, 1987.

27. This is notably the argument of Weil, *Qu'est ce qu'un français?*, p. 177. For the debates during the *auditions* of the Nationality Commission, see Long Report, Vol. 1.

28. Schnapper, *France de l'Intégration*, p. 62.

29. *Ibid.*, p. 68.

30. *Ibid.*, pp. 355, 351.

31. Cf. Brubaker *Citizenship and Nationhood in France and Germany*, p. 10, for a similar idea: 'in the French conception of the nation, political unity was constitutive, and cultural unity expressive'.

32. It is worth pointing out that state-centered cultural assimilationism was not an exclusively republican commitment. Republicans were the (often enthusiastic) heirs to a long-standing, pervasive and multifaceted assimilationist tradition. For an excellent survey of French 'national assimilation', see Gérard Noiriel, *Population, Immigration et Identité Nationale en France, XIXème-XXème siècle.* Paris: Hachette, 1992, pp. 85–126. First, as suggested above, France's objective cultural, linguistic, and ethnic diversity had meant that historically nation-building had been much more state-centred and state-promoted than was the case in more homogeneous societies: the French state, in a sense, had 'instituted' the nation from above. Second, the interventionist and centralizing mission of the state was further enhanced in the nineteenth century in response to the perceived risk of social fragmentation and anomie arising out of the individualistic reforms of the 1789 Revolution, which had weakened all intermediary groups between the individual and the state. Historian Pierre Rosanvallon has suggested that the state in France was *'l'instituteur du social'.* (*L'État en France, De 1798 à nos jours.* Paris: Seuil, 1990, pp. 95–135). Third, nineteenth-century French elites' confidence in the virtues of cultural assimilation was rooted in a belief in the intrinsic superiority of French culture: the universal ideals of rational progress and individual autonomy, central to the perfectionist ideal of *laïcité* analysed in Chapter 5, were easily conflated with the particular genius of French civilization. Fourth, French rulers were keen to foster the cultural solidarity of nationalism between social classes, as a foil to social conflict and the class struggle.

33. Jürgen Habermas, 'Citizenship and National Identity: Some Reflections on the Future of Europe', in Ronald Beiner (ed.), *Theorizing Citizenship.*

New York: State University of New York Press, 1999, pp. 255–68, at p. 263.

34. Quentin Skinner, 'On Justice, the Common Good and the Priority of Liberty', in C. Mouffe (ed.), *Dimensions of Radical Democracy*. London: Verso, 1992, pp. 211–24.

35. Danièle Lochak, 'Les minorités et le droit public français: du refus des différences à la gestion des differences', in Alain Ferret and Gérard Soulier, *Les minorités et leurs droits depuis 1789*. Paris: Harmattan, 1989, pp. 111–84.

36. Jack Hayward, 'Solidarity: the Social History of an Idea in Nineteenth-Century France', *International Review of Social History*. Vol. IV, 1959, pp. 261–84. On the relevance of the theme of solidarity to contemporary debates about reforms of the welfare state, see Daniel Béland and Randall Hansen, 'Reforming the French Welfare State: Solidarity, Social Exclusion and the Three Crises of Citizenship', *West European Politics*. Vol. 23, No. 1, Jan. 2000, pp. 47–64. For a comprehensive update on the use of the concept of solidarity in debates in the social sciences, see Serge Paugam (ed.), *Repenser la solidarité. L'apport des sciences sociales*. Paris: Presses Universitaires de France, 2007.

37. Maurizio Viroli, *For Love of Country: An Essay on Nationalism and Patriotism*. Oxford: Oxford University Press, 1995.

38. Jürgen Habermas, *The New Conservatism. Cultural Criticism and the Historians' Debate*. Boston: MIT, 1989; Jürgen Habermas, 'Citizenship and National Identity. Some Reflections on the Future of Europe', in Ronald Beiner (ed.), *Theorizing Citizenship*. New York: State University of New York Press, 1999, pp. 255–68. For an alternative interpretation, which situates Habermas within the tradition of republican patriotism, see Cécile Laborde, 'From Constitutional to Civic Patriotism', *British Journal of Political Science*, Vol. 32, 2002, pp. 591–612; Maurizio Viroli, *For Love of Country. An Essay on Patriotism and Nationalism*. Oxford: Oxford University Press, 1995, pp. 169–77 and Jan-Werner Müller, *Another Country. German Intellectuals, Unification and National Identity*. New Haven and London: Yale University Press, 2000, pp. 96–7.

39. Gérard Noiriel, *État, Nation et Immigration. Vers une Histoire du Pouvoir*. Paris: Belin, 2001, p. 1136.

40. Long Report, Vol. 2, 24. For a classic statement, see Ernest Gellner, *Nations and Nationalism*. Ithaca, NY: Cornell University Press, 1983.

41. Fred Constant, *La citoyenneté*. Paris: Montchrestien, 1998, p. 28.

42. Schnapper, *Communauté des citoyens*, p. 78. For discussions of this claim see Paul Thibaud and Jean-Marc Ferry, *Discussion sur l'Europe*. Paris: Calmann-Lévy, 1992; Lacroix, *L'Europe en procès*; Patrick Savidan (ed.), *La République ou l'Europe?* Paris: Livre de Poche, 2004.

43. Schnapper, *France de l'intégration*, p. 361.

44. Eugen Weber, *Peasants into Frenchmen*. Stanford, CA: Stanford University Press, 1976.

45. Noiriel, *Immigration et identité nationale en France; État, Nation et Immigration.*

46. Note that the French republican philosophy of education is not as internally incoherent as this schematic analytical presentation suggests: 'neutralist', '*laïciste*', and 'national' concerns are no more than different interpretations of a shared republican commitment to the primarily political and civic purpose of education. All agree that republican education must create citizens, but there is disagreement as to what makes a good republican citizen.

47. François Dubet, 'La laïcité dans les mutations de l'école', in Michel Wieviorka (ed.), *Une société fragmentée? Le multiculturalisme en débat.* Paris: La Découverte, 1996, pp. 85–112, at p. 87.

48. But see François Chanet, *L'école républicaine et les petites patries.* Paris: Aubier, 1996; Anne-Marie Thiesse, *Ils apprenaient la France. L'exaltation des régions dans le discours patriotique.* Paris: Éditions de la MSH, 1997, for more nuanced accounts of the extent of cultural assimilation during the Third Republic.

49. For a rich historical account of the 'sacralisation' of the republic, see Yves Déloye and Olivier Ihl, 'Deux figures singulières de l'universel: la république et le sacré', in Marc Sadoun (ed.), *La démocratie en France.* Vol. 2, Paris: Gallimard, 2000. For critical commentaries, see Jean-Louis Willaime, 'La religion civile à la française et ses métamorphoses', *Social Compass*, Vol. 40, No. 4, 1993, pp. 571–80, Joël Roman, 'La laïcité comme religion civile', *Esprit*, Vol. 175, 1991, pp. 108–15.

50. See, critically, Susanne Citron, *Le Mythe national: l'histoire de France en question.* Paris: Editions Ouvrieres/Etudes et Documentation Internationales, 1987.

51. Olivier Ihl, *La fête républicaine.* Paris: Gallimard, 1996.

52. Yves Deloye, *Ecole et citoyenneté. L'individualisme républicain de Jules Ferry à Vichy: controverses.* Paris: Presses de la Fondation Nationales des Sciences Politiques, 1994, p. 22.

53. Robert Goodin, 'Folie Républicaine', *American Review of Political Science*, Vol. 6, 2003, pp. 55–76, p. 62; Hughes Jallon and Pierre Mounier, *Les enragés de la République.* Paris: La Découverte, 1999, pp. 105–10.

54. Etienne Balibar, 'Propositions sur la citoyenneté', in Wihtol de Wenden, *La citoyenneté et les changements de structures*, pp. 223–34, at pp. 228–9.

55. Marc Lazar, 'La République à l'épreuve du social', in Marc Sadoun (ed.), *La démocratie en France.* Vol. 2, Paris: Gallimard, 2000, Vol. 2, pp. 309–406, at p. 358, *passim.*

56. Although political polemics invoking this contrast have been fierce, few serious attempts have been made to give it strong philosophical or empirical grounding. The idealized 'republican' model is a social-democratic model, which emphasizes principles of equality and universality of rights. Yet, as the classic study by Andersen Esping has shown, the actual institutions of the French welfare state are closer to the 'corporatist' model, which is less egalitarian and less individualist. See Gøsta Esping-Anderson, *The Three Worlds of Welfare Capitalism.* Cambridge:

Polity Press and Princeton, NJ: Princeton University Press, 1990. The differences between the republican and corporatist models on the one hand, and the 'liberal' model, which only provides a 'safety net' for the worst-off, are perhaps clearer. For a speculative essay which contrasts 'republican solidarity' with 'the Anglo-Saxon model of tolerance cum indifference', and makes intriguing connections with national politics of immigrant integration, see Philippe D'Iribarne, 'Du rapport à l'autre. Les singularités françaises dans l'intégration des immigrés', *Le Débat*, Vol. 129, mars-avril 2004, pp. 122–35.

57. Gilbert Vincent (ed.), *Services Publics, solidarité et citoyenneté*. Paris: L'Harmattan, 1998; Severine Decreton, *Service Public et Lien Social*. Paris: Harmattan, 1999.

58. Social rights in France have traditionally been attributed to foreigner residents and citizens alike. Cf. Haut Conseil à l'Intégration, *L'intégration à la française*, pp. 53–5. There are, however, forms of legalized discrim-inations, particularly concerning civil service jobs, and an increasingly stratified system of access to welfare provision. For details, see Danièle Lochak, 'Discriminations against Foreigners under French Law', in Donald Horowitz and Gérard Noiriel (eds), *Immigrants in Two Democracies. French and American Experiences*. New York: New York University Press, 1992, pp. 391–410; Freedman, *Immigration and Insecurity in France*, pp. 98–103.

59. Bernard Toulemonde, 'La discrimination positive dans l'éducation: des ZEP à Sciences Po,' *Pouvoirs*, Vol. 111, 2004, pp. 87–99; Marie-Christine Weidmann Koop, 'Discrimination positive en France: l'expérience de l'éducation prioritaire', *Contemporary French Civilization*, Vol. 24, No. 1, Winter/Spring 2005, pp. 85–104; Éric Keslassy, *De la discrimination posi-tive*. Rosny-sous-bois: Bréal, 2004; Thomas Kirszbaum, 'La discrimination positive territoriale: de l'égalité des chances à la mixité urbaine', *Pouvoirs*, Vol. 111, 2004, pp. 101–18.

60. For an implicitly critical assessment of the 'ethnic welfare state', see Dominique Schnapper, *La Démocratie providentielle. Essai sur l'égalité contem-poraine*. Paris: Gallimard, 2002, pp. 175–209. For a normative critique, which combines two arguments which I have distinguished in this book: 'neutralist' (which targets the morally arbitrary nature of racial or cultural difference) and 'solidarity-based' (which is concered about the divisive nature of 'culturally sensitive' policies) see Brian Barry, *Culture and Equality*. Cambridge: Polity, 2001.

61. This is a direct reference to the title of a typical book on the subject, by Jacqueline Costa-Lascoux, *De l'immigré au citoyen*. Paris: La Documentation Française, 1989.

62. Brubacker, *Citizenship and Nationhood in France and Germany*, pp. 108–9. See also Cohen, 'Intégration: théories, politiques et logiques d'État', p. 37.

63. Noiriel, *Population, Immigration et identité nationale*, p. 120.

64. *Ibid.*, pp. 119–20.
65. For a nuanced account, see Noiriel, *Le Creuset français; Immigration et Identité Nationale.*
66. Donald Horowitz, 'Immigration and group relations in France and America', in Horowitz and Noiriel (ed.), *Immigrants in Two Democracies*, pp. 3–37, at pp. 8–9.
67. Schnapper, *France de l'Intégration*, p. 300.
68. See Henri Giordan, *Démocratie culturelle et droit à la différence.* Paris: La Documentation Française, 1982; William Safran, 'The Mitterrand Regime and its Policies of Ethnocultural Accommodation', *Comparative Politics*, Vol. 18, No. 1, 1985, pp. 41–63 and Miriam Feldblum, *Reconstructing Citizenship. The Politics of Nationality Reform and Immigration in Contemporary France.* New York: State University of New York Press, 1999, pp. 32–4.
69. Pierre-André Taguieff, *La Force du préjugé: Essai sur le racisme et ses doubles.* Paris: La Découverte, 1987; Pierre-André Taguieff, *Les fins de l'antiracisme.* Paris: Michalon, 1995.
70. See Jeremy Jennings, 'Citizenship, Republicanism and Multiculturalism in Contemporary France', *British Journal of Political Science*, Vol. 2000, No. 30, pp. 575–98; Feldblum, *Reconstructing Citizenship*; Adrian Favell, *Philosophies of Integration. Immigration and the Idea of Citizenship in France and Britain.* Basingtoke: Macmillan, 1998; Max Silverman, *Deconstructing the Nation. Immigration, Racism and Citizenship in Modern France.* London & New York: Routledge, 1992; Patrick Weil, *La République et sa Diversité. Immigration, Intégration, Discriminations.* Paris: Seuil, 2005; Brubaker, *Citizenship and Nationhood in France and Germany*; Patrick Ireland, *The Policy Challenge of Ethnic Diversity. Immigrant Politics in France and Switzerland.* Cambridge, MA: Harvard University Press, 1994, ch. 2, pp. 47–99. For a synthesis in English of the national republican position by one of its most sophisticated exponents, see Dominique Schnapper, 'Making Citizens in an Increasingly Complex Society: Jacobinism Re-Visited', in Sudhir Hazareesingh (ed.), *The Jacobin Legacy in Modern France.* Oxford: Oxford University Press, 2002, pp. 196–216.
71. On the American counter-model, see Marie-Christine Granjon, 'Le regard en biais. Attitudes françaises et multiculturalisme américain', *Vingtième Siècle*, Vol. 43, 1994, pp. 18–29; Éric Fassin, 'Two Cultures? French Intellectuals and the Politics of Culture in the 1980s', *French Politics and Society*, Vol. 14, No. 2, Spring 1996; Eric Fassin, '"Good to Think". The American Reference in French Discourses of Immigration and Ethnicity', in Christian Joppke and Steven Lukes (eds), *Multicultural Questions.* Oxford: Oxford University Press, 1999, pp. 224–41; Todorov, 'Du culte de la différence à la sacralisation de la victime', *Esprit*, Vol. 6, June 1995, pp. 90–102; Jim Cohen, 'Les "modèles d'intégration" face aux particularismes: malentendus et dialogues France/Etat Unis', *Mouvements*, Vol. 38, Mar.–Apr. 2005, pp. 41–9.
72. De Rudder, 'Jalons pour une histoire socio-politique', p. 85.

73. See Schnapper, *La Relation à l'Autre*, 352–3 and *passim* on the relative continuity of national traditions of reflection about pluralism and 'Otherness'.

74. In the words of the Long report, cited in René Gallissot, 'Épouvantail ethnique et méli-mélo culturel', in Ida Simon-Barouch and Véronique de Rudder (eds), *Migrations Internationales et Relations Interethniques.* Paris: Harmattan, 1997, pp. 267–95, at p. 286.

75. Françoise Lorcerie, 'Les sciences sociales au service de l'identité nationale', in Denis Constant Martin (ed.), *Cartes d'identité. Comment dit-on "nous" en politique?* Paris: Presses de la Fondation Nationale des Sciences Politiques, pp. 245–81, 1994.

76. Feldblum, *Reconstructing Citizenship*, p. 56, *passim.*

77. *Ibid.*, ch. 4, ch. 6; Long Report.

78. Long Report, *passim.* For an analysis, see Schnapper, *La France de l'Intégration*, pp. 348–58. The Commission later became the Hant Conseil à l'Intégration, whose annual reports give a fascinating insight into the elaboration of the republican theory of immigrant integration.

79. Cited in Feldblum, p. 106.

80. The term is a contested one in France, as it is associated with a communitarian, *souverainiste,* and Eurosceptic movement. See notably Lacroix, *L'Europe en procès*, chs. 2 and 3; Justice Lacroix, 'Les Nationaux-Républicans de gauche et la construction et la construction européenne', *Le Banquet*, Vol. 15, Nov. 2000, pp. 157–68. I use the term in a broader, more neutral and less politicized sense (which I clarify throughout this chapter) to refer to a broader consensus of republican opinion in France on the subject of the integration of immigrants and the rejection of the public recognition of cultural differences. For good synthetic analyses of the emergence of this national republican consensus, see Favell, *Philosophies of Integration*; Feldblum, *Reconstructing Citizenship.* For a critical analysis of some of its internal contradictions, see Cécile Laborde, 'The Culture(s) of the Republic'. Nationalism and Republicanism in Contemporary French Republican Thought', *Political Theory*, Vol. 29, No. 5, 2001, pp. 716–35.

81. Schnapper, *La Communauté des Citoyens*; *La France de l'Intégration*; Costa-Lascoux: *De l'Immigré au Citoyen*; Todd, *Le Destin des Immigrés*; Taguieff, *La Force du Préjugé*; Noiriel, *Le Creuset Français*; Michèle Tribalat, *Faire France. Une enquête sur les immigrés et leurs enfants*, Paris: La Découverte, 1995; *De l'immigration à l'assimilation. Enquête sur les populations d'origine étrangère en France.* Paris: La Découverte 1996.

82. Long Report, Vol. 1, p. 24.

83. *Ibid.*, 24.

84. Haut Conseil à l'Intégration, *L'intégration à la française*, p. 34.

85. *Ibid*, p. 35.

86. Christian Jelen, *Les casseurs de la République.* Paris: Plon 1997, esp. at p. 174; Todd, *Le destin des immigrés*, esp. at pp. 442–3.

87. Schnapper, *Communauté des citoyens*, p. 37. The expression 'tolerant republicans' is used by Jennings, 'Citizenship, Republicanism and Multiculturalism in Contemporary France' and Michel Wieviorka 'Le multiculturalisme est-il la réponse?', *Cahiers Internationaux de Sociologie*, Vol. 105, 1998, pp. 233–60, pp. 245–7), both of which offer useful typologies of French republican attitudes towards multiculturalism.

88. On the controversy provoked by Tribalat's use of seemingly 'ethnic' categories, see Alain Blum 'Comment décrire les immigrés? A propos de quelques recherches sur l'immigration', *Population*, Vol. 3, 1998, pp. 569–87; Henri Le Bras, *Le Démon des Origines. Démographie et Extrême Droite*. Paris: Éd. de L'Aube, 1998.

89. Tribalat, *De l'immigration à l'assimilation*, pp. 254–67. This is not dissimilar to the approach promoted by the Chicago School, following the pionneering works of Robert Park in the 1920s and 1930s. According to this functionalist assimilationist theory dominant the 1950s, assimilation is a situation whereby individuals' ethnic origin is irrelevant to the prediction of their social trajectory, and where cultural uniformization signifies the progressive erosion of minority cultures. See Philippe Poutignat and Jocelyne Streiff-Fenart, *Théories de l'ethnicité*. Paris: Presses Universitaires de France, 1995, pp. 70–4. For a theoretical comparison between the French 'Durkheimian' and the American 'Chicago' approaches, see Stéphane Beaud and Gérard Noiriel, 'Penser l'intégration des immigrés', *Hommes et Migrations*, Vol. 1133, 1990, pp. 43–54. For a synthetic survey of the varying modes of acculturation of immigrants in France, see Alec Hargreaves, *Immigration, 'Race' and Ethnicity in Contemporary France*. London: Routledge, 1995, pp. 85–148.

90. Long Report, Vol. 2, p. 27.

91. *Ibid.*, pp. 26–7.

92. See, for a far more speculative essay by another demographer, Todd, *Le destin des immigrés*.

93. Long Report, Vol. 2, pp. 41–50; Haut Conseil à l'Intégration, *L'intégration à la française*, pp. 15–35.

94. Weil Taguieff, 'Immigration, fait national et citoyenneté', p. 93. For a different view, which focuses more on the systemic and institutional aspects of the French melting pot, see the works of Noiriel, and his statement (with Stéphane Beaud) that 'willingly or otherwise, assimilation takes place'. Beaud, Noiriel, 'Penser l'intégration des immigrés', p. 47.

95. Favell, *Philosophies of Integration*, pp. 163–4.

96. Touraine, cited in Feldblum, *Reconstructing Citizenship*, p. 112.

97. Long Report, Vol. 2, p. 85.

98. Schnapper, *La France de l'integration*, p. 95.

99. *Ibid.*, p. 183; Noiriel, *Le creuset français*, p. 341.

100. Todd, *Le Destin des Immigrés*, p. 444.

101. We saw in Chapter 2 that this was the strategy of those neutralist *laïque* republicans concerned with the preservation of a secular public sphere and concomitant privation of religious and cultural identities.

102. Noiriel, *Le creuset français*, p. 344.

103. Haut Conseil à l'Intégration, *Liens culturels et intégration*. Paris: Documentation Française, 1995, pp. 21–2, 42.

104. *Ibid.*, p. 19.

105. *Ibid.*, p. 53.

106. *Ibid.*, pp. 17–18.

107. Schnapper, *La France de l'integration*, pp. 168, 302–3.

108. Haut Conseil à l'Intégration, *L'intégration à la française*, pp. 118–20; Haut Conseil à l'Intégration, *Liens culturels et intégration*, 24, Long Report, Vol. 2, p. 88. For a more nuanced account, see Françoise Lorcerie, 'Laïcité 1996. La République à l'école de l'immigration?', *Revue Française de Pédagogie*, Vol. 117, Oct.–Nov.–Dec., 1996, pp. 53–86.

109. Presentation of the Report by the Commission chairman, Marceau Long, cited in Feldblum, *Reconstructing Citizenship*, p. 109 (underlining in the original).

110. Haut Conseil à l'Intégration, *L'intégration à la française,* p. 9.

111. Will Kymlicka, *Multicultural Citizenship. A Liberal Theory of Minority Rights*. Oxford: Oxford University Press, 1995.

112. *Ibid.*, pp. 30–1, 113–15, 119–20. The issue of cultural equality was discussed at greater length in relation to the neutralist strand of republicanism in chs. 2 and 3. National republicans, like neutralist republicans, endorse a difference-blind conception of equality but, in addition, tend to prioritize the value of social cohesion over that of equality. These two commitments militate against the recognition of cultural rights.

113. Haut Conseil à l'Intégration, *Affaiblissement du lien social, enfermement dans les particularismes et intégration dans la cité*. Paris: La Documentation Française, 1997.

114. Didier Lapeyronnie, *L'individu et les minorités. La France et la Grande-Bretagne face à leurs immigrés*. Paris: Presses Universitaires de France, 1993, p. 46.

115. The most concise survey is Schnapper, *La France de l'intégration*, ch. 6, 'L'Emiettement des Institutions Nationales'. See also François Dubet and Danilo Martucelli, *Dans quelle société vivons-nous?* Paris: Seuil 1998, chs. 5 and 6.

116. Long Report, Vol. 2, p. 27.

117. Jeanne-Hélène Kaltenbach and Michèle Tribalat, *La République et l'Islam. Entre crainte et aveuglement*. Paris: Gallimard, 2002; Shmuel Trigano, *La démission de la République. Juifs et Musulmans en France*. Paris: Presses Universitaires de France, 2003.

118. Marcel Gauchet, 'L'école à l'école d'elle-même. Contraintes et contradictions de l'individualisme démocratique', *Le Débat*, Vol. 36, 1985,

pp. 55–78. Reprinted in his *La Démocratie contre elle-même*. Paris: Gallimard, 2002, pp. 109–69.

119. On this theme, see Schnapper, *La Démocratie providentielle*.

120. See, for example, Jeanne-Hélène Kaltenbach and Michèle Tribalat, *La République et l'Islam. Entre crainte et aveuglement*. Paris: Gallimard, 2002.

121. Régis Debray, Max Gallo, Jacques Julliard, Blandine Kriegel, Olivier Mongin, Mona Ozouf, Anicet Le Pors, and Paul Thibaud, 'Républicains, n'ayons plus peur!', *Le Monde*, 4 Sept. 1998, p. 13.

122. Haut Conseil à l'Intégration, *Affaiblissement du lien social, enfermement dans les particularismes...*, p. 64.

123. Pierre-André Taguieff, *La République menacée*. Paris: Textuels, 1996.

124. Long Report, Vol. 2, p. 90.

125. But see Schnapper, *La France de l'Intégration*, p. 238, *passim*, for the suggestion, that the difficulties with integration must be addressed not through a culpabilization of immigrants, but through a reassessment of the decline of the integrative functions of national institutions.

126. Farhad Khosrokhavar, *L'islam des jeunes*. Paris: Flammarion, 1997, p. 39.

127. This is the definition Schnapper gives of 'integration' in *France de l'Intégration*, p. 95. Yet she puts the burden on institutions to foster such attitudes over time, and does not present them as virtues that can be directly expected of citizens.

128. Julia Kristeva, *Nations without Nationalism*. New York: Columbia University Press, 1993, p. 60.

129. Kaltenbach, Tribalat, *La République et l'Islam*, p. 47.

130. Horowitz, 'Immigration and Goup Relations in France and America', p. 28. See, for republican assimilationist arguments of this type, Jelen, *Les Casseurs de la République*; Todd, *Le Destin des Immigrés*, Debray, 'Du rapport à l'autre', Régis Debray, *Contretemps. Eloge des idéaux perdus*. Paris: Gallimard, 1992; Régis Debray, *Le Code et le Glaive. Après l'Europe, la Nation*. Paris: Albin Michel, 2000.

131. Marcel Gauchet, *La religion dans la démocratie. Parcours de la laïcité*. Paris: Gallimard, 1998; *Le désenchantement du monde. Une histoire politique de la religion*. Paris: Gallimard, 1985.

132. On Muslim identity politics, see Feldblum, *Reconstructing Citizenship*, ch. 7; Catherine Wihtol de Wenden, *Les immigrés et la politique*. Paris: Presses de la FNSP, 1988; Riva Kastoryano: *Negotiating Identities: States and Immigrants in France and Germany*. Princeton: Princeton University Press, 2002; Nezar Al Sayyad and Manuel Castells (eds), *Muslim Europe or Euro-Islam: Politics, Culture and Citizenship in an Age of Globalisation*. London: Lexington Books, 2002; Jocelyne Cesari, *When Islam and Democracy Meet: Muslims in Europe and in the United States*. New York: Palgrave, 2004; Yvonne Yazbeck Haddad (ed.), *Muslims in the West. From Sojourners to Citizens*. Oxford: Oxford University Press, 2002; Gilles Kepel, *Allah in the West: Islamic movements in America and Europe*. Cambridge: Polity, 1997; Gilles Kepel, *The War for Muslim Minds: Islam and the West*. Cambridge, MA and London:

Belknap Press, 2004; Dale F. Eickelman and James Piscatori, *Muslim Politics*. Princeton, NJ: Princeton University Press, 2004; Jytte Klausen, *The Islamic Challenge. Politics and Religion in Western Europe*. Oxford: Oxford University Press, 2005.

133. Rémy Leveau, cited in Feldblum, *Reconstructing Citizenship*, p. 137.
134. Schnapper, *La France de l'Intégration*, p. 143.
135. Slang for *français*.
136. Haut Conseil à l'Intégration, *Affaiblissement du lien social, enfermement dans les particularismes*, p. 23.
137. Jean-Louis Debré, *La laïcité à l'école: un principe républican à réaffirmer. Rapport fait au nom de la mission d'information sur la question du port des signes religieux à l'école*. Paris: Assemblée Nationale, 2003, p. 73.
138. See, for example, Régis Debray, *Ce que nous voile le voile*. Paris: Folio, 2004, p. 17.
139. Note, however, the context of terrorist attacks in Algeria and Paris in 1994–5.
140. Bernard Stasi, *Laïcité et République. Rapport de la commission de réflexion sur l'application du principe de laïcité dans la République remis au Président de la République le 11 décembre 2003*. Paris: La Documentation Française, 2004, thereafter 'Stasi Report'. Available at <http://www.iesr.ephe.sorbonne.fr/docannexe/file/3112/rapport_laicite.Stasi.pdf> (last accessed 27 July 2007), pp. 7, 58.
141. Cited in Vincent Geisser, *La nouvelle Islamophobie*. Paris: La Découverte, 2003, p. 18.
142. Emmanuel Brenner (ed.), *Les Territoires Perdus de la Republique: Milieu scolaire, antisémitisme, sexisme*. Paris: Mille et Une Nuits, 2002; Shmuel Trigano, *La démission de la République. Juifs et Musulmans en France*, Paris: Presses Universitaires de France, 2003.
143. This is a reference to Jean-Marie le Pen, the leader of the racist, rightist party *Front National*.
144. Taguieff, *La République menacée*, p. 30.
145. Debré, *La laïcité à l'école: un principe républican à réaffirmer*, p. 72.
146. Schnapper, *La France de l'Intégration*, p. 305, *La Relation à l'Autre*, p. 406.
147. Stasi Report, p. 44.

Notes to Chapter 9

1. Christine Delphy, 'Le foulard islamique: une affaire française', in Charlotte Nordmann (ed.), *Le foulard islamique en questions*. Paris: Editions Amsterdam, 2004, pp. 64–71.
2. As the journal of the *Hizb ut-tahrir* puts it. Cited in Olivier Roy, *L'Islam mondialisé*. Paris: Seuil, 2004, 1st edn 2002, p. 168.
3. Dominique Schnapper, *La Relation à l'Autre, Au cœur de la pensée sociologique*. Paris: Gallimard, 1998, p. 486.

4. Schnapper, *La Relation à l'Autre*, pp. 450, 454.

5. On the historical origins of this *citoyenneté capacitaire*, see Blandine Kriegel, *Philosophie de la République*. Paris: Plon, 1998, pp. 196–206.

6. Farhad Khosrokhavar, 'L'universel abstrait, le politique et la construction de l'islamisme comme une forme d'altérité', in Michel Wieviorka (ed.), *Une société fragmentée. Le multiculturalisme en débat*. Paris: La Découverte, 1996, pp. 113–51, p. 148, Adrian Favell, *Philosophies of Integration. Immigration and the Idea of Citizenship in France and Britain*. Basingstoke: Macmillan, 1998, pp. 183–90.

7. Schnapper, *La Relation à l'Autre*, p. 450.

8. Susanne Citron, *Le Mythe national: l'histoire de France en question*. Paris: Éditions Ouvrières/Études et Documentation Internationales, 1987.

9. As recommended by Renan. Ernest Renan, 'Qu'est ce qu'une nation?' (extracts in English), in John Hutchinson and Anthony Smith (eds), *Nationalism*. Oxford: Oxford University Press, 1994, pp. 17–18.

10. Saïd Bouamama, 'Derrière le "beur", l'indigène colonial', *Les Cahiers de l'Orient*, Vol. 71, 2003, pp. 15–22, at p. 19.

11. Symptomatically, some demands of naturalization have been rejected on the grounds that the applicant wore signs of Muslim allegiance, and therefore was deemed to display 'insufficient assimilation' to French culture. Haut Conseil à l'Intégration, *Lutte contre les discriminations: faire respecter le principe d'égalité*. Paris: La Documentation Française, 1998, p. 66.

12. As Stéphane Beaud and Gérard Noiriel point out, the Durkheimian tradition has traditionally underplayed the importance of the family as a prime locus of socialization for children in general, and for children of immigrants in particular. Stéphane Beaud and Gérard Noiriel, 'L' "assimilation", un concept en panne', *International Review of Community Development*, Vol. 61–2, Sept. 1989, pp. 63–76, at p. 72.

13. Charles Taylor, 'Multiculturalism and the "Politics of Recognition"', in Amy Gutmann (ed.), *Multiculturalism and the Politics of Recognition*. Princeton, NJ: Princeton University Press, 1994, 25–36.

14. Françoise Lorcerie, 'Les habits neufs de l'assimilation en France', in Ida Simon-Barouch and Véronique de Rudder (eds), *Migrations Internationales et Relations Interethniques*. Paris: Harmattan, 1997, pp. 297–344, at p. 304.

15. Haut Conseil à l'Intégration, *Affaiblissement du lien social, enfermement dans les particularismes et intégration dans la cité*. Paris: La Documentation Française, 1997, p. 66.

16. Joël Roman, 'Un multiculturalisme à la française?', *Esprit*, Vol. 6, June 1995, pp. 145–60, at pp. 153; Hughes Jallon and Pierre Mounier, *Les enragés de la République*. Paris: La Découverte, 1999, p. 76, *passim*.

17. Patrick Simon, 'L'arbre du racisme et la forêt des discriminations', in Nacira Guénif-Souilamas (ed.), *La république mise à nu par son immigration*. Paris: La Fabrique Édition, 2006, pp. 160–77, at p. 166.

18. René Gallissot, 'Épouvantail ethnique et méli-mélo culturel', in Simon-Barouch, de Rudder, *Migrations Internationales et Relations Interethniques*, pp. 267–95, at pp. 292–3.

19. On the difficult integration of Italians, see, for example, Marie-Claude Blanc-Chaléard, 'L'intégration des Italiens hier: quels enseignements pour aujourd'hui?', in Philippe Dewitte (ed.), *Immigration et intégration. L'état des savoirs*. Paris: La Découverte, 1999, pp. 165–72.

20. Abdelmalek Sayad, 'Qu'est ce que l'intégration?', *Hommes et Migrations*, Vol. 1182, Dec. 1994, pp. 8–14.

21. Patrick Ireland, *The Policy Challenge of Ethnic Diversity. Immigrant Politics in France and Switzerland*. Cambridge, MA: Harvard University Press, 1994, pp. 76, 92–3; Laurent Mucchielli and Véronique Le Goaziou (eds), *Quand les banlieues brûlent... Retour sur les émeutes de novembre 2005*. Paris: La Découverte, 2006.

22. Philippe Genestier, 'Pour une intégration communautaire', *Esprit*, Feb. 1991, pp. 48–59, at p. 58.

23. Bernard Stasi, *Laïcité et République. Rapport de la commission de réflexion sur l'application du principe de laïcité dans la République remis au Président de la République le 11 décembre 2003*. Paris: La Documentation Française, 2004, thereafter 'Stasi Report'. Available at <http://www.iesr.ephe.sorbonne. fr/docannexe/file/3112/rapport_laicite.Stasi.pdf> (last accessed 27 July 2007), p. 49.

24. On the ambiguous relationship between 'socio-economic' and 'ethnicist' explanations for immigrants' problems, see Vincent Geisser, 'L'émotion comme "norme" d'une nouvelle politique laïque', Quand Huntington s'invite chez les "Sages"', *Migrations Société*, Vol. 16, No. 96, Nov.–Dec. 2004, pp. 131–56, p. 154.

25. See Emmanuel Terray, 'La question du voile: une hystérie politique', *Mouvements*, Vol. 32, 2004/2, pp. 96–104.

26. Khosrokhavar, 'L'universel abstrait, le politique et la construction de l'islamisme comme forme d'altérité', p. 115.

27. Sayad, 'Qu'est ce que l'intégration?

28. On the 'tournant sécuritaire' of national republicans, see, notably, Pierre Tevanian, *Le Racisme républicain*, ch. 3; Jallon, Mounier, *Les enragés de la République*; Françoise Lorcerie, 'Les sciences sociales au service de l'identité nationale', in Denis C. Martin (ed.), *Cartes d'identité. Comment dit-on "nous" en politique?* Paris: Presses de la Fondation Nationale des Sciences Politiques, 1994, pp. 245–81; Michael F. Leruth, 'The Neo-Republican Discourse on French National Identity', *French Politics and Society*, Vol. 16, No. 4, 1998, pp. 46–61; Daniel Lindenberg, *Le rappel à l'ordre. Enquête sur les nouveaux réactionnaires*. Paris: Seuil, 2002; Jane Freedman, *Immigration and Insecurity in France*. Aldershot: Ashgate, 2004; Mustafa Dikeç, 'Two Decades of French Urban Policy: From Social Development of Neighbourhoods to the Republican Penal State', *Antipode*, Vol. 38, No. 1, 2006, pp. 59–81.

29. Joël Roman, 'Pourquoi la laïcité?', in Nacira Guénif-Souilamas (ed.), *La république mise à nu par son immigration*. Paris: La Fabrique Édition, 2006, pp. 62–80, at p. 78.

30. Collectif, 'Oui à la laïcité, non aux lois d'exception', *Pro-Choix*, Vol. 25, Eté 2003, pp. 14–17. On this theme, see Jane Freedman, 'Secularism as a Barrier to Integration? The French Dilemma', *International Migration*, Vol. 42, No. 3, 2004, pp. 5–27.

31. See, for example, Schnapper, *La Relation à l'Autre*, p. 444.

32. Véronique De Rudder, Christian Poiret, and François Vourc'h, *L'Inégalité Raciste. L'universalité républicaine è l'épreuve*. Paris: Presses Universitaires de France, 2000, p. 194.

33. See, notably, Pierre-André Taguieff, *Les fins de l'antiracisme*. For a good analysis of French anti-racist legislation, see Erik Bleich, *Race Politics in Britain and France. Ideas and Policy-Making since the 1960s*. Cambridge: Cambridge University Press, 2003.

34. Didier Fassin, 'L'invention française de la discrimination', *Revue Française de Science Politique*, Vol. 52, No. 4, Aug. 2002, pp. 403–23, at p. 411. See also Philippe Bataille, *Le racisme au travail*. Paris: La Découverte, 1997.

35. Michèle Tribalat, *De l'immigration à l'assimilation. Enquête sur les populations d'origine étrangère en France*. Paris: La Découverte, 1996, pp. 254–67.

36. Claude-Valentin Marie, 'Enjeux actuels de la lutte contre les discriminations en France', in Daniel Borrillo (ed.), *Lutter contre les discriminations*. Paris: La Découverte, 2003, pp. 125–38, at p. 126.

37. Françoise Lorcerie (ed.), *L'école et le défi ethnique. Éducation et intégration*. Institut de la Recherche Pédagogique/ESF: Paris, 2003, p. 9.

38. Alec G. Hargreaves, *Immigration, 'Race' and Ethnicity in Contemporary France*. London: Routledge, 1995, p. xvi.

39. On the denial, and denegation, of the importance of discriminations in France, see Didier Fassin, 'Du déni à la dénégation. Psychologie politique de la représentation des discriminations', in Didier Fassin, Éric Fassin (eds), *De la question sociale à la question raciale. Représenter la société française*. Paris: La Découverte, 2006, pp. 133–57.

40. See Gwénaële Calvès, 'Pour une analyse (vraiment) critique de la discrimination positive', *Le Débat*, Vol. 117, Nov.–Dec. 2001, pp. 164–74, at p. 165; De Rudder, Poiret, and Vourc'h, *L'inégalité raciste*, p. 13, *passim*.

41. Véronique De Rudder and Christian Poiret, '*Affirmative Action* et "discrimination justifiée": vers un universalisme en acte', in Dewitte, *Immigration et Intégration*, pp. 397–406; Schnapper, *Relation à l'Autre*, pp. 200–9.

42. See Damian Moore, *Ethnicité et politique de la ville en France et GB*. Paris: Harmattan, 2001; Elise Palomares, 'L'ethnicisation des politiques locales et sociales', *Contretemps*, Vol. 13, 2005, pp. 92–102; Vincent Geisser, 'Ethnicité républicaine versus République ethnique?', *Mouvements*, Vol. 38, Mar.–Apr. 2005, pp. 19–25, 22.

43. See the criticisms of De Rudder, Poiret, amd Vourc'h *L'inégalité raciste*, pp. 21, 139.

44. This is recognized by Dominique Schnapper, *La Communauté des Citoyens*. Paris: Gallimard, 1994, pp. 80–2, *passim*, as well as by other defenders of the republican ideal of nationality such as David Miller, *On Nationality*. Oxford: Oxford University Press, p. 123, *passim*, and Maurizio Viroli, *For Love of Country. An Essay on Patriotism and Nationalism*. Oxford: Oxford University Press, 1995, *passim*.

45. Sophie Wahnich, *L'Impossible Citoyen: l'étranger. dans le discours de la Révolution française*. Paris: Albin Michel, 1997.

46. Gérard Noiriel, *La Tyrannie du national. Le droit d'asile en Europe (1793–1993)*. Paris: Calmann-Lévy, 1991.

47. Marxist critiques point out racism and xenophobia were instrumental to the inter-classist ideology of national solidarity. See Etienne Balibar, 'Racisme et nationalisme', in Etienne Balibar and Immanuel Wallerstein (eds), *Race, Nation, Classe. Les Identités Ambiguës*. Paris: La Découverte, 1988, pp. 54–92. For a recent reformulation, see Patrick Simon, 'Les apories de l'universalisme à la française', *Contretemps*, Vol. 12, Feb. 2005, pp. 31–40, and for a Marxist-influenced interpretation of the hijab controversy, Saïd Bouamama, *L'affaire du foulard islamique. La production d'un racisme respectable*. Paris: Le Geai Bleu, 2004.

48. Maxim Silverman, *Deconstructing the Nation. Immigration, Racism and Citizenship in Modern France*. London and New York: Routledge, 1992, pp. 20–2.

49. Stasi Report, p. 6.

50. Balibar and Wallerstein, *Race, nation, classe*, p. 127.

51. De Rudder, Poiret, and Vourc'h, *L'inégalité raciste*, pp. 9–10.

52. Simone Bonnafous, 'Mots et paroles de l'immigration', *Revue Française des Affaires Sociales*, Vol. 39, 1992, No. 3, pp. 5–15, at p. 12.

53. Françoise Lorcerie, 'Penser l'intégration nationale après l'État-nation', *Migrations Société*, Vol. 15, No. 86, Mar.–Apr. 2003, pp. 43–52, at p. 48.

54. Abdelmalek Sayad, *La double absence. Des illusions de l'émigré aux souffrances de l'immigré*. Paris: Seuil, 1999, p. 359.

55. See, for example, the report of the Haut Conseil à l'Intégration, *L'intégration à la française*. Paris: Union Générale d'Éditions, 1993 which, after drawing distinctions between 'foreigner' and '*immigré*', quickly reverts to common terminology, setting 'French society' in contrast to '*immigrés*'.

56. Gérard Noiriel, 'Les jeunes "d'origine immigrée" n'existent pas', *État, Nation et immigration, vers une histoire du pouvoir*. Paris: Belin, 2001, pp. 221–9.

57. Favell, *Philosophies of Integration,* p. 73.

58. Michel Giraud, 'Portrait de l'intégration en Arlesienne', *Recherche Socialiste*, No. 23, June 2003, pp. 17–26 at p. 19, Silverman, *Deconstructing the Nation*, p. 145.

59. Yazid Sabeg, Yacine Sabeg, *Discrimination positive. Pourquoi la France ne peut y échapper*. Paris: Calmann-Lévy, 2004, p. 73.

60. Sayad, *La double absence*; Didier Lapeyronnie, 'De l'altérité a la différence. L'identité, facteur d'intégration ou de repli ?', in Dewitte, *Immigration et Intégration*, pp. 252–9.

61. Adbelmalek Sayad, cited in Lorcerie, *L'école et le défi ethnique*, 2003, p. 8.
62. Benjamin Stora, *Le transfert d'une mémoire. De l' "Algérie française" au racisme anti-arabe*. Paris: La Découverte, 1999; Sami Naïr, *Le regard des vainqueurs: les enjeux français de l'immigration*. Paris: Grasset, 1992; Giraud, 'Portrait de l'intégration en Arlesienne'.
63. Nicolas Bancel, Pascal Blanchard, and Françoise Vergès, *La République Coloniale. Essai sur une utopie*. Paris: Albin Michel, 2003, p. 36.
64. This, notoriously, listed special crimes of which only natives could be accused, and was in force between 1881 and 1945. See Emmanuelle Saada, 'La République des Indigènes', in Vincent Duclert and, Christophe Prochasson (eds), *Dictionnaire Critique de la République*. Paris: Flammarion, 2002, pp. 364–70.
65. Bancel, Blanchard, and Vergès, *La République Coloniale*, p. 110.
66. Ahmed Boubeker, *Les mondes de l'ethnicité. La communauté d'expérience des héritiers de l'immigration maghrébine*. Paris: Balland, 2003, p. 55.
67. Bancel, Blanchard, and Vergès, *La République Coloniale,* p. 110, *passim*. For a similar analysis concerning women and citizenship, entitled 'only paradoxes to offer', see Joan Scott, *La Citoyenne paradoxale. Les féministes et les droits de l'homme*. Paris: Albin Michel, 1998. American edition: *Only Paradoxes to Offer.* (Cambridge, MA: Harvard University Press, 1996).
68. Silverman, *Deconstructing the Nation*; René Gallissot 'Nationalisme et racisme', in Martine Fourier and Geneviève Vermes (eds), *Ethnicisation des rapports sociaux. Racismes, nationalismes, ethnicismes et culturalismes*. Paris: Harmattan, 1994, pp. 7–29; Catherine Lloyd, *Discourses of Antiracism in France*. Aldershot: Ashgate, 1998, p. 134, Ch. 5.
69. Bonnafous, *L'immigration prise aux mots*; Silverman, *Deconstructing the Nation*, Ch. 3, 'The problem of immigration'; Daniele Lochak, 'Usages et mésusages d'une notion polémique. La référence à l'identité nationale dans le débat sur la réforme du Code de la Nationalité, 1985–1993', in Jacques Chevalier (ed.), *L'identité politique*. In *Sciences Humaines*, No. 15, Special Issue, Dec. 1996–Jan. 1997, pp. 306–23; Lorcerie, 'Les sciences sociales au service de l'identité nationale'; Pierre Tevanian, *Le Racisme Républicain. Réflexions sur le modèle français de discrimination*. Paris: L'Esprit Frappeur, 2002.
70. For criticisms of 'law-and-order republicanism', see bibliography in footnote 28 above.
71. Francois Burgat, 'Veils and Obscuring Lenses', in John L. Esposito and François Burgat (eds), *Modernizing Islam. Religion in the Public Sphere*. London: Hurst & Co, 2003, pp. 17–41, at p. 21.
72. Sabeg and Sabeg, *Discrimination Positive*, p. 194.
73. Bouamama, 'L'affaire du foulard islamique', pp. 20–6; Alain Gresh, *L'Islam, la République et le monde*. Paris: Fayard, 2004.
74. Geisser, 'L'émotion comme "norme" d'une nouvelle politique laïque'; Françoise Lorcerie, *La politisation du voile en France, en Europe et dans le monde arabe*. Paris: Harmattan, 2005.
75. Vincent Geisser, *La nouvelle islamophobie*. Paris: La Découverte, 2003.

76. EUMC (European Monitoring Centre on Racism and Xenophobia) Newsletter, June 2002, 13, p. 1, cited in Valérie Amiraux, 'Existe-t-il une discrimination religieuse des Musulmans en France?', *Maghreb-Machrek*, Vol. 183, Spring 2005, pp. 67–82, at p. 73n26.

77. Tevanian, *Le racisme républicain*; Bouamama, *L'affaire du foulard islamique*.

78. Françoise Lorcerie, 'L'école au prisme du paradigme de l'ethnicité. Etat des travaux', in Lorcerie (ed.), *L'école et le défi ethnique*, pp. 163–85, at p. 167; Geisser, 'Ethnicité républicaine versus République ethnique?'.

79. Erving Goffman, *Stigmate. Les usages sociaux des handicaps*. Paris: Minuit, 1975; Nilüfer Göle, 'The Voluntary Adoption of Islamic Stigma Symbols', *Social Research*, Vol. 70, No. 3, Fall 2003, pp. 809–28.

80. Slang for 'français'.

81. For an analysis of the media reception of the manifesto, see Jade Lindgaard, 'L'appel des indigènes de la République: Contestation ou consécration du dogme républicain? Etude de cas', in Vincent Bourdeau and Roberto Merril (eds), *La république et ses démons. Essais de républicanisme appliqué*. Paris: Éditions Eres, 2007, pp. 123–35.

82. Michel Wieviorka, 'Faut-il en finir avec la notion d'intégration?', *Les Cahiers de la Sécurité Intérieure*, Vol. 45, 3rd Trimester, 2001, pp. 9–20.

83. Philippe Poutignat and Jocelyne Streiff-Fenart, *Théories de l'ethnicité*. Paris: Presses Universitaires de France, 1995, p. 192.

84. See for example the seminal works of Fredrik Barth and Milton Gordon. For recent surveys in French, see Poutignat and Streiff-Fenart *Théories de l'ethnicité*. Schnapper, *La Relation à l'Autre*; Lorcerie, *L'école et le défi ethnique*, Part I; Eric Fassin, 'Penser la discrimination positive', in Daniel Borrillo (ed.), *Lutter contre les discriminations*. Paris: La Découverte, 2003, pp. 55–68; De Rudder, Poiret, and Vourc'h, *L'inégalité raciste*, pp. 31–3. An early, still influential account of the ways in which 'racism creates race' can be found in Colette Guillaumin, *L'idéologie raciste. Genèse et langage actuel*. Paris and La Haye: Mouton, 1972.

85. Dounia Bouzar, 'Islam et reconstruction identitaire des jeunes en difficulté', *Les Cahiers de la Sécurité Intérieure*, Vol. 45, 3rd Trimester, 2001a, pp. 21–44, at p. 36.

86. See notably Nathan Glazer and Daniel Patrick Moynihan, *Beyond the Melting Pot. The Negroes, Puerto Ricans, Jews, Italians and Irish of New York City*. Cambridge, MA: MIT Press and Harvard University Press, 1964; and Milton Myron Gordon, *Assimilation in American Life. The Role of Race, Religion and National Origins*. New York: Oxford University Press, 1964. For commentaries, see Poutignat and Streiff-Fenart, *Théories de l'ethnicité*, pp. 74–86, Schnapper, *Relation à l'Autre*, pp. 260–4.

87. Vincent Geisser, *Ethnicité républicaine*. Paris: Presses de Sciences Po, 1997; Ireland, *The Policy Challenge of Ethnic Diversity*.

88. De Rudder, Poiret, and Vourc'h, *L'Inégalité Raciste*; Lorcerie (ed.), *L'école et le défi ethnique*; Borrillo, *Lutter contre les discriminations*; Didier Fassin and

Éric Fassin (eds), *De la question sociale à la question raciale. Représenter la société française*. Paris: La Découverte, 2006.

89. See Dominique Schnapper, *La Relation à l'Autre*; Dominique Schnapper, 'Lutte contre les discriminations et lien social', in Serge Paugam (ed.), *Repenser la solidarité. L'apport des sciences sociales*. Paris: Presses Universitaires de France, 2007, pp. 515–30.

90. See Haut Conseil à l'Intégration, *Lutte contre les discriminations: faire respecter le principe d'égalité*. Paris: La Documentation Française, 1998; Jean-Michel Belorgey, *Lutter contre les discriminations. Stratégies institutionnelles et normatives*. Paris: Éditions de la Maison des Sciences de l'Homme, 2001.

91. Notably Employment Minister Martine Aubry from 1998 and Interior Ministers Jean-Pierre-Chevènement from 1999 and Nicolas Sarkozy from 2002–2004 and 2005–2007.

92. Gwénaële Calvès, *La discrimination positive*. Paris: Presses Universitairese de France, 2004, p. 117.

93. Jim Cohen, 'Les "modèles d'intégration" face aux particularismes: malentendus et dialogues France/Etat Unis', *Mouvements*, Vol. 38, Mar.–Apr. 2005, pp. 41–9, at p. 43.

94. Fassin, 'L'invention française de la discrimination', p. 410.

95. Belorgey, *Lutter contre les discriminations*, p. 14.

96. Gwénaële Calvès, ' "Il n'y as pas de race ici". Le modèle français à l'épreuve de l'intégration européenne', *Critique Internationale*, Vol. 17, Oct. 2002, pp. 173–85; Fassin, 'L'invention française de la discrimination'.

97. Fassin, 'L'invention française de la discrimination', pp. 408–9.

98. Costa-Lascoux is one rare author to place anti-discrimination at the heart of her account of traditional republican principles of integration. See Jacqueline Costa-Lascoux, 'L'intégration à la française: une philosophie, des lois', in Dewitte (ed.), *Immigration et intégration*, pp. 328–40, at p. 333.

99. For a recent survey, see the special issue of *Pouvoirs* 111 (2004) and Luc Ferry (ed.), *Pour une société de la nouvelle chance. Une approche républicaine de la discrimination positive*. Paris: Documentation française, 2005.

100. See the ground-breaking report of the Conseil d'État, *Sur le principe d'égalité. Extrait du rapport public 1996*. Paris: Documentation Française, 1998, 87, *passim*. See also Thierry Lambert *et al.* (eds), *Egalité ou Equité. Antagonisme ou complémentarité? Actes du colloque CERAP Paris 13*. Paris: Economica, 1999; Joëlle Affichard and Jean-Baptiste de Foucault (eds), *Justice sociale et inegalités*. Paris: Esprit, 1993.

101. This was seen as a common interpretation of the controversial Minc Report on the subject. Alain Minc (ed.), *La France de l'an 2000*. Paris: Odile Jacob/La Documentation Française, 1994. For a republican critique of *équité*, see Michel Borgetto, 'La réforme de la Sécurité Sociale: continuité ou déclin du modèle républicain', *Droit Social*, 1997, pp. 877–84, p. 881.

102. Gwénaële Calvès, 'Les politiques françaises de discrimination positive: trois spécificités', *Pouvoirs*, Vol. 111, 2004, pp. 29–40.

103. See the excellent analysis of Éric Deschavanne, 'La discrimination positive face à l'idéal républicain: définition, typologie, historique, arguments', in Luc Ferry (ed.), *Pour une société de la nouvelle chance. Une approche républicaine de la discrimination positive*. Paris: Documentation française, 2005, pp. 63–192; and Fassin, 'Penser la discrimination positive'.

104. Thomas Kirszbaum, 'La discrimination positive territoriale: de l'égalité des chances à la mixité urbaine', *Pouvoirs*, Vol. 111, 2004, pp. 101–18; Jacques Donzelot (with Catherine Mevel and Anne Wyvekens) *Faire société. La politique de la ville aux Etats-Unis et en France*. Paris: Seuil, 2003.

105. Sabeg and Sabeg, *Discrimination positive*, pp. 118–33.

106. Claude Bébéar, *Des entreprises aux couleurs de la France. Minorités visibles: relever le défi de l'accès à l'emploi*. Paris: Institut Montaigne, 2004. See Éric Keslassy, *De la discrimination positive*. Rosny-sous-bois: Bréal, 2004, p. 20n.

107. Marie-Claire Laval-Reviglio, 'Égalité et éducation: les discriminations justifiées, l'exemple de Sciences-Po', in Claude Courvoisier and Patrick Charlot (eds), *Actualité Politique et Juridique de l'Égalité*. Dijon: Éditions Universitaires de Dijon, 2003, pp. 115–31.

108. Prefects are high civil servants representing the state in each of France's regions.

109. For a review, see Calvès, *La discrimination positive*, pp. 115–17.

110. For the argument that multiculturalist themes emerged as a corrective for some of the ambiguities of egalitarian affirmation action policies in the USA, see Daniel Sabbagh, *L'égalité par le droit. Les paradoxes de la discrimination positive aux Etats-Unis*. Paris: Economica, 2003. A powerful critique of the substitution of 'cultural' for racial difference as the basis for positive action programmes is Richard Ford, *Racial Culture: A Critique*. Princeton: Princeton University Press, 2005.

111. Alain Touraine, *Pourrons-nous vivre ensemble? Égaux et différents*. Paris: Fayard, 1997, 240, *passim*.

112. François Dubet and Danilo Martucelli, *Dans quelle société vivons-nous?* Paris: Seuil, 1998, p. 202.

113. Slang for Arab.

114. See Saïd Bouamama, *Dix ans de marche des Beurs*. Paris: Desclée de Brouwer, 1991.

115. Bouzar, 'Islam et reconstruction identitaire des jeunes en difficulté'.

116. Delphy, 'Une affaire française', 66.

117. As the journal of the *Hizb ut-tahrir* puts it, 'our fraternity is real and their citizenship is fake.' Cited in Roy, *L'Islam mondialisé*, p. 168.

118. Khosrokhavar, *Islam des jeunes*, *passim*.

119. Nancy Venel, *Musulmans et citoyens*. Paris: Presses Universitaires de France, 2004, ch. 4. Venel's work is based on in-depth interviews with young people of immigrant origin. Venel identifies four ways of being 'Muslim and citizen': '*Français pratiquants*' (who broadly fit the national republican ideal of assimilation described in the previous chapter), '*contractants*' (who shun all identification with a larger community, be it French or Muslim

in the name of critical individualist citizenship), *néo-communautaires* (who prioritize their Muslim identity over their nationality) and *accommodateurs* (who seek to reconcile the two). This section and the next roughly correspond to Venel's last two groups—that is, those who advocate and practise forms of Muslim identity politics.

120. Khosrokhavar, 'L'universel abstrait, le politique et la construction de l'islamisme comme forme d'altérité', p. 136; Olivier Roy, 'Ethnicité, bandes et communautarisme', *Esprit*, Feb. 1991, pp. 37–47, at p. 42.

121. Olivier Roy, *La laïcité face à l'Islam*. Paris: Stock, 2005, pp. 138–40.

122. Venel, *Musulmans et citoyens*, Vol. 186, pp. 190–201.

123. 'Haroun', interviewed by Venel, *Musulmans et citoyens*, p. 165.

124. Venel, *Musulmans et citoyens*, pp. 170–4.

125. On Salafism or de-deterritorialized 'neo-fondamentalism', see Roy, *Islam mondialisé*, ch. 6.

126. The 1991 Iraq War, the Algerian troubles and wave of terrorist attacks in France in 1995, the 2001 World Trade Centre attacks, the 2004 Iraq hostage crisis.

127. Abderrahim Lamchichi, 'Les musulmans de France à l'épreuve de la laïcité', *Cahiers de l'Orient*, Vol. 71, 2003, pp. 35–53, at p. 45.

128. In the autumn of 1995 French police killed Khaled Kelkal, the chief suspect in a traumatic terrorist bombing campaign. The incident sparked public debate about the phenomenon of alienated young French Muslims joining violent Islamist groups—a debate which was echoed ten years later in the UK, in the aftermath of the London bombings of July 2005. See Tahir Abbas (ed.), *Islamic Political Radicalism. A European Perspective*. Edinburgh: Edinburgh University Press, 2007.

129. Xavier Ternisien, *La France des mosquées*. Paris: Albin Michel, 2002.

130. On the Islam of the excluded, see Khosrokhavar, *L'islam des jeunes*.

131. Roy, 'Ethnicité, bandes et communautarisme'. On Jihadist radicalism generally, see ch. 8 of his *Islam mondialisé*.

132. De Rudder, Poiret, and Vourc'h, *L'inégalité raciste*, pp. 74–5.

133. Khosrokhavar, 'L'universel abstrait, le politique et la construction de l'islamisme comme une forme d'altérité', p. 139.

134. Jocelyne Cesari, 'De l'islam en France à l'islam de France', in Dewitte, *Immigration et intégration. L'état des savoirs*, pp. 222–31.

135. Jerome Vidal, 'La République à l'épreuve des discriminations', in Nordmann (ed.), *Le foulard islamique en questions*, pp. 5–14, at p. 11.

136. Cited in Bouzar, 'Islam et reconstruction identitaire des jeunes en difficulté', pp. 32–3.

137. Nancy Venel, *Musulmanes françaises. Des pratiquantes voilées à l'université*. Paris: Harmattan, 1999, p. 106, *passim*.

138. Venel, *Musulmans et Citoyens*, ch. 2.

139. Dounia Bouzar, '"*Monsieur Islam*" n'existe pas. Pour une dé-islamisation des débats'. Paris: Hachette, 2004, pp. 50n, 81.

140. Cesari Jocelyne, *Etre musulman en France aujourd'hui.* Paris: Hachette Littératures, 1997, pp. 123–4; Venel, *Musulmans et citoyens*, p. 252.
141. Dounia Bouzar, *L'Islam des banlieues, les prédicateurs musulmans, nouveaux travailleurs sociaux.* Paris: Syros-La Découverte, 2001; Cesari, *Etre musulman en France aujourd'hui.*
142. Terray, 'La question du voile: une hystérie politique'.
143. Lorcerie, *L'école et le défi ethnique.* p. 73; Christophe Bertossi, *Les frontières de la citoyenneté en Europe. Nationalité, residence, appartenance.* Paris: Harmattan, 2001, p. 20.
144. Françoise Gaspard and Farhad Khoroskhavar, *Le Foulard et la République.* Paris: La Découverte, 1995; Venel, *Musulmanes françaises*; Venel, *Musulmans et citoyens*; Jocelyne Césari, *Musulmans et républicains: les jeunes, l'Islam et la France.* Paris: Complexe, 1998; Dounia Bouzar and Saida Kada, *L'une voilée, l'autre pas. Le témoignage de deux musulmanes françaises.* Paris: Albin Michel, 2003.

Notes to Chapter 10

1. See, for example, the otherwise exemplary Didier and Eric Fassin (eds), *De la question sociale à la question raciale. Représenter la société française.* Paris: La Découverte, 2006.
2. See, for example, Alec G. Hargreaves, *Immigration, 'Race' and Ethnicity in Contemporary France.* London: Routledge, 1995.
3. Iris Marion Young, *Justice and the Politics of Difference.* Princeton, NJ: Princeton University Press, 1990, p. 47.
4. David Miller, 'Multiculturalism and the Welfare State: Theoretical Reflections', in Keith Banting and Will Kymlicka (eds), *Recognition and Redistribution in Contemporary Democracies.* Oxford: Oxford University Press, 2006, pp. 323–38. Miller draws attention to the negative impact of multicultural *ideology* (the over-emphasis of cultural difference in public discourse) rather than of particular multicultural policies. For (admittedly inconclusive) empirical studies of the impact of multicultural policies on social solidarity, see the other contributions in Banting and Kymlicka's volume.
5. Christian Joppke, 'The Retreat of Multiculturalism in the Liberal State: Theory and Policy', *The British Journal of Sociology*, Vol. 55, No. 2, 2004, pp. 237–57.
6. Nancy Fraser, 'From Redistribution to Recognition? Dilemmas of Justice in a "Postsocialist" Age', *New Left Review*, Vol. 212, July/Aug. 1995, pp. 68–93.
7. Young, *Justice and the Politics of Difference*, p. 190.
8. Jeffrey C. Alexander, 'Theorizing the "Modes of Incorporation": Assimilation, Hyphenation and Multiculturalism as Varieties of Civil Participation', in Peter Kivisto (ed.), *Incorporating Diversity: Rethinking Assimilation in a Multicultural Age.* Boulder, CO: Paradigm Publisher, 2005, pp. 320–37;

Jeffrey C. Alexander, *The Civil Sphere*. Oxford: Oxford University Press, 2006, pp. 398–402. See also David Miller, 'Is Deliberative Democracy Unfair to Disadvantaged Minorities?', in David Miller (ed.), *Citizenship and National Identity*. Cambridge: Polity Press, 2000, pp. 142–60.

9. Alexander, *The Civil Sphere*. He defines the civil sphere as 'one whose members are symbolically represented as independent and self-motivating persons individually responsible for their actions, yet also as actors who feel themselves, at the same time, bound by collective obligations to all the other individuals who compose this sphere'.

10. The expression is from Will Kymlicka, *Multicultural Citizenship. A Liberal Theory of Minority Rights*. Oxford: Oxford University Press, 1995, p. 108.

11. See, notably, Jürgen Habermas, *The Theory of Communicative Action*. Boston: Beacon Press, 1987; Jürgen Habermas, *Droit et démocratie. Entre faits et normes*. Paris: Gallimard, 1997; Alex Honneth, *The Struggle for Recognition: The Grammar of Social Conflicts*. Cambridge: Polity, 1995; Ernesto Laclau, *La guerre des identités. Grammaire de l'émancipation*. Paris: La Découverte, 2000; Etienne Balibar, *Les frontières de la démocratie*. Paris: La Découverte, 1992; Etienne Balibar, *La crainte des masses. Politique et philosophie après Marx*. Paris: Galilée, 1997; Jacques Bidet, *Théorie de la modernité*. Paris: Presses Universitaires de France, 1990; Jacques Bidet, *John Rawls et la théorie de la justice*. Paris: Presses Universitaires de France, 1995; Jacques Rancière, *La Mésentente*. Paris: Galilée, 1995; Jacques Rancière, *Aux bords du politique*. Paris: La Fabrique Éditions, 1998; Emmanuel Renault, *Mépris social. Éthique et politique de la reconnaissance*. Bègles: Éditions du Passant, 2000.

12. Emmanuel Renault and Yves Sintomer (eds), *Où en est la théorie critique?* Paris: La Découverte, 2003, p. 25. The volume as a whole offers a useful survey of the contemporary agenda of critical theory. For a critical sociology of the experience of injustice, see Laurent Bolstanski and Luc Thévenot, *De la justification. Les économies de la grandeur*. Paris: Gallimard, 1991; Luc Boltanski and Eve Chiapello, *Le nouvel esprit du capitalisme*. Paris: Gallimard, 1999. On the relationship between social critique and liberal egalitarianism, see Alex Callinicos, 'Egalitarisme et critique sociale', *Actual Marx*, Vol. 202, No. 31, pp. 147–58.

13. This insight is found in the writings of, notably, Machiavelli, Rousseau, Tocqueville, Durkheim, and Arendt. See also, more recently, Jean-Fabien Spitz, *La Liberté Politique*. Paris: Presses Universitaires de France, 1995; Jean-Fabien Spitz, *Le Moment Républicain en France*. Paris: Gallimard, 2005; Gérard Raulet, *Apologie de la Citoyenneté*. Paris: Cerf, 1999; Chantal Mouffe (ed.), *Dimensions of Radical Democracy*. London: Verso Press, 1992; Benjamin Barber, *Strong Democracy. Participatory Politics for a New Age*. Berkeley, CA: University of California Press, 1984; David Miller, 'Citizenship and Pluralism', *Political Studies*, Vol. 43, 1995, pp. 432–50; David Miller, 'Republican Citizenship, Nationality and Europe', in Cécile Laborde and John Maynor (eds), *Republicanism and Political Theory*, pp. 133–58. Oxford: Blackwell, 2007;

Richard Bellamy, *Liberalism and Pluralism: Towards a Politics of Compromise.* London: Routledge, 1999; Richard Bellamy, *Political Constitutionalism.* Cambridge: Cambridge University Press, 2007.

14. See, notably, Jürgen Habermas, 'Reconciliation through the Public Use of Reason: Remarks on John Rawls's Political Liberalism', *Journal of Philosophy*, Vol. 92, 1995, pp. 109–31; *Entre faits et normes*, p. 73; Will Kymlicka, 'The New Debate Over Minority Rights', in his *Politics in the Vernacular. Nationalism, Multiculturalism, and Citizenship.* Oxford: Oxford University Press, 2001, pp. 17–38.

15. Ronald Dworkin, 'Bakke's Case: Are Quotas Really Unfair?' and 'What Did *Bakke* Really Decide?', in Ronald Dworkin (ed.), *A Matter of Principle.* Cambridge, MA: Harvard University Press, 1985; 'Affirming Affirmative Action', *New York Review of Books*, Oct. 22, 1998.

16. Brian Barry, *Political Argument.* London: Routledge, 1965, p. 66.

17. On social equality, see David Miller, 'Complex Equality', in David Miller and Michael Walzer (eds), *Pluralism, Justice and Equality.* Oxford: Oxford University Press, 1995, pp. 197–225; David Miller, *Principles of Social Justice*, pp. 15–16, 240–41.

18. On the importance of good-quality city life to republican citizenship, see Richard Dagger, *Civic Virtues: Rights, Citizenship and Republican Liberalism.* Oxford: Oxford University Press, 1997, pp. 154–72.

19. Renault, *Mépris social.*

20. This 'Rawlsian', social democratic interpretation of the republicanism of Durkheim and the *solidaristes*, which contrasts with the more communitarian reading propounded by official republicans, is convincingly defended by Jean-Fabien Spitz, *Le Moment Républicain en France.* Paris: Gallimard, 2005, notably at pp. 294–5.

21. For a survey of this theme in contemporary political philosophy, see Anne Phillips, ' "Really" Equal: Opportunities and Autonomy', *Journal of Political Philosophy*, Vol. 14, No. 1, 2006, pp. 18–32.

22. Rancière, *La Mésentente.*

23. For an analysis of how trans-ethnic solidarity emerges from the possibility to 'resist ethnic identification', see Rachel A. D. Bloul, 'Beyond Ethnic Identities: Resisting Exclusionary Identification', *Social Identities*, Vol. 5, No. 1, 1999, pp. 7–30. For a comparison of Rancière's radical universalist theory of democracy and Axel Honneth's theory of recognition along these lines, see Jean-Phillipe Deranty, 'Jacques Rancière's Contribution to the Ethics of Recognition', *Political Theory*, Vol. 31, No. 1, Feb. 2003, pp. 136–56.

24. Sylvain Brouard and Vincent Tiberj, *Français comme les autres? Enquête sur les citoyens d'origine maghrébine, africaine et turque.* Paris: Presses de Sciences Po, 2005; Jytte Klausen, *The Islamic Challenge. Politics and Religion in Western Europe.* Oxford: Oxford University Press, 2005.

25. Good analyses include Vincent Geisser, *La nouvelle Islamophobie.* Paris: La Découverte, 2003; Alain Gresh, *L'Islam, la République et le monde.* Paris,

Fayard, 2004; Aziz Al-Azmeh, *L'Obscurantisme postmoderne et la question musulmane*. Paris: Actes Sud, 2004; Alain Roussillon, 'Islam et mondialisation. État des lieux (provisoire) des débats suscités en France par les attentats du 11 septembre 2001', *Maghreb-Machrek*, Vol. 174, Oct. 2001, pp. 75–89; Jocelyne Cesari, 'Islam de l'extérieur, musulman de l'intérieur. Deux visions après le 11 septembre 2001', *Cultures & Conflits*, Vol. 44, 2001, pp. 97–115.

26. Nicolas Sarkozy, *La République, les religions, l'espérance*. Paris: Cerf, 2004, pp. 21–2, 104–7.

27. My account is heavily indebted to Daniel Sabbagh, 'Affirmative Action at Sciences Po', *French Politics, Culture and Society*, Vol. 20, No. 3, Fall 2002, pp. 52–64. See also Marie-Claire Laval-Reviglio, 'Égalité et éducation: les discriminations justifiées, l'exemple de Sciences-Po', in Claude Courvoisier and Patrick Charlot (eds), *Actualité Politique et Juridique de l'Égalité*. Dijon: Éditions Universitaires de Dijon, 2003, pp. 115–31.

28. Éric Keslassy, *De la discrimination positive*. Rosny-sous-bois: Bréal, 2004, p. 80.

29. *Ibid.*, p. 20; Gwénaële Calvès, 'Les politiques françaises de discrimination positive: trois spécificités', *Pouvoirs*, Vol. 111, 2004, pp. 29–40, p. 31.

30. On the labour market, see Roxane Silberman and Irène Fournier, 'Les enfants d'immigrés sur le marché du travail. Les mécanismes d'une discrimination sélective', *Formation Emploi*, Vol. 65, 1999, pp. 31–55; on schools, see Serge Boulot and Danièle Boyzon-Fradet, *Les Immigrés et l'Ecole, une course d'obstacles*. Paris: Harmattan, 1988; and L. P. Vallet and J. P Caille, 'Les élèves étrangers ou issus de l'immigration dans l'école et le collège français. Une étude d'ensemble', *Les Dossiers d'éducation et formations*, No. 67. Paris: Direction de l'évaluation et de la prospective, ministère de l'Éducation nationale, 1996; and on public services, see Gwénaële Calvès, *Renouvellement démographique de la fonction publique de l'État: vers une intégration prioritaire des Français issus de l'immigration?* Paris: La Documentation française, 2005.

31. See the full programme report at <http://www.sciences-po.fr/presse/zep/index.htm> (last accessed 31 July 2007).

32. Sabbagh, 'Affirmative Action at Sciences Po', p. 58.

33. On the unfairness of the *concours*, see the Sciences-Po-commissioned study: <http://www.sciences-po.fr/presse/zep/enquete.pdf>.

34. Pierre Bourdieu and Jean-Claude Passeron, *Reproduction in Education, Society and Culture*. London: Sage, 1990.

35. Boyzon-Fradet Boulot, *Les Immigrés et l'École*.

36. Patrick Weil, *La République et sa diversité. Immigration, Intégration, Discriminations*. Paris: Seuil, 2005, pp. 94–7.

37. Weil, *La République et sa diversité*, p. 97.

38. Eric Maurin, *Le ghetto français. Enquête sur le séparatisme social*. Paris: Seuil, 2004. See also Éric Maurin, 'La ségrégation urbaine, son intensité et ses

causes', in Serge Paugam (ed.), *Repenser la solidarité. L'apport des sciences sociales.* Paris: Presses Universitaires de France, 2007, pp. 621–34.

39. For the view that segregation undermines democracy as inclusion, see Iris Marion Young, 'Residential Segregation and Regional Democracy', in her *Inclusion and Democracy.* Oxford: Oxford University Press, 2000, pp. 154–95. Young, however, explicitly rejects the republican ideal of social and racial mixity in favour of a 'differentiated solidarity' compatible with the territorial clustering of racial, cultural, and religious groups.

40. See Jacques Donzelot (with Catherine Mevel and Anne Wyvekens), *Faire société. La politique de la ville aux États-Unis et en France.* Paris: Seuil, 2003. See also Jacques Donzelot, 'Un État qui rend capable', in Serge Paugam (ed.), *Repenser la solidarité. L'apport des sciences sociales.* Paris: Presses Universitaires de France, 2007, pp. 87–109.

41. Laurent Mucchielli and Véronique Le Goaziou (eds), *Quand les banlieues brûlent... Retour sur les émeutes de novembre 2005.* Paris: La Découverte, 2006. For a good synthesis of the press coverage of the riots, see Dominic McGoldrick, *Human Rights and Religion: the Islamic Headscarf Debate in Europe.* Oxford and Portland: Hart, 2006, pp. 56–60. An insightful article in English is Jason Burke 'France and the Muslim Myth', *The Observer*, 13 Nov. 2005.

42. Éric Deschavane offers a useful typology of egalitarian policies. He distinguishes between (i) fairness (*équité*) policies, which provide special help to disadvantaged groups, without however altering formal opportunity sets and competition rules; (ii) socio-economic positive discrimination, which provides preferential treatment in the form of guaranteed places to socially disadvantaged groups (examples are the Science-Po conventions); (iii) counter-discriminatory positive discrimination, which guarantees places to groups defined by otherwise illegitimate criteria such as race or gender; and (iv) active non-discrimination, which uses techniques such as testing and monitoring to identify groups that are potentially victim of structural discrimination, and encourage employers to change their recruitment practices. He implicitly suggests that only the third type is incompatible with republican principles. Éric Deschavanne, 'La discrimination positive face à l'idéal républicain: définition, typologie, historique, arguments', in Luc Ferry (dir.) *Pour une société de la nouvelle chance. Une approche républicaine de la discrimination positive.* Paris: Documentation Française, 2005, pp. 63–192, at p. 96.

43. Catherine Wihtol de Wenden, 'Les "jeunes issus de l'immigration", entre intégration culturelle et exclusion sociale', in Philippe Dewitte (ed.), *Immigration et intégration. L'état des savoirs*, Paris: La Découverte, 1999, pp. 232–37.

44. Joël Roman, 'Pourquoi la laïcité?', in Nacira Guénif-Souilamas (ed.), *La république mise à nu par son immigration.* Paris: La Fabrique Édition, 2006, pp. 62–80, at p. 74. See also Brouard and Tiberj, *Français comme les autres?*

45. See, for example, Elizabeth Meehan, *Citizenship and the European Community*. London: Sage, 1993; Justine Lacroix, *L'Europe en procès. Quel patriotisme au-delà des nationalismes?* Paris: Cerf, 2004.

46. Yasemin Nuhoğlu Soysal, *Limits of Citizenship: Migrants and Postnational Membership in Europe*. Chicago: Chicago University Press, 1994, p. 166.

47. Soysal, *Limits of Citizenship*, pp. 8, 140.

48. Jürgen Habermas, 'Citizenship and National Identity: Some Reflections on the Future of Europe', in Ronald Beiner (ed.), *Theorizing Citizenship*. New York: State University of New York Press, 1999, pp. 255–68, at p. 263.

49. Andrew Mason, 'Political Community, Liberal-Nationalism, and the Ethics of Assimilation', *Ethics*, Vol. 109, Jan. 1999, pp. 261–86.

50. Michael Walzer, *Spheres of Justice*. Oxford: Blackwell, 1985, pp. 52–61, David Miller, *On Nationality*. Oxford: Oxford University Press, 1995, p. 143. The question of whether the ideal of republican citizenship imposes limits on immigration is a distinct but connected one, which I shall not address here.

51. For an analysis of 'identity assignation' as a form of domination, see Guenif-Souilamas, *La république mise à nu par son immigration*.

52. See, for example, Attracta Ingram, 'Constitutional Patriotism', *Philosophy and Social Criticism*, Vol. 22, No. 6, 1996, pp. 1–18; Etienne Tassin, 'Identités Nationales et Citoyenneté Politique', *Esprit*, Vol. 198, 1994, pp. 97–111.

53. Jürgen Habermas, 'Un débat sur *Droit et Démocratie*', in Jürgen Habermas (ed.), *L'intégration républicaine. Essais de théorie politique*. Paris: Fayard, 1998, pp. 289–375, at p. 308.

54. Jürgen Habermas, *The New Conservatism. Cultural Criticism and the Historians' Debate*. Boston: MIT Press, 1989, p. 236.

55. See Cécile Laborde, 'From Constitutional to Civic Patriotism', *British Journal of Political Science*, Vol. 32, 2002, pp. 591–612.

56. Anthony Simon Laden, *Reasonably Radical: Deliberative Liberalism and the Politics of Identity*. Ithaca, NY: Cornell University Press, 2001, p. 136, *passim*.

57. Nancy Fraser, 'Social Justice in the Age of Identity Politics: Redistribution, Recognition and Participation', in Nancy Fraser and Axel Honneth (eds), *Redistribution or Recognition? A Political-Philosophical Exchange*. London: Verso, 2003, pp. 7–109, at pp. 29–30, *passim*. Note that, by targeting the dominating structure of institutional social arrangements, instead of diffuse discursive cultural representations, Fraser avoids the illiberal consequences associated with the 'thought police' of political correctness. *Ibid.*, p. 31.

58. Nancy Fraser, 'Social Justice in the Age of Identity Politics: Redistribution, Recognition and Participation', p. 36, *passim*.

59. Margalit, *The Decent Society*. Cambridge, MA: Harvard University Press, 1996, pp. 163, 169. Humiliation does not include just anything which happens to give offence, nor is it tied to the self-esteem of particular persons or groups. Margalit defines it as 'any sort of behaviour or conditions that constitutes a sound reason for a person to consider his or her self-respect injured' (p. 9) and intend the 'sound reason' clause to

imply that claims of humiliation are to be morally evaluated, not simply accepted.

60. As our analysis of the Debré and Stasi Reports have shown.
61. Habermas, *The New Conservatism*, p. 236.
62. Pierre Nora, *Les lieux de mémoire*, Vol. I: *La République*. Vol. II. *La Nation* (1986), Vol. III *Les France* (1992). Paris: Gallimard, 1984; Julian Jackson, 'Historians and the Nation in Contemporary France', in Stefan Berger, Mark Donovan, and Kevin Passmore (eds), *Writing National Histories. Western Europe since 1800*. London: Routledge, 1999, pp. 239–51; Susanne Citron, *Le Mythe national: l'histoire de France en question*. Paris: Éditions Ouvrières/Etudes et Documentation Internationales, 1987; Françoise Lorcerie, 'Penser l'intégration nationale après l'Etat-nation', *Migrations Société*, Vol. 15, No. 86, Mar.–Apr. 2003, pp. 43–52.
63. Dounia Bouzar and Saida Kada, *L'une voilée, l'autre pas. Le témoignage de deux musulmanes francaises*. Paris: Albin Michel, 2003, Françoise Gaspard and Farhad Khoroskhavar, *Le Foulard et la République*. Paris: La Découverte, 1995.
64. Benjamin Stora, *La Gangrène et l'Oubli, la mémoire de la guerre d'Algérie*. Paris: La Découverte, 1998; Dounia Bouzar, ' "*Monsieur Islam*" n'existe pas. Pour une dé-islamisation des débats'. Paris: Hachette, 2004, pp. 174–80; Yazid Sabeg and Yacine Sabeg, *Discrimination positive. Pourquoi la France ne peut y échapper*. Paris: Calmann-Lévy, 2004, pp. 219–28.
65. Ian MacMullen, *Faith in Schools? Autonomy, Citizenship, and Religious Education in the Liberal State*. Princeton: Princeton University Press, 2007. See the arguments in Chapter 4, pp. 92–3 Chapter 7, pp. 159–60
66. Eamonn Callan, *Creating Citizens. Political Education and Liberal Democracy*. Oxford, Oxford University Press, 1997, p. 177.
67. Meira Levinson, *The Demands of Liberal Education*. Oxford: Oxford University Press, 1999, p. 114.

BIBLIOGRAPHY

Abbas, Tahir, 'Recent Developments to British Multicultural Theory, Policy and Practice: The Case of British Muslims', *Citizenship Studies*, Vol. 9, No. 2, 2005, pp. 153–66.

—— (ed.), *Islamic Political Radicalism. A European Perspective*. Edinburgh: Edinburgh University Press, 2007.

Affichard, Joëlle, and de Foucault, Jean-Baptiste (eds), *Justice sociale et inegalités*. Paris: Esprit, 1993.

Ahdar, Rex, and Leigh, Lan, *Religious Freedom in the Liberal State*. Oxford: Oxford University Press, 2005.

Ahmed, Leïla, *Women and Gender in Islam. Historical Roots of a Modern Debate*. New Haven and London: Yale University Press, 1992.

Al-Azmeh, Aziz, *L'obscurantisme postmoderne et la question musulmane*. Paris: Actes Sud, 2004.

Alexander, Jeffrey C., 'Theorizing the "Modes of Incorporation": Assimilation, Hyphenation and Multiculturalism as Varieties of Civil Participation', in Peter Kivisto (ed.), *Incorporating Diversity: Rethinking Assimilation in a Multicultural Age*. Boulder: Paradigm Publisher, 2005, pp. 320–37.

—— *The Civil Sphere*. Oxford: Oxford University Press, 2006.

Allen, Danielle, 'Invisible Citizens: Political Exclusion and Domination in Arendt and Ellison', in Melissa S. Williams and Stephen Macedo (eds), *Political Exclusion and Domination. Nomos*, Vol. 46. New York: New York University Press, 2005, pp. 29–76.

Al Sayyad, Nezar, and Castells, Manuel (eds), *Muslim Europe or Euro-Islam: Politics, Culture and Citizenship in an Age of Globalisation*. London: Lexington Books, 2002.

Altschull, Elisabeth, *Le voile contre l'école*. Paris: Seuil, 1995.

Amera, Fadela, *Ni putes, ni soumises*. Paris: La Découverte, 2003.

Amiraux, Valérie, 'Les musulmans dans l'espace politique européen. La délicate expérience du pluralisme confessionnel', *Vingtième Siècle. Revue d'Histoire*, Vol. 82, April–June 2004, pp. 119–30.

—— 'Existe-t-il une discrimination religieuse des musulmans en France?', *Maghreb-Machrek*, No. 183, Spring 2005, pp. 67–82.

Amselle, Jean-Loup, *Vers un multiculturalisme français. L'empire de la coutume*. Paris: Aubier, 1996.

Anderson, Benedict, *Imagined Communities. Reflections on the Origins and Spread of Nationalism*. London: Verso, 1991.

Anderson, Elizabeth, 'What is the Point of Equality?', *Ethics*, Vol. 109, 1999, pp. 287–337.

Appiah, Anthony K., 'Multicultural Misunderstanding', *New York Review of Books*, Vol. 44, No. 15, 9 October 1997, pp. 30–6.

——and Gutmann, Amy, *The Political Morality of Race*. Princeton, NJ: Princeton University Press, 1996.

Arendt, Hannah, *On Revolution*. London: Faber, 1963.

Audard, Catherine 'Rawls in France', in Cécile Laborde (ed.), 'Rawls in Europe', *European Journal of Political Theory*, Vol. 1, No. 2, 2002, pp. 215–27.

Audi, Robert, 'The Separation of Church and State and the Obligations of Citizenship', *Philosophy and Public Affairs*, Vol. 18, No. 3, Summer 1989, pp. 259–96.

——'Religious Commitment and Secular Reason: A Reply to Professor Weithman', *Philosophy and Public Affairs*, Vol. 20, No. 1, Winter 1991, pp. 66–76.

——*Religious Commitment and Secular Reason*. Cambridge: Cambridge University Press, 2000.

Audidière, Sophie, 'L'école républicaine à l'épreuve d'une révision républicaine', in Vincent Bourdeau and Roberto Merril (eds), *La république et ses démons. Essais de républicanisme appliqué*. Paris: Éditions Eres, 2007, pp. 85–107.

Audier, Serge, *Les théories de la république*. Paris: La Découverte, 2004.

Babès, Leïla, *L'islam positif. La religion des jeunes musulmans en France*. Paris: Éditions de l'Atelier, 1997.

——*Le voile démystifié*. Paris: Bayard, 2004.

Bader, Veit, 'The Cultural Conditions of Transnational Citizenship. On the Interpenetration of Political and Ethnic Cultures', *Political Theory*, Vol. 25, No. 6, 1997, pp. 771–813.

——'Religious Pluralism: Secularism or Priority for Democracy?', *Political Theory*, Vol. 27, No. 5, October 1999, pp. 597–633.

——'Religious Diversity and Democratic Institutional Pluralism', *Political Theory*, Vol. 31, No. 2, April 2003, pp. 265–94.

Badinter, Elizabeth, Debray, Régis, Finkielkraut, Alain, de Fontenay, Elisabeth, and Kintzler, Catherine, 'Profs, ne capitulons pas', *Nouvel Observateur*, 2–8 November 1989. Reprinted in Kintzler, *La République en Questions*, 78–81.

Badiou, Alain, 'Derrière la loi foulardière, la peur', *Le Monde*, 21 February 2004.

Baker Keith, M. (ed.), *The French Revolution and the Creation of Modern Political Culture*. Oxford: Pergamon Press, 1987.

——*Inventing the French Revolution*. Cambridge: Cambridge University Press, 1990.

Balibar Etienne, 'Racisme et nationalisme', in Etienne Balibar and Immanuel Wallerstein (eds), *Race, nation, classe. Les identités ambiguës*. Paris: La Découverte, 1988, pp. 54–92.

——'Propositions sur la citoyenneté', in Catherine Wihtol de Wenden (ed.), *La citoyenneté et les changements de structures sociale et nationale de la population française*. Paris: Fondation Diderot, 1988, pp. 223–34.

——'Faut-il qu'une laïcité soit ouverte ou fermée?', *Mots*, Vol. 27, June 1991, pp. 73–9.

——*Les frontières de la démocratie*. Paris: La Découverte, 1992.

——*La crainte des masses. Politique et philosophie après Marx*. Paris: Galilée, 1997.

Balibar Etienne, 'Dissonances dans la laïcité', *Mouvements*, Vols. 33–4, May–August 2004, pp. 148–61.

——and Wallerstein, Immanuel, *Race, nation, classe. Les identités ambiguës*. Paris: La Découverte, 1988.

Bancel, Nicolas, Blanchard Pascal, and Vergès Françoise, *La République Coloniale. Essai sur une utopie*. Paris: Albin Michel, 2003.

Banting, Keith, and Kymlicka, Will (eds), *Recognition and Redistribution in Contemporary Democracies*. Oxford: Oxford University Press, 2006.

Barber, Benjamin, *Strong Democracy. Participatory Politics for a New Age*. Berkeley, CA: University of California Press, 1984.

Barbier Maurice, *La laïcité*. Paris: L'Harmattan, 1995.

——'Laïcité: questions à propos d'une loi centenaire', *Débat*, Vol. 127, Nov–Dec 2003, pp. 160–74.

Barret-Kriegel, Blandine, 'La formation de l'esprit laïque', in Hubert Bost (ed.), *Genèses et enjeux de la laïcité. Christiannismes et laïcité*. Paris: Labor et Fides, 1990, pp. 139–49.

Barry, Brian, *Political Argument*. London: Routledge and Kegan Paul, 1965.

——*Justice as impartiality*. Oxford: Clarendon Press, 1995.

——*Culture and Equality*. Cambridge: Polity, 2001.

Barthélémy, Jean, 'La liberté de religion et le service public', *Revue française de droit administratif*, Vol. 6 November–December 2003, pp. 1066–73.

Barthélémy, Martine, 'La logique d'ouverture de l'école publique: une fragilisation de la laïcité française', in Jean Baudouin and Philippe Portier (eds), *La laïcité, valeur d'aujourd'hui? Contestations et renégociations du modèle français*. Rennes: Presses Universitaires de Rennes, 2001, pp. 297–314.

Basdevant-Gaudemet, Brigitte, 'The Legal Status of Islam in France', in Silvio Ferrari and Anthony Bradney (eds), *Islam and European Legal Systems*. Aldershot: Ashgate, 2000, pp. 97–124.

Bataille, Philippe, *Le racisme au travail*. Paris: La Découverte, 1997.

——'Racisme institutionnel, racisme culturel et discriminations', in Philippe Dewitte (ed.), *Immigration et intégration. L'état des savoirs*. Paris: La Découverte, 1999, pp. 285–93.

Baubérot, Jean, *Vers un nouveau pacte laïque?* Paris: Seuil, 1990.

——'Aux fondements de la laïcité scolaire. Réponse à Catherine Kintzler', *Les Temps Modernes*, January–February 1991, pp. 163–71.

——(ed.), *Religions et laïcité dans l'Europe des Douze*. Paris: Syros, 1994.

——'Le débat sur la laïcité', *Regards sur l'Actualité*, Vol. 298 March–April 1995, pp. 51–62.

——'L'affaire des foulards et la laïcité à la française', *L'Homme et la Société*, Vol. 120, April–June 1996, pp. 9–16.

——*La morale laïque contre l'ordre moral*. Paris: Seuil, 1997.

——*Histoire de la laïcité en France*. Paris: PUF, 2000 (4th edn 2007).

——'La laïcité comme pacte laïque', in Jean Baudouin and Philippe Portier (eds), *La laïcité, valeur d'aujourd'hui? Contestations et renégociations du modèle français*. Rennes: Presses Universitaires de Rennes, 2001, pp. 39–50.

—— 'Laïcité, le grand écart', *Le Monde*, 4 January 2004.

—— *Laïcité 1905–2005, entre passion et raison*. Paris: Seuil, 2004.

Baudouin, Jean, and Portier, Philippe (eds), *La laïcité, valeur d'aujourd'hui? Contestations et renégociations du modèle français*. Rennes: Presses Universitaires de Rennes, 2001.

Bayes, Jane H., and Tohidi, Nayereh (eds), *Globalization, Gender and Religion. The Politics of Women's Rights in Catholic and Muslim Contexts*. Basingstoke: Palgrave, 2001.

Beaud, Stéphane, and Noiriel, Gérard, 'L' "assimilation", un concept en panne', *International Review of Community Development*, Vol. 61–2, September 1989, pp. 63–76.

—— and —— 'Penser l'intégration des immigrés', *Hommes et Migrations*, Vol. 1133, 1990, pp. 43–54.

Bébéar, Claude, *Des entreprises aux couleurs de la France. Minorités visibles: relever le défi de l'accès à l'emploi*. Paris: Institut Montaigne, 2004.

Bedouelle, Guy, and Costa, Jean-Paul, *Les laïcités à la française*. Paris: Presses Universitaires de France, 1998.

Béji, Hélé, 'Radicalisme culturel et laïcité', *Le Débat*, Vol. 58, January–February 1990, pp. 45–9.

Béland, Daniel, and Hansen, Randall, 'Reforming the French Welfare State: Solidarity, Social Exclusion and the Three Crises of Citizenship', *West European Politics*, Vol. 23, No. 1, January 2000, pp. 47–64.

Bellamy, Richard, *Liberalism and Pluralism: Towards a Politics of Compromise*. London: Routledge, 1999.

—— *Political Constitutionalism*. Cambridge: Cambridge University Press, 2007.

Belorgey, Jean-Michel, *Lutter contre les discriminations. Stratégies institutionnelles et normatives*. Paris: Éditions de la Maison des Sciences de l'Homme, 2001.

Benbassa, Esther, *Histoire des Juifs de France*. Paris: Seuil, 1997.

—— *La République face à ses minorités. Les Juifs hier, les Musulmans aujourd'hui*. Paris: Fayard, 2004.

Bencheikh, Soheib, *Marianne et le Prophète. L'Islam dans la France laïque*. Paris: Livre de Poche, 2003.

Benhabib, Seyla (ed.), *Democracy and Difference. Contesting the Boundaries of the Political*. Princeton, NJ: Princeton University Press, 1996.

—— *The Claims of Culture: Equality and Diversity in the Global Era*. Princeton, NJ: Princeton University Press, 2002.

Bensaïd, Daniel, and Corcuff, Philippe, 'Consensus républicain contre République sociale', *Le Monde*, 11 September 1998.

Benslama, Fethi, *La psychanalyse à l'épreuve de l'islam*. Paris: Aubier-Montaigne, 2002.

Bergounioux, Alain, 'La laïcité, valeur de la République', *Pouvoirs*, Vol. 75, 1995, pp. 17–26.

Beriss, David, 'Scarves, Schools and Segregation: The Foulard Affair', *French Politics and Society*, Vol. 8, No. 1, 1990, pp. 1–13.

Berten, André, and Pourtois, Hervé (eds), *Libéraux et communautariens*. Paris: Presses Universitaires de France, 1997.

Bertheleu, Hélène, 'De l'unité républicaine à la fragmentation multiculturelle: le débat français en matière d'intégration', *L'Homme et la Société*, Vols. 123–4, January–June 1997, pp. 27–38.

Bertho, Alain, 'Malaise dans la République', *Mouvements*, Vol. 38, March–April 2005, pp. 14–8.

Bertossi, Christophe, *Les frontières de la citoyenneté en Europe. Nationalité, résidence, appartenance*. Paris: Harmattan, 2001.

Bessis, Sophie, 'Pauvre main de Fatma!', *Le Monde*, 15 March 2004.

Bhargava, Rajeev, 'Introduction' to Rajeev Bhargava (ed.), *Secularism and its Critics*. Delhi: Oxford University Press, 1998, pp. 1–28.

——(ed.), *Secularism and its Critics*. Delhi: Oxford University Press, 1998.

Bidet, Jacques, *Théorie de la modernité*. Paris: Presses Universitaires de France, 1990.

——*John Rawls et la théorie de la justice*. Paris: Presses Universitaires de France, 1995.

Bihr, Alain, 'Marianne et le voile', *Revue Politique Mensuelle*, January–February 2004, at: www.alencontre.org/page/page/print/france14.html, 6 pp.

Billig, Michael, *Banal Nationalism*, London: Sage, 1997.

Birnbaum, Pierre, *Les Fous de la République. Histoire politique des Juifs d'Etat de Gambetta à Vichy*. Paris: Fayard, 1992.

Blais, Marie-Claude, *Au principe de la République. Le cas Renouvier*. Paris: Bibliothèque des Idées, Paris: Gallimard, 2001.

——*Pour une philosophie politique de l'éducation*. Paris: Bayard, 2002.

Blanc-Chaléard, Marie-Claude, 'L'intégration des Italiens hier: quels enseignements pour aujourd'hui?', in Philippe Dewitte (ed.), *Immigration et intégration. L'état des savoirs*. Paris: La Découverte, 1999, pp. 165–72.

Bleich Erik, *Race Politics in Britain and France. Ideas and Policy-Making since the 1960s*. Cambridge: Cambridge University Press, 2003.

Bloul, Rachel, 'Engendering Muslim Identities: Deterritorialization and the Ethnicization Process in France', in Barbara Daly Metcalf (ed.), *Making Muslim Space in North America and Europe*. Berkeley: University of California Press, 1996, pp. 234–50.

——'Beyond Ethnic Identity: Resisting Exclusionary Identification', *Social Identities*, Vol. 5, No. 1, 1999, pp. 7–30.

Blum, Alain, 'Comment décrire les immigrés? A propos de quelques recherches sur l'immigration', *Population*, Vol. 3, 1998, pp. 569–87.

Bohman, James, 'Public Reason and Cultural Pluralism', *Political Theory*, Vol. 23, No. 2, 1995, pp. 253–79.

Bolstanski, Laurent, and Thévenot, Luc, *De la justification. Les économies de la grandeur*. Paris: Gallimard, 1991.

Boltanski, Luc, and Chiapello, Luc, *Le nouvel esprit du capitalisme*. Paris: Gallimard, 1999.

Bonnafous, Simone, *L'immigration prise aux mots. Les immigrés dans la presse au tournant des années 1980*. Paris: Kimé, 1980.

—— 'Mots et paroles de l'immigration', *Revue Française des Affaires Sociales*, Vol. 39, No. 3, 1992, pp. 5–15.

Borella, François, 'Nationalité et citoyenneté', in Dominique Colas, Claude Emeri, and Jacques Zylberberg (eds), *Citoyenneté et nationalité: perspectives en France et au Québec*. Paris: Presses Universitaires de France, pp. 209–29.

Borgetto, Michel, 'La réforme de la Sécurité Sociale: continuité ou déclin du modèle républicain', *Droit Social*, Vols. 9–10, September–October 1997, pp. 877–84.

Borrillo, Daniel (ed.), *Lutter contre les discriminations*. Paris: La Découverte, 2003.

Bouamama, Saïd, *Dix ans de Marche des Beurs*. Paris: Desclée de Brouwer, 1991.

—— *Vers une nouvelle citoyenneté. Crise de la pensée laïque*. Lille: La boîte de Pandore, 1991.

—— 'Derrière le "beur", l'indigène colonial', *Les Cahiers de l'Orient*, Vol. 71, 2003, pp. 15–22.

—— *L'affaire du foulard islamique. La production d'un racisme respectable*. Paris: Le Geai Bleu, 2004.

—— Cordeiro, Albano, and Roux, Michel, *La citoyenneté dans tous ses états. De l'immigration à la nouvelle citoyenneté*. Paris: L'Harmattan, 1992.

Boubakeur, Dalil, 'L'État et les cultes: le cas de l'Islam', *Administration*, Vol. 161, October–December 1993, pp. 133–45.

Boubeker, Ahmed, *Les mondes de l'ethnicité. La communauté d'expérience des héritiers de l'immigration maghrébine*. Paris: Balland, 2003.

—— 'Sous le voile, la mascarade de l'identité', in Jean-Michel Helvig (ed.), *La laïcité dévoilée. Quinze années de débat en quarante Rebonds*. Paris: Libération and Éditions de l'Aube, 2004, pp. 168–71.

Boucher, Manuel, *Les théories de l'intégration. Entre universalisme et différentialisme*. Paris: Harmattan, 2000.

Bouleau, Michel, 'La démission du Conseil d'État dans l'affaire du foulard', in Charles Zarka (ed.), *L'Islam en France*. Special issue of *Cités*, March 2004, pp. 277–85.

Boulot, Serge, and Boyzon-Fradet, Danièle, *Les Immigrés et l'école, une course d'obstacles*. Paris: Harmattan, 1988.

Bourdeau, Vincent, and Merril, Roberto (eds), *La république et ses démons. Essais de républicanisme appliqué*. Paris: Éditions Eres, 2007.

Bourdieu, Pierre, *La domination masculine*. Paris: Seuil, 1998.

—— and Passeron, Jean-Claude, *Reproduction in Education, Society and Culture*. London: Sage, 1990.

Boussinesq, Jean, 'Une nouvelle laïcité?', *Projet*, Vol. 225, Spring 1991, pp. 7–15.

—— *La laïcité française. Mémento juridique*. Paris: Seuil, 1994.

Bouzar, Dounia, 'Islam et reconstruction identitaire des jeunes en difficulté', *Les Cahiers de la Sécurité Intérieure*, Vol. 45, 3rd Trimester, 2001, pp. 21–44.

—— *L'Islam des banlieues, les prédicateurs musulmans, nouveaux travailleurs sociaux*. Paris: Syros-La Découverte, 2001.

—— 'Pas de débat réchauffé sur le foulard', *Le Monde*, 25 April 2003.

—— *'Monsieur Islam' n'existe pas. Pour une dé-islamisation des débats*. Paris: Hachette, 2004.

Bouzar, Dounia, and Kada, Saïda, *L'une voilée, l'autre pas. Le témoignage de deux musulmanes françaises.* Paris: Albin Michel, 2003.

Bowen, John R., 'Two Approaches to Rights and Religion in Contemporary France', in Richard Ashby Wilson and Jon P. Mitchell (eds), *Human Rights in Global Perspective. Anthropological Studies of Rights, Claims and Entitlements.* London: Routledge, 2003, pp. 33–53.

—— 'Muslims and Citizens. France's Headscarf Controversy', *Boston Review*, February–March 2004 <http://bostonreview.net/BR29.1/bowen.html>.

—— *Why the French Don't Like Headscarves. Islam, the State and Public Space.* Princeton, NJ: Princeton University Press, 2007.

Boyer, Alain, Le *droit des religions en France.* Paris: Presses Universitaire de France, 1993.

Brenner, Emmanuel (ed.), *Les territoires perdus de la république: Milieu scolaire, antisémitisme, sexisme.* Paris: Mille et Une Nuits, 2002.

Brighouse, Harry, 'Civic Education and Liberal Legitimacy', *Ethics*, Vol. 108, No. 4, July 1998, pp. 719–45.

—— *School Choice and Social Justice.* Oxford: Oxford University Press, 2000.

—— 'Faith-Based Schools in the United Kingdom: An Unenthusiastic Defence of a Slightly Reformed Status Quo', in Roy Gardner, Jo Cairns and Denis Lawton (eds), *Faith Schools. Consensus or Conflict?* London: Routledge, 2005, pp. 83–9.

Brouard, Sylvain, and Tiberj, Vincent, *Français comme les autres? Enquête sur les citoyens d'origine maghrébine, africaine et turque.* Paris: Presses de Sciences Po, 2005.

Brubaker, Rogers, *Citizenship and Nationhood in France and Germany.* Cambridge, MA: Harvard University Press, 1992.

—— 'The Return of Assimilation? Changing Perspectives on Immigration and its Sequels in France, Germany and the United States', *Ethnic and Racial Studies*, Vol. 24, No. 4, July 2001, pp. 531–48.

Brunerie-Kauffmann, Joëlle, Désir, Harlem, Dumont, René, Perrault, Gilles, and Touraine, Alain, 'Pour une laïcité ouverte', *Politis*, 9–15 November 1989.

Burgat, François, 'Veils and Obscuring Lenses', in John L. Esposito and François Burgat (eds), *Modernizing Islam. Religion in the Public Sphere.* London: Hurst & Co, 2003, pp. 17–41.

Burke, Jason, 'France and the Muslim Myth', *The Observer*, November 13, 2005.

Bussy, Florence, 'Le débat sur la laïcité et la loi', *Recueil Dalloz*, Vol. 37, 2004, pp. 2666–74.

Callan, Eamonn, *Creating Citizens. Political Education and Liberal Democracy.* Oxford: Oxford University Press, 1997.

Callinicos, Alex, 'Egalitarisme et critique sociale', *Actual Marx*, Vol. 202, No. 31, pp. 147–58.

Calvès, Gwénaële, 'Pour une analyse (vraiment) critique de la discrimination positive', *Le Débat*, Vol. 117, November–December 2001, pp. 164–74.

—— ' "Il n'y a pas de race ici". Le modèle français à l'épreuve de l'intégration européenne', *Critique Internationale*, Vol. 17, October 2002, pp. 173–85.

—— 'Les politiques françaises de discrimination positive: trois spécificités', *Pouvoirs*, Vol. 111, 2004, pp. 29–40.

—— *La discrimination positive*. Paris: Presses Universitaires de France, 2004.

—— *Renouvellement démographique de la fonction publique de l'Etat: vers une intégration prioritaire des Français issus de l'immigration?* Paris: La Documentation Française, 2005.

Canivez, Patrick, *Eduquer le citoyen?* Paris: Hatier, 1995.

Canto-Sperber, Monique (ed.), *Dictionnaire d'éthique et de philosophie morale*. Paris: Presses Universitaires de France, 1996.

—— 'Les ambitions de la réflexion éthique', *Esprit*, Vol. 5, May 2000, pp. 114–36.

—— and Ricoeur, Paul, 'Des philosophes contre une loi', *Le Monde*, 10 December 2003.

Carbonnier, Jean, 'La culture française: une culture "catholique" laïcisée?', *Parole et Société*, Vol. 34, 1993, pp. 173–87.

—— *Culture, Citizenship and Community. A Contextual Exploration of Justice as Even-Handedness*. Oxford: Oxford University Press, 2000.

—— 'Démocratie, multiculturalisme et *hijab*', *Esprit*, Vol. 311, January 2005, pp. 54–61.

—— and Williams, Melissa S., 'Muslim Minorities in Liberal Democracies: The Politics of Misrecognition', in Rajeev Bhargava (ed.), *Secularism and its Critics*, Delhi: Oxford University Press, Delhi, 1998, pp. 137—173.

Caron, François, *La France des patriotes, de 1851 à 1918*. Paris: Fayard, 1985.

Castoriadis, Cornélius, *La montée de l'insignifiance. Les carrefours du labyrinthe IX*. Paris: Seuil, 1996.

Césari, Jocelyne, *Etre musulman en France. Associations, militants et mosquées*. Paris: Hachette, 1997.

—— *Musulmans et républicains: les jeunes, l'Islam et la France*. Paris: Complexe, 1998.

—— 'De l'islam en France à l'islam de France', in Philippe Dewitte (ed.), *Immigration et Intégration. L'état des savoirs*. Paris: La Découverte, 1999, pp. 222–31.

—— 'Musulmans français et intégration socio-politique', in Pierre Bréchon, Bruno Duriez, and Jacques Ion (eds), *Religion et action dans l'espace public*. Paris: Harmattan, 2000, pp. 59–73.

—— 'L'unité républicaine menacée par les idéologies multiculturelles', in Jean Baudouin and Philippe Portier (eds), *La laïcité, valeur d'aujourd'hui? Contestations et renégociations du modèle français*. Rennes: Presses Universitaires de Rennes, 2001, pp. 117–31.

—— 'Islam de l'extérieur, musulman de l'intérieur. Deux visions après le 11 septembre 2001', *Cultures & Conflits*, Vol. 44, 2001, pp. 97–115.

—— 'Muslim Minorities in Europe: The Silent Revolution', in John L. Esposito and François Burgat (eds), *Modernizing Islam. Religion in the Public Sphere*. London: Hurst & Co, 2003, pp. 251–70.

—— *L'Islam à l'épreuve de l'Occident*. Paris: La Découverte, 2004.

Césari, Jocelyne, *When Islam and Democracy Meet: Muslims in Europe and in the United States*. New York: Palgrave, 2004.

——and Baubérot, Jean, 'Laïcité, communautarisme et foulard: vrais et faux débat', *Libération*, 4 September 2003.

——and McLoughlin, Seán (eds), *European Muslims and the Secular State*. Aldershot: Aldgate, 2005.

Chaïb, Yassine, 'Le rite funéraire de l'intégration', in Yves-Charles Zarka (ed.), *L'Islam en France. Hors série de la revue Cités*. Paris: Presses Universitaires de France, March 2004.

Chambers, Clare, 'Are Breast Implants Better Than Female Genital Mutilation? Autonomy, Gender Equality, and Nussbaum's Political Liberalism', *Critical Review of International Social and Political Philosophy*, Vol. 7, No. 1, 2004, pp. 1–33.

Champion, Françoise, 'Entre laïcisation et sécularisation. Des rapports Église-État dans l'Europe communautaire', *Le Débat*, Vol. 77, 1993, pp. 46–63.

Chanet, François, *L'école républicaine et les petites patries*. Paris: Aubier, 1996.

Changeux, Jean-Pierre, 'Comité Consultatif National d'Ethique', *Une même éthique pour tous?* Paris: Odile Jacob, 1997.

Cingolani, Patrick, *La république, les sociologues et la question politique*. Paris: La Dispute, 2003.

Cinquième Zone, 'Derrière le voile... un tout autre combat', 1994, at <http://www.sisyphe.org/article.php3?id_article=709>, pp. 1–7.

Citron, Susanne, *Le Mythe national: l'histoire de France en question*. Paris: Éditions Ouvrières/Etudes et Documentation Internationales, 1987.

Cohen, Gerald Allan, 'Incentives, Inequality, and Community', in Grethe Peterson (ed.), *The Tanner Lectures on Human Values*, Vol. 13. Salt Lake City, UT: University of Utah Press, 1992.

——'Where the Action Is: On the Site of Distributive Justice', *Philosophy and Public Affairs*, Vol. 26, No. 1, 1997, pp. 3–30.

——*If You're An Egalitarian, How Come You're So Rich?* Cambridge, MA: Harvard University Press, 2000.

——'Facts and Principles', *Philosophy and Public Affairs*, Vol. 31, No. 3, 2003, pp. 211–45.

Cohen, Jim, 'Intégration: théories, politiques et logiques d'État', in Philippe Dewitte (ed.), *Immigration et intégration. L'état des savoirs*. Paris: La Découverte, 1999, pp. 32–55.

——'Les "modèles d'intégration" face aux particularismes: malentendus et dialogues France/État Unis', *Mouvements*, Vol. 38, March–April 2005, pp. 41–9.

Cohen, Joshua, 'Deliberation and Democratic Legitimacy', in Alan Hamlin and Philippe Pettit (eds), *The Good Polity*. Oxford: Oxford University Press, 1989, pp. 17–34.

——'Taking People as They Are?', *Philosophy and Public Affairs*, Vol. 30–4, Fall 2001, pp. 363–86.

Cohen, Martine, 'L'intégration de l'islam et des musulmans en France: modèles du passé et pratiques actuelles', in Jean Baudouin and Philippe Portier (eds), *La laïcité, valeur d'aujourd'hui? Contestations et renégociations du modèle français.* Rennes: Presses Universitaires de Rennes, 2001, pp. 315–30.

——'La laïcité française en débat', *Migrations Société*, Vol. 16, No. 96, November–December 2004, pp. 31–41.

Collectif 'Oui à la laïcité, non aux lois d'exception', *Pro-Choix*, Vol. 25, Summer 2003, pp. 14–7 (published in *Libération* 20 May 2003 as 'Oui au foulard dans l'école laïque').

Collin, Thibaud, 'Quel enseignement moral dans une société laïque?', *Liberté Politique*, Vol. 24, Winter 2003–4, pp. 71–85.

Commission de la Nationalité, *Etre Français aujourd'hui et demain. Rapport présenté par Marceau Long au Premier Ministre*, Vol. 2. Paris: Union Générale d'Éditions, 1988.

Condorcet, Marie-Jean-Antoine de Caritat, *Esquisse d'un tableau historique des progrès de l'esprit humain.* Paris: Flammarion, 1988.

Conklin, Alice L., *A Mission to Civilize. The Republican Idea of Empire in France and West Africa, 1895–1930.* Stanford, CA: Stanford University Press, 1997.

Connolly, William, *Identity/Difference: Democratic Negotiations of Political Paradox.* Ithaca, NY: Cornell University Press, 1991.

Conseil d'Etat, Section de l'Intérieur, 27 Novembre 1989, no. 346893, Avis "Port du foulard islamique", at <http://www.rajf.org/article.php3?id_article=1065> (last accessed 17 July 2007).

——*Sur le principe d'égalité. Extrait du rapport public 1996.* Paris: Documentation Française, 1998.

Constant, Fred, *La citoyenneté.* Paris: Montchrestien, 1998.

Coq, Guy, *Laïcité et république. Le lien nécessaire.* Paris: Edition du Félin, 1995.

Costa-Lascoux, Jacqueline, *De l'immigré au citoyen.* Paris: La Documentation Française, 1989.

——*Les trois âges de la laïcité. Débat avec Joseph Sitruk, Grand Rabbin de France.* Paris: Hachette, 1996.

——'L'intégration à la française: une philosophie, des lois', in Philippe Dewitte (ed.), *Immigration et intégration. L'état des savoirs.* Paris: La Découverte, 1999, pp. 328–40.

Coutel Charles (ed.), *La République et l'école. Une anthologie.* Paris: Presses Pocket, 1991.

Dagger, Richard, *Civic Virtues: Rights, Citizenship and Republican Liberalism.* Oxford: Oxford University Press, 1997.

——'Communitarianism and Republicanism', in Gerald Gaus and Chandran Kukathas (eds), *Handbook of Political Theory.* London: Sage, 2004, pp. 167–79.

——'Domination and the Republican Challenge to Liberalism', in John Christman and Joel Anderson (eds), *Autonomy and the Challenges to Liberalism.* Cambridge: Cambridge University Press, 2005, pp. 177–203.

Dargent, Claude, 'Les musulmans déclarés en France: affirmation religieuse, subordination sociale et progressisme politique', *Cahiers du CEVIPOF*, Vol. 34, February 2003, pp. 40–93.

Dayan-Herzbrun, Sonia, 'The Issue of the Islamic Headscarf', in Jane Freedman and Carrie Tarr (eds), *Women, Immigration and Identities in France*. Oxford: Berg, 2000, pp. 69–82.

Debray, Régis, *Vive la République*. Paris: Odile Jacob, 1989.

—— 'Etes-vous démocrate ou républicain?', *Nouvel Observateur*, Vol. 30, November–6 December 1989, pp. 115–21.

—— 'La laïcité: une exception française', in Hubert Bost (ed.), *Genèses et enjeux de la laïcité. Christianismes et laïcité*. Paris: Labor et Fides, 1990, pp. 199–208.

—— *Contretemps. Eloge des idéaux perdus*. Paris: Gallimard, 1992.

—— *Le Code et le Glaive. Après l'Europe, la Nation*. Paris: Albin Michel, 2000.

—— *L'enseignement du fait religieux dans l'école laïque*. Paris: Documentation Française, 2002. Available at <http://www.education.gouv.fr/rapport/debray/debray.pdf> [accessed, 11 December 2004].

—— *Ce que le voile nous voile. La République et le sacré*. Paris: Folio/Gallimard, 2004.

—— Max, Gallo, Jacques, Julliard, Blandine, Kriegel, Olivier, Mongin, Mona, Ozouf, Anicet, Le Pors, and Paul, Thibaud, 'Républicains, n'ayons plus peur!', *Le Monde*, 4 September 1998, p. 13.

Debré, Jean-Louis, *La laïcité à l'école: un principe républicain à réaffirmer. Rapport fait au nom de la mission d'information sur la question du port des signes religieux à l'école La laïcité à l'école: un principe républicain à réaffirmer. Rapport fait au nom de la mission d'information sur la question du port des signes religieux à l'école*. Paris: Assemblée Nationale, 2003.

Decreton, Severine (ed.), *Service Public et Lien Social*. Paris: Harmattan, 1999.

Defrance, Bernard, 'Contre le voile *et donc* contre l'exclusion de l'école des jeunes filles qui le portent', <http://www.bernard-defrance.net/bin/imprim.php?from=textesperso&where=156&PHPSESSID=896ffc5882745d667b5738e4ed087973> (last accessed 27 July 2007).

de Galembert, Claire, 'La gestion publique de l'islam en France et en Allemagne. De l'improvisation des pratiques *in situ* à l'amorce d'un processus de régulation nationale', *Revue Internationale et Stratégique*, Vol. 52, Winter 2003–4, pp. 67–78.

Delafaye, François, *Laïcité de combat. Laïcité de droit*. Paris: Hachette, 1997.

Déloye, Yves, *Ecole et citoyenneté. L'individualisme républicain de Jules Ferry à Vichy: controverses*. Paris: Presses de la Fondation Nationales des Sciences Politiques, 1994.

—— 'L'instruction', in Vincent Duclert and Christophe Prochasson (eds), *Dictionnaire Critique de la République*. Paris: Flammarion, 2002, pp. 183–8.

—— and Ihl, Olivier, 'Deux figures singulières de l'universel: la république et le sacré', in Marc Sadoun (ed.), *La démocratie en France*. Vol. I. Paris: Gallimard, 2000, pp. 138–246.

Delphy, Christine, 'Egalité, équivalence et équité: la position de l'Etat français au regard du droit international', *Nouvelles Questions Féministes*, Vol. 16, No. 1, February 1995, pp. 5–58.

——'La suppression d'une liberté contre la défense d'une *autre* liberté?', *Revue Politique Mensuelle*, January–February 2004. Available at <http://www.alencontre.org/page/page/print/france16.html>.

——'Le foulard islamique: une affaire française', *Hommes et Libertés*, Vol. 125, January–March 2004, pp. 40–1.

——'Antisexisme ou antiracisme? Un faux dilemme', in Nacira Guénif-Souilamas (ed.), *La république mise à nu par son immigration*. Paris: La Fabrique Edition, 2006, pp. 81–108.

Delsenne, Ludivine, 'De la difficile adaptation du principe républicain de laïcité à l'évolution socio-culturelle française', *Revue du Droit Public*, Vol. 2, 2005, pp. 427–62.

Deranty, Jean-Phillipe, 'Jacques Rancière's Contribution to the Ethics of Recognition', *Political Theory*, Vol. 31, No. 1, February 2003, pp. 136–56.

De Rudder, Véronique, 'Jalons pour une histoire socio-politique sur les relations interethniques en France', in Ida Simon-Barouch and Véronique de Rudder (eds), *Migrations Internationales et Relations Interethniques*. Paris: Harmattan, 1997, pp. 73–96.

——and Poiret, Christian, '*Affirmative Action* et discrimination justifiée: vers un universalisme en acte', in Philippe Dewitte (ed.), *Immigration et Intégration. L'état des savoirs*. Paris: La Découverte, 1999, pp. 397–406.

——Poiret, Christian, and Vourc'h Francois, *L'inégalité raciste. L'universalité républicaine à l'épreuve*. Paris: Presses Universitaires de France, 2000.

De Salvia, Michel, 'La laïcité française et les principes du droit européen', *Tranversalités*, Vol. 93, January–March 2005, pp. 1–16.

Deschavanne, Eric, 'La discrimination positive face à l'idéal républicain: définition, typologie, historique, arguments', in Luc Ferry (ed.), *Pour une société de la nouvelle chance. Une approche républicaine de la discrimination positive*. Paris: Documentation Française, 2005, pp. 63–192.

de Tocqueville, Alexis, *De la démocratie en Amérique*. Paris: Gallimard, 1992.

Deveaux, Monique, *Gender and Justice in Multicultural Liberal States*. Oxford: Oxford University Press, 2007.

De Wenden, Catherine, *Citoyenneté, nationalité et immigration*. Paris: Éditions Arcantère, 1987.

Dewitte, Philippe (ed.), *Immigration et Intégration. L'état des savoirs*. Paris: La Découverte, 1999.

Dikeç, Mustafa, 'Two Decades of French Urban Policy: From Social Development of Neighbourhoods to the Republican Penal State', *Antipode*, Vol. 38, No. 1, 2006, pp. 59–81.

D'Iribarne, Philippe, 'Du rapport à l'autre. Les singularités françaises dans l'intégration des immigrés', *Le Débat*, Vol. 129, March–April 2004, pp. 122–35.

——*L'étrangeté française*. Paris: Seuil, 2006.

Djavann, Chahdortt, *Bas les voiles!* Paris: Gallimard, 2003.

Donaldson, Laura E., and Pui-lan, Kwok (eds), *Postcolonialism, Feminism and Religious Discourse.* London and New York: Routledge, 2002.

Donzelot, Jacques (with Catherine Mevel and Anne Wyvekens), *Faire société. La politique de la ville aux États-Unis et en France.* Paris: Seuil, 2003.

——'Un État qui rend capable', in Serge Paugam (ed.), *Repenser la solidarité. L'apport des sciences sociales.* Paris: Presses Universitaires de France, 2007, pp. 87–109.

Dord, Olivier, 'Laïcité à l'école: l'obscure clarté de la circulaire Fillon du 18 mai 2004', *Actualité Juridique du Droit Administratif,* Vol. 26 July 2004, pp. 1523–29.

Drago, Roland, 'Laïcité, neutralité, liberté?', *Archives de Philosophie du Droit,* Vol. 38, 1993, 221–30.

Drysek, John, *Deliberative Democracy and Beyond. Liberals, Critics, Contestations.* Oxford: Oxford University Press, 2000.

Dubet, François, *Immigration: Qu'en savons-nous?* Paris: La Documentation Française, 1989.

——*Sociologie de l'expérience.* Paris: Seuil, 1994.

——'La laïcité dans les mutations de l'école', in Michel Wieviorka (ed.), *Une société fragmentée? Le multiculturalisme en débat.* Paris: La Découverte, 1996, pp. 85–112.

——and Martucelli, Danilo, *Dans quelle société vivons-nous?* Paris: Seuil, 1998.

——'Les "différences" a l'école: entre l'égalité et la performance', in Michel Wieviorka and Jocelyne Ohana (eds), *La différence culturelle. Une reformulation des débats.* Paris: Balland, 2001, pp. 100–17.

Duclert, Vincent, and Prochasson, Christophe (eds), *Dictionnaire Critique de la République.* Paris: Flammarion, 2002.

Durkheim, Emile, *Professional Ethics and Civil Morals.* Transl. C. Brookfield, preface B.S. Turner. London: Routledge, 1957.

Dworkin, Ronald, *A Matter of Principle.* Cambridge, MA: Harvard University Press, 1985.

——'Affirming Affirmative Action', *New York Review of Books,* 22 October 1998.

Dyson, Kenneth H.F., *The State Tradition in Western Europe: A Study of an Idea and Institution.* Oxford: Martin Robertson, 1980.

Edwards, John, and Révauger, Jean-Paul (eds), *Discourse on Inequality in France and Britain.* Aldershot: Ashgate, 1998.

Ehrenberg, Alain, *L'individu incertain.* Paris: Calmann-Lévy, 1995.

Eickelman, Dale F., and Piscatori, James, *Muslim Politics.* Princeton, NJ: Princeton University Press, 2004.

Eisenberg Avigail, and Spinner-Halev Jeff (eds), *Minorities within Minorities.* Cambridge: Cambridge University Press, 2005.

El Guindi, Fadwa, *Veil. Modesty, Privacy and Resistance.* Oxford: Berg, 1999.

El Hamel, Chouki, 'Muslim Diaspora in Western Europe: The Islamic Headscarf (*Hijab*), the Media and Muslims' Integration in France', *Citizenship Studies,* Vol. 6, No. 3, 2002, pp. 293–308.

Elster Jon, *Sour Grapes. Studies in the Subversion of Rationality.* Cambridge: Cambridge University Press, 1983.

Esping-Anderson, Gøsta, *The Three Worlds of Welfare Capitalism.* Cambridge: Polity Press & Princeton, NJ: Princeton University Press, 1990.

Esposito, John L., and Burgat, François (eds), *Modernizing Islam. Religion in the Public Sphere.* London: Hurst & Co, 2003.

Estlund, David, 'Liberalism, Equality and Fraternity in Cohen's Critique of Rawls', *Journal of Political Philosophy*, Vol. 6, 1998, pp. 99–112.

Evans, Carolyn, *Freedom of Religion under the European Convention on Human Rights.* Oxford: Oxford University Press, 2001.

Ewald, François, *L'Etat-Providence.* Paris: Fayard, 1986.

Fabre-Alibert, Véronique, 'La loi française du 15 mars 2004 encadrant, en application du principe de *laïcité,* le port de signes ou de tenues manifestant une appartenance religieuse dans les écoles, collèges et lycées publics: vers un pacte social laïque?', *Revue Trimestrielle des Droits de l'Homme*, Vol. 59, July 2004, pp. 575–609.

Fanon, Frantz, *A Dying Colonialism.* New York: Grove Press, Inc., 1965.

Farrelly, Colin, 'Dualism, Incentives and the Demands of Rawlsian Justice', *Canadian Journal of Political Science*, Vol. 38, No. 3, September 2005, pp. 675–95.

——'Justice in Ideal Theory: A Refutation', *Political Studies*, Vol. 55, No. 4, December 2007, 844–64.

Fassin, Didier, 'L'invention française de la discrimination', *Revue Française de Science Politique*, Vol. 52, No. 4, August 2002, pp. 403–23.

——'Du déni à la dénégation. Psychologie politique de la représentation des discriminations', in Didier Fassin and Éric Fassin (eds), *De la question sociale à la question raciale. Représenter la société française.* Paris: La Découverte, 2006, pp. 133–57.

——and Fassin, Éric (eds), *De la question sociale à la question raciale. Représenter la société française.* Paris: La Découverte, 2006.

Fassin, Éric, 'Two Cultures? French Intellectuals and the Politics of Culture in the 1980s', *French Politics and Society*, Vol. 14, No. 2, Spring 1996, pp. 9–16.

——'Du multiculturalisme à la discrimination', *Le Débat*, Vol. 97, November–December 1997, pp. 130–6.

——' "Good to Think". The American Reference in French Discourses of Immigration and Ethnicity', in Christian Joppke and Steven Lukes (eds), *Multicultural Questions.* Oxford: Oxford University Press, 1999, pp. 224–41.

——'Penser la discrimination positive', in Daniel Borrillo (ed.), *Lutter contre les discriminations.* Paris: La Découverte, 2003, pp. 55–68.

——'Questions sexuelles, questions raciales. Parallèles, tensions et articulations', in Didier Fassin and Éric Fassin (eds), *De la question sociale à la question raciale. Représenter la société française.* Paris: La Découverte, 2006, pp. 230–48.

——and Feher, Michel, 'Parité et PACS: anatomie d'un rapport', in Daniel Borrillo and Éric Fassin (eds), *L'expertise familiale à l'épreuve de l'homosexualité.* PUF, 1999, pp. 13–43.

Favell, Adrian, *Philosophies of Integration. Immigration and the Idea of Citizenship in France and Britain*. Basingstoke: Macmillan, 1998.

——and Modood, Tariq, 'Multiculturalism and Normative Political Theory', in Alan Finlayson (ed.), *Contemporary Political Thought: A Reader and Guide*. Edinburgh: Edinburgh University Press, 2003, pp. 484–513.

Feldblum, Miriam, *Reconstructing Citizenship. The Politics of Nationality Reform and Immigration in Contemporary France*. New York: State University of New York Press, 1999.

Femmes Publiques, 'Etre féministe, ce n'est pas exclure!', at <http://lmsi.net/article.php3?id_article=181>.

Ferrari, Alessandro, 'Laïcité et voile islamique en France au début du nouveau millénaire', *Migrations Société*, Vol. 16, No. 96, November–December 2004, pp. 63–129.

Ferrari, Silvio, 'Islam and the Western European Model of Church and State Relations', in Wasif Shadid and Sjoerd van Koningsveld (eds), *Religious Freedoms and the Neutrality of the State: The Position of Islam in the European Union*. Leuven: Peeters, 2002, pp. 6–19.

——'The Secularity of the State and the Shaping of Muslim Representative Organizations in Western Europe', in Jocelyne Césari and Seán McLoughlin (eds), *European Muslims and the Secular State*. Aldershot: Aldgate, 2005, pp. 11–23.

Ferret, Alain, and Soulier, Gérard (eds), *Les minorités et leurs droits depuis 1789*. Paris: Harmattan, 1989.

Ferry, Jean-Marc, *Philosophie de la communication. Vol. 2: Justice politique et démocratie procédurale*. Paris: Cerf, 1994.

Ferry, Jules 'Lettre aux instituteurs', 27 November 1883, reprinted in *Pouvoirs*, Vol. 75, 1995, pp. 109–16.

Ferry, Luc (ed.), *Pour une société de la nouvelle chance. Une approche républicaine de la discrimination positive*. Paris: Documentation Française, 2005.

——and Renaut, Alain, *La Pensée 68. Essai sur l'anti-humanisme contemporain*. Paris: Gallimard, 1985.

——and Renaut, Alain, *68–86. Itinéraires de l'individu*. Pari: Gallimard, 1987.

——and Renaut, Alain, *From the Rights of Man to the Republican Idea*. Chicago: Chicago University Press, 1992.

Fetzer, Joel S., and Soper, Christopher, *Muslims and the State in Britain, France and Germany*. Cambridge: Cambridge University Press, 2005.

Filali-Ansary, Abdou, 'Islam, laïcité, démocratie', *Pouvoirs*, Vol. 104, 2003, pp. 5–19.

Finkielkraut, Alain, *La défaite de la pensée*. Paris: Gallimard, 1987. (English translation: *The Undoing of Thought*), London: Claridge Press, 1988.

——'Le foulard et l'espace sacré de l'école', *L'Arche*, No. 544–545, 2003, at <http://lmsi.net/spip.php?article192> (last accessed 27 July 2007).

Ford, Caroline, *Divided Houses. Religion and Gender in Modern France*. Ithaca, NY: Cornell University Press, 2005.

Forey, Elsa, 'L'égalité des cultes: un principe en évolution?', in Claude Courvoisier and Patrick Charlot (eds), *Actualité politique et juridique de l'égalité*. Dijon: Éditions Universitaires de Dijon, 2003, pp. 41–65.

Fort, Richard, *Racial Culture: A Critique*. Princeton, NJ: Princeton University Press, 2005.

Forquin, Jean-Claude, 'L'école et la question du multiculturalisme: approches françaises, américaines et britanniques', in Agnès Van Zanten (ed.), *L'école. L'état des savoirs*. Paris: La Découverte, 2000, pp. 151–60.

Foucault, Michel, *Discipline and Punish. The Birth of the Prison*. New York: Vintage Books, 1979.

——'Afterward: The Subject and Power', in Hubert Dreyfus and Paul Rabinow (eds), *Michel Foucault: Beyond Structuralism and Hermeneutics*. Chicago: University of Chicago Press, 2nd ed., 1983.

Fourest, Caroline, *Frère Tariq: Discours, stratégie et méthode de Tariq Ramadan*. Paris: Grasset, 2004.

——and Venner, Fiametta, *Tirs Croisés. La laïcité à l'épreuve des intégrismes juif, chrétien et musulman*. Paris: Calmann-Lévy, 2003.

——and Venner, Fiametta, 'Les enjeux cachés du voile à l'école', *Pro-Choix*, Vol. 25, Summer 2003, pp. 19–31.

Fourier, Martine, and Vermes, Geneviève (eds), *Ethnicisation des rapports sociaux. Racismes, nationalismes, ethnicismes et culturalismes*. Paris: Harmattan, 1994.

Fraser, Nancy, 'Foucault on Modern Power: Empirical Insights and Normative Confusions', *Praxis International*, Vol. 1, No. 3, 1981, pp. 272–87.

——'From Redistribution to Recognition? Dilemmas of Justice in a "Post-socialist" Age', *New Left Review*, Vol. 212, July–August 1995, pp. 68–93.

——'Social Justice in the Age of Identity Politics: Redistribution, Recognition and Participation', in Nancy Fraser and Axel Honneth (eds), *Redistribution or Recognition? A Political-Philosophical Exchange*. London: Verso, 2003, pp. 7–109.

——and Honneth, Alex, *Redistribution or Recognition? A Political-Philosophical Exchange*. London: Verso, 2003.

Freeden, Michael, *Ideologies and Political Theory. A Conceptual Approach*. Oxford: Clarendon Press, 1996.

Freedman, Jane, *Immigration and Insecurity in France*. Aldershot: Ashgate, 2004.

——'Secularism as a Barrier to Integration? The French Dilemma', *International Migration*, Vol. 42, No. 3, 2004, pp. 5–27.

——and Tarr, Carrie (eds), *Women, Immigration and Identities in France*. Oxford: Berg, 2000.

Frégosi, Frank, 'L'Islam d'Europe', *Esprit*, Vol. 1, January 1998, pp. 109–35.

Friedman, Marilyn, *Autonomy, Gender, Politics*. Oxford: Oxford University Press, 2003.

——'Pettit's Civic Republicanism and Male Domination', in Cécile Laborde and John Maynor (eds), *Republicanism and Political Theory*. Oxford: Blackwell, 2007, pp. 246–68.

Furet, François, *Penser la Révolution française* (with Denis Richet). Paris: Fayard, 1978.

Furet, François, *La gauche et la Révolution au 19ème siècle. Edgar Quinet et la question du jacobinisme*. Paris: Hachette, 1986.

——and Ozouf, Mona, *Le siècle de l'avènement républicain*. Paris: Gallimard, 1993.

Galeotti, Elisabetta, 'Citizenship and Equality. The Place for Toleration', *Political Theory*, Vol. 21, No. 4, 1993, pp. 585–605.

—— *Toleration as Recognition*. Cambridge: Cambridge University Press, 2002.

Gallissot, René, *Misère de l'antiracisme*. Paris: Arcantère, 1985.

——'Épouvantail ethnique et méli-mélo culturel', in Ida Simon-Barouch and Véronique de Rudder (eds), *Migrations Internationales et Relations Interethniques*. Paris: Harmattan, 1997, pp. 267–95.

——'Nationalisme et racisme', in Martine Fourier and Geneviève Vermes (eds), *Ethnicisation des rapports sociaux. Racismes, nationalismes, ethnicismes et culturalismes*. Paris: Harmattan, 1994, pp. 7–29.

Garay, Alain, 'La laïcité, principe érigé en valeur de la Convention Européenne des Droits de l'Homme', *Recueil Dalloz*, Vol. 2, No. 7231, 2006, pp. 103–10.

Gaspard, Françoise, and Khoroskhavar, Farhad, *Le Foulard et la République*. Paris: La Découverte, 1995.

Gauchet, Marcel, *Le désenchantement du monde*. Paris: Gallimard, 1985.

—— *La révolution des droits de l'homme*. Paris: Gallimard, 1989.

—— *La religion dans la démocratie. Parcours de la laïcité*. Paris: Gallimard, 1998.

—— *La démocratie contre elle-même*. Paris: Gallimard, 2002.

Gautherin, Jacqueline, 'L'universalisme de l'école laïque à l'épreuve', in Agnès Van Zanten (ed.), *L'école. L'état des savoirs*. Paris: La Découverte, 2000, pp. 381–8.

Gauthier, Guy, and Nicolet, Claude (eds), *La laïcité en mémoire*. Paris: Edilic, 1987.

Gay, Peter, *The Enlightenment: An Interpretation*. London: Weidenfeld and Nicolson, 2 Vols, 1967–70.

Geisser, Vincent, *Ethnicité républicaine*. Paris: Presses de Sciences Po, 1997.

—— *La nouvelle islamophobie*. Paris: La Découverte, 2003.

——'L'émotion comme "norme" d'une nouvelle politique laïque'. Quand Huntington s'invite chez les "Sages"', *Migrations Société*, Vol. 16, No. 96, November–December 2004, pp. 131–56.

——'Ethnicité républicaine versus République ethnique?', *Mouvements*, Vol. 38, March–April 2005, pp. 19–25.

Gellner, Ernest, *Nations and Nationalism*. Ithaca, NY: Cornell University Press, 1983.

Genestier, Philippe, 'Pour une intégration communautaire', *Esprit*, Vol. 163, No. 2 February 1991, 48–59.

——and Laville, Jean-Louis, 'Au-delà du mythe républicain. Intégration et socialisation', *Le Débat*, Vol. 82, November–December 1994, pp. 154–72.

Giddens, Anthony, *Modernity and Self-Identity*. Cambridge: Polity Press, 1991.

Giordan, Henri, *Démocratie culturelle et droit à la différence*. Paris: La Documentation Française, 1982.

Giraud, Michel, 'Portrait de l'intégration en Arlésienne', *Recherche Socialiste*, Vol. 23, June 2003, pp. 17–26.

Glazer, Nathan, and Moynihan, Daniel Patrick, *Beyond the Melting Pot. The Negroes, Puerto Ricans, Jews, Italians and Irish of New York City*. Cambridge, MA: M.I.T. Press and Harvard University Press, 1964.

Goffman, Erving, *Stigmate. Les usages sociaux des handicaps*. Paris: Minuit, 1975.

Goldberg Moses, Claire, *French Feminism in the Nineteenth Century*. New York: State University of New York Press, 1984.

Goldberg-Salinas, Anette, and Zaidman, Claude, 'Les rapports sociaux de sexe et la scolarité des enfants de parents migrants. Une étude exploratoire', *Recherches Féministes*, Vol. 11, No. 1, 1998, pp. 47–59.

Göle, Nilüfer, *Musulmanes et Modernes: voile et civilisation en Turquie*. Paris: La Découverte, 1993.

—— 'The Voluntary Adoption of Islamic Stigma Symbols', *Social Research*, Vol. 70, No. 3, Fall 2003, pp. 809–28.

Goodin, Robert, 'Folie Républicaine', *Annual Review of Political Science*, Vol. 6, 2003, pp. 55–76.

Gordon, Milton Myron, *Assimilation in American Life. The Role of Race, Religion and National Origins*. New York: Oxford University Press, 1964.

Granjon, Marie-Christine, 'Le regard en biais. Attitudes françaises et multiculturalisme américain', *Vingtième siècle*, Vol. 43, 1994, pp. 18–29.

Greenawalt, Kent, *Religious Convictions and Political Choice*. Oxford: Oxford University Press, 1988.

Gresh, Alain, *L'Islam, la République et le Monde*. Paris: Fayard, 2004.

—— 'Les faux-semblants de la commission Stasi', *Revue Politique Mensuelle*, January–February 2004, at: www.alencontre.org/page/page/print/france15.html.

Gros, Dominique, 'La séparation de l'Eglise et de l'école (1878–1886). Principes juridiques fondateurs de la laïcité scolaire', in Jean Baudouin and Philippe Portier (eds), *La laïcité, valeur d'aujourd'hui? Contestations et renégociations du modèle français*. Rennes: Presses Universitaires de Rennes, 2001, pp. 51–63.

Guénif Souilamas, Nacira, 'La fin de l'intégration, la preuve par les femmes', *Mouvements*, Vol. 29–30, May–August 2005, pp. 150–7.

—— *Des beurettes*. Paris: Grasset & Fasquelle, 2000.

—— (ed.), *La république mise à nu par son immigration*. Paris: La Fabrique Edition, 2006.

—— and Macé, Éric, *Les féministes et le garçon arabe*. Paris: editions de l'Aube, 2004.

Guillaumin, Colette, *L'idéologie raciste. Genèse et langage actuel*. Paris/La Haye: Mouton, 1972.

Guillebaud, Jean-Claude, *La trahison des Lumières. Enquête sur le désarroi contemporain*. Paris: Seuil, 1995.

Gutmann, Amy, 'Children, Education and Autonomy: A Liberal Argument', *Philosophy and Public Affairs*, Vol. 9, No. 4, Summer 1980, pp. 338–58.

Gutmann, Amy, *Democratic Education*. Princeton, NJ: Princeton University Press, 1987.

—— 'Civic Education and Social Diversity', *Ethics*, Vol. 105–3, April 1995, pp. 557–79.

—— 'Responding to Racial Injustice', in K. Anthony Appiah and Amy Gutmann (eds), *The Political Morality of Race*. Princeton, NJ: Princeton University Press, 1996.

—— *Identity in Democracy*. Princeton, NJ: Princeton University Press, 2003.

Gutting, Gary, *French Philosophy in the Twentieth Century*. Cambridge: Cambridge University Press, 1991.

Haakonssen Knud, 'Republicanism', in Philip Pettit and Robert Goodin (eds), *Handbook of Contemporary Political Philosophy*. Oxford: Blackwell, 1993, pp. 568–74.

Haarscher, Guy, *La laïcité*. Paris: Presses Universitaires de France, 1996.

Habermas, Jürgen, *The Theory of Communicative Action*. Boston: Beacon Press, 1987.

—— *The New Conservatism. Cultural Criticism and the Historians' Debate*. Boston, MA: M.I.T., 1989.

—— 'Citizenship and National Identity: Some Reflections on the Future of Europe', *Praxis International*, Vol. 12, No. 1, 1992, pp. 171–206. Reprinted in Ronald Beiner (ed.), *Theorizing Citizenship*. New York: State University of New York Press, 1999, pp. 255–68.

—— 'Three Normative Models of Democracy', *Constellations*, Vol. 1, No. 1, 1994, pp. 1–10.

—— 'Reconciliation Through the Public Use of Reason: Remarks on John Rawls's Political Liberalism', *Journal of Philosophy*, Vol. 92, 1995, pp. 109–31.

—— *Between Facts and Norms: Contributions to a Discourse Theory of Law and Democracy*. Boston, MA: M.I.T. Press, 1996.

—— *L'intégration républicaine. Essais de théorie politique*. Paris: Fayard, 1998. English version: *The Inclusion of the Other: Studies in Political Theory*. Cambridge: Polity Press, 1999.

—— 'De la tolérance religieuse aux droits culturels', *Cités*, Vol. 13, 2003, pp. 150–70.

—— 'Religion in the Public Sphere', *European Journal of Philosophy*, Vol. 14, No. 1, 2006, pp. 1–25.

Haddad, Yvonne Yazbeck (ed.), *Muslims in the West. From Sojourners to Citizens*. Oxford: Oxford University Press, 2002.

—— and Esposito John L. (eds), *Islam, Gender and Social Change*. New York and Oxford: Oxford University Press, 1998.

Hadjam, Mimouna, 'L'islamisme contre les femmes, partout dans le monde'. *Respublica, Journal de la Gauche Républicaine*, Vol. 2, September 2004, pp. 1–4.

Halimi, Gisèle, 'Laïcité: une loi pour la cohésion', 23 October 2003, at <http://www. Sisyphe.org/article.php3?id_article=730>.

Hamel, Christelle, 'De la racialisation du sexisme au sexisme identitaire', *Migrations Société*, Vol. 17, No. 99–100, May–August 2005, pp. 91–104.

Hargreaves, Alec G., *Immigration, 'Race' and Ethnicity in Contemporary France*. London: Routledge, 1995.

Harvard Law Review Note (n.a), 'Developments in the Law: Religion and the State', *Harvard Law Review*, Vol. 100, 1987, pp. 1606–781.

Haut Conseil à l'Intégration, *Pour un modèle français d'intégration*. Paris: Documentation Française, 1991.

—— *L'intégration à la française*. Paris: Union Générale d'Éditions, 1993 (Synthesis of the following reports: *Pour un modèle français d'intégration* [1991], *Conditions juridiques et culturelles de l'intégration* [1992], *Les étrangers et l'emploi* [1993], *La connaissance de l'immigration et de l'intégration* [1991, 1993]).

—— *Liens culturels et intégration*. Paris: Documentation Française, 1995.

—— *Affaiblissement du lien social, enfermement dans les particularismes et intégration dans la cité*. Paris: La Documentation Française, 1997.

—— *Lutte contre les discriminations: faire respecter le principe d'égalité*. Paris: La Documentation Française, 1998.

—— *L'Islam dans la République. Rapport au 1er ministre*. Paris: Documentation Française, 2001.

Hayat, Pierre, *La passion laïque de Ferdinand Buisson*. Paris: Kimé, 1999.

Hayward, Jack, 'Solidarity: The Social History of an Idea in Nineteenth-Century France', *International Review of Social History*, Vol. 4, 1959, pp. 261–84.

Hazareesingh, Sudhir, *Political Traditions in Modern France*. Oxford: Oxford University Press, 1994.

—— *From Subject to Citizen: The Second Empire and the Emergence of Modern French Democracy*. Princeton, NJ: Princeton University Press, 1998.

—— *Intellectual Founders of the Republic. Five Studies in Nineteenth-Century French Political Thought*. Oxford: Oxford University Press, 2001.

Helvig, Jean-Michel (ed.), *La laïcité dévoilée. Quinze années de débat en quarante Rebonds*. Paris: Libération and Éditions de l'Aube, 2004.

Hervieu-Léger, Danièle, *Le pèlerin et le converti*. Paris: Flammarion, 1999.

—— 'Le miroir de l'Islam en France', *Vingtième Siècle. Revue d'Histoire*, Vol. 66, April–June 2000, pp. 79–89.

Hervieu-Léger, Danièle, *La religion en miettes ou la question des sectes*. Paris: Calmann-Lévy, 2001.

Higonnet, Patrice, *Sister Republics. The Origins of French and American Republicanism*. Cambridge, MA: Harvard University Press, 1988.

Hill, Thomas E., *Autonomy and Self-Respect*. Cambridge: Cambridge University Press, 1991.

Hirschmann, Nancy J., 'Western Feminism, Eastern Veiling, and the Question of Free Agency', *Constellations*, Vol. 5, No. 3, 1998, pp. 345–68.

Honohan, Iseult, *Civic Republicanism*. London: Routledge, 2002.

Honneth, Alex, *The Struggle for Recognition. The Grammar of Social Conflicts*. Cambridge: Polity, 1995.

Hoodfar, Homa, 'The Veil in Their Minds and on our Heads: Veiling Practices and Muslim Women', in Elizabeth A. Castelli (ed.), *Woman, Gender, Religion: A Reader*. Basingstoke: Palgrave, 2001, pp. 420–40.

Hoodfar, Homa, 'More than Clothing: Veiling as Adaptive Strategy', in Sajida Sultana Alvi, Homa Hoodfar, and Sheila McDonough (eds), *The Muslim Veil in North America. Issues and Debates*. Toronto: Women's Press, 2003, pp. 3–40.

Horowitz, Donald, and Noiriel, Gérard (eds), *Immigrants in Two Democracies. French and American Experiences*. New York: New York University Press, 1992.

Horton, John, 'Liberalism and Multiculturalism. Once More Unto the Beach', in Bruce Haddock, and Peter Stuch (eds), *Multiculturalism, Identity and Rights*. London: Routledge, 2003, pp. 25–41.

Houle, François, 'La communauté partagée. Patriotisme et sociétés pluralistes', *Politique et Sociétés*, Vol. 20, No. 1, 2001, pp. 97–122.

Hulliung, Mark, *Citizens and Citoyens: Republicans and Liberals in America and France*. Cambridge, MA: Harvard University Press, 2002.

Humanist Philosophers' Group, *Religious Schools: The Case Against*. London: British Humanist Association, 2001.

Ihl, Olivier, *La fête républicaine*. Paris: Gallimard, 1996.

Ingram, Attracta, 'Constitutional Patriotism', *Philosophy and Social Criticism*, Vol. 22, No. 6, 1996, pp. 1–18.

Ireland, Patrick, *The Policy Challenge of Ethnic Diversity. Immigrant Politics in France and Switzerland*. Cambridge, MA: Harvard University Press, 1994.

Isaac, Jeffrey C., 'Republicanism vs. Liberalism? A Reconsideration', *History of Political Thought*, Vol. 9, No. 2, Summer 1988, pp. 349–77.

Ivison, Duncan, *The Self at Liberty: Political Argument and the Arts of Government*. Ithaca, NY: Cornell University Press, 1997.

Jackson, Julian, 'Historians and the Nation in Contemporary France', in Stefan Berger, Mark Donovan, and Kevin Passmore (eds), *Writing National Histories. Western Europe since 1800*. London: Routledge, 1999, pp. 239–51.

Jallon, Hughes, and Mounier, Pierre, *Les enragés de la République*. Paris: La Découverte, 1999.

Jambert, Christian, and Meddeb, Abdelwahab, 'Voile et dévoilement', *Esprit*, Vol. 305, June 2004, pp. 131–47.

James, Susan, 'The Good-Enough Citizen: Female Citizenship and Independence', in Gisela Bock and Susan James (eds) *Beyond Equality and Difference. Citizenship, Feminist Politics and Female Subjectivity*. London: Routledge, 1992, pp. 48–65.

Jami, Irène, Perriaux, Anne-Sophie, Sintomer, Yves, and Wasserman, Gilbert, 'Ne pas émanciper les filles de force', in Jean-Michel Helvig (ed.), *La laïcité dévoilée. Quinze années de débat en quarante Rebonds*. Paris: Libération and Éditions de l'Aube, 2004, pp. 59–62.

Jamous, Haroun, 'Les jeunes filles au foulard', *L'Homme et la Société*, Vol. 120, April–June 1997, pp. 17–23.

Jasser, Ghaïss, 'Le voile en deux maux', *Nouvelles Questions Féministes*, Vol. 16, No. 4, 1995, pp. 51–72.

Jaume, Lucien, *L'individu effacé, ou le paradoxe du libéralisme français*. Paris: Fayard, 1997.

Jelen, Christian, *Les casseurs de la République*. Paris: Plon, 1997.

—— 'La régression multiculturaliste', *Le Débat*, Vol. 97, 1997, pp. 137–43.

Jennings, Jeremy, 'Citizenship, Republicanism and Multiculturalism in Contemporary France', *British Journal of Political Science*, Vol. 30, 2000, pp. 575–98.

—— 'L'Egalité', 'La Liberté', 'L'Universalisme', in Vincent Duclert and Christophe Prochasson (eds), *Dictionnaire Critique de la République*. Paris: Flammarion, 2002, pp. 169–76, 216–23, 275–82.

—— and Honohan, Iseult (eds), *Republicanism in Theory and Practice*. London: Routledge, 2005.

Jones, Peter, 'Bearing the Consequences of Belief', *Journal of Political Philosophy*, Vol. 2, No. 1, 1994, 24–43.

—— 'Equality, Recognition and Difference', *Critical Review of International Social and Political Philosophy*, Vol. 9, No. 1, March 2006, pp. 23–46.

Joppke, Christian, 'The Retreat of Multiculturalism in the Liberal State: Theory and Policy', *The British Journal of Sociology*, Vol. 55, No. 2, 2004, pp. 237–57.

Julia, Dominique, 'La République, l'Eglise et l'immigration. La laïcité dans l'histoire', *Le Débat*, January–February 1990, Vol. 58, pp. 33–7.

Kacimi, Mohamed, 'Voile, une antique aliénation', in Jean-Michel Helvig (ed.), *La laïcité dévoilée. Quinze années de débat en quarante Rebonds*. Paris: Libération and Éditions de l'Aube, 2004, pp. 79–84.

Kahn, Pierre, 'La laïcité entre la philosophie et l'histoire', *Le Télémaque*, Vol. 14, 1998, pp. 31–9.

Kaltenbach, Jeanne-Hélène, and Tribalat, Michèle, *La République et l'Islam. Entre crainte et aveuglement*. Paris: Gallimard, 2002.

Kaltenbach, Pierre-Patrick, 'Entre Urnes et Croissant: électeurs ou musulmans?', *Liberté Politique*, Vol. 24, Winter 2003–4, pp. 119–24.

Kastoryano, Riva, *La France, l'Allemagne et leurs immigrés. Négocier l'identité*. Paris: Armand Colin, 1996.

—— 'Religion and Incorporation: Islam in France and Germany', *International Migrations Review*, Vol. 38, No. 3, Fall 2004, pp. 1234–55.

Kebabza, Horia, 'Au croisement de la "race" et du "genre": les "jeunes de quartiers"', *Migrations Société*, Vol. 17, No. 99–100, May–August 2005, pp. 77–89.

Kepel, Gilles, *La Revanche de Dieu*. Paris: Seuil, 1991.

—— *Allah in the West: Islamic Movements in America and Europe*. Cambridge: Polity, 1997.

—— *The War for Muslim Minds: Islam and the West*. Cambridge, MA and London: Belknap Press, 2004.

Keslassy, Éric, *De la discrimination positive*. Rosny-sous-bois: Bréal, 2004.

Kessler, David, 'Neutralité de l'enseignement public et liberté d'opinion des élèves (à propos du port des signes distinctifs d'appartenance religieuse dans les établissements scolaires'. Conclusions du Conseil d'État, 2 novembre 1992', *Revue Française de Droit Administratif*, Vol. 9, No. 1, January–February 1993, 112–8.

Kessler, David, 'Laïcité: du combat au droit', *Le Débat*, November–December 1993, Vol. 77, 95–101.

Khan, Shahnaz, 'Muslim Women: Negotiations in the Third Space', in Therese Saliba, Carolyn Allen, and Judith A. Howard (eds), *Gender, Politics and Islam*. Chicago: University of Chicago Press, 2002, pp. 305–36.

Khosrokhavar, Farhad, 'L'universel abstrait, le politique et la construction de l'islamisme comme forme d'altérité', in Michel Wieviorka (ed.), *Une société fragmentée? Le multiculturalisme en débat*. Paris: La Découverte, 1996, pp. 113–51.

——*L'islam des jeunes*. Paris: Flammarion, 1997.

——and Gaspard, Françoise, *Le foulard et la République*. Paris: La Découverte, 1995.

Kian-Thiébaut, Azadeh, 'L'Islam, les femmes et la citoyenneté', *Pouvoirs*, Vol. 104, 2003, pp. 71–84.

Kilani, Mondher, 'Equivoques de la religion et politiques de la laïcité en Europe: réflexions à partir de l'islam', *Archives de Sciences Sociales des Religions*, Vol. 121, January–March 2003, 69–86.

Kintzler, Catherine, *Condorcet: l'instruction publique et la formation du citoyen*. Paris: Éditions du Sycomore, 1984.

——'Aux fondements de la laïcité scolaire. Essai de décomposition raisonnée du concept de laïcité', *Les Temps Modernes*, Vol. 527, 1990, pp. 82–90.

——*La république en questions*. Paris: Minerve, 1996.

Kirszbaum, Thomas, 'La discrimination positive territoriale: de l'égalité des chances à la mixité urbaine', *Pouvoirs*, Vol. 111, 2004, pp. 101–18.

Kivisto, Peter, 'The Revival of Assimilation in Historical Perspective', in Peter Kivisto (ed.), *Incorporating Diversity: Rethinking Assimilation in a Multicultural Age*. Boulder: Paradigm Publisher, 2005, pp. 3–29.

Klausen, Jytte, *The Islamic Challenge. Politics and Religion in Western Europe*. Oxford: Oxford University Press, 2005.

Koubi, Geneviève, 'Le droit à la différence, un droit à l'indifférence?', *Revue de la Recherche Juridique. Droit Prospectif*, Vol. 2, No. 53, 1993, pp. 451–63.

——'La laïcité dans le texte de la Constitution', *Revue de Droit Public*, Vol. 5, September–October 1997, pp. 1301–22.

——'Des propositions de loi relatives à la laïcité dans les établissements publics scolaires', *Revue de la Recherche Juridique. Droit Prospectif*, Vol. 73, 1998, pp. 577–85.

——'Le juge administratif et la liberté de religion', *Revue française de droit administratif*, Vol. 19, November–December 2003, pp. 1055–61.

Kriegel, Blandine, *Philosophie de la République*. Paris: Plon, 1996.

Kristeva, Julia, *Nations Without Nationalism*. New York: Columbia University Press, 1993.

Kukathas, Chandran, 'Are There Any Cultural Rights?', *Political Theory*, Vol. 20, No. 1, 1992, pp. 105–39.

——'Cultural Toleration', in Will Kymlicka and Ian Shapiro (eds), *Ethnicity and Group Rights. Nomos*, Vol. 39. New York: New York University Press, 1997, pp. 69–104.

Kwok Pui-Lan 'Unbinding our Feet: Saving Brown Women and Feminist Religious Discourse', in Laura E. Donaldson and Kwok Pui-lan (eds), *Postcolonialism, Feminism and Religious Discourse*. London and New York: Routledge, 2002, pp. 62–81.

Kymlicka, Will, 'Liberal Individualism and Liberal Neutrality', *Ethics*, Vol. 99, July 1989, pp. 883–905.

——*Multicultural Citizenship*. Oxford: Oxford University Press, 1995.

——*Politics in the Vernacular. Nationalism, Multiculturalism, and Citizenship*. Oxford: Oxford University Press, 2001.

Laacher, Smaïn (ed.), *Questions de Nationalité. Histoire et enjeux d'un code*. Paris: Harmattan, 1987.

——'L'Islam des nouveaux Musulmans en terre d'immigration', *Mouvements*, Vol. 38, March–April 2005, pp. 50–1.

Laborde, Cécile, *Islam et culture traditionnelle en Afrique. La confrérie layenne et les Lébous du Sénégal*. Bordeaux: Centre National pour la Recherche Scientifique-CEAN, 1995.

——*Pluralist Thought and the State in Britain and France (1900–1925)*. Basingstoke: Macmillan, 2000.

——'The Concept of the State in British and French Political Thought', *Political Studies*, Vol. 48, 2000, pp. 540–57.

——'On Republican Toleration', *Constellations. An International Journal of Critical and Democratic Theory*, Vol. 9, July 2002, pp. 167–83. Reprinted as 'Toleration and Laïcité', in Catriona McKinnon, and Dario Castiglione (eds), *The Cultures of Toleration in Diverse Societies. Reasonable Tolerance*. Manchester: Manchester University Press, 2003, pp. 161–77.

——'The Culture(s) of the Republic'. Nationalism and Republicanism in Contemporary French Republican Thought', *Political Theory*, Vol. 29, No. 5, 2001, pp. 716–35.

——'From Constitutional to Civic Patriotism', *British Journal of Political Science*, Vol. 32, 2002, pp. 591–612.

——'La citoyenneté', in Vincent Duclert, and Christophe Prochasson (eds), *Dictionnaire Critique de la République*. Paris: Flammarion, 2002, pp. 116–23.

——(ed.), 'Rawls in Europe', *European Journal of Political Theory*, Vol. 1, No. 2, 2002.

——'Republican Citizenship and the Crisis of Integration in France', in Richard Bellamy, Dario Castiglione, and Emilio Santoro (eds), *Lineages of Citizenship*. Basingstoke: Palgrave, 2004, pp. 46–72.

——'Secular Philosophy and Muslim Headscarves in Schools', *Journal of Political Philosophy*, Vol. 13, No. 3, 2005, pp. 305–29.

——'Female Autonomy, Education and the *Hijab*', *Critical Review of International Social and Political Philosophy*, Vol. 9, No. 3, September 2006, pp. 351–77.

——and Maynor, John (eds), *Republicanism and Political Theory*. Oxford: Blackwell, 2008.

Laclau, Ernesto, *La guerre des identités. Grammaire de l'émancipation*. Paris: La Découverte, 2000.

Lacorne, Denis, *La crise de l'identité américaine, du melting pot au multiculturalisme*. Paris: Fayard, 1997.

—— 'Pour un multiculturalisme modéré', *Le Débat*, Vol. 97, 1997, pp. 158–67.

Lacroix, Justine, 'Les Nationaux-Républicains de gauche et la construction européenne', *Le Banquet*, Vol. 15, November 2000, 157–68.

—— *L'Europe en procès. Quel patriotisme au-delà des nationalismes?* Paris: Cerf, 2004.

Laden, Anthony Simon, *Reasonably Radical: Deliberative Liberalism and the Politics of Identity*. Ithaca, NY: Cornell University Press, 2001.

Lalouette, Jacqueline, *La République anti-cléricale. XIXème-XXème siècles*. Paris: Seuil 2002.

Lambert, Thierry *et al.* (ed.) *Egalité ou Equité. Antagonisme ou complémentarité? Actes du colloque CERAP Paris 13*. Paris: Economica, 1999.

Lamchichi, Abderrahim, 'Les musulmans de France à l'épreuve de la laïcité', *Cahiers de l'Orient*, Vol. 71, 2003, pp. 35–53.

Lamine, Anne-Sophie, *La cohabitation des dieux. Pluralité religieuse et laïcité*. Paris: Presses Universitaires de France, 2004.

Lapeyronnie, Didier, *L'individu et les minorités. La France et la Grande-Bretagne face à leurs immigrés*. Paris: Presses Universitaires de France, 1993.

—— 'Les deux figures de l'immigré', in Michel Wieviorka (ed.), *Une société fragmentée. Le multiculturalisme en débat*. Paris: La Découverte, 1996, pp. 251–65.

—— 'De l'altérité à la différence. L'identité, facteur d'intégration ou de repli?', in Philippe Dewitte (ed.), *Immigration et Intégration. L'état des savoirs*. Paris: La Découverte, 1999, pp. 252–59.

Larabi Hendaz, Louisa, *Le voile humilié, ou les auditions manquées de la commission Stasi. Avec le témoignage de femmes musulmanes*. Paris: Éditions Marjane, 2005.

Latraverse, Sophie, 'Le droit français en matière de discrimination', at <http:// iom.fi/files/legal_training/french/french_anti-discrimination_handbook_ chap4.pdf> (last accessed 31 July 2007).

Laurence, Jonathan (ed.), *Le Conseil français du culte musulman*. Special Issue of *French Politics, Culture and Society*, Vol. 23, No. 1, Spring 2005.

—— and Veisse, Justin, *Integrating Islam. Political and Religious Challenges in Contemporary France*. Washington, DC: Brookings Institution Press, 2006.

Laval-Reviglio, Marie-Claire, 'Égalité et éducation: les discriminations justifiées, l'exemple de Sciences-Po', in Claude Courvoisier, and Patrick Charlot (eds), *Actualité Politique et Juridique de l'Égalité*. Dijon: Éditions Universitaires de Dijon, 2003, pp. 115–31.

Lazar, Marc, 'La République à l'épreuve du social', in Marc Sadoun (ed.), *La démocratie en France*. Paris: Gallimard, 2000, Vol. 2, pp. 309–406.

Lægaard, Sune, 'Galeotti on Recognition as Inclusion', *Critical Review of International Social and Political Philosophy*, Vol. II, No. 3, September 2008.

Le Bras, Hervé, *Le Démon des origines: démographie et extrême droite*. Paris: Aube, 1998.

—— 'La confusion des origines', *Les Temps Modernes*, Vol. 603, March–April 1999, pp. 228–41.

Leca, Jean, 'Questions sur la citoyenneté', *Projet*, Vols. 171–2, January–February 1983, pp. 113–25.

—— 'Individualisme et citoyenneté', in Pierre Birnbaum, and Jean Leca (eds), *Sur l'individualisme*. Paris: Presses de la Fondation Nationale des Sciences Politiques, 1986, 2nd ed., 1991, pp. 185–98.

Leclerc, Arnauld, 'La contribution de la théorie procédurale de John Rawls à la redéfinition de la laïcité', in Jean Baudouin, and Philippe Portier (eds), *La laïcité, valeur d'aujourd'hui? Contestations et renégociations du modèle français*. Rennes: Presses Universitaires de Rennes, 2001, pp. 229–46.

Lemoyne de Forges, Jean-Michel, 'Laïcité et liberté religieuse en France' in Joël-Benoît d'Onorio (ed.), *La liberté religieuse dans le monde. Analyse doctrinale et politique*. Paris: Éditions Universitaires, 1991, pp. 149–70.

Le Pourhier, Anne-Marie, 'Pour une analyse critique de la discrimination positive', *Le Débat*, Vol. 114, March–April 2001, pp. 166–77.

Lequin, Yves, *Histoire de la laïcité*. Besancon: CRDP de Franche-Comté, 1994.

Leruth, Michael F., 'The Neo-Republican Discourse on French National Identity', *French Politics and Society*, Vol. 16, No. 4, 1998, pp. 46–61.

Leveau, Rémy, and Zghal, Abdelkader, 'Islam et laïcité en France', *Etudes*, Vol. 370, No. 5 May 1989, pp. 679–88.

Levinson, Meira, 'Liberalism versus Democracy? Schooling Private Citizens in the Public Square', *British Journal of Political Science*, Vol. 27, 1997, pp. 333–60.

—— *The Demands of Liberal Education*. Oxford: Oxford University Press, 1999.

Levy, Jacob T., *The Multiculturalism of Fear*. Oxford: Oxford University Press, 2000.

Lieberman, Robert C., 'A Tale of Two Countries. The Politics of Color-Blindness in France and the United States'. *French Politics, Culture and Society*, Vol. 19, No. 3, Fall 2001, pp. 32–59.

Lilla, Mark, 'The Legitimacy of the Liberal Age', in Mark Lilla (ed.), *New French Thought: Political Philosophy*. Princeton, NJ: Princeton University Press, 1994, pp. 3–34.

Lindenberg, Daniel, *Le rappel à l'ordre. Enquête sur les nouveaux réactionnaires*. Paris: Seuil, 2002.

Lindgaard, Jade, 'L'appel des indigènes de la République: Contestation ou consécration du dogme républicain? Etude de cas', in Vincent Bourdeau, Roberto Merril (eds), *La république et ses démons. Essais de républicanisme appliqué*. Paris: Éditions Eres, 2007, pp. 123–35.

Lipovestsky, Gilles, *L'ère du vide. Essai sur l'individualisme contemporain*. Paris: Gallimard, 1983.

Lloyd, Catherine, *Discourses of Antiracism in France*. Aldershot: Ashgate, 1998.

Lochak, Danièle, 'Les minorités et le droit public français: du refus des différences à la gestion des différences', in Alain Ferret, and Gérard Soulier, *Les minorités et leurs droits depuis 1789*, Paris: Harmattan, 1989, pp. 111–84.

—— 'Discriminations against Foreigners under French Law', in Donald Horowitz, and Gérard Noiriel (eds), *Immigrants in Two Democracies. French and*

American Experiences. New York: New York University Press, 1992, pp. 391–410.

—— 'Usages et mésusages d'une notion polémique. La référence à l'identité nationale dans le débat sur la réforme du Code de la Nationalité, 1985–1993', in Jacques Chevalier (ed.), *L'identité politique. Sciences Humaines*, No. 15, Special Issue, December 1996–January 1997, pp. 306–23.

—— (ed.), *La lutte contre les discriminations. Entre théorie et pratique, entre droit et politique*. Actes du séminaire du 21 juin 2000. Paris: CREDOF, 2001.

Lorcerie, Françoise, 'L'école pourrait être un laboratoire de civilité', *Hommes et Migrations*, Vol. 1129–1130, February–March 1990, pp. 41–6.

—— 'Les sciences sociales au service de l'identité nationale', in D.C. Martin (ed.), *Cartes d'identité. Comment dit-on "nous" en politique?* Paris: Presses de la Fondation Nationale des Sciences Politiques, 1994, pp. 245–81.

—— 'Dissonance normative. A propos de la crise de la laïcité en France', *Printemps*, Vol. 2, 1996, pp. 7–20.

—— 'Laïcité 1996. La République a l'école de l'immigration?', *Revue Française de Pédagogie*, Vol. 117, October–December, 1996, pp. 53–86.

—— 'Les habits neufs de l'assimilation en France', in Ida Simon-Barouch, and Véronique de Rudder (eds), *Migrations Internationales et Relations Interethniques*. Paris: Harmattan, 1997, pp. 297–344.

—— 'Penser l'intégration nationale après l'Etat-nation', *Migrations Société*, Vol. 15, No. 86, March–April 2003, pp. 43–52.

—— (ed.), *L'école et le défi ethnique. Education et intégration*. Paris: Institut de la Recherche Pédagogique/ESF, 2003.

—— (ed.), *La politisation du voile en France, en Europe et dans le monde arabe*. Paris: Harmattan, 2005.

Luca, Nathalie, 'Quelles politiques face aux sectes? La singularité francaise', *Critique Internationale*, Vol. 17, October 2002, pp. 105–25.

Lyotard, Jean-François, *La Condition post-moderne*. Paris: Éditions de Minuit, 1979.

Macedo, Stephen, 'Liberal Civic Education and Religious Fundamentalism: The Case of God v. John Rawls?', *Ethics*, Vol. 105, April 1995, pp. 468–96.

—— *Diversity and distrust. Civic Education in a Multicultural Democracy*. Cambridge, MA: Harvard University Press, 2000.

Machelon, Jean-Pierre, *Les relations des cultes avec les pouvoirs publics*. Paris: La Documentation Française, 2006.

Macherey, Pierre, 'Philosophies laïques', *Mots*, Vol. 27, 1991, pp. 5–21.

MacMullen, Ian, *Faith in Schools? Autonomy, Citizenship, and Religious Education in the Liberal State*. Princeton, NJ: Princeton University Press, 2007.

Madeley, John T.S., 'European Liberal Democracy and the Principle of State Religious Neutrality', *West European Politics*, Vol. 26, No. 1, 2003, pp. 1–22.

Madiot, Yves, 'Le juge et la laïcité', *Pouvoirs*, Vol. 75, 1995, pp. 73–84.

Mahajan, Gurpreet, 'Can Intra-Group Equality Co-exit with Cultural Diversity? Re-examining Multicultural Frameworks of Accommodation', in

Avigail Eisenberg, and Jeff Spinner-Halev (eds), *Minorities within Minorities*. Cambridge: Cambridge University Press, 2005, pp. 90–112.

Malaurie, Philippe, 'Laïcité, voile islamique et réforme législative. Loi No. 2004–228 du 15 mars 1994', *JCP-La Semaine Juridique Edition Générale*, Vol. 14, 31 March 2004, pp. 607–10.

Manuel de Queiroz, J., 'Pédagogie et pédagogues contre le savoir', in Agnès Van Zanten (ed.), *L'école. L'état des savoirs*. Paris: La Découverte, 2000, pp. 374–80.

March, Andrew F., 'Liberal Citizenship and the Search for an Overlapping Consensus: The Case of Muslim Minorities', *Philosophy and Public Affairs*, Vol. 34, No. 4, 2006, 373–421.

Marie, Claude-Valentin, 'Enjeux actuels de la lutte contre les discriminations en France', in Daniel Borrillo (ed.), *Lutter contre les discriminations*. Paris: La Découverte, 2003, 125–38.

Margalit, Avishai, *The Decent Society*. Cambridge, MA: Harvard University Press, 1996.

Markell, Patchen, *Bound by Recognition*. Princeton, NJ: Princeton University Press, 2003.

Martucelli, Danilo, 'Retour sur la domination', *Recherches Sociologiques*, Vol. 34, 2003–2, pp. 3–11.

——*Dominations Ordinaires. Explorations de la condition moderne*. Paris: Balland, 2001.

Marx, Karl, 'The Jewish Question', in David McLellan, *Karl Marx: Selected Writings*. Oxford: Oxford University Press, 1977, pp. 51–7.

——(with Friedrich Engels), *The German Ideology*. Amherst, NY: Prometheus Books, 1998.

Mason, Andrew, 'Political Community, Liberal-Nationalism, and the Ethics of Assimilation', *Ethics*, Vol. 109, January 1999, pp. 261–86.

——'Just Constraints', *British Journal of Political Science*, Vol. 34, 2004, pp. 251–68.

Massignon, Bérengère, 'Laïcité et gestion de la diversité religieuse à l'école publique en France', *Social Compass*, Vol. 47, No. 3, 2000, pp. 353–66.

Maurin, Eric, *Le ghetto français. Enquête sur le séparatisme social*. Paris: Seuil, 2004.

——'La ségrégation urbaine, son intensité et ses causes', in Serge Paugam (ed.), *Repenser la solidarité. L'apport des sciences sociales*. Paris: Presses Universitaires de France, 2007, pp. 621–34.

Maynor, John, *Republicanism in the Modern World*. Cambridge: Polity, 2003.

——'Without Regret: The Comprehensive Nature of Non-Domination', *Politics*, Vol. 22, 2002, pp. 51–8.

Mazet, Pierre, 'La construction contemporaine de la laïcité par le juge et la doctrine', in Jean Baudouin, and Philippe Portier (eds), *La laïcité, valeur d'aujourd'hui? Contestations et renégociations du modèle français*. Rennes: Presses Universitaires de Rennes, 2001, pp. 263–83.

McBride, Cillian, 'Deliberative Democracy and the Politics of Recognition', *Political Studies*, Vol. 53, No. 3, 2005, pp. 497–515.

McCarthy, Thomas, 'Political Philosophy and Racial Injustice: From Normative to Critical Theory', in Seyla Benhabib, and Nancy Fraser (eds), *Pragmatism, Critique, Judgement*. Boston: MIT, 2004, pp. 154–66.

McConnell, Michael 'Believers as Equal Citizens', in Nancy L. Rosemblum (ed.), *Obligations of Citizenship and Demands of Faith. Religious Accommodation in Pluralist Democracies*. Princeton, NJ: Princeton University Press, 2000, pp. 90–110.

McGoldrick, Dominic, *Human Rights and Religion: The Islamic Headscarf Debate in Europe*. Oxford and Portland: Hart, 2006.

McKinnon, Catriona, *Liberalism and the Defence of Political Constructivism*. New York: Palgrave, 2002.

—— 'Democracy, Equality and Toleration', *Journal of Ethics*, Vol. 11, No. 2, June 2007, pp. 125–46.

Meehan, Elizabeth, *Citizenship and the European Community*. London: Sage, 1993.

Melliès, Chantal, Deramchi, Salima, and Dubois, Bernice, 'La pointe de l'iceberg intégriste visible sur la scène altermondialiste. La question du voile', 22 October 2003, at <http://www.sisyphe.org/article.php3?id_article=711>.

Mernissi, Fatima, *Beyond the Veil. Male-Female Dynamics in a Modern Muslim Society*. Bloomington: Indiana University Press, Revised edition, 1987.

—— *Women and Islam. An Historical and Theological Enquiry*. Oxford: Blackwell, 1991.

—— *The Veil and the Male Elite. A Feminist Interpretation of Women's Rights in Islam*. Oxford: Blackwell, 1991.

Messner, Francis, 'Laïcité imaginée et laïcité juridique', *Le Débat*, Vol. 77, 1993, pp. 88–94.

—— 'La législation cultuelle des pays de l'Union européenne face aux groupes sectaires', in Françoise Champion et Martine Cohen (eds), *Sectes et démocratie*. Paris: Seuil, 1999, pp. 331–58.

Mesure, Sylvie, and Renaut, Alain, *La guerre des dieux. Essai sur la querelle des valeurs*. Paris: Grasset, 1996.

—— and Renaut, Alain, *Alter Ego. Les paradoxes de l'identité démocratique*. Paris: Flammarion, 1999.

Meuret, Denis, 'Intérêt, justice, laïcité', *Le Télémaque*, Vol. 14, 1998, pp. 67–77.

Miet, Jacques, 'Le droit local des cultes en Alsace-Moselle', *Les Cahiers de la Fonction Publique*, Vol. 13, April 2004, pp. 14–16.

Mill, John Stuart, *The Subjection of Women*. London: Dent and Everyman, 1985.

—— *On Liberty*. Cambridge: Cambridge University Press, 1989.

Miller, David, 'Citizenship and Pluralism', *Political Studies*, Vol. 43, 1995, 432–50.

—— 'Complex Equality', in David Miller and Michael Walzer (eds), *Pluralism, Justice and Equality*. Oxford: Oxford University Press, 1995, pp. 197–225.

—— *On Nationality*. Oxford: Oxford University Press, 1995.

—— *Citizenship and National Identity*. Cambridge: Polity Press, 2000.

—— *Principles of Social Justice*. Cambridge, MA: Harvard University Press, 2001.

——'Republican Citizenship, Nationality and Europe', in Cécile Laborde and John Maynor (eds), *Republicanism and Political Theory*. Oxford: Blackwell, 2007.

Milner, Jean-Claude, *De l'école*. Paris: Seuil, 1984.

Minc, Alain (ed.), *La France de l'an 2000*. Paris: Odile Jacob and La Documentation Française, 1994.

Modood, Tariq, 'Establishment, Multiculturalism and British Citizenship', *The Political Quarterly*, Vol. 65, No. 1, 1994, pp. 53–73.

——(ed.), *Church, State and Religious Minorities*. London: Policy Studies Institute, 1997.

——'Anti-Essentialism, Multiculturalism and the "Recognition" of Religious Groups', *Journal of Political Philosophy*, Vol. 6, No. 4, 1998, pp. 378–99.

——'La place des musulmans dans le multiculturalisme laïc en Grande-Bretagne', *Social Compass*, Vol. 47, No. 1, 2000, pp. 41–55.

——*Multiculturalism, Muslims and the British State*. London: British Association for the Study of Religion, 2003.

——Triandafyllidou, Anna, and Zapata-Barrero, Ricard, *Multiculturalism, Muslims and Citizenship. A European Approach*. London: Routledge, 2006.

Moghadam Valentine M., *Modernizing Women. Gender and Social Change in the Middle East*. London and Boulder, CO: Lynne Rienner, 2003.

——'Islamic Feminism and its Discontents: Toward a Resolution of the Debate', in Therese Saliba, Carolyn Allen, and Judith A. Howard (eds), *Gender, Politics and Islam*. Chicago: University of Chicago Press, 2002, 15–51.

Molokotos Liederman, Lina, 'Religious Diversity in Schools: The Muslim Headscarf Controversy and Beyond', *Social Compass*, Vol. 47, No. 3, 2000, pp. 367–81.

Monsma, Stephen V., and Soper, Christopher, *The Challenge of Pluralism. Church and State in Five Democracies*. Lanham, MD: Rowman and Littlefield, 1997.

Moore, Damian, *Ethnicité et politique de la ville en France et en Grande-Bretagne*. Paris: Harmattan, 2001.

Morin, Edgar, 'Le trou noir de la laïcité', *Le Débat*, Vol. 58, January–February 1990, pp. 38–41.

Moruzzi, Norma Claire, 'A Problem with Headscarves: Contemporary Complexities of Political and Social Identity', *Political Theory*, Vol. 22, No. 4, 1994, pp. 653–72.

Mouffe, Chantal (ed.), *Dimensions of Radical Democracy*. London: Verso Press, 1992.

Mucchielli, Laurent, and Le Goaziou, Véronique, *Quand les banlieues brûlent... Retour sur les émeutes de Novembre 2005*. Paris: La Découverte, 2006.

Muglioni, Jacques, 'Philosophie, école, même combat?', in Charles Coutel (ed.), *La République et l'école. Une anthologie*. Paris: Presses Pocket, 1991, pp. 74–80.

——*L'Ecole ou le loisir de penser*. Paris: Éditions du CNDP, 1993.

Müller, Jan-Werner, *Another Country. German Intellectuals, Unification and National Identity*. New Haven and London: Yale University Press, 2000.

Murphy, Liam B., *Moral Demands in Nonideal Theory*. Oxford: Oxford University Press, 2000.

Naïr, Sami, *Le regard des vainqueurs: les enjeux français de l'immigration*. Paris: Grasset, 1992.

Neidleman, Jason, *The General Will is Citizenship. Inquiries into French Political Thought*. Lanham, MD: Rowman & Littlefield, 2001.

Nelson, Alan, 'Explanation and Justification in Political Philosophy', *Ethics*, Vol. 97, No. 1, October, 1986, pp. 154–76.

Nicolet, Claude, *L'idée républicaine en France (1789–1924). Essai d'histoire critique*. Paris: Gallimard, 1982.

Nicolet, *Histoire, Nation, République*. Paris: Odile Jacob, 2000.

Nieuwenhuis, Aernout, 'European Court of Human Rights: State and Religion, Schools and Scarves. An Analysis of the Margin of Appreciation as Used in the Case of Leyla Sahin v. Turkey, Decision of 29 June 2004, Application Number 44774/98, *European Constitutional Law Review*, Vol. 1, 2005, pp. 495–510.

Nique, Christian, and Lelièvre, Claude, *La République n'éduquera plus*. Paris: Plon, 1993.

Noiriel, Gérard, *Le creuset français. Histoire de l'immigration, XIX-XXème siècles*. Paris: Seuil, 1988.

——*La Tyrannie du national. Le droit d'asile en Europe (1793–1993)*. Paris: Calmann-Lévy, 1991.

——*Population, Immigration et identité nationale en France, XIX-XXè siècle*. Paris: Hachette, 1992.

——*État, nation et immigration. Vers une histoire du pouvoir*. Paris: Belin, 2001.

Nora, Pierre, *Les lieux de mémoire*, Vol. 1: *La République*. Vol. 2. *La Nation* (1986), Vol. 3. *Les France* (1992). Paris: Gallimard, 1984.

Nordmann, Charlotte (ed.), *Le foulard islamique en questions*. Paris: Éditions Amsterdam, 2004.

Nussbaum, Martha, 'Adaptive Preferences and Women's Options', *Economics and Philosophy*, Vol. 17, 2001, pp. 67–88.

Ognier, Pierre, 'Ancienne ou nouvelle laïcité? Après dix ans de débats', *Esprit*, Vol. 1904, April–September 1993, pp. 202–21.

Okin, Susan Moller, with respondents, *Is Multiculturalism Bad for Women?* Princeton, NJ: Princeton University Press, 1999.

——'"Mistress of Their Own Destiny". Group rights, Gender and Realistic Rights of Exit', *Ethics*, Vol. 112, No. 2, 2002, pp. 205–30.

——'Multiculturalism and Feminism: No Simple Question, No Simple Answers', in Avigail Eisenberg and Jeff Spinner-Halev (eds), *Minorities within Minorities*. Cambridge: Cambridge University Press, 2005, pp. 67–89.

Oldfield, Adrian, *Citizenship and Community: Civic Republicanism and the Modern World*. London: Routledge, 1990.

O'Neill, Onora, *Towards Justice and Virtue: A Constructive Account of Practical Reasoning*. Cambridge: Cambridge University Press, 1996.

Ozouf, Mona, *L'école de la France*. Paris: Gallimard, 1984.

Ozouf, Jacques, and Ozouf, Mona, *La République des Instituteurs*. Paris: Gallimard, 1992.

Palau, Yves, 'La Ligue de l'enseignement depuis les années 1980: nouvelle réflexion sur la laïcité et position dans l'espace politique', in Jean Baudouin and Philippe Portier (eds), *La laïcité, valeur d'aujourd'hui? Contestations et renégociations du modèle français*. Rennes: Presses Universitaires de Rennes, 2001, pp. 205–19.

Palomares, Elise, 'L'ethnicisation des politiques locales et sociales', *Contretemps*, Vol. 13, 2005, pp. 92–102.

Parekh, Bhikhu, *Rethinking Multiculturalism*. Basingstoke: Macmillan, 2000.

—— 'Hate Speech', *Public Policy Research*, Vol. 12, No. 4, December 2005– February 2006, pp. 213–23.

Patten, Alan, 'Liberal Neutrality and Language Policy', *Philosophy and Public Affairs*, Vol. 31, No. 4, 2003, pp. 356–86.

Paugam, Serge (ed.), *Repenser la solidarité. L'apport des sciences sociales*. Paris: Presses Universitaires de France, 2007.

Payet, Jean-Paul, 'L'ethnicité et la citoyenneté dans l'espace scolaire', in Agnès Van Zanten (ed.), *L'école. L'état des savoirs*. Paris: La Découverte, 2000, pp. 389–97.

Pellissier, Gilles, *Le principe d'égalité en droit public*. Paris: LGDJ, 1996.

Pena-Ruiz, Henri, *Dieu et Marianne. Philosophie de la laïcité*. Paris: Presses Universitaires de France, 1999.

—— *La laïcité pour l'égalité*. Paris: Mille et Une Nuits, 2001.

—— *Qu'est ce que la laïcité?* Paris: Gallimard, 2003.

—— *La laïcité. Textes choisis et présentés*. Paris: Flammarion, 2003.

Pettit, Philip, 'Negative Liberty, Liberal and Republican', *European Journal of Philosophy*, Vol. 1, No. 1, 1993, pp. 15–38.

—— 'Freedom as Antipower', *Ethics*, Vol. 106, No. 3, 1996, pp. 576–604.

—— *Republicanism: A Theory of Freedom and Government*. Oxford: Oxford University Press, 1997.

—— 'Republican Political Theory', in Andrew Vincent (ed.), *Political Theory: Tradition, Diversity and Ideology*. Cambridge: Cambridge University Press, 1997, pp. 112–32.

—— 'Republican Freedom and Contestatory Democratization', in Ian Shapiro and Casiano Hacker-Cordon (eds), *Democracy's Value*. Cambridge: Cambridge University Press, 1999, pp. 63–90.

—— 'Democracy, Electoral and Contestatory', *Nomos*, Vol. 42, New York: New York University Press, 2000, pp. 105–44.

—— *A Theory of Freedom: From the Psychology to the Politics of Agency*. Cambridge: Polity Press, 2001.

—— 'Deliberative Democracy, the Discursive Dilemma, and Republican Theory', in James Fishkin, and Peter Laslett (eds), *Philosophy, Politics and Society*, Vol. 7. New York: Cambridge University Press, 2003, pp. 138–62.

Pettit, Philip, 'The Domination Complaint', in Melissa S. Williams and Stephen Macedo (eds), *Political Exclusion and Domination. Nomos*, Vol. 46. New York: New York University Press, 2005, pp. 87–117.

Phillips, Anne, 'In Defense of Secularism', in Tariq Modood (ed.), *Church, State and Religious Minorities*. London: Policy Studies Institute, 1997, pp. 23–8.

——'Feminism and Republicanism: Is this a Plausible Alliance?', *Journal of Political Philosophy*, Vol. 8, No. 2, 2000, pp. 279–93.

——'"Really" Equal: Opportunities and Autonomy', *Journal of Political Philosophy*, Vol. 14, No. 1, 2006, 18–32.

——*Multiculturalism without Culture*. Princeton, NJ: Princeton University Press, 2007.

Pierré-Caps, Stéphane, 'Les "nouveaux cultes" et le droit public', *Revue de Droit Public*, Vol. 4, 1990, pp. 1073–119.

Plenel, Edwy, *La République Inachevée. L'État et l'école en France*. Paris: Stock, 1997.

Pocock, John Greville Agard, *The Machiavellian Moment. Florentine Political Thought and the Atlantic Republican Tradition*. Princeton, NJ: Princeton University Press, 1975.

Policar, Alain, 'Libéraux et communautariens: un antagonisme irréductible?', *Les Temps Modernes*, Vol. 603, March–April 1999, pp. 204–27.

Poulat, Emile, *Liberté-Laïcité. La guerre des deux France et le principe de modernité*. Paris: Cerf/Cujas, 1987.

——*Notre laïcité publique. 'La France est une République laïque'*. Paris: Berg, 2003.

Poulter, Sebastian, 'Muslim Headscarves in School: Contrasting Legal Approaches in England and France', *Oxford Journal of Legal Studies*, Vol. 17, No. 1, 1997, pp. 43–74.

Poutignat, Philippe, and Streiff-Fenart, Jocelyne, *Théories de l'ethnicité*. Paris: Presses Universitaires de France, 1995.

Pratt Ewing, Katherine, 'Legislating Religious Freedom: Muslim Challenges to the Relationship between "Church" and "State" in Germany and France', *Daedalus*, Vol. 129, No. 4, Fall 2000, pp. 31–54.

Prost, Antoine, 'La République et l'école', *Projet*, Vol. 213, 1988, pp. 85–95.

Quong, Jonathan, 'Cultural Exemptions, Expensive Tastes and Equal Opportunities', *Journal of Applied Philosophy*, Vol. 23, No. 1, 2006, pp. 53–71.

Ramadan, Tariq, *Les Musulmans dans la laïcité. Responsabilités et droits des musulmans dans les sociétés occidentales*. Lyon: Tawid, 1994.

——*Les musulmans d'Occident et l'avenir de l'Islam*. Paris: Actes Sud, 2003.

Rancière, Jacques. *La mésentente*. Paris: Galilée, 1995.

——*Aux bords du politique*. Paris: La Fabrique Éditions, 1998.

Raulet, Gérard, *Apologie de la Citoyenneté*. Paris: Cerf, 1999.

——'L'exotisme de l'intérieur. Tentative d'état des lieux épistémologique', *L'Homme et la Société*, Vol. 149, July–September 2003, pp. 75–103.

Rawls, John, *A Theory of Justice*. Cambridge, MA: Harvard University Press, 1971 (1973 edition).

—— 'The Idea of Public Reason Re-Visited', *The University of Chicago Law Review* Vol. 64, No. 3, 1997, pp. 765–807.

—— *Political Liberalism.* New York: Columbia University Press, 1993.

Reichenbach, Hans, *Experience and Prediction.* Chicago, IL: University of Chicago Press, 1961.

Rémond, René. 'La laïcité n'est plus ce qu'elle était', *Etudes*, Vol. 120, April 1984, 439–48.

Renan, Ernest, 'Qu'est ce qu'une nation?' (extracts in English), in John Hutchinson and Anthony Smith (eds), *Nationalism.* Oxford: Oxford University Press, 1994, pp. 17–18.

Renard, Michel, 'Lois de l'islam, lois de la République: l'impossible conciliation', in Charles Zarka (ed.), *L'Islam en France.* Special issue of *Cités*, March 2004, pp. 387–95.

Renault, Emmanuel, *Mépris social. Éthique et politique de la reconnaissance.* Bègles: Éditions du Passant, 2000.

—— and Sintomer, Yves (eds), *Où en est la théorie critique?* Paris: La Découverte, 2003.

Renaut, Alain, *L'ère de l'individu.* Paris: Gallimard, 1989.

—— 'Les discussions républicaines du républicanisme moderne', in Alain Renaut (ed.), *Histoire de la philosophie politique.* Vol. 4, Paris: Calmann-Lévy, 1999, pp. 317–59.

Renaut, Alain and Mesure Sylvie, *Alter Ego. Les paradoxes de l'identité démocratique.* Paris: Aubier, 1999.

—— *Qu'est ce qu'une politique juste? Essai sur la question du meilleur régime.* Paris: Grasset, 2004.

—— *Qu'est ce qu'un peuple libre? Libéralisme ou républicanisme.* Paris: Grasset, 2005.

Richardson, Henry S. *Democratic Autonomy: Public Reasoning about the Ends of Policy.* Oxford: Oxford University Press, 2002.

Ricoeur, Paul, *Soi-même comme un autre.* Paris: Seuil, 1990.

—— *Temps et récit.* Vol. 3. Paris: Seuil, 1991.

Rivero, Jean, 'La notion juridique de laïcité', *Chronique du Recueil Dalloz*, Vol. 31, 1949, 137–40.

Robert, Jacques, 'La notion juridique de laïcité et sa valeur constitutionnelle', in Hubert Bost (ed.), *Genèses et enjeux de la laïcité. Christianismes et laïcité.* Paris: Labor et Fides, 1990, pp. 89–100.

Rochefort, Florence, 'Foulard, genre et laïcité en France', *Vingtième Siècle, Revue d'Histoire*, Vol. 75, July–September 2002, pp. 145–56.

Rolland, Patrice, 'Le phénoméne sectaire au regard de la laicite francaise', in BP, pp. 331–44.

Roman, Joël, 'La laïcité comme religion civile', *Esprit*, Vol. 175, 1991, pp. 108–15.

—— 'Un multiculturalisme à la française?', *Esprit*, Vol. 6, June 1995, pp. 145–60.

—— *La démocratie des individus.* Paris: Calmann-Lévy, 1998.

—— *Chronique des idées contemporaines.* Rosny: Bréal, 2000.

Roman, Joël, 'Pourquoi la laïcité?', in Nacira Guénif-Souilamas (ed.), *La république mise à nu par son immigration*. Paris: La Fabrique Edition, 2006, pp. 62–80.

Rosanvallon, Pierre, *La crise de l'État-Providence*. Paris: Seuil, 1981.

—— *L'État en France. De 1798 à nos jours*. Paris: Seuil, 1990.

—— *Le sacre du citoyen. Histoire du suffrage universel en France*. Paris: Gallimard, 1992.

—— *Le peuple introuvable. Histoire de la représentation démocratique en France*. Paris: Gallimard, 1998.

—— *La démocratie inachevée. Histoire de la souveraineté du peuple en France*. Paris: Gallimard, 2000.

—— 'Political Rationalism and Democracy in France in the 18th and 19th Centuries', *Philosophy and Social Criticism*, Vol. 28, No. 6, 2002, pp. 687–701.

—— *Le modèle politique français. La société civile contre le jacobinisme de 1789 à nos jours*. Paris: Seuil, 2004.

—— *La contre-démocratie, la politique à l'âge de la défiance*. Paris: Seuil, 2006.

Rosenblum, Nancy, 'Introduction. Pluralism, Integralism, and Political Theories of Religious Accommodation', in Nancy L. Rosemblum (ed.), *Obligations of Citizenship and Demands of Faith. Religious Accommodation in Pluralist Democracies*. Princeton, NJ: Princeton University Press, 2000, pp. 3–31.

—— (ed.), *Obligations of Citizenship and Demands of Faith. Religious Accommodation in Pluralist Democracies*. Princeton, NJ: Princeton University Press, 2000.

Rouland, Norbert, 'La tradition juridique française et la diversité culturelle', *Droit et Société*, Vol. 27, 1994, pp. 381–419.

Roussel, Francois, 'Le sens du commun: dissonances des voix laïques', *Rue Descartes*, Vol. 42, 2003, pp. 64–83.

Roussillon, Alain, 'Islam et mondialisation. Etat des lieux (provisoire) des débats suscités en France par les attentats du 11 septembre 2001', *Maghreb-Machrek*, Vol. 174, October 2001, pp. 75–89.

Roy, Olivier, 'Ethnicité, bandes et communautarisme', *Esprit*, February 1991, pp. 37–47.

—— *L'Islam mondialisé*. Paris: Seuil, 2004 (1st ed. 2002).

—— 'L'islam est le miroir où la société française se regarde aujourd'hui', *Libération*, Vol. 6, November 2004.

—— *La laïcité face à l'Islam*. Paris: Stock, 2005.

—— 'Fondamentalisme et *laïcité* en miroir', in Charles Zarka (ed.), *L'Islam en France*. Special issue of *Cités*, March 2004, pp. 143–50.

Saada, Emmanuelle, 'La République des Indigènes', in Vincent Duclert and Christophe Prochasson (eds), *Dictionnaire Critique de la République*. Paris: Flammarion, 2002, pp. 364–70.

Sabbagh, Daniel, 'Affirmative Action at Sciences Po', *French Politics, Culture and Society*, Vol. 20, No. 3, Fall 2002. Paris: Economica, 2003, pp. 52–64.

—— *L'égalité par le droit. Les paradoxes de la discrimination positive aux États-Unis*. Paris: Economica, 2003.

Sabeg, Yazid, and Sabeg, Yacine, *Discrimination positive. Pourquoi la France ne peut y échapper.* Paris: Calmann-Lévy, 2004.

Sadoun, Marc (ed.), *La démocratie en France.* Vol. 2. Paris: Gallimard, 2000.

Safran, William, 'The Mitterrand Regime and its Policies of Ethnocultural Accommodation', *Comparative Politics*, Vol. 18, No. 1, 1985, pp. 41–63.

Sahgal, Gita, and Nira Yuval-Davis (eds), *Refusing Holy Orders. Women and Fundamentalism in Britain.* Paris: Virago, 1992.

Saliba, Therese, 'Introduction' to Therese Saliba, Carolyn Allen, and Judith A. Howard (eds), *Gender, Politics and Islam.* Chicago: University of Chicago Press, 2002, pp. 1–14.

Sandel, Michael, *Democracy's Discontent: America in Search of a Public Philosophy.* Cambridge, MA: Harvard University Press, 1996.

Sangiovanni, Andrea, 'Justice and the Priority of Politics to Morality', *Journal of Political Philosophy*, Vol. 16, No. 2, June 2008, pp. 137–64.

Sarkozy, Nicolas, *La République, les religions, l'espérance.* Paris: Cerf, 2004.

Savidan, Patrick (ed.), *La République ou l'Europe?* Paris: Livre de Poche, 2004.

Sayad, Abdelmalek, 'Qu'est ce que l'intégration?', *Hommes et Migrations*, Vol. 1182, December 1994, pp. 8–14.

—— *La double absence. Des illusions de l'émigré aux souffrances de l'immigré.* Paris: Seuil, 1999.

Séve, Bernard, 'Les convictions d'autrui sont-elles un argument?' *Le Débat*, Vol. 58, January 1990.

Schlegel, Jean-Louis, 'Laïcité et religion dans la société française d'aujourd'hui', in Catherine Wihtol de Wenden (ed.), *La citoyenneté.* Paris: Fondation Diderot, 1988, pp. 295–306.

Schnapper, Dominique, *La France de l'intégration. Sociologie de la nation en 1990.* Paris: Gallimard, 1990.

—— *La Communauté des Citoyens.* Paris: Gallimard, 1994. English translation: *Community of Citizens. On the Modern Idea of Nationality.* Piscataway, NJ: Transaction, 1998.

—— *La relation à l'autre. Au cœur de la pensée sociologique.* Paris: Gallimard, 1998.

—— *La Démocratie providentielle. Essai sur l'égalité contemporaine.* Paris: Gallimard, 2002.

—— 'Making Citizens in an Increasingly Complex Society: Jacobinism Re-Visited' in Sudhir Hazareesingh (ed.), *The Jacobin Legacy in Modern France.* Oxford: Oxford University Press, 2002, pp. 196–216.

—— 'Citoyenneté européenne et démocratie providentielle', in Patrick Savidan (ed.), *La République ou l'Europe?* Paris: Livre de Poche, 2004, pp. 337–60.

—— 'Lutte contre les discriminations et lien social', in Serge Paugam (ed.), *Repenser la solidarité. L'apport des sciences sociales.* Paris: Presses Universitaires de France, 2007, pp. 515–30.

Scott, David, 'Culture in Political Theory', *Political Theory*, Vol. 31, No. 1, February 2003, pp. 92–115.

Scott, Joan W., *La Citoyenne paradoxale. Les féministes et les droits de l'homme.* Paris: Albin Michel, 1998. American edition: *Only Paradoxes to Offer.* Cambridge, MA: Harvard University Press, 1996.

Scott, John, and Zaretsky, Robert, 'Rousseau and the Revival of Humanism in Contemporary French Political Thought', *History of Political Thought*, Vol. 24, No. 4, Winter 2003.

Semprini, Andrea, *Le multiculturalisme.* Paris: Presses Universitaires de France, 1997.

Seglow, Jonathan, 'Theorizing Recognition', in Bruce Haddock and Peter Stuch (eds), *Multiculturalism, Identity and Rights.* London: Routledge, 2003, pp. 78–93.

Shachar, Ayelet, 'On Citizenship and Multicultural Vulnerability', *Political Theory*, Vol. 28, No. 1, February 2000, pp. 64–78.

Shadid, Wasif, and van Koningsveld, Sjoerd (eds) *Religious Freedoms and the Neutrality of the State: The Position of Islam in the European Union.* Leuven: Peeters, 2002.

Shepard, Todd, 'La "bataille du voile" pendant la guerre d'Algérie', in Charlotte Nordmann (ed.), *Le foulard islamique en questions.* Paris: Éditions Amsterdam, 2004.

Sher, George, *Approximate Justice. Studies in Non-Ideal Theory.* Lanham, MD: Rowman & Littlefield, 1997.

Shiose, Yuki, and Zylberberg, Jacques, 'L'univers flou de la laïcité. The Fuzzy World of Laicity', *Social Compass*, Vol. 47, No. 3, 2000, pp. 299–316.

Shukrallah, Hala, 'The Impact of the Islamic Movement in Egypt', in Darlene M. Juschka (ed.), *Feminism in the Study of Religion. A Reader.* London: Continuum, 2001.

Sieffert, Denis, *Comment peut-on être (vraiment) républicain?* Paris: La Découverte, 2006.

Silberman, Roxane, and Fournier, Irène, 'Les enfants d'immigrés sur le marché du travail. Les mécanismes d'une discrimination sélective', *Formation Emploi*, No. 65, 1999, pp. 31–55.

Silverman, Maxim, *Deconstructing the Nation. Immigration, Racism and Citizenship in Modern France.* London & New York: Routledge, 1992.

Simon, Patrick, 'L'encombrante visibilité', in Jean-Michel Helvig (ed.), *La laïcité dévoilée. Quinze années de débat en quarante Rebonds.* Paris: Libération and Éditions de l'Aube, 2004, pp. 91–5.

—— 'Les apories de l'universalisme à la française', *Contretemps*, No. 12, February 2005, pp. 31–40.

—— 'L'arbre du racisme et la forêt des discriminations', in Nacira Guénif-Souilamas (ed.), *La république mise à nu par son immigration.* Paris: La Fabrique Edition, 2006, pp. 160–77.

Skhlar, Judith, 'The Liberalism of Fear', in Nancy Rosemblum (ed.), *Liberalism and the Moral Life.* Cambridge, MA: Harvard University Press, 1989.

Skinner, Quentin, 'Meaning and Understanding in the History of Ideas', *History and Theory*, Vol. 8, 1969, pp. 3–53.

—— 'The Paradoxes of Political Liberty', in Sterling M. McMurrin (ed.), *The Tanner Lectures on Human. Value*, Vol. VII, Salt Lake City, UT: University of Utah Press, 1986, pp. 227–50.

—— 'Machiavelli's *Discorsi* and the Pre-humanist Origins of Republican Ideas', in Gisela Bock, Quentin Skinner, and Maurizio Viroli (eds), *Machiavelli and Republicanism*. Cambridge: Cambridge University Press, 1990.

—— (ed.), *The Return of Grand Theory in the Social Sciences*. Cambridge: Cambridge University Press, 1990.

—— 'On Justice, the Common Good and the Priority of Liberty', in Chantal Mouffe (ed.), *Dimensions of Radical Democracy*. London: Verso Press, 1992, pp. 211–24.

—— *Liberty before Liberalism*. Cambridge: Cambridge University Press, 1997.

—— 'The Idea of Negative Liberty: Machiavellian and Modern Perspectives', in *Vision of Politics*, Vol. 2, *Renaissance Virtues*. Cambridge: Cambridge University Press, 2002.

—— *Visions of Politics. Vol. 2: Renaissance Virtues*. Cambridge: Cambridge University Press, 2002.

Slama, Alain-Gérard, 'La peur du conflit engendre la violence', in Charles Zarka (ed.), *L'Islam en France*. Special issue of *Cités*, March 2004, pp. 151–7.

Smith, Paul, *Feminism and the Third Republic*. Oxford: Oxford University Press, 1996.

Smith, Peter J., 'Le désaveu postmoderne du républicanisme', *Politique et Sociétés*, Vol. 20, No. 1, 2001, pp. 71–95.

Stasi, Bernard, *Laïcité et République. Rapport de la commission de réflexion sur l'application du principe de laïcité dans la République remis au Président de la République le 11 décembre 2003*. Paris: La Documentation Française, 2004. Available at: <http://www.iesr.ephe.sorbonne.fr/docannexe/file/3112/rapport_laicite.Stasi.pdf.>

Stasse, François, 'Pour les discriminations positives', *Pouvoirs*, Vol. 111, 2004, 119–32.

Southwood, Nicholas, 'Beyond Pettit's Neo-Roman Republicanism: The Deliberative Republic', *Critical Review of International Social and Political Philosophy*, Vol. 5, No. 1, 2002, pp. 16–42.

Soysal, Yasemin Nuhoğlu, *Limits of Citizenship: Migrants and Post-national Membership in Europe*. Chicago: Chicago University Press, 1994.

—— 'Changing Parameters of Citizenship and Claims-Making: Organized Islam in European Public Spheres', *Theory and Society*, Vol. 26, No. 4, August 1997, pp. 509–27.

Spinner-Halev, Jeff, 'Feminism, Multiculturalism, Oppression, and the State', *Ethics*, Vol. 112, October 2001, pp. 84–113.

Spitz, Jean-Fabien, *La Liberté Politique*. Paris: Presses Universitaires de France, 1995.

—— 'Voile au lycée: non à l'intolérance!', *Le Monde*, 17 October 2003.

—— *Le Moment Républicain en France*. Paris: Gallimard, 2005.

Spivak, Gayatri Chakravorty, 'Can the Subaltern Speak?', in Cary Nelson and Lawrence Grossberg (eds), *Marxism and the Interpretation of Culture*. Champaign, IL: University of Illinois Press, 1988.

Spragens, Thomas A., *Civic Liberalism. Reflections on our Democratic Ideals*. Lanham, MD: Rowman and Littlefield, 1999.

Stock-Morton, Phyllis, *Moral Education for a Secular Society. The Development of Morale Laïque in Nineteenth Century France*. New York: State University of New York Press 1988.

Stora, Benjamin, *La Gangrène et l'Oubli, la mémoire de la guerre d'Algérie*. Paris: La Découverte, 1998.

—— *Le transfert d'une mémoire. De l' 'Algérie francaise' au racisme anti-arabe*. Paris: La Découverte, 1999.

Sunstein, Cass R., 'Beyond the Republican Revival', *Yale Law Journal*, Vol. 97, 1988, pp. 1623–31.

—— *The Partial Constitution*. Cambridge, MA: Harvard University Press, 1993.

—— 'Preferences and Politics', in *Free Markets and Social Justice*. Oxford: Oxford University Press, 1997, pp. 13–31.

Sylvestre, Jean-Pierre, 'Les fondements de la conception laïque du lien social', *Raison Présente*, Vol. 122, 1997, pp. 79–96.

Tamsali, Wassyla, 'Féministes, je vous écris d'Alger. Le port du voile n'est pas une affaire de culture', *Libération*, 14 January 2004.

Taguieff, Pierre-André, *La Force du préjugé: Essai sur le racisme et ses doubles*. Paris: La Découverte, 1987.

—— *Les fins de l'antiracisme*. Paris: Michalon, 1995.

—— *La République menacée*. Paris: Textuels, 1996.

—— 'Universalisme et racisme évolutionniste: le dilemme républicain', *Hommes et Migrations*, Vol. 1207, 1997, pp. 90–8.

—— and Weil, Patrick, ' "Immigration", fait national et "citoyenneté" ', *Esprit*, May 1990, pp. 245–81.

Tassin, Etienne, *Le trésor perdu. Hannah Arendt, l'intelligence de l'action politique*. Paris: Payot, 1999.

—— *Hannah Arendt, L'humaine condition politique*. Paris, Harmattan, 2001.

—— 'Identités Nationales et Citoyenneté Politique', *Esprit*, Vol. 198, 1994, pp. 97–111.

Taylor, Charles, *Sources of the Self. The Making of Modern Identity*. Cambridge: Cambridge University Press, 1989.

—— 'Multiculturalism and the "Politics of Recognition', in Amy Gutmann (ed.), *Multiculturalism and the Politics of Recognition*. Princeton, NJ: Princeton University Press, 1994, pp. 25–36.

—— 'Modes of Secularism', in Rajeev, Bhargava (ed.), *Secularism and its Critics*. Delhi: Oxford University Press, 1998, pp. 31–53.

Terchek, Ronald J., *Republican Paradoxes and Liberal Anxieties: Retrieving Neglected Fragments of Political Theory*. Lanham, MD: Rowman and Littlefield, 1996.

Ternisien, Xavier, *La France des mosquées*. Paris: Albin Michel, 2002.

Terray, Emmanuel, 'L'hystérie politique', in Charlotte Nordmann (ed.), *Le foulard islamique en questions*. Paris: Éditions Amsterdam, 2004, pp. 103–17.

Tersigni, Simona 'La pratique du hijab en France. Prescription, transmission horizontale et dissidence', in Françoise Lorcerie (ed.), *La politisation du voile en France, en Europe et dans le monde arabe*. Paris: Harmattan, 2005, pp. 37–52.

Tevanian, Pierre, *Le racisme républicain. Réflexions sur le modèle français de discrimination*. Paris: L'Esprit Frappeur, 2002.

——'De la laïcité égalitaire à la laïcité sécuritaire', *Les mots sont importants*, 15 May 2004 (accessed at: <http://www.lmsi.net>).

Thibaud, Paul, and Ferry, Jean-Marc, *Discussion sur l'Europe*. Paris: Calmann-Lévy, 1992.

Thiesse, Anne-Marie, *Ils apprenaient la France. L'exaltation des régions dans le discours patriotique*. Paris: Éditions de la MSH, 1997.

Thiriot, Agnès, 'Le principe de neutralité et l'enseignement', *Savoir Education–Formation*, Vol. 3, 1993, pp. 403–23.

Thomas, Elaine, 'Keeping Identity at a Distance: Explaining France's New Legal Restrictions on the Islamic Headscarf', *Ethnic and Racial Studies*, Vol. 29, No. 2, March 2006, pp. 237–59.

Todorov, Tzvetan, 'Du culte de la différence à la sacralisation de la victime', *Esprit*, 6 June 1995, pp. 90–102.

Todd, Emmanuel, *Le destin des immigrés. Assimilation et ségrégation dans les démocraties occidentales*. Paris: Seuil, 1994.

Toulemonde, Bernard 'La discrimination positive dans l'éducation: des ZEP à Sciences Po', *Pouvoirs*, Vol. 111, 2004, pp. 87–99.

Touraine, Alain, *Le retour de l'acteur*. Paris: Fayard, 1984.

—— *Critique de la modernité*. Paris: Fayard, 1992.

—— *Qu'est ce que la démocratie?* Paris: Fayard, 1994.

—— *Pourrons-nous vivre ensemble? Egaux et différents*. Paris: Fayard, 1997.

Tribalat, Michèle, *Faire France. Une enquête sur les immigrés et leurs enfants*. Paris: La Découverte, 1995.

—— *De l'immigration à l'assimilation. Enquête sur les populations d'origine étrangère en France*. Paris: La Découverte 1996.

——'Un sentiment de trahison', *Le Figaro*, 24 September 2003.

Trigano, Shmuel, *La démission de la République. Juifs et Musulmans en France*. Paris: Presses Universitaires de France, 2003.

Tully, James, *Strange Multiplicity: Constitutionalism in an Age of Diversity*. Cambridge: Cambridge University Press, 1995.

——'La conception républicaine de la citoyenneté dans les sociétés multi-culturelles et multinationales', *Politique et Sociétés*, Vol. 21, No. 1, Fall 2001, pp. 204–8.

Valadier, Paul, *Inévitable morale*. Paris: Seuil, 1990.

Vallet L.P., and Caille, J.P., 'Les élèves étrangers ou issus de l'immigration dans l'école et le collège français. Une étude d'ensemble', *Les Dossiers d'éducation et formations*, No. 67. Paris: Direction de l'évaluation et de la prospective, ministère de l'Éducation nationale, 1996.

Van Kley, Dale (ed.), *The French Idea of Freedom. The Old Regime and the Declaration of Rights of 1789*. Stanford, CA: Stanford University Press, 1994.

Van Zanten, Agnès (ed.), *L'école. L'état des savoirs*. Paris: La Découverte, 2000.

Venel, Nancy, *Musulmanes françaises. Des pratiquantes voilées à l'université*. Paris: Harmattan, 1999.

——*Musulmans et citoyens*. Paris: Presses Universitaires de France, 2004.

Verrier, Raphaël, 'Loi anti-secte. Le remède empoisonné d'un mal imaginaire', Site *Les mots sont Importants*, at <http://lmsi.net/spip.php?article58> (last accessed 20 July 2007).

Vertovec, Steven and, Peach, Ceri (eds), *Islam in Europe. The Politics of Religion and Community*. Basingstoke: Macmillan, 1997.

Vidal, Jérôme, 'La République à l'épreuve des discriminations', in Charlotte Nordmann (ed.), *Le foulard islamique en questions*. Paris: Éditions Amsterdam, 2004, pp. 5–14.

Vincent, Gilbert (ed.), *Services Publics, solidarité et citoyenneté*. Paris: L'Harmattan, 1998.

Viroli, Maurizio, *For Love of Country. An Essay on Patriotism and Nationalism*. Oxford: Oxford University Press, 1995.

——*Republicanism*. New York: Hill and Wang, 2001.

Vivien, Alain, *Les sectes en France. Expression de la liberté morale ou facteurs de manipulation? Rapport au Premier Ministre*. Paris: Documentation Française, 1983.

Voisin, Marcel, *Vivre la laïcité. Essai de méthodologie de la philosophie et de la morale laïque*. Bruxelles: Éditions de l'Université de Bruxelles, 1981.

Wahnich, Sophie, *L'impossible citoyen. L'étranger dans le discours de la révolution française*. Paris: Albin Michel, 1997.

Walker, Graham, 'Illusory Pluralism, Inexorable Establishment', in Nancy L. Rosemblum (ed.), *Obligations of Citizenship and Demands of Faith. Religious Accommodation in Pluralist Democracies*. Princeton, NJ: Princeton University Press, 2000, pp. 111–26.

Wall, Steven, and Klosko, George, *Perfectionism and Neutrality. Essays in Liberal Theory*. Lanham, MD: Rowman & Littlefield, 2003.

Walzer, Michael, *Spheres of Justice*. Oxford: Blackwell, 1985.

Wauquiez-Motte, Laurent, 'Laïcité et neutralité de l'État', *Les Cahiers de la Fonction Publique*, April 2004, pp. 7–9.

Weber, Eugen, *Peasants into Frenchmen*. Stanford, CA: Stanford University Press, 1976.

Weber, Max, *Economy and Society: An Outline of Interpretive Sociology*. New York: Bedminster Press, 1968.

Weibel, Nadine B., *Par-delà le voile. Femmes d'Islam d'Europe*. Paris: Éditions Complexe, 2000.

Weidmann Koop, Marie-Christine 'Discrimination positive en France: l'expérience de l'éducation prioritaire', *Contemporary French Civilization*, Vol. 24, No. 1, Winter/Spring 2005, pp. 85–104.

Weil, Patrick, *Qu'est ce qu'un Français? Histoire de la nationalité française depuis la Révolution*. Paris: Grasset, 2002.

—— 'La crise du principe d'égalité dans la société française', *Recherche Socialiste*, No. 23, June 2003, pp. 5–16.

—— *La République et sa diversité. Immigration, Intégration, Discriminations.* Paris: Seuil, 2005.

—— 'Lever le voile', *Esprit*, Vol. 311, January 2005, pp. 45–53.

Weinstock, Daniel, 'Beyond Exit Rights: Reframing the Debate', in Avigail Eisenberg and Jeff Spinner-Halev (eds), *Minorities within Minorities.* Cambridge: Cambridge University Press, 2005, pp. 227–47.

Weithman, Paul J., 'The Separation of Church and State: Some Questions for Professor Audi', *Philosophy and Public Affairs*, Vol. 20, No. 1, Winter 1991, pp. 52–65.

—— (ed.), *Religion and Contemporary Liberalism.* Notre Dame: University of Notre Dame Press, 1997.

—— *Religion and the Obligations of Citizenship.* Cambridge: Cambridge University Press, 2002.

Wieviorka, Michel, *L'espace du racisme.* Paris: Seuil, 1991.

—— (ed.), *Racisme et modernité.* Paris: La Découverte, 1993.

—— (ed.), *Une société fragmentée? Le multiculturalisme en débat.* Paris: La Découverte, 1996.

—— 'Identity and Difference. Reflections on the French Non-Debate on Multiculturalism', *Thesis Eleven*, No. 47, November 1996, pp. 49–71.

—— 'Le multiculturalisme est-il la réponse?', *Cahiers Internationaux de Sociologie*, Vol. 105, 1998, pp. 233–60.

—— 'Faut-il en finir avec la notion d'intégration?', *Les Cahiers de la Sécurité Intérieure*, Vol. 45, 3rd Trimester, 2001, pp. 9–20.

—— and Ohana, Jocelyne (eds), *La différence culturelle. Une reformulation des débats.* Paris: Balland, 2001.

Wihtol de Wenden, Catherine (ed.), *La citoyenneté et les changements de structures sociales et nationales de la population française.* Paris: Edilig and Fondation Diderot, 1988.

—— Catherine, 'Les "jeunes issus de l'immigration", entre intégration culturelle et exclusion sociale', in Philippe Dewitte (ed.), *Immigration et intégration. L'état des savoirs.* Paris: La Découverte, 1999, pp. 232–37.

William, Jean-Claude, 'Le Conseil d'État et la laïcité. Propos sur l'avis du 27 novembre 1989', *Revue Française de Science Politique*, Vol. 41, No. 1, February 1991, pp. 28–57.

Willaime, Jean-Paul, 'Le religieux dans l'espace public', *Projet*, Vol. 225, 1991, pp. 71–9.

—— 'La laïcité française au miroir du foulard', *Le Supplément*, No. 181, July 1992, pp. 71–83.

—— 'La religion civile à la française et ses métamorphoses', *Social Compass*, Vol. 40, No. 4, 1993, pp. 571–80.

—— 'Eglises, laïcité et intégration européenne', in Alain Dierkens (ed.), *Pluralismes religieux et laïcités dans l'Union Européenne.* Bruxelles: éditions de l'Université de Bruxelles, 1994, pp. 153–65.

—— *Europe et religions. Les enjeux du XXème siècle.* Paris: Fayard, 2004.

Williams, Andrew, 'Incentives, Inequality and Publicity', *Philosophy and Public Affairs,* Vol. 27, No. 3, Summer 1998, pp. 225–47.

Williams, Melissa S., *Voice, Trust and Memory. Marginalized Groups and the Failings of Liberal Representation.* Princeton, NJ: Princeton University Press, 1998.

——and Macedo, Stephen (eds), *Political Exclusion and Domination. Nomos,* Vol. 46. New York: New York University Press, 2005.

Wittgenstein, Ludwig, *Philosophical Investigations.* Oxford: Blackwell, 2001.

Wolf, Patrick J., Macedo, Stephen (eds), *Educating Citizens. International Perspectives on Civic Values and School Choice.* Washington, DC: Brookings Institution Press, 2004.

Wolff, Jonathan 'Fairness, Respect, and the Egalitarian Ethos', *Philosophy and Public Affairs,* Vol. 27, No. 2, Spring 1998, pp. 97–122.

Wright, Johnson K., *A Classical Republican in the XVIIIth Century: The Political Thought of Mably.* Stanford, CA: Stanford University Press, 1997.

Wright, Susan, 'The Politicization of "Culture"', *Anthropology Today,* Vol. 14, No. 1, February 1998, pp. 7–15.

Yankelevich, Hector, 'Trois fillettes voilées peuvent-elles émouvoir Marianne?', in Jean-Michel Helvig (ed.), *La laïcité dévoilée. Quinze années de débat en quarante Rebonds.* Paris: Libération and Éditions de l'Aube, 2004, pp. 103–7.

Yeğenoğlu, Meyda, 'Sartorial Fabric-ations: Enlightenment and Western feminism', in Laura E. Donaldson and Kwok Pui-lan (eds), *Postcolonialism, Feminism and Religious Discourse.* London and New York: Routledge, 2002, pp. 82–99.

Yonnet, Paul, *Voyage au cœur du malaise français. L'antiracisme et le roman national.* Paris: Gallimard, 1993. *Justice and the Politics of Difference.* Princeton, NJ: Princeton University Press, 1990.

Young, Iris Marion, *Inclusion and Democracy.* Oxford: Oxford University Press, 2000.

Young, Robert, 'Autonomy and Socialization', *Mind,* Vol. 89, 1980, pp. 565–76.

Zakariya, Fouad, *Laïcité ou islamisme: les Arabes à l'heure du choix.* Paris: La Découverte, 1990.

Zarka, Charles (ed.), *L'Islam en France.* Hors série de revue *Cités,* March 2004.

Zarka, Yves-Charles, and Fleury, Cynthia, *Difficile Tolérance.* Paris: Presses Universitaires de France, 2004.

Zelensky, Anne, and Vigerie, Anne, 'Laïcardes, puisque féministes', *Pro-Choix,* Vol. 25, Summer 2003, pp. 11–13. Originally published in *Le Monde,* 30 May 2003.

Zouari, Fawzia, *Le voile islamique.* Paris: Favre, 2002.

——*Ce voile qui déchire la France.* Paris: Ramsay, 2004.

Zylberberg, Jacques, 'Laïcité, connais pas: Allemagne, Canada, États-Unis, Royaume-Uni', *Pouvoirs,* Vol. 75, 1995, pp. 37–52.

Index

Ingram Content Group UK Ltd.
Milton Keynes UK
UKHW020210210423
420545UK00004B/62